POLITICS AND ETERNITY

STUDIES IN THE HISTORY
OF
CHRISTIAN THOUGHT

EDITED BY

HEIKO A. OBERMAN, Tucson, Arizona

IN COOPERATION WITH
ROBERT BAST, Knoxville, Tennessee
HENRY CHADWICK, Cambridge
BRIAN TIERNEY, Ithaca, New York
ARJO VANDERJAGT, Groningen

VOLUME XCII

FRANCIS OAKLEY

POLITICS AND ETERNITY

POLITICS AND ETERNITY

STUDIES IN THE HISTORY OF MEDIEVAL AND EARLY-MODERN POLITICAL THOUGHT

BY

FRANCIS OAKLEY

BRILL
LEIDEN · BOSTON · KÖLN
1999

This book is printed on acid-free paper.

Library of Congress Cataloging-in-Publication Data

Oakley, Francis.
    Politics and eternity : studies in the history of medieval and
early-modern political thought / by Francis Oakley.
        p.   cm. — (Studies in the history of Christian thought, ISSN
0081–8607 ; v. 92)
    Includes bibliographical references and index.
    ISBN 9004113274 (cloth : alk. paper)
    1. Political science—History.   2. Philosophy, Medieval.
3. Church history—Middle Ages, 600-1500.   1. Title.   II. Series.
JC111.O18   1999
320'.09'02—dc21
                                                                99–29170
                                                                    CIP

Die Deutsche Bibliothek - CIP-Einheitsaufnahme

Oakley, Francis:
Politics and eternity : studies in the history of medieval and early-
modern political thought / by Francis Oakley. – Leiden ; Boston ;
Köln : Brill, 1999
    (Studies in the history of Christian thought ; Vol. 92)
    ISBN 90–04–11327–4

ISSN   0081-8607
ISBN   90 04 11327 4

PRINTED IN THE NETHERLANDS

To

Ian and Creina

CONTENTS

ACKNOWLEDGMENTS

Of the studies gathered together below, Chapters 1 and 10 were written specifically for this book, and Chapter 9 is the original, somewhat fuller, version of a long essay which appeared in the form of two articles published in the *Journal of the History of Ideas*, LIX (No. 3, 1998), 437–61, and LIX (No. 4, 1998), 669–90. I should like to thank the Journal of the History of Ideas, Inc. for permission to reprint both this material and, as Chapter 8, a further article "Jacobean Political Theology: The Absolute and Ordinary Powers of the King," *Journal of the History of Ideas*, XXIX (No. 3, 1968), 323–46. I must also thank the following publishers, journals and learned societies for permitting me to reprint articles originally published under their auspices: The Past and Present Society, 175 Banbury Road, Oxford, England, holder of the World Copyright of "Celestial Hierarchies Revisited: Walter Ullmann's Vision of Medieval Politics," *Past and Present: A Journal of Historical Studie*s, 60 (August, 1973), 3–48 (Chapter 2), and "'Anxieties of Influence': Skinner, Figgis, Conciliarism and Early Modern Constitutionalism," *ibid.*, 151 (May, 1996), 60–110 (Chapter 5), both reprinted with the permission of the Society; Brill Academic Publishers for *"Verius est licet difficilius*: Tierney's *Foundations of the Conciliar Theory after Forty Years," Nicholas of Cusa on Christ and the Church*, ed. G. Christianson and T.M. Izbicki (Leiden, 1996), 15–34 (Chapter 3); The Center for Medieval and Renaissance Studies, University of California, Los Angeles, for "Legitimation by Consent: The Medieval Roots," *Viator*, XIV (1983), 303–35 (Chapter 4); The Catholic University of America Press for "Complexities of Context: Gerson, Bellarmine, Richer and the Venetian Interdict of 1606–1607," *Catholic Historical Review*, LXXXII (1996), 369–96 (Chapter 6); Imprint Academic for "Locke, Natural Law and God—Again," *History of Political Thought*, XVII (1997), 624–51 (Chapter 7).

For his kind assessment of the manuscript and for including it in the series *Studies in the History of Christian Thought* I should like to thank Professor Heiko A. Oberman. And for research support most generously extended at one point or another during the long years I was working on these studies, I am indebted to the American Council of Learned Societies, The National Endowment for the

Humanities, The Institute for Advanced Studies, Princeton, The Woodrow Wilson International Center for Scholars, Washington, D.C., The National Humanities Center, Research Triangle, North Carolina, and the President and Trustees of Williams College. The College was also kind enough to provide a subvention in support of publication. I would be remiss if I did not acknowledge, too, that I was fortunate enough to be able to share earlier drafts of several of these pieces with my colleagues in the History Department and at the Oakley Center for the Humanities and Social Sciences, Williams College. For their help, criticism, advice and colleagueship I am most deeply grateful.

F.O.
Williamstown, Massachusetts
January, 1999

CHAPTER ONE

INTRODUCTION: TEXT, CONTEXT, TEMPERAMENT AND TRADITION

The essays gathered together in this book and written across the past three decades were conceived, in general, as contributions to the history of ideas and, in particular, as interventions in that currently very lively (if stubbornly loose-limbed) subfield that we are accustomed to calling "the history of political thought." Although their chronological reach extends at its most ambitious from Graeco-Roman antiquity down to the late-seventeenth century, and although they range broadly across theories of kingship, prerogative law, natural-law thinking, ecclesiology, constitutionalist ideas, consent theory and the like, the individual essays are linked together by three shared characteristics.

First, and as the book's title suggests, all of them explore the important, if persistently underestimated, continuities that existed in the medieval and early-modern centuries between religious and theological notions, on the one hand, and patterns of legal and political thinking on the other. Second, nearly all of them focus their attention on the period running from the fourteenth to the seventeenth centuries and insist, accordingly, on transgressing the sharp dividing line that for long it was customary to draw between "the medieval" and "the modern," and that served to introduce so many distortions into our understanding of sixteenth- and seventeenth-century intellectual developments.[1] Third, all of the essays, at one level of abstraction or another, address historiographic questions or touch upon the interpretative debates that have come of late to characterize the field.

From pagan Germanic *Geblütsheiligkeit*, for example, or the quasi-divinity that hedged even Christian kings (ch. 2), to the harmonics in prerogative law and natural-law thinking of scholastic attempts to grapple with the divine attribute of omnipotence (chs. 7, 8 and 9)[2]—

---

[1] Distortions still evident in some of the most recent contributions to the field. See below, ch. 5.

[2] Or again, from the parallels between conciliarist ecclesiology and the arguments

between such seemingly disparate phenomena, once comfortably cabined and confined by scholars within their discrete disciplinary domains, the interconnections have become increasingly evident. And as so many of the chapters contributed, for example, to *The Cambridge History of Political Thought: 1450–1700* have made abundantly clear, historians of the subject have become increasingly willing, of late, to acknowledge that fact."[3]

Something similar may also be said about the frontier, once so well-patrolled, that sealed off the medieval from the modern. Classificatory rigidities, curricular tradition and professional formation notwithstanding, the frontier guards have now begun to relax their vigilance, and scholars have demonstrated an increasing willingness in their work, not only to transgress that frontier, but also to raise questions about the essentially humanistic presuppositions that led to its erection in the first place. Observing that right at the end of the period covered by *The Cambridge History* "we find the stubborn persistence of theological issues that had preoccupied late medieval scholastics," and emphasizing the unprecedented nature of the "mass societies" brought into existence in Europe by the eighteenth- and nineteenth-century population explosion, J.H. Burns noted the implication of such facts for the way in which we should go about periodizing the history of political thought. If the differentiation between "early modern" and "late modern" has sharpened, that between "early modern" and "medieval," he says, has softened.[4] Similarly, Brian Tierney has argued that "it is hardly possible to understand" the European tradition of constitutional thinking "unless we consider the whole period from 1150 to 1650 as a single era of essentially continuous development."[5] And Anthony Black has likewise urged that we would do well to go about our task of historical interpretation on the assumption that "the truly epochal shifts in European political thought occurred in the eleventh and eighteenth centuries," so

of sixteenth- and seventeenth-century resistance theorists (chs. 3, 5 and 6) to the reverberations in early-modern notions of legitimation by consent of the religious individualism that had emerged in Cistercian and Franciscan spirituality (ch. 4).

[3] *The Cambridge History of Political Thought: 1450–1700*, ed. J.H. Burns and Mark Goldie (Cambridge, 1991).

[4] J.H. Burns in his introduction to *The Cambridge History of Political Thought: 1450–1700*, 1–3.

[5] Brian Tierney, *Religion, Law, and the Growth of Constitutional Thought: 1150–1650* (Cambridge, 1982), p. 1. Cf. below, ch. 3.

that the whole period in between should properly be understood, therefore, as "essentially a single epoch."[6]

During the thirty years since I wrote the first of these essays,[7] then, the direction characteristically taken by scholarship in the field has tended in some very important ways to converge with the trajectory of my own scholarly preoccupations and intellectual predilections. In some ways, that is, but not necessarily in all. If the exploration of historiographical issues as it is pursued in so many of these essays is essentially in line with the norm of professional historical practice already well-established in the years immediately following the Second World War, the metahistorical and methodological concerns evident in some of them[8] reflect the subsequent advent of preoccupations whose rise to prominence could not readily have been predicted during my own formative student years in the 1950s. The times are not long since gone, after all, when (in the Anglophone world at least) it was a matter of rueful commentary that philosophers, while feeling it their duty to deliver themselves of opinions concerning the logic and methodology of the natural sciences (to which they had characteristically had little direct exposure), appeared stubbornly uninterested in addressing themselves to the philosophical and quasi-philosophical issues that lurk just below the surface of historical discourse (in which they had frequently been immersed via a course of advanced study).[9]

Gone, however, those times certainly are. The past three decades have witnessed a veritable flowering of interest in such metahistorical concerns. And not only among the ranks of the philosophers. Historians, too, and especially those concerned with the history of ideas, have come to share those concerns and to busy themselves also with affiliated methodological questions. Among historians of political thought, indeed, the current level of methodological self-consciousness is such as to threaten to swamp the upper threshold of available interest beneath an unassimilable overflow of commentary and debate. And J.G.A. Pocock, whose stimulating contributions have done so much

---

[6] Antony Black, *Political Thought in Europe: 1250–1450* (Cambridge, 1992), p. 191.
[7] See below, ch. 8.
[8] See below, chs. 5 and 6.
[9] A situation on which R.G. Collingwood had remarked with some asperity in his *An Autobiography* (Oxford, 1939), p. 74, and the persistence of which led W.H. Walsh in 1950 to write a book with the purpose of demonstrating to his fellow philosophers "that there are problems about history to which philosophers might well give their attention"—see his *Philosophy of History: An Introduction* (New York, 1958), p. 7.

to energize that debate, in boldly proclaiming "the emergence of a truly autonomous method" for the history of political thought, has also ventured the daunting judgment that even "good work done in a context of methodological confusion is in some sense done by chance, or by some coincidence of *virtù* and *fortuna*; it is done despite the available methods, and lacks the critical autonomy which comes only when the method is operating positively to produce the work."[10]

About the rectitude of that judgment, however, I myself am not so sure.[11] Nor, I suspect, are most historians whose insistent energies and compelling interests drive them less readily to metahistorical concerns than to engagement in historical work itself. Struggle though they may have to with the destabilizing undertow generated by the great tidal wave of theory which has come of late to engulf the humanities, their interest and sympathy, like that of Lucien Febvre half a century ago, tend to be quickened more by "achieved results" than by "theoretical disquisitions" and methodological prescription.[12] Despite its deceptive proximity to the rhythms and tactic of ordinary day-to-day discourse (perhaps, indeed, because of it), the historical enterprise is in fact the outcome of an intellectual effort at once more artful, more complex, and more difficult than its practitioners are often prone to acknowledge or their colleagues in contiguous disciplines usually willing to concede. The very intricacy, flexibility, richness and variety of the historical tactic have persistently escaped the conceptual nets in which philosophers and historians alike have struggled so frustratingly to capture them.[13] Accurate generalization on this matter being so difficult to achieve, and even marginally adequate *description* of the intellectual moves characteristic of historical endeavor

---

[10] J.G.A. Pocock, *Politics, Language and Time: Essays on Political Thought and History* (New York, 1971), p. 11.

[11] As I indicated in Francis Oakley, *Omnipotence, Covenant, and Order: An Excursion in the History of Ideas from Abelard to Leibniz* (Ithaca and London, 1984), pp. 39–40, the point being made there in the course of a (perhaps quixotic) attempt, by pursuing an essentially Lovejovian project, to vindicate the efficacy and power of Arthur O. Lovejoy's improperly maligned approach to the history of ideas.

[12] As Febvre indicated in introducing the first issue of the *Annales*. See Fernand Braudel, "Personal Testimony," *Journal of Modern History*, XLIV (No. 4, 1974), 448–67 (at 462).

[13] The classic example of which is the long and ultimately unsuccessful effort of analytical philosophers to assimilate historical thinking to the natural scientific model of explanation by means of general laws. For some agreeably pungent comments on which, see J.H. Hexter, *Doing History* (Bloomington and London, 1972), pp. 67–76.

itself posing so daunting a challenge, the temptation to indulge in exercises of methodological *prescription* is for most of us, accordingly, not very pressing.[14]

In the particular case presented, however, by the history of political thought, the very intensity of interpretative disagreement across the past three decades[15] and the concomitant level of methodological unease is such as to suggest the need to locate for the reader one's own position amid the confusing point-counterpoint of debate. Or, put more diffidently, the desirability of making an attempt, however fumbling, to give at least the general coordinates of one's position, to plot out one's chosen course through the countervailing currents of disagreement, perhaps also to signal the broad philosophical sympathies which methodological claims so often reflect but which their proponents not infrequently fail to acknowledge. And in my own attempt to respond to that imperative, perhaps I may be permitted to speak with a somewhat more personal voice than that customary for the historian and instinctively adopted in the chapters ensuing.

Mariners by calling on the mysterious oceans of time, historians have long since become experienced navigators of the demanding passage from present to past. In effecting that treacherous transit they have always had to stop their ears to the siren calls of the present. But not until the great linguistic turn in humanistic studies characteristic of the past quarter-century have they had to cope with so insistent a displacement to the present of the magnetic north on which their

---

[14] Here I am struck by the pertinence of the remarks concerning the relation of theory to the enterprise of interpretative anthropology which Clifford Geertz made in *The Interpretation of Cultures: Selected Essays* (New York, 1975), p. 25: "The major theoretical interpretations not only lie in specific studies . . . but they are very difficult to abstract from such studies and integrate into anything one might call 'culture theory' as such. Theoretical formulations hover so low over the interpretations they govern that they don't make much sense or hold much interest apart from them. This is so, not because they are general (if they are not general, they are not theoretical), but because, stated independently of their applications, they seem either commonplace or vacant."

[15] A good sense of the unfolding of these disagreements can be garnered from James Tully ed., *Meaning and Context: Quentin Skinner and his Critics* (Oxford, 1988); Richard Tuck, "History," in *A Companion to Contemporary Political Philosophy*, ed. Robert E. Goodin and Philip Pettit (Oxford, 1993), 72–89; John Dunn, "The History of Political Theory and other essays" (Cambridge, 1996), pp. 11–38; David Boucher, *Texts in Context: Revisionist Methods for Studying the History of Ideas* (Dordrecht-Boston-Lancaster, 1985)—this last not only focusing on Dunn, Pocock and Skinner but also setting them in the context of the revisionist historiography of W.H. Greenleaf and of the British tradition of idealist philosophy from which he drew his inspiration.

interpretative compasses are set. Never before, certainly, (at least since
the emergence of history as a university discipline in the nineteenth
century) have they witnessed in neighboring disciplines so widespread
a subversion of "the hard and fast distinction between text and interpretation," so impetuous an "overturning of the opposition between
reading and writing," so blithe a willingness, concomitantly, to place
interpretation "within an economy of production rather than consump-
tion."[16] That such intellectual moves serve to privilege the present
over the past has not altogether precluded their appealing to historical
practitioners themselves. Rarely before, therefore, have historians
encountered within their own ranks so serene a willingness to let the
cognitive anchor drag, to abandon "referentiality," to concede that
"knowledge and meaning are not discoveries but constructions," neither grounded in nor limited by any access to "an unmediated world
of objective things and processes," and to elide, as a result, the traditionally sharp distinction between fiction and history.[17]

In the early 1980s I myself reacted to such developments with a
degree of historicist astringency and a certain hardening of the interpretative arteries. And having since encountered no argument compelling enough to induce me to modify the position I took at that time,[18]
it is not my intention here to dwell further on the poststructuralist

---

[16] Mark C. Taylor, "Deconstruction: What's the Difference," *Soundings*, LXVI
(No. 4, 1983), 387–403 (at 401), a concise and lucid comment on the significance
of the project and on the philosophic milieu in which it made its appearance.

[17] John E. Toews, "Intellectual History after the Linguistic Turn: The Autonomy
of Meaning and Irreducibility of History," *American Historical Review*, XCII (No. 4,
1987), 879–907 (at 901–2). This review article provides a calm assessment of the
countervailing currents that now make it difficult to forecast the future direction of
studies in intellectual history. See also the subsequent forums on intellectual history,
with contributions by David Harlan, David A. Hollinger, Russell Jacoby, and
Domenick LaCapra, in *American Historical Review*, XCIV (No. 3, 1989), 581–626,
and *ibid.*, XCVII (No 2, 1992), 405–39. Similarly, Anthony Pagden, "Rethinking
the Linguistic Turn: Current Anxieties in Intellectual History," *Journal of the History
of Ideas*, XLIX (No. 3, 1988), 519–29; Joyce Appleby, Lynn Hunt and Margaret
Jacob, *Telling the Truth about History* (New York and London, 1994), and the forum,
"Truth, Objectivity and History: An Exchange," devoted to that book (with con-
tributions by Martin Bunzl, Bonnie G. Smith, John Higham and a response by
Appleby, Hunt and Jacob) in *Journal of the History of Ideas*, LVI (No. 4, 1995), 651–80.
See also for another informative review article and one which reaches out helpfully
to scan the positions characteristic of the "new historicists" in literary studies, John
H. Zammito, "Are We Being Theoretical Yet? The New Historicism, the New
Philosophy of History, and Practicing Historians," *Journal of Modern History*, XLV
(No. 4, 1993), 783–814.

[18] For which, see Oakley, *Omnipotence, Covenant, and Order*, pp. 22–27.

aspect of the linguistic turn or what it implies for historical studies. My concern is somewhat narrower in scope. It is, rather, with a different aspect of that protean interpretative shift, one no less linguistic and philosophical in inspiration, but Anglophone in its origins and more directly focused on the degree to which the unreflective intrusion of present-day concerns may have served to distort the way in which the history of political thought has traditionally been written. And I wish to approach the matter via a somewhat indirect route.

I wish to do so because I now realize, in retrospect, that my own sensitivity to the imperiousness with which present-day commitments and concerns can trench upon the integrity of the historian's effort to recover past meanings had been quickened long before I came to be acquainted with poststructuralist modes of thinking and in a very different (and narrower) intellectual setting. During the latter half of the 1960s, and in the course of writing a book whose topic had taken me right up to the borderline between history and theology, I had been forced to a startled recognition of the fact that ecclesiastical historians even of the caliber of Hubert Jedin and Joseph Gill (not to mention such lesser luminaries as Remigius Bäumer and August Franzen) were willing to respond in matters essentially historical to the alien exigencies of nineteenth- and twentieth-century doctrinal, theological and canonistic commitments.[19] The "neuralgic point"[20] involved in this particular instance of the subordination of past to present was ecclesiological in nature. Nothing other, in fact,

---

[19] Hubert Jedin was the distinguished historian of the Council of Trent and Joseph Gill of the Council of Florence. I refer here to the interpretative gymnastics to which both resorted in their attempts to cope with the decree *Haec sancta synodus* (1415) of the Council of Constance. See Hubert Jedin, *"Bischöfliches Konzil oder Kirchenparlament? Ein Beitrag zur Ekklesiologie der Konzilien von Konstanz und Basel"* (2nd ed., Basel und Stuttgart, 1965), and Joseph Gill, "The fifth session of the Council of Constance," *Heythrop Journal*, V (1964), 131–43, and *idem*, "Il decreto *Haec sancta synodus* del concilio di Costanza," *Revista di storia della Chiesa in Italia*, XII (1967), 123–30. For an essentially "historicist" critique of their positions (as also of those adapted by August Franzen and by the Canadian sociologist/theologian, Gregory Baum) see Francis Oakley, *Council over Pope?* (New York, 1969), pp. 105–31, and *idem*, "The 'New Conciliarism' and its Implications: A Problem in History and Hermeneutics," *Journal of Ecumenical Studies* VIII (1971), 815–40. For the hermeneutic challenge these issues have posed for twentieth-century Catholic theologians, see Helmut Riedlinger, "Hermeneutische Überlegungen zu den Konstanzer Dekreten," in *Das Konzil von Konstanz: Beiträge zu seiner Geschichte und Theologie*, eds. A. Franzen and W. Müller (Freiburg, 1964), 214–38.

[20] I owe this phrase to the ecclesiastical historian K.A. Fink, "Zur Beurteilung des Grossen Abendländischen Schismas," *Zeitschrift für Kirchengeschichte*, LXXIII (1962), 335–43 (at 335).

than the perceived threat to ultramontane views of papal authority posed by fifteenth-century conciliar decrees asserting the jurisdictional superiority under certain conditions of general council to pope. A somewhat limited and recondite issue, it may well be. But the threat posed to the painstaking work of historical reconstruction by a hermeneutic that, in effect, legitimated the subordination of historical judgment to the unfolding in the decrees of the First Vatican Council (1870) of an allegedly timeless ecclesiological vision had intellectual ramifications that reached well beyond the immediate issue. And the ecclesiological debates that raged in Catholic circles during the late-1960s and early-1970s made that unmistakably clear. For in the course of those debates, and responding to the exigencies of contemporary doctrinal strife and the needs of their own competing versions of an updated *theologia perennis*, theological liberals and conservatives alike were able by resort to a comparably compromising hermeneutic to erase (or at least ignore) the stubborn untidinesses and confusions of the historical past.[21]

Had not, then, a long-standing admiration for the work of Dilthey and Collingwood itself disposed me to do so, I now think that this particular moment of historicist epiphany would probably have inclined me to react with sympathy to the interpretative position which, around the same time, Quentin Skinner was carving out in relation specifically to the history of political thought. For he was doing so partly by way of reaction to the persistent anachronism of the type of present-oriented and philosophized histories of political thought which he and some of his Cambridge colleagues depicted as the characteristic product of political philosophers accustomed to treating the classical political texts as repositories of timeless answers to perennial problems.

---

[21] For some subsequent historiographic reverberations of these historico-theological tensions, see below, ch. 3. See below, ch. 6, for a similar resort in the seventeenth century by Cardinal Bellarmine to what (for want of a better label) might be called a hermeneutic of dogmatic desperation. And for an analogous, though entirely modern and secular, move, see what E.D. Hirsch, Jr., calls "the Gadamerian way of avoiding datedness [i.e. 'pastness' viewed as 'an obstacle to the present relevance of a text'], under which we can save the text, any text, by the expedient of *making* it true according to our current beliefs." While he concedes that "this way of dealing with traditional texts has the advantage of giving surface continuity to our culture," he also views it as unacceptable "in a learned activity which pretends to historical and scholarly accuracy."—See his "Meaning and Significance Reinterpreted," *Critical Inquiry*, XI (1984), 202–25 (at 216–19).

Viewed now with the benefit of hindsight, with the help of the subsequent flood-tide of commentary and debate,[22] and not, it must be confessed, without a measure of simplification, the great and vivifying effort which Skinner and his colleagues launched (and to which, even at moments of disagreement, I should properly acknowledge my own indebtedness) may be said to have been fueled by three principal factors First, by the desire to extend into the domain of intellectual history the methods and procedures that, during the postwar years, had come to be characteristic of professional history in general, to naturalize in that domain, therefore, the sensitivity to anachronism that Herbert Butterfield had so powerfully evinced in *The Whig Interpretation of History*, and, by so doing, "to wrest the history of political thought from the hands of contemporary political philosophers."[23] Second, by the "Romantic" hermeneutical approach mediated directly via Collingwood but deriving from the historicism of Vico and Dilthey and with roots in the soil of British, Italian and (ultimately) German philosophical idealism. That approach characteristically distinguished between the "outside" and "inside" of historical events, between, that is, the external physical expression of an action, and the internal play of purpose and intention on the part of the author of that action. And, in interpreting those complex human actions that we call texts, it characteristically placed its emphasis on the intentional and purposive "inside" of the action.[24] Third, and

---

[22] The unfolding of Skinner's position in his principal articles from the 1960s and 1970s, the attacks on that position launched by his leading critics, and his own updated restatement of his views along with a lucid and lengthy response to those critics (a sort of exercise of emotion recollected in quasi-tranquillity) are all now helpfully gathered together in Tully ed., *Meaning and Context: Quentin Skinner and his Critics*. See also the works by Tuck, Dunn and Boucher cited above, n. 15. Note Dunn's rueful comment [*The History of Political Theory and other essays*, p. 2]: "After more than thirty years of reflecting on . . . [the history of political thought], the weightiest judgments about it now seem to me less often clear and negative than I used intuitively to suppose."

[23] Thus David Wootton, ed., *Divine Right and Democracy: An Anthology of Political Writing in Stuart England* (Harmondsworth, Middlx., 1986), Preface, 12—a general appraisal than Skinner himself endorses in "A reply to my critics," in *Meaning and Context*, ed. Tully, 233 (and 327 nn. 9, 12 and 13), where he adds: "One way of describing my original essays would be to say that I merely tried to identify and restate in more abstract terms the assumptions on which Pocock's, and especially Laslett's scholarship seemed to me to be based."

[24] Boucher, *Texts in Context*, pp. 197–98; Dunn, *The History of Political Theory and other essays*, p. 20. Skinner has more than once acknowledged his indebtedness to Collingwood—see "A reply to my critics," in *Meaning and Context*, ed. Tully, 233–34, 274–75.

congruent with that emphasis, by the insights of Anglo-American analytic philosophy into the performative nature of language. In particular, the speech-act theory which J.L. Austin developed and P.F. Strawson and John R. Searle expanded and which bears directly on the interpretative task of identifying "intentions *in* acting" and teasing out the illocutionary force of utterances—that is to say, "what an agent may have intended or meant by speaking or writing in a certain way."[25]

When, in the early 1980s, in hot (and perhaps quaint) pursuit of an essentially Lovejovian project, I first had occasion to comment on Skinner's approach. I indicated my broad sympathy with its goals and my gratitude for the measure of protection it afforded against both the reductionism characteristic of some of the sociologists of knowledge and the interpretative excesses of some, at least, of the then fashionable theorists of poststructuralism—people who did not hesitate to intimate the very bankruptcy of historical endeavor itself or to leave the reader adrift, without benefit of chart, compass or anchor, on "the communal sea of linguicity."[26] But like many another of similar disposition my sympathy was not altogether unalloyed. Though at the time I had no reason to develop the first of them and focused exclusively on the second, my principal reservations were, in fact, two in number.

First, reacting to the unqualified formulations and sweeping rejections characteristic of Skinner's early articles (not least among them the blunt dismissal from the history of ideas of "perennial problems" or of "'universal truths' to be learned from the classic texts"),[27] I shared the worry expressed most forcefully by such critics as Joseph Femia and John Gunnell. Namely, that so deep a gulf was being dug between "past-minded" and "present-minded" approaches as to cast doubt on the very pertinence of the *history* of political thought

---

[25] For an account of this aspect of his thinking, see Skinner, "A reply to my critics," in *Meaning and Context*, ed. Tully, 259–73. The words cited appear at 263. For the distinction between the *locutionary* and *illocutionary* aspects of utterances, see below, n. 48.

[26] Oakley, *Omnipotence, Covenant, and Order*, pp. 27–31. The arresting phrase I borrow from Edward W. Said, *Beginnings: Intention and Method* (New York, 1975), p. 338.

[27] Skinner, "Meaning and Understanding in the History of Ideas," in *Meaning and Context*, ed. Tully, 65. First published in 1969, this article is the most sweeping, wide-ranging and hard-hitting of Skinner's statements. Cf. the comment in Boucher, *Texts in Context*, pp. 233–38.

to our contemporary political and philosophical concerns.[28] Second (and the point is not unrelated), reacting this time to the seeming exclusivity of Skinner's contextualist preoccupations with linguistic conventions and ideological concerns contemporaneous with the lifetime of the historical author under scrutiny, and given also the bluntness of his affiliated rejection of Lovejoy's classic approach to the history of ideas, I was led to conclude that he was guilty of overlooking (or, at least, of deemphasizing in historiographically counterproductive fashion) the presence in the past of persistent intellectual traditions marked by a good deal of continuity and conceptual stability, themselves pertinent to the enterprise of interpreting the meaning of historical texts. And I was encouraged in this conclusion by the sharpness of his initial criticism of the way in which the notion of "influence" had traditionally been employed by historians of ideas.[29] These two principal reservations I propose to address in turn.

So far as the first of them is concerned, further clarifications on Skinner's part, as well as the lapse of time and the general settling of the argumentative dust, suggest that it was not really warranted. In launching his influential attack on anachronism and "the subordination of the past to the present," Butterfield had addressed the matter as "an aspect of the psychology of the historian" rather than as "a problem in the philosophy of history," and he had certainly been willing to concede that there was at least *some* sense in which "history must also be written from the point of view of the present."[30] And Collingwood, speaking of what he termed "the question-answer complex which constitutes what people call 'real' life, the superficial or obvious present of the mind in question," had insisted that "every historical question ultimately arises out of 'real' life," that "we study history in order to see more clearly into the situation in which we

---

[28] Joseph V. Femia, "An Historicist critique of 'revisionist' methods for studying the history of ideas," in *Meaning and Context*, ed. Tully, 156–75 (and first published in 1981); John G. Gunnell," Interpretation and the history of political theory: apology and epistemology," *American Political Science Review*, LXXVI (No. 2, 1982), 317–27 (at 319).

[29] As I have pointed out elsewhere, his rejection of the Lovejovian project as wrong in principle, as resting "on a fundamental philosophical mistake" (see Tully ed., *Meaning and Context*, 54–55) appeared to stem from a mistaken alignment of Lovejoy's interpretative stance with that of the proponents of the New Criticism in literary studies. See Oakley, *Omnipotence, Covenant*, and *Order*, pp. 30–36. For Skinner's approach to the question of influence, see below, ch. 5.

[30] Herbert Butterfield, *The Whig Interpretation of History* (London, 1931), pp. vi, 16, 92.

are called upon the act."[31] It would have been odd, then, if a neo-
Collingwoodian of Skinner's stamp had ever really intended altogether
to deny the presence, even in the most "purist" of historical endeavors,[32] of that complex and baffling interplay between past and present
on which theorists like Hans-Georg Gadamer and (more recently)
Domenick LaCapra have dwelt so insistently.[33]

No such denial, certainly, is foregrounded in his theoretical writing. While understandably not prone to evoking the prospect of a
Gadamerian "fusion of horizons" between the interpreter locked in
his own historicity and the past texts he is studying or to emphasizing,
as does LaCapra, the necessity of moving beyond a merely "documentary" approach in the direction of a more "dialogic" reading of
historical texts,[34] Skinner is careful to concede that "all forms of history are bound to be 'whiggish'" in the sense that the problems historians choose to address will necessarily "reflect their own sense of
intellectual priorities."[35] Nor, it should be acknowledged, does that
concession reflect any recent shift in his position. Right at the start,
when attacking what he called "the mythology of prolepsis," his concern had not been to deny the significance that an argument embedded in some historical text might well have for us today. Nor was
it to deny the legitimacy of an historian's being "more interested . . .
in the retrospective significance of a given historical work or action
than in its meaning for the agent himself." Instead, his purpose was
to deplore what he saw as a tendency to turn judgments about such
a work's significance into affirmations about its contents.[36]

---

[31] Collingwood, *An Autobiography*, pp. 113–14, "Hence," he continues, "the plane
on which ultimately all problems arise is the plane of 'real' life: that to which they
referred for their solution is history."

[32] For the distinction between historical "purists" and "impurists" see Boucher,
Texts in Context, pp. 237–43.

[33] Hans-Georg Gadamer *Truth and Method*, trans. Garrett Barden and John Cumming (New York, 1986); Domenick LaCapra, "Rethinking Intellectual History and
Reading Texts," in *Modern European Intellectual History: Reappraisals and New Perspectives*,
eds. Domenick LaCapra and Steven L. Kaplan (Ithaca and London, 1982), 47–85;
idem, History and Criticism (Ithaca and London, 1985).

[34] Gadamer, *Truth and Method*, pp. 267–74, 325–41; LaCapra, "Rethinking
Intellectual History," 50–55, 78–85; *idem, History and Criticism*, pp. 36–44. Similarly
John Keane, "More theses on the philosophy of history," in *Meaning and Context*, ed.
Tully, 204–17.

[35] Skinner, "A reply to my critics" (1988), in *Meaning and Context*, ed. Tully, 248.
Cf. the similar statement he had made in 1974, "Some problems in the analysis of
political thought and action," in *ibid.*, 100–101.

[36] Skinner, "Meaning and Understanding in the history of ideas," in *Meaning and
Context*, ed. Tully, 44–45.

During the 1960s when Skinner was beginning to formulate these views, the literary theorist E.D. Hirsch, Jr. had drawn attention to the fact that something similar was going on in interpretative controversies at large. What was so often involved, he pointed out, was less any "conflict over original versus anachronistic meanings" than a confusion between meaning and significance.[37] He went on, then, and responding in this to the promptings of Gottlob Frege and Edmund Husserl, to discriminate firmly in interpretative endeavors between meaning and significance,[38] and I believe that the likelihood of Skinner's having been misunderstood by such critics as Femia and Gunnell would have been diminished had he himself deployed and foregrounded that distinction. For I believe also that the distinction is both fundamental and clarifying and certainly deserving of close attention on the part of anyone concerned, as historians must necessarily be, with the very *pastness* of texts.

The term "meaning" Hirsch used to refer to "the whole verbal meaning of a text," and "significance" to denote "textual meanings in relation to a larger context, i.e. another mind, another era, a wider subject-matter, an alien system of values, and so on."[39] Significance, therefore, "is meaning-as-related-to-something-else," and "while meaning is a principle of stability in interpretation, significance," accordingly, "embraces a principle of change."[40] For Hirsch, the great advantage of this distinction is the degree of ambassadorial flexibility

---

[37] E.D. Hirsch, Jr., *The Aims of Interpretation* (Chicago and London, 1976), pp. 85–88, reproducing material first published in 1972. For earlier statements of his on the matter, see below, n. 38.

[38] Hirsch first focused on the distinction and discussed its roots in Frege and Husserl in "Objective Interpretation," *PMLA*, LXXV (Sept., 1960), 463–79, and in his "Gadamer's Theory of Interpretation," *The Review of Metaphysics*, XVIII (No. 3, 1965), 488–509, *Validity in Interpretation* (New Haven and London, 1967), pp. 8, 51, 62–63, 127, and *Aims of Interpretation*, pp. 1–13, 79–92. He has since refined and/or modified it in "Meaning and Significance Reinterpreted," 202–25, and "Transhistorical Intentions and the Persistence of Allegory," *New Literary History*, XXV (No. 3, 1994), 549–67. In 1972 Skinner, noting that Hirsch's understanding of the term "meaning" (what a writer means by saying what he says in a work) coincided with his own, alluded to the meaning/significance distinction but without passing any judgment on its validity. See "Motives, Intentions and the Interpretation of Texts," in *Meaning and Context*, ed. Tully, 70.

[39] Hirsch, *Aims of Interpretation*, pp. 2–3, or, as he has put it more recently: "Meaning ... may be conceived as a self-identical schema whose boundaries are determined by an originating speech event, which *significance* may be conceived as a relationship drawn between that self-identical meaning and something, anything else." See "Meaning and Significance Reinterpreted," 204.

[40] Hirsch, *Aims of Interpretation*, p. 80.

it affords us as we go about the complex negotiation between past and present that is part and parcel of all humanistic endeavor but quintessentially so of historical work. It permits us, that is, to acknowledge the force of the claim that "not just our texts but also our [own] understandings are historical" without being led thereby to concede to the extreme "perspectivists," "dogmatic relativists," or (as he prefers to call them) "cognitive atheists," that "all attempts accurately to reconstruct past meanings are doomed to failure."[41] It authorizes us to find the significance of a past utterance *for us* (as did the medieval allegorist, as do current readers of poststructuralist sympathies, and as do most of us at least some of the time) in the way in which the text which embodies it can be seen (or made) to speak to our present condition.[42] But it does so without forcing us thereby to abandon the countervailing humanist conviction that it is in principle within our power, should we so desire and should the pertinent enabling evidence be available, to penetrate to the original, "historical" meaning intended by the author. Without such a "stable determinacy of meaning," Hirsch argues, "there can be no *knowledge* in interpretation, nor any knowledge in the many humanistic disciplines based upon textual interpretation."[43]

It is the distinction's further advantage, I myself would add, that it permits one the historian's traditionally robust commitment to the historicity of the meanings he believes himself to have wrested from the documents of the past, without at the same time binding one to the odd notion that in accepting "history the way it was" the historian must necessarily share his "ideas of 'significance'" with those of actors in the history itself."[44] While it is undoubtedly part of the enterprise

---

[41] *Ibid.*, pp. 3, 5, 81 and 13, where he labels Jacques Derrida as "currently the most fashionable of the theologians of cognitive atheism in the domain of literary theory."

[42] Hirsch, *Aims of Interpretation*, p. 85, where he refers to the medieval allegorists as "the Heideggerians of an earlier day." Cf. his more extended discussion of the allegorical mode and its pertinence to the application of texts in law as well as in other domains in his "Transhistorical Intentions and the Persistence of Allegory," 549–67.

[43] Hirsch, *Aims of Interpretation*, p. 1 (italics mine).

[44] J.G.A. Pocock, "Political Theory, History, and Myth: A Salute to John Gunnell," *Annals of Scholarship*, II (1980), 3–25 (at 15), canvasses this notion while commenting on Judith Schklar's impatience with the "insignificance" of so many of the writers he had discussed in the introduction to his edition, *The Political Works of James Harrington* (Cambridge, 1997). Schklar's review appears in *Political Theory*, VI (No. 4, 1978), 558–61. Butterfield, *The Whig Interpretation of History*, p. 25, defends a similar

of historical reconstruction to labor to discover what actions, achievements, authors, texts, ideas contemporaries in a given era themselves judged significant, it is far from being the whole of that enterprise. Indeed, to urge that in choosing his own emphases and constructing his own account the historian should be bound by such criteria drawn from the period under investigation would be a cripplingly restrictive move. It would also involve a stance very much at odds not only with the traditional but also with the current practice of historians.[45] Any history of political thought, certainly, that was really shaped by so odd a commitment would be open to criticism no less fierce than that directed over the past quarter-century and more at histories that were taken to have been constructed in accordance with the notion of a "great tradition" of canonical works in political philosophy.[46]

Hirsch's insistence on discriminating clearly between meaning and significance appears to have fared reasonably well in the marketplace of ideas.[47] His handling of the nature of meaning itself, however, has encountered a certain amount of critical turbulence. In discussing that issue, and brushing aside dismissive talk about the "intentional fallacy," Hirsch had committed himself firmly to the position that, so far as the interpretation of texts goes, the only "genuinely discriminatory norm" or "compelling normative principle" is "the old-fashioned ideal of rightly understanding what the author meant." So that, as he put it in a later formulation, "authorial intention" is "the only practical norm for a *cognitive* discipline of interpretation."[48] From

position, as also does W.H. Greenleaf, *Oakeshott's Philosophical Politics* (London, 1966), p. 28. Skinner, however, expressly distances himself from such a position, arguing that in choosing what problems to focus on in the past we inevitably involve our own present-day criteria of rationality and significance. See his "A reply to my critics," in *Meaning and Context*, ed. Tully, 248, and "Some problems in the analysis of political thought and action," in *ibid.*, 100–101.

[45] And certainly with mine. See the assumptions concerning the assessment of historical significance embedded in chs. 3 and 4 below, as well as the explicit specification of a present-day criterion of historical significance in Francis Oakley, *The Medieval Experience: Foundations of Western Cultural Singularity* (New York, 1974), pp. 1–8.

[46] See John G. Gunnell, *Political Theory: Tradition and Interpretation* (Cambridge, Mass., 1979).

[47] See Hirsch's comments in "Meaning and Significance Reinterpreted."

[48] Hirsch, *Validity in Interpretation*, p. 27. Cf. pp. 11–14, where he discusses the celebrated essay, "The Intentional Fallacy," which W.K. Wimsatt and Monroe Beardsley had published in *The Sewanee Review*, LIV (1946), 468–88; *idem, Aims of Interpretation*, p. 7.

that position, however, similarly preoccupied with authorial intention though he has been, Skinner has sought, nonetheless, to distance
himself. He has done so partly, it would seem, because he appears
to have understood it as involving the claim that the *entire* object of
the interpretative effort in decoding texts is the recovery of authorial
intention, whereas he himself had simply insisted that it should be
among those interpretative tasks. He has done so, again and in part,
because he has taken Hirsch to be committed to a position involving the outright *identification* of the meaning of a text with the author's
intention, whereas, in focusing upon authorial intention, his own
"principal concern had not been with meaning, but with the per-
formance of illocutionary acts."[49]

In a celebrated article and subsequent elaborations, however, Knapp
and Michaels have criticized Hirsch on the very different ground
that he fails to recognize that "meaning and intended meaning are
already [and simply] the same," and that by distinguishing between
"author's meaning" and "reader's meaning" he opens up a broader
interpretative enterprise that invites the debilitating intrusion of theory.[50] Vulnerable to criticism he may well be, but Hirsch can hardly
be guilty of *both* of these diametrically opposed transgressions. He
certainly did not regard the recovery of authorial intention as the
whole story, nor has he persisted in viewing that intention as simply
identical with meaning. But it may well be reasonable to fault him
for having left himself open to misinterpretation by the broad nature
of his original claim and by subsequent fluctuations in the way in

---

[49] And some of Hirsch's earliest formulations in his "Gadamer's Theory of
Interpretation" and "Objective Interpretation" do indeed lend themselves to such
a reading. Cf. Skinner, "A reply to my critics," in *Meaning and Context*, ed. Tully,
270, using here the terminology of speech-act theory, and distinguishing the locutionary aspects of utterances ("what S meant by his utterance") and the illocutionary (or "what S meant in uttering his utterance"). See J.L. Austin, *How To Do Things
with Words* (Oxford, 1975), p. 101. The argument here is quite intricate and *may*
be in tension with some of Skinner's earlier assertions, but of that I must permit
the reader to be judge—see esp. his "Motives, intentions and the interpretation of
texts," in *Meaning and Context*, ed. Tully, 68–78. There is a clear and succinct discussion of this aspect of Skinner's approach and of the degree to which it has been
misunderstood by his critics in Peter L. Janssen, "Political Thought as Traditionary
Action: The Critical Response to Skinner and Pocock," *History and Theory*, 24 (1985),
115–46 (at 130–33).

[50] Steven Knapp and Walter Benn Michaels, "Against Theory," *Critical Inquiry*,
VIII (Summer, 1982), 723–42 (at 725–36). For a sharp (and effective) rebuttal, see
John R. Searle, "Literary Theory and Its Discontents," *New Literary History*, XXV
(No. 3, 1994), 637–67.

which he has formulated his position. Whatever the case, and these intricate skirmishes notwithstanding, I would judge his approach to be roughly aligned with Skinner's—at least to the degree to which both acknowledge that the meaning of a text is more capacious than, and not simply to be identified with (or collapsed into) what it was that the author himself had intended to say. Their approaches are also roughly aligned in that both nevertheless ascribe to the recovery of authorial intention a centrally important role in the business of interpreting texts. And Hirsch's own concern with intentionality is not incompatible, at least, with Skinner's more specific emphasis on the importance, in attempting to recover the meaning of a text, of identifying the illocutionary force of the author's utterances—what, that is, "he may have been intending to do *in* writing what he wrote."[51]

Of course, those who sympathize with or subscribe to such commitments (and I would count myself as one of them) necessarily find themselves forging along on a collision course with some of the most striking of poststructuralist maneuvers—not least among them the celebratory ascription to texts of "an irreducible plurality" of meanings,[52] the blunt rejection of the role of creative subject,[53] the flamboyant proclamation, accordingly, of the "death" or "disappearance" of the author.[54] But, then, such challenges notwithstanding, and as Dunn rightly points out, "the idea that authorship itself is a form of agency . . . has proved comparatively robust."[55] So robust, ironically (and embarrassingly), that even persistent proclaimers of the author's sad demise have been prone, when it comes to alleged misrepresentations by others of their own arguments, to themselves evincing an aggrieved solicitude for the despised principle of authorial intentionality.[56]

---

[51] Skinner, "Motives, intentions and the interpretation of texts," in *Meaning and Contexts* ed. Tully, 75.

[52] Roland Barthes, "From Work to Text," in *Textual Strategies: Perspectives in Post-Structuralist Criticism*, ed. Josué V. Harari (Ithaca and London, 1979), 76–81.

[53] And of the attempt "to restore what has been thought, wished, aimed at, experienced, desired by men in the very moment when they expressed it in discourse"—thus Michel Foucault, *The Order of Things* (New York, 1970), p. 275; *The Archaeology of Knowledge*, trans. A. Sheridan Smith (New York, 1972), pp. 138–39.

[54] Michel Foucault, "What is an Author?" in *Textual Strategies*, ed. Harari, 141–60; Barthes, "From Work to Text," in *ibid.*, 73–81.

[55] Dunn, *The History of Political Theory and other essays*, pp. 23–24.

[56] Karlis Racevskis, *Michel Foucault and the Subversion of the Intellect* (Ithaca and London, 1983), p. 39, argues (somewhat paradoxically, it may be) that "to objectify Foucault by making him the subject of his own discourse would amount to adopting

But if the much-abused figure of the author is alive and well and unlikely soon to retire from the interpretative scene, "the idea of a context of authorship," as Dunn also remarks, has by no means fared as well. Instead, that idea, so beloved of historians in general that LaCapra has been led to deride it as "cracker-barrel logocentrism,"[57] and despite the efforts of such as Pocock and Skinner to specify and refine it, "has proved, on closer consideration, remarkably elusive."[58] That observation may serve as a bridge to the second of my two reservations concerning Skinner's approach. And if, as we have seen, the lapse of years has happily worked to dissipate the first of those reservations, it must now be acknowledged that it has served also, and less happily, to intensify the second. What is at issue in this second case is not simply the problematic nature of the specific types of linguistic contextualism which Pocock and Skinner have advocated and which have recently been subjected to some very sharp criticism.[59] Even if that particular line of criticism turns out in the end to be misplaced, the notion of context itself (see below, ch. 6) has proved to be less clear, less focused, less universal and less problem-free than historians in general and the Skinner of the early articles in particular appear to have assumed.

a strategy of interpretation that Foucault explicitly intends to discredit." But even if Foucault has indeed "frequently reiterated his wish to minimize his own authorial presence as much as possible," his actions belie his words. In a revealing exchange with Lawrence Stone he rebuked the latter for having misread or misinterpreted his line of argument in *Histoire de la folie à l'age classique*. "Don't you agree," he says, "that only by respecting the thought of an author can one prevent criticism from falling prey to the bad habits of hurried journalism?" See "An Exchange with Michel Foucault," in *New York Review of Books*, XXX, no. 5 (March 31, 1983), 42. See also Hirsch, *Aims of Interpretation*, p. 91, on the displeasure of Roland Barthes at having his *intended* meaning distorted by another scholar. Cf. Hirsch, "The Politics of Theories of Interpretation," *Critical Inquiry*, IX (No. 1, 1982), 235–47 (at 240, n. 5).

[57] LaCapra, *History and Criticism*, p. 105, where he complains of the interpretative maneuver whereby "an ill-defined notion of 'the historical context' is constituted as an external, extra-discursive ground and assumed to solve all basic problems in interpretation, including those that may have been disclosed by one's own reading of a text." For his own "problematicization" of the notion of context, see *ibid.*, pp. 117–34.

[58] Dunn, *The History of Political Theory and other essays*, p. 23. Skinner himself, "A reply to my critics," in *Meaning and Context*, ed. Tully, 274, has been led to concede the notion's "great complexity."

[59] See Mark Bevir, "The Errors of Linguistic Contextualism," *History and Theory*, XXXI (1992), 276–98, where, criticizing both the "hard linguistic contextualism" of Pocock and the "soft linguistic contextualism" of Skinner, he argues that while "intentions fix hermeneutical meanings" and while "intentions are recoverable," there is "in the face of human creativity . . . "no definite procedure that historians must follow" and no "fixed method" in going about that process of recovery.

Of late, it has become something of a cliché to point out that contexts are not simply given but are chosen, constructed—indeed, themselves textually mediated.[60] And central to my own reservations in the early 1980s about Skinner's approach was the concern that the very insistence with which he had chosen in his own interpretative endeavor to privilege the ideological and linguistic context contemporaneous with the author of a text under study had blinded him to the pertinence of a very different type of context. Namely, that provided by those long-enduring intellectual continuities, often possessed of a considerable measure of conceptual stability, to which the term "tradition" has often been applied. My concern was by no means to question the pertinence of the various and contemporaneous social, linguistic and ideological contexts of past utterances to the classically *historical* interpretative task of deciding what a given author, "in writing at the time he did write for the audience he intended to address, could in practice have been intending to communicate by the utterance of [a] . . . given utterance."[61] It was, rather, to insist on the importance, especially for anyone interested in the history of ideas, of recognizing the degree to which the authors whose texts are to be interpreted inhabited a world peopled through books with the dead, to the urgency of whose promptings they were quite capable in their thinking of responding no less directly than to the pressures, limitations and exigencies of their contemporary predicament.[62]

Quintessential people of the book though they themselves may be, intellectuals are often (and oddly) prone to overlooking that particular fact. But long exposure to the minds of medieval and modern scholastic thinkers has served to strengthen my own conviction that it is perfectly possible for an author to have more in common, both intellectually and in terms of linguistic conventions followed, with writers of the past than with many of his own contemporaries. It has similarly sensitized me to the possibility that the particular intellectual matrix, with its tacit presuppositions and dominant questions

---

[60] See the discussion below in ch. 6, and the comments of Charles Bernheimer in Bernheimer ed., *Comparative Literature in the Age of Multiculturalism* (Baltimore and London, 1995), p. 16, to the effect that "contexts can be just as ambiguous as texts, from which, given that contexts are to a large extent textually mediated, their difference is not clear." Cf. LaCapra, *History and Criticism*, p. 128.

[61] Skinner, "Meaning and Understanding in the History of Ideas" in *Meaning and Context*, ed. Tully, 63.

[62] A point on which LaCapra has some interesting things to say—"Rethinking Intellectual History and Reading Texts," 69–70.

in terms of which alone an author's work will become fully intelligible, may well be shaped by, or even coincide with, some intellectual tradition stretching back, it may be, to a very distant past. A similar sensitivity, of course, informed Lovejoy's approach to the history of ideas, and if Skinner has commented only glancingly and in dismissive general terms on that specific approach,[63] he still appears to be adamant in his opposition to any historiographical tactic that smacks of "the history of concepts." And that opposition extends, if Pocock is correct, to *any* such approach, whether it derives from the native Anglophone variants of the species or draws its inspiration from the school of *Begriffsgeschichte* pioneered in Germany by Otto Brunner, Werner Conze and Reinhart Koselleck.[64]

It is not surprising, then, that in his early articles Skinner was led to mount a veritable onslaught on the notion of "influence" that had played so important a role in the traditional history of ideas. As noted below in ch. 5, however, he has since backed away from that early hostility and has gone on, indeed, to use the "*influence*-model" to magisterial effect in his own historical work. In response to criticism, moreover, he has also been at pains to insist that his own particular contextualist mode of interpretation by no means committed him to the view that the only "appropriate context for understanding the point of . . . [a] . . . writer's utterances" must necessarily be "an immediate one." That writer, after all, might well be responding to questions "raised at a remote period." Nor was he to be taken

---

[63] Skinner, "Meaning and Understanding in the History of Ideas" in *Meaning and Context*, ed. Tully, 34, and his "What is intellectual history?" *History Today*, XXXV (Oct., 1985), 50–52. In neither case does his brief depiction of allegedly Lovejovian histories of ideas coincide with what Lovejoy himself actually did—though they might catch something of the approach favored by J.B. Bury, whose work Lovejoy treated with some disdain. See Oakley, *Omnipotence, Covenant, and Order*, pp. 29–40.

[64] See Skinner, "A reply to my critics," in *Meaning and Context*, ed. Tully, 283: ". . . [I]n spite of the long continuities that have undoubtedly marked our inherited patterns of thought, I remain unrepentant in my belief that there can be no histories of concepts as such; there can only be histories of their uses in argument." Skinner does not appear to have addressed himself to *Begriffsgeschichte* but Pocock represents his position as being at odds with that approach. See J.G.A. Pocock, "Concepts and Discourses: A Difference in Culture," in Hartmut Lehmann and Melvin Richter eds., *The Meaning of Historical Terms and Concepts: New Studies in Begriffsgeschichte*, Occasional Paper No. 15 (German Historical Institute: Washington, D.C., 1996), 47–58. Reinhart Koselleck's interesting response (*ibid.*, 59–70, and esp. 62–63) suggests a greater measure of agreement with Skinner's approach than Pocock concedes. See also Melvin Richter, "Opening a Dialogue and Recognizing an Achievement," *Archiv für Begriffsgeschichte*, XXXIX (1996), 19–26.

to be denying the presence in "Western traditions of philosophy" of "long continuities . . . reflected in the stable employment of a number of key concepts and modes of argument." Nor again, and accordingly, was he hostile to the study of "traditions of discourse" or even to the project of taking such traditions "as a unit of study."[65] These are interesting concessions, and perhaps I may be forgiven if I take them to suggest (countervailing rhetoric to the contrary) that the gulf which divides Skinner's project from Lovejoy's actual historical practice (and even from some, at least, of his methodological priorities) is not in fact as wide as it might once have appeared to be.[66]

Whether or not that turns out to be the case, I myself have been led, by a combination of temperament and training, to devote much of my own historical endeavor to the identification and tracking of the sort of long-term continuities in the history of ideas that preoccupied Lovejoy and that may be said to constitute traditions. And those traditions I have treated both as appropriate contexts for the understanding of particular texts[67] and as subjects of historical investigation in their own right.[68] That being so, and "tradition" itself being as pliable, multi-faceted and elusive a notion as is "context," it behooves me, by way of conclusion, to attempt a clarification or (at least) a specification of what I myself have in mind when I invoke the idea of traditions in the history of political thought.

If I have, indeed, invoked that notion,[69] let it be said that I have not done so out of any wish to raise the ghost of "the great tradition" in which the canonical texts were seen to be embedded and which played so prominent a role in mid-century discussion of political philosophy.[70] In addition to its more celebrated shortcomings that notion, after all, characteristically gave short shrift to the medieval phase in

---

[65] Skinner, "A reply to my critics," in *Meaning and Context*, ed. Tully, 83, 75; *idem*, "Some problems in the analysis of political thought and action," in *ibid.*, 106–7.

[66] For this point, see Oakley, *Omnipotence, Covenant, and Order*, pp. 31–39.

[67] See e.g. below, chs. 5, 6, and 7.

[68] See esp. *Omnipotence, Covenant, and Order*, and below, chs. 4, 5, 7, 8 and 9.

[69] Oakley, *Omnipotence, Covenant, and Order*, pp. 121–22.

[70] The notion is discussed at some length, and with especial reference to Leo Strauss, Eric Voegelin, Hannah Arendt and Sheldon Wolin, by John G. Gunnell, *Political Theory: Tradition and Interpretation* (Cambridge, Mass., 1979). Cf. his subsequent exchange with J.G.A. Pocock in *Annals of Scholarship*, I (No. 4, 1980), 3–62 (Pocock, "Political Theory, History and Myth: A Salute to John Gunnell," 3–25; Gunnell, "Method, Methodology, and the Search for Traditions in the History of Political Thought: A Reply to Pocock's Salute," 26–56; Pocock, "Intentions, Traditions, and Methods: Some Sounds on a Fog-Horn," 57–62).

European political thinking which has claimed the bulk of my own attention as an historian. In its specifically Straussian version, moreover, it tended to minimize the vitalizing, theologically-induced tensions in European intellectual life which have so fascinated me, and it did so in part by the casual extrusion into the outer philosophical darkness of that whole voluntarist strand of thinking to which I devote so much attention in the essays which follow.[71]

That said, I should nevertheless acknowledge something of an unrepentant commitment to the notion that such unity as the long history of political thinking in the West does indeed possess springs from the fact that it itself constitutes a sinuous and enduring tradition of argument or discourse. Not, if I understand him correctly, the sort of "tradition of discourse" that Sheldon Wolin has evoked so eloquently. For that he describes as a "continuous tradition of political thought," a "tradition . . . of meanings extended over time."[72] What I have in mind is something looser than that, not a tradition centered on shared values or beliefs but one of argument or discourse, one pivoting on "a related set of questions or common concerns" and reflected in "a body of authoritative literature defining problems [and] proffering a range of solutions."[73] Or to put it in Oakeshottian terms, it being characteristic of those whose reflection on political life reaches out beyond the merely instrumental to "deal in darkness," "the unity of the history of political philosophy lies in a pervading sense of human life as a predicament," however differently that predicament may have been conceived across time, and however various the redemptive schemes political philosophers may have proposed by way of deliverance from that predicament.[74]

Further than that, I harbor the view that within the overall tradition of argument or discourse which loosely links together Western political philosophizing taken as a whole, are lodged a number of

---

[71] See below, chs. 4, 7, 8, and 9.

[72] Sheldon Wolin, *Politics and Vision: Continuity and Innovation in Western Political Thought* (Boston and Toronto, 1961), pp. 22–27.

[73] Adopting here the helpful distinction that Andrew Lockyer, "'Traditions' as Context in the History of Political Thought," *Political Studies*, XXVII (No. 2, 1979), 201–17 (at 202–3), draws between "traditions of argument or discourse" (implying "minimally a shared subject matter") and "traditions of thought" (which "minimally involve similar conceptions of man and the state, informed by shared moral or metaphysical beliefs, giving rise to a certain appropriate terminology."

[74] Michael Oakeshott ed., *The Leviathan of Thomas Hobbes* (Oxford, 1946), Introduction, pp. x–xi.

specific *traditions of thought*. By that I mean historical constellations of shared philosophical commitment, constellations of shared values and beliefs marked by their own distinctive terminologies to which thinkers adhere with "some degree of self-consciousness."[75] Preserving across (sometimes long) periods of time a certain identity, continuity and authority, such traditions are by no means static or unchanging. As Cardinal Newman argued long ago, it is "by trial" that the content of an idea is "elicited and expanded." It may have to change somewhat "in order to remain the same" and its "force and depth, and the argument for its reality" are sharpened "in proportion to the variety of aspects under which it presents itself to various minds."[76] In some eras such traditions attain a dominating force (as did the ideology of sacral kingship in late antiquity and the early Middle Ages).[77] In others they coexist with rival traditions (as did the Romano-canonistic tradition of consent theory during the late-medieval and early-modern eras when high papalist views revived and the ideology of sacral kingship, modulated into a new, and specifically Christian, key began to recover some of its former vigor).[78] Sometimes such traditions even enter across time into complex liaisons with successive patterns of thought of very different provenance and import (as did the extraordinarily resilient tradition of natural-law thinking, spanning the late-antique, medieval and early modern centuries).[79] All such traditions, moreover, and as I have tried to demonstrate in several of the following essays, can not only themselves constitute intelligible and viable subjects of historical investigation (thus Lovejoy's great chain of being as well as its rival, the vision of order as grounded not in the very nature of things but in will, promise and covenant).[80]

---

[75] Lockyer, "'Traditions' as Context in the History of Political Thought," 202.

[76] John Henry Cardinal Newman, *An Essay on the Development of Christian Doctrine* (London, 1885), pp. 34 and 40. My attention was drawn to the pertinence of Newman's remarks by Richard Vernon, "Politics as Metaphor: Cardinal Newman and Professor Kuhn," *Review of Politics*, XLI (No. 4, 1979), 513–35, and by Jannsen, "Political Thought as Traditionary Action," esp. 137–40. In order to catch the element of development and to emphasize the wisdom of speaking "not of traditions as objects carried on, but of the nature of that carrying on, that activity of handing down through language," Jannsen proposes the substitution for "tradition" of the term "traditionary action."

[77] See below, ch. 2.

[78] See below, chs. 4 and 6.

[79] See below, ch. 7.

[80] Or so I have long argued. See below, chs. 9 and 10; also Oakley, *Omnipotence, Covenant, and Order* and *idem*, "Lovejoy's Unexplored Option," *Journal of the History of Ideas*, XLVIII (No. 2, 1987), 231–45.

They can also provide "an appropriate framework for the understanding of linguistic performances (words and texts)."[81] In the construction of narrative accounts focused on the unfolding and development of such traditions of thought, moreover, the notion of "influence" understandably plays a central role. And my own preoccupation with them undoubtedly served to stiffen my resistance to the (happily) evanescent fashion of trying to banish the "influence model" from the methodological armory of historians of ideas.[82]

Finally, though reposing more confidence in the genuine historicity of traditions of discourse and traditions of thought as described above, I find myself reluctant wholly to exclude from consideration the rather different type of tradition not infrequently invoked by historians of philosophically idealist sympathies and, so far as the history of political thought is concerned, classically identified with Michael Oakeshott's wonderfully illuminating schematization of that history in accordance with the "master-conceptions" of Reason and Nature, Will and Artifice, and Rational Will.[83] Like many another, I myself have been inclined to bracket such "traditions" as reflecting the historian's own organizing principles rather than embodying identifiably *historical* traditions.[84] About the rectitude of that bracketing, however, I am no longer as sure as I once was, and am now inclined to situate these Oakeshottian traditions in the at least arguably historical territory falling somewhere between the ground occupied, respectively, by traditions of thought and traditions of discourse as described above. For any attempt to come to terms with this issue, however, exposure to concrete exemplification is crucial, and illumination is more likely to be forthcoming from commentary that is retrospective rather than prospective. Further discussion of the issue, then, I propose to defer until such exemplification has indeed been forthcoming. I will return to it, accordingly, in the *Epilogue* to the book.

---

[81] The words are Lockyer's, "'Traditions' as Contexts," 216. What I wish to suggest is that the identification of such traditions can serve both to enrich and specify the context that holds the key to an author's intentions, enabling us not only to identify the dominant questions or concerns he was confronting or the characteristic beliefs or values he was bringing to their solution, but also to discern how he was responding to (or departing from) that intellectual inheritance when he said what he had to say. For pertinent illustrations relating to the thinking of Robert, Cardinal Bellarmine, Robert Boyle, John Locke and James I of England, see below, chs. 6, 7 and 8.

[82] See below, ch. 5.

[83] Oakeshott ed., *The Leviathan of Thomas Hobbes*, Introduction, pp. x–xiii.

[84] Oakley, *Omnipotence, Covenant, and Order*, p. 121.

CHAPTER TWO

CELESTIAL HIERARCHIES REVISITED:
ULLMANN'S VISION OF MEDIEVAL POLITICS

Over the course of the last dozen years, with a contempt for his critics at once both admirable and deplorable, Walter Ullmann has set out to reshape our understanding of medieval political and constitutional thinking. He has done so in a series of overlapping but far-ranging studies, which, though they take as their point of departure the line of argument developed already in his *Growth of Papal Government in the Middle Ages*, have not evoked the degree of scholarly dissent which that earlier work succeeded in stimulating.[1] It is true that Ullmann has had his persistent critics, but as book has succeeded book—the *Principles of Government and Politics in the Middle Ages* (since 1966 in its second edition), the *History* of *Political Thought: The Middle Ages*, the *Individual and Society in the Middle Ages*, and now (with a scholar of Ullmann's energy and imagination one hesitates to say "finally") *The Carolingian Renaissance and the Idea of Kingship*—the voices of acclaim have more than balanced those of dissent. Again and again, reviewers have felt moved to laud his "mastery of the sources," the "richness" of his ideas, the "profundity" and "range" of his learning, the "subtlety" and "penetration" of his analyses, the "force" of his argumentation.[2] References to "the magisterial sweep of Professor

---

[1] Walter Ullmann, *The Growth of Papal Government in the Middle Ages* (London, 1955; 3rd ed., 1970), cited hereafter as *Growth*. In this essay I address myself to the views expressed in the following studies of Ullmann: "Law and the Medieval Historian," in *XIe Congrès International des Sciences Historiques: Rapports* (5 vols., Göteborg, 1960), III, 34–74; *Principles of Government and Politics in the Middle Ages* (London, 1961; 2nd ed., 1966), cited hereafter as *Principles; A History of Political Thought: The Middle Ages* (Harmondsworth, 1965) cited hereafter as *History; The Individual and Society in the Middle Ages* (Baltimore, Md., 1966), cited herafter as *Individual; The Carolingian Renaissance and the Idea of Kingship* (London, 1969), cited hereafter as *Kingship*.

[2] Thus R. Folz on *Principles* in *Revue des sciences religieuses*, XXXVII (No. 1, 1963), 31; unsigned note on *Individual* in *The Virginia Quarterly Review*, XLIII (No. 3, 1967), cxxiii; Karl Schnitt on *Principles* in *Historisches Jahrbuch*, LXXXII (1963), 361; J.M. Wallace-Hadrill on *Principles* in *Journal of Theological Studies*, new series, XIII (Part 2, 1962), 442; T.M. Parker on *Individual* in *Journal of Ecclesiastical History*, XX (No. 1, 1969), 124; R.C. van Caenegem on *Individual* in *Le Moyen Age*, LXXVI (No. 1, 1970), 177; D.A. Bullough on *Kingship* in *History*, LVI (Feb., 1971), 82.

Ullmann's scholarship" and even to "the preternatural brilliance of his vision"[3] represent merely the less restrained modulations of a laudatory theme to which his ear must long since have become no stranger. That such compliments have sometimes only grudgingly been conceded strengthens, if anything, the power of their witness, and their cumulative effect is to make it clear that in these studies Ullmann has achieved a novel and powerful synthesis, with the fearful symmetries of which anyone seriously interested in medieval political and constitutional thinking must now come to terms. Hence my own attempt at an appraisal. Hence, too, the fact that the very necessity of essaying such an appraisal itself stands as a tribute to the magnitude of his scholarly achievement.[4]

Of course, like many another intellectual pace-setter, Ullmann is now in danger of being both quoted and criticized more often than he is read. But I have read him; I have read him at length, with attention, and with deepening bewilderment. For if the density of his scholarship nearly always succeeds in intimidating, with surprising frequency it also fails to convince. The omissions and mistakes of fact are simply too striking; some of the most confident assertions simply too bizarre. The interpretations given to familiar texts are all too frequently idiosyncratic, and, "semantic method" notwithstanding,[5] the meanings accorded to such crucial terms as "nature" and "grace" are altogether too pliable. In studies as wide-ranging as these, it is true, omissions and mistakes are fully to be expected. What surprises, however, in Ullmann, is their nature and importance.

That in these studies we should hear so little, for example, of Ockham or of the Anglo-Norman Anonymous, if striking,[6] is perhaps explicable. But the absence of any direct treatment of Augustine is harder to understand—the more so because there is much reliance on the confusing and shop-worn label, "Augustinian," and because a tag of Augustine's, read, it would seem, via Gratian and taken out of context, is quoted as "a neat statement concerning the descend-

---

[3] Thus M. Wilks on *Individual* in *English Historical Review*, LXXXIV (Jan., 1969), 159; P. Wormald on *Kingship*, *ibid.*, LXXXVI (April, 1971), 350.

[4] And here it would be appropriate to acknowledge with respect not only Ullmann's own achievement but also that of a whole series of distinguished pupils. The impact upon medieval studies of their extensive contributions has undoubtedly been a vitalizing one.

[5] See *Principles*, 16–17.

[6] The more so given his discussion of the latter's thought in *Growth*, pp. 394–403.

ing thesis of government and law," leaving us thereby with the impression that Augustine was unambiguously a proponent of that thesis.[7] Again, it is perhaps understandable that one who does not claim to be a seventeenth-century specialist should apparently take it for granted (despite the counter-example of Locke) that in the modern period the tradition of grounding the natural law in the divine will had necessarily been pushed to one side.[8] More surprising, however, is the ascription to Aquinas of the first break (presumably under Aristotelian influence) with what he calls "the traditional medieval doctrine" in accordance with which "the order of a superior, whether just or unjust had to be obeyed."[9] In the *Decretals* themselves, after all, there are two letters of Innocent III asserting that under certain conditions one must humbly accept excommunication at the hands of one's ecclesiastical superior rather than go against one's conscience by obeying him.[10]

Nor are these isolated instances. Why is it, for example, that Ullmann, in asserting that the political views of John of Paris "might well have appeared revolutionary" at the time, notes that when he died he was expecting "definitive sentence for heresy," giving us thereby the impression that the heresy involved had something to do with his political views whereas in fact it concerned his teaching on the Eucharist?[11] And what exactly are we to make of the bland assertion that the Latin language in the thirteenth century "could quite clearly no longer cope . . . with the subtle variations of human feelings, passions and motives,"[12] or, again, that there is "an antinomy"

---

[7] *Principles*, p. 21; "Law and the Medieval Historian," 73 note 8. The reference is to Augustine, *In Joannis Evangelium Tractatus* CXXIV, Tract. VI ad cap. 1 § 25; ed. J.-P. Migne, *Patrologiae cursus completus: series latina* (221 vols., Paris, 1844–64), XXV, 1437. The text is included in the *Decretum*, D. 8, c. 1; ed. A. Friedberg, *Corpus Juris Canonici* (2 vols., Leipzig, 1879–81), I, 13.

[8] This is certainly implied in *Principles*, p. 253, and *History*, pp. 184–85, 204–205. Indeed, Ullmann's statement that "as nature and the natural law were conceived to be manifestations of divinity, a formidable bar to the fully-fledged autonomy of the citizen and of the State was erected" (*History*, p. 204), is particularly odd on the lips of one who clearly regards John Locke as *the* spokesman for the fully-fledged "populist" or "ascending" theme (see *Individual*, pp. 132, 150–51). For Locke's understanding of the divine foundation of natural law see Francis Oakley and Elliot W. Urdang, "Locke, Natural Law, and God," *Natural Law Forum*, XI (1966), 92–109.

[9] *Individual*, pp. 126–27, cf. p. 13; *Principles*, p. 107.

[10] X, 2, 13, 13; ed. Friedberg, II, 287–88. X, 5, 39, 44; *ibid.*, II, 908.

[11] *History*, p. 204. See *Lexikon für Theologie und Kirche*, ed. Josef Höfer and Karl Rahner (10 vols., Freiburg, 1957–65), V, 1068, *s.v.* "Johannes v. Paris"; Frederick J. Roensch, *Early Thomistic School* (Dubuque, Iowa, 1964), pp. 98–100.

[12] *Individual*, pp. 106–107.

between "the laws of logical reasoning" and "the laws of human natural reasoning?"[13]

And so on. To extend the list would not necessarily be difficult,
but it would certainly be tedious, perhaps also profitless. Above all,
it would be unfair. For if, on the one hand, Ullmann's most trou-
bling allegations are frequently unclear,[14] on the other, we should
not fail to remind ourselves that what an interpreter gets out of the
medieval legal and political texts depends in no small degree upon
what he brings to them. It would be improper, therefore, to pass
too swift a judgment upon Ullmann's reading of any particular text
without having attempted to evaluate the general interpretative structure in terms of which it has been understood—the more so, as the
late Ernst Kantorowicz pointed out, since the *Principles of Government
and Politics in the Middle Ages*, the book on which all of the others
build, is "a study whose conceptual framework was apparently the
author's chief concern."[15] It is, then, to the adequacy of this conceptual framework, the component central to Ullmann's whole contribution, that I propose in this essay to address myself.

Fortunately enough, its main outlines stand out in bold relief.[16]
Despite much talk about the importance during the Middle Ages of
what he refers to as "the so-called teleological conception of law,"[17]
Ullmann's fundamental preoccupation when he approaches medieval
politics is not with the end or purpose but rather with the source
of law and of governmental power. Though nowhere does he quite
say as much he clearly shares the modern liberal-democratic assumption that it is with reference to efficient rather than to final causa-

---

[13] *Principles*, pp. 105–106.

[14] E.g., see above, notes 12 and 13. As a result of this lack of clarity, the would-be
critic has all too often to weigh the daunting realization that a perfectly defensible
meaning *could* be given to a particular assertion against the firm conviction that *that*
is not the meaning which Ullmann has in mind at all.

[15] Ernst Kantorowicz in a review of *Principles, Speculum*, XXXIX (No. 2, 1964),
344–51 at 344. He had begun by saying: "In our days when technical skills so
often prevail and dominate the field, books based upon a genuine and original
conception have become rare. Dr. Ullmann's latest study belongs to that rarer
category."

[16] I follow here the succinct statements given in *Principles*, pp. 19–26 and *History*,
pp. 11–18. Cf. *Individual*, pp. 3–6; his inaugural lecture, *The Relevance of Medieval
Ecclesiastical History* (Cambridge, Eng., 1966), esp. pp. 16–36; and his *Papst und König:
Grundlagen des Papsttums und der englischen Verfassung im Mittelalter* (Salzburg u. München,
1966), pp. 49–55. But see below, note 22.

[17] *Principles*, pp. 19, 221–222; *History*, p. 15.

tion that political authority must be legitimated.[18] Despite much evidence to the contrary, he also clearly believes that one can without anachronism presume medievals themselves to have shared that assumption. This being so, medieval political thinking was in his view dominated by two competing "conceptions of government and law," conceptions which, being "diametrically opposed" to one another, were mutually exclusive.[19] These he refers to as the "ascending" and "descending" themes or theses.[20] According to the former of these, which he designates also as the "populist" conception, "governmental authority and law-creating competence" are attributed to the people or community and ascend to the top of the political structure "from the broad base in the shape of a pyramid." With this theme are associated consent, representation, and the notion of the individual as citizen, as participant in public government, occupying within society a status characterized by autonomy and independence, endowed, therefore, with a battery of "inalienable rights" proof even against the encroachments of the powers that be. According to the latter thesis, on the other hand, all power is located ultimately in God, who, by means of an earthly vicegerent himself endowed to this end with a plenitude of power, distributes it downwards *via* a hierarchy of officials "again in the shape of a pyramid."[21] In the context of this theme, faith is substituted for consent, the notion of office delivered from above replaces that of representation, and instead of the autonomous, right-bearing individual, we encounter the faithful

---

[18] The reference here as elsewhere in this essay is to two of the four "necessary conditions" or "reasons for" any process which Aristotle described, which Cicero rendered in Latin as the four *causae*, and which have since been known in the Western philosophical tradition as the "four causes." See Aristotle, *Physics*, ii.3.194b–195a; *Metaphysics*, v. 2. I,0I3a–b; cf. J.H. Randall, *Aristotle* (New York and London, 1962), pp. 54, 65–7, 123–9. Randall (p. 124) describes the *Formal Cause* as responding to the question: "What is it?," the *Material Cause* to the question: "Out of what is it made?"; the *Efficient Cause* to the question: "By what agent?"; and the *Final Cause* to the question: "For what end?." And he illustrates the causes as follows: "Thus we can ask, What is it? It is a flag. Out of what is it made? Bunting. By what was it made? The firm of Rosenkranz and Guildenstern. For what was it made? To serve as a patriotic symbol."

[19] *Principles*, p. 20.

[20] All of the studies under consideration presuppose this typology and elaborate upon it. For its genesis in Ullmann's work, see below, pp. 68–70.

[21] *Principles*, pp. 20–23; *Individual*, pp. 6–9. It was Ullmann's stress on the role of Pseudo-Dionysius's *De coelesti hierarchia* in providing a "theosophic and philosophic foundation" for the descending theme that suggested to me the title of the present essay. See *Principles*, pp. 46–48; *History*, pp. 30–32.

Christian, recipient of the favors of an absolutist government, subject rather than citizen.[22]

Of the two, the ascending theme is taken by Ullmann to be the more fundamental—prevalent, it would seem, both over longer stretches of time and over broader expanses of space, rooted more deeply in the soil of mundane human existence, attached more firmly to the very bedrock of the human psyche. Thus, in "unadulterated" form, it has prevailed in the modern era, in republican Rome, and also (or so one must presume) in the world of the Greek *polis* as well.[23] It prevailed likewise among the Germanic peoples of the pre-Christian era among whom kingship was "based on the popular will"—so much so, indeed, that long after the descending thesis had triumphed over "the whole of Southern and Western Europe," not only did the "populist kingship" survive in the Scandinavian north, but even in the West, at the village level and in the "lower regions of society," remnants of populism eked out "a somewhat subterranean existence throughout the medieval period."[24] And, in the thirteenth and early-fourteenth centuries, it was those populist remnants, fortified long since by the growth of feudalism, which made possible the full-scale appropriation of "Aristotelian naturalism"— itself the single most important factor making for the recovery of the ascending theme, and, as a result, for the "advance of political reasoning toward what might well be called a Lockean position."[25]

The expressions which Ullmann uses in connection with the ascending or populist theme, and the adjectives with which he qualifies it, suggest very strongly that there was nothing accidental about either its popularity or its staying power. On the contrary, he seems to

---

[22] It should be noted, however, that more recently in *Kingship*, esp. pp. 111–34, 167–90, Ullmann has been at pains to stress the degree to which the adoption of the ceremony of royal unction, by opening the way to clerical intervention and supervision, in effect promoted "the stunting of the king's sovereignty" (121) and the spread of the conviction that "the Ruler was subjected to a law" (134). This being so, he must now be taken to wish to qualify somewhat his earlier alignment of the descending thesis with monarchical absolutism. Pushed far enough, of course, such qualifications would undermine the coherence of his whole interpretative schema. But it is not yet clear that he would wish to push them that far.

[23] As is suggested by his interpretation of Aristotle—see the remarks below, pp. 63–66. See also *Principles*, pp. 21–23, and *History*, p. 14, where he says that the "very strong ecclesiastical character of early political thought marked it off both from ancient—Greek and Roman—as well as modern political thinking."

[24] *Principles*, pp. 22–23, 215–30; *History*, pp. 53, 159–61.

[25] *Individual*, p. 132; cf. *Relevance of Medieval Ecclesiastical History*, pp. 24–25.

view it as nothing other than the "natural" way of thinking about matters political.[26] Thus, he speaks of its "earthiness," its "practicality," its immediate appeal to the "unsophisticated," to "ordinary humanity." He associates it with "subjectivity," with "individualism," with "humanism," with the vernacular languages, with the working of "natural forces," with the lay rather than the clerical mind. Grounded in nature itself rather than in any notion of the divine, it is, accordingly, "realistic," flexible, "unspeculative," "earth-bound," reflecting the "ordinary laws of nature" and the natural diversities and "variations of human development," pressing itself imperatively upon those who are open to the promptings of "empirical" or "inductive" reason—or responsive, as he puts it elsewhere,[27] to "the laws of human natural reasoning."

In contrast with the homely features of this naturalistic norm, the rival "descending" thesis is of grander mien, conveying a sense of majesty, evoking a feeling of awe. For it stands out as extremely "doctrinaire," a characteristic product of the clerical mind, associated with "the Latin of the academics," with the "a-natural," the "objective," the "extra-human," the world of spirit, the divine. It is "sophisticated," "monolithic," "a rarified doctrine," a "speculative theorem" deduced from "abstract principles," the outcome, in fact, of rigid adherence to "the laws of logical reasoning."[28] This being so, the fact that it succeeded in dominating Byzantine political thinking and in displacing the ascending theme in southern and western Europe so effectively and for so long[29] clearly calls for some extraordinary explanation. And that explanation Ullmann finds in the influence exerted upon political thinking by Christianity in general and by certain New Testament motifs in particular. Thus, given the papal claim to a "direct link" with divinity, "a provable title-deed" provided by the very words of Christ as reported in the Bible, it is no accident that in medieval papal government we meet with "the descending theme

---

[26] For the contrasting words and expressions which he characteristically uses of the two theses see *Principles*, pp. 236–37, 304–305; *History*, pp. 116, 159–60, 230–31; *Kingship*, pp. 6–9, 41–42, 53–54, 71, 95–96, 112, 115, 163; *Individual*, pp. 14, 53, 55, 57, 59, 61, 66, 95–96, 98, 101–104, 115–18, 123, 129, 131–32, 141.

[27] *Principles*, pp. 105–6.

[28] I.e. as opposed to "the laws of human natural reasoning." See the texts cited above, notes 26 and 27.

[29] So much so, indeed, that Ullmann, *Individual*, p. 46, can even refer to it as "the properly medieval doctrine." Cf. *History*, p. 160.

in its purest form."[30] Again, although "the unadulterated ascending thesis" prevailing in republican Rome was modified under the Principate, it was only "through the adoption of Christianity" that it finally gave way to "the fully-fledged descending (theocratic)" doctrine which "gained momentum from the late fourth century onwards" and triumphed at Byzantium.[31] Finally, in the early Middle Ages it was again "as a result of the overpowering influence of Christianity" that the Germanic people's adopted the descending or theocratic theory "inherent in Christian doctrine" and that the ascending theme was "driven underground, not to emerge as a theoretical proposition until the late thirteenth century."[32] It is true that the Western theocratic monarchs who thus emerged lacked, like their Byzantine counterparts, that direct link with divinity which the papacy possessed in its Biblical title-deeds. Nevertheless, the West Frankish bishops of the ninth century, by introducing the practice of anointing and crowning these monarchs, did much to remedy that deficiency, effecting nothing less, indeed, than "the visible and concrete sacralization of the kingly office." By so doing, they finally succeeded then in substituting "the ecclesiastical unction and coronation as king-creating agencies in place of conquest and election." So that, from the mid-ninth century onwards, these Western monarchs, unlike their Byzantine counterparts, enjoyed in the sacrament of unction an outward and public sign of the divine grace transmitted to them as "kings by the grace of God," *via* the mediation of the clerical hierarchy.[33]

Such, then, is the general conceptual framework upon which Ullmann constructs his interpretation of medieval political thinking. It is easy enough to perceive its value as an explanatory tool when confronting the differences between the medieval political vision and those of the modern world or of classical antiquity; or, again, when confronting the more specific differences between Scandinavia and Southern and Western Europe, or between the earlier and later Middle Ages. But within the outlines of his main ideological drama Ullmann inserts, as it were, a sub-plot, and, modifying somewhat his typol-

---

[30] *Principles*, p. 23. On the alleged Biblical underpinnings of the descending theme, see the remarks below, pp. 45–47.

[31] *Principles*, pp. 21–22.

[32] *History*, pp. 13, 57–58, 91, 130; *Principles*, p. 23.

[33] *Kingship*, esp. pp. 62–64, 72–73, 80–81. Thus "the unction and coronation of Charles the Bald at Orléans in 848 marked the birth of the fully-fledged sacral-theocratic kingship in Western realms."

ogy by contrasting feudal forms of monarchy with theocratic, he uses it to explain the differences between the late-medieval English and French conceptions of kingship, and even to propose his own solution to one of the most persistently and hotly-disputed issues of Bractonian scholarship—namely, the precise import of Bracton's view of kingship.[34] This is, perhaps, a little more surprising and it is, I would suggest, by grasping the nettle, by focussing first on the sub-plot, on Ullmann's Bracton and the historical context in which he understands him, that we begin our assessment of the degree to which his conceptual apparatus succeeds in illuminating the intricacies of medieval political thinking.

I

a. *Bracton on Kingship*

According to Ullmann, the problem with some of the most recent studies on Bracton's view of kingship is that they have grievously underestimated the impact upon his thinking of feudal law and practice. Rectify this imbalance, and the apparent inconsistency between Bracton's "absolutism" and "constitutionalism" becomes readily explicable. For Bracton's king was in fact an "amphibious creature" (*Zwitterding*), at once both theocratic monarch and feudal king. It is the theocratic function, therefore, that Bracton has in mind when "he makes the king the true sovereign by saying that he has no equal and no superior; that no one may question the legality of his acts; that the king is the vicar of God, because the king's power *solius Dei est* [is from God alone]."[35] On the other hand, it is the

---

[34] *Principles*, pp. 176–78, 310–11, and his lengthier statement (cited henceforth as *Tijdschrift*) in *Tijdschrift voor Rechtsgeschiedenis*, XXXI (1963), 289–99, a review-article on Wiebke Fesefeldt, *Englische Staatstheorie des 13. Jahrhunderts: Henry de Bracton und sein Werk* (Göttingen, 1962). For the more recent lines of interpretation concerning Bracton's theory of kingship see, in addition to Fesefeldt, Fritz Schulz, "Bracton on Kingship," *English Historical Review*, CCXXXVI (Jan. 1945), 136–76; Ernst Kantorowicz, *The King's Two Bodies* (Princeton, 1957), pp. 143–92; Brian Tierney, "Bracton on Government," *Speculum*, XXXVIII (No. 2, 1963), 295–317; Ewart Lewis, "King above Law? 'Quod principi placuit' in Bracton," *ibid.*, XXXIX (No. 2, 1964), 240–69; Gaines Post, "Bracton on Kingship," *Tulane Law Review*, XLII (No. 3, 1968), 519–54.

[35] *Principles*, p. 176, citing Henry de Bracton, *De Legibus et Consuetudinibus Angliae*, fol. 107–107b; *Bracton: On the Laws and Customs of England*, rev. ed. and trans. by Samuel E. Thorne (5 vols., Cambridge, Mass., 1968–), II, 305. All references will

feudal function that is involved when Bracton insists that the king
is subject to the law, that he cannot make or change the law without the assent of his barons,[36] that he has a superior not only in
God and the law but also in the earls and barons of his court—for,
on this last claim, that made by the famous and disputed passage
known usually as the *Addicio de cartis*, Ullmann brushes aside the
problem of authorship as making "little difference" on the grounds
that the passage in question "is in Bracton's temper."[37] Moreover,
it is again with reference to these two royal functions, theocratic and
feudal, that Bracton in his discussion of franchises "very clearly distinguishes" between "governance" (*gubernaculum*) and "jurisdiction" (*jurisdictio*). For *gubernaculum* denotes the theocratic sphere, within which
the king as vicar of God and free, therefore, to exercise his "executive
power" to the full, has "no equal, much less a superior" and "is not
responsible to anyone" so that *"no compulsion can be envisaged"* (italics
mine). And *jurisdictio* denotes the feudal sphere within which the king
is bound by the law. And to say that, Ullmann adds, is to say also
that "the authority of making and therefore changing the law does
not reside solely with him, but with the magnates *and* him."[38]

Now despite the persistence among contemporary Bractonian scholars of some highly intricate disagreement concerning the meaning
and significance of these crucial texts on kingship, their interpretations have been harmonious enough to underscore the dissonance
of Ullmann's approach. Its peculiarities, certainly, are both numerous and striking. Thus, taken seriatim: In the first place, the force-

---

be given to this edition. Happily it maintains the same pagination as the Woodbine
edition of which it is a revision. Cf. *Tijdschrift*, 295.

[36] *Principles*, pp. 176–77; *Tijdschrift*, 295–96—citing *De Legibus*, fols. 1 (II, 19), 1b
(II, 21), 5b (II, 33), 107–107b (II, 305). In relation to the references to the *lex regia*
in fols. 1 (II, 19) and 107–107b (II, 305) Ullmann further argues that Bracton "tries
to reconcile the contemporary English point of view with that of Roman law, . . . by
equating the *populus* of the Roman law passage with the feudal baronage in England."—
Principles, p. 176; cf. p. 191 and *Tijdschrift*, 296. The reference is to two Roman
legal texts which assert that the emperor's legislative enactments possess the force
of law precisely because by a "regal law" the people has conferred upon him all
its authority and power. See *Digest*, I, 4, 1; *Institutes*, I, 2, 6.

[37] *Principles*, p. 176 note 3, referring to *De Legibus*, fol. 34 (II, 110). Cf. *History*,
p. 153, where he clearly assumes "Bracton's view that the king was under the law"
to involve the notion that the barons "had become partners of the law-creative
process" and possessed, as a result, the "legal possibility to *force* the king" to observe
the law (Italics mine).

[38] *Principles*, pp. 177–78 (Italics in the original); *Tijdschrift*, 296–97. The crucial
text is *De Legibus*, fol. 55b (II, 166).

ful insistence on the importance of feudal conceptions in Bracton's theory of kingship is puzzling. Maitland may well have portrayed him as a blundering incompetent when it came to Roman law, no more indeed than a self-taught beginner, but the steady accumulation of scholarly evidence in subsequent years has finally imposed the conclusion that Maitland, self-confessedly himself no Romanist, was simply mistaken."[39] That on this point Ullmann should turn to him for support, therefore, is odd, the more so in that nearly all the crucial texts are drawn from the sections of Bracton's treatise which even Maitland thought to have been Romanist in inspiration.[40] In the second place, Ullmann renders folio 107 as saying that "the king is the vicar of God, *because* the king's power *solius Dei est*" (italics mine). But this is misleading. According to the text, it is only the power to do justice that is from God; only in so doing is the king the Vicar of God. "[T]he power of *injuria*, however, is from the devil," and when the king "deviates into injustice" he becomes, accordingly, the minister not of God but of the devil.[41] Here, as so often elsewhere, Bracton's predominant concern is not with the source of royal power as Ullmann would have us believe, but rather with the use to which that power is put. Ullmann's forcing of the text, then, is a good illustration of his persistent tendency to focus on efficient rather than on final causes.[42] In the third place, when Bracton asserts, as he frequently does, that the king is "under the law," he is concerned not with the location in the realm of legislative competence but with the king's exercise of his executive and judicial power. Ullmann, however, more or less equates the king's subordination to the law with the fact that he can neither make nor alter the law without the consent of the barons.[43] And it is this, presum-

---

[39] Frederic W. Maitland ed., *Bracton and Azo* (London, 1895), "Introduction," pp. xiv–xxiv; cf. the definitive judgment of Thorne, summing up the work of Woodbine, H. Kantorowicz, Schulz and others, and adding thereto his own findings concerning the nature of Bracton's text and the number of excerpts from both the *Digest* and the *Code* which it contains—*Bracton: On the Laws and Customs of England*, I, "Translator's Introduction," pp. xxxii–xlviii. Bracton now emerges (xxxvi) as "a civil lawyer who had received his formal training at a university."

[40] I.e. *De Legibus*, fols. 1–10, 98b–107, 112–15 (II, 19–47, 282–305, 317–26). See Maitland, *Bracton and Azo*, pp. xv–xvi; Ullmann, *Principles*, p. 311. Cf. the remarks of Schulz, "Bracton on Kingship," 175–76: "It is noteworthy that no part of this exposition is influenced by feudal law."

[41] *De Legibus*, fol. 107b (II, 305).

[42] See the remarks below, pp. 68–70.

[43] *Principles*, pp. 176, 178; *Tijdschrift*, 295–96. For the relevant Bractonian texts,

ably, which leads him to assert, without any support at all from Bracton's text, that when Bracton cites the *lex regia* he equates the feudal baronage of England with the people (*populus*), which, according to the Roman law, confers all its power and authority on the prince."[44] In the fourth place, a related point, to be able to assume, as does Ullmann, that the Bractonian king's subordination to the law necessarily implies his subordination also to the coercive power of a superior, one must be prepared to establish either Bracton's authorship of the *Addicio de cartis* or at least the claim that that passage is truly "in Bracton's temper." But Ullmann himself makes no attempt to do so, nor does he cite any of the attempts made by others. Instead (and oddly) he contents himself with giving a reference to Maitland and McIlwain who had both in fact concluded that the passage was "no part of the original text" and who had doubted its Bractonian authorship precisely because it ran counter to the position repeatedly stated elsewhere in the treatise.[45] In the fifth place, I would concur in Ewart Lewis's judgment that the crucial distinction between *gubernaculum* and *jurisdictio*, which, on McIlwain's authority, Ullmann like many another finds in Bracton, is "the product of McIlwain's classificatory acumen rather than of Bracton's."[46] Bracton's text will simply not sustain it—no more, indeed (as I have argued elsewhere), than will the texts of those seventeenth-century

---

see above, note 36. Cf. the remarks of Tierney, "Bracton on Government," 304–305; Lewis, "King Above Law?," 263, 268–9.

[44] See above, note 36. Lewis, "King Above Law?," 248 note 28, comments: "Since I cannot imagine what this means and how it is related to Bracton's words, I do not know how to refute it."

[45] *Principles*, p. 176. Cf. Frederic W. Maitland, ed., *Bracton's Note Book* (3 vols., London, 1887), I, 29–33; Charles H. McIlwain, *Constitutionalism: Ancient and Modern* (rev. ed., Ithaca, N.Y., 1958), pp. 157–8 note 2. For attempts to defend Bracton's authorship of the *Addicio* or, if not, to interpret the views it expresses as consistent with those expressed by Bracton in the other texts, see Ludwik Ehrlich, *Proceedings Against the Crown (1217–1377)*, in Sir Paul Vinogradoff ed., *Oxford Studies in Social and Legal History*, VI (Oxford, 1921), 49 note 4, 202–205; H. Kantorowicz, *Bractonian Problems* (Glasgow, 1941), pp. 49–52; Tierney, "Bracton on Government," 310–16. For an interesting recent comment, Charles M. Radding, "The Origins of Bracton's *Addicio de Cartis*," *Speculum*, XLIV (No. 2, 1969), 239–46.

[46] Lewis, "King Above Law?," 266; cf. Tierney's lengthier criticism, "Bracton on Government," 306–10. Also Post, "Bracton on Kingship," 545; Fesefeldt, *Englische Staatstheorie*, pp. 73–4, note 84, and Schulz, "Bracton on Kingship," 172, who certainly found no such distinction in *De Legibus*, fol. 55b (II, 166). For McIlwain's analysis and his broader application of the distinction to early-modern constitutional history in general, see *Constitutionalism: Ancient and Modern*, chs. 4 and 5, pp. 67–122.

English authors in which McIlwain also detected the same distinction.[47] In any case, and in the sixth place, even if McIlwain were right and the Bractonian text could sustain the weight of his distinction, it would have to be noted that with Ullmann that distinction takes on a somewhat different meaning.[48] Thus, unlike McIlwain, who did not regard the *Addicio de cartis* as authentically Bractonian, he seems to subsume under *jurisdictio* the element of coercive political control furnished by the claim that the king had a superior in the barons of his court. Again, McIlwain's use of the distinction was correlated with his more fundamental belief that medieval kings lacked a true law-making capacity, being subordinate to the law precisely because law, in its highest sense, was something "found" not "made."[49] Ullmann, on the other hand, has no such doubts.[50] His central concern is with the source of "law-creating competence" and of governmental authority, and, though he does so rather loosely, he correlates *gubernaculum* and *jurisdictio* with contrasting theses of legislative competence—the "descending" and the "feudal." Finally, whereas McIlwain regarded Bracton's distinction as "nothing but a commonplace of late-thirteenth century European political thought" and as lying at the very heart of medieval constitutionalism in general,[51] Ullmann certainly does not. For him, indeed, the whole point of focussing on Bracton is that he delineates the characteristics of a type of feudal kingship peculiarly English, one that stands out in sharp contrast to the theocratic monarchy of late-medieval France, one that bears witness to the profound impact of feudalism on English constitutional history from Magna Carta onwards.

Now, if at this point we pause to ask what more general lessons can be gleaned from the markedly peculiar fashion in which Ullmann

---

[47] Francis Oakley, "Jacobean Political Theology: The Absolute and Ordinary Powers of the King." *Journal of the History of Ideas*, XXIX (No. 3, 1968), 323–46 (below, ch. 8).

[48] As he himself seems partly to recognize when he speaks of being able to "go a small step further" than McIlwain—*Principles*, p. 177; cf. *Tijdschrift*, 297 note 28.

[49] It was "a substantive customary law within which private rights and royal powers were set"—Lewis, "King Above Law?," 241; cf. Tierney, "Bracton on Government," 305, and the incisive critique of McIlwain's view by Frederic Cheyette, "Custom, Case Law, and Medieval 'Constitutionalism': A re-examination," *Political Science Quarterly*, LXXVIII (No. 3, 1963), 362–90. McIlwain himself states his view clearly in *The Growth of Political Thought in the West*. (New York, 1932), pp. 170–75, 185–95.

[50] See esp. his remarks in the review cited below, note 161 (esp. at pp. 363–64).

[51] McIlwain, *Constitutionalism: Ancient and modern*, pp. 77–78; note, too, his claim on p. 74: "The riddle of Bracton is in reality the riddle of our medieval constitutionalism."

handles these Bractonian materials, the key to the' answer lies in recognizing clearly the rôle he has already assigned to feudalism when
he approaches not only Bracton but also the history of the English
and French monarchies in the later Middle Ages. That rôle is an
important one. Having depicted the world of medieval political thinking as an arena dominated by the clash between two diametrically
opposed and mutually exclusive conceptions, theocratic and populist, and having defined constitutional government not simply as "the
limitation of government by law"[52] but as "the establishment of controls, measures and checks on the exercise of theocratic monarchic
functions," he is understandably forced to conclude that a transition
from a "royal theocracy" which knows no control and embodies in
itself the principles of legislative sovereignty to "a constitutional or
limited monarchy" in which populist consental elements could have
their place "lay notionally [i.e. conceptually] beyond what was humanly
possible."[53] This being so, he is led to stress the presence, even during the early-medieval theocratic phase, of factors by definition alien
to theocracy and capable ultimately of easing the passage to late-
medieval populism. Among these factors, feudalism stands out as
being of crucial importance.

That it should do so is readily comprehensible. Faithful to his fundamental preoccupation with the source of "law-making competence"
and to his understanding of constitutionalism in terms of sanction
or coercive control, Ullmann lays great emphasis on the fact that
the king, set as theocrat in lonely and impregnable eminence above
his subjects, his will serving as their law, is as feudal suzerain removed
to a "fundamentally different" level. On that level he is bound by
"the contractual nature of the feudal nexus," limited in his governing and in the making or changing of law by the fact that he must
needs "proceed by consultation and agreement with the other par-
ties in the feudal contract" if he does not wish to provoke them into
invoking the sanction which is legitimately theirs to invoke—namely,
the right of resistance.[54] Thus Ullmann is willing to speculate that

---

[52] This is McIlwain's definition, *ibid.*, pp. 21–22: ". . . [I]n all its successive phases,
constitutionalism has one essential quality: it is legal limitation on government; it
is the antithesis of arbitrary rule; its opposite is despotic government, the government of will instead of law."

[53] An affirmation which, given Ullmann's definitional structure, would appear to
be tautologous. See *Principles*, pp. 24 and 150; cf. *History*, p. 146.

[54] *Principles*, pp. 150–53. Note the hesitation on p. 24 where he says that "in

"a further analysis of the passage from the populist kind of kingship to the medieval king might well show that a good many elements of this earlier kingship were transformed and reappeared on the feudal side of the medieval king."[55] And throughout he is insistent on the contribution which feudalism made, "where it became an effective means of government," in fostering "those elements which were later to reappear as true populism" and in smoothing "the transition from royal theocracy to constitutional or limited monarchy." Hence the ringing assertion which with little change he repeats no less than five times in these studies: "The road leading from the theocratic *point d'appui* to constitutional government is bloodstained and signposted by revolutions; the road leading from the feudal *point d'appui* to constitutionalism is marked by steady evolution."[56]

This approach, it should be acknowledged, works well enough when Ullmann uses it to elucidate such documents as Magna Carta or the coronation oath of Edward II.[57] But it works less well with Bracton, and it is only when one recognizes the tenacity of Ullmann's commitment to it that such oddities in his interpretation of Bracton as his endorsement (and modification) of McIlwain's questionable distinction or his handling of Bracton's references to the *lex regia*, or, again, his insistence on the doctrinal authenticity of the *Addicio de cartis* fall into a comprehensible and revealing pattern. For the texts are being stretched in fact on a conceptual framework sufficiently

---

itself feudalism was indifferent to either the theocratic or the populist form of government."

[55] For this and for the quotations that follow, see *Principles*, pp. 24, 152–53 and 215. Cf. "Law and the Medieval Historian," 59; *Individual*, p. 81.

[56] *Principles*, pp. 24 and 152–54 (cf. 211); *History*, pp. 148–49; *Individual*, p. 69; "Law and the Medieval Historian," 59 (an incomplete version). Cf. *Papst und König*, p. 55.

[57] In saying this I do not wish to imply that Ullmann's readings of those texts (and esp. of *Magna Carta*, cap. 39) are necessarily incontestable or have not, in fact, been contested, but simply that they clearly fall within the range of plausible scholarly option. And this I do not believe to be true of the way in which he reads several of the crucial Bractonian texts discussed above. For Ullmann's understanding of *Magna Carta*, cap. 39 and of the fourth clause of Edward II's coronation oath, see *Principles*, pp. 164–73, 186–89; *History*, pp. 149–53; *Individual*, pp. 70–79; cf. the introduction to his edition of *Liber Regie Capelle*, Henry Bradshaw Society, XCII (London, 1961), pp. 29–33, and *Papst und König*, pp. 60–64. For differing interpretations, see e.g. James C. Holt, *Magna Carta* (Cambridge, 1965), pp. 226–30; Percy E. Schramm, *A History of the English Coronation Oath*, trans. Leopold G. Wickham Legg (Oxford, 1937), pp. 206–11; H.G. Richardson, "The English Coronation Oath," *Speculum*, XXIV (No. 1, 1949), 44–75; Bertie Wilkinson, *Constitutional History of Medieval England: 1216–1399* (3 vols., London, 1948–58), II, 86–107.

ill-fitting to cause no little distress. In order to fit that framework
Bracton simply *has* to be concerned with the source of legislative
competence, his theory of kingship *has* to have a strong feudal component, his subordination of king to law *has* to be the outcome of
that feudal component—this last claim even though the texts themselves characteristically link that subordination not with the existence
of any coercive sanction, or with the source of the law, or even with
the fact that the king as suzerain is bound by the terms of the feudal contract, but rather with what Ullmann would call the "theocratic" function. Not that Bracton himself uses that expression. Instead,
he tells us that "there is no *rex* where will rules rather than *lex*."
Without equal in his realm and freed from all this-worldly legal
coercion, the king must still reckon with the vengeance which God
visits upon the unjust ruler. For it is only insofar and as long as he
does the work of justice that he can truly claim to be "the minister
and vicar of God on earth." It is his duty, therefore, to follow the
example of Christ, "whose vicegerent on earth he is," and freely to
submit himself to the law.[58] So that, once again, the predominant
concern is with final rather than efficient causes, with the end or
purpose of authority rather than with its source.

b. *Kingship in England and France*

Of course, the question which immediately arises is to what degree
Ullmann's handling of the Bractonian texts is characteristic of his
work as a whole. Certainly, if we broaden our focus just enough to
include along with Bracton the context in which he is understood—
namely, that of the growing divergence in character during the later
Middle Ages of the English and French monarchies—the drawbacks
of Ullmann's approach are again disturbingly evident.[59] It is true

---

[58] *De Legibus*, fols. 5b (II, 33) and 107–107b (II, 305–306); cf. fol. 55b (II, 166).
On this point see Ernst Kantorowicz, *King's Two Bodies*, pp. 155–59; Tierney, "Bracton
on Government," 296–305; Lewis, "King Above Law?," 260–65; and especially,
Post, "Bracton on Kingship," 519–54. Although these recent commentators disagree
among themselves as to whether Bracton regarded the king as in some sense "unfettered by the laws" (*legibus solutus*) and his obligation to obey the law as legal or
moral, they do concur in affirming the connection between the king's "theocratic"
status and his submission to the law. Similarly, they all stress the degree to which
Bracton's discussion of this point is conditioned by Civilian commentaries on *Inst.*
I, 2, 6; *Digest*, I, 4, 1 (the *Quod principi placuit* text) and *Cod.* I, 14, 4 (the *Digna vox*).
[59] It is this phase of his interpretation rather than any other that has drawn fire
most persistently from his critics.

that the seventeenth century finally witnessed the emergence of contrasting forms of monarchy, absolute and constitutional, in France and England, but Ullmann himself indicates that "at the turn of the twelfth and thirteenth centuries" the similarities between them outweighed the differences, and this would certainly still hold true during Bracton's lifetime. Doubtless, if we insist, as does Ullmann, that true constitutionalism involves not merely the limitation of executive power by law but also the presence of coercive sanction, the operation of effective institutional controls, then the case for characterizing the two late-medieval monarchies, French and English, as "absolute" and "constitutional" respectively becomes concomitantly (if not unquestionably) stronger. Thus Bryce Lyon rejects the alleged "constitutionality" of the late-medieval French kings precisely because "it was not theory, not professed belief in tradition and established institutions and law, not admiration of a saintly monarch, and not counsel from a council, but political pressure become constant and institutionalized that made medieval kings constitutional."[60] Distinguished historians, however, can still contrive to debate, and in good faith, that most intriguing of questions: Was Philip IV a constitutional king?[61] And given all the subtleties and complexities in the respective historical development of the two monarchies, the relevance of factors rooted deep in the disparate national histories, the importance of matters as fundamental and intractable as the differing geographic extent of the two kingdoms, to attempt, as does Ullmann, to cram all these variables within the narrow confines of the theocratic-feudal typology is truly breathtaking.

After all, even if we concede the fact that under Louis IX the French monarchy took on an especially strong religious coloration, even if we admit (with Fawtier) the propriety of characterizing Philip IV as a "devotee of the religion of monarchy,"[62] may we not still

[60] Bryce Lyon, "What Made a Medieval King constitutional?," in T.A. Sandquist and M.R. Powicke eds., *Essays in Medieval History presented to Bertie Wilkinson* (Toronto, 1969), 175. But for a forceful counter-case in relation to the French kings of the late-fifteenth century, see J. Russell Major's succinct statement, "The French Renaissance Monarchy as Seen through the Estates General," *Studies in the Renaissance*, IX (1962), 113–25.

[61] See Joseph R. Strayer, "Philip the Fair—A 'Constitutional' King," *American Historical Review*, LXII (Oct., 1956), 18–32; Lyon, "What Made a Medieval King Constitutional?", 157–75. Cf. Ferdinand Lot and Robert Fawtier, *Histoire des institutions françaises au Moyen Âge: Institutions royales* (2 vols., Paris, 1958), II, 555–57.

[62] Robert Fawtier, *L'Europe Occidentale de 1270 à 1380*, Part I (vol. VI; pt. 1 of *Histoire Générale*, ed. Gustave Glotz, Paris, 1940), p. 301.

cavil at the lengths to which Ullmann takes his insistence on the
"unparalleled accentuation of the theocratic kingship" in France, and
begin to wonder, indeed, if we have been mistaken in believing that
English kings right down to the eighteenth century had themselves
continued by their sacred touch to dispense cures for "the king's
evil?"[63] Again, even if we concede that feudalism did indeed flourish
in England and that representative institutions did indeed succeed
in thrusting permanent roots into English soil, may we not still query
such tendentious contrasts as that between "the feudally soaked
English ground" and "the feudal veneer with which the thirteenth-
century French kings knew how to surround themselves?"[64] And are
we not justified in beginning to wonder if, after all, the Estates
General never did succeed in wielding real power, or, more important, if, in return for a grudging consent to subsidies, provincial
assemblies never did manage to drive hard bargains with French
royal officials?

But, then, these are regrettably untidy phenomena. Ullmann's
equations, it must be remembered, have already been drawn, and
their terms admit of no modification. The French monarchy which
emerged in the early modern era was an absolute one; in later-
medieval France, therefore, "feudal kingship" *must* have been "stunted,"
theocratic kingship *must* have been accentuated. And, given the even-
tual outcome, the reverse *must* clearly have been the case in England.
Moreover, "the doctrine of representation containing" in its essence
all the features of the ascending (populist) conception of government
and law" and being, indeed, its offshoot, it simply *had to be* "antag-
onistic to the whole tenor and substance of theocratic kingship."
Between such ideas of representation and a "correctly understood
theocratic conception" "no reconciliation . . . [was] . . . possible." Hence,
the representative assemblies of medieval France must needs be dismissed as "populist phantoms" possessed only of "pseudo-functions."[65]
Hence, too, the vitality of the English parliament must needs be
accounted for by the fact that its roots were feudal, and the easy

---

[63] See Marc Bloch, *Les rois thaumaturges: Étude sur le caractère surnaturel attribué à la
puissance royale particulièrement en France et en Angleterre* (Strasbourg and Paris, 1924).
[64] *Individual*, p. 92; *History*, p. 227; *Principles*, p. 194; cf. 202–203, where he speaks
of "the stunting of feudal kingship in France" and of "the tenuous feudal relationship between the king and the baronage."
[65] *Principles*, pp. 190–91, 207–10; cf. "Law and the Medieval Historian," 64–65.

penetration into England of the "idea of representation" by the fact that it was "no strange bedfellow" to feudalism.[66]

The peculiarities which emerge in Ullmann's treatment of medieval representation, however, have a broader significance and one that points us beyond the subsidiary plot on which we have been focussing. His tacit assumption that. the consent which representatives were called upon to give had necessarily to be "popular or sovereign" rather than "compulsory," "procedural" or "judicial-conciliar,"[67] his related assumption that the initiative of kings could hardly have played a role, therefore, in the development of authentic representative machinery, his unwillingness to admit that the initial establishment and success of such machinery might well reflect the effective strength of kings rather than the limitations on their power, above all, his failure to note the emergence of representative procedures on the political level both in the papal states and in the constituting of provincial and general councils of the Latin Church—in the very heart, therefore, of theocratic-descending territory—,[68] these shortcomings raise issues that take us beyond the provincial perspectives dictated by the tension between theocratic and feudal kingship and lead on into the broader arena dominated by the more fundamental antagonism between the descending or theocratic and ascending or populist conceptions. And to this fundamental antagonism,

---

[66] *Principles*, pp. 189–90; *History*, p. 154.

[67] The terminology is that of Gaines Post whose fundamental studies have done so much to illuminate the development and role of medieval representaive ideas and institutions. These studies, which appeared in article form from 1934 onwards, have now been collected and reprinted in his *Studies in Medieval Legal Thought: Public Law and the State, 1100–1322* (Princeton, 1964), pp. 3–328, 562–70. It is one of the more striking oddities of the books under discussion that in them Ullmann seems nowhere to have cited these studies of Post's. In the second edition or *Principles*, however, there are (309–10) a couple of condescending references to a later study of Post's which Ullmann had also criticized rather severely in *Historische Zeitschrift*, CCII (No. 1, 1966), 104–6. Cf. the work in question, Gaines Post, "Status Regis," in William M. Bowsky ed., *Studies in Medieval and Renaissance History*, I (Lincoln, Nebr., 1964), 3–103.

[68] Thus, e.g., already in 1200 and 1207 Innocent III summoned to Rome to meet with his *curia* mandated representatives from the communes of the Marches. He also summoned proctors to represent convents and cathedral chapters at the Fourth Lateran Council in 1215. See Post, *Studies*, pp. 85–90; Antonio Marongiu, *Medieval Parliaments: A Comparative Study*, trans. S.J. Woolf (London, 1968), pp. 117–18. And yet, in *Individual*, p. 58, Ullmann can speak of "the idea of representation, which within the descending scheme of government, could never make its appearance." Cf. *Principles*, pp. 20–21.

the principal plot, as it were, in Ullmann's ideological drama, we must now turn.

II

As his treatment of representation and representative institutions sug-gests, the value of Ullmann's interpretative schema is undercut by his failure to perceive that "consent" is a word with more than one meaning and by his related insistence on denying it any role within those forms of monarchy—papal, imperial, "national"—which he wishes to call "theocratic" and to view as manifestations exclusively of the descending theme. Hence, having asserted that it is in the papal government that we encounter the theocratic-descending theme "in its purest form," he is understandably reluctant to admit that late-medieval Conciliarism marked any unambiguous assertion of his ascending theme. But noting the fact that his interpretation of medieval papalist ideology has already been subjected to detailed criticism,[69] and noting, too, that I myself have elsewhere taken exception to his view of Conciliar theory,[70] I propose here to exclude from consid-eration what he has to say about ecclesiastical government and to concentrate instead on his picture of the rise of imperial and royal theocracy and of the challenge posed to it by that later re-emergence of the ascending or populist theme. More precisely, I propose to focus first on what he has to say about the emergence and re-emergence of the fully-fledged theocratic-descending theme in the latter years of the Roman empire and in the monarchies of the early-medieval Latin West; second, on what he has to say about the decisive reasser-tion of the populist-ascending theme by the Aristotelian thinkers of the later Middle Ages.

---

[69] See A.M. Stickler, "Concerning the Political Theories of the Medieval Canonists," *Traditio*, VIII (1949–51), 450–63 (criticizing Ullmann's *Medieval Papalism: The Political Theories of the Medieval Canonists* [London, 1949]); Friedrich Kempf, "Die päpstliche Gewalt in der mittelalterlichen Welt: Eine Auseinandersetzung mit Walter Ullmann," *Miscellanea Historiae Pontificiae*, XXI (1959), 117–69 (criticizing Ullmann's *Growth*).

[70] Francis Oakley, "Figgis, Constance, and the Divines of Paris," *American Historical Review*, LXXV (Dec., 1969), 376–86, criticizing the second thoughts on Conciliarism expressed in *Principles*, pp. 313–15 (in additional notes appended to the second edi-tion), and in *History*, pp. 219–25. Earlier on he had been willing to classify Conciliarism as a "classic application" of the populist-ascending theme—see "Law and the Medieval Historian," 41; *Principles*, p. 289.

a. *The Triumph of Theocracy*

Although Ullmann nowhere really addresses himself to them, he is apparently willing to concede some role to the Principate and to "the sacral nature of pagan Germanic kingship," respectively, in promoting the ultimate victory of the theocratic-descending theme in the Roman empire and later on in the early-medieval Latin West.[71] But, as we have seen, the truly vital factor he believes to have been the influence of Christianity. It was, he says, "the overpowering force of the Christian idea" which "itself was responsible for the very institution of theocratic kingship." By the Christian "idea" or "theme" he means, in effect, the Pauline teaching that "there is no power but of God," a teaching which, in his discussion of medieval kingship by the grace of God, he links up with the other Pauline statement: "What I am, I am by the grace of God."[72] And at once we encounter a puzzle of major proportions concerning the way in which he goes about constructing his conceptual framework.

When speaking of "the principles with which and on which the medieval papacy" functioned, he is careful to insist that "the prerequisite . . . for a proper historical presentation . . . is to see the institution from within itself." Thus "the question whether a particular papal tenet can be squared with biblical data" is one that belongs, not to the historian but to the theologian. The question which "comes within the precinct of the historian's quest" is a rather different one—namely, whether or not "the papacy based the tenet on the Bible."[73] Now Ullmann does not repeat this *caveat* when he comes to discuss medieval theocratic monarchy,[74] but even had he done so, we should still be entitled to accuse him of using this attractively economical division of scholarly labor to avoid facing up to a quite properly historical question, and an important one at that.

In some of his most interesting passages he illustrates the ingenious ways in which medieval propagandists aligned on the side of the "theocratic" idea the Pauline texts to which he refers. But nowhere

---

[71] *Principles*, pp. 22–23.
[72] *History*, pp. 91, 53–54, where he cites also John 19:10–11.
[73] *Principles*, p. 29.
[74] Though one remark in his latest book at least suggests that he might now wish to do so. Thus in *Kingship*, p. 17, he says: "In pursuit of the ecclesiological theme Frankish society was to be clothed in the basic characteristics of christian religion *as understood at the time*." (Italics mine)

does he really explain what it was that disposed them to manipu-
late those texts in such a fashion. And yet this cries out for an explanation. For despite the use to which they could often be (and frequently
were) put during the medieval and early modern centuries, these
texts say nothing at all about monarchy, still less about absolute
monarchy. Nor, Passerin d'Entrèves has insisted,[75] does Romans XIII
necessarily say anything more about the historical origin or derivation of power than it does about its form. Instead, it simply asserts
that there is something sacred about the authority which rulers possess. Moreover, it reflects only the most positive of the several attitudes towards political authority which find expression in the New
Testament. Side by side with it should be placed those other New
Testament texts which cover a whole doctrinal spectrum, ranging
from the more guarded affirmations of Peter's First Epistle to the
blank hostility of the Apocalypse of John, which, in the name of the
Kingship of God, denounces as Satanic the blasphemously deified
emperors of Rome.[76] If these texts are to be regarded as any less
"Christian" than those of Paul, then the reason for so discriminating should clearly be stated. As it is, their existence should serve to
remind us that New Testament political views (including the Pauline)
were predicated upon the assumption that the empire was a heathen power. It should serve to remind us, too, that when compared
with the classical political vision, those views are markedly negative
in tone—certainly ill-designed to engineer the triumph of the type
of theocratic-descending conception which Ullmann describes. A far
better index of the nature of their influence, it may be urged, is the

---

[75] Alexander Passerin d'Entrèves, *The Notion of the State: An Introduction to Political
Theory* (Oxford, 1967), pp. 182–90—see esp. 187: "[T]he excellence of monarchy
in no way follows from the sacredness of authority. The gist of the Christian view
is simply that all legitimately constituted power has a sacred character; that whatever its historical origin or form, it must be viewed as ultimately going back to God's
will, and hence as possessing, under certain conditions, divine sanction." Given these
views, d'Entrèves has understandably questioned the link which Ullmann attempts
to forge between Romans xiii and theocratic kingship. See his review of *Principles*
in *Rivista Storica Italiana*, LXXV (fasc. 2, 1963), 385–90.
[76] I Peter 2:13–17 (cf. I Tim. 2:1–2, Titus 3:1); John, 12:31, 14:30–31, 16:11;
I John, 5:18–19; and esp. Rev. 12 and 13, (cf. Rev. 17:10, 12–14) where the Roman
Empire is portrayed as a Beast deriving its authority from Satan. See the interesting analysis by L. Cerfaux, "Le Conflit entre Dieu et le souverain divinisé dans
l'Apocalypse de Jean," in *The Sacral Kingship: Contributions to the Central Theme of the
VIIIth International Congress for the History of Religions* (Rome, 1955), in *Studies in the
History of Religions*, IV (Leiden, 1959), 459–70.

fundamentally negative political vision that found expression, long
after the accession of the Christian emperors, in Augustine's *De civitate dei*,[77] and one cannot help wondering if Ullmann's silence on
that work is indicative of his inability to align it with his general
conceptual framework.

If, then, we wish at all to speak in terms of the dominance of the
theocratic-descending theme in "the later Roman and Christianized
empire," we must look elsewhere for its origins than in the pages of
the New Testament. Instead, we must ask ourselves what it was that
led such Christian thinkers as Eusebius of Caesarea (whom Ullmann
cites) to ignore the more negative aspects of New Testament political teaching and to marshal in support of absolute sacral monarchy
those Biblical texts susceptible of a sympathetic interpretation. And
the critical factor at work, as Eusebius's writings make abundantly
clear, was the pervasive influence of those Hellenistic ideas of kingship which, awakening native resonances, had by the fourth century
A.D. triumphed in the Roman world, and which, themselves in tension with Judaic and Christian beliefs, had their roots deep both in
Pythagorean-Platonic speculation and in ancient Near Eastern notions
of divine or sacral monarchy.[78]

Ullmann, it is true, is uneasily aware of the importance of such
Romano-Hellenistic conceptions.[79] But he appears unconscious of the

---

[77] In saying this, of course, I do not wish to deny that the *De civitate dei* was
characteristically interpreted by medievals in a "clericalist" fashion. But I would
agree with Arquillière and others that the medieval "augustinisme politique" involved
a distortion of Augustine's own thinking. See H.-X. Arquillière, *L'Augustinisme politique: Essai sur la formation des théories politiques du Moyen Âge* (2nd ed., Paris, 1955).
Reference should be made, however, to the interesting but (I think) unconvincing
attempt to rehabilitate the medieval interpretation made recently by Michael J.
Wilks, "Roman empire and Christian State in the De civitate Dei," *Augustinus*, XII
(1967), 489–510. Wilks, whose general views on medieval political thought come
very close to those of Ullmann, concludes (510): "When viewed in the perspective
of the Anglo-Saxon mission, Gregory I's negotiations with the Lombards, Stephen
II's approaches to the Franks, and the *renovatio Romani imperii* of 800, Augustine's
hopes might be said to be a prophetic indication of the future course of development of the papal-hierocratic system."

[78] See Erwin R. Goodenough, "The Political Philosophy of Hellenistic Kingship,"
Yale Classical Studies, I (1928), 55–102; *idem, The Politics of Philo Judaeus* (New Haven,
1938), pp. 86–120; Francis Dvornik, *Early Christian and Byzantine Political Philosophy*
(2 vols., Washington, D.C., 1966), I, 205–77, II, 453–658. For the Near Eastern
background see Ivan Engnell, *Studies in Divine Kingship in the Ancient Near East* (2nd
ed., Oxford, 1967); Henri Frankfort, *Kingship and the Gods* (Chicago, 1948).

[79] *History*, pp. 32–36; cf. *Growth*, pp. 14–18, 31–36.

degree to which they preempted motifs which he regards as manifestations of "the specifically Christian idea." Thus when he attributes to Eusebius in the fourth century the chief responsibility for
"linking monotheism with the concept of the Roman emperorship"
he makes no mention of Eusebius's well-attested indebtedness to the
political thinking of Philo Judaeus, who, four centuries earlier and
without benefit, it need hardly be added, of the Pauline epistles, had
not only correlated monarchy with monotheism and described ruler-
ship as a special gift of God but also, in remarks actually quoted by
Eusebius, introduced what it is tempting to think of as the characteristically "Pauline" notion that God permits even the rule of tyrants
as punishment for a people's wickedness.[80] Similarly, while Ullmann
makes much of the importance of Paul's description of the ruler as
a "servant of God" (*minister dei*) he makes no mention, for example,
of Pliny the Younger's description of the emperor Nerva's acting as
a "servant of the gods" (*minister deorum*) or of the fact that the notions
expressed by this and by such related titles as *vicarius dei* and *imago
dei* were of Hellenistic provenance, or, indeed, more ancient still.[81]
And to say this is to say also that even if "king by the grace of
God" did not become a standard royal title until the eighth century,
the idea which it conveyed was a much more ancient one and by
no means the creation of Christian thinkers.[82] Ullmann can say that

---

[80] Dvornik, *Early Christian and Byzantine Political Philosophy*, II, 559–65, 614–22;
Goodenough, *Politics of Philo Judaeus*, pp. 1–120; Per Beskow, *Rex Gloria: The Kingship
of Christ in the Early Church* (Uppsala, 1962), pp. 189–202, 261–68, 317–20, where
he discusses the fragment of Philo's lost work on Providence expounding his political metaphysics in general and his teaching on tyranny in particular. Cf. Eusebius,
Praeparatio Evangelica, VIII, xiv; ed. J.-P. Migne, *Patrologiae cursus completus: series graeca*
(161 vols., 1857–66), XXI, 651–56. See also Norman H. Baynes, "Eusebius and
the Christian Empire," in *Mélanges Bidez: Annuaire de l'Institut de Philologie et d'Histoire
Orientale*, II (1934), 13–18.

[81] *Panegyricus Plini Secundi Dictus Traiano Imp.*, viii, 2; in R.A.B. Mynors ed., *XII
Panegyrici Latini* (Oxford, 1964), 7. See also the works cited above, note 78, and esp.
Frankfort, pp. 229, 248 and 309, for the Mesopotamian king as the chosen servant
of the gods and for the royal style: "appointed of Enlil"; Engnell, p. 67 for the
Hittite royal title: "Image of the god," and 169 (cf. 131, 137, 163, 171) for "serv-
ant of god" as a "primordial royal title of honour" among the Canaanites. For the
Hittite king as the servant of the god, see O.R. Gurney, "Hittite Kingship," in S.H.
Hooke ed., *Myth, Ritual and Kingship* (Oxford, 1958), pp. 111–12.

[82] *History*, pp. 54 and 130; Principles, esp. pp. 23, 117–37; *Individual*, pp. 18–38.
Also *Kingship*, pp. 45–46, where Ullmann seems to regard the title *rex dei gratia* as
reflecting or springing from a combination of "the two fundamental Pauline principles—'all power comes from God' and 'What I am I am by the grace of God.'"
But see W. Ensslin, "The End of the Principate," *Cambridge Ancient History* (12 vols.,

"the first pictorial representation" of the appointment of the emperor by God "occurred in fact soon after Constantine the Great, when on a medallion a hand was seen to reach down from the clouds and put a crown on the head of the emperor."[83] But in this he is simply mistaken. For the same notion finds visual expression on numerous Roman coins ranging from the time of the emperor Trajan (d. 117) to that of Galerius Maximianus, many of them bearing the legend "by the providence of the gods" (*providentia deorum*)[84] and depicting Jupiter conferring upon the emperor the imperial insignia.[85] Alföldi has suggested a coin dating back to the last century of the Republic as a Roman prototype for this motif and has noted its deeper roots in a more ancient iconographic tradition of Assyro-Babylonian origin.[86]

That Ullmann misconceives not only the importance but also the nature of the ancient pattern of divine or sacral monarchy to which these iconographical materials witness, is evidenced by his summary formulation that with their adoption of Christianity the Roman emperors "changed from considering themselves divine emperors to

---

Cambridge, Eng., 1923–39), XII, 352–82—esp. 354, 360–61, 370; Dvornik, *Early Christian and Byzantine Political Philosophy*, II, 500–506.

[83] *History*, p. 37.

[84] One is reminded of the title which the usurper Lothar I adopted in October 831, only (as Ullmann stresses) after the bishops had pronounced on the withdrawal of the divine grace from his father—namely, "By the ordination of divine providence, Emperor Augustus." See *Kingship*, p. 66.

[85] See Harold Mattingly, *Coins of the Roman Empire in the British Museum* (5 vols., London, 1936; repr. 1966), III, 417, No. 1203 (Pl. 79.3), 421, No. 1236 (Pl. 79.12), IV, 754, No. 347, 833, No. 678. There is a discussion of the significance of these coins in Dvornik, *Early Christian and Byzantine Political Philosophy*, II, 500–506.

[86] Andreas Alföldi, "Die Geburt des kaiserlichen Bildsymbolik: Kleine Beiträge zur ihrer Enstehungsgeschichte," *Museum Helveticum*, VII (Fasc. 1, 1950), 1–13; cf. H.A. Grueber, *Coins of the Roman Republic in the British Museum* (3 vols., London, 1910), I, 407. André Grabar argues that the medallion in question witnesses to the substitution for the older pagan representation of the gods of a more acceptable motif drawn from Jewish iconography of the previous century—*L'Art de la fin de l'Antiquité et du Moyen Âge* (3 vols., Paris, 1968), II, 791–94. For a very close parallel of ancient Assyrian provenance, see, in addition to Alföldi (p. 10), Henri Frankfort, *Cylinder Seals: A Documentary Essay on the Art and Religion of the Ancient Near East* (London, 1939), pp. 210–11; René Labat, *Le caractère religieux de la royauté Assyro-Babylonienne* (Paris, 1939), pp. 89–94. If, as would seem to be the case, the medallion Ullmann has in mind is the one to which he refers also in *Growth*, p. 17 note 3, then it *may* be that it was his intention here to make the less sweeping assertion that the medallion is the first pictorial representation of divine appointment as evidenced specifically by the act of *coronation*. But even this more modest claim would run into difficulties. See Andreas Alföldi, "Insignien und Tracht der Römischen Kaiser," *Mitteilungen des Deutschen Archaeologischen Instituts*, Röm. Abt., I (1935), 1–171 at 56.

considering themselves emperors by the grace of God," the significance of that change lying in the fact that they "abandoned their claim to be true divinity on earth and recognized instead in God the origin of their power."[87] For to put the matter in such a way is erroneously to assume that the attribution of a divine status to a ruler, on the one hand, and the derivation of his authority from a god on the other are incompatible ideas. And to assume that is, in turn, to be committed to the prior assumption that pagan notions of what it is to be divine are commensurate with that narrower, more exclusive, and historically much more peculiar conception of divinity which emerges in the pages of the Bible—the conception, that is, of a unique God, a single and impenetrable entity, who, suffering no alienation and admitting of no degree, transcends the natural world which of his omnipotence he has created out of nothing and at every moment sustains in being.[88] In making this assumption Ullmann is by no means alone. But the assumption itself is no less misleading for being commonly or even unconsciously held, and it vitiates much of what he has to say about the triumph of his "theocratic-descending theme" not only in the later Roman world but also in the early-medieval Latin West. For there, too, analogous considerations apply.

Evidence concerning the nature of kingship in ancient and early-medieval Scandinavia, though late in date, is comparatively abundant. As a result, there is enough of a scholarly consensus for one scholar recently to assert: "That kingship in Old Scandinavia was entirely sacral is nowadays considered as a mere matter of fact."[89] Certainly, it is clear that the Scandinavian monarchs of the early medieval period played a prominent role in the religious cult, were

---

[87] *Principles*, p. 57.

[88] For the background to these remarks, see the essays gathered together in Daniel O'Connor and Francis Oakley eds., *Creation: The Impact of an Idea* (New York, 1969). More specifically, note Engnell's insistence (*Studies in Divine Kingship*, pp. 131 and 171) that though the expression "servant of god" was used of the Canaanite king there was still an identity between the king and the god. The expression, he says, "reflects a typical oscillation in the totality formed by the king and the god, who are identical, it is true, but at the same time two different persons."

[89] Ake V. Ström, "The King God and His Connection with Sacrifice in the Old Norse Religion," in *The Sacral Kingship*, 702; cf. E.O.G. Turville-Petrie, *Myth and Religion of the North: The Religion of Ancient Scandinavia* (New York, 1964), esp. ch. 9, pp. 190–95. In light of the views since expressed by Walter Baetke, *Yngvi und die Ynglinger: Eine quellenkritische Untersuchung über das nordische "Sakralkönigtum"* (Berlin, 1964), the confidence evident in Ström's judgment now seems to have been a little premature.

sometimes revered as gods after their death, were regarded as being of divine descent, and, in accordance with a pattern familiar also to the ancient Near East (and, indeed, at one time or another to most parts of the world) were held responsible for the rotation of the seasons, the fertility of the crops, and the general prosperity and well-being of their subjects. Consensus evaporates, however, when one turns to the Germanic kingship in Southern and Western Europe during the early imperial age and during the later era of barbarian migrations. The picture is more complex, the evidence much scantier. Moreover, how it is interpreted depends very much on the position taken concerning the admissibility of evidence based on later Scandinavian parallels. It depends, too, upon the preconceptions concerning the nature of the divine with which it is approached. Now Ullmann clearly sides with those who argue that pagan Germanic kingship did indeed possess some sort of sacral dimension. In this he is, I believe, quite correct.[90] And in his most recent and impressive analysis of "the clericalization of the royal office" in the Carolingian era he asserts that it was precisely because Pepin the Short lacked the "blood charisma" possessed by his Merovingian predecessors and needed, if his title was to be legitimized in the eyes of the people, some substitute religious character, that unction was administered to him in 751.[91] Here again, I believe, he is not mistaken. Unfortunately, however, he nowhere addresses himself explicitly to the nature of Germanic sacral monarchy. And what little he does say about it—even more, what he implies—may be criticized on three grounds at least.

In the first place, while he assigns some vague role to the sacral nature of Germanic kingship in accounting for the triumph of the

---

[90] *Principles*, pp. 23, 129 note 2; *Kingship*, pp. 10, 53–55, 77, 112. Otto Höfler has been the least inhibited exponent of the sacral character of Germanic kingship—see his *Germanisches Sakralkönigtum: I: Der Runenstein von Rök und die germanische Individualweihe* (Tübingen, 1952), and "Der Sakralcharakter des germanischen Königtums," in *The Sacral Kingship*, 664–701. In order to accept the sacral character of that kingship, however, one does not have to go the whole way with Höfler. See, e.g., H.M. Chadwick, *The Heroic Age* (Cambridge, Eng., 1926), esp. ch. 17, pp. 366–92; Hans Naumann, "Die magische Seite der altgermanischen Königtums und ihr Fortwirken in christlicher Zeit," in Gian Piero Bognetti *et al.*, *Wirtschaft und Kultur: Festschrift zum 70. Geburtstag von Alfons Dopsch* (Leipzig, 1938), pp. 1–12; Georges Dumézil, *Mythes et Dieux des Germains: Essai d'interprétation comparative* (Paris, 1939); Jan de Vries, "Des Königtum bei den Germanen," *Saeculum*, VII (1956), 289–309; William A. Chaney, *The Cult of Kingship in Anglo-Saxon England* (Berkeley and Los Angeles, 1970).

[91] *Kingship*, p. 77.

theocratic-descending theme in Southern and Western Europe, he can still assert that "there was no trace of a theocratic-descending form of government" in Scandinavia until "very much later" and that "in the Scandinavian countries the populist kingship never died out."[92] It is surely not unreasonable to infer from this that he ascribes no sacral character to Scandinavian kingship. And given the strength of the evidence to the contrary, it seems legitimate, therefore, to wonder why.

In the second place, he characterizes the contrast which he draws between the Carolingian monarchy and the Merovingian and older Germanic kingship as being cognate at least to the distinctions between the spiritual and material, the supernatural and natural. Thus he persistently correlates the so-called pagan *Geblütsrecht* (or *Geblütsheiligkeit*) not with the Germanic notion of royal descent from divinity, not, indeed, with any notion of divinity at all, but rather with the human, the physical, the biological, the natural.[93] So that, over and against the "theocratic" kings of the Carolingian era and later—divine appointees, ruling by "gift of God," by virtue of "divine intervention" and the "transmission of divine grace," he sets those earlier Germanic rulers whom he characterizes as the products of merely "natural-biological forces," their kingship resting only on foundations "of a physical and purely human kind."[94] In so doing, in attempting to assimilate to "the natural" the godsprung, priestly kings of the Germanic world—mana-filled mediators between their gods and their peoples[95]—he is once more guilty of anachronistically imposing on a less differentiated world of thought to which it was alien that firm distinction between the realms of nature and supernature which is grounded in the Hebraic and Christian doctrine of creation and the peculiarly exclusive conception of God which that doctrine, philosophically speaking, both presupposes and entails.[96]

---

[92] *History*, p. 53; *Principles*, p. 22.

[93] Though, less characteristically, he does say: "The Germanic Ruler embodied a sacred and magical mythos because of his blood kinship with distant ancestors; this was now replaced by an equally sacred mythos that was derived from divine sanction and grace."—*Kingship*, p. 54.

[94] For these contrasts, see *Kingship*, pp. 8–10, 53–55, 59, 96–6, 163.

[95] Chaney, *Cult of Kingship*, pp. 55–56, points out that it was precisely the parallelism between the pagan *mana* and the Christian *grace* that "facilitated the conversion of the Anglo-Saxons. . . . Paganism gave way to a triumphant Christianity but the king still remained a central and sacral figure."

[96] See esp. Hans Jonas, "Jewish and Christian Elements in the Western Philosophical Tradition," in O'Connor and Oakley eds., *Creation*, 241–58.

The fact that he should be betrayed into so doing should be correlated, moreover, with the implicit assumption which constitutes the third ground for criticizing his handling of these issues—the assumption, namely, that the conceptual relationship between forms of kingship rooted in the divine and those rooted in popular election and limited in some sense by popular will must necessarily be one of opposition or contradiction.[97] So that, because medieval Scandinavian kings and their ancient Germanic forebears were often "elected," or because there were limitations of some sort upon their power, the implication is that they cannot be regarded as truly sacral kings.[98] And yet, despite the example of ancient Near Eastern monarchies or of early-modern divine right theory, there is nothing *a priori* necessary about the opposition presupposed in this assumption. After all, in what has been called "the first Indo-European contribution" to the development of ideas of kingship, the Hittite *pankuš*, or assembly of nobles, which we know to have existed at least in the Old Kingdom, may have had a voice in the making of the Hittite kings (on this there is some scholarly disagreement),[99] and certainly "had jurisdiction over the king if the latter committed a crime."[100] And this despite the fact that the Hittite king was unquestionably a fundamentally sacral figure "regarded during his lifetime as the incarnation of his deified ancestor" and himself worshipped after death as a god.[101] Nor should we slip into the anachronistic assumption that the *thing*, or popular assembly, which is described as "electing" Germanic or Scandinavian kings was necessarily itself some sort of "secular" and "democratic" body, lacking a sacral status and bereft of sacral functions, or that the act of "election"—even apart from the limitation of choice to members of royal families claiming divine descent—was itself devoid of a sacred dimension.[102] And as for

---

[97] E.g., *Principles*, pp. 22–24, 137; *History*, pp. 53–54; *Kingship*, pp. 52–53.

[98] See Baetke, *Yngvi und die Ynglinger*, pp. 8–10, 171ff. For a particularly blunt statement of this view.

[99] H.G. Güterbock, "Authority and Law in the Hittite Kingdom," *Supplement to the Journal of the American Oriental Society*, No. 17 (July–Sept., 1956), 16–24, rejects this theory. Albrecht Goetze, *Kulturgeschichte des Alten Orients: Kleinasien*, Handbuch der Altertumswissenschaft, III, 1, 3, 3, 1, ed. Herman Bengtson (2nd ed., München, 1957), 85–87, affirms it. Cf. Dvornik, *Early Christian and Byzantine Political Philosophy*, I, 52.

[100] Güterbock, "Authority and Law," 19.

[101] Gurney, "Hittite Kingship," 115, 121.

[102] On the *Thing* or assembly as itself a sacral institution or as an institution compatible with sacral monarchy, see Chadwick, *Heroic Age*, pp. 368–70; Dumézil, *Mythes*

allegedly populist limitations on the power of pre-Christian Germanic
kings in western and southern Europe, the most definite evidence
that has come down to us again suggests very strongly that such
limitations, like those alleged to have been suffered also by some of
the Irish and Scandinavian kings, sprang precisely from their sacral
status. The king of the Burgundians, as the fourth-century Roman
historian, Ammianus Marcellinus, tells us,

> according to an ancient custom, lays down his power and is deposed,
> if under him the fortune of war has wavered, or the earth has denied
> sufficient crops; just as the Egyptians commonly blame their rulers for
> such occurrences.[103]

Just as consent could in the Middle Ages signify many things, so,
too, it should be remembered, could accountability.

But if the pagan Germanic and Scandinavian kingship was by no
means as unqualifiedly "populist" (in Ullmann's sense of that word)
as he claims, are we not entitled, then, to feel some misgivings about
the allegedly "theocratic" purity of the medieval Christian monarchy which he contrasts with it as a manifestation of the descending
rather than the ascending theme? Ullmann is not alone in stressing
the fact that the Christian emphasis on the derivation of the king's
powers from God, symbolized so effectively in the reception of unction and the adoption of the title "king by the grace of God," involved
also an emphasis on the independence of the king in his relations
with his people. Fritz Kern said as much long ago, and in a statement of classic balance.[104] But, then, Kern was also at pains to stress
the interdependence during the greater part of the Middle Ages of

---

et Dieux des Germaines, pp. 41–43; de Vries, "Des Königtum bei den Germanen,"
298; Höfler, "Der Sakralcharakter des germanischen Königtums," 692–96; Chaney,
Cult of Kingship, p. 17. On "election" as possessing a religious significance, see
Chadwick, p. 368; Höfler, 694–96; Walter Schlesinger, "Uber germanisches Heerkönigtum," in Th. Mayer ed., *Das Königtum: Seine geistigen und rechtlichen Grundlagen* (Lindau
u. Konstanz, 1956), 105–41 at 140 (speaking of the making of kings in Sweden).
On both points, see Wallace-Hadrill, *Early Germanic Kingship*, pp. 8–16.

[103] Ammianus Marcellinus, *Res gestae*, xxviii, 5, 14; ed. and trans. John C. Rolfe,
Ammianus Marcellinus (3 vols. Cambridge, Mass., 1935), III, 168–69. Cf. Bloch, *Les
rois thaumaturges*, p. 58; Schlesinger, "Uber germanisches Heerkönigtum," 135; Turville-
Petrie, *Myth and Religion of the North*, pp. 191–92; Maartje Draak, "Some Aspects of
Kingship in Pagan Ireland," *The Sacral Kingship*, 651–63.

[104] Fritz Kern, *Kingship and Law in the Middle Ages*, trans. S.B. Chrimes (Oxford,
1939), p. 43; cf. Walter Schlesinger, "Herrschaft und Gefolgschaft in der germanisch-
deutschen Verfassungsgeschichte," *Historische Zeitschrift*, CLXXVI (No. 2, 1953),
225–75 (at 251–52), along with the literature he cites in note 1.

the divine and popular sanctions which the monarchy enjoyed, insisting that the monarch's dependence upon God "was broadly enough conceived to allow the monarch to be dependent also upon the will of the community insofar as monarchy itself was based upon a popular as well as a divine mandate."[105] This formulation, however ill it sets with the categorical exclusiveness of the ascending-descending schema, surely accords better with the complexities of the actual medieval situation. Certainly, it carries greater conviction than does Ullmann's characteristic dismissal of the intitulation: "king by the grace of God and through election by the people" as a futile attempt "to reconcile . . . two irreconcilables," or his attempt, by means of definitional legerdemain, retroactively to immunize his purely theocratic kingship against even the low-grade "populist" infection which is all that the medieval royal electoral process could convincingly be held to convey.[106]

b. *Aristotelian naturalism and the recovery the ascending theme*

The rigidities, however, of Ullmann's overarching conceptual framework are not only exclusivist; they are also interlocking. It follows, therefore, that the price which he must pay for them, evident as it is in his depiction of the triumph of the theocratic-descending thesis in the late Roman and early medieval eras, must accordingly be manifest also in what he has to say in general about the recovery of the populist—ascending theme in the later-medieval period, and, in particular about the role of what he calls "Aristotelian naturalism" in sponsoring that recovery. Having set up his purely theocratic kingship in stark contrast to the supposedly pure populism of the archaic Germanic past, he must now turn to the dramatic intervention of a novel factor to render intelligible that "return" to the populist ascending theme which, he argues, characterized late-medieval

---

[105] Kern, Kingship *and Law*, p. 10; cf. the similar sentiment expressed by Marc Bloch, *Feudal Society*, trans. L.A. Manyon (2 vols., Chicago, 1964), II, 383–84.

[106] *Kingship*, pp. 96–97, where he categorizes as "an emergency solution" the title "Louis, King by the mercy of our Lord God and the election of the people." Cf. *Principles*, p. 260, where, speaking of the medieval Aristotelians later on, he says: "It was no more than a comforting device to maintain that the people were the organ which made known God's will. To say that the people or some of its organs in elections mediated the divine will was merely to bow to an ancient and traditional way of thinking." Also *Principles*, pp. 145–47; *History*, p. 135.

political thinking. The novel factor he has in mind is, of course, the recovery of the works of Aristotle, and he argues that the attitude they conveyed was able to make so profound an impact upon later-medieval political thinking because of the prior undermining of the theocratic descending theme by factors indigenous to Western Europe, most notably by feudalism.

Now we have already seen that the assignment of this role to feudalism leads Ullmann in his account of feudal institutions to impose upon them an explanatory burden which they cannot convincingly be made to sustain. It remains only to demonstrate, then, that the role he ascribes to the recovery of Aristotelian views sponsors comparably severe distortions—in his assessment of the nature and importance of their impact, in his treatment of the medieval Aristotelian thinkers on whom he repeatedly focuses, and even in his understanding of the political thinking of Aristotle himself. For, given his insistent correlation of the descending thesis with the supernatural and the ascending with the natural, Ullmann's Aristotle and his medieval disciples must bear the burden of accounting at the same time for the recovery of a "naturalistic" view of political life and for the emphasis on popular consent as the source of political power that is assumed to go with it. This despite the fact that canonist and civilian authors, long before the translation of Aristotle's *Politics* had undoubtedly begun to appropriate the notion that man is by nature a political animal.[107] This despite the fact, too, that "Aristotelian naturalism" notwithstanding, it was possible to employ Aristotelian ideas to buttress the theocratic descending theme.[108] Thus the papalist theologian, James of Viterbo, while adopting the Aristotelian teleological approach and agreeing with Aristotle and Aquinas that the state was natural and possessed a positive ethical value of its own, argued from the superior end pursued in the Christian society by the spiritual power to its ultimate supreme control over the temporal, believing that only in this way could nature be perfected.[109]

---

[107] On which see Post, *Studies*, ch. 11 ("The Naturalness of Society and the State"), 494–561, and the literature referred to therein.

[108] As Ullmann himself recognizes in *Growth*, p. 455. See Georges de Lagarde, *La Naissance de l'esprit laïque au déclin du Moyen Âge* (new ed., 5 vols. Louvain and Paris, 1956–70), I, 195–98.

[109] He did so in his tract *De regimine christiano*; ed. H.-X. Arquillière, *Le plus ancien traité de l'église. Jacques de Viterbo, De Regimine Christiano (1301–1302)* (Paris, 1926), pp.

But we hear little from Ullmann about political "naturalism" in medieval Europe before the advent of Aristotle's *Politics* and nothing at all about James of Viterbo.[110] His chosen Aristotelians, instead, are Aquinas, John of Paris, Dante and Marsilius of Padua, and he uses them to illustrate the process by which Aristotelian ideas, after an initital phase of hostility, were first received and absorbed "into Christian cosmology" and then, in the fourteenth century, released "from the Christian garb." So that, whether or not John of Paris is taken to be more "progressive" or advanced than Dante,[111] we are given to understand that what occurred on the road from Aquinas to Marsilius was a progressive de-Christianizing of Aristotle. "The Christian elements faded into the background more and more, and what remained was Aristotle," or, as Ullmann adds in one place with perhaps uncharacteristic caution, "what was believed to be Aristotle."[112]

Unfortunately, even though they are of his own choosing, the first three of his Aristotelians prove to be ungratefully recalcitrant and he elicits the desired answers from them only by dint of applying considerable pressure to their texts. Thus, though he is quite correct in his emphasis on the Thomistic commitment to the viewpoint that man is by nature a social and political animal, may one not cavil, even while admitting the complexity of Dante's thought, at a reading of the *De monarchia* which, because of an obsessive preoccupation with Dante's "naturalism," refuses any recognition to the

---

83–310. In doing so James based himself on Thomistic principles but conflated the two principal texts of Aquinas on the relationship of the two powers—see I.T. Eschmann, "St. Thomas Aquinas on the Two Powers," *Mediaeval Studies*, XX (1958), 177 note 4.

[110] Thus, he points out (*History*, p. 183) that Aquinas did not have "any words of condemnation for the States of the infidels or pagans: they exercised their authority legitimately, because their State was as much a product of nature as any other State was." But he does not note that Innocent IV without benefit of Aristotle had expressed similar ideas—see Brian Tierney, *The Crisis of Church and State: 1050–1300* (Englewood Cliffs, N.J., 1964), pp. 152, 155–56. Nor does he note that, at least according to one reading of the crucial texts in Books II and XIX of the *De civitate dei*, a comparable claim can be made for St. Augustine.

[111] In *Principles* and *History* the order of exposition is: Aquinas, Dante, John of Paris, Marsilius. In *Individual*, John of Paris is treated before Dante.

[112] *Principles*, pp. 231–32; *History*, p. 167. See Gordon Leff, "The Apostolic Ideal in Later Medieval Ecclesiology," *Journal of Theological Studies*, n.s. XVIII (April, 1967), 58–82, for a sharp attack on this point of view and on the whole role ascribed to "Aristotelian naturalism" by Ullmann and by Michael Wilks in his book, *The Problem of Sovereignty in the Later Middle Ages* (Cambridge, 1963).

quasi-religious character of his world-empire.[113] And noting the fact that Isidore of Seville, in a famous passage included in Gratian's *Decretum*, had long since stressed that laws should vary in accordance with place, time, differences in local custom and so on,[114] one cannot help wondering at the repeated emphasis on John of Paris's remark to the effect that the disposition of temporal power must reflect or accommodate itself to such natural diversities, a remark on the basis of which Ullmann can conclude that "the rigidity of political thought" was giving way to a more naturalistic "flexibility" and that "into the place of the hitherto prevalent monolithic thesis of absoluteness" was now stepping "the dominant note of relativity."[115]

But, then, it should be noted that the context in which he addresses himself to this issue has been set by his prior insistence that John of Paris, even more sharply it would seem than Aquinas before him, distinguished between "the natural body politic and the supranatural mystical body of Christ," so that to him, as Ullmann puts it,

> The Church . . . was a mystical body pure and simple—a concept that had come more and more in evidence in the thirteenth century—and as such contrasted sharply with the natural body politic. Since the Church was purely mystical, its ministers had similarly purely sacramental functions. Negatively expressed, the Church was, for John of Paris, no organic juristic body in the traditional sense.[116]

Unfortunately, the chapter of the (*De potestate regia et papal*) to which he refers in support of this claim is not itself concerned at all to distinguish between the Church and the "natural body politic" nor does

---

[113] *Principles*, pp. 258–63; *History*, pp. 189–95; *Individual*, pp. 133–35. See Dante, *De Monarchia*, esp. III, cap. 16; ed. Dr. E. Moore (Oxford, 1916), pp. 375–76. Cf. the remarks of A. Passerin d'Entrèves, *Dante as a Political Thinker* (Oxford, 1952), pp. 49–51, and Etienne Gilson, *Dante the Philosopher*, trans. David Moore (New York, 1949), pp. 179–80.

[114] *Decretum*, 4, c. 2; ed. Friedberg, I, 5. Post, *Studies*, p. 502, draws attention to this text.

[115] *Individual*, pp. 131–32; cf. *History*, pp. 201–202; *Principles*, pp. 263–64. The relevent text is in John of Paris, *Tractatus de potestate regia et papali*, cap. 3; ed. Jean Leclercq, *Jean de Paris et l'ecclésiologie du XIIIᵉ siècle* (Paris, 1942), pp. 179–82, where he is simply concerned to establish (and rather less on the basis of any stark contrast between "nature" and "supernature" than on practical grounds—see esp. 181) that it is not as necessary for temporal rulers to be subjected to one supreme head as it is for ecclesiastical.

[116] *History*, p. 201; cf. *Principles*, p. 263. See *Principles*, pp. 252–53 and *History*, pp. 179–80, for Aquinas's alleged distinction between the Church as a "mystical body" (*corpus mysticum*) and the "natural State" as a "moral and political body" (*corpus politicum et morale*). Ullmann cites no text of Aquinas on this point.

it make any reference to the Church as a mystical body.[117] Indeed, in John's entire treatise only three such references occur, and they tell a story directly opposed to Ullmann's—as also, for that matter, does the way in which Aquinas sometimes uses that term. For, as Henri de Lubac and others have pointed out, from the mid-twelfth century onwards, in their anxiety to stress the doctrine of the Real Presence, theologians had begun to designate the eucharist no longer as the "mystical" but as "the true body of Christ [*verum corpus Christi*]."[118] As a result, the expression "mystical body of Christ" (*corpus Christi mysticum*), reserved now for the Church, began to lose its sacramental associations and to acquire political and juristic connotations, so that by the early-fourteenth century, as Kantorowicz has put it, the *corpus mysticum* had been integrated "very neatly . . . into the Aristotelian scheme" and "*corpus mysticum* and *corpus morale et politicum* ['moral and political body'] had become almost interchangeable notions."[119]

This development is evident already in Aquinas who can even speak of the "mystical body of the Church" (*corpus ecclesiae mysticum*), an expression almost devoid of sacramental connotations.[120] It is evident also in the way in which Aegidius Romanus can argue from the position of the pope as head of "the mystical body" to his lordship over temporal goods and to his plenitude of power.[121] And it is evident equally in John of Paris, who, while accepting the juridicized understanding of the term *corpus mysticum*, rejects the sort of conclusion Aegidius draws from it, arguing that it is Christ alone

---

[117] *Tractatus*, cap. 2; ed. Leclercq, pp. 178–79.

[118] Henri de Lubac, *Corpus Mysticum: L'Eucharistie et l'église au Moyen Âge* (Paris, 1944), esp. ch. 5, pp. 117–37. Also Gerhart B. Ladner, "Aspects of Medieval Thought on Church and State," *Review of Politics*, IX (No. 4, 1947), 403–22, and Kantorowicz, *King's Two Bodies*, pp. 193–206 (noting the relevance of the change to secular political thinking). For the way in which the canonists capitalized upon the juristic implications of the doctrine of the Mystical Body, see Brian Tierney, *Foundations of the Conciliar Theory* (Cambridge, 1955), pp. 132–41.

[119] Kantorowicz, *King's Two Bodies*, pp. 211–12.

[120] De Lubac, *Corpus Mysticum*, pp. 129–31, notes 55–63 for the pertinent texts. Kantorowicz, *King's Two Bodies*, p. 201, comments on these texts: "The change in terminology was not haphazardly introduced. It signified another step in the direction of allowing the clerical corporational institution of the *corpus ecclesiae juridicum* to coincide with the *corpus ecclesiae mysticum* and thereby to 'secularize' the notion of 'mystical body.' In that development Aquinas himself holds a key position."

[121] Aegidius Romanus, *De ecclesiastica potestate*, Lib. II, cap. 4; Lib. III, cap. 2; ed. Richard Scholz (Weimar, 1929), pp. 50 and 152; cf. Lib. II, cap. 14; ed. Scholz, p. 132.

who is "properly and in the highest degree" head of the Church and that even as his principal vicar the pope does not have the disposition of temporals.[122] Ullmann to the contrary, then, the Church for John of Paris was very much a "juristic body," a corporational entity, and, *as such*, a mystical body. Similarly, the sacramental power of the priesthood—its primary though certainly not its sole function[123]—he can see as pertaining both (by way of consecration) to "the true body of Christ," and also (by way of administration and, therefore, of jurisdiction) to "the mystical body of Christ."[124]

Ironically enough, it is in connection with the power of jurisdiction which popes and prelates exercise in the ecclesiastical mystical body which is the Church that Ullmann can find his most striking evidence of John of Paris's advocacy of the populist-ascending thesis. For, by consistently applying canonistic corporational theory to the structure of the whole Church, John developed what has been called "by far the most consistent and complete formulation of conciliar doctrine before the outbreak of the Great Schism."[125] In comparison, what he has to say about the popular source of royal power is not very extensive. But it is clear and, indeed, traditional enough. Royal power is from God and from the people.[126] What he wishes to exclude by this formula is not, as Ullmann seems to imply,[127] the derivation of royal power from God, but the high papalist claim that that power was mediated to the king via the pope, and he drives his point home appropriately by reminding us that Paul in his famous

---

[122] *Tractatus*, cap. 11 and 18; ed. Leclercq, pp. 204 and 230. The third reference to the *corpus mysticum* occurs in cap. 12; ed. Leclercq, p. 209, where it is contrasted with the *corpus Christi verum*.

[123] Ullmann certainly exaggerates when he says (*History*, p. 201) that for John the only functions of ecclesiastical ministers were sacramental. See John's analysis of ecclesiastical power in *Tractatus*, cap. 12 and 13; ed. Leclercq, pp. 207–16.

[124] *Tractatus*, cap. 12; ed. Leclercq, pp. 208–209. On this distinction and its correlation with the "true" and "mystical" bodies of Christ, see the pertinent remarks of Michael Wilks, *The Problem of Sovereignty*, pp. 375–80. He, too, finds the distinction in John Paris (378 note 1).

[125] Tierney, *Foundations*, p. 177.

[126] *Tractatus*, cap. 10; ed. Leclercq, p. 199: ". . . neither in itself nor in its mode of exercise does the royal power come from the pope but from God and from the people choosing a king either in person or as a member of a dynasty (. . . [P]otestas regia nec secundum se nec quantum ad executionem est a papa sed a Deo et a populo regem eligente in persona vel in domo)." Cf. cap. 15 and 19; ed. Leclercq, pp. 222 and 235.

[127] *Principles*, p. 260.

statement to the Romans had not said that the ruler was a "servant of the pope" but a "servant of God."[128]

That Ullmann, however, should make so much of these statements is understandable enough. Fragmentary though they are, they constitute by far the most explicit affirmations of the derivation of political power from the people to be found in the first three of his Aristotelians. For it is only by sailing rather too close to the dialectical wind that he can elicit from Aquinas and Dante truly convincing intimations of his populist-ascending thesis. Thus, for example, he classifies as an enviably clear elaboration of the populist-ascending theme Aquinas's commentary on Aristotle's genetic account of the emergence of the *polis* as the completion of such other natural associations as the family, village and so on—an analysis which is, in fact, concerned rather with the goal than with the derivation of power.[129] Or, again, he stresses Aquinas's definition of democracy in *Summa Theologica*[130] without noting that elsewhere Aquinas, following Aristotle, classifies democracy as one of the unjust or perverted forms of government.[131] At the same time, he implies that the words "and this was established by the divine law" apply to democracy when in fact they apply to the "mixed" form of constitution, and then, not because Aquinas was himself willing to describe it (here and in one other text) as the "best polity," but simply because it was the constitutional form which he believed to have been instituted among the Jews under Moses and his successors.[132] Moreover, Ullmann's

---

[128] *Tractatus*, cap. 10; ed. Leclercq, p. 199.

[129] *Principles*, p. 249. See the pertinent comments of Ewart Lewis, *Medieval Political Ideas* (2 vols., London, 1954), I, 151: "The details of the human process through which the state arose were not important for Aquinas. Apparently the consent of the subjects might be a factor in particular situations; but the general basis of the legitimacy of governments was, for Aquinas, their rationally demonstrable necessity to the natural needs of man."

[130] *Principles*, p. 255; *History*, p. 178. Thomas Aquinas, *Summa theologica*, I, 2a, qu. 105, art. 1; printed in A. Passerin d'Entrèves ed., *Aquinas: Selected Political Writings* (Oxford, 1959), pp. 149–51.

[131] *De regimine principum*. I, cap. 1 and 3; ed. d'Entrèves, pp. 2–9, 15–19. Also *Commentarium in libros Politicorum*, III, 5–6, in *Sancti Thomae Aquinatis . . . Opera Omnia* (25 vols., Parma, 1852–73), XXI, 464–66. Ullmann does in fact cite this last text but with the odd comment: "Thomas very clearly approached the ascending or populist theory, and this quite especially when he spoke of the *status popularis* in connexion with democracy and 'the will of the people.'"—*History*, p. 178; cf. *Principles*, p. 255.

[132] The other text is *Summa theologica*, I, 2a, qu. 95, art. 4; ed. d'Entrèves, pp. 131–33.

further suggestion that "the principle of representation" necessarily
follows from Aquinas's alleged flirtation with democracy involves the
imposition of a further strain on two unrelated texts which, while
they certainly reflect the older medieval view of representation as
personification, in no way indicate any adhesion to the newer notion
of representation as delegation—a notion which one would have
thought to be more germane to his concern with popular consent.[133]
Similarly, in an effort to imply (he never quite says as much) that
Dante, too, can be numbered among the supporters of the populist-
ascending thesis, he sharply contrasts Dante's description of the ruler
as the "servant of all" (*minister omnium*) with the Pauline statement
that he was the "servant of God" (*minister dei*). He frames this contrast, however, without signalling the fact (perhaps, even, without
realizing it) that in so doing he is contrasting a final cause of ruler-
ship with an efficient.[134] He does so, again, without noting that in
the *De monarchia* Dante himself clearly regards the emperor as the
servant or minister of God and elsewhere explicitly describes Henry
VII as such.[135] He does so finally, and despite all his stress on the
importance of the Latin Vulgate in shaping medieval political conceptions, without noting that the expression *minister omnium*, which
he says is "a far cry" from the earlier Pauline conception, can itself
lay claim to be of equally Biblical provenance.[136]

---

[133] See *History*, p. 178, and *Principles*, p. 255, where he cites *Summa theologica*, II 2a,
qu. 67, art. 2 *ad* 1 and *Ibid.*, Ia, qu. 75, art. 4 *ad* 1.

[134] *Principles*, p. 261; *History*, p. 195; *Individual*, p. 135. *De monarchia*, I, cap. 12;
ed. Moore, pp. 347–48. Here Dante's concern is explicitly with ends. He admits
that kings may be the lords of others with respect to means, but insists that with
respect to ends they are "the servants of others (*aliorum ministri*)." This, he adds, is
especially true of the world-ruler who is to be regarded as "the servant of all." In
any case, the sentiment expressed here is hardly incompatible with that of Paul
who can describe the ruler, after all, as the minister of God *for the good of his subjects*: Rom. 13:4.

[135] See esp. *De monarchia*, III, cap. 16; ed. Moore, pp. 374–76. Cf. III, cap. 4;
ed. Moore, p. 366, where he describes such things as governments as "remedies
for the infirmity of sin (remedia contra infirmitatem peccati)." *Epistola VII* (to Henry
VII), pp. 36–37; ed. Paget Toynbee, *Dantis Alagheri Epistolae* (2nd ed., Oxford, 1966),
pp. 90 and 101: ". . . nevertheless we believe and hope in thee, declaring thee to
be the minister of God, the son of the Church, and the furtherer of the glory of
Rome (. . . nihilominus in te credimus et speramus, asseverantes te Dei ministrum,
et Ecclesiae filium, et Romanae gloriae promotorem)." Cf. *Ep. VI*, 32; ed. Toynbee,
p. 68.

[136] Mark 9:35 (Vulgate 9:34): "If anyone would be first, he must be last of all
and servant of all (Si quis vult primus esse, erit omnium novissimus, et *omnium min-*

It may be, of course, that Ullmann would account for his difficulties with these three Aristotelians on the grounds that their views were transitional ones which, "precisely because they set out from the theocentric origin, could not exhibit a genuine populism, could not arrive at a genuine popular sovereignty." This could not emerge "as long as there was, conceptually at least, the idea of nature being created by God, as long as the natural inclination of man to form the State was eventually of divine provenance."[137] Aristotelian ideas had still, therefore, to be released from "their Christian garb." What was needed was "a radical operation." And what better a candidate for that task than Marsilius of Padua who "set out from the axiom that the link between nature and God was a matter of faith, and not a matter capable of rational proof," and, as a result, not "an operational principle in political science?"[138]

Certainly, with Marsilius, Ullmann has no difficulty in documenting the political "naturalism" and the preoccupation with popular consent which he regards as integral to the populist-ascending theme. Instead, the trouble here is that we are given the impression, and overwhelmingly so, that with Marsilius we encounter once more the political teaching of Aristotle himself,[139] an impression bolstered by a highly tendentious reading of Aristotle's *Politics* which succeeds in transforming even the Stagirite himself into an advocate of "Aristotelian naturalism." For, to take only three crucial points which Ullmann emphasizes, it must be insisted that neither in his separation of law and politics from morals, nor in his attribution of legislative sovereignty to the people, nor in his own particular version of political naturalism is Marsilius at one with Aristotle.[140]

Thus, in the first place, if, by distinguishing between "transient" and "immanent" acts and limiting government almost entirely to the

---

ister)." Cf. Matt. 20:25–27. For his thinking concerning the application of biblical themes to government in the Middle Ages, see Walter Ullmann, "The Bible and Principles of Government in the Middle Ages," in *La Bibbia nell' alto medioevo* (Spoleto, 1963), 181–227.

[137] *Principles*, p. 268; *History*, pp. 204–205.

[138] *Ibid.*

[139] An impression modified only by the single qualification noted above, note 112.

[140] For Ullman's version of Aristotle, see *Principles*, pp. 231–35; *History*, pp. 167–70. Cf. *Individual*, pp. 117–19—esp. 119 where he commits himself to the generalization that "... Aristotelianism [was] characterized by the clean separation of ethics and politics." And for Marsilius, *Principles*, pp. 268–79; *History*, pp. 204–14; *Individual*, pp. 135–39.

moderation of "the excesses" of men's "transient" acts,[141] or, again,
if by identifying enforceable, coercive command as the very essence
of law, one can argue that Marsilius did indeed engineer a separation between politics and morals,[142] Aristotle most certainly did not.
On the contrary, so closely related are the subjects of ethics and
politics that with him, Barker has said, "political philosophy becomes
a sort of moral theology."[143] A state which limited itself to "pre-
venting mutual injustice and easing exchange" would be for him no
state at all. For "the end of the state is not mere life; it is, rather,
a good quality of life." That is to say, the state exists to make possible not merely man's physical survival but also his moral and spiritual perfection. Hence the "spiritualizing" of politics which Gewirth
discerns in Aristotle, and the "totalitarian" character of the *polis* on
which many commentators have remarked. Hence, too, the oddity
of Ullmann's claim that Aristotle's approach "broke down the one-
ness and 'totalitarian' or wholeness point of view."[144]

In the second place, if Marsilius defines law as in its very essence
enforceable, coercive command and regards the people as alone
endowed with the power so to command, Aristotle really does neither. For him law is the voice of Reason and of God. It can be

---

[141] *Defensor Pacis*, I, v, 4 and 7; ed. C.W. Previté-Orton (Cambridge, 1928), pp.
16–17. By "immanent" acts Marsilius means those private "movements" of the
human mind—cognitions, emotions and so on—which remain within the agent himself and are not externalized in actions affecting other persons. By "transient" acts,
then, he means those movements which pass over into motions of the body's external organs affecting other persons. Cf. the remarks of Alan Gewirth, *Marsilius of
Padua: The Defender of Peace* (2 vols., New York, 1951–56), I, 101–104.

[142] *Defensor Pacis.*, I, x, 4; ed. Previté-Orton, pp. 38–39. Gewirth, *Marsilius of Padua*,
II, 36, translates thus: "[Law] . . . may be considered according as with regard to
its observance there is *a command coercive through punishment and reward to be distributed
in the present world*, or according as it is handed down by way of such a command;
and considered in this way it most properly is called, and is, a law." (Italics mine.)
See Gewirth, *Marsilius of Padua*, I, esp. 34–42, 102–104, 134–39; cf. the rather
different appraisal of Georges de Lagarde, *La naissance de l'esprit laïque au déclin du
Moyen Âge*, III, 103–104, 173–77.

[143] Ernest Barker, in the introduction to his translation *The Politics of Aristotle*
(Oxford, 1948), p. li; cf. App. I, pp. 353–59, for Aristotle's understanding of the
relationship between the two subjects.

[144] *Politics*, III, 9, 1280a–b; trans. Barker, pp. 118–19. (Note the stress placed on
this text by Mario Grignaschi and the related contrast he draws between the views
of Marsilius and Aristotle—"Le rôle de l'aristotélisme dans le 'Defensor Pacis' de
Marsile de Padoue," *Revue d'histoire et de philosophic religieuses*, XXXV [1955], 312–13.)
Gewirth, *Marsilius of Padua*, I, 103; Ullmann, *History*, p. 169; cf. *Principles*, p. 234.
The text to which Ullmann refers (*Pol.* III, 4, 1276b; trans. Barker, p. 102) cannot
sustain the burden he places upon it.

defined as "Reason free from all passion," and the qualities essential to the art of legislation are, therefore, intelligence and "right judgment."[145] The texts which Ullmann cites to support his own contention that for Aristotle it is the "will" of the people which "determines what should be law" say nothing of the sort—even if Marsilius, before him, had thought that they did.[146] What they convey, instead, is a rather tentative statement coming from an Aristotle who has just classified democracy as a perverted constitution, to the effect that there may be something to be said after all for the idea that the people at large should wield the dominant authority in the state. At least, even if they should not be permitted "themselves in their individual capacity" to hold office, it would be appropriate to let them "share in the deliberative and judicial functions"—in particular, to elect the magistrates to office and to call them "to account at the end of their tenure of office."[147] Of course, given Aristotle's rationalistic conception of law, that the text should say nothing about legislative sovereignty in particular or about the source of law in general is hardly surprising. Still less is it surprising given, too, the markedly teleological orientation of so much of his political thinking and especially of the section of the *Politics* from which the particular texts are drawn. For his whole classification of constitutions into those which are "right" and those which are "perverted" depends fundamentally on the ends to which they are dedicated.[148] In contrast with this, and despite his frequently attested dependence on Aristotle, Marsilius persistently reorients his own political thinking from final to efficient causes; it is "an efficient cause called the 'legislator'" which occupies "the dominant position" in his doctrine.[149]

---

[145] *Politics* III, 16, 1287 a; trans. Barker, p. 146; *Nichomachean Ethics*, X, 9, 1181a; trans. W.D. Ross in W.D. Ross ed., *The Works of Aristotle Translated into English* (12 vols., Oxford, 1930–52), IX, 1181a, 18. See Barker's introduction, pp. lxix–lxxli and App. I, pp. 362–72; also Huntington Cairns, *Legal Philosophy from Plato to Hegel* (Baltimore, 1949), pp. 77–126, who underlines (92) the "partial" nature of Aristotle's definitions of law as well as the fact that "we are without any analysis of his conducted for the express purpose of stating a general and ultimate theory of law."

[146] *Politics* III, 11, 1281a–b; trans. Barker, pp. 123–25. See Marsilius, *Defensor Pacis*, I, 12, 3; ed. Previté-Orton, 49; Ullmann, *Principles*, p. 233; *History*, p. 169.

[147] *Politics* III, ii, 1281b; trans. Barker, p. 125.

[148] *Politics* III, 6–12, 1278b–1284b; trans. Barker, pp. 110–36. Cf. the comments of Richard McKeon, "Aristotle's Conception of Moral and Political Philosophy," *Ethics*, LI (No. 3, 1940–41), 253–90.

[149] Gerwith, *Marsilius of Padua*, I, 36 (cf. 31–37, 52–53, 139–47). This reorientation forms perhaps the central theme of Gewirth's interpretation. He also stresses

And this in turn, it should be noted, reflects (or accounts for) the difference, in the third place, between the types of political "naturalism" espoused by the two thinkers.

In embarking upon his discussion of Aristotle, Ullmann rightly stresses the relevance of his natural philosophy to his political thinking.[150] He does so in order to stress Aristotle's fundamental "empiricism," but fails to note that, unlike modern behaviorist empiricism, Aristotle's is not of the "mechanistic" or "instrumental" variety. For him the concern with efficient causality, though necessary, can never by itself suffice to convey an adequate understanding of any process. As he makes clear in his analysis of causality, in order to find a process intelligible we must know in addition to its efficient cause, its formal, material, and, above all, its final cause.[151] For it is in the end or outcome of a process that the nature of a thing resides; it is on ends or outcomes, therefore, that Aristotles emphasis characteristically lies—and in his political as well as his natural philosophy.[152] So that right at the beginning of the *Politics* he can say:

> It [the polis] is the end or consummation to which those [earlier natural] associations move, and the "nature" of things consists in their end or consummation; for what each thing is when its growth is completed we call the nature of that thing, whether it be man or a horse or a family.[153]

On this matter, Marsilius provides a striking contrast. For along with his orientation of politics to efficient causes goes a cognate inclination to interpret the "natural" less as the completed or perfect than as the primitive.[154] This inclination was promoted already by the use of the Latin word *natura* to translate the Greek *physis*,[155] but it is

---

the fact that Marsilius, unlike the other medieval Aristotelians, "adopted the orientation of that portion of the *Politics* which is at opposite pole from the finalistic: the book [V] on revolutions." See also Grignaschi, "Le rôle de l'aristotlélisme," esp. 334–40.

[150] See esp. *Individualism*, pp. 117–18.

[151] See above, note 18.

[152] With some felicity Randall, *Aristotle*, p. 126, puts it thus: "So to the old question, which comes first, the chicken or the egg? Aristotle has a clear answer: the chicken comes first—in understanding eggs, the chicken that is to be."

[153] *Politics* I, 2, 1252b; trans. Barker, p. 5.

[154] On this point see Gewirth, *Marsilius of Padua*, I, 54–56, and the texts cited therein.

[155] As Barker comments, *The Politics of Aristotle*, pp. lxxii–lxxlii: "[A]n English translator [*a fortiori* a translator into Latin] is bound to render *physis* and *physikos* by the Latin words 'nature' and 'natural,' and . . . he is equally bound to alter the exact

much less marked in other medieval Aristotelians and least of all, perhaps, in Aquinas who faithfully sought to echo Aristotle's own teleological understanding of the "nature" of things. It is still, however, wholly misleading to say, as does Ullmann, that Aquinas's "concept of nature was no different from Aristotle's."[156] To endorse that sentiment would be to assume that what would remain if we subtracted the realm of the supernatural from the Thomistic scheme of things entire would be the realm of the natural as Aristotle understood it. If Ullmann never quite makes that suggestion explicitly, he comes very close to so doing and it is his unstated assumption that it holds true which sows the seed of so much confusion in his repeated discussions of nature, natural law and the role of "Aristotelian naturalism" during the later Middle Ages.[157]

The point at issue here concerns fundamental metaphysical assumptions. Ullmann, it would seem, in his concern with the destructive impact of Aristotelian ideas on traditional Christian modes of thought, has underestimated the degree to which those ideas were themselves transformed into something rich and strange under the impress of the profoundly alien metaphysic into which the scholastic thinkers strove to insert them. It should not be forgotten that Aristotle's world of nature, before it was "absorbed into the Christian cosmology," was a world which in its ceaseless striving to emulate the perfection of God itself pulsated to the rhythm of the divine. It was a restless but intelligible world, one in which final causes were ceaselessly at work, one dependent for its very motion upon that ultimate final cause, the unmoved mover, the final good which he himself calls God. For "upon such a principle," he tells us, "depend the heavens and the world of nature."[158] It was not, therefore, the natural world

---

significance of the Greek by using those Latin terms. The Latin *natura*, connected with a verb which indicates the idea of birth, suggests the primitive: the Greek *physis* . . . suggests the whole process that leads . . . to the completion of the 'grown' man." Cf. the pertinent remarks of Thomas Gilby, *Principality and Polity: Aquinas and the Rise of State Theory in the West* (London, 1958), pp. 109–10.

[156] *History*, p. 175.

[157] *Principles*, pp. 233–34, 253, 268–69; *History*, pp. 169, 184, 204–206. (Note esp. his misleading attribution to Aristotle of the notion of the "natural rights" of the citizen.)

[158] *Metaphysics*, XII, 7, 1072b; trans. Ross, in Ross ed., *The Works of Aristotle*, VIII, 1072b, 17–18. For the doctrine of the unmoved mover, see esp. *Metaph.*, XII, 6–10, 1071b–1076a, and *Physics*, VIII, 5, 9–10, 256a–258b, 265a–267b. For some helpful comments on *Metaph.*, XII, 8, and the doctrine of the plurality of unmoved movers, see R.G. Collingwood, *The Idea of Nature* (New York, 1960), pp. 89–91.

which the Hebraic and Christian tradition bequeathed to the modern era, a world which, precisely because it was regarded as having
been created out of nothing by an omnipotent and transcendent God
was a "disenchanted" one—one from which the divine had finally
been banished. Instead, it was a world which at once both yearned
towards the divine, the transcendent good which was its final end,
and, at the same time, by virtue of its immanent order, was in some
sense suffused with it.[159] As a result, if we choose to talk at all about
"Aristotelian naturalism," we must be careful to do so in the knowledge that Aristotle's idea of "the natural" was one which can itself
be said in some degree to have comprehended that which under the
influence of the Christian tradition we ourselves have become accustomed to classify as "the supernatural."[160]

III

Remote considerations, it may be, but important ones nonetheless—
the more so in that they may serve also to give us some insight,
however speculative and partial, into the reasons which have moved
Ullmann to shape his historical materials on so manifestly uneasy a
conceptual framework. And if they succeed in so doing, it will be
because the most admirable (if, also, perhaps, the most damaging)
feature of Ullmann's approach is its marked consistency. For however long the journey from Bracton to Aristotle, and however diverse
the materials examined *en route*, it is still possible to discern in the
peculiarities of his interpretations the rudiments of a pattern. Thus,
in the first place, even when least appropriate to the materials under

---

[159] I have in mind here Aristotle's teaching that the unmoved mover, the ultimate final cause, and, therefore, the highest good, while it transcends the universe
is also immanent in it "as the order of the parts."—*Metaph.* XII, 10 trans. Ross,
1075a, 10–24. Also *ibid.*, XII, 8, 1074b, 1–15, where he characterizes as "inspired"
the old myth that the first substances "are gods and that the divine encloses the
whole of nature." See the pertinent remarks of Collingwood, *Idea of Nature*, pp.
88–89, and of G.E.R. Lloyd, *Aristotle: The Growth and Structure of his Thought* (Cambridge,
1968), pp. 157–58. For the general perspective from which these remarks are framed,
I venture to refer again to O'Connor and Oakley eds., *Creation*, esp. pp. 1–12,
241–58.
[160] For the notion of the supernatural and the late date at which the word itself
emerged during the Christian era, see Henri de Lubac, *Surnaturel: Études historiques*
(Paris, 1946), pp. 325–428.

discussion—as, for example, in the cases of Bracton and Aquinas—
his dominant, if not exclusive, concern remains with the *sources* of
legal and governmental power; that is to say, with the realm of efficient causes. In the second place, even when it is most anachronistic
and confusing—as in the case of the pagan Germanic and Scandinavian kingship—his approach is also framed by the sharp contrast
between natural and supernatural; that is to say, by a motif of Christian provenance. And the explanation for this, I would suggest, is
ultimately to be sought in the nature of the perspectives, both disciplinary and historical, which prompted him to propose his ascending-
descending schema and progressively to elaborate its ramifications.

Taking first the disciplinary perspective. It is no accident, I believe,
that the context in which Ullmann was first moved to propose his
schema was that of legal history, or the history of legal theory.
Although some of the ideas involved were in fact adumbrated in the
closing pages of his *Growth of Papal Government*, he himself tells us that
he first used "this terminology of the ascending and descending
themes" in 1958. He did so in the course of reviewing a book the
subject of which was the rise to prominence of the late-medieval and
modern eras of the conception of law as the product of a consciously
legislating will [*das gesetzte Recht*].[161] Again, the paper delivered in
1960 at the *International Congress of Historical Sciences* in which he went
on to elaborate his schema was also concerned with the history of
legal rather than of political theory and did not address itself to the
medieval political philosophers or to their characteristic concerns.[162]
Only in the following year, in his *Principles of Government and Politics*,
did he broaden the scope of his inquiries to include the contributions of Aristotle and of the medieval Aristotelians. Even then, he
did so by fitting them into the conceptual framework already constructed to accommodate the very different preoccupations of modern legal theorists and historians—notably that central concern with
the constitutive moment of law, with the factor that distinguishes law

---

[161] *Growth*, pp. 454–57; the review is of M.J. Odenheimer, *Der Christliche—Kirchliche
Anteil an der Verdrangung der mittelalterlichen Rechtsstruktur und an der Entstehung der Vorherrschaft
des staatlich gesetzten Rechts im deutschen und französischen Rechtsgebiet* (Basel, 1957), in
Tijdschrift voor Rechtgeschiendenis, XXVI (No. 3, 1958), 360–66. Cf. *Principles*, p. 20
note 1; *Papst und König*, p. 49 note 5.
[162] "Law and the Medieval Historian," 34–74, where there are only a couple of
glancing references to the impact of Aristotle (65, and 74 note 17).

properly so called from other regulations of a merely moral or extra-
legal type. This concern has usually conspired to focus attention on
the realm of efficient causation, and if, in all of these studies, Ullmann
remains remarkably faithful to that focus, I believe his particular
disciplinary perspective goes at least part of the way to account for
the fact.

A similar role can be ascribed to the general *historical* perspective
from which he views the history of medieval political thought. His
identification of the ascending thesis with the natural and the descending with the supernatural, the adjectives he characteristically applies
to both, and the periods during which he asserts them to have been
prevalent[163] suggest very strongly that for him there is, despite all
surface differences, a fundamental continuity between the modes of
political thinking characteristic of the modern world and those characteristic of the classical world, at least from Aristotle onwards—
both periods being committed, presumably, to the "natural" and
"secular" modes of explanation appropriate to any properly *political*
thinking. In addition, they suggest, too, that for him the medieval
period stands out in the history of Western political thinking as
an exceptional one, something of an interruption, a deviation from
the norm, a period during which the "natural" categories of political philosophy as we know it were pushed to one side by motifs of
supernatural bent. In assuming this picture of the larger historical
process Ullmann is by no means alone. Its tidiness continues, it would
seem, to beguile. And yet it is now a hundred years and more since
Fustel de Coulanges, in a classic evocation of the centrality of religion to the political life of the ancient world, warned his own contemporaries of the dangers of anachronism, of historical narcissism,
of finding their own attitudes reflected all too readily in those of
ancient peoples whose modes of thought were in reality fundamentally alien to theirs. Since he wrote, moreover, the findings of the
cultural anthropologists, the sociologists, the students of primitive and
comparative religion have converged to confirm the precocious acute-
ness of his vision and to make clear that the transition from the
archaic and classical outlook to the Christian was not so much a
shift from a "secular" to a "religious" viewpoint as from one ancient
and widespread mode of religious consciousness to another and rad-

---

[163] See above, pp. 28–32.

ically different one.[164] The same is true of the transition from the
world of Germanic paganism to that of early-medieval Christianity.[165]
Once this is understood, of course, it is no longer, *pace* Ullmann,
the "religious" nature of medieval political thinking that cries out
for explanation, but rather the emergence in the modern era of that
uniquely secularized political vision which has so succeeded in shaping the common political sense of the Western world that we are
persistently tempted, even at the cost of rampant anachronism, to
see it as something grounded in the very nature of man. But, then,
it is properly the task of historical reflection rather to deliver us from
such delusions than to strengthen our bondage to them. That in this
respect it should fail us may well, therefore, be the gravest defect in
Ullmann's whole overarching conceptual apparatus.

Harsh judgments, perhaps, and ones made, it must certainly be
admitted, with intimations of fallibility more than usually insistent.
Nonetheless, they are judgments I am prepared to stand by—not
unmindful, however, of the need to insist that they are judgments
the specific concern of which is the adequacy of Ullmann's conceptual apparatus as a guide to the intricacies of medieval political
thought. Even at their most negative, therefore, they should not be
taken to impugn either the desirability or the significance of the
whole interpretative enterprise upon which he has been bold enough
to embark. Nor, for that matter, should the persistent identification
of weaknesses which precedes them be taken to preclude the admir-
ing recognition of strengths. For, in this respect, I am struck with
the pertinence of a remark once made by John Stuart Mill. "For
our own part," he said,

> we have a large tolerance for one-eyed men, provided their one eye
> is a penetrating one: if they saw more, they probably would not see
> so keenly, nor so eagerly pursue one course of inquiry. Almost all rich

---

[164] Numa Denis Fustel de Coulanges, *The Ancient City*, trans. Willard Small (New
York, 1955), p. 11; cf. W.K.C. Guthrie, *The Greek Philosophers; From Thales to Aristotle*
(New York, 1960), pp. 3–4, where, acknowledging the indebtedness of classicists to
anthropological studies, he remarks of the Greeks that they remain "in many respects
a remarkably *foreign* people, and to get inside their minds . . . means unthinking much
that has become part and parcel of our mental equipment so that we carry it about
with us unquestioningly and for the most part unconsciously." For Christianity
among the other religions, see Arend Th. Van Leeuwen, *Christianity in World History*,
trans. H.H. Hoskins (New York, 1965).

[165] Thus Höfler, "Der Sakralcharakter des germanischen Königtums," 700–701.

veins of original and striking speculation have been opened up by systematic half-thinkers.[166]

Taking this statement, then, and applying it to Ullmann's vision of
medieval politics, my own verdict overall would run very much as
follows: Rich? Undoubtedly. Striking? Without question. Original?
In no small degree. Speculative? More, perhaps, than he would care
to admit. But fundamentally valid as a key to the understanding of
medieval political thought? I would argue not.

---

[166] John Studart Mill, *Essays on Ethics, Religion and Society*, ed. J.M. Robson (Toronto,
1969), p. 95. My attention was drawn to this remark by Herbert A. Deane, *The
Political and Social Ideas of St. Augustine* (New York, 1963), p. 332.

CHAPTER THREE

"VERIUS EST LICET DIFFICILIUS:" TIERNEY'S *FOUNDATIONS OF THE CONCILIAR THEORY* AFTER FORTY YEARS

The trouble with the writers of classic historical works, or so Felix Gilbert once suggested, is that however much their critics feel obliged to come to terms with the authority of their names, those critics often fail to read them—or, at least, to read them with the close attention they deserve. When he suggested that, Gilbert was ruminating about the fate of von Ranke, almost a century after that great historian's death.[1] But when, in the late 1960s, I encountered Quentin Skinner's withering critique of Lovejoy's approach to the history of ideas, I was forced to wonder if the process in question had accelerated and was now overtaking that author only thirty years after the publication of his classic *Great Chain of Being*.[2] And, more recently, after digesting Hermann Josef Sieben's oblique criticism of Tierney's *Foundations of the Conciliar Theory*, I began to worry that the same fate might now be threatening that distinguished work, too.[3] Sieben's rather wooden cataloguing of selected decretist and decretalist views on general councils and the relationship of pope to council did not even come close to engaging the intricacy, suppleness and restraint of the argument set forth in *Foundations*, nor did it take account (or, at least, take much accurate account) of the historiographic context

---

[1] See the introduction to Felix Gilbert and Stephen Graubard eds., *Historical Studies Today* (New York, 1972), p. xv.

[2] Discussed in Francis Oakley, *Omnipotence, Covenant and Order: An Excursion in the History of Ideas from Abelard to Leibniz* (Ithaca and London, 1984), pp. 27–29.

[3] Hermann Josef Sieben, *Die Konzilsidee des lateinischen Mittelalters (847–1378)* (Paderborn, 1984), pp. 232–76 (esp. 253–55). Constantin Fasolt, *Council and Hierarchy: The Political Thought of William Durant the Younger* (Cambridge, 1991), pp. 17–19, takes a somewhat more positive view of Sieben's critique. He views it as "an outright assault on the central element of Tierney's thesis" and says: ". . . Sieben has tried to cut the 'foundations' of the conciliar theory down to size by showing that the decretists and decretalists of the twelfth and thirteenth centuries overwhelmingly considered general councils to be subordinate to papal authority, so that their thought could hardly have been the immediate source of the conciliar theory."

in which that book had been written.[4] It is with this last matter that
I propose to begin.

It would be hard, I think, fully to sense the importance of the
contribution *Foundations* made, without having had some personal
acquaintance with the state of the field prior to its publication. "In
Conciliar studies," E.F. Jacob had grumbled in 1943, "we are frequently told that this or that view 'is to be found in Ockham,' and
there the matter is unsatisfactorily left."[5] On that score, nothing much
had changed prior to the appearance of *Foundations* in 1955. By then
nobody was any longer content, with the earliest writers on the history of conciliarism, to regard the positions staked out by Conrad
of Gelnhausen and Henry of Langenstein at the start of the schism
as simply the outcome of their attempts to come to terms with the
grievous difficulties occasioned thereby.[6]

---

[4] Thus he exaggerates the degree to which Tierney's case had been preempted
by earlier scholars. Similarly Fasolt, *Council and Hierarchy*, p. 19, where, invoking the
authority of Seidlmayer and Bäumer, he states that "Tierney's emphasis on the
canonists had been anticipated by Bliemetzrieder." Franz Bliemetzrieder, *Das
Generalkonzil im Grossen Abendländischen Schisma* (Paderborn, 1904), pp. 75–76, basing
himself on Otto Gierke, had indeed suggested that in Gratian's *Decretum* and the
canonistic glosses would be found "die Hauptquelle" of conciliar thinking, and that
historians would be wise to pay attention to them. But it was no more than a suggestion that was involved, and in his important review article on *Foundations*, Michael
Seidlmayer does not suggest that it was anything other than that—see *Zeitschrift der
Savigny-Stiftung für Rechtsgeschichte. Kanonistische Abteilung*, XLIII (1957), 374–87 (at 377).
But Remigius Bäumer, who three years earlier had launched a distressingly personal
attack on Tierney (in a review of the latter's *Origins of Papal Infallibility*—see his
"Um die Anfänge der päpstlichen Unfehlbarkeitslehre," *Theologische Revue*, LXIX
[1973], 441–50), does make more of it. He gives the impression, indeed, of being
determined to minimize the originality of Tierney's contribution in *Foundations*—see
his "Die Erforschung des Konziliarismus," in Remigius Bäumer ed., *Die Entwicklung
des Konziliarismus: Werden und Nachwirken der konziliaren Idee* (Darmstadt, 1976), 3–50
(at 29–34). It should be noted, too, that this report is marked also by some odd
emphases and exclusions. Hans Küng's lengthy discussion of conciliarism in *Strukturen
der Kirche* (Freiburg, 1962) gets no more, for example, than a glancing, critical reference. Francis Oakley, *Council over Pope? Towards a Provisional Ecclesiology* (New York
and London, 1969), gets no mention at all, though other works of his are cited.
And John T. McNeill's concluding discussion of that book in his "The Relevance
of Conciliarism," *The Jurist*, XXXI (1971), 81–112, is without explanation deleted
in the translation of the article which appears as "Die Bedeutung des Konziliarismus"
in Bäumer's edited volume, *Die Entwicklung des Konziliarismus* 91–106.

[5] E.F. Jacob, *Essays in the Conciliar Epoch* (2nd ed., Manchester, 1953), p. 85.

[6] For the pertinent scholarly literature, see the introductory survey of the field
as it stood in the 1950s in Tierney, *Foundations of the Conciliar Theory*, pp. 1–14. See
also Karl August Fink, "Zur Beurteilung des grossen abendländischen Schismas,"
Zeitschrift für Kirchengeschichte, LXXIII (1962), 335–43 (despite its brevity, a very important article), and the updated (to 1976 and 1978, respectively) and lengthier discussions

Nor did much enthusiasm attach to John Neville Figgis's unargued assertion that what conciliar theory, in effect, reflected was the bold extension to the universal church of constitutionalist principles long since hammered out in the secular kingdoms of Europe.[7] E.F. Jacobs's twinge of asperity notwithstanding, more sympathy was extended to the efforts of later historians to push back beyond the immediate context in which Gelnhausen and Langenstein had framed their views, and to claim an earlier source for conciliarist views in the great efflorescence of publicistic literature occasioned in the first half of the fourteenth century by the bitter clash between the Avignon papacy and Lewis of Bavaria—and especially in the tracts contributed by those two imperial publicists, William of Ockham and Marsiglio of Padua. For those made uneasy by fact that it was Juan de Torquemada, in his role as leading papalist ideologist at the Council of Basel, who (as Thomas Izbicki has recently reminded us)[8] had first attached this suspect radical genealogy to conciliar theory—for such historians recourse was not readily available. They might conceivably turn to the suggestions advanced periodically over the years by such scholars as Gierke, Bliemetzrieder, Arquillière, Martin and Ullmann to the effect that, behind the works of publicists like Ockham and Marsiglio, beckoned an even deeper and more promising source in the *Decretum Gratiani* itself and in the ocean of glosses written by decretists and decretalists alike. But such suggestions, however intriguing, were no more than suggestions, and, for most historians, given the fact that the bulk of those glosses (many of them unprinted) still awaited investigation, forbiddingly unmanageable suggestions at that.

It was Tierney's great achievement, then, not only to have embarked hopefully on the vast glossatorial ocean (more than one historian had done that), but also, with the publication of *Foundations*, to have brought his ship safely into port, laden with a wealth of pertinent evidence and propelled forward by the power of a sustained argument.

---

in Bäumer, "Die Erforschung des Konziliarismus," 1–34, and Guiseppe Alberigo, "Il movimento conciliare (xiv–xv sec.) nella ricerca storica ricente," *Studi medievali*, XIX (1978), 913–50. Cf. *idem, Chiesa conciliare: Identità e significato del conciliarismo* (Brescia, 1981), pp. 340–54.

[7] John Neville Figgis, *Political Thought from Gerson to Grotius: 1414–1625. Seven Studies* (New York, 1960), pp. 41–70. The book was first published in 1907.

[8] Thomas M. Izbicki, "Papalist Reaction to the Council of Constance: Juan de Torquemada to the Present," *Church History*, LV (No. 1, 1986), 7–20—a very helpful account.

That argument was as economical as it was elegant (the book, after all, is less than three hundred pages long), as lucid as it was compelling, and no less bold for being so carefully delimited and so diffidently restrained. This last point deserves particular emphasis. Not all of the critics have chosen to acknowledge the quite explicit limitations Tierney set for himself[9] when he eschewed any claim to be offering a "complete history" of conciliar thinking prior to the outbreak of the schism, or a "complete account" of the thinking of the canonists on matters pertaining to ecclesiastical government. Instead, it was his explicit intention to focus only on "those elements in canonistic thought that contributed to the growth of Conciliar Theory" (ix).[10]

That tightness of focus paid off. Leaning strongly against "the tendency to treat the Conciliar Movement as something accidental or external thrust upon the Church from the outside," Tierney portrayed it instead as "the logical culmination of ideas that were embedded in the law and doctrine of the Church itself" (15). During the century and more preceding the onset of the Great Schism, the decretalists, in their attempts to rationalize the structure both of the individual churches of Christendom and of the universal Church itself, had been led to develop not one but two separate doctrines concerning the Church's unity. "The more conspicuous one, which has usually been regarded as the canonistic doctrine *par excellence* insisted that the unity of the Church would be secured only by a rigorous subordination of all the members to a single head" (240). Hence the doctrine of absolute papal monarchy that admittedly dominated most of the canonistic glosses of the fourteenth century:

> But side by side with this [familiar doctrine of papal sovereignty] there existed another theory, applied at first to single churches and then at the beginning of the fourteenth century, in a fragmentary fashion, to the Roman Church and the Church as a whole, a theory which stressed the corporate association of the members of the Church as

---

[9] Though Seidlmayer certainly did so—see his review in *ZSSR, Kan. Abt*, XLIII (1957), at 377. Similarly, Fasolt, *Council and Hierarchy*, p. 19, n. 75. Sieben, *Die Konzilsidee des lateinischen Mittelalters*, pp. 253–55, however, did not. Nor, I would judge, did Bäumer, "Die Erforschung des Konziliarismus," 29–34. Nor, perhaps, did Helmut G. Walther, *Imperiales Königtum, Konziliarismus und Volkssouveränität: Studien zu den Grenzen des mittelalterlichen Souveränitätsgedankens* (Munich, 1976), pp. 186–87.

[10] Here (and later) the numbers in brackets refer to the pagination of Brian Tierney, *Foundations of the Conciliar Theory: The Contributions of the Medieval Canonists from Gratian to the Great Schism* (Cambridge, 1955).

the true principle of ecclesiastical unity and which envisaged the exercise of corporate authority by the members of a Church even in the absence of a collective head (240).

That theory, along with an older strand in canonistic thinking going back to the twelfth- and early thirteenth-century commentators on Gratian's *Decretum* (and especially to their discussions of the case of the heretical pope), laid the essential foundations for conciliar theory. The ambivalence of the canonistic heritage blocked the crystallization of a coherently constitutionalist understanding of the Church's unity until the imperative necessities of a protracted schism called such an understanding into being in the formulations of the great conciliarists of Pisa, Constance and Basel, theologians no less than canonists—not least of all those characteristic of "the most mature and harmonious of the conciliar theories, that of Nicolaus Cusanus" himself (36). But it remains nonetheless true that what made those formulations possible was nothing other than "the impregnation of Decretist ecclesiology by Decretalist corporation concepts" (245).

The case Tierney made was at once both powerful and subtly nuanced and, despite the subsequent surfacing of some oblique (and not so oblique) scholarly grumbling,[11] I would judge that the great tide of literature on conciliar and related matters that has been flowing during the forty years since he propounded his thesis has really done little or nothing to shake it. As our knowledge of the thinking of individual conciliarists has grown, so, too, has the body of evidence for the deep impress made on the full range of conciliarist literature by arguments drawn (either directly or at one remove or another) from the glosses of decretists and decretalists alike. That this should be so in works written by those who were themselves lawyers is hardly surprising;[12] more striking is the degree to which some of the theologians, too, reveal their acquaintance with, or indebtedness to, the canonistic literature.[13] And if we are willing to

---

[11] See above, nos. 3, 4 and 9.

[12] Though some of these works come close at times to being a veritable tissue of canonistic citation—see Philippus Decius, *Consilium . . . de auctoritate papae et concilii* (1511), printed in Melchior Goldast ed., *Monarchia S. Romani Imperii* (3 vols., Frankfurt, 1614), II, 1662–76, and Matthias Ugonius, *Synodia Ugonia Episcopi Phamagustani de Conciliis* (Venice, 1532).

[13] That is true even of a Pierre d'Ailly, in whose writings the blunt expression of his contempt for lawyers and for the study of law is a recurrent motif. Or of a Jean Gerson, whose commentators have more than once remarked on his indifference

accord a measure of deference to the understanding of conciliar theory shown by commentators who lived closer in time to the conciliar epoch than do we and who had themselves not even a remotely
conciliar axe to grind, we may wish to take note of the fact that
the English Protestant divines, John Ponet in the mid-sixteenth century and John Bramhall in the mid-seventeenth, unhesitatingly labelled
the conciliar theory as a canonistic teaching. And so, too, did the
seventeenth-century English parliamentarian, William Prynne.[14]

If that is my assessment of the case made by a book which is
concerned to make a contribution to the *history* of ecclesiology, how
then would I appraise its significance beyond that for our understanding of the history of constitutional and political thought, or, for
that matter, its significance for the development of contemporary
Catholic ecclesiology? Let me take up those two matters in turn,
though reversing their order and beginning with ecclesiology and
concluding with the history of political thought.

Almost two centuries ago now, when in his *View of the State of Europe
during the Middle Ages* the English historian, Henry Hallam, came to
write about the ending of the Great Schism at the Council of Constance by the deposition of the rival pontiffs, he spoke of "the Whig
principles of the Catholic church" embodied in the superiority decree
Haec sancta, and described that decree as one of "the great pillars of
that moderate theory with respect to papal authority which . . . is
embraced by almost all laymen and the major part of ecclesiastics

---

to canonistic argumentation. See Francis Oakley, *The Political Thought of Pierre d'Ailly:
The Voluntarist Tradition* (New Haven and London, 1964), pp. 163–64, 209–10, for
d'Ailly's not inconsiderable canonistic erudition. For commentary on Gerson, see
John B. Morrall, *Gerson and the Great Schism* (Manchester, 1960), p. 120; G. Posthumus
Meyjes, *Jean Gerson: Zijn Kerkpolitick en ecclesiologie* (The Hague, 1963), pp. 277–84;
and Oakley, "Gerson and d'Ailly: An Admonition," *Speculum,* XL (No. 1, 1965),
74–83 (at 81), for an argument that Gerson was more familiar with canonistic
modes of thought than his citations might suggest.

[14] John Ponet, *A Shorte Treatise of Politicke Power* (1556)—facsimile reprint in W.S.
Hudson, *John Ponet (1516?–1556): Advocate of Limited Monarchy* (Chicago, 1942), pp.
[103]–[104]; John Bramhall, *The Serpent-Salve,* in A.W.H. ed., *The Works of the Most
Reverend Father in God, John Bramhall, D.D.* (5 vols., Oxford, 1842–45), III, 316; cf.
his *A Just Vindication of the Church of England, ibid.,* I, 248; *A Replication to the Bishop
of Chichester, ibid.,* II, 249; William Prynne, *The Soveraigne Power of Parliaments and
Kingdoms* (London, 1643), p. 73. Bramhall used the fact that the general council's
power to depose criminous popes was "grounded," as he said, "in a known law,"
to argue for the inapplicability of the conciliar analogy to the relationship of king
and parliament.

on this side of the Alps."[15] By the end of the century, however, in the wake of the ecclesiastical and theological developments that had culminated in 1870 in the First Vatican Council, what Hallam had seen as a live ecclesiological option for the Catholics of his day had become a matter of interest only to the archaeologists of defunct ideologies. Vatican I's definitions of papal primacy and infallibility seemed to leave Catholic historians with little choice but to treat the conciliar movement as nothing more than a revolutionary moment in the life of the Church, and Catholic theologians with no alternative but regard the conciliar theory—the malign contribution, it was thought, of those dangerous radicals Marsiglio of Padua and William of Ockham—as a dead issue, an ecclesiological fossil, something lodged deep in the lower carboniferous of the dogmatic geology.[16]

Upon this whole matter—very much one of the "neuralgic points" in Catholic ecclesiology, as Karl August Fink has since labelled it[17]—there descended an ecclesiastical version of the "politics of oblivion." It was only the fortuitous intersection of advances in historical knowledge and John XXIII's unexpected convocation in 1959 of the Second Vatican Council that shattered the silence. Six years before *Foundations* was published, in the long, opening section of his great *History of the Council of Trent*, Jedin gave a powerful impetus to the surge of historical work on the persistence of conciliarism into the Age of Reformation which has continued down to the present, which has long since established the fact that the demise of conciliar theory after the dissolution of Basel was neither as sudden nor as final as we once were led to suppose, and which has powerfully suggested that it is only our familiarity with the papalist outcome that has contrived to suggest the apparent necessity of the process.[18] Six years

---

[15] Henry Hallam, *View of the State of Europe during the Middle Ages* (3 vols., London, 1901), III, 243 and 245. The work was first published in 1818.

[16] So much so, indeed, that in 1908 the editors of *The Catholic Encyclopedia* did not even judge it worthwhile to include in that work an article on conciliarism. For the extraordinary degree of contradiction, confusion, disingenuousness and disarray evident well into the 1960s in the treatment by Catholic encyclopedias of such topics as conciliarism, the Councils of Pisa, Constance and Basel, and the status of the popes of the Avignonese and Pisan lines, see Oakley, *Council over Pope*, pp. 27–29, 123–24. Cf. Izbicki, "Papalist Reaction to the Council of Constance," 17–20.

[17] Fink, "Zur Beurteilung des grossen abendländischen Schismas," 335.

[18] Hubert Jedin, *Geschichte des Konzils von Trient* (4 vols., Freiburg, 1951–75), I, chs. 1–7. Since the publication of Jedin's first volume there has been a steady flow of scholarly literature illuminating the continuing history of conciliarist ideas in the centuries after Basel. For which, see Francis Oakley, "Constance, Basel, and the

later it was likewise (if more dramatically) the contribution of Tierney to have made it abundantly clear that the conciliar theory was neither as recent nor as revolutionary in its origins as it had long been customary to believe.

With the excitement surrounding the convocation of Vatican II, then, and the concomitant renewal of interest in matters conciliar, it is not surprising that during the 1960s Catholic theologians (and those Catholic historians prone to scratching a theological itch) should quickly be forced to come to terms with the implications of all these new historical interpretations for contemporary Catholic ecclesiology. To this development Tierney himself was no stranger, pointing up the pertinence of medieval canonistic teaching to the much-discussed doctrine of episcopal collegiality, and, beyond that, emphasizing at large the constitutionalist implications for the Church of the conciliar tradition.[19]

By the time he did so, however, things had taken a somewhat more radical turn and attention had come to focus rather tightly upon the ecclesiological significance of the Council of Constance itself and of its decrees *Haec sancta* and *Frequens*. As a result, within less than a decade of the publication of *Foundations*, Joseph Gill, of the Pontifical Oriental Institute at Rome, reiterating the long-since traditional rejection of Constance's legitimacy at the time it enacted *Haec sancta*, and warning that "the principle of the superiority of council over pope, forgotten and denied in the intervening centuries [since Constance and Basel], is being revived," ruminated gloomily about what he called "the conciliarists of today" and nominated the Belgian Benedictine, Paul de Vooght, for that forbidding title.[20] In that de Vooght, already in 1960 (and referring to the work of Ullmann

two Pisas: The Conciliar Legacy in Sixteenth and Seventeenth Century England," *Annuarium Historiae Conciliorum*, XXVI (1994), 1–32. Reference should be made especially to Remigius Bäumer, *Nachwirkungen des Konziliaren Gedankens in der Theologie und Kanonistik des frühen 16. Jahrhunderts* (Münster, 1971); Hans Schneider, *Der Konziliarismus als Problem der neueren katholischen Theologie* (Berlin, 1976); Hermann Josef Sieben, *Die katholische Konzilsidee von der Reformation bis zur Aufklärung* (Paderborn, 1988).

[19] Brian Tierney, "Collegiality in the Middle Ages," in *Concilium* (Glenn Rock, N.J.), VII (1965), 5–14 and "Roots of Western Constitutionalism in the Church's Own Tradition: The Significance of the Council of Constance," in James A. Coriden ed., *We, The People of God: A Study of Constitutional Government for the Church* (Huntington, Ind., 1968), 113–28. These points were picked up, e.g., by Richard P. McBrien, *The Remaking of the Church: An Agenda for Reform* (New York, 1973), pp. 86–87, 143–46.

[20] Joseph Gill, "The Fifth Session of the Council of Constance," *Heythrop Journal*, V (1964), 131–43 (at 131). Cf. his later, more general, statement: "Il decreto *Haec*

and Tierney), had been the first to have reopened, once more, the question of the dogmatic status of the Constance superiority decree *Haec sancta*, the nomination was not entirely inappropriate. But it should be noted that in his initial statement de Vooght had restricted himself almost entirely to the role of historian and had hesitated to draw any precise theological conclusions. Only in the final restatement of his position in 1965, and after the appearance of Hans Küng's *Structures of the Church*, did he draw the obvious theological conclusions from his own historical arguments and conclude that *Haec sancta* fulfilled all the conditions necessary to make it a binding dogmatic decree. So that, he concluded, "there is no longer today any motive for maintaining the [traditional] ostracism of a dogmatic decree which clarifies a point of doctrine always admitted in the Church and always taught in the schools."[21]

That conclusion had, in effect, been anticipated by Küng in 1962. Pointing out that "the (traditionally understood) legitimacy of Martin V and all other subsequent popes up to the present day depends on the legitimacy of the Council of Constance and its procedure in the question of popes," he had argued that the question of papal approbation of the decree is not to be "posed anachronistically" and had stated flatly that "the binding character of the decrees of Constance is not to be evaded." But "what was defined," he hastened to add, was not a "radical conciliarism" (his words) reducing the pope to "a subordinate executive organ of a conciliar parliament," but rather "a distinct kind of superiority of the council ... according to which an ecumenical council has the function of 'control authority,' not only in connection with the emergency situation of that time, but

sancta synodus del concilio di Constanza" *Rivista di storia della Chiesa in Italia*, XII (1967), 123–30.

[21] Paul de Vooght, *Les pouvoirs du concile et l'autorité du pape au Concile de Constance* (Paris, 1965), p. 198. In that book, de Vooght restated the case he had developed in the following articles: "Le Conciliarisme aux conciles de Constance et Bâle," in B. Botte *et al.*, *Le Concile et les Conciles: Contribution à l'histoire de la vie conciliaire de l'église* (Chevetogne-Paris, 1960), 143–181; "Le Conciliarisme aux conciles de Constance et Bâle (Compléments et précisions), *Irénikon*, XXXVI (1963), 61–75; "Le concile œcumenique de Constance et le conciliarisme," *Istina*, IX (1963), 57–86; "Le Cardinal Cesarini et le Concile de Constance," in A. Franzen and W. Müller, *Das Konzil von Konstanz: Beiträge zu seiner Geschichte und Theologie* (Freiburg, 1964), 357–81. Hans Küng, *Strukturen der Kirche* (Freiburg, 1962). This was translated into English by Salvatore Attanasio as *Structures of the Church* (New York, 1964). The references below are given to this edition.

also for the future in the premise that a possible future pope might lapse into heresy, schism, or the like."[22]

In light, however, of Küng's subsequent and masterly ecclesiological treatise, with its almost agnostic appraisal of the whole question of a scripturally-validated papal primacy, and his rejection (even before he wrote his book on infallibility), as "something that is not directly demonstrable from the New Testament," of "the *a priori*, unquestionable and *verifiable* infallibility of particular 'doctrinal statements,'—in light of these subsequent, more radical, positions, what is striking is the extreme caution with which, in *Structures of the Church*, he interpreted the implications of his own affirmation of the dogmatic validity of *Haec sancta*. In that book, indeed, he came close, in effect, to understanding *Haec sancta* in terms of the teaching of Vatican I, or, more precisely, to understanding it in terms of the room left by that teaching and by the 1917 Code of Canon Law for the existence of limitations upon the exercise of papal authority.[23] As a result, in the years prior to the appearance in 1970 of his book on infallibility, it was left to others to push into more novel territory the implications of the "new conciliarism." And, along that route, the outer limits were reached with the insistence that Constance's *Haec sancta* and Vatican I's *Pastor aeternus*—both of them meeting the tests for valid conciliar, doctrinal pronouncements—were in almost direct conflict one with another, that not even the most agile of hermeneutical gymnastics made it possible to effect a credible reconciliation between them, that, as a result, the absolutist claims traditionally made (and currently being made) by the official Church for the *magisterium* had simply to be dropped, and that it was necessary to admit, with full candor, the essential historicity and reformability of all doctrinal pronouncements, conciliar no less than papal, as well as, concomitantly, the reformability of all ecclesiologies, conciliar no less than ultramontane.[24]

---

[22] Küng, *Structures of the Church*, pp. 270–71, 284–85. Cf. pp. 288–302, where he makes heavy use of *Foundations* and pays generous tribute to the importance of its contribution.

[23] See Küng, *Die Kirche* (Freiburg-Basle-Vienna, 1967), translated by Ray and Rosaleen Ockenden as *The Church* (New York, 1968)—see esp. pp. 342–43, 471–72, and his *Unfehlbar? Eine Anfrage* (Zürich, 1970) translated by Edward Quinn as *Infallible? An Inquiry* (New York, 1971). For the pertinent sections of *Structures of the Church*, see pp. 224–341, and esp. pp. 281–85, 310ff. For a contemporary criticism of Küng's "deductive timidity" in this last book, see Oakley, *Council over Pope*, pp. 134–41.

[24] This is the position set forth by Oakley in *Council over Pope*, pp. 132–85, and

In the history of interpreting the ecclesiological significance of *Haec sancta*, however, that position stood out as something of an isolated extreme.[25] The 1960s and 1970s saw an extensive body of scholarly literature produced concerning the status and interpretation of *Haec sancta*, but no viable historical or theological consensus was generated thereby.[26] The mainstream of interpretation flowed, instead, through less broken countryside than that occupied by the extreme position; it pursued, on the one hand, a course more cautious than that adopted by Küng, even in *Structures of the Church*, while on the other still departing in varying degree from the rejectionist high ground defended by Gill and others of similarly traditionalist sympathies. But here the story becomes even more tangled and, feeling a sharp tug on the tether confining me to the topic at hand, I must

in his "The 'New Conciliarism' and its Implications: A Problem in History and Hermeneutics," *Journal of Ecumenical Studies*, VIII (No. 4, 1971), 815–40. That ecclesiological stance enjoyed a distinctly mixed reception. The responses of Catholic commentators ranged from uneasy approval (variously qualified), via distaste, to silence. See the reviews of the book by Felix Malmberg in *Bijdragen*, XXXI (No. 1, 1970), 98–99, and his "Naar ein Wezenlijk-provisorische Ecclesiologie?" *ibid.*, 33–52; Brian Tierney, in *The Jurist*, XXX (No. 3, 1970), 398–99; Richard P. McBrien, review in *Commonweal* (Jan. 30, 1970), 490–92; Michael J. Walsh, S.J., review in *The Month*, CCXXIX (Feb., 1970), 121–22. For the politics of silence, see above, n. 4. The single most negative reaction, however, was of Protestant provenance. See the oddly (and sloppily) irascible review by Albert C. Outler in *Journal of Ecumenical Studies*, VII (1970), 804–6, and the response (puzzled and belligerent!) of Oakley, *ibid.*, VIII (1971), 382–83. There is an accurate and balanced appraisal in Schneider, *Der Konziliarismus als Problem der neueren katholischen Theologie*, pp. 264–73.

[25] That is the judgment of Schneider, *ibid.*, pp. 270–71.

[26] Much of the pertinent literature up to the mid-1970s is summarized, criticized, or commented on in Oakley, *Council over Pope*, pp. 105–71, Paul de Vooght, "Les controverses sur les pouvoirs du concile et l'autorité du pape au Concile du Constance," *Revue theologique de Louvain*, I (1970), 45–75, and Schneider, *Der Konziliarismus als Problem der neuren Katholischen Theologie*, pp. 239–339. Complete listing up to 1981 in Francis Oakley, "Natural Law, the *Corpus Mysticum*, and Consent in Conciliar Theory from John of Paris to Matthias Ugonius," *Speculum*, LVI (No. 4, 1981), 786–810 (at 788–89 n. 9). Cf. the interesting account of the way in which the decree was evaluated in the half-century prior to Vatican I in Hermann Josef Sieben, *Katholische Konzilsidee im 19. und 20. Jahrhundert* (Paderborn, 1993), pp. 36–71. Among the most judicious contributions (occupying ground between that staked out by Küng and Jedin, respectively) are those of Brian Tierney, "Hermeneutics and History: The Problem of *Haec Sancta*," in T.A. Sandquist and Michael Powicke eds., *Essays in Medieval History for Presentation to Bertie Wilkinson* (Toronto, 1969), pp. 354–70. His position in this article was criticized by Oakley, "The 'New Conciliarism' and its Implications," 831–33, and there is a persuasive (if not necessarily conclusive) response to that criticism in Tierney, "'Divided Sovereignty' at Constance: A Problem of Medieval and Early Modern Political Theory," *Annuarium Historiae Conciliorum*, VII (1975), 338–56 (see esp. 242–48).

restrict myself to focusing on the revealingly selective way in which some of the scholars involved made use of the thesis propounded in *Foundations*.

In an address which he himself identified, not as a work of history, but as a contribution to ecclesiological discourse,[27] Jedin himself signalled the general direction that was to be followed by this stream of interpretation. While at one with Küng in his desire to avoid posing anachronistically the question of subsequent papal approbation of *Haec sancta*, he insisted (invoking the definitions of Vatican I) that the fact that John XXIII was not an indisputably legitimate pope was "decisive" for the doctrinal status of the decree. Despite the later efforts of the Council of Basel to accord it such a status, therefore, it was not to be viewed as a "universal, as it were, free-floating definition of belief," but rather as "an emergency measure to meet a quite definite exceptional case" of the type that the decretists had envisaged and in which, they had insisted, the interest of the Church had to come before that of the pope. Only (and for the first time) in 1439, he said, when it was attempting to depose an unquestionably legitimate pope, and when it had become a rump council bent on turning itself into a "church parliament" in a manner wholly alien to the conciliar tradition, did Basel accord to *Haec sancta* an absolute dogmatic value and declare the superiority of council to pope a truth of the faith.

Shortly thereafter, in a *Concilium* article that enjoyed a very wide circulation, claiming oddly to be in broad agreement with *both* Küng and Jedin and insisting that *Haec sancta* was "not the kind of dogmatic definition which Vatican I described," August Franzen argued that Constance "did not intend the decree . . . to be a norm of faith."[28] Only because the fathers assembled at Basel moved in 1439

---

[27] Hubert Jedin, *Bischöfliches Konzil oder Kirchenparlament? Ein Beitrag zur Ecklesiologie des Konzilien von Konstanz und Basel* (2nd ed., Basel and Stuttgart, 1965), a revision and extension of the first version published in 1962. See esp. pp. 6–8, 12–15, 37–39.

[28] August Franzen, "The Council of Constance: Present State of the Problem," *Concilium*, VII (1965), 29–68, esp. 45–68. This lengthy article is largely dependent upon two earlier articles of his: "Zur Vorgeschichte des Konstanzer Konzils vom Ausbruch des Schismas bis zum Pisanum," and "Das Konzil der Einheit: Einigung bemühungen und Konziliaren Gedanken auf dem Konstanzer Konzil. Die Dekrete 'Haec sancta' und 'Frequens'," in *Das Konzil von Konstanz*, ed. Franzen and Müller, 3–35, 69–112. It should be noted that while Jedin's argument is marked by its own confusions (in the second edition he ruefully conceded the manifest difficulties attendant upon it—see *Bischöfliches Konzil oder Kirchenparlament*, pp. 38–39), they are over-

to reinterpret the decree "in a radical conciliarist sense" was it taken to be a dogmatic statement. What it really was, instead, was a measure for emergencies, a piece of legislation designed to give formal, legal force to the traditional decretist teaching that a general council was superior in authority to a pope who, by lapsing into heresy or by fostering schism had ceased *ipso facto* to be anything more than a pseudo-pope.[29]

With this approach Remigius Bäumer, in his subsequent study of the reverberations of conciliar thinking in the theology and canonistics of the early sixteenth century, was clearly sympathetic.[30] But his treatment of these matters, in common with Franzen's, was marked by one striking characteristic. Though they both invoked the argument of *Foundations* (Franzen referred to it as Tierney's "brilliant study"), they appear to have assimilated that argument only in a reduced or truncated form. Thus, they misleadingly insisted on distinguishing between, on the one hand, a "conciliarism" or "radical conciliarism" which they viewed as stemming from Marsiglio and Ockham and as having been adopted by Basel, and, on the other, a "conciliar theory" or "moderate conciliarism" which they viewed as having been affirmed at Constance in the decree *Haec sancta* and as being nothing other than an expression of the decretist teaching on the extraordinary case of the heretical pope.[31] Tierney's stress on the contribution of decretalist corporation theory to conciliar thinking was passed over in silence. So, too, by and large, the decretist school of thought which insisted that a heretical pope had to be subjected as pope to conciliar trial, judgment and deposition. Instead,

---

shadowed by the incoherence of the case Franzen makes here. For a discussion and critique of both, see Oakley, *Council over Pope*, pp. 113–20.

[29] Franzen, 57–58, 67.

[30] Bäumer, *Nachwirkungen des Konziliaren Gedankens.*

[31] Franzen, "The Council of Constance," 45–61; Bäumer, *Nachwirkungen des konziliaren Gedankens*, pp. 14–15, 261, 265. For the inadequacy of such categorizations of conciliarism see Ulrich Bubenheimer's review of Bäumer's book in *Zeitschrift der Savigny-Stiftung für Rechtsgeschichte*, XC (1973), *Kanonistische Abteilung* 59, 455–63; Heiko A. Oberman, both in his introduction to the Facet Books edition of Brian Tierney, *Ockham, the Conciliar Theory and the Canonists* (Philadelphia, 1971), pp. xii–xvii, and in his "Et tibi dabo claves regni coelorum" *Nederlands Theologisch Tijdschrift*, XXXIX (No. 2, 1975), 97–118 (at 103–9); Francis Oakley, "Conciliarism in the Sixteenth Century: Jacques Almain Again," *Archiv für Reformationsgeschichte*, LXVIII (1977), 111–32 (at 130–32); Alberigo, *Chiesa conciliare*, p. 345. Fasolt, *Council and Hierarchy*, p. 20, n. 77, takes Alberigo at this point to be criticizing Oakley, but in this he is mistaken.

they focused on the alternative teaching that a heretical pope ceased *ipso facto* to be pope and, as a result, could be subjected as a private person to a merely declaratory process of judgment.[32] But that latter view, of course, was close to being a commonplace, even among such staunch papalists as Torquemada in the fifteenth century and Bellarmine over a century later.[33] And, as even Robert Persons, the Elizabeth Jesuit controversialist readily acknowledged, it was still at the end of the sixteenth century a matter taught publicly in the schools, even at Rome itself.[34]

So diminished (or domesticated) the ecclesiological importance of the Council of Constance on which Küng had insisted, and for the recognition of which by the theological community Tierney's historical work in *Foundations* had blazed the trail, became understandably less obvious.[35] Perhaps accordingly, as the 1970s and 1980s wore on, the attention of Catholic ecclesiologists appears to have drifted away somewhat from such matters—mainly, I would judge, and after a brief period of intense focus on the question of papal infallibility, back in the direction of the more fundamental (or, at least, more abstract and theoretical) dimensions of their field.[36] Doubtless, there

---

[32] For these two approaches to the case of the heretical pope, see Tierney, *Foundations of the Conciliar Theory*, pp. 8–9, 56–65, 212–18.

[33] And Thomas de Vio, Cardinal Cajetan, went further than that, attributing an actual power of deposition to the general council—see Vincent-Marie Pollet, "La doctrine de Cajetan sur l'Église," *Angelicum*, XII (No. 2, 1935), 223–44 (at 224–29).

[34] Thus "Philopater" (Robert Persons), *Elizabethae Angliae Reginae Haeresim Calvinianam propagantis saevissimum in Catholicos sui regni Edictum* (Lyons, 1592), § 221, p. 152; similarly, his *A Treatise tending to Mitigation towards Catholicke Subjectes in England* (St. Omer, 1607), §§ 52–53, pp. 180–81. Cf. William Allen, *A true, sincere and modest defence of English Catholiques that suffer for their Faith* (Ingolstadt [?], 1586), p. 73, where he argues that "... no more [would] the Popes Holines ... count anie of his own subiectes Traitors for houlding, that in case of Heresie or Apostasie, he might be deposed or loose the right of his place and dignitie."

[35] Reflecting perhaps the sense, too, even among historians, that the claim of Küng and De Vooght to the effect that *Haec sancta* constituted a dogmatic definition had been forcefully and successfully contradicted and had come, as a result, to represent by the late 1970s no more than a "marginal" position—thus Erich Meuthen, "Das Basler Konzil in "römisch-katholischer Sicht," *Theologische Zeitschrift*, XXXVIII (1982) 274–308 (at 277–78 n. 8). Note, on the other hand, that Yves Congar had judged Tierney's *Foundations* to be "le livre décisif"—see his "La collégialité de l'épiscopat et la primauté de l'évêque de Rome dans l'histoire," in Congar, *Ministères et communion ecclésiale* (Paris, 1971), p. 116 n. 32. Cf. Küng, *Structures of the Church*, pp. 268–88.

[36] For a useful review of the state of Catholic ecclesiological discussion in the immediate aftermath of Vatican II, see Richard P. McBrien, *Church: The Continuing Quest* (New York, 1970). The flurry of interest in the infallibility question was stim-

were many factors involved in that shift. In 1970 Gregory Baum had berated Catholics at large for their "institutional hang-up," their instinctive tendency to ecclesiasticize religion, their obsessive concern with questions relating to "defined doctrine, sacramental legislation or ecclesiastical jurisdiction."[37] His sentiments may well have been

---

ulated almost immediately thereafter by the publication of Hans Küng's *Unfehlbar? Eine Anfrage* (Zürich, 1970) and Brian Tierney's *Origins of Papal Infallibility: 1150–1350* (Leiden, 1972). The argument of the former was vigorously engaged, for example, in Karl Rahner ed., *Zum Problem Unfehlbarkeit. Antworten auf die Anfrage von H. Küng* (Freiburg, 1971)—see especially Rahner's own contributions to that volume, pp. 9–70, 174–95. Cf. Yves Congar, "Infallibilité et Indéfectibilité," in Congar, *Ministères et Communion Ecclésiale*, pp. 141–65. There is a useful discussion of the debate stimulated by Küng's book in Sieben, *Katholische Konzilsidee im 19. und 20. Jahrhundert*, pp. 386–407. And for a sense of the range of debate concerning the thesis of the latter, see Alfons M. Stickler, "Papal Infallibility—a Thirteenth-Century Invention," *Catholic Historical Review*, LXV (No. 3, 1974), 427–41, Tierney's reply "Infallibility and the Medieval Canonists: A Discussion with Alfons Stickler," *ibid.*, LXVI (No. 2, 1975), 265–73, and Stickler's "Rejoinder to Professor Tierney," *ibid.*, 274–77, as well as Tierney's exchange with Remigius Bäumer: See Bäumer, "Um die Anfänge der päpstlichen Unfehlbarkeitslehre," *Theologische Revue*, 69 (1973), 441–50; Tierney's response, "On the History of Papal Infallibility: A Discussion with Remigius Bäumer," *ibid.*, 70 (1974), 185–93; and Bäumer again, "Antwort an Tierney," *ibid.*, 193–94.

This general issue is the focus of a forthright discussion (under the rubric of "infallibility or indefectibility" and with reference to the contributions of Yves Congar, Küng and Rahner) in a recent, comprehensive survey of modern Catholic ecclesiological thinking by Miguel M. Garijo-Guembe, *Communion of the Saints: Foundation, Nature, and Structure of the Church* (Collegeville, Minnesota, 1994), pp. 182–86. (The book is a translation by Patrick Madigan of *Gemeinschaft der Heiligen: Grund, Wesen und Struktur der Kirche*, first published in 1988). But in the same work the conciliar issue gets only the most glancing of references and then (p. 223) via the final report of the Anglican-Roman Catholic International Commission. There are similarly glancing references to the medieval teaching on the case of the heretical pope (see pp. 190, 227). But this is incorrectly interpreted (as was the case with Franzen, see above n. 29) as a "unanimous teaching" asserting that a pope who lapsed into heresy ceased *ipso facto*, as a result, to be pope, and that teaching is incorrectly ascribed to Cajetan (see p. 190, n. 27). For that interpretation the authority of both Congar and Küng is invoked, though Küng in fact proffers a more accurately nuanced view. See Küng, *Structures of the Church*, pp. 261–63, 296, 308–10. Garijo-Guembe's bibliographical listings are quite rich, but he slights in general the contributions of historians on this topic and, in particular, makes no reference to any of Tierney's writings. In this respect, Patrick Granfield, *The Papacy in Transition* (New York, 1980), pp. 78–85, 166–74, is somewhat more helpful and reliable—though he does follow the *Annuario Pontificio* in appearing to recognize the exclusive legitimacy of the Roman line of claimants during the Great Schism—see p. 198.

[37] Gregory Baum, "The Institutional Hang-Up," *Commonweal* (May 15, 1970), 212–13. While the particular set of hermeneutical principles Baum himself was bringing to the interpretation of papal and conciliar magisterial pronouncements might be expected to liberate him from the necessity of harboring any such distracting "hang-ups" (on which, see Oakley, "The 'New Conciliarism' and its Implications," 834–40), he had in fact indicated in the previous year his own worry that collegiality was destined to be "a dead word unless the Pope . . . [changed] . . .

shared by many a theologian at the time, though it is tempting to
speculate that the shift at Rome over the past two decades into an
unambiguously Thermidorian phase may have rendered somewhat
less than appealing as a sub-specialty the more institutional or constitutional aspects of ecclesiological work. Certainly, on the latter
(perhaps ungenerous) note, there come irresistibly to mind from the
late fourteenth century the words of the Parisian theologian, Jean
Courtecuisse (Johannes Breviscoxe). After ruminating provocatively
about the source of some aspects of the papal power of coercive
jurisdiction, he wryly added, tongue firmly in scholastic cheek: "But
this I do not assert. For it is perilous to speak of this matter—more
perilous, perhaps, than to speak of the Trinity, or the Incarnation
of Jesus Christ our Savior."[38]

When one turns, however, to the significance of the contribution of
Foundations to our understanding of the history of political thought,
one finds oneself on more welcoming terrain. The principal reason
for that is the subsequent (and congruent) development of Tierney's
own thinking evident in a very impressive body of scholarly work
published over the course of the past forty years. And the subsidiary
reason: the unfolding of events during the same period in the world
at large—the chastening experience of decolonization and its aftermath, the restoration over the past decade and more of constitutionalist regimes in so many parts of Latin America, and, most
recently, the collapse of communism and the attempt to establish
and consolidate liberal democratic regimes in eastern Europe and in
the successor states to the Soviet Union. I will return to this latter
development by way of conclusion to this paper. What I should like
to do now is to focus briefly on the direction taken by Tierney's
work in the aftermath of *Foundations*.

Right at the start of that book (p. 1) he noted that late-medieval
political thinking was dominated by "two major problems concern-

---

the understanding of his own office," and, referring to Constance and *Haec sancta*,
had argued that "it should . . . be possible to have papal primacy and episcopal collegiality guaranteed by some sort of constitutional law"—see his "Suenens Crying
in the Wilderness," *The Catholic World*, No. 210 (Dec., 1969), 103–107.

    [38] Johannes Breviscoxe, *Tractatus de fide et ecclesia, romano pontifice et concilio generali*,
in Jean Gerson, *Opera omnia*, ed. Louis Ellies Dupin (6 vols., Antwerp, 1706), I, 882.
Cf. Francis Oakley, "The 'Tractatus de Fide et Ecclesia, Romano Pontifice, et
Concilio Generalis' of Johannes Breviscoxe," *Annuarium Historiae Conciliorum*, X (1978),
99–130.

ing the nature and limits of ecclesiastical authority," problems often, in their development across time, closely associated one with another but logically quite distinct. The first was the long drawn-out conflict between *regnum* and *sacerdotium*. The second concerned matters internal to the structure of the Church itself and the distribution of authority among head and members. Among historians, the first had always attracted a great deal of interest and attention. The second, much less so. It was, of course, with the second that *Foundations* was concerned. And commenting in that book on Figgis's thesis about the origins of conciliar theory Tierney had emphasized the further point that the interactions of the rival governmental structures of state and church may have been even more significant than the state of conflict that so often enveloped them.[39] Indeed, "one might . . . argue," he said, "that the resemblance between the conciliar theories and the constitutional experiments of secular states was due partly to canonistic influence in the secular sphere" (pp. 11–12, n. 2).

Much of his subsequent work—most notably his Wiles lectures on religion, law, and the growth of constitutional thought from the mid-twelfth to the mid-seventeenth centuries (along with the earlier work it drew upon), and, more recently, the continuing series of articles he has devoted to an investigation of the origins and development of theories of individual natural rights in European legal and political thought—much of that work has focused on these "more complex and more important" problems of interaction. It has been directed, in effect, to a probing exploration of the proposition that the juridical culture of the twelfth century—the works of the Roman and canon lawyers, especially those of the canonists where religious and secular ideas most obviously intersected—formed a kind of seedbed from which "[eventually] grew," not only "the whole tangled forest of early modern constitutional thought,"[40] but also the notion of natural rights which played so central a role in early modern political theory.[41] The project, of course, is mightily ambitious,

---

[39] A point made with great clarity in Tierney, "Medieval Canon Law and Western Constitutionalism," *The Catholic Historical Review*, LII (No. 1, 1966), 1–17 (at 8).

[40] The words cited are those of Brian Tierney, *Religion, Law, and the Growth of Constitutional Thought: 1150–1650* (Cambridge, 1982), p. 1. Among the earlier articles of his that this book builds upon, attention should be drawn especially to "Medieval Canon Law and Western Constitutionalism," "The Roots of Western Constitutionalism in the Church's Own Tradition," and "'Divided Sovereignty' at Constance: A Problem of Medieval and Early Modern Political Theory."

[41] Since the publication of *Religion, Law, and the Growth of Constitutional Thought* in

and the topic hugely complex. Here I must content myself with making no more than a handful of observations about what it has involved,
observations focused, in particular, on its investigation of the development of constitutional thinking.

The basic assumptions underlying the whole project are two-fold.
First, that "it is impossible really to understand the growth of Western
constitutional thought unless we consider constantly, side by side,
ecclesiology and political theory, ideas about the church and ideas
about the state." And, again, that "it is hardly possible to understand" that tradition of constitutional thinking "unless we consider
the whole period from 1150 to 1650 as a single era of essentially
continuous development."[42]

In relation to the former assumption, it should be noted that the
claims Tierney makes, developing further a tradition of scholarship
represented notably in the United States by such scholars as Gaines
Post and Ernst Kantorowicz,[43] link closely with the thesis argued in
Foundations, especially as it relates to the specific contribution of canonistic corporation theory to the development of a form of ecclesiastical constitutionalism.[44] For that corporation theory, preoccupied as
it was with the distribution of authority among head and members
of a complex collegiate body, and insisting as it did on the ability

---

1982, Tierney has produced a notable series of articles on the origins of the notion
of individual rights. See his "Tuck on Rights: Some Medieval Problems," *History of
Political Thought*, IV (1983), 429–41; "Religion and Rights: A Medieval Perspective,"
Journal of Law and Religion, V (1987), 163–75; "Villey, Ockham and the Origins of
Individual Rights," in John Witte and Frank S. Alexander eds., *The Weightier Matters
of the Law: A Tribute to Harold J. Berman* (Atlanta, 1988), 1–31; "Origins of Natural
Rights Language: Texts and Contexts," *History of Political Thought*, X (1989), 615–46;
"Marsilius on Rights," *Journal of the History of Ideas*, LII (1991), 3–17; "Natural Rights
in the Thirteenth century: A *Quaestio* of Henry of Ghent," *Speculum*, LXVII (1992),
58–68. While with this line of investigation Tierney moves away somewhat from
his earlier preoccupation with conciliar thought, he brings the two interests together
in "Conciliarism, Corporation and Individualism: The Doctrine of Individual Rights
in Gerson," *Cristianesimo nella storia*, IX (1988), 81–110, where among other things
he points out (93) that "medieval conciliarism is the truly significant . . . context that
makes Gerson's theory of rights intelligible," and suggests (at 107–8) the desirability of re-evaluating "the individualist element in the whole body of conciliarist literature . . . in relation to the Western natural rights tradition."
    [42] Tierney's *Religion, Law, and the Growth of Constitutional Thought*, p. 1.
    [43] See, especially, Gaines Post, *Studies in Medieval Legal Thought* (Princeton, 1964),
and Ernst Kantorowicz, *The King's Two Bodies* (Princeton, 1957).
    [44] The aspect of his argument, in effect, that Franzen and Bäumer, in down-
playing the significance of that constitutionalist thrust, contrived somehow to push
to one side.

of the members to exercise the corporate authority even absent the presence of an effective head—that specifically canonistic variant of corporation theory was assimilated, he argues, not only into ecclesiastical but also into secular thinking. And assimilated also during the later medieval centuries, along with such notions, was in addition a whole battery of affiliated constitutionalist ideas pertaining to representation, consent, rights of resistance, collegiate and "divided" sovereignty, ideas which coalesced into "an unusual structure of constitutional thought that was common to medieval law, to fifteenth century conciliarism, and to seventeenth century constitutional theory."[45] In relation to Tierney's affiliated assumption that in matters constitutional the period from the late-twelfth to the late-seventeenth centuries must be understood as a single epoch, more than one approach is pertinent. The older one was pioneered by Figgis and pursued more recently by those who, while rejecting his thesis about the origins of conciliar theory, have endorsed his claim about the influence of conciliar theory upon the thinking of the secular resistance theorists and constitutionalists of the sixteenth and seventeenth centuries, and have busied themselves with the task of mapping out that process more precisely. While not unduly dismissive of that approach, Tierney himself, however, has persistently nudged us to probe somewhat deeper, to recognize that "resemblances which cannot be explained as a result of the influence of one writer on another may be at least as important for the historian as those that can be so explained." For they reflect "a continued preoccupation of many thinkers with essentially similar problems of constitutional theory through more than five centuries of Western history."[46]

---

[45] Tierney, *Religion, Law, and the Growth of Constitutional Thought*—the words cited appear at p. 103. See also his "'Divided Sovereignty' at Constance," 238–56, a fine article with a broader significance than its title might suggest.

[46] Tierney, "'Divided Sovereignty' at Constance," 254–55, where he adds: "It follows . . . that the task of a historian is not simply to pursue threads of influence from one author to another down the course of the centuries. The further, more difficult task for future research will be to understand what elements of continuity existed in social, political and religious life (during a period of such incessant change) which might explain the continued preoccupation of so many thinkers with the same constitutional problems over such a long period of time." Cf. *Religion, Law, and the Growth of Constitutional Thought*, pp. 103–8. Given this emphasis, I find it odd that Cary J. Nederman, in a recent critique of the Figgis influence thesis and its latter-day defenders appears to regard Tierney as one of those defenders and reserves one or two of his sharpest barbs for him—see Nederman, "Conciliarism and Constitutionalism: Jean Gerson and Medieval Political Thought," *History of European*

Of course, in a project of such scale and complexity it is only to be expected that disagreement should arise on this or that particular point. On the interpretation, for example, of Aegidius Romanus, writing in the fourteenth century.[47] Or on the use made of Julian Franklin's interpretation of George Lawson, writing in the seventeenth.[48] Or on whether one can really, without anachronism, speak of thirteenth-century lawyers as having "asked Rousseau's questions" and addressed explicitly the problem of political obligation.[49] Or, for that matter, whether one should not, after all, persist in ascribing a somewhat greater importance than does Tierney to the really quite extensive use made of the conciliar precedent by the Protestant resistance theorists and constitutionalists of the sixteenth and seventeenth centuries—if only because of what that usage reveals about the ideological demands of the religious and political context in which they found themselves.[50]

So far as the general approach is concerned, however, I would predict that in the stakes of historiographic reputation it will pros-

---

Ideas, XII (No. 3, 1990), 189–209. I have always thought that the powerful case Tierney has made for an essentially continuous unfolding of constitutionalist ideas from the canonistic literature of the twelfth century to the political thinkers of the seventeenth tended rather to diminish than enhance the significance that Figgis (and later sympathizers like myself) attached specifically to the conciliar legacy.

[47] On which, see J.H. Burns, review of *Religion, Law, and the Growth of Constitutional Thought*, in *Journal of Ecclesiastical History*, XXXIV (No. 2, 1983), 271–73.

[48] That interpretation (see J.H. Franklin, *John Locke and the Theory of Sovereignty* [Cambridge, 1978]) has been sharply criticized by James H. Tully, "Current Thinking about Sixteenth- and Seventeenth-Century Political Theory," *The Historical Journal*, XXIV (No. 2, 1981), 475–84 (at 480–83), and by Conal Condren, "Resistance and Sovereignty in Lawson's *Politica*: An Examination of a Part of Professor Lawson, his Chimera," *ibid.*, XXIV (No. 3, 1981), 673–81. Tierney discusses Lawson in *Religion, Law, and the Growth of Constitutional Thought*, pp. 97–102, and p. 81 where he cites Franklin.

[49] As does Tierney in *Religion, Law, and the Growth of Constitutional Thought*, pp. 34–39. For a different (perhaps more old-fashioned) view of the matter, see Francis Oakley, "Legitimation by Consent: The Question of the Medieval Roots," *Viator*, XIV (1983), 303–35, and "Disobedience, Consent, Political Obligation: The Witness of Wessel Gansfort (c. 1419–1489)," *History of Political Thought*, IX (No. 2, 1988), 211–21.

[50] I addressed these issues some years ago in "Figgis, Constance, and the Divines of Paris," and "Natural Law, the *Corpus Mysticum*, and Consent in Conciliar Thought," and have since returned to them in "Constance, Basel, and the Two Pisas," in which I conclude that, in the early-seventeenth century, "the access of English people to the conciliarist literature was easier . . . (and their knowledge of that literature concomitantly greater) than at any time preceding, the fifteenth century not excluded." And "*Anxieties of Influence*: Skinner, Figgis, Conciliarism and early-modern Constitutionalism," see below, ch. 5.

per, and increasingly so as the new picture being generated by current investigations of the natural rights tradition comes progressively
into focus. In one of a notable series of articles emphasizing important discontinuities between late-medieval political thinking and distinctively modern preoccupations, Cary J. Nederman, it is true, has
recently launched a sweeping attack on the claims being made for
the impact of medieval ecclesiology in general and conciliar theory
in particular upon the shaping of early-modern constitutionalism.[51]
That attack, however, depends for its force on something of a mis-
representation of what those claims actually involved, as well as upon
the deployment of an over-rigid and essentially anachronistic definition
of "modern constitutionalism," one as ill-matched to the realities of
the seventeenth century as it is to those of the fifteenth.[52] Indeed,
Nederman's greatest contribution in this article, or so I conclude,
may well have been other than he intended. Namely, that of lend-
ing unwitting support to those—A.J. Black, J.H. Burns and others—
who, like Tierney, have argued that we would do well to go about
our task of historical interpretation on the assumption that "the truly
epochal shifts in European political thought occurred in the eleventh
and eighteenth centuries," so that the whole period in between should
properly be understood, therefore, as "essentially a single epoch."[53]

   These being the centuries which witnessed, as Tierney has argued,
the crystallization in Europe of a body of constitutional thinking that

---

[51] See Nederman, "Conciliarism and Constitutionalism: Jean Gerson and Medieval
Political Thought," 189–209. Cf. Nederman, "Nature, Sin and the Origins of Society:
The Ciceronian Tradition in Medieval Political Thought," *Journal of the History of
Ideas*, XLIX (No. 1, 1988), 3–26; *idem*, "Knowledge, Consent and the Critique of
Political Representation in Marsiglio of Padua," *Political Studies*, XXXIX (No. 1,
1991), 19–35.

[52] For a discussion and critique of Nederman's case, see Francis Oakley, "Nederman,
Gerson, Conciliar Theory and Constitutionalism: *Sed contra*," *History of Political Thought*,
XVI (No. 1, 1995), 1–19.

[53] The words are those of Antony Black, *Political Thought in Europe: 1250–1450*
(Cambridge, 1992), p. 191. See also the comments of J.H. Burns in his introduction to J.H. Burns and Mark Goldie eds., *The Cambridge History of Political Thought:
1650–1700* (Cambridge, 1991), 1–3. There he notes that "as the differentiation
between 'early modern' and 'later modern' has sharpened, that between 'early modern' and 'medieval' has softened." Right at the end of the period covered by the
volume we find, after all "the stubborn persistence of theological issues that had
preoccupied late medieval scholastics." Certainly, the amount of emphasis placed
on such issues by the historians contributing to the volume itself signals a significant
shift in the way in which, over the past quarter century, we have come to understand the ideological underpinnings of early-modern political thinking.

we now recognize as distinctively Western,[54] let me return, by way of conclusion, to my earlier suggestion that the unfolding of events world-wide over the past half-century has served to underline the significance of the particular course of historical investigation which Tierney, building upon the argument in *Foundations*, has been pursuing during the forty years since that book appeared. If it was easy enough for Figgis and historians of his generation to suppose that "constitutional government was a kind of normal, natural end toward which human history inevitably progressed,"[55] that degree of optimism is hardly available to us today. The flowering in the very heartland of Europe of totalitarian despotisms of the most squalid kind, the failure in so many parts of the decolonized world of the Western-style constitutional forms so confidently bequeathed to them, and, more recently, the mounting challenges currently being confronted by the countries of eastern Europe and Latin America in their struggle to consolidate liberal democratic regimes and to rebuild the institutions and practices of a viable civil society—such developments hardly encourage us to take at all for granted the emergence of constitutionalism in medieval and early-modern Europe. What they do encourage, instead, is a forthright acceptance of the historical singularity of that development,[56] as well as an energetic investigative effort to identify and understand its roots and presuppositions. And that must take us back, of course, as Tierney has again and again insisted, to the medieval centuries, to the aspects of medieval civilization which are "extremely abnormal by the standards of other societies," and, above all, therefore, to the religious aspect and "the exceptional role" played by "the Christian church in the organization of medieval society."[57]

The technical nature of so much of the scholarly work demanded by this effort, and the intricacy and subtlety of argumentative tactic

---

[54] The importance of that recognition was underlined by the papers produced by scholars from all over the world for the international conferences sponsored between 1987 and 1989 as part of the American Council of Learned Societies' Comparative Constitutionalism project. See Douglas Greenberg *et al.* eds., *Constitutionalism and Democracy: Transitions in the Contemporary World* (New York and Oxford, 1993).

[55] Tierney, *Religion, Law, and the Growth of Constitutional Thought*, p. 5.

[56] For an attempt to evoke the dimensions of that political singularity and to set them in a broader and comparative cultural context, see Francis Oakley, *The Medieval Experience: Foundations of Western Cultural Singularity* (New York, 1974), esp. pp. 1–8, 103–35, 209–12.

[57] *Religion, Law, and the Growth of Constitutional Thought*, pp. 8–13.

necessarily pursued, have been such as to retard the absorption of the interpretative shift involved into the habitual thinking of the generalists or of modernists whose minds still revolve within the Ptolemaic cycles and epicycles of the traditional periodization of European history.[58] But time, I would judge, is on its side; it explains more, and explains it more profoundly. At the end of his long review of *Foundations*, and by way of concluding judgment on the power of its thesis compared with the historiography preceding it, Michael Seidlmayer borrowed four words from the great decretalist, Hostiensis. They were words which Hostiensis had used when he insisted, against the view of Innocent IV, that it is in its membership taken as a whole, and not in its head alone, that the authority of a corporation resides. Those words apply with equal felicity to the argument Tierney has since developed concerning the shaping, not simply of medieval ecclesiastical constitutionalism, but of European constitutional thought in general. *Verius est*, Hostiensis had said, *licet difficilius*.[59]

---

[58] For a brief (but telling) comment on one illustrative case, see Brian Tierney, "Hierarchy, Consent and the 'Western Tradition'," *Political Theory*, XV (1987), 646–52.

[59] Seidlmayer, 387; cf. Tierney, *Foundations of the Conciliar Theory*, p. 107.

CHAPTER FOUR

LEGITIMATION BY CONSENT:
THE QUESTION OF THE MEDIEVAL ROOTS

The medieval roots of modern consent theory: If the subject has an old-fashioned ring to it, it is not without reason. For long it (or something akin to it) was one of the standard *topoi* in the old debates of confessional scholarship over the significance to be attached to the Protestant Reformation in the achievement of modern political liberties. Because of that, for some, indeed, the subject may well be immediately evocative less of current scholarly discussion than of the more unambiguously confessional effusions to be found in some of the older issues of the *Catholic Historical Review* and the *Papers of the American Society of Church History*,[1] of triumphal talk about "the thirteenth, greatest of centuries," of proud intimations that it was in the Middle Ages that "modern democracy [truly] had its rise,"[2] of suggestions that "the sources of world democracy are to be found, not in the political doctrine of the Reformation, but in the writings of [those] Catholic thinkers" who "like Bellarmine" mediated to the modern world the democratic legacy of the Middle Ages,[3] of more precise assertions, indeed, that "the immediate source of that part of the Virginia Declaration of Rights and the Declaration of Independence which proclaimed the equality of man and sovereignty by consent of the people, is to be found in the political theories of Cardinal Bellarmine,"[4] of bold claims, even, flung in the teeth of outraged Protestant denials, that "the Declaration of Independence is an accurate transcript of the Catholic mind."[5]

---

[1] See e.g. Gaillard Hunt, "The Virginia Declaration of Rights and Cardinal Bellarmine," *Catholic Historical Review*, III (No. 3, 1917), 276–89; David S. Schaff, *The Bellarmine—Jefferson Legend the Declaration of Independence* (New York and London, 1927)—reprinted from *Papers of the American Society of Church History*, vol. VIII.

[2] Thus James J. Walsh, *The Thirteenth: Greatest of Centuries* (New York, 1929), p. 391, cf. pp. 375 and 388.

[3] John C. Rager, *Political Philosophy of Blessed Cardinal Bellarmine* (Washington, D.C., 1926), pp. 10–11.

[4] Thus Rager, *Bellarmine*, pp. 132 and 152, summarizing the case made by Hunt, "The Virginia Declaration of Rights," 276–89.

[5] Alfred Rahilly, "The Sources of English and American Democracy," *Studies*,

But if old-fashioned in some of its dimensions, the topic is by no means old-fashioned in them all. For debate about the so-called "democratic" legacy of the Middle Ages to modern European and American political thinking has never been wholly confessional in its inspiration. Stimulated equally by the distortions sponsored in scholarship and graduate education alike by the traditional periodization of European history into ancient, medieval and modern (that most regrettable of humanist legacies), it was pursued also by scholars who, if they may well have had axes to grind, do not appear to have been grinding them with specifically Protestant or Catholic targets in mind. Gierke and Figgis, McIlwain and Carlyle, Laski, Gough, Sabine and Lecler—all of them (and others too)[6] were at pains to stress the importance of the legacy which the medieval theorists of popular sovereignty, contract and consent passed down, across the ideological turbulence of the age of Reformation and religious war, to the constitutionalists and consent theorists of the early modern era. It was left for Walter Ullmann, that doughty defender of the relevance of medieval studies and among our contemporaries possibly the most distinguished student of medieval political thinking, simply

VIII (June, 1919), 189–209 at 209. This general approach was summed up in somewhat more moderate fashion and popularized among generations of Catholic students in the United States by the successive editions of John A. Ryan and Moorhouse F.X. Millar, *The State and the Church* (New York, 1922). See pp. 114–20, 134–37, 160–65, 172–77, and esp. p. 174, where it is said: "The Declaration of Independence was not the assertion of new principles or new arguments. It contains the true medieval and Christian norm of all just governments."

[6] Otto von Gierke, *The Development of Political Theory*, trans. Bernard Freyd (New York, 1939), esp. pp. 91–240; J.N. Figgis, *Political Thought from Gerson to Grotius: 1614–1625. Seven Studies* (New York, 1960), esp. Lecture II, pp. 41–70; Charles H. McIlwain, *Constitutionalism: Ancient and Modern* (rev. ed., Ithaca, New York, 1958), esp. pp. 67–122; R.W. and A.J. Carlyle, *A History of Medieval Political Thought in the West* (6 vols., London, 1903–36),—see esp. V, 457–74; H.J. Laski, "Political Theory in the Later Middle Ages," in *The Cambridge Medieval History* (8 vols., Cambridge, 1911–36), VIII, esp. 638; J.W. Gough, *The Social Contract: A Critical Study of its Development* (Oxford, 1936); George H. Sabine, *A History of Political Theory*, rev. ed. (New York, 1950), esp. ch. 16, pp. 313–28; Joseph Lecler, "Les théories démocratiques au Moyen Age," *Études*, 225 (Oct.–Dec., 1935), 5–26, 168–92. In these articles, though Lecler is reacting to the casual assumption of an opposition between the thinking of Renaissance and Middle Ages (p. 191), he is also, admittedly, seeking to rebut the identification with Catholicism of monarchical absolutism and theories of divine right, and with Protestantism of popular sovereignty and contract theory (see p. 6). His treatment, however, is anything but confessional in tone. Paul Janet, *Histoire de la science politique dans ses rapports avec la morale*, 3rd ed. (2 vols., Paris, 1887), stands out as a notable exception by virtue of his willingness to minimize the medieval legacy. (See e.g., I, 675: "En morale, nulle originalité. Aristote uni à Saint Augustin, voilà la scholastique!".)

to reaffirm that stress, to put the point with characteristic force and
to relate it even to the American revolutionary experience. "There
is, to my mind," he has said, "a direct lineage from Locke back to
the feudal compact and consent in the Middle Ages and forward to
the Declaration of Independence.... The government for which
Locke supplied the theory was in its essentials the heir of a government originally based on feudal law, principles, and practice and the
feudal contract."[7]

Its importance mounts, moreover, if one is moved, not inappropriately, to attempt to view that legacy from some sort of world-historical
perspective. From such a perspective one is less likely to miss the
singularity of those features of our Western cultural landscape whose
familiarity is such that it persistently betrays us into assuming them
to be the deliverances of nature.[8] Not least of all that theory of legitimation by consent which, though it dominated European political
philosophizing only from the era of Hobbes to that of Kant, has contrived so to shape our liberal democratic common sense that we are
persistently tempted to take it for granted. And yet, historically speaking, it stands out as a very singular theory, the outcome of a very particular coalescence of disparate developments, one not at all to be
taken for granted, one that calls urgently for historical illumination.

I

In his book, *The Notion of the State*, Passerin d'Entrèves (following
closely on the heels of Max Weber) draws a distinction between the
state regarded as "might" or mere force, the state regarded as "power,"
and the state regarded as "authority."[9] In the first place, as the word

---

[7] Walter Ullmann, *The Individual and Society in the Middle Ages* (Baltimore, Md.,
1966), pp. 150–51; cf. pp. 96–97.

[8] For a general attempt to assess from this perspective the historical significance
of the European Middle Ages, see Francis Oakley, *The Medieval Experience: Foundations
of Western Cultural Singularity* (New York, 1974).

[9] Alexander Passerin d'Entrèves, *The Notion of the State* (Oxford, 1967). The distinction in question, which provides the framework for the whole book, is outlined
on pp. 1–11, where the citations which follow occur. Cf. pp. 141–49. For the distinction between *Macht, Herrshcaft* and *legitime Herrschaft*, which d'Entrèves notes (pp.
10–11) is closely related though not identical with his, see Max Weber, *The Theory
of Social and Economic Organization*, trans. A.M. Henderson and Talcott Parsons (New
York, 1947), esp. pp. 152–53.

itself suggests, the state is viewed in purely factual terms as the expression of force, an entity capable of imposing its commands despite resistance; and the important attribute, accordingly, is effectiveness, the ability to see those commands obeyed. In the second and third places, however, while choosing to employ the words "power" and "authority," d'Entrèves chooses also to give them very specific meanings. "The State regarded as 'power,'" he says, "is the State of legal theorizing, where power means force qualified by law, force with the sign 'plus' attached to it." Here the concern is primarily "with the validity or 'legality' of commands. The power of the State is a legal power, conditioned by the existence and the observance of law, 'valid' only insofar as it is legally determined and appointed. Where law ends, power ends." But "legality" is not to be confused with "legitimacy." And we can speak of legitimacy only when the power of the state, however legally exercised, is so grounded in a justification of moral and philosophical nature that the acquiescence of the subject or citizen deepens now into obligation. As d'Entrèves puts it: "We should not assume that we have fully unravelled the notion of the State unless we are able to explain how force, first legalized as power, becomes in turn legitimate as authority."

Employing that terminology, then, it is with "authority" that this essay will be concerned, with the line of thought that set out to explain political obligation or legitimacy not predominantly in terms of divine or prescriptive right, of aristocratic superiority, of the necessities of the common interest, convenience, or the "natural" status of political life, but rather in terms of the consent of the governed. More specifically, it is concerned with the line of thinking that sought to ground political legitimacy and obligation in consent conceived now in a very particular way—namely, as a concatenation of individual acts of willing. So far as political life is concerned, that is to say, this line of thinking sought to ground the obligation of the subject or citizen in the realm not of final but of efficient causes, not in the ends governments exist to promote but in the source from which they derive their powers. And resonating to the Hobbesian view that there is "no obligation on any man, which ariseth not from some Act of his own; for all men equally, are by nature free"[10]

---

[10] Thomas Hobbes, *Leviathan*, Part II, ch. 21; ed. Michael Oakeshott (Oxford, 1946), p. 141. Cf. Carole Pateman, *The Problem of Political Obligation: A Critical Analysis of Liberal Theory* (New York, 1979) p. 6: "Liberal theory, and its conception of self-

it regarded that obligation, accordingly, in some very significant measure, as self-assumed.

In order to set in bold relief the uncommon nature of this way
of thinking it is not even necessary to reach for comparisons with
political notions prevalent in cultures which have not fed directly
into our own civilizational heritage.[11] Reference to the pioneering
political speculation of the classical Greek world should suffice. That
speculation had characteristically focussed on the realm of final rather
than efficient causation, upon the dimensions of the "good" state
rather than upon the presuppositions of the "legitimate" state.[12] The
modern conceptions of will and autonomous individuality were adumbrated only in the haziest of fashions, the problem of political obligation, accordingly, can scarcely be said to have arisen, and consent (when
involved) was assigned, as a result, a merely instrumental role.[13] In
comparison, then, with that world of thought the novelty and singularity of the essentially "voluntaristic" modern approach—which,
by the late-eighteenth century, the spokesmen for the revolutionary
generation in America, for example, could take to be no more than

assumed obligation, was born in conflict with divine right and patriarchalist theorists who insisted that relationships of subordination and authority were God-given
or natural. It is absolutely basic to liberal theory that political authority is conventional. The conception of political 'obligation' as a relationship that individuals
voluntarily take upon themselves—and so can refuse, reject or change—makes no
sense outside of a conventionalist view of at least a large number of human relationships and, most especially, of political relationships."

[11] Though such comparisons would unquestionably sustain the point being made.

[12] Put in somewhat different terms, it rejected an "ethics of virtue" rather than
an "ethics of obligation"—see Stephen G. Salkever, "Virtue, Obligation and Politics,"
American Political Science Review, LXVIII (No. 1, 1974), 78–92.

[13] Behind this political speculation lay an epistemology in accordance with which
the individual entity was regarded as apprehensible by the intellect only insofar as
it was a "particular"—that is, a participation in a universal, eternal archetype.
Behind it also, though at a further remove, lay a psychology that, lacking a clearly-
differentiated concept of individual personality, saw no sharply-defined boundaries
between the self and the collectivity to which it belonged. For these points see the
essays by Daniel O'Connor, Emil Brunner, Erich Franck, and Hans Jonas in Daniel
O'Connor and Francis Oakley eds., *Creation: The Impact of an Idea* (New York, 1969),
pp. 105–56 and 241–58 (stressing the fundamental inter-relationship persisting among
the shifting notions of time, personality, will, freedom and responsibility). Also, the
classic study of Bruno Snell, *The Discovery of Mind*. trans. T.G. Rosenmeyer (Cambridge,
Mass., 1953), esp. ch. 1, and a fine recent work that shares something of Snell's
perspective—Arthur W.H. Adkins, *Merit and Responsibility: A Study in Greek Values*
(Oxford, 1960). Cf. E.R. Dodds, *The Greeks and the Irrational* (Berkeley and Los
Angeles, 1951); A.W.H. Adkins, *From the Many to the One: A Study of Personality and
Views of Human Nature in the Context of Ancient Greek Society, Values, and Beliefs* (Ithaca,
1970).

enlightened common sense[14]—in comparison, that novelty is not to be gainsaid.[15] Hence the importance of the question of historical origins. Hence, too, or so one would assume, the relevance of the medieval intellectual and political experience to such modern political convictions at their most fundamental.

Unfortunately, it is here, precisely, that discussions of the medieval contribution have not always been very helpful. Framed by altogether too hazy a perception of the specific features distinguishing modern theories of legitimation by consent, they have frequently betrayed an overeager willingness to detect the roots of modern freedoms, perhaps even the very well-springs of modern liberal democracy, not only in the teachings of a whole series of medieval thinkers from Thomas Aquinas to Nicholas of Cusa or in the great medieval contributions to representative theory and practice, or, again, in the feudal limitations on monarchical power that those contributions presupposed, but also in the fundamental role which the Roman law had ascribed to the Roman *populus* in the legislative process and the conferring of the imperial power, and even in the allegedly "populist" procedures whereby the various Germanic *Völker* had chosen their kings and called them to account.[16]

---

[14] Thus Jefferson could speak of it as expressing the "harmonizing sentiments of the day: and of "the elementary books of public right, as Aristotle, Cicero, Locke, Sidney, etc.," as placing "before mankind the common sense of the subject in terms so plain and firm as to command their assent." Letter to Lee in 1825; see *The Works of Thomas Jefferson*, ed. H.A. Washington, (9 vols., 1884), VII, 407.

[15] Patrick Riley explores the ramifications of this point in a truly notable series of articles: "A Possible Explanation of Rousseau's General Will," *American Political Science Review*, LXIV (March, 1970), 86–97; "Will and Legitimacy in the Philosophy of Hobbes: Is he a Consent Theorist?" *Political Studies*, XXI (1973), 500–522; "On Kant as the Most Adequate of the Social Contract Theorists," *Political Theory*, I (No. 4, 1973), 450–71; "Hegel on Consent and Social-Contract Theory: Does he 'cancel and preserve' the Will?" *The Western Political Quarterly*, XXVI (no. 1, 1973), 140–161; "How Coherent is the Social Contract Tradition?" *Journal of the History of Ideas*, XXXIV (No. 4, 1973), 543–62; "On finding an Equilibrium between Consent and Natural Law in Locke's Political Philosophy," *Political Studies*, XXII (1974), 432–52; "Locke on 'voluntary agreement' and Political Power," *Western Political Quarterly*, XXIX (No. 1, 1976), 136–45. See also Pateman, *The Political Theory of Possessive Individualism* (Oxford, 1962), pp. 1–4; Steven Lukes, *Individualism* (Oxford, 1973), esp. pp. 73–87; Isaiah Berlin, "Two Concepts of Liberty," reprinted in his *Four Essays on Liberty* (Oxford, 1977), esp. pp. 127–29.

[16] In the course of their monumental *History of Medieval Political Theory*, though their formulations are marked by a cautious sobriety, the Carlyles do in effect contrive to touch upon all of these bases. See especially the summary at the end of vol. V, 457–74. Similarly, Lecler, "Les théories democratiques au Moyen Age," touches upon most of them.

However questionable it has come to seem today, this last theory is the oldest of them all, predating the English civil wars of the seventeenth century but first rising to prominence in the Leveller literature spawned by those conflicts, enjoying widespread popularity among the Revolutionary generation in the American colonies,[17] gaining renewed momentum during the course of the nineteenth century, and finding perhaps its most engaging expression in Bishop Stubbs' great *Constitutional History of England*. That *History* ends in 1485, but the date it leads up to is 1688. "When," Stubbs says, "under the Stuarts, the time came for the maturity of national organization to stand face to face with the senility of medieval royalty, the context was decided as all previous history had pointed the way and all subsequent history justifies."[18] And in that "previous history" he clearly included the national prehistory in the continental Germanic homeland. From the very start of his work he was at pains to insist that "the English are not aboriginal" but a people of Teutonic origin, a people which from time immemorial had rejoiced in the possession of what he calls "the common germs of Germanic institutions." And, for Stubbs, the word "Teutonic" clearly generated as its harmonics the words "national" and "free." "Freedom," he says, "was inherent in the blood. Caesar had seen it in the ancient Germans." Hence, along with a similar extract from the *Germania* of Tacitus, he placed at the start of his *Select Charters Illustrative of English Constitutional History* (the Procrustean bed on which the minds of generations of Oxford undergraduates have been stretched—and narrowed), in incongruous

---

[17] Thus James Otis declared that "the present civil constitution of England derives its original from those Saxons who . . . established a form of government in [England] similar to that they had been accustomed to live under in their native country. . . . This government, like that from whence they come, was founded upon principles of the most perfect liberty."—*Rights of the British Colonies* (John Harvard Library, 7, p. 31) as cited in Bailyn, *Ideological Origins of the American Revolution*, p. 80. Cf. H. Trevor Colbourn, *The Lamp of Experience: Whig History and the Intellectual Origins of the American Revolution* (Chapel Hill, N.C., 1965), pp. 21–39. For the English background to this view, see Christopher Hill, *Puritanism and Revolution: Studies in Interpretation of the English Revolution of the Seventeenth Century* (London, 1958), pp. 50–122, and J.G.A. Pocock, *The Ancient Constitution and the Feudal Law* (Cambridge, 1957), pp. 30–70. If the American colonists tended to equate such English consensual constitutional arrangements with the *natural* order of things, some of their English predecessors had done likewise (see Hill, *Puritanism and Revolution*, p. 55).
[18] William Stubbs, *The Constitutional History of England*, 3rd ed. (3 vols., Oxford, 1887), II, 322; 1, 2, 231.

juxtaposition with the laws of Ethelbert and Wihtred and Ine and Alfred, a passage from the *De bello gallico*.[19]

Though in more refined form it has not been without strong resonances in some of the most recent literature devoted to medieval political thought,[20] it is only by dint of a rather casual anachronism that the credentials of this theory can still be presented in a truly favorable light. Whatever the force of the "elective" process so often associated with the older Germanic kings—in Scandinavia, in west and south Europe, in England—it certainly did not involve legitimation by consent, whether that consent be viewed as an expression of the corporate will of the community or as a concatenation of individual wills. Nor was the limitation of royal power or even the dismissal of royal incumbents based upon the implications of such a legitimating consent. Given the sacral status of the ancient Germanic kings, which scholars have become increasingly willing to concede, the true grounds of their legitimacy must be seen to have lain elsewhere—in the *Geblütsheiligkeit* possessed by the entire dynasty by virtue of its divine descent, and in the ability of the individual chosen from that dynasty by virtue of his "luck," *heil* or *mana* successfully to mediate between his people and their gods, to hold their world together "by relating it to the cosmic forces in which that world was enmeshed," and to ensure thereby their well-being and prosperity in peace as well as war.[21] This being so, "the tribal election of the sacral ruler

---

[19] William Stubbs, *Select Charters and other Illustrations of English Constitutional History*, 9th ed., rev. H.W.C. Davis (Oxford, 1913), pp. 56–74.

[20] E.g., in Walter Ullmann's several discussions of what he calls the "ascending" or "populist" thesis of government and law—see Francis Oakley, "Celestial Hierarchies Revisited: Walter Ullmann's Vision of Medieval Politics," *Past and Present*, 60 (August, 1973), 3–48 at 7–9, 18–21, 27–32 (see above, ch. 2). The old "democratic" interpretation of the ancient Germanic and Scandinavian kingship also finds some echoes in Bernhard Kummer, "Ein Lebenspiel zur Frage nach Ursprung und Fortwirkung Demokratischen und Sakralen Königtums in Skandinavien," in *The Sacral Kingship: Studies in the History of Religions*, IV (Leiden, 1959), pp. 716–33, and in Walter Baetke, *Yngvi und die Ynglinger: Eine quellenkritische Untersuchung über das nordische "Sakralkonigtum"* (Berlin, 1964).

[21] Citing William A. Chaney, *The Cult of Kingship in Anglo-Saxon England: The Transition from Paganism to Christianity* (Berkeley and Los Angeles, 1970), p. 15. See also H.M. Chadwick, *The Heroic Age* (Cambridge, 1926), esp. pp. 366–92; D.A. Binchy, *Celtic and Anglo-Saxon Kingship* (Oxford, 1970); Marc Bloch, *Les rois thaumaturges: Étude sur le caractère surnaturel attribué á la puissance royale particulièrement en France et en Angleterre* (Strasbourg and Paris, 1928); Hans Naumann, "Die magische Seite der altgermanischen Königtums und ihr Fortwirken in christlicher Zeit," in Gian Piero Bognetti *et al.*, *Wirtschaft und Kultur: Festschrift zum 70. Geburtstag von Alfons Dopsch* (Leipzig, 1938), pp. 1–12; Georges Dumézil, *Mythes et Dieux des Germains: Essai d'interprétation comparative* (Paris, 1939); Jan de Vries, "Das Königtum bei den Germanen,"

was not so much a 'democratic' institution" as an attempt to assure
"the possession of the *mana*-filled, god-sprung king, selected from the
royal race for his obvious 'luck.'"[22] Moreover, that attempt is described
as being made, it should be noted, by the *thing* or popular assembly,
itself no "secular" or "democratic" body, but clearly sacral in character, dedicated, it may be to *Tiwaz*, sky god and god of the entire
order of the universe, and charged with the maintenance of an order
which is itself part of that sacred world-order.[23] Hence, in Otto
Höfler's formulation: "The *Thing* was not 'free' in the sense that its
members possessed an unlimited freedom of decision—even the inherited norms and customary laws could not be taken for human inven-
tions and products of will, but as a part of the total world-order, as
independent of men as the structure of the world, but entrusted to
men and their consecrated assembly for protection and for continuing
realization."[24]

If, then, one wishes to speak about a specifically Germanic contribution to the rise of modern consent theory (thinking perhaps of
the royal electoral practices that lingered on into the Middle Ages
or the sense that kings were in some fashion accountable to their
peoples for serious betrayal of their trust), one must do so with an

---

Saeculum VII (1956), 289–309; see also his useful comment "The Present State of
Studies on Germanic Religion," *Diogenes*, No. 18 (1957), 78–92; Otto Höfler, "Der
Sakralcharakter des germanischen Königtums," in *The Sacral Kingship*, pp. 664–701;
J.M. Wallace-Hadrill, *Early Germanic Kingship in England and on the Continent* (Oxford,
1971), pp. 1–20, where he announces his own shift to a stress on the sacral status
of the Germanic Kings. Not all scholars, admittedly, have been willing to concede
the point. Baetke, *Yngvi und die Ynglinger*, is an extreme and unbalanced manifesto
of opposition, but a more cautious scepticism is evinced by František Graus, *Volk,
Herrscher und Heiliger im Reich der Merowinger* (Prague, 1965), pp. 313–16. There is an
attempt to come to terms with the methodological problems involved in the study
of sacral kingship in H. Wolfram, "Methodische Fragen zur Kritik am 'Sacralen'
Königtum germanischer Stämme," in H. Birkhan and O. Gschwantler, eds., *Festschrift
für Otto Höfler* (2 vols., Vienna, 1968), II, 473–90. The lectures printed in P.H.
Sawyer and I.N. Wood, eds., *Early Medieval Kingship* (Leeds, 1977), convey a good
sense of the difficulties confronting those investigating the topic.

[22] Chaney, *Cult of Kingship*, p. 16.

[23] See Chadwick, *Heroic Age*, p. 368; Dumézil, *Mythes et Dieux des Germains*, pp.
41–43; de Vries, "Das Königtum bein den Germanen," 298, and *Altgermanische
Religionsgeschichte* (2 vols., Berlin, 1957), II, 11–14, Höfler, "Der Sakralcharakter des
germanischen Königtums," 692–96; Wallace-Hadrill, *Early Germanic Kingship*, pp.
8–16; cf. Walter Schlesinger, "Über germanisches Heerkönigtum," in Th. Mayer,
ed., *Das Königtum: Seine geistige und rechtlichen Grundlagen* (Lindau u. Konstanz, 1956),
pp. 105–41 at 140.

[24] An extreme formulation, admittedly, but also illuminating. See Höfler, "Der
Sakralcharakter des germanischen Königtums," 694.

important qualification in mind. For one must recognize that such a contribution can have occurred only after those originally religious mechanisms for selecting rulers or calling them to account had come to be understood in a fundamentally different way by being filtered through the conceptual screen which the novel religious and political conditions prevailing during the Latin Middle Ages had interposed between them and their original source.

Something similar must also be said of the currently more fashionable invocation of the contribution stemming from the republican constitution of Rome and mediated by the Roman law. The more strident affirmations of the importance and beneficence of the Teutonic political legacy having frequently gone hand in hand with solemn denunciations of the *damnosa haereditas* of Roman law and its contribution to the rise of modern absolutism, it is comprehensible that the onset of disenchantment with the former should have coincided with a more positive appraisal of the latter. Thus it was to the accompaniment of references to "the recent deplorable exhibitions of tribalism in Germany" that Charles Howard McIlwain in 1939 himself made the most forceful of his claims to the effect that "the true essence of Roman constitutionalism does not lie in those late statements of absolutism to which so much currency has since been given, such as the maxim, *Quod principi placuit legis vigorem habet*, or Ulpian's assertion, *Princeps legibus solutus est* . . . [but] in the older, deeper principle that the *populus*, and none but the whole *populus*, can be the ultimate source of legal authority."[25] And, in so doing, he referred to those earlier texts (incorporated and preserved in the sixth-century compilation which we know as the *Corpus Juris Civilis*) indicating that "law (lex) is what the people orders and has established,"[26] and that the prince's decisions have the force of law precisely in virtue of the fact that by a special sort of law concerning his government, that is by a *lex regia*, "the people confers upon him the whole of *its* government and power [*imperium et potestatem*]."[27]

As McIlwain himself notes, however, Cicero is the "first expositor"

---

[25] McIlwain, *Constitutionalism: Ancient and Modern*, p. 57.
[26] Thus Gaius in the second century A.D.: *Inst.* 1, 2–7.
[27] Thus Ulpian is the third century: *Digest*, 1, 4, 1, where the word "conferat" is used; in *Inst.*, 1, 2, 6, "concessit" replaces "conferat." C. 1, 17, 1, 7, has "translata sunt." Cf. McIlwain, *Constitutionalism: Ancient and Modern*, pp. 45–46, 156 n. 5; Ernst H. Kantorowicz, *The King's Two Bodies: A Study in Political Theology* (Princeton, N.J., 1957), pp. 103–06.

of Roman republican institutions "whose works we know in any great detail."[28] As a result it is extremely difficult to determine with any degree of confidence what the principle of the derivation of all power from the people can originally have meant.[29] Three points, however, may briefly be noted. In the first place, we should recall that in relation to such internal matters the *populus Romanus* meant, quite specifically, the assembly in one form or another of the people of Rome itself, the prerogatives of which were subject to extensive limitation, both direct and indirect, by the rival power of the magistrates.[30] In the second place, the popular assembly in the early period clearly had some sacral appurtenances and religious functions analogous to those of the Germanic *thing* or folk assembly. Thus, for example, organized as the *comitia centuriata* it met usually (and, as the *comitia tributa*, occasionally) on the *Campus Martius* where there was a very ancient altar to Mars,[31] and could do so only after the auspices were taken by the appropriate magistrate. Organized as the *comitia curiata*, moreover, it sometimes met under the presidency of the *pontifex maximus* to deal with matters pertaining to the sacral law or to those areas of private law (e.g., will-making) possessed of religious significance, and to witness the inauguration of the *flamines majores* (priests) and of the *rex sacrorum*, the king whom the Romans of the republican period felt it was necessary to appoint for religious purposes.[32] In

---

[28] McIlwain, *Constitutionalism: Ancient and Modern*, p. 42.

[29] Though the Carlyles, *History of Medieval Political Theory*, 1, 64, did not hesitate to characterize *Digest*, 1, 4, 1, as "an almost paradoxical description of an unlimited personal power founded on a purely democratic basis," or to add: "We consider the Roman lawyers as expressing one aspect of the theory out of which the medieval and modern democratic conception of the state has grown."

[30] See Ch. Wirszubski, *Libertas as a Political Idea at Rome during the Late Republic and Early Principate* (Cambridge, 1950), pp. 17–22, 31–40, 47–50. Note the four forms that these assemblies could take: the *comitia curiata*, the *comitia centuriata*, the *comitia tributa*, and the *concilium plebis*—each with its own principle of organization. See Lily Ross Taylor, *Roman Voting Assemblies: From the Hannibalic War to the Dictatorship of Caesar* (Ann Arbor, 1966), esp. the helpful diagram facing p. 5, and the older study by George W. Botsford, *The Roman Assemblies: From their origin to the end of the Republic* (New York, 1909).

[31] On which, see Georges Dumézil, *Archaic Roman Religion* (2 vols., Chicago and London, 1970), 1, 206. Note, by way of analogy, that in order to be valid a *senatus consultum* had to be held in a temple. See *ibid.*, 316.

[32] See Taylor, *Roman Voting Assemblies*, esp. pp. 1–14, 62–64; Botsford, *The Roman Assemblies*, esp. pp. 155–56, H.F. Jolowicz, *Historical Introduction to the Study of Roman Law* (Cambridge, 1932), pp. 17–18, 86–87; Fritz Schulz, *History of Roman Legal Science* (Oxford, 1946), pp. 14–22; Wolfgang Kunkel, *An Introduction to Roman Legal and Constitutional History*, trans. J.M. Kelly (Oxford, 1966), pp. 9–14. On the office of

the third place, religious matrix apart, it has been remarked that even to the Roman lawyers later on "the principle of the derivation of power from the people has a markedly 'juridical' or legal, not a political, meaning." That is to say, it served as a principle enabling them, if only by recourse to fiction,[33] to represent all the various sources of what we would call law—whether customary, plebescital, senatorial or imperial—as flowing ultimately from a common source. Thus, by appealing to a *lex regia* whereby the people had conferred the whole of its power on the *princeps*, they were able to maintain that principle even during the later Empire "after all the sources of law had dried up . . . [and] . . . the Imperial 'constitution' had come to be the sole expression of positive law."[34]

If, then, such memories of republican constitutional theory and practice were later to be at the disposal of those—medieval civilians, canonists and publicists alike—who for one reason or another and in one way or another wished to argue for the grounding of the law and of the royal authority itself in the consent of the people,[35] it

rex sacrorum, Kunkel (*ibid.*, pp. 13–14) has the following pertinent comment to make: "[T]his was not a new office, different from the Kingship, but was the old kingship itself; for as long as a Roman state cult remained it continued to exist in its sacral function because only a king possessed the necessary magic power. The way in which this *rex sacrorum* was chosen obviously goes back to ancient ideas about the rightful king's closeness to the gods and about his magical powers, and may therefore be applied to the early Roman kingship with a high degree of probability. The king was neither elected nor nominated by his predecessor but was revealed by the gods through a sign (especially through the flight of birds). Thus the *rex sacrorum* of republican and imperial times, having been taken (*captus*) by the president of the college of pontiffs learned in the sacral law (the *pontifex maximus*), was presented to the gods, in the presence of the *comitia curiata*, for their approval by means of a sign. . . . A special, partly religious, partly magical charisma, similar to the old Germanic *Königsheil*, was thus the basis of the kingly power, and the sacral function of the king was originally just as essential as his political and military functions, with which it was indissolubly connected."

[33] See Jolowicz, *Historical Introduction*, pp. 370–71; Kunkel, *Introduction to Roman Legal and Constitutional History*, p. 119, who characterizes as "the purest fiction" Ulpian's view (D. 1, 4, 1) that "the emperor himself received his power from the Roman people through the *lex de imperio*, and that his decrees therefore rested at least indirectly on the popular will."

[34] Thus d'Entrèves, *Notion of the State*, p. 78.

[35] Ways that were sometimes conflicting. Thus, Walter Ullmann, *Medieval Papalism: The Political Theories of the Medieval Canonists* (London, 1949), p. 105, claims that whereas the civilians argued that by the *lex regia* "the people had transferred all power to the emperor and that this transfer was irrevocable," the canonists usually regarded the transfer merely as a revocable concession. At the same time, some of the Decretists also applied the idea of the *lex regia* to the Pope, but apparently with

would appear to have been very much by virtue of the fact that they, too, like the analogous Germanic notions, were instinctively reinterpreted in more explicitly "political" a fashion by those whose horizon of expectations had been determined by the religious and political conditions prevailing during the centuries subsequent to the fall of Rome. In particular, the comparative de-sacralization of the political,[36] the traditionally communitarian nature of ecclesiastical life, the feudal ties binding kings to their chief subjects in a genuinely contractual relationship, the emergence of a myriad of corporate bodies and of cities enjoying de facto an extensive measure of self-governance, the high status accorded everywhere to the old customary laws, the general sense that the principles and practices, political and religious, then prevailing had existed time out of mind—all of these and more conduced powerfully to the conviction that established legal and doctrinal patterns, as well as customary governmental and fiscal arrangements, could be altered only with the agreement of all concerned. Hence an understandable preoccupation in theory with the notion of consent and in practice with the means whereby it could be secured.

To identify this religio-political complex of principles and practices as the matrix of later consent theories is by no means to suggest the irrelevance of more ancient notions or practices to the historical development of such theories. Least of all, perhaps, for those thinkers writing in the context of the small city republics of northern Italy, who, with a glad if often overhasty recognition, were persistently tempted as they peered anxiously into the past to discern in the republican institutions of Greek and Roman antiquity and in the political principles of the classical authors the looming outlines of their own cherished ideals. Thus in the fourteenth century, for example, so influential a figure as the great jurist, Bartolus of Sassoferato (d. 1357), could proceed from a denial that the transfer by the *lex regia* of legislative authority from *populus* to emperor was an irrevocable one, to his own further claim that in a city which recognizes de facto no superior in temporal affairs jurisdiction continues to reside in the body of the people.[37] So that their magistrates

---

the object of enhancing rather than diminishing his authority; see Brian Tierney, *Foundations of the Conciliar Theory* (Cambridge, 1955), pp. 55–56.

[36] For a brief comment on which, see Oakley, *The Medieval Experience*, pp. 105–15.

[37] *Tractatus de regimine civitatis*, §§ 15–20; in Bartolus of Sassoferrato, *Opera omnia* (11 vols., Basel, 1588–89), X, 417–20. Cf. the discussions of Bartolus's advocacy of

exercise their powers only by delegation as representatives of the people which retains the right to withdrawn those powers or to limit their exercise.[38] Similarly, Marsiglio of Padua, who could claim to ground in the third book of Aristotle's *Politics* his own blunt definition of law as the coercive command of the whole people.[39] Doubtless, this was a not inconsiderable achievement, but given the authoritative status of Aristotle and the Roman law, such arguments carried great weight.

Though they were invoked, of course, with great frequency—and especially by the defenders of republican values in northern Italy—the pertinence of such classical preoccupations to the political conditions prevailing in the *monarchies* of Europe was much less marked. And yet it was within the context of those monarchies, I would argue—including the papal monarchy, the universal Church—that the principal line of development of medieval consent theory was laid down. Upon that line of development this essay will focus.

II

Bartolus himself had conceded that popular sovereignty, however appropriate for city-states of the right size, was a mode of governance ill-suited to the needs of really large political societies which might well require monarchical governments. But it was in connection with those larger polities, and with the great flowering of representative institutions, all over Europe, that from the twelfth to the fourteenth centuries the revived Roman law and the canon law so closely linked with it made a most significant contribution to the development of the theory and practice of consent. I have in mind

"popular sovereignty" in C.N.S. Woolf, *Bartolus of Sassoferrato* (Cambridge, 1913), pp. 174–80; Walter Ullmann, "De Bartoli Sententia: Concilium repraesentat mentem populi," in *Bartolo da Sassoferrato: Studi e Documenti* (2 vols., Milan, 1962), II, 705–33; Quentin Skinner, *Foundations of Modern Political Thought* (2 vols., Cambridge, 1978), I, 61–65, II, 181–84. M.H. Keen gives a lucid general introduction to the political thinking of the postglossators in his "The Political Thought of the Fourteenth-Century Civilians," in Beryl Smalley, ed., *Trends in Medieval Political Thought* (Oxford, 1965), pp. 105–26.

[38] See Ullmann, "De Bartoli Sententia," esp. 714–22.

[39] See *Defensor Pacis*, I, 12, 3; ed. C.W. Previté-Orton, *The Defensor Pacis of Marsilius of Padua* (Cambridge, 1928), p. 49, where Marsiglio adduces the authority of Aristotle, *Politics*, III, 11, 1281a–b. For a comment on Marsiglio's use (and abuse) of Aristotle in this connection, see Oakley, "Celestial Hierarchies Revisited," 40–42—above, ch. 2.

the complex process whereby the canonists and civilians appropriated for their own purposes principles and procedures drawn from Roman private law and pertaining, in effect, to what we would call "due process." Those principles and procedures concerned the defense of joint rights in court cases and the representation of the co-tutors or corporate bodies, whose rights were being affected, by attorneys possessed of powers sufficient to see through to a definite conclusion the business at hand. Having first deployed such procedures in connection with the increasing amount of litigation involving monastic and cathedral chapters and other ecclesiastical corporations, the canonists then boldly transferred them from the restricted realm of private law into the public constitutional sphere. By so doing they were able to fashion viable mechanisms whereby such corporate bodies could be summoned to send to provincial and general councils of the Church representatives possessed of legally delegated authority to give their advice and consent concerning policy changes that touched the interests of their "constituents." Thus Innocent III, who in 1200 and 1207 had summoned to Rome to meet with his *curia* mandated representatives from the communes of the Marches, in 1215 summoned from every part of the universal Church proctors to represent convents and cathedral chapters at the Fourth Lateran Council. During the course of the two centuries following, as representative assemblies of one sort or another made their appearance all over Europe, national monarchs and territorial princes came to adopt similar procedures in order to secure for their increasingly rigorous and ambitious governmental activities, and for the mounting taxation needed to finance them, the requisite consent not only of the noblemen who could attend their assemblies as individuals but of the increasingly powerful corporate or quasi-corporate groupings which could not.[40]

---

[40] See especially, Gaines Post, *Studies in Medieval Legal Thought: Public Law and the State, 1100–1322* (Princeton, N.J., 1964), pp. 3–328, 562–70; cf. Antonio Marongiu, *Medieval Parliaments: A Comparative Study*, trans. S.J. Woolf (London, 1968). For a useful report on work concerning both the political theory of representation and the development of representative assemblies, see H.M. Cam, A. Marongiu, G. Stökl, "Recent Work and Present Views on the Origins and Development of Representative Assemblies," in *Relazioni del X Congresso Internazionale di Scienze Storiche* (3 vols., Florence, 1955), 1, 1–101. There are useful discussions of the maxim *Quod omnes tangit ab omnibus approbetur* both in Post and in the following articles: Yves M.J. Congar, "Quod omnes tangit, ab omnibus tractari et approbari debet," *Revue d'histoire de droit français et étranger*, 4 me sér., XXXVI (1958), 210–59; A. Marongiu, "Il Principio

By their imaginative transfer of such principles and procedures from the realm of private into public law the medieval lawyers had clearly taken a creative step that it does not appear to have occurred to their Roman predecessors to take. By taking that step, moreover, they had made possible the effective eliciting of the consent of the governed, not merely in cities or in small corporate bodies, but in large national and territorial states and even in an international body like the universal Church itself. It is not to be supposed, however, that the consent secured thereby, even when it involved consent to new taxation, was necessarily the type of consent that can truly be called "political" or "democratic"—the type of consent that expresses the sovereign will of the people and implies the presence of some sort of limitation on the ruler's prerogative. True instead to its roots in private law and legal due process, and especially so at the outset, it remained very much consultative and procedural, in some ways akin, if you wish, to the process that occurs today in cases where the state exercises its right to take property by eminent domain. In d'Entrèves' terminology, that is, it pertained to legality rather than legitimacy, to power rather than authority. Thus, behind the Romano-canonical maxim cited so frequently in writs of summons to representative assemblies—*Quod omnes tangit ab omnibus approbetur*—lay the traditional commitment to the view that "all whose rights were touched by an issue should have every opportunity to prepare the defense of their rights, to take advantage of all means within the law and to consent to the court's decision on the legality of the rights after a full defense . . . discussion and debate had taken place." The consent to that decision itself, however, was in effect compulsory. Similarly, behind the persistent attempts of rulers to insist that delegated representatives should come, not with limited mandates from constituents whose rights were being touched, but with *plena et sufficiens potestas*, lay the need of the courts to ensure that the agent or attorney had the requisite power to conclude the business at hand and that his conclusion would have the concurrence of his principal or constituent. That concurrence or consent, therefore, was given in advance. And as Gaines Post puts it: "*Plena potestas* . . . was to an assembly what it was to a court, it was in theory an expression of

fondamentale della democrazia nel XIII secolo," *Paideia*, I (No. 5, 1946), 257–62, and "Il principio della democrazia e del consenso nel XIV secolo," *Studia Gratiana*, VIII (1962), 555–75.

consent, given before the action, to the decision of the court and council of the king."[41]

Given the very prevalence of representative assemblies, however, the accumulation of experience by representatives, and the fluctuations in relative strength between rulers and the communities from which they were demanding consent, it is readily comprehensible that by the mid-fourteenth century representative procedures should have come to function less exclusively in the interest of the ruler. The challenge to papal prerogatives issued at the Councils of Pisa (1409), Constance (1414–18), Pavia-Siena (1423–24) and Basel (1431–49) is only one of the most dramatic manifestations of the ways in which consent of a procedural-consultative nature could deepen into consent that was genuinely political-sovereign. At one time or another, most representative assemblies were able to make their weight felt in a whole range of governmental activities, notably in the legislative process, and the English Parliament was far from being alone in using the power of the purse, its control over taxation, in order to enhance its legislative authority and to limit the ruler's freedom of action.[42]

Against this background it is readily comprehensible, too, that theories of consent pertaining now to legitimacy rather than legality, authority rather than power, should begin to surface, and with growing frequency, in the writings of theologians, lawyers, publicists and political thinkers both prominent and obscure alike. Not, admittedly, to any marked degree in Aquinas, despite the claims sometimes made by commentators to the contrary and despite also his own intimate acquaintance with the elaborate consentual and representative mechanisms enshrined in the constitutional arrangements of his own Dominican Order. The faithfulness of his commitment to Aristotle's essentially teleological approach to political life was such that he was not disposed to bestow more than passing attention on the human

---

[41] I follow here the interpretation of Post (n. 40 above). The passages cited occur in *Studies* at pp. 180 and 116. The latter passage, focussing on the example of a royal request for a subsidy on the grounds of necessity or emergency, continues: "The case of necessity was, as it were, tried in the assembly, and the representatives were, in a sense, attorneys protecting the rights and interests of the Communities against the royal claim of public utility and binding the communities by their consent to the decision."

[42] See the useful comparative account by Marongiu, *Medieval Parliments: A Comparative Study*.

sources, at least, of political authority.[43] Brandish Aristotle though they might, few other medieval thinkers, however, were so clear-sighted in their apprehension of what the Aristotelian political vision involved or quite so thoroughgoing in their assimilation to it. Accordingly, they were disposed to respond much more markedly than had Aquinas to the preoccupation with consent and the modalities of consent that was do deeply rooted in Romano-canonical corporational-thinking and so evident in the day-to-day political and ecclesiastical life of their own era.

This is true in some small degree even of Aegidius Romanus and James of Viterbo in the opening years of the fourteenth century and of John of Turrecremata in the mid-fifteenth, all of them thinkers highly responsive to the Thomistic version of Aristotelianism and all of them papalists anxious to stress that in the Church, at least, power is distributed downwards from papal head to subordinate members.[44] It is true in much greater degree of John of Paris and William of Ockham, again in the early fourteenth century, for both of whom consent played an important validating role in the Church as well as in the secular polity.[45] It is true most of all of Ockham's fellow controversialist, Marsiglio of Padua, whose famous treatise, the *Defensor*

---

[43] See the pertinent comments of Ewart Lewis, *Medieval Political Ideas* (2 vols., London, 1954), I, 151: "The details of the human process through which the state arose were not important for Aquinas. Apparently the consent of the subjects might be a factor in particular situations; but general basis of the legitimacy of governments was, for Aquinas, their rationally demonstrable necessity to the natural needs of man." The "consent texts" in Aquinas usually cited as *Summa theologica*, Ia IIae, qu. 90, art. 3; IIa IIae, qu. 57, art. 2; *In quatuor libros Sententiarum*, II, dist. 44, qu. 2, art. 2.

[44] See the remark of Aegidius Romanus, *De renunciatione papae*, xvi, I: "Et sicut, per assensum hominum perficitur et completur, ut quis aliis praeficiatur, sic per consensum hominum contrario modo factum fieri potest, quod prefectus cedat, vel quod etiam deponatur." Cited in Carlyle, *History of Medieval Political Theory*, V, 88, who comments: "The position of Egidius is the more noticeable because he preferred an absolute to a constitutional monarchy, and he thinks of government as being the natural consequence of difference in wisdom and capacity." James of Viterbo, *De regimine christiano*, Pt. II, caps. 3 and 10; ed. H.X. Arquillière, *Le plus ancien traité de l'Église* (Paris, 1926), pp. 179, and 303. John of Turrecremata, *Summa contra Ecclesie et Primatus Apostoli Petri Adversarios* (Rome, 1489), Lib. II, cap. 41 (I have been unable to recheck this text). Lewis, *Medieval Political Ideas*, I, 160, comments that while Turrecremata "repudiated in horror any suggestion that the essence of ecclesiastical authority could possibly be mediated by popular consent, he now accepted as an established principle the idea that secular authority came from God by way of the community."

[45] John of Paris, *Tractatus de potestate regia et papali*, caps. 10, 15, and 19; ed. Fritz Bleienstein, *Johannes Quidort von Paris: Über königliche und päpstliche Gewalt* (Stuttgart,

pacis (1324), has not improperly been described as "the first systematic statement of the popular basis of authority."[46]

These are, all of them, commanding figures, and Marsiglio, especially,
stands out because of the boldness, clarity and specificity with which
he endorses the role of consent in the political process.[47] He stands
out also, however, as an exceptional figure, as a thinker too individual and complex, it seems, by himself to exert much of a direct
influence either upon his contemporaries or his successors.[48] The
main burden of consent theory was borne through the later Middle
Ages, instead, by a stream of thought with which he was admittedly
affiliated but which drew much more directly than did his thinking
upon the great watershed of Romano-canonistic corporational thought,
and flowed through more generally familiar territory and at a much
more measured pace. I have in mind that particular tradition of theorizing about the nature of the Church which was associated with
the Conciliar movement and which made possible in 1417 the ending
of the crippling schism which had divided the Latin Church since
the disputed papal election of 1378—first into two rival "obediences,"
each with its own pope, and then into three.

It is not always realized that the scandal of the Great Schism confronted Europe with a truly major and protracted constitutional crisis,
one that had been brewing since the latter decades of the thirteenth
century and one that the triumph of the papacy over the Council
of Basel in 1449 did not fully resolve. That crisis brought into sharp
focus the question of the location of ultimate authority within the

---

1969), pp. 106–17, 150–53, 169–76. Both Bleienstein (pp. 33–34, 38–40) and
Thomas J. Renna, "The Populus in John of Paris' Theory of Monarchy," *Revue
d'histoire du droit*, XLII (1974), 243–68, correctly stress the limited fashion in which
John of Paris applies consent theory to the secular polity. William of Ockham,
Breviloquium de potestate papae, Lib. III, caps. 7–11, Lib. IV, cap. 10; ed. L. Baudry
(Paris, 1937), pp. 85–91, 119–22. For a most helpful assessment, see Arthur S.
McGrade, *The Political Thought of William of Ockham: Personal and Institutional Principles*
(Cambridge, 1974), pp. 103–09.

[46] Thus, Lewis, *Medieval Political Ideas*, I, 159. See esp. *Defensor pacis*, I, caps. 12
and 15; ed. C.W. Previté-Orton, pp. 48–54, 66–74. Cf. the excellent commentary
in Alan Gewirth, *Marsilius of Padua: The Defender of Peace* (2 vols., New York, 1951–56),
I, 167–225.

[47] See esp. *Defensor pacis*, I, cap. 12, 6; ed. Previté-Orton, pp. 51–52.

[48] Though the Conciliarists Dietrich of Niem (d. 1418) and Nicholas of Cusa
(1401–64) both draw (without acknowledgment) some material from him—see Paul
E. Sigmund, Jr., "The Influence of Marsilius of Padua on XVth-Century Conciliarism,"
Journal of the History of Ideas, XXIII (No. 3, 1962), 392–402. For later citations of
the *Defensor pacis*, see Gewirth, *Marsilius of Padua*, I, 303–04.

universal Church, and, in particular, the matter of the relative powers of pope and general council. And the Conciliar theory was, in effect, a constitutionalist theory which provided the doctrinal underpinnings enabling the Council of Constance to end the schism by trying, sentencing and deposing the rival pontiffs. At its heart lay the belief that the pope was not an absolute monarch but rather in some sense a constitutional ruler, that he possessed a merely ministerial authority delegated to him for the good of the Church, that the final authority in the Church (at least in certain critical cases) lay not with him but with the whole body of the faithful or with their representatives gathered together in a general council. This being so, and Conciliar theory being, in effect, a constitutionalist doctrine, its rise to prominence during the course of the Great Schism is entirely understandable for it offered a way out of what had become a scandalous impasse. It is important to realize, however, that it long predated the tragic onset of the schism and long survived its happy demise. Thus, twenty-five years ago, pursuing in systematic fashion scattered suggestions made over the years by Otto von Gierke, H.X. Arquillière, Walter Ullmann and others, Tierney was able to establish the fact that Conciliar theory was the logical outgrowth of certain strands of canonist thought, both Decretist and Decretalist, the outcome of attempts by generations of canonists imbued with the principles and categories of Roman corporation law to rationalize the structure both of the individual churches of Christendom and of the universal Church itself. Side by side with "the familiar theory of papal sovereignty," some of them had developed a different theory which stressed "the corporate association of the members of a church" rather than the "rigorous subordination of all the members to a single head" as "the true principle of ecclesiastical unity." That theory "envisaged an exercise of corporate authority by the members of a church [as also by the members of the universal Church] even in the absence of an effective head" and, in so doing, laid the essential foundations for the later development of Conciliar theory.[49]

---

[49] Brian Tierney, *Foundations of the Conciliar Theory*, pp. 240, 10–11; cf. Gierke, *Political Theories of the Middle Age*, p. 50; H.X. Arquillière, "L'appel au concile sous Philippe le Bel et le genèse des theories conciliares." *Revue des questions historiques*, XLV (No. 1, 1911), 51–55; Walter Ullmann, *The Origins of the Great Schism* (London, 1948), pp. 185–86, and *The Growth of Papal Government in the Middle Ages* (London, 1955), pp. 652–53. Cf. John Watt, "The Early Medieval Canonists and the Formation of Conciliar Theory," *Irish Theological Quarterly*, XXIV (Jan. 1957), 13–31; James

Some aspects of that Conciliar position are present in the ecclesiologies of William Durantis the Younger (d. 1328) and William of Ockham, while Marsiglio of Padua enunciated a related but far more radical formulation in his *Defensor pacis*.[50] A few years earlier, however, John of Paris had developed what has been called "by far the most consistent and complete formulation of conciliar doctrine before the outbreak of the Great Schism."[51] And from the latter point onwards formulations that are at least comparable and at best more sophisticated and systematic come thick and fast. They are to be found at the start of the schism in the tracts written by Conrad of Gelnhausen and Henry of Langenstein, during its course in the Conciliar writings of (among others) Pierre d'Ailly, Jean Gerson, Dietrich of Niem and Francesco Zabarella, and after its end in the works of John of Ragusa, Panormitanus, Andrew of Escobar, Heimerich van de Velde, Jean Beaupère, John of Segovia, Matthias Doering, Gregor Heimburg, Aenius Sylvius Piccolomini, Denys van Rijkel and, of course, Nicholas of Cusa.[52] Nor, as of late Klotzner, Jedin, Bäumer and others have

Moynihan, *Papal Immunity and Liability in the Writings of the Medieval Canonists* (Rome, 1961). There is a useful review article on some of the recent scholarship by Giuseppe Alberigo. "Il movimento conciliare (xiv–xv sec.) nella ricerca storica recente," *Studie Medievali*, 3rd series, XIX (No. 2, 1978), 213–50.

[50] For the contribution of Durandus to the growth of Conciliar thought, see Tierney, *Foundations of Conciliar Theory*, pp. 190–98. Of Ockham's contributions, however important, Georges de Lagarde, *La naissance de l'esprit laïque an déclin du moyen âge*, new edn. (5 vols., Louvain and Paris, 1956–70), V, 53, comments that it would be futile to look in his works for "a coherent theory of the rights of a general council." For my own sense that Marsiglio's views were so radical that it would be a salutary clarification if, by general agreement, we could decide henceforth to withhold from him the designation of "Conciliarist," see Francis Oakley, "Conciliarism in the Sixteenth Century: Jacques Almain Again," *Archiv für Reformationsgeschichte*, LXVIII (1977), 111–32.

[51] Tierney, *Foundations of Conciliar Theory*, p. 177. See *Tractatus de postestate regia et papali*, caps. 22–25; ed. Bleienstein, pp. 192–211.

[52] See esp. Conrad of Gelnhausen, *Epistola concordie*, in Franz Bliemetzrieder, *Literarische Polemik zur Beginn des grossen abendländischen Schismas* (Vienna and Leipzig, 1910), pp. 111–40; Henry of Langenstein, *Epistola concilii pacis*, in H. von der Hardt, *Magnum oecumenicum Constantiense Concilium* (7 vols., Leipzig, 1697ff.), II, 1, 3–60. Pierre d'Ailly, *Tractatus de ecclesiastica potestate* and Jean Gerson, *Tractatus de unitate ecclesiae*—both in Jean Gerson, *Opera omnia*, ed. Louis Ellies Dupin (5 vols., Antwerp, 1706), II, 925–60 and 113–80; Dietrich of Niem, *De modis uniendi et reformandi ecclesiam in concilio universali*, ed., Hermann Heimpel, *Dietrich von Niem: Dialog über Union und Reform der Kirche* (Leipzig und Berlin, 1933); Franciscus Zabarella, *De ejus temporis schismate tractatus* (Strasbourg, 1609); for the relevant texts quarried from the commentaries of Panormitanus (Nicholas de Tudeschis), see K.W. Nörr, *Kirche und Konzil bei Nicholaus de Tudeschis* (Cologne, 1964); Andrew of Escobar, *Gubenaculum Conciliorum*, in von der Hardt, VI, 139–333; John of Segovia, *Amplificatio disputacionis* (forms Lib. XVII, caps.

reminded us, did the failure of the Conciliarists to engineer a constitutional revolution in the Church necessarily mean the demise of Conciliar theory after the dissolution of the Council of Basel in 1449.[53] Much work remains to be done, but quite enough is known about such men as Philippus Decius, Zacharius Ferreri, Jacques Almain, John Major, Pierre Cordier, Giovanni Gozzadini and Matthias Ugonius—all of them writing in the early sixteenth century—to classify them unambiguously as Conciliarists.[54]

From John of Paris, then, writing in 1301, to Matthias Ugonius, writing in 1532, the tradition is a lengthy one. Those contributing to it—lawyers, theologians, ecclesiastical publicists—wrote under differing circumstances one from another, with shifting preoccupations and confronting changing problems, and those differentials are

---

25–60, of his *Historia gestarum generalis synodi Basiliensis*), in F. Palacky *et al.*, *Monumenta conciliorum generalium seculo decimi quinti* (4 vols., Vienna-Basel, 1857–1935), III, 635–941; Aenius Sylvius Piccolominus, *De Gestis Concilii Basiliensis Commentariorum: Libri II*, ed. Denys Hay and W.K. Smith (Oxford, 1967); Nicholas of Cusa, *De Concordantia Catholica*, ed. Gerhard Kallen, in *Nicolai de Cusa Opera omnia* (14 vols., Leipzig-Hamburg, 1932–63), XIV (I cite from the 1963 reissue).

[53] Hubert Jedin, *A History of the Council of Trent*, trans. Ernst Graf (2 vols., London, 1957–61), I, 1–165; Josef Klotzner, *Kardinal Domenikus Jacobazzi und sein Konzilswerk* (Rome, 1948); Francis Oakley, "Almain and Major: Conciliar Theory on the Eve of the Reformation," *American Historical Review*, LXX (April, 1965), 673–90; *idem.*, "Conciliarism at the Fifth Lateran Council?" *Church History*, XLI (1973), 652–63; *idem.*, "Conciliarism in the Sixteenth Century"; Olivier de la Brosse, *Le Pape et le Concile: La comparaison de leurs pouvoirs à la veille de la Réforme* (Paris, 1965); Remigius Bäumer, *Nachwirkungen des konziliaren Gedankens in der Theologie und Kanonistik des frühen 16. Jahrhunderts* (Münster, 1971), and "Die Konstanzer Dekrete 'Haec sancta' und 'Frequens' in Urteil Katholischer Kontroverstheologen des 16. Jahrhunderts," in Remigius Bäumer, ed., *Von Konstanz nach Trient: Beitrage zur Geschichte der Kirche von den Reformkonzilien bis zum Tridentinum* (München, Paderborn, Wien, 1972), pp. 547–74.

[54] See Philippus Decius, *Consilium ... de auctoritate papae et concilii*, in Goldast, *Monarchia*, II, 1667–76; also his *Sermo ... pro justificatione Concilii Pisani, ibid.*, 1677–82; Zacharius Ferreri, *Apologia Sacri Pisani Concilli*, Goldast, II, 1654–65; the relevant tracts of Jacques Almain and John Major are printed in Dupin, II, 961–1145; Pierre Cordier, *De potestate generalis concilii supra papam*, Ms Leiden BPL 41, fols. 395v–408v; Giovanni Gozzadini, *De Romani Pontificis electione*, Ms. Vat. lat. 4414, fols. 1–307r; Matthias Ugonius, *Synodia Ugonia episcopi Phamagustani de Conciliis* (Venice, 1532). For brief comments on all of these writers and others, see Klotzner, *Kardinal Domenikus Jacobazzi*, pp. 209–87, as well as Bäumer, *Nachwirkungen* and "Die Konstanzer Dekrete" (the latter devotes considerable attention to Ugonius). For Almain and Major, see Francis Oakley, "From Constance to 1688: The Political Thought of John Major and George Buchanan," *Journal of British Studies*, I (No. 2, 1962), 1–31 at 12–19, as well as *idem.*, "Almain and Major," and "Conciliarism in the Sixteenth Century." Hubert Jedin analyzes the Conciliar thinking of Gozzadini in his "Giovanni Gozzadini, ein Konziliarist am Hofe Julius II," in Jedin, *Kirche das Glaubens, Kirche der Geschichte Ausgewälte Aufsätze und Voträge* (2 vols., Freiburg-Basel-Wien, 1966), II, 17–74.

certainly reflected in their thinking. All of them, nonetheless, in one
degree or another and at one remove or another, witness to the profound impact of the Romano-canonistic tradition of representation
and consent. And if, as John Neville Figgis put it in a classic appraisal,
some of them "appear to have discerned more clearly than their
predecessors the meaning of the constitutional experiments which the
last two centuries had seen in considerable profusion, to have thought
out the principles that underlay them, and based them upon reasoning that applied to all political societies,"[55] it was not, it should
now be insisted, because they rejected that corporatist tradition of
consent but because they brought it into contact with notions of
philosophic provenance.[56] By so doing they succeeded in formulat-
ing the theoretical principles underlying medieval constitutionalism
in general with such clarity and universality that their formulations
reverberated right down to the mid-seventeenth century, generating
explicit echoes especially among the Protestant resistance theorists of
the sixteenth century (English, French, Scottish) and among the
Parliamentary opponents of Charles I of England during the civil
war. And, among the latter, "the conciliar precedent . . . was invoked
frequently enough to force the Royalist writers into a polemic, and
thus came to form a distinct strand of the controversy over the right
of resistance in the years 1642–44."[57]

---

[55] Figgis, *Gerson to Grotius*, p. 47. It should be noted that Figgis was unaware of
the canonistic background and judged the Conciliarists, therefore, to have been
applying to the Church constitutionalist arguments drawn from the world of secular politics. For comments on his view, see Tierney, *Foundations*, pp. 10–11, and
Francis Oakley, "Figgis, Constance, and the Divines of Paris," *American Historical
Review*, LXXV (No. 2, 1969), 368–86 at 369–73.

[56] For a more systematic treatment of the point being outlined here, see Francis
Oakley, "Natural Law, the *corpus mysticum*, and consent in Conciliar Thought from
John of Paris to Matthias Ugonius," *Speculum*, LVI (No. 4, 1981), 786–810.

[57] Citing Zofia Rueger, "Gerson, the Conciliar Movement, and the Right of
Resistance," *Journal of the History of Ideas*, XXV (no. 4, 1964), 467–86 at 486. For
the relevance of Conciliar thought to the later development of secular constitutionalism and/or evidence of its explicit employment by later political thinkers, see
in addition to Figgis, *Gerson to Grotius*, pp. 41–70, and Rueger's article, James H.
Burns, "The Conciliarist Tradition in Scotland," *Scottish Historical Review*, XLII (Oct.,
1963), 89–104; Francis Oakley, "From Constance to 1688," *The Political Thought of
Pierre d'Ailly: The Voluntarist Tradition* (New Haven and London, 1964), 217–32; "From
Constance to 1688 Revisited," *Journal of the History of Ideas*, XXVII (No. 2, 1966),
429–32, and "Figgis, Constance, and the Divines of Paris," 371–76 (notes 16–32
of this article contain full references to the pertinent primary literature and to the
secondary literature up to 1969); A.J. Black, *Monarchy and Community: Political Ideas
in the Later Conciliar Controversy: 1430–1450* (Cambridge, 1970), esp. pp. 7–51, 130–35;

Although a distinguished canonist like Zabarella was by no means incapable of invoking the authority of philosophers or, indeed, necessarily averse to so doing,[58] it was the philosopher theologians among the Conciliarists and proto-Conciliarists, understandably, who moved most clearly and persistently to bring theories of consent deriving from Romano-canonistic corporational thinking into contact with more universal principles of a philosophic nature.

In the context of the history of political thought, therefore, some segments of the vast Conciliarist or proto-Conciliarist literature must bulk larger than the rest. In that context, or so it may be suggested, a particular interest attaches to the formulations of John of Paris, William of Ockham, Pierre d'Ailly, Jean Gerson, Nicholas of Cusa, Jacques Almain and John Major. All of these men were to be cited by the English political writers of the early-seventeenth century, and some of them with considerable frequency.[59] All of them saw the grounding of governmental authority in the consent of the governed as a principle pertaining not merely to the Church but rather to all "rightly ordained" political communities. In making their case for the continuing as well as the original possession of ultimate authority by the community as a whole, all felt free to move to and fro between the secular and ecclesiastical polities, drawing their illustrations from both. All were moved, therefore, at least in part, to disengage their theories of consent from the particularizing elements of ecclesiastical, national and regional law or custom, and nearly all to bring them into firm connection with the more universal mandates

---

idem., *Council and Commune: The Conciliar Movement and the Fifteenth-century Heritage* (London and Sheperdstown, 1979), esp. pp. 194–209; Brian Tierney, "'Divided Sovereignty' at Constance: A Problem of Medieval and Early Modern Political Theory," *Annuarium Historiae Conciliorum*, VII (1975), 238–56. There is an excellent synthetic statement in Skinner, *Foundations of Modern Political Thought*, II, 36–47, 114–23, 227–28, 235, 321.

[58] Zabarella, *De ... schismate tractatus*, p. 541,—though Tierney, *Foundations*, pp. 223–26, notes that "he chose to emphasize the juristic foundations of his theory at this point. . . ."

[59] The bulk of the references are d'Ailly, Gerson, Major and (especially) Almain. The names of John of Paris, William of Ockham and Marsiglio of Padua crop up less frequently. I have found only a handful of references to Nicholas of Cusa— see Oakley, "Figgis, Constance, and the Divines of Paris," 375–76. It should be noted that Gerson, d'Ailly and Cusa appear to have been the thinkers that Figgis had especially in mind when he said of the Conciliarists that it was their distinction to have "raised the constitutionalism of the past three centuries to a higher power, expressed it in a more universal form, and justified it on grounds of reason, policy and Scripture"—*Gerson to Grotius*, p. 47.

of the natural law. And by so doing they were in effect suggesting
that the natural law which had long been understood to prescribe
theoretical and moral limits to a ruler's exercise of his power should
now be understood as indicating also the practical instrumentality
whereby such limits could in the last resort be enforced. Thus,
Nicholas of Cusa, basing consent on the natural freedom and equality
of men, crisply asserted that "if by nature men are equally powerful
and equally free, the valid and ordained power of one man equal
in power with the others cannot naturally be established except by
the election and consent of the others."[60] Thus Ockham, taking as
a fundamental axiom the notion that by natural law any free people can elect its own head, argued: "All mortals have from God and
from the nature the right of freely giving themselves a head, for they
are born free and subject to no one by human law; whence every
city and ever people can establish law by itself."[61] Thus d'Ailly,
Gerson, Almain, Major—all of them repeatedly insisted that the right
of the Church as a whole to rid itself of an incorrigible head and
to prevent its own destruction was not simply a right based on ecclesiastical custom or derived from canon law but was an inalienable
right pertaining to all "free communities" and grounded in the dictates of natural law itself.[62]

The notably universal expression which these men gave to the
principles underlying the medieval constitutionalist tradition took
them into philosophical territory that lay outside the more parochial

---

[60] Nicholas of Cusa, *De Concordantia Catholica*, Lib. II, cap. 14: "Nam si natura
aeque potentes et aeque liberi homines sunt, vera et ordinata potestas unius com-
munis aeque potentis naturaliter non nisi electione et consensu aliorum constitui
potest"; ed. Kallen, XIV, 162. For a discussion of this and of other passages in the
De Concordantia Catholica that stress consent, see Paul E. Sigmund, *Nicholas of Cusa
and Medieval Political Thought* (Cambridge, Mass., 1963), pp. 137–57.

[61] Guillelmi de Occam, *Breviloquium de potestate papae*, Lib. IV, cap. 10; ed. Baudry,
p. 21: "A Deo enim et a nature habent omnes mortales, qui nascuntur liberi et
jure humano nequaquam alteri sunt subjecti, quod sponte possunt sibi rectorem
preficere, quemadmodum quisque populus et queqe civitas jus sibi constituere
potest. . . ." Cf. his *Dialogus*, III, II, III, cap. 6; in Goldast, *Monarchia*, II, 932–35.
Similarly, Pierre d'Ailly, *Tractatus de ecclesiastica potestate*, in Dupin, II, 936B, where
he grounds the right of the Romans to elect the pope in ". . . jure illo naturali,
large sumpto, quod omnibus competit, quibus est aliqua praeficienda potestas, sive
saecularis sive ecclesiastica, videlicet eligendi sibi rectorem. . . ."

[62] Gerson, *Tractatus de unitate*, in Dupin, II, 114D–115D, and *De auferabilitate papae*,
ibid., 215C–216A; Almain, *Tractatus de auctoritate ecclesiae*, *ibid.*, 1009A–B; Major,
Disputatio de auctoritate concilli, *ibid.*, 1134D–35A, 1136A, d'Ailly, *Propositiones utiles*, *ibid.*,
112–13, and *Tractatus de ecclesiastica potestate*, *ibid.*, 956A.

vision of many a later constitutionalist including some whose memory has been more widely honored than theirs. One need think only of the historically-minded traditionalism of a François Hotman or a Chief Justice Coke, or again, of the rather conservative radicalism of an Oliver Cromwell or a Henry Ireton.[63] It may well have been that universality, indeed, that accounted for some of the appeal of Conciliarist ideas to the Protestant resistance theorists of the sixteenth century. John Ponet, certainly, in some ways the most precocious of them all, drew attention in 1556 to the fact that "the canonists," in arguing that wicked popes "maie be depryved by the body of the churche," grounded themselves upon "this lawe of nature to depose and punishe wicked governours," and added: "By this lawe [of nature] and argumentes of the Canonistes and example of deprivacion of a Pope, are all clokes (wherewith Popes, bishoppes, priestes, kaisers and Kinges use to defende their iniquitie) utterly taken away."[64] It is understandable, then, that in what has since become something of a classic formulation H.J. Laski should have been moved to assert that "the road from Constance to [the Glorious Revolution of] 1688 is a direct one."[65]

III

But not quite. If the constitutionalist tradition to which the Conciliarists had given so powerful an expression flowed on into the sixteenth, seventeenth and, indeed, eighteenth centuries, it undoubtedly lacked

---

[63] Note the evident alarm with which Ireton and Cromwell greeted the efforts of the Levelers during the course of the Putney Debates in 1647 to base their demand for the vote not in the traditional rights of Englishmen grounded in the "fundamental part of the civil constitution," but in the law of nature itself. See A.S.P. Woodhouse, ed., *Puritanism and Liberty: Being the Army Debates (1647–49)* . . . *with Supplementary Documents*, 2nd ed. (Chicago, 1951), pp. 53–60. As Cromwell exclaimed (p. 59): "[W]here is there any bound or limit set if you take away this [limit], that men that have no interest but the interest of breathing [shall have no voice in elections]?" For an illuminating comment on the reluctance of resistance theorists like Hotman "to talk about the law of nature as the foundation of their resistance theory," see Richard Tuck, *Natural Rights Theories: Their Origin and Development* (Cambridge, 1979), pp. 42–43.
[64] *A Shorte Treatise of Politicke Power* (1556): facsimile edition printed in Winthrop S. Hudson, *John Ponet (1516?–1556): Advocate of Limited Monarchy* (Chicago, 1942), pp. [103] and [105].
[65] Laski, "Political Theory in the Later Middle Ages," 638.

one element crucial to the modern theory of legitimation by consent.[66] For what truly distinguishes the modern contractarian tradition of political thinking running from Hobbes to Kant, is the fact that it ascribes to the autonomous individual will a real choice as to whether or not to implicate itself in politics, that it ascribes to the free authorizing act of that individual will "an importance . . . which never appeared before in the history of political philosophy."[67] Despite the confusing ambiguities undoubtedly attaching to the notion of will, and despite the divergent conclusions contract theorists like Hobbes and Locke drew from their stress on consent, this, it has well been argued, provides "a thread which holds the modern tradition together," "setting it off from the classical tradition,"[68] and setting it off, too, it must now be insisted, even from that great tradition of consent theorizing which ran from the fourteenth- and fifteenth-century Conciliarists on to the Protestant constitutionalists and resistance theorists of the sixteenth and early seventeenth centuries—French, Scottish, English, Dutch—as well as to their counterparts among the ideologists of the Catholic *Ligue* in France and among the Spanish writers on matters political, Jesuit as well as Dominican.

Doubtless, these are large claims. But for even the most philosophically-minded among the representatives of this latter tradition (and despite some formulations arrestingly modern in their intonation), consent appears finally to have remained what it had been even for the most "advanced" of medieval consent theorists: not, that is, the assent of a concatenation of free and equal individuals imposing on themselves an obligation which of their ultimate autonomy they could well avoid, but the consent instead of free communities, possessed at a minimum of the original right to choose their rulers, perhaps also to choose the form of government under which they

---

[66] Note the cognate but not quite parallel contrast which Harro Höpfl and Martyn P. Thompson draw between what they call "constitutional contractarianism" and "philosophical contractarianism" in the late-seventeenth and early-eighteenth centuries. "The History of Contract as a Motif in Political Thought," *American Historical Review*, XCIV (No. 4, 1979), 919–44 at 941–44.

[67] Riley, "How Coherent is the Social Contract Tradition?," 561; cf. Pateman, *The Problem of Political Obligation*, esp. pp. 1–2, 12–13, 98–102.

[68] Riley, *ibid.*, 561. See the same article (549–53) for the lack of clarity attaching to the notion of will (and especially the blending of psychological meanings) in all the great contract theorists with the exception of Kant. On this same point, see also his "Will and Legitimacy in the Philosophy of Hobbes," esp. 521–22, and "On Kant as the Most Adequate of the Social Contract Theorists," esp. 456–60.

were to live, maybe even to participate on some sort of continuing basis in the governmental process—those choices, however, "conditioned by the principle that authority must exist," that it was "necessary and in some sense natural to man."[69] This is clearly true, for example, of John of Paris; only a little less clearly is it true also of William of Ockham, whose doctrine of consent, it has recently been argued, was "far less developed than that of some of his contemporaries."[70] It is true of the Conciliar thinkers in general, and again, perhaps more surprisingly, of Marsiglio of Padua and Nicholas of Cusa.[71] In the sixteenth century it is true of the famous Huguenot tract, the *Vindiciae contra tyrannos,* and of its Catholic counterpart, the *De justa reipublicae Christianae . . . authoritate* of William Reynolds (Rossaeus),[72] of Spanish thinkers like Francisco de Vitoria, Domingo

---

[69] Lewis, *Medieval Political Ideas,* I, 160.

[70] McGrade, *The Political Thought of William of Ockham,* p. 108, adding (n. 82): "So far as I have been able to determine, Ockham never construes political consent as a matter of individual agreement to the powers and laws of government." Cf. the discussion in Georges de Lagarde, *Naissance,* IV, 227–34.

[71] This, in Marsiglio's case, despite his explicit stress on the role of will in legislation and the constitution of governments. For he advances no doctrine of individual natural rights and the consenting will he has in mind is that of the *populus* or the *universitas civium* or the *valentior pars* thereof (*Defensor pacis,* I, xii, 3; ed. Previté-Orton, p. 49), the expression *valentior pars* referring to a qualitative as well as a quantitative preponderance. The critical passages on this point occur at I, xii, 3, 5, and 6 (ed. Previté-Orton, pp. 49–52). Gewirth, *Marsilius of Padua,* I, 218–25, while conceding that the legislating *populus* or *universitas* "is a corporate whole rather than simply a collection of individuals," makes much of *Defensor pacis,* I, xii, 6 (unconvincingly, I think) as adding an emphasis on "freedom and individualism [that] is not . . . contradictory to the naturalistic determinism and corporatism of Marsilius' other arguments." Cf. Previté-Orton, "Marsilius of Padua," *Proceedings of the British Academy,* XXI (1935), 137–83 at 153–54, and Lewis, *Medieval Political Ideas,* I, 160. Similarly, Nicholas of Cusa, for all his acknowledgment of the freedom and equality of men, ends by placing his emphasis on the freedom of the corporate community to give its consent, that consent being given, moreover, to "a fixed political and ecclesiastical order, which is part of the natural order of the universe designed by God."—Sigmund, *Nicholas of Cusa,* pp. 155–56. See esp. *De Concordantia Catholica,* Lib. III, proemium, ed. Kallen, pp. 313–26.

[72] See *Vindiciae contra tyrannos,* Qu. 2 and 3; in the English translation of 1689 reprinted by Harold J. Laski, *A Defense of Liberty against Tyrants* (New York, 1972), pp. 87–213. This work was attributed to Hubert Languet and more recently, at least in part to Philippe du Plessis Mornay. See Raoul Patry, *Philippe du Plessis Mornay, un huguenot homme d'état* (Paris, 1933), pp. 275–82. G. Rossaeus, *De justa reipublicae christianae in reges impios et haereticos authoritate* (Paris, 1590), cap. I, fols. 1r–20r (see esp. fols. 1r, 2r, 4r, 5r–v, 20r). For a definitive case in favor of attributing this work to William Rainolds, see Charles H. McIlwain, *Constitutionalism in the Changing World* (New York, 1939), pp. 178–83.

de Soto and Luis de Molina,[73] and even (though with some qualifications) of the Scottish humanist, George Buchanan, about whose
radicalism so much has often been made.[74] In the seventeenth century it is true of the political thinking of the Jesuits Francisco Suarez[75]
and Juan de Mariana,[76] of the *Politica methodice digesta* of Johannes
Althusius,[77] and of the Parliamentarian tract, *Lex, Rex: The Law and the
Prince*, which Samuel Rutherford, the Scottish Presbyterian, published

---

[73] On whom see Guenter Lewy, *Constitutionalism and Statecraft during the Golden Age
of Spain: A Study of the Political Philosophy of Juan de Mariana, S.J.* (Geneva, 1960), esp.
pp. 37–42; Bernice Hamilton, *Political Thought in Sixteenth-Century Spain* (Oxford, 1963);
J.A. Fernández-Santamaria, *The State, War and Peace: Spanish Political Thought in the
Renaissance: 1516–1559* (Cambridge, 1977), who discusses Vitoria at some length, as
well as such thinkers as Alonso de Castrillo, Alfonso de Valdés, and Juan Ginés de
Sepúlveda. Cf. Skinner, *Foundations of Modern Political Thought*, II, 135–73 (esp. 148–66),
and the older discussion by Figgis, *Gerson to Grotius*, pp. 190–217.
[74] Most recently by Skinner, *Foundations of Modern Political Thought*, II, 339–44,
who overemphasizes somewhat, or so I would judge, Buchanan's individualism. Cf.
Francis Oakley, "On the Road from Constance to 1688," 1–31, esp. 23–26; also
the remarks of Tuck, *Natural Rights Theories*, pp. 43–44. While strongly sympathiz-
ing with Skinner's stress on the continuities binding the sixteenth-century resistance
theorists to their scholastic predecessors, I remain uneasy about his ascription to
members of both groups of a "'subjective' theory of rights" and of the individualist sympathies that would appear to attach to such a theory. On which, see below,
note 91.
[75] See Francisco Suarez, *Tractatus de Legibus ac Deo Legislatore* (Coimbra, 1612), Lib.
I, cap. 3, § 3; cap. 6, §§ 18–22; Lib. III, cap. 2, esp. §§ 3–5; cap. 3, esp. §§ 1–6
(pp. 14–15, 36–37, 201–205). These texts are all reprinted in facsimile in James
Brown Scott, ed., *Selections from Three Works of Francisco Suarez, S.J.* (Washington,
D.C., 1944), I, original pagination. Cf. Reijo Wilenius, *The Social and Political Theory
of Francisco Suarez* (Helsinki, 1963), esp. pp. 101–112, where he describes Suarez's
theory of the state and society as "intensely anti-individualistic"; Hamilton, *Political
Thought in Sixteenth-Century Spain*, pp. 30–43; Lewy, *Constitutionalism and Statecraft*, pp.
41–42, where he comments: "It is . . . a mistake to see in Suarez a spokesman for
an individualistic social contract theory. This interpretation is invited by some of
the expressions Suarez used, but is untenable if seen in the total context of his
work." Cf. Heinrich Rommen, *Die Staatslehre des Franz Suarez, S.J.* (München Gladbach,
1926), p. 112.
[76] Joannis Marianae, *De Rege et Regis Institutione, Libri III* (Toledo, 1599), Lib. I,
caps. 1 and 8 (Note that the work was published first in 1599; subsequent editions
appeared in 1605, 1611 and 1640). Cf. Lewy, *Constitutionalism and Statecraft*, esp.
p. 47 where he stresses the fact that Mariana's doctrine is not "very harmonious."
While sometimes reminding one of Hobbes, his argument "also leans toward the
organic tenets of the Thomists who insisted that man's life in society is natural and
a means to attain the full development of the human personality. . . . With all of
Mariana's voluntarism, society remains for him, in an important sense, a necessity
inspired by God, and not dependent exclusively on man's will."
[77] And despite Gierke's portrayal of Althusius as having brought out "into the
sharpest relief the last philosophical consequence of the idea of contract," as having derived "all the rights of the community from the inborn rights of the human

in 1644.[78] And despite the fact that Locke invoked his authority so profusely and misleadingly in the *Second Treatise*, it is true also even of Richard Hooker. For while Locke invokes Hooker's references to the natural equality of men to support his own highly individualistic doctrine of consent. Hooker himself saw equality as "a source of duties, not of rights, and consent [as] . . . the expression of the corporate life of the whole society, not of single individual wills."[79]

That this should be so, of course, confronts us with something of a puzzle and one that demands solution. For some, the basic components of such a solution lie readily at hand—in the burgeoning development of the early-modern capitalist market economy and in the abstraction from its conditions that led the great seventeenth-century political theorists to conceive of the individual in "possessive" terms, "as essentially the proprietor of his own person, and possessions, owing nothing to society for them," and, accordingly, to conceive of freedom as "a function of possession."[80] But whether or not they

---

individual," and as having portrayed even "the State's rights of superiority" as "in the last analysis simply the product of individual rights which are voluntarily given up and communalized."—See *Development of Political Theory*, pp. 102–103, and, for a telling and persuasive critique, Höpfl and Thompson, "The History of Contract as a Motif in Political Thought," 919–944. For pertinent texts see Carl J. Friedrich, ed., *Politica Methodice Digesta of Johannes Althusius* (Cambridge, Mass., 1932), caps. 1–4 and 9, pp. 15–38, 87–94 (esp. cap. 1, pp. 18–19). Gierke's high estimate of Althusius notwithstanding, it is hard not to feel a twinge of sympathy for Kossman's exasperated comment: "According to Althusius, absolute legislative sovereignty did not reside in the king but in the people. But what is the people? Althusius did not tire of answering this elementary question again and again. Whenever he had to use the words 'people' or 'popular sovereignty' he poured out an endless stream of synonyms—synonyms . . . that neither explain nor define his position very much."—see E.H. Kossman, "The Development of Dutch Political Theory in the Seventeenth Century," in J.S. Bromley and E.H. Kossman, eds., *Britain and the Netherlands*, 2 vols. (London, 1960), I, 91–110 at 93.

[78] Samuel Rutherford, *Lex, Rex: The Law and the Prince. A dispute for the just Prerogative of King and People* (London, 1644), esp. pp. 1–5, 8–9, 50–51 (where he cites Jacques Almain), 66. J.F. Maclear, "Samuel Rutherford: the Law and the King," in George L. Hunt, ed., *Calvinism and the Political Order* (Philadelphia, 1965), pp. 65–87, gives a useful general discussion of the background to this work.

[79] Citing d'Entrèves, *Notion of the State*, p. 197, n. 2. For a lengthier statement of this view, see *idem.*, *The Medieval Contribution to Political Thought* (Oxford, 1939), pp. 125–35. Cf. Richard Hooker, *Of the Laws of Ecclesiastical Polity*, I, viii, 7 (for natural equality), and I, x, 3–4 (for consent); Everyman's Library Edition (2 vols., London, 1954), I, 177–81, 189–91.

[80] So that "Society becomes a lot of free equal individuals related to each other as proprietors of their own capacities and of what they have acquired by their exercise."—McPherson, *The Political Theory of Possessive Individualism*, p. 4; cf. Pateman, *The Problem of Political Obligation*, pp. 11–12, 24–25. McPherson's general thesis as it

helped mold the abstract individualism of such thinkers as Hobbes and Locke—and that remains a *quaestio disputata*—such factors certainly did not lie at its roots. These were engaged, instead, in soil far deeper and by far more ancient. And in our attempt to trace those roots we could do much worse, I would suggest, than turn for help to Hegel.

In one of those lucid shafts of historical insight that pierce the gloom of his philosophical discourse, Hegel made a series of inter-related claims. First, that "the principle of the self-subsistent inher-ently infinite personality of the individual, the principle of subjective freedom . . . is historically subsequent to the Greek world," that it is "the pivot and the center of the difference between antiquity and modern times." Second, that it was Christianity that gave it full expression, making it "the universal effective principle of a new form of civilization."[81] Third, that that principle arose first in religion and was introduced into the secular world only "by a long and severe effort of civilization." Fourth, that during the Middle Ages the author-itarianism and externalism of the hierarchical Church had the effect of blunting that effort, taking itself the place of man's conscience, laying its stress on "outward actions" that were not "the promptings of his own good will" but were performed at *its* command, and suc-ceeding in obscuring the fundamental principle of subjective freedom until that principle was finally thrown into bold relief by "the all-enlightening *Sun*" of the Protestant Reformation.[82]

On the first three of these claims Hegel was, I believe, almost cer-tainly correct. The deepest roots of what he calls "the principle of subjective freedom," along with the related emphases on will and responsibility, are indeed engaged, not in Hellenic soil, but in the

---

relates to Locke has been acutely criticized by John Dunn, "Justice and the Interpretation of Locke's Political Theory," *Political Studies*, XVI (No. 1, 1968), 68–87; *idem.*, The *Political Thought of John Locke* (Cambridge, 1969), much of which is writ-ten in implicit or explicit dialogue with McPherson's views. Also, from a different angle, Tuck, *Natural Rights Theories*, pp. 2–3.

[81] For these two points, see *Hegel's Philosophy of Right*, trans. T.M. Knox (New York, 1967), pp. 84 § 124, 124 § 185; cf. p. 51 § 62, p. 133 §§ 206, p. 195 §§ 299, and pp. 267–68, *Add.* 118, where, among other things, he mentions the differing roles ascribed to "the subject's arbitrary will" in the political life of the ancient and modern worlds. For the further link with the Christian notion of conscience, see Knox's editorial comment on p. 339. On this latter point, see also the interesting analysis of Ernest L. Fortin, "The Political Implications of St. Augustine's Theory of Conscience," *Augustinian Studies*, I (1970), 133–52.

[82] G.W.F. Hegel, *Reason in History: A General Introduction to the Philosophy of History*, trans. Robert S. Hartman (New York, 1953), pp. 23–24.

Biblical doctrine of divine omnipotence and the historically peculiar doctrine of creation that goes with it.[83] Moreover, that principle and its related emphases were indeed felt first in matters religious and it was centuries before they touched the secular sensibilities and began to revolutionize the modalities of Western political thinking. At the same time, Hegel distorted the picture somewhat, I would judge, when he confined that process almost entirely to the period after the Reformation.

The stretch of history involved encompasses some formidable obstacles to understanding and has never been satisfactorily mapped. Nonetheless, access to it can in some measure be secured if (conceding the importance of the distinction between *normative* and *historical* Christianity) one realizes the degree to which Hegel's "principle of subjective freedom" and its related emphases, rooted admittedly in "those biblical norms about human nature and human destiny that give to Christianity whatever identity it may possess," were muffled— even, for centuries, lost—in that *historical* Christianity which "though much of it is not specifically Christian," still "reflects the composite of those cultural impulses that make up what is commonly thought of as Christian civilization."[84]

Thus, even in the Patristic era and even in matters religious, the individualism which we think of as quintessentially Christian was able to make its way but slowly in the teeth of such alien notions as that of the cyclicity of time or that of the divine soul and its primordial fall into matter. With the collapse of the Roman world, moreover, and the transformation of Latin Christianity through its encounter with religious sensibilities shaped in the mold of Celtic and Germanic paganism, the characteristically Christian concern with the relationship of the individual soul to God was to a remarkable degree submerged in the collective rhythms of a devotional life that was communal rather than personal, external rather than internal, public rather than private.[85]

---

[83] For these claims, I venture to refer again to O'Connor and Oakley, *Creation*, esp. pp. 1–12, 107–89, 239–58. See also the literature referred to above in note 24.

[84] See William J. Bouwsma, "Christian Adulthood." *Daedalus* (Spring, 1976), 77–92 at 77, from whom I borrow this useful distinction.

[85] For this point and for the transformation of medieval spirituality in the twelfth century, see R.W. Southern, *The Making of the Middle Ages* (New Haven, 1961); Colin Morris, *The Discovery of the Individual: 1050–1200* (New York, 1973); brief accounts in Francis Oakley, *The Medieval Experience: Foundations of Western Cultural Singularity* (New York, 1974), ch. 6, pp. 173–189; *idem.*, *The Western Church in the Later Middle*

Only in the late eleventh century did that concern begin to surface once more in the spiritual literature. Linked now, however with
a marked emotionalism and a firm stress on the role of the individual will in the encounter with the divine, and borne far and wide
by the proponents first of the Cistercian spirituality and then of the
Franciscan, it came to reside at the very heart of late-medieval religion,[86] blunting in the process what little there survived of the originally collective thrust of the eucharistic liturgy, and, by virtue of its
voluntarism, even setting limits to the extent to which some of the
mystics were able to assimilate Neoplatonic modes of thought.[87]
During the fourteenth and fifteenth centuries, moreover, that voluntarism was paralleled in moral philosophy and theology by the
heightened stress which thinkers of the Franciscan school came to
place on the role of will, duty and intention in matters ethical.[88] And

---

Ages (Ithaca and London, 1979), pp. 80–91. See also the recent pertinent exchange
(with full references to the earlier contributions of André Wilmart, Walter Ullmann,
Peter Dronke, R.W. Hanning, John Benton, C.M. Radding and others) in Caroline
W. Bynum, "Did the Twelfth-Century Discover Individualism?," *The Journal of
Ecclesiastical History*, XXXI (No. 1, 1980), 1–17, and Colin Morris, "Individualism
in Twelfth-Century Religion. Some Further Reflections," *ibid.*, XXXI (No. 2, 1980),
195–206.

[86] On which see esp. the two important articles by Giles Constable, "Twelfth-Century
Spirituality and the Late Middle Ages," in O.B. Hardison, Jr., ed., *Proceedings of the
Southeastern Institute of Medieval and Renaissance Studies*, 5 (1971), 27–60, and "The
Popularity of Twelfth-Century Spiritual Writers," in Anthony Molho and John A.
Tedeschi, eds., *Renaissance Studies in Honor of Hans Baron* (Florence and De Kalb,
1971), pp. 5–28.

[87] Thus the two Victorine authors who were very influential in mediating the
thinking of Pseudo-Dionysius to the later-medieval world—Richard of St. Victor in
the twelfth century and Thomas Gallus, Abbot of St. Andrew's at Vercelli in the
thirteenth—reshaped that thinking by substituting for the characteristically Greek
and Neoplatonic preoccupation with the role of intellect in the mystical ascent the
more traditional Augustinian emphasis on will and love both in the life of contemplation and in the final ecstasy of communion with God. On which see Oakley,
The Western Church in the Later Middle Ages, pp. 96–97.

[88] But, then, at least in contrast with the ancients, there was nothing novel about
such a stress. Despite his rationalism, it was evident already in Aquinas and can
be observed, though not necessarily without close scrutiny, in the subtle modifications
he introduces when citing as his authority passages drawn from Aristotle's *Nichomachean
Ethics*. Thus compare Aquinas, *Summa Theologica*, Ia IIae, qu. 100, art. 9, with
Aristotle, *Nichomachean Ethics*, II, 4, 1105a–b. Aquinas cites the latter text, but with
an added stress on the necessity of a *duplex motus, scilicet voluntatis et intentionis* for the
practice of virtue. Cf. the illuminating comment of Adkins, *Merit and Responsibility*,
pp. 334ff., on the Aristotelian text in question, with a warning to the effect that
we should not be misled by the seeming "modernity" of his words into thinking
that it expresses an adequate notion of moral responsibility. Though he does not
discuss these texts, Riley, "How Coherent is the Social Contract Tradition?," 546–47,

because that voluntarism was extended also to the understanding of God and of the divine psychology, it was accompanied also in the thinking of William Ockham and of those who trod in his footsteps by the vision of a world radically contingent on the divine will, a world from which any metaphysic of essences had been banished, a world that amounted, therefore, to a collection of singular existents linked solely by relations of an external type and comprehensible each in isolation from the rest. Because of this, scholars have sometimes concluded that the radical individualism of Ockham's nominalist philosophy must necessarily have entailed in his political thinking a comparable "individualism" and a comparable adhesion to a doctrine of subjective natural rights cognate to that affiliated with the early-modern doctrine of legitimation by consent. Not an unreasonable expectation, one might think, but what Ockham himself actually has to say on matters political does not quite meet that expectation.[89] And the same is true, as Richard Tuck properly concedes, in those later nominalists—D'Ailly, Gerson, Major, Almain—in whose moral theologizing he has recently detected, though on different grounds, what he calls "the first theory of rights."[90]

Such a theory notwithstanding, then, and whatever the prominence of the role ascribed to the individual will in religious and moral living, one would search the medieval world in vain, it seems, for any parallel insistence that the political life, like the life of moral

---

does point out that while in the *Ethics* Aristotle did indeed discuss "legal responsibility in terms of whether a given action is voluntary or not," he "never suggested a theory of moral personality which required that all legitimate actions be voluntary, or chosen by private individuals." Aquinas, however, "needed to apply the idea of the voluntary not only to law, but also to sin and to 'good acts.'" There is a fine discussion of the Christian preoccupation with will, intention, and duty and its transformation of the ancient Greek ethics in Etienne Gilson, *The Spirit of Mediaeval Philosophy*, trans. A.H.C. Downes (London, 1950), pp. 343–63. In relation to Duns Scotus, perhaps the greatest of the Franciscan philosophers, Hannah Arendt, *The Life of the Mind* (2 vols., New York, 1978), vol. 1: *Willing*, 125–46, provides a perceptive discussion of the treatment of creation, contingency, freedom, selfhood, and the primacy of the will in his thinking.

[89] On which, see Arthur S. McGrade, "Ockham and the Birth of Individual Rights," in Brian Tierney and Peter Lineham, eds., *Authority and Power: Studies of Medieval Law and Government* (Cambridge, 1980), 149–65, where, in highly persuasive fashion, he takes issue directly with the views of Michel Villey (see esp. the latter's "La Genèse du droit subjectif chez Guillaume d'Occam," *Archives de Philosophie du Droit*, IX [1964], 97–127), and indirectly with the interpretation of Ockham and his times advanced by Georges de Lagarde, *La Naissance de l'esprit laïque au déclin du Moyen Age*, rev. ed. (5 vols., Paris, 1956–70).

[90] See below, n. 91.

virtue, requires moral assent, requires, that is, "the implication of the individual in politics through his own volition."[91] What we do find, nevertheless, stated already and with classic force by St. Augustine, is the negative side of that coin, the insistence that we must exercise our individual will, choose to suspend our political allegiance, and opt for disobedience if the civil ruler exceeds the limits of his authority and commands us to do something that contravenes the divine law.[92] In such cases, we must follow the Biblical injunction and "obey God rather than man" (*Acts* 5:29). And what that meant, it must be insisted, even for the Middle Ages, was not simply that the individual believer must place the moral and spiritual guidance of the hierarchically ordered Church ahead of the legal authority of the state (though that in itself was a novel departure fraught with revolutionary implications), but also that it may be necessary for him *in extremis* to follow the promptings of his own conscience rather than the mandates of any authority whatsoever including that of the Church.

Thus Aquinas himself insisted that the orders of an ecclesiastical superior are not to be equated with divine precept and that the dictates of the individual conscience must be followed even in the teeth

---

[91] Riley, "How Coherent is the Social Contract Tradition?," 544. In this connection, attention should be drawn to the rectitude of Tuck's insistence that the theory of subjective rights which he finds in d'Ailly, Major, Almain and (above all) in Gerson belonged rather to their moral theology than to their political thinking. Thus (see his *Natural Rights Theories*, p. 30): "The Theory [of subjective natural rights] in fact seems to have played very little part in the communitarian, conciliarist case to arguing which d'Ailly, Gerson, Almain and Major all devoted so much of their time. Its implications were, after all, potentially individualistic, while it was a crucial feature of their kind of conciliarism that a community was the source of political authority." Skinner, on the other hand, ascribes to Gerson, Major, Goodman, Buchanan, the author of the *Vindiciae* and Suarez the invocation even in matters political of the theory of "subjective" rights (see *Foundations of Modern Political Thought*, II, 117, 121, 176–77, 320, 328–29, 338–39, 343–44). But in almost every instance (there is conceivably room for argument about the formulations of Goodman and Buchanan) the rights referred to would appear to be the rights of rulers or communities. And in the latter case the use of the term "subjective right" is surely misleading. For Tuck and for Villey to whom Skinner also refers ("La genèse du droit subjectif chez Guillaume d'Occam," 97–127), the transition involved is not simply one from duties or obligations to rights, but also the further and less readily explicable transition to the rights of *individuals*.

[92] E.g., Augustine, *De civitate dei*, XIX, 17. Cf. Aquinas, *Summa theologica*, IIa IIae, qu. 104, art. 5: "Alio modo non tenetur inferior suo superiori obedire, si ei aliquid praecipiat in quo ei non subdatur.... Et ideo in his quae pertinent ad interiorem motum voluntatis, homo non tenetur homini obedire, sed solum Deo."

of a contrary order emanating from such a superior.[93] A few years earlier, Innocent III had written two letters (later included in the *Corpus Juris Canonici*) asserting that under certain circumstances one must humbly accept excommunication at the hands of one's ecclesiastical superior rather than go against one's conscience by obeying him.[94] Two centuries later, it was in the context of discussing this precise issue that Wessel Gansfort came closer than any other medieval thinker of whom I know to grounding the legitimacy of political as well as ecclesiastical authority in the freely-given consent of the individuals subjected to it. For in one passage of his *Tractatus de dignitate et potestate ecclesiastica*, considering how much "the subject owes to his prelate and the inferior to his superior," he portrays the relationship as a contractual one grounded in free consent and argues that if the prelate breaks the terms of the contract, then the subject's obligation ceases. "All such subjection," he says, "ought to be voluntary and spontaneous," undertaken only after deliberation, and "it is generally of the nature of this obligation that the subjects elect as their superior one in whom and through whom they expect most nearly to attain the cause and fruit of their deliberation." The same, he adds, applies to kings in "every well-framed commonwealth."[95] Indeed, if one did not take into account the imprecision and fluctuations in position evident in the tract as a whole, where he can also ground the legitimate title of a prelate in the corporate consent of his flock or even in the collation of a superior,[96] it would be easy to suppose that Gansfort had made some sort of definitive breakthrough in the direction of the doctrine of consent that came to the fore in the thinking of Locke and the modern contract theorists.

---

[93] Aquinas, *Quaestiones disputatae de veritate* qu. 17, art. 5 *resp.* The whole of *quaestio* 17 concerns the role and status of conscience.

[94] X, 2, 13, 13 and X, 5, 39, 44; ed., A. Friedberg, *Corpus Juris Canonici* (2 vols., Leipzig, 1879–81), II, 287–88, 908.

[95] Wessel Gansfort, *Tractatus de dignitate et potestate ecclesiastica, de vera et recta obedientia*, cap. XVIII; in Goldast, *Monarchia*, I, 569–70: "Omnis enim illa subjectio voluntaria et spontanea esse debet, quare non subeunda nisi cum deliberatione. Deliberatio autem causam considerabit et fructum. Unde quandoque causa cum fructu ejuscemodi sunt, ut movere possent deliberantem ante contractum, pari ratione solvunt obligatum, quando alter contrahentium deficit in promisso. Fere enim ex natura hujus obligationis est, ut subditi superiorem sibi eligant, quatenus talem eligant, in quo et ex quo suae deliberationis fructum et causam proxime conjectent."

[96] And can even link the obligation of the inferior with the power of the superior to edify his flock—see *Tractatus de dignitate*, caps. VII, XXI and XXIII, ed., Goldast, *Monarchia*, I, 565, 570–71.

But this he failed to do. So, too, notwithstanding their stress on
conscience and the priesthood of all believers, did the magisterial
Protestant Reformers, as well as the Protestant and Catholic monarchomachs of the late-sixteenth century, who never went further than
Gansfort and often did not go as far. It was not, in fact, until the
seventeenth century that the transition occurred that a Gansfort had
not quite succeeded in making—the transition from the traditional
ascription of a negative role to the individual will in the face of
ecclesiastical and civil authority to the more novel attribution of a
positive role to that same will in the constitution and legitimation
of that authority. And when that finally happened, it did so by a
complex process (or series of processes) that remains both uncertain
and obscure.[97]

The fact that the magisterial reformers and sixteenth-century resistance theorists never went further than Gansfort itself suggests, however, the identity of at least *one* very important strand in that process.
Given the intensely religious focus of their concerns, there is no cause
for surprise that in relation to the *state* they should have spent so
much of their energies in exploring the implications of the necessity
of obeying God rather than man.[98] In relation to the Church, however, their failure to move beyond Gansfort's position is perhaps best
explained by the fact that all of them, Protestant and Catholic alike,
continued by and large to think in terms of an all-inclusive Church,
a compulsory body in the medieval mold embracing society as a
whole—in terms that is, of Ernst Troeltsch's "church-type" Christianity.
Only when some of the Elizabethan Puritans had finally abandoned
their earlier scruples and had come to think in terms of reform "without tarrying for any" did the sectarianism of the Radical Reformation
begin to make truly significant inroads upon one of the established

---

[97] While it is impossible within the compass of the present essay even to attempt
a preliminary sketch, it is already clear that any putative history of that process, if
it aspires to be at all complete, will have to come to terms not only with MacPherson's
controversial thesis concerning the advent of "possessive individualism" but also with
Richard Tuck's recent and intriguing claims (*Natural Rights Theories*, pp. 58–142) concerning the contributions of Hugo Grotius, John Selden, and the latter's followers
to the development of the theory of individual natural rights, and the degree to
which Hobbes should be seen against the background of those contributions.

[98] Of the work, for example, of the Marian exile, Christopher Goodman—*How
Superior Powers Oght to be Obeyd* (Geneva, 1558)—Christopher Morris has commented
that it is "a long and tedious sermon on the text: 'We must obey God rather than
man.'"—*Political Thought in England from Tyndale to Hooker* (Oxford, 1953), p. 152.

strongholds of Protestantism, bringing with it the idea of the Church as a voluntary society of true believers who have entered it "on the basis of conscious conversion," a restricted fellowship or sect that eschews talk of institutional sanctity, stressing instead the subjective holiness of its individual members and demanding of them the type of freely-undertaken life commitment to which the many may periodically aspire but which only the few can long sustain.[99] Such sectarians

> . . . interpreted their churches as free and voluntary associations founded on covenants. And, by a process that has yet to be fully explained, they appear, having compared their congregations to bodies politic, to have gone on to interpret bodies politic as if they were sectarian congregations. In so doing, they attributed to citizens, as natural rights, the rights of moral autonomy and self-government that they had demanded for themselves as members of the congregation.[100]

Thus, as early as 1613 and 1616, English Separatist writings indicate that that process was already underway, the "visible church" (itself "a Spirituall Body Politicke"), like "all Civill perfect Corporations," being described as constituted by "free mutuall consent."[101] By 1638, John Lilburne, the future Leveler leader, was describing the visible Church in similarly sectarian fashion, as a voluntary society grounded in the free consent of its members, who, "by virtue of their . . . uniting and joyning themselves together each to the other and so unto

---

[99] For the church-sect categorization, see Ernst Troeltsch, *The Social Teaching of the Christian Churches*, trans., Olive Wyon (2 vols., New York, 1960), I, 331–43, 378–82; II, 461–65. It would seem, then, that in this matter as on many another, the critical disjuncture was engineered not so much by Luther's challenge to the authority of Rome in particular, or by the doctrines of the magisterial Reformers in general. It was, instead, the failure in the sixteenth and seventeenth centuries of all the great religious groupings (old as well as new) to command a universal allegiance, and the appearance, as a result, of beleaguered religious minorities nudged along the road to sectarianism no less by the stresses and strains of the political situation in which they found themselves than by their own heartfelt beliefs.

[100] Höpfl and Thompson, "The History of Contract as a Motif in Political Thought," 938.

[101] Winfried Förster, *Thomas Hobbes und der Puritanismus: Grundlagen und Grundfragen seiner Staatslehre* (Berlin, 1969), pp. 95–97, and Höpfl and Thompson, "The History of Contract as a Motif in Political Thought," 938, all draw attention to assertions made by Henry Jacob to the effect that a "visible church" (defined as "a Spirituall Body Politicke") is constituted by "a free mutuall consent of Believers joyning and covenanting to live as members of a holy Society togeather in all religious and vertuous duties as Christ and his Apostles did institute and practice in the Gospell. By such free mutuall consent also all Civill perfect Corporations did first beginne."

the Lord . . . become a true visible Church of Jesus Christ" with power "to chuse elect and ordaine" as well as "to reprove her owne Officers."[102] By 1645–46, in the wake of the first civil war, Lilburne and his colleagues, Richard Overton and William Walwyn, had begun to apply that same voluntaristic, consentual and implicitly contractarian model to secular political society.[103] Thus, in the classic invocation of natural rights with which he opens his pamphlet, *An Arrow against all Tyrants*, Overton argues:

> To every Individuall in nature, is given an individuall property by nature, not to be invaded or usurped by any: for every one as he is himselfe, so he hath a selfe propriety, else coulde he not be himselfe, and on this no second may presume to deprive any of, without manifest violation and affront to the very principles of nature, and of the Rules of equity and justice between man and man; mine and thine cannot be, except this be: No man hath power over my rights, and liberties, and I over no man's. . . . For by naturall birth, all men are equally and alike borne to like propriety, liberty and freedome, and as we are delivered of God by the hand of nature into this world, every one with a naturall, innate freedome and propriety . . . even so we are to live, every one equally and alike to enjoy this Birthright and priviledge; even all whereof God by nature hath made him free.
>
> . . . And from this fountain or root, all just humaine powers take their original; not immediately from God (as Kings usually plead their prerogative) but mediatly by the hand of nature, as from the represented to the representors; for originally, God hath implanted them in the creature, and from the creature those powers immediately proceed; . . . Every man by nature being a King, Priest and Prophet in his owne naturall circuite and compasse, whereof no second may partake, but by deputation, commission, and free consent from him, whose naturall right and freedome it is.[104]

---

[102] John Lilburne, *An answer to nine arguments* (a work written in 1638 but published in 1645), 28; cited in Perez Zagorin, *A History of Political Thought in the English Revolution* (London, 1954), p. 9. Zagorin (p. 14) rightly points out that "a church in these terms may be created at any time because it is merely a grouping within society"—hence the radical nature of the move to apply similar ideas to society at large. Similarly, Höpfl and Thompson, "The History of Contract as Motif in Political Thought," 938. Cf. Woodhouse, *Puritanism and Liberty*, Introduction, esp. pp. [71]–[77], where he discusses the *Agreement of the People* and the covenant idea as applied in the Puritan churches. Also Gough, *Social Contract*, pp. 88–99.

[103] For these men, their writings, and the history of the development of their respective positions, see esp. Joseph Frank, *The Levellers. A History of the Writings of Three Seventeenth-Century Democrats: John Lilburne, Richard Overton, William Walwyn* (Cambridge, Mass., 1955).

[104] Richard Overton, *An Arrowe Against All Tyrants And Tyranny*, October 12, 1646;

In similar fashion, Lilburne argued that "God, the absolute Soveraigne Lord and King of all things," having endowed man his creature "with a rationall soule or understanding, and thereby created him after his own image," made him lord over the rest of his creatures, but not "over the individuals of Mankind, no further than by free consent, or agreement, by giving up their power, each to the other, for their better being."[105] For "all and every particular man and woman that ever breathed in the world" since the time of Adam and Eve, their progenitors, "are, and were, by nature all alike in power, dignity, authority, and majesty, none of them having any authority, dominion or magisterial power, one over or above another, but by institution or donation, that is to say, by mutuall agreement or consent. . . ."[106] Hence his argument that when government threatens "their Fundamentall naturall Liberties" men are freed from the obligation of obedience; hence, too, his insistence that all men, poor as well as rich, must have the right as individuals, to vote;[107] hence, again, his role in framing the *Agreement of the People* of 1647, which, Zagorin has argued, was "a democratic constitution and much more." "It was also the reenactment of the great myth of the social contract, indeed, the very pact by which political society was to be created anew and England removed from the state of nature into which Lilburne believed she had now been dissolved." And removed, it should be added, by the free consent of every individual, for "men

---

extract printed in G.E. Aylmer, ed., *The Levellers in the English Revolution* (Ithaca, 1975), pp. 68–69.

[105] John Lilburne, *Regall Tyrannie Discovered* (London, 1647), pp. 6–7; cf. *idem*, *London's Liberty in Chains Discovered* (London, 1646), p. 17, and the "Postscript" from his *The Free Man's Freedom Vindicated* (1646), reprinted in Woodhouse, *Puritanism and Liberty*, pp. 317–18.

[106] Lilburne, *Regall Tyrannie discovered*, p. 7; cf. Woodhouse, *Puritanism and Liberty*, p. 317. See the discussion of some of these texts (and of others I have been unable to see) in Zagorin, *History*, pp. 10–14.

[107] With the possible exclusion of servants, beggars and alms-takers, and, according to MacPherson, wage-earners (*Political Theory of Possessive Individualism*, pp. 107–59). For critiques of MacPherson's thesis concerning the qualifications the Levelers allegedly imposed on *manhood* suffrage see e.g., J.C. Davis, "The Levelers and Democracy," *Past and Present*, 40 (1968), 174–80, and Keith Thomas, "The Levelers and the Franchise," in G.E. Aylmer, ed., *The Interregnum: The Quest for Settlement, 1646–1660* (London, and Hamden, 1972), pp. 57–78. It should be noted here that, their theoretical premises notwithstanding, not even the clearest proponents of abstract individualism, Hobbes and Locke no more than the Levelers, envisaged the extension of the suffrage to women. See Teresa Brennan and Carole Pateman, "'Mere Auxiliaries to the Commonwealth': Women and the Origins of Liberalism," *Political Studies*, XXVII (No. 2, 1979), 183–200.

in a state of nature retain their natural rights entire, and can give up a portion of them only by their own consent."[108]

Lilburne, Overton and the other Levelers were, of course, extremists. So too, though in a different fashion, was Thomas Hobbes, who, during the same decade, and via a somewhat different route, had broken through to a similarly individualistic and voluntaristic conception of the foundations of political legitimacy—placing it, however, in service to the cause of governmental absolutism and in opposition to the traditional constitutionalism which Lilburne sought to radicalize, simplify and purify.[109] John Locke, writing nearly half a century later, was to share the voluntarism and radical individualism that was central to the political thinking of both of these men. Unlike Hobbes, however, he contrived to wed it to the constitutionalist tradition. At the same time, unlike the Levelers, too, he clearly did not feel unduly compelled to radicalize that tradition and to develop it in a more democratic direction.[110] And to say that is to say also that Locke, his individualism notwithstanding, stood somewhat closer than did they to the tradition of consent-thinking that was ultimately medieval in its origins, had attained its most universal formulation at the hands of the Conciliarists, had been mediated to the seventeenth century especially by the resistance theorists of the sixteenth, and was still finding expression during the English civil war in the Parliamentarian thinking of a man like Rutherford.

If, therefore, we seek the historical origins of that peculiar approach to the problem of political authority and obligation which sought to ground legitimacy in the free consent of a concatenation of individual wills, and if the case I have been making is at all correct, then I would suggest the following general conclusion. That we must

---

[108] Zagorin, *History*, pp. 15–16.

[109] Though in the future I may wish to do so, I cannot enter here into any extended discussion of Hobbes, the interpretation of whose thinking has become, in the last few years, the focus of a great deal of controversy. But perhaps I should indicate my sympathy with the general approach shared by those who, like Oakeshott, Warrender, and Glover, argue that he can best be understood if read, at least in some measure, in a theological context, and, more specifically, in the context of late medieval and Calvinist voluntarism. For a lucid introduction to the current tangle of competing interpretations, see W.H. Greenleaf, "Hobbes: The Problem of Interpretation," in Maurice Cranston and Richard S. Peters, eds., *Hobbes and Rousseau: A Collection of Critical Essays* (New York, 1972), pp. 5–36.

[110] In this respect, Dunn's stress on "the gap between Locke's conventional constitutionalism and his more distinctive religious individualism" is apposite—*The Political Thought of John Locke*, p. 57.

seek those origins in two great processes (neither of them to be taken at all for granted) whereby ideas of very different provenance come into creative contact with one another. In the first place, the process whereby doctrines of consent called into being by the practical exigencies of medieval political and ecclesiastical life and shaped by Romano-canonistic corporational thinking, connected with a tradition of natural-law theorizing originating in the Hellenistic era and were nudged thereby along a line of theoretical development more abstract and philosophical in its texture and more universal in its import. In the second, that further, more halting, and much more obscure process whereby the resulting synthesis was itself impregnated by Christian notions of moral autonomy, by an individualism and a voluntarism that were ultimately of Biblical derivation. The critical phase of the former process occurred during the later Middle Ages. That of the latter, which had had its point of departure already in the Patristic era and had quickened during the later Middle Ages, appears to have occurred only in the wake of the Reformation, and then only after considerable delay, perhaps only, indeed, when the turmoil of religious and civil unrest had generated within one of the main branches of Protestantism an unambiguously sectarian impulse.

CHAPTER FIVE

"ANXIETIES OF INFLUENCE:" SKINNER, FIGGIS, CONCILIARISM AND EARLY-MODERN CONSTITUTIONALISM

If, as Harold Bloom claims, "strong" poets struggling to escape the long shadows cast by their powerful predecessors have characteristically been dogged by "anxieties of influence,"[1] so too, of late, have historians of ideas and especially those who aspire to contribute to the history of political thought. It is true that literary theorists of more Francophone sympathies than Bloom's, people long since attuned to the ceaseless murmur of "the infinite text," have evinced no such apprehensions. For them, instead, the traditional scholarly preoccupation with identifying the influences at work on a text involves altogether too constricting an effort at narrow contextualization. Themselves happily adrift on "the communal sea of linguicity,"[2] they see such an effort as missing the crucial fact that a text is itself *heterotextual*, cannot but be a potpourri of traces, "a tissue of quotations drawn from the innumerable centers of culture"—in Roland Barthes's words again, "a multidimensional space in which a variety of writings, none of them original, blend and clash."[3] But at the very moment when

---

[1] Harold Bloom, *The Anxiety of Influence: A Theory of Poetry* (Oxford and New York, 1973). I borrow the title of this essay from the title and theme of Bloom's splendid book, though, by an appropriate misprision, I use it to denote, not anxiety about the *fact* of influence itself, but rather the anxiety currently generated among historians by the very *suggestion* that one thinker may have influenced another.

[2] I draw this arresting phrase from Edward W. Said, *Beginnings: Intention and Method* (New York, 1975), p. 338.

[3] The term "heterotextual" is Claudio Guillen's. Discussing Julia Kristeva's introduction of the term "intertextuality" to describe the phenomenon in question, he says: "It might just as well have been suggested that the text of a literary work is heterotextual, penetrated by alterity, by words other than its own." Claudio Guillén, *The Challenge of Comparative Literature*, trans. Cola Franzen (Cambridge, Mass. and London, 1993), p. 245. Or, as Kristeva herself put it: "Any text is constructed as a mosaic of quotations; any text is the absorption and transformation of another"—see her essay "Word, Dialogue and Novel" in *The Kristeva Reader* (Oxford, 1986), p. 37. The essay was published originally in 1966 as "Le mot, le dialogue et le roman." Roland Barthes, *Image, Music, Text* (New York, 1977), pp. 146, 148, cited in Jonathan Culler, *On Deconstruction: Theory and Criticism after Structuralism* (Ithaca and New York, 1982),

theorists of such stripe were bent on evoking the degree to which this very phenomenon of intertextuality transgresses and subverts the limitations of context, the members of what is sometimes referred to as "the Cambridge School" among historians of political thought were urging, to the contrary, that the challenge confronting the interpreter is precisely that of limiting the context[4] and insisting that the project of tracking influences had necessarily to be "irreducibly arbitrary." And not because it is too cautious, narrow or constricted in the method usually employed, but on the contrary because it is altogether too vague, loose and sloppy.[5]

It is with the latter claim that I am concerned in this essay. The problems it raises are important ones; they are not casually to be dismissed by anyone concerned with the history of ideas in general or the history of political thought in particular. And those problems can best be explored, I believe, by an exercise which combines some general methodological reflection with an attempt to assess a specific case of some significance in which influence has been both alleged and contested. In what follows, then, I propose to address myself to two matters. First, to the recent body of methodological writing (much of it critical) concerning the viability of the influence model as an explanatory tactic in the history of ideas and the histories of literature and art. Second, to the validity of the long-standing claim that the conciliar movement and conciliar ideas of the fifteenth century later exerted a demonstrable and important influence on the shaping of early-modern political and constitutional thinking.

---

pp. 32–33. Elsewhere Barthes put it thus: "Every text is an *intertext*; other texts are present in it, at varying levels, in more or less recognizable forms; earlier cultural texts and those of the surrounding culture, every text is a new texture of passing citations. . . . Intertextuality, the condition of every text, no matter what it is, is obviously not limited to a problem of sources or influences;"—"Texte (théorie du)," in *Encyclopedia universalis* (20 vols., Paris, 1968–75), XV, 1,015c, cited from Guillén, *The Challenge of Comparative Literature*, p. 246.

[4] Thus John Dunn, "The Identity of the *History of Ideas*," *Philosophy*, XLIII (April, 1968), 65–104 (at 98), where he had just asserted that "If a statement is considered in a fully open context, its meaning may be any lexically possible set of colligations of the uttered proposition. A man might mean by it anything that a man might mean by it."

[5] See Quentin Skinner, "The Limits of Historical Explanation," *Philosophy*, XLI (July, 1966), 179–215. (The sentence cited appears at 210.)

I

It was Quentin Skinner who, in three characteristically lively articles published in the mid-1960s, succeeded in generating the current
wave of anxiety among historians of political thought about the
employment (as, ironically, in this sentence!) of the influence model
of historical explanation, as well as a degree of timidity about the
very use of the word "influence" itself, and a tendency, among those
actually employing the model, to resort to clumsy circumlocutions
in order to avoid acknowledging that fact.[6] It was in the first of these
articles that the attempt to trace influences was most sweepingly condemned. If such affiliations are to be established, "the connection
has to be close enough to be separable from chance but sufficiently
loose-limbed to be separable from causality." "The philosophical status of this activity . . . is by no means so self-evidently clear," the
assumptions on which it depends are frequently questionable, and
the practical obstacles it encounters (not least among them the lack
of sufficient evidence to permit convincing corroboration) are truly
formidable. This is the case even when we have the apparently independent corroboration constituted by an author's himself claiming
to have been influenced by another. For the validity of *that* claim,
too, has itself to be established. The author in question may, after
all, be lying, boasting, sheltering behind the authority of a great
name, trying to conceal his real sources, and so on.[7] And where we
lack even the possibility of independent corroboration of that sort,
we are in constant danger of supposing, when an argument in a
later work calls to mind a similar line of reasoning in an earlier one,
that the later writer was deliberately referring to the earlier one when
what may be involved is nothing but a random parallelism. In such

---

[6] Note the affiliated tendency to avoid the use of the word without resort to the
protective obliquity of quotation marks—see, e.g., Donald Winch, *Adam Smith's
Politics: An Essay in Historiographic Revision* (Cambridge, 1978), pp. 48–49, 174–75.
For a good example of Skinner's influence in these respects see Thomas F. Mayer,
Thomas Starkey and the Commonweal: Humanist politics and religion in the reign of Henry VIII
(Cambridge, 1989), pp. 9–10, where he is careful to deny that he is "concerned to
track 'influences' on Starkey's mind," noting that "both Skinner and Condren have
shown this concept" to be "nearly devoid of explanatory power." Ironically, Mayer
is himself willing to speak (p. 9, n. 15) of "Quentin Skinner's influential emphasis
on context."

[7] For the especially difficult challenge presented in this respect by the medieval
author, see Francis Oakley, *The Political Thought of Pierre d'Ailly: The Voluntarist Tradition*
(New Haven and London, 1964), pp. 198–200.

matters, proof is stubbornly elusive. "The attempt to trace influences *must be irreducibly arbitrary*" (my emphasis), and "explanations in this mode at best not evidently convincing and often evidently false."[8]

Given the scathing nature of his dismissal in the second of these articles of the use made by one respected literary scholar of the influence model,[9] it is noteworthy that in the third, published only two years later, Skinner backed off a little from the sweeping, theoretically-based nature of his earlier denunciations, conceding now that in his earlier "critique of the influence model I perhaps stressed too much the impossibility of making the model work, rather than its sheer elusiveness." That model, in fact, is "far from being empty of explanatory force." The problem with it is of a practical nature: "it can very rarely be made to work," and, "even when it can . . ., there is scarcely ever any point in doing so." As so often used in the past it has been based, indeed, on "nothing better than the capacity of the observer to foreshorten the past by filling it with his own reminiscences." That being so, and in order to avoid the generation of "purely mythological explanations," Skinner proposed three minimal "necessary conditions" which would have to be met if we wanted "to explain the appearance in any given writer B of any given doctrine, by invoking the 'influence' of some earlier given writer, A." Namely, (i) that there should be the presence of "a genuine similarity between the doctrines of A and B;" (ii) "that B could not have found the relevant doctrine in any writer other than A;" (iii) "that the probability of the similarity being random should be very low." And he clearly inclined to the conclusion that investigations of influence in the history of ideas have characteristically failed to meet those conditions.[10]

---

[8] Skinner, "Limits of Historical Explanation," 204–7, 210–11.

[9] Quentin Skinner, "More's Utopia," *Past and Present*, No. 38 (Dec., 1967), 152–68, where the target is Edward Surtz's discussion of the literary influences on Thomas More's *Utopia*. Skinner's crushing conclusion in this case is that "the only real information to come out of Surtz's study . . . concerns Surtz himself. He is clearly an extremely widely-read scholar, who while reading More has very often been *reminded* of other books he has read. But this suggests that at best the whole business of studying influences is nothing more than a scholar's game; at worst, moreover, it clearly leads to the assertion of many claims which there is no reason to suppose are true, and which are very likely false."

[10] Quentin Skinner, "Meaning and understanding in the history of ideas," *History and Theory*, VIII (1969), 3–53; reprinted conveniently in James Tully ed., *Meaning and Context: Quentin Skinner and his Critics* (Cambridge, 1988), pp. 30–67, to which my references will be given. Skinner discusses the problem of influence under the general rubric of "the mythology of parochialism" at pp. 45–47.

So, too, did others who followed in his wake—notably Conal Condren.[11] Condren, indeed, moved by the practical difficulties attendant upon the employment of the influence model, and arguing that "anything influence can do, use can do better," urged the replacement of "influence" with "usage." Usage, after all, "by being a general term with a multitude of possibilities" has, among other things the advantage of inviting "immediate specification—how and in what way and to what extent did *y* in fact use *x*?"[12] But Skinner, in his only subsequent comment on the matter of which I am aware, made no mention of this interesting suggestion. Instead, and having without any apology made extensive (and very effective) use of the influence model in his *Foundations of Modern Political Thought*,[13] he continued the process of backing away from his earlier strictures, and, by the unconscious irony of an implicit invocation of the notion of influence, attributed his own initial skepticism about "the use of the concept of 'influence' in the history of ideas" to the impact on him of Peter Laslett's skepticism about "the capacity of Hobbes's alleged influence to explain any features of Locke's *Two Treatises*."[14] Not altogether a satisfactory conclusion to the hue and cry of the two decades preceding, and for a more consistent discussion of the matter it is necessary to look in a somewhat different direction.

In one of his earlier discussions, Skinner had noted that, apart from some glancing remarks by Philip Wiener, he was unaware of any previous attempt to analyze the range of problems attaching to the use of the concept of influence.[15] But such discussions had, indeed, occurred—quite singular in the case of André Gide in 1900, and

---

[11] Conal Condren, *The Status and Appraisal of Classic Texts: An Essay on Political Theory, Its Inheritance, and the History of Ideas* (Princeton, N.J., 1985), esp. 129–41.

[12] *Ibid.*, pp. 136 and 137–39.

[13] On which, and for the influence-claims involved, see David Boucher, "New Histories of Political Thought for Old," *Political Studies*, XXXI (No. 1, 1983), 112–21 (at 118–19). Boucher lists many of the pertinent pages in Quentin Skinner's *The Foundations of Modern Political Thought* (2 vols., Cambridge, 1978). To that list should be added *ibid.*, II, 112, 114–18, 321, 346. Reference should also be made to Quentin Skinner, "The Origins of the Calvinist Theory of Revolution," in B.C. Malament, ed., *After the Reformation* (Manchester, 1980), pp. 309–30 (see esp. 324–26).

[14] Quentin Skinner, "A Reply to my Critics," in Tully ed., *Meaning and Context*, pp. 233, 327 n. 13. Peter Laslett himself appears to have had no reservations about the influence model as such. He stated that "the prime reason for the importance attached to [Locke's *Second Treatise*] . . . is its enormous historical influence." See the introduction to his edition of *John Locke: Two Treatises of Government* (rev. ed., New York and London, 1965), pp. 16ff.

[15] Skinner, "Meaning and Understanding in the History of Ideas," 298 n. 116,

admittedly fragmentary in the case of Louis Cazamian in 1912 and R.G. Collingwood in 1945,[16] but becoming more thoroughgoing and widespread in Comparative Literature circles as that field rose to prominence during the years after the Second World War.[17]

For those of us who have tracked the degree to which "anxieties of influence" have dogged historians of ideas over the course of the past two decades, the nervousness and discontent with the employment of the concept evident in these earlier discussions and underlined by "the enclosure of the word 'influence' within guarded and ironic quotes"[18] will be all too familiar—so familiar, indeed, as to threaten to conceal from us that something intriguingly different was

referring to Philip P. Wiener, "Some Problems and Methods in the History of Ideas," *Journal of the History of Ideas*, XXII (No. 4, 1961), 531–48 (at 537).

[16] André Gide, "De l'influence en littérature," in *Oeuvres complètes d'André Gide*, ed. L. Martin-Chauffier (15 vols., Paris, 1932–39), III, 269–73. Gide's purpose was not to explore the difficulties posed by the notion of influence but to celebrate its importance for artistic creativity. The epoch and the writer most profoundly influenced are likely to be the most fertile in creativity and the most profoundly original. Cf. Henri Peyre, "André Gide et les problèmes d'influence en littérature," *Modern Language Notes*, LVII (1942), 558–67; R.G. Collingwood, *The Idea of Nature* (Oxford, 1945), p. 128; Louis Cazamian, "Goethe en Angleterre. Quelques réflexions sur les problèmes d'influence," *Revue Germanique*, XII (1921), 371–78 (at 375–77).

[17] Of the pertinent literature (which is quite extensive), I have found the following discussions in varying degree helpful: James Robert Hightower, "Chinese Literature in the Context of World Literature," *Comparative Literature*, V (1953), 117–24; H. Hassan, "The Problem of Influence in Literary History: Notes Towards a Definition," *The Journal of Aesthetics and Art Criticism*, XIV (No. 1, 1955), 66–76; Claudio Guillén, "Literatura Como Sistema," *Filologia Romanza*, IV (1957), 1–29; *idem*, "The Aesthetics of Influence Studies in Comparative Literature" (1959), reprinted in his *Literature as System: Essays Toward the Theory of Comparative Literature* (Princeton, N.J., 1971), pp. 17–52 (see also "A Note on Influences and Conventions," *ibid.*, pp. 53–68). Guillén has recently returned to those issues in his *The Challenge of Comparative Literature*, esp. pp. 24–62 and 240–87. Haskell M. Block, "The Concept of Influence in Comparative Literature," *Yearbook of Comparative and General Literature*, VII (1958), 30–57; *idem*, *Nouvelles tendances en littérature comparée* (Paris, 1963), pp. 13–49; René Etiemble, *Comparaison n'est pas raison: La Crise de la littérature comparée* (Paris, 1963), pp. 61–73; René Wellek, *Concepts of Criticism*, ed. Stephen G. Nichols, Jr. (New Haven and London, 1963), pp. 282–95; Goran Hermerén, *Influence in Art and Literature* (Princeton, N.J., 1975); Robert J. Clements, *Comparative Literature as Academic Discipline: A Statement of Principles, Praxis, Standards* (New York, 1978). Cf. Henry Peyre, "A Glance at Comparative Literature," *Yearbook of Comparative and General Literature*, I (1952), 1–8; Harry Levin, "La littérature comparée: point de vue d'Outre-Atlantique," *Revue de littérature comparée*, XXVII (1953), 17–26; F.W. Bateson, "Editorial Commentary," *Essays in Criticism*, IV (1954), 436–40; R.W. Stallman, "The Scholar's Net: New Literary Sources," *College English*, XVII (1955), 20–27.

[18] A tactic, Hassan says, that did not entirely resolve the "ambivalence that students of literature had come to feel about the problem of influence": Hassan, "The Problem of Influence in Literary History," 66.

going on. Whereas for Skinner it was the elusiveness, imprecision, and lack of historicity in the way in which the influence model was characteristically employed that fueled his discontent with the model itself, for the students of comparative literature the source of discontent lay in an almost diametrically opposed direction. For them, as they began to respond to the promptings of structuralist modes of literary analysis or of the New Criticism and to give, accordingly, a higher priority to formal values and aesthetic judgment, it was the traditional domination of the discipline by historical concerns that itself stimulated their dismay. Or, more precisely, its domination by the type of literary history associated quintessentially with the "French School" of comparatists.[19] This school, students of comparative literature—in Europe and Asia as well as in America[20]—had increasingly come to view as overwhelming positivistic, as laboring under "the dead hand of nineteenth-century factualism, scientism, and historical relativism."[21] And its preoccupation with a typically mechanical and externalistic investigation of sources and influences they saw as "springing from an essentially scientistic attempt" to understand the course of literary history as "a series of cause and effect relationships."[22] In their reaction to this approach some were led either to abandon the customary investigation of influences in favor of a probing of "tradition" or "development,"[23] or, without rejecting it, to seek to supplement it in order to take into account the broader phenomenon for which Julia Kristeva was later to propose the term "intertextuality."[24]

---

[19] Wellek, *Concepts of Criticism*, ed. Nichols, pp. 282–90; Block, *Nouvelles tendances*, pp. 13–20.

[20] See Etiemble, *Comparaison n'est pas raison*, pp. 61–65, where he notes the discontent of Japanese comparatists with what they referred to as the "positivism" and "historicism" of the French method.

[21] Wellek, *Concepts of Criticism*, ed. Nichols, pp. 282–83; cf. Block, *Nouvelles tendances*, pp. 16–18.

[22] Block, "The Concept of Influence in Comparative Literature," 30–31.

[23] Thus Hassan, "The Problem of Influence in Literature History," 74–76.

[24] This, if I understand him correctly, was the position of Claudio Guillén in 1959: "Note on Influences and Conventions," 58, 83; "Aesthetics of Influence Studies," 34 n. 28; cf. his earlier "Literatura Como Sistema," esp. 4, 27–29. More recently, certainly, Guillén has endorsed "the concept of *intertextuality* . . . as especially useful for comparatists. We believe that here we have at last a way to dissipate the many ambiguities and errors such as those brought along in the wake of the notion of influences"—*The Challenge of Comparative Literature*, p. 246. It may be remarked, however, that as scholars currently deploy it new *intertextuality* can sometimes appear to be nothing other than old *influence* writ large—and not always all that large. See, e.g. Evelyn Ellerman, "Intertextuality in the Fiction of Camus and Wendt," in Cornelia

Most, however, at least at the time, appear to have been reluctant to go that far. As Haskell M. Block pointed out, their discontent with traditional investigations of influence sprang not simply from abstract methodological worries but also from the unsatisfactory, mechanical and even trivial nature of so many of those studies.[25] They did not believe that literary studies could dispense entirely with the use of the influence model. Influence, after all, was "an intrinsic part of literary experience" and it was altogether "too valuable, too essential a notion to be discarded." The problem, rather, was that in the literary history of the older mould the concept of influence had been "obliged to bear more than it [could] . . . properly bear." What it needed was sharpening, "redefinition," and employment by literary historians in the future "with a precise understanding of its scope and limits."[26]

It was with the specific objective of reaching such an understanding that Göran Herméren, a Swedish philosopher, later picked up on these discussions among the comparatists and, extending his inquiry to embrace history of art as well as literature, embarked on the project that was to eventuate in the longest, fullest, most intricate, and certainly most relentless treatment of the issue available.[27] Noting that when one uses the word "influence" according "to the rules of ordinary English" one tends to be stating or implying "a weak causal connection," he proceeded, unlike Skinner, to treat influence statements as susceptible to analysis as "a particular kind of causal explanation."[28] But beyond indicating his awareness of the likelihood of disagreement on that point and affirming his own sense that there are

---

N. Moore and Raymond A. Moody eds., *Comparative Literature East and West: Traditions and Trends* (Honolulu, 1989), 43–50.

[25] And in 1961 Philippe Van Tieghem, *Les Influences étrangères sur la littérature française (1550–1880)* (Paris, 1961), had pointed out that there were no less than twelve hundred such studies devoted to the relations between foreign literatures and French alone—cited in Block, *Nouvelles tendances en littérature comparée*, p. 17.

[26] Block, "The Concept of Influence in Comparative Literature," 34–36.

[27] Herméren, *Influence in Art and Literature*, over three hundred pages of analysis replete (in the analytic philosophical mode) with sequences of numbered propositions—e.g. p. 93: "(R1) *Ontological Requirement 2*. If x influenced the creation of y with respect to a, then x and y are visual or literary works of art or, alternatively, certain kinds of actions." Herméren appears to have been unaware of Skinner's articles on the subject.

[28] *Ibid.*, p. 119. The particular kind of causal explanation he has in mind is the "counterfactual conditional," though he emphasizes (pp. 126–7) that the counterfactual conditions involved may be of more than one kind—all of this embedded in a highly technical set of arguments running, in effect, from pp. 104–155.

"good arguments supporting the causal analysis of [human] action,"
he passed no judgment on "the crucial distinction between reasons
and causes" and sidestepped the philosophical debate on the whole
issue.[29] Conscious of the degree to which "exaggeration and lack of
subtlety" in investigations dating back to the earlier part of the century had "given the term 'influence research' a bad connotation" in
art history as well as literary studies,[30] it was his primary concern
to bring some precision to the whole effort, and to identify via a
painstaking analysis of a myriad of examples drawn from both fields
the problems it raises and the practical obstacles it encounters.

In so doing, he elaborated in intricate detail a set of some thirteen
restrictions on "the family of concepts of influence" he proposed to
examine,[31] and followed it up with a set of five necessary conditions
"for artistic influence to have taken place."[32] These overlap or link
with Skinner's three necessary conditions but do so in rather complex fashion. Thus whereas Skinner simply presupposed the temporal priority of the work doing the influencing to that influenced,
Herméren felt it necessary to spell it out explicitly, and in two different
ways.[33] He similarly spelled out the necessity for there having been
direct or indirect contact between the creator of the work influenced
and the work influencing him,[34] folded in along with the stipulation
of genuine similarity that of "systematic differences" in the case of
negative influence,[35] and appended the condition that the work
influenced should in the pertinent respects be discernibly different
from what it would have been had it not been influenced.[36]

All of which serves to underline the number of difficulties involved
at every stage even of the process of deciding whether the stipulated
requirements and conditions have been met. But in common with
Block and the other comparatists discussed earlier, he came to the
conclusion that "studies of influence can be worthwhile," that "hypotheses of influence can be corroborated" just as well, indeed, "as most
other empirical hypotheses," that the value of such hypotheses has

[29] *Ibid.*, pp. 104–106.
[30] *Ibid.*, p. 8.
[31] *Ibid.*, p. 14.
[32] For these, see *ibid.*, ch. 2, pp. 156–262.
[33] *Ibid.*, pp. 152 and 177.
[34] *Ibid.*, p. 165.
[35] *Ibid.*, p. 194.
[36] *Ibid.*, p. 246; see also pp. 247–57.

to be assessed in terms of the significance of their "payoff," and that such (essentially historical) questions are not to be "decided by philosophers, at least not by them alone."[37] Thus, despite their differing points of departure, there is in the end something of a convergence in the line of argument pursued by Skinner and others sympathetic to his approach to the history of political thought[38] and that pursued by scholars in comparative literature and art history who were likewise preoccupied with the influence problem. While undoubtedly sharpening a critical awareness of the pitfalls involved in the use of the influence model, the long drawn-out critique of that model appears to have eventuated in the somewhat grudging concession that it is capable, after all, of yielding worthwhile results, as also in the implicit recognition that in its absence it would be difficult to construct effectively explanatory historical narratives. The proof of the pudding, it seems, is most likely to be found in the eating. With that in mind, then, it is time now to address the specific case. And, as is only fitting, it is one itself signalled by Skinner's own major contribution to the interpretation of early modern political and constitutional thought.

II

In a review of *The Foundations of Modern Political Thought* Julian Franklin identifies as "the most general [if contestable] new interpretation" in that book Skinner's location of "the direct ancestors of the great resistance theorists of the 1570s in the conciliarist writers of the late fifteenth and early sixteenth centuries,"[39] with their remote ancestors, one should add, being the distinguished early fifteenth-century conciliarists, Pierre d'Ailly and Jean Gerson. Franklin is right to emphasize this particular interpretative move. It is a very important one and exceedingly well executed. Though the word itself is not used, it involves the deployment of nothing other than the influence model, the bold assertion that, strictly speaking, "no such entity" as the

---

[37] *Ibid.*, pp. 320–21.

[38] See David Boucher, "New Histories of Political Thought for Old," *Political Studies*, XXXI (No. 1, 1983), 111–21 (at 118–20).

[39] Julian A. Franklin, review of Skinner, *Foundations of Political Thought, Political Theory*, VII (No. 1, 1979), 552–58 (at 557–58).

"Calvinist theory of revolution exists." That is to say, that when the Calvinists of the late-sixteenth century elaborated a constitutionalist resistance theory (traditionally regarded as distinctively Calvinist and as one of the "startling innovations of sixteenth century political history"),[40] they were in fact doing nothing other than drawing upon "the existing theories of revolution [long before] developed by their Catholic adversaries."[41] The claim itself is striking enough, but without in any way wishing to diminish its importance as an interpretative move, it has to be insisted that Franklin is simply wrong to label it as "novel." That he can do so, indeed, is a jolting reminder of the fact that the traditional periodization of European history into ancient, medieval and modern, and the degree of mutually exclusive scholarly specialization it has helped sponsor, continue to exact an unacceptable historiographic toll.

Almost two hundred years ago now, when in his *View of the State of Europe during the Middle Ages* the English historian, Henry Hallam, came to write about the scandal occasioned during the Great Schism of the West by the spectacle of three rival claimants obdurately contending for the papal office, he interpreted the success of the Council of Constance in ending the schism by the deposition in 1415 of the rival pontiffs as "a signal display of a new system . . . which I may venture to call the whig principles of the catholic church." And the Constance decree *Haec sancta* (which provided the theoretical basis for such a deposing power by asserting the subordination under certain conditions of pope to general council) and *Frequens* (which mandated for the future the assembly of such councils at frequent and regular intervals)—those decrees he went on to describe as "the great pillars of that moderate theory with respect to papal authority which [not only] distinguished the Gallican church, ... "but] is embraced by almost all laymen and the major part of ecclesiastics on this side of the Alps."[42]

Hallam wrote those words in 1816. When, later on in the century

---

[40] The words which Skinner cites are those of Michael Walzer, *The Revolution of the Saints* (Cambridge, Mass., 1965), pp. 1–2.

[41] Following here the "brief epitome" of the argument in Skinner, "The Origins of the Calvinist Theory of Revolution," esp. 312, 324–26. The argument is developed at much greater length in his *Foundations of Modern Political Thought*, II, chs. 2, 4 and 9.

[42] Henry Hallam, *View of the State of Europe during the Middle Ages* (3 vols., London, 1901), III, 243 and 245. The work was originally published in 1818.

Lord Acton came to allude to the conciliar issue, what Hallam had seen as a live ecclesiological option for the Catholics of his day had become a matter of interest only to the archaeologists of defunct ideologies. But Acton, nonetheless, was clearly stuck by the pertinence of "the whig principles" embedded in conciliar theory to the history of *secular* political thought.[43] So, too, around the same time, was Otto Gierke.[44] And, a few years later, Acton's distinguished pupil, John Neville Figgis, in one of his brilliant series of Birkbeck Lectures at Cambridge, went on to urge very forcefully the significance of the role he took the conciliar movement to have played in the history of European political and constitutional thinking.

That is should be cast in such a role at all is not to be taken for granted. Conciliar theory, after all, was an ecclesiological doctrine. Its rise to prominence was occasioned by a crisis in the life of the Church: the disputed papal election of 1378, the subsequent protracted schism, and the failure of repeated attempts to end it. Its immediate appeal sprang from the fact that if offered a way out of what had become a scandalous impasse, for it was, in effect, a constitutionalist theory. At its heart lay the belief that the pope was not an absolute monarch but rather in some sense a constitutional ruler, that he possessed a merely ministerial authority conferred upon him for the good of the Church, that the final authority in the Church (at least in certain cases) lay not with him but with the whole body of the faithful or with their representatives gathered in a general council. In response to that belief the Councils of Pisa (1409) and Constance (1414–18) assembled to put an end to the schism, the conciliarists at the Council of Basel (1431–49) defied unsuccessfully the authority of a pope the validity of whose title was not in question, and the cardinals of the opposition convoked (May, 1511) the dissident and abortive assembly derided by the papalists of the day as the *conciliabulum* of Pisa.

---

[43] Lord Acton, *Lectures on the French Revolution*, ed. J.N. Figgis and R.V. Laurence (London, 1910), p. 17. The lectures were delivered at Cambridge in the 1890s. J.H. Burns, *Lordship, Kingship, and Empire: The Idea of Monarchy, 1400–1525* (Oxford, 1992), p. 10, n. 14, notes that Acton's position in the matter had shifted somewhat across the previous forty years and that, earlier on, he had been "unimpressed by Gerson's 'attempt to apply the principles of secular polity to the Church'"—see Lord Acton, *The History of Freedom and Other Essays*, ed. J.N. Figgis and R.V. Laurence (London, 1907), pp. 191–92.

[44] Otto Gierke, *Political Theories of the Middle Age*, ed. and trans. F.W. Maitland (Cambridge, 1900), pp. 49–58.

If conciliar theory was indeed a form of constitutionalism, it was ecclesiastical constitutionalism that was involved, and its claim to a place in the history of political thought may not be immediately evident. But on this matter Figgis's opinions were characteristically robust. "Probably the most revolutionary document in the history of the world," he said,

> is the decree of the Council of Constance [*Haec sancta*] asserting its superiority to the Pope, and striving to turn into a tepid constitutionalism the Divine authority of a thousand years. The movement is the culmination of medieval constitutionalism. It forms the watershed between the medieval and the modern world.[45]

And why is this so? Because, in the first place, the scandal of the Great Schism had the effect of turning attention from the old familiar dispute between the two powers, temporal and spiritual, and focusing it upon the nature of the Church itself. Because in the second, "[s]peculation on the possible power of the Council as the true depositary of sovereignty within the Church drove the [conciliar] thinkers to treat the Church definitely as one of a class, political societies."[46] Because, in the third, the conciliar theorists of Constance

> appear to have discerned more clearly than their predecessors the meaning of the constitutional experiments which the last two centuries had seen in considerable profusion, to have thought out the principles that underlay them, and based them upon reasoning that applied to all political societies; to have discerned that arguments applicable to governments in general could not be inapplicable to the Church. In a word, they raised the constitutionalism of the past three centuries to a higher power, expressed it in a more universal form, and justified it on grounds of reason, policy and Scripture.[47]

According, then, to Figgis, if the conciliar movement was more properly to be regarded as "medieval rather than modern in spirit," it was also to be regarded as "having helped forward modern constitutional tendencies." Why? Because it asserted "the principles that underlay acts like the deposing of Richard II in a far more definite and conscious way than had yet been done" and stripped "the arguments for constitutional government of all elements of the provincialism

---

[45] J.N. Figgis, *Political Thought from Gerson to Grotius: 1414–1625. Seven Studies* (New York, 1960), pp. 41–70 (at 41).

[46] *Ibid.*, p. 56.

[47] *Ibid.*, p. 47.

which might have clung to them for long had they been concerned only with the internal arrangements of the national states." Conciliar theorists expressed their principles "in a form in which they could readily be applied to politics," and so applied they were. "Even [sixteenth-century] Huguenot writers like DuPlessis Mornay," said Figgis,

> were not ashamed of using the doctrine of the Council's superiority over the Pope to prove their own doctrine of the supremacy of the estates over the king . . . Emperors might be the fathers of the Council [of Constance], and Kings its nursing mothers, but the child they nurtured was Constitutionalism, and its far off legacy to our own day was "the glorious revolution."[48]

Three main claims are made in this argument, claims that I will distinguish one from another and take up separately. The first, that the source of fourteenth and early fifteenth-century conciliar theory is to be found in the secular constitutional developments of the previous centuries. The second, that conciliar theory exerted a demonstrable influence on the constitutionalists and resistance theorists of the sixteenth and seventeenth centuries. The third, that it did so (and herein lies its historical significance) because of the precision with which it discerned the theoretical principles underlying medieval constitutionalism, the universality with which it formulated those principles, and the clarity and force with which it restated them. And to say that was to say also that conciliar theory was not only an ecclesiological option but also a political theory.

The evidence which Figgis actually adduced in support of these assertions was, in fact, quite scanty.[49] Nonetheless, his claims were received enthusiastically in the interwar years by a series of widely-read historians of political thought—from H.J. Laski, Figgis's pupil, to R.G. Gettell, R.H. Murray, C.H. McIlwain, and George H. Sabine.[50]

---

[48] *Ibid.*, pp. 46–48, 63.

[49] Though he had clearly read widely in the pertinent sources and, had he so chosen, could undoubtedly have extended the evidentiary foundations of his claim.

[50] Figgis himself advanced his thesis on more than one occasion. See his "Political Thought in the Sixteenth Century," in A.W. Ward, G.W. Prothero and Stanley Leathes, eds., *The Cambridge Modern History* (13 vols., Cambridge, 1902–11), III, 736; also his "Politics at the Council of Constance," *Transactions of the Royal Historical Society*, New. Ser., XIII (1899), 103–15. Cf. Raymond G. Gettell, *History of Political Thought* (London, 1924), pp. 133–35; R.H. Murray, *The History of Political Science* (2nd ed., New York, 1930), p. 101; Charles H. McIlwain, *The Growth of Political Thought in the West* (New York, 1932), p. 348 n. 2; George H. Sabine, *A History of Political Theory* (New York, 1937; rev. ed., 1950), pp. 326–27; H.J. Laski, "Political

But interest in conciliar *theory* at least languished somewhat in the years after Figgis wrote, and it was only in the years after the Second World War that concern with the subject began to quicken again.[51] And when it did, the validity of his first claim—which concerned the influence of earlier *secular* constitutional developments upon the formation of conciliar theory—was brought into question.

Figgis had made little effort to ground that claim, and one can only assume that he was nudged into making it in part because of the frequent use the conciliar theorists themselves made of analogies drawn from secular political and constitutional practice.[52] But while the popularity of such analogies certainly lends powerful support to his assertion that the conciliarists were viewing the Church as "one of a class, political societies," it does little or nothing to help substantiate the claim that they developed these conciliar ideas on the basis of secular models. Perhaps because of this E.F. Jacob, as long ago in 1943, had begun to wonder about the widespread tendency to regard conciliar theory as simply a transference to the Church of ideas of secular political origin.[53] And in 1955 Brian Tierney, pursuing suggestions made over the years by Otto Gierke, H.X. Arquillière, Walter Ullmann and others, made the claim that conciliar theory, far from being a reaction against canonistic views or an importation of secular constitutionalist ideas onto ecclesiastical soil, was in fact the logical outgrowth of canonistic thought itself, reflecting a subtle and complex amalgam of older Decretist discussions of the case of the heretical pope and the subsequent attempts of generations of Decretalists to rationalize in terms of corporation law the structure of both the individual churches of Christendom and of the Universal Church itself. Side by side with "the familiar theory of papal sovereignty," he argued, "there had developed another theory," one that was "applied at first to single churches and then at the beginning of the fourteenth century . . . to the Roman Church and the Church as a whole." This theory stressed "the corporate association of the

---

Theory in the Later Middle Ages," in H.M. Gwatkin *et al.* eds., *The Cambridge Medieval History* (8 vols., Cambridge, 1911–36), VIII, 838.

[51] See the useful discussions of conciliar scholarship listed in Francis Oakley, "Natural Law, the *Corpus Mysticum*, and Consent in Conciliar Thought from John of Paris to Matthias Ugonius," *Speculum*, LVI (No. 4, 1981), 786–810 (at 787, n. 5.). See, especially, Guiseppe Alberigo, "Il movimento conciliare (xiv–xv sec.) nella ricerca storica recente," *Studi Medievali*, 3rd series, XIX (1978), 213–50.

[52] See below, n. 144.

[53] E.F. Jacob, *Essays in the Conciliar Epoch* (Manchester, 1943), pp. 2–3.

members of a church" rather than the "rigorous subordination of all the members to a single head" as "the true principle of ecclesiastical unity." It "envisaged an exercise of corporate authority by the members of a church even in the absence of an effective head," and in so doing laid the essential foundations for the later development of conciliar theory.[54]

The case Tierney makes is at once both powerful and subtly nuanced and, despite the surfacing of some oblique scholarly grumbling,[55] I would judge that the great tide of literature on conciliar and related matters that has been flowing during the forty years since he propounded his thesis has done nothing to shake it and a good deal to confirm it.[56]

As a result, Figgis's first influence claim falls victim to redundancy. It does so primarily as a result of the research of the past half-century into the vast body of canonistic glosses to which Figgis himself had little access (many of those glosses, indeed, have still to be edited). And it does so secondarily because the contemporaneous progress in our knowledge of the full range of conciliar literature has familiarized us with the extent to which the conciliarists themselves were consciously dependent on earlier canonistic formulations for their central commitments.[57]

---

[54] Brian Tierney, *Foundations of the Conciliar Theory: The Contribution of the Medieval Canonists from Gratian to the Great Schism* (Cambridge, 1955), pp. 240, 10–11; cf. Gierke, *Political Theories of the Middle Age*, ed. Maitland, p. 50; Franz Bliemetzrieder, *Das Generalkonzil im grossen abendländischen Schisma* (Paderborn, 1904), pp. 75–76; H.X. Arquillière, "L'appel au concile sous Philippe le Bel et la genèse des théories conciliaires," *Revue des questions historiques*, XLV (No. 1, 1911), 51–55; Walter Ullmann, *The Origins of the Great Schism* (London, 1948), pp. 184–85, and *idem*, *The Growth of Papal Government in the Middle Ages* (London, 1955), pp. 452–53.

[55] See Helmut G. Walther, *Imperiales Königtum, Konziliarismus und Volkssouveranität* (Munich, 1976), pp. 187–88; Hermann Josef Sieben, *Die Konzilsidee des lateinischen Mittelalters (847–1378)* (Paderborn, 1984), pp. 232–76 (esp. 255). I would judge Sieben's treatment of the canonists as a rather wooden, literal-minded account that does not even begin to address the subtlety and complexity of Tierney's formidable argument. But for a rather more positive appraisal of his (implicit) critique of Tierney, see Constantin Fasolt, *Council and Hierarchy: The Political Thought of William Durant the Younger* (Cambridge, 1991), pp. 18–20.

[56] See Francis Oakley, "*Verius est licet difficulius*: Tierney's *Foundations of the Conciliar Theory* after Forty Years," in Thomas M. Izbicki and Gerald Christianson eds., *Nicholas of Cusa on Christ and the Church* (Leiden, 1996), pp. 1–20. See above, ch. 3.

[57] I would suggest, as one striking illustration, the use the theologian Pierre d'Ailly made of the canonistic glosses of Guido de Baysio, Hostiensis and Johannes Monachus in developing a conception of the Church as a mixed monarchy that is very close in intention (if not in legal precision) to that developed on a similar basis by his fellow conciliarist, the distinguished canonist Francesco Zabarella. For Zabarella's

The same cannot be said, however, of his second claim, that pertaining to the subsequent influence of conciliar theory on the constitutionalists and resistance theorists of the sixteenth and seventeenth centuries. It is true that interest in this historical issue has been almost exclusively an Anglophone affair.[58] Nor should we miss the degree to which indifference to (or ignorance of) Figgis's argument has persisted among historians. Pierre Mesnard, the Carlyles, J.W. Allen, Christopher Morris and, more recently, Julian Franklin—all of them, if they betray any consciousness at all of conciliar thinking, appear to have regarded it, in its sixteenth- no less than its fifteenth-century expression, as irrelevant, strictly speaking, to the history of political thought.[59] Nonetheless, during the years after the Second World War, when in conciliar studies attention shifted from matters diplomatic and political to ecclesiological and doctrinal issues, the case Figgis had made drew renewed and sometimes vigorous support from a whole series of scholars interested in late-medieval political thought.[60] And, of course, with the publication in 1978 of Quentin Skinner's *Foundations of Modern Political Thought*, a forceful acknowledgement of

version, see Tierney, *Foundations of the Conciliar Theory*, pp. 220–37. Cf. *The Political Thought of Pierre d'Ailly*, pp. 114–29. For conciliarist views of mixed monarchy in general, see James M. Blythe, *Ideal Government and the Mixed Constitution in the Middle Ages* (Princeton, 1992), pp. 243–59.

[58] Though Otto Gierke stands out as an important exception to that generalization. And, for a more recent exception, see Juan Beneyto Pérez, *Historia de las doctrinas políticas* (4th ed., Arguilar, 1964), pp. 161–64.

[59] Pierre Mesnard, *L'Essor de la philosophie politique au XVIᵉ siècle* (Paris, 1936); J.W. Allen, *A History of Political Thought in the Sixteenth Century* (London, 1928), and his *English Political Thought 1603–1660* (London, 1938); Christopher Morris, *Political Thought in England: Tyndale to Hooker* (London, 1953); R.W. and A.J. Carlyle, *A History of Political Thought in the West* (6 vols., London, 1903–36), VI, 163–67, and 247 where the author (A.J. Carlyle) *contrasts* "the ecclesiastical questions of the relation between the Pope and the General Council," which he excludes from consideration, with the remarks of the conciliarists concerning properly "political principles." For Franklin, see above n. 39.

[60] Zofia Rueger, "Gerson, the Conciliar Movement and the Right of Resistance (1642–1644)," *Journal of the History of Ideas*, XXV (No. 4, 1964), 467–80; A.J. Black, "The Conciliar Movement," in J.H. Burns ed., *The Cambridge History of Medieval Political Thought c. 350–c. 1450* (Cambridge, 1988), 573–87 (esp. 586–87); *idem*, *Political Thought in Europe: 1250–1450* (Cambridge, 1992), pp. 169–78; J.H. Burns, "The Conciliarist Tradition in Scotland," *Scottish Historical Review*, XLII (Oct., 1963), 89–104; *idem*, *Lordship, Kingship, and Empire*, pp. 10–12; Francis Oakley, "From Constance to 1688: The Political Thought of John Major and George Bushanan," *Journal of British Studies*, I (No. 2, 1962), 1–31; *idem*, *The Political Thought of Pierre d'Ailly*, pp. 217–32; *idem*, "Figgis, Constance, and the Divines of Paris," *American Historical Review*, LXXV (No. 2, 1969), 368–86; *idem*, "Natural Law, the *Corpus Mysticum*, and Consent in Conciliar Thought," 786–810.

the importance of the contributions made by conciliar theorists to early-modern political thinking was, in effect, "mainstreamed" among historians of modern political thought.[61] It is time, then, to turn to the nature and accuracy of the case being made.

III

That that case should *need* to be made at all, however, is not simply to be taken for granted. And to say that is to insist also that in any assessment of its strengths and weaknesses the appropriate point of departure should be the sober recognition of the degree to which our traditional understanding of the nature and career of conciliarism was shaped by the micropolitics of late nineteenth-century Catholic historiography. As we have seen, it was still possible for an English commentator like Hallam as late as the end of the Napoleonic era to speak of "the Whig principles" endorsed by the Council of Constance, and to view the conciliarist position as having survived since then as a live ecclesiological option to which most northern European Catholics subscribed. But in the wake of the ecclesiastical and theological developments that culminated in 1870 in the First Vatican Council's definition of papal primacy and infallibility, all that was changed. Those definitions seemed to leave Catholic theologians with no alternative but to regard the conciliar theory as a dead issue, an ecclesiological fossil, something lodged deep in the Lower Carboniferous of the dogmatic geology. More tellingly—or, at least, more pertinent to the matter with which we are concerned—it also seemed to leave Catholic historians with little choice but to treat the conciliar movement as nothing more than a revolutionary episode in the life of the Church. And, in striking degree, the historiographic tradition emerging from that realization has framed (and in some residual measure continues to frame) the picture of the subject conveyed in our general histories.[62]

---

[61] As is reflected in the quite generous degree of attention recently afforded it by the contributors to J.H. Burns and Mark Goldie eds., *The Cambridge History of Political Thought: 1450–1700* (Cambridge, 1991). For Skinner, see above, n. 41.

[62] Thus, for example, and less than a quarter of a century ago, Paul Ourliac could still depict the year 1440 as the great turning point after which theologians turned energetically to the "constructive task" of vindicating the papal monarchy. See Paul Ourliac and Henri Gilles, "La problématique de l'époque: les sources,"

That historiographic tradition had its ultimate origins in the historical arguments hammered out by Juan de Torquemada in defence
of Eugenius IV's cause during the Council of Basel and subsequently
embedded in his great *Summa de ecclesia* (*ca.* 1453). Those arguments
were further developed and refined by Thomas de Vio, Cardinal
Cajetan, in the early sixteenth century and put in canonical form a
century later by Robert, Cardinal Bellarmine.[63] The conciliar movement was portrayed as an unfortunate aberration spawned by the
crisis and confusion of the Great Schism and brought to an end in
the 1440s by the papal triumph over the conciliarist onslaught at Basel.
And the ecclesiology on which the conciliarists had taken their stand
came to be seen as an extreme position with little or no basis in
the orthodox doctrinal tradition, and, according to some, with suspect
origins in the speculations of those dangerous fourteenth-century radicals, William of Ockham and Marsiglio of Padua. Pius II's bull
Execrabilis had clearly proscribed it in 1460, and in 1516 the Fifth
Lateran Council's decree *Pastor aeternus* banished it definitively into
the outer darkness of heterodoxy. That being so, and even with due
recognition accorded to the twilight existence conciliar theory continued to eke out in Gallican propaganda, it is understandable that
something of a burden of proof should have come to rest on the
shoulders of anyone wishing to claim that the continuing memory
of the fifteenth-century councils and the continuing availability of
conciliarist writings were such even in the sixteenth and seventeenth
centuries as to have made it possible for conciliar theories to play
a role in the shaping of constitutionalist and political thinking.

The postwar blossoming of conciliar studies, however, has lessened
that burden considerably. If, as part of that development it was the
contribution above all of Tierney to have made it abundantly clear
that the conciliar theory was neither as recent nor as revolutionary

---

in Gabriel le Bras ed., *Histoire du Droit et des Institutions de l'Église en Occident* (18 vols.,
Paris, 1956–84), XIII, 1, 51; cf. Paul Ourliac, "La victoire de la papauté," in
A. Fliche and V. Martin eds., *Histoire de l'Église* (26 vols., Paris, 1934–64), XIV,
285. The intrusion into history of theological and canonistic criteria is evident in
the way in which the pertinent encyclopedias have treated the fifteenth-century
councils and the claim to legitimacy of the Avignonese and Pisan popes during the
Schism. For which, see the remarks in Francis Oakley, *Council over Pope?* (New York,
1969), pp. 121–26.

[63] See the helpful historiographical discussion in Thomas M. Izbicki, "Papalist
Reaction to the Council of Constance: Juan de Torquemada to the Present," *Church
History*, LV (No. 1, 1986), 7–20.

in its origins as it formerly was customary to believe, it was likewise the achievement especially of Hubert Jedin, Josef Klotzner, Olivier de la Brosse, Remigius Bäumer, and Hans-Jürgen Becker to have established the fact that the demise of that theory in the years after the dissolution of Basel was neither as rapid nor as final as we once were led to assume.[64] Similarly, and more recently, Hans Schneider and Hermann Joseph Sieben have focussed renewed attention on the long and unexpectedly vital "half-life" that conciliarist views continued to enjoy (and not only in Gallican France) for two centuries and more after the great changes wrought by the Council of Trent.[65]

[64] Hubert Jedin, *A History of the Council of Trent*, trans. Ernest Graf (2 vols., London, 1957–61), I, 1–165; Josef Klotzner, *Kardinal Domenikus Jacobazzi und sein Konzilswerk* (Rome, 1948); Olivier de la Brosse, *Le Pape et le Concile: La comparaison de leurs pouvoirs à la veille de la Réforme* (Paris, 1965); Remigius Bäumer, *Nachwirkungen des Konziliaren Gedankens in der Theologie und Kanonistik des frühen 16. Jahrhunderts* (Münster, 1971), *idem*, "Die Konstanzer Dekrete 'Haec sancta' und 'Frequens' im Urteil katholischer Kontroverstheologen des 16. Jahrhunderts," in Remigius Bäumer ed., *Von Konstanz nach Trient: Beiträge zur Geschichte der Kirche von den Reformkonzilien bis zum Tridentinum* (Munich, 1972), pp. 547–74, and "Silvester Prierias und seine Ansichten über das ökumenische Konzil," in Georg Schwaiger ed., *Konzil und Papst, Historische Beiträge zur Frage des höchsten Gewalt in der Kirche* (Munich, 1975), pp. 277–301; Hans-Jürgen Becker, *Die Appellation vom Papst an Allegemeines Konzil. Historisches Entwicklung und kanonistische Diskussion im späten Mittelalter und der frühen Neuzeit* (Vienna, 1988), pp. 339–84. See also J.H. Burns, "The Conciliarist Tradition in Scotland," *The Scottish Historical Review*, XLII (1963), 89–104; K.A. Fink, "Die konziliare Idee im späten Mittelalter," in Th. Mayer ed., *Die Welt zur des Konstanzer Konzils* (Constance, 1965), pp. 119–34; Josef Macek, "Le mouvement conciliaire, Louis XI et Georges de Podebrady," *Historica*, XV (1967), 5–63, *idem*, "Der Konziliarismus in der böhmischen Reformation, besonders in der Politik Georgs von Podiebrad," *Zeitschrift für Kirchengeschichte*, LXXX (1969), 312–30; Paul W. Knoll, "The University of Cracow and the Conciliar Movement," in James M. Kittelson and Pamela J. Transue eds., *Rebirth, Reform and Resilience: Universities in Transition: 1300–1700* (Columbus, Ohio, 1986), 190–202; Heiko A. Oberman, Daniel E. Zerfoss and William J. Courtenay eds., *Defensorium obedientiae apostolicae et alia documenta* (Cambridge, Mass., 1968), introductory essay, "The Twilight of the Conciliar Era," pp. 3–55; Francis Oakley, "Almain and Major: Conciliar Theory on the Eve of the Reformation," *American Historical Review*, LXX (1965), 673–90; *idem*, "Conciliarism at the Fifth Lateran Council?" *Church History*, XLI (1972), 452–63; *idem*, "Conciliarism in the Sixteenth Century: Jacques Almain Again," *Archiv für Reformationsgeschicte*, LXVIII (1977), 111–32; *idem*, "Natural Law, the *Corpus Mysticum*, and Consent in Conciliar Thought from John of Paris to Matthias Ugonius;" Thomas F. Mayer, "Marco Mantova, a Bronze Age conciliarist," *Annuarium historiae conciliorum*, XIV (1984), 385–408; James V. Mehl, "The First Printed Editions of the History of Church Councils," *ibid.*, XVIII (1986), 128–43; *idem*, "Ortwin Gratius, Conciliarism, and the Call for Church Reform," *Archiv für Reformationsgeschichte*, LXXVI (1985), 169–94.

[65] Hans Schneider, *Der Konziliarismus als Problem der neueren katholischen Theologie* (Berlin and New York, 1976), esp. chs. 2, 3 and 4, pp. 27–119; Hermann Josef Sieben, *Die katholische Konzilsidee von der Reformation bis zur Aufklärung* (Paderborn, 1988).

It is now clear, certainly, that we can no more take for granted the weakening of the conciliarist impulse in the late-fifteenth and early-sixteenth centuries than could the popes of the period. It may well be that it is only our familiarity with the papalist outcome that suggests the necessity of the process. Without the marked persistence of ecclesiological tensions into the Age of Reformation it would be hard, for example, to explain the failure of the Council of Trent, despite the challenges laid down by the novel Protestant ecclesiologies of the day, to promulgate any decree on the nature of the Christian Church. *Execrabilis*, we now know, was viewed less in its own day as an authoritative pronouncement than as a statement of the views of one particular faction; in the older histories it was clearly accorded a much exaggerated significance.[66] Similarly, the crucial phrases of the 1516 decree *Pastor aeternus* are simply too restricted in meaning to constitute any unambiguous condemnation of conciliar theory.[67] No surprise, then, should be occasioned by the vigorous reassertion of conciliarist principles in the early-sixteenth century by such Parisian theologians as John Mair (d. 1550) and Jacques Almain (d. 1515)—the thinkers on whose closely affiliated constitutionalist theories of resistance Skinner has rightly placed so much emphasis. Nor, similarly, should we be surprised by the degree of acquaintance Luther—or, for that matter, Bullinger—showed with conciliar views,[68] or by the efforts in Germany of Ortwin Gratius on the very eve of Trent to make the history of the fifteenth-century councils and the writings of some of the leading conciliarists readily available in new editions,[69] or by the fact that the Scottish Calvinist, George Buchanan (like John Knox, a former

---

[66] For a recent reiteration of this older view, see Steven Ozment, *The Age of Reform 1250–1550: An Intellectual and Religious History of Late Medieval and Reformation Europe* (New Haven and London, 1980), pp. 176 and 398–99.

[67] See Oakley, "Conciliarism at the Fifth Lateran Council?," 462–63, where I conclude that Bishop Boussuet's "Gallican" interpretation of this particular piece of history is more plausible than that of his ultramontane critics.

[68] Thus in November, 1518, in anticipation of a papal condemnation, Luther appealed from the judgment of the pope to that of a future general council, drawing some sections of his text from the earlier appeal launched by the theologians of the Sorbonne in response to the compromising Franco-papal concordat of 1516—see Jules Thomas, *Le Concordat de 1516* (3 vols., Paris, 1919), III, 72–74. Heinrich Bullinger, *Of the Holy Catholic Church*, in *Zwingli and Bullinger*, ed. and trans. G.W. Bromiley (Philadelphia, 1953), pp. 283–325 (at p. 317).

[69] For which, see Mehl, "The first printed editions of the history of church councils," *passim*.

pupil of John Mair's) later confessed to having held conciliarist ideas in his own younger Catholic days.[70]

France, Germany, Scotland, Poland, Italy even—[71] in all of them the conciliarist tradition endured on through the late-fifteenth and sixteenth centuries, and though in his recent account Sieben oddly does not dwell on the fact,[72] it was in marked degree revitalized during the first two decades of the seventeenth century. The Europewide ideological warfare of those years concerning the indirect power of the papacy in matters temporal has not received the attention it deserves and still awaits its historian.[73] That warfare was occasioned in England by the discovery in 1605–1606 of the Gunpowder Plot and the subsequent Oath of Allegiance controversy, in Venice in 1606 by the papal imposition of an interdict, in France in 1610 by the assassination of Henri IV at the hands of a Catholic and by the

---

[70] Buchanan admitted his earlier adherence to the conciliarist position when he was in the hands of the Lisbon Inquisition in 1550. See James M. Aitken, *The Trial of George Buchanan before the Lisbon Inquisition* (Edinburgh, 1939), pp. 22–25. Cf. Burns, "The Conciliarist Tradition in Scotland," 101–104.

[71] One of the more unexpected conciliarist survivals in Italy is the presence of more than one conciliarist in the court of Julius II himself. See Hubert Jedin, "Giovanni Gozzadini, ein Konziliarist am Hofe Julius II," in Hubert Jedin, *Kirche des Glaubens, Kirche der Geschichte: Ausgewählte Aufsätze und Vorträge* (2 vols., Freiburg, 1966), II, 17–74; Nelson H. Minnich, "Girolamo Massaino: Another Conciliarist at the Papal Court, Julius II to Adrian VI," in Nelson H. Minnich *et al., Studies in Catholic History in Honor of John Tracy Ellis* (Wilmington, 1985), pp. 520–65. For other Italian exponents of conciliarist ideas in the mid-sixteenth century, see Mayer, "Marco Mantova, a Bronze Age Conciliarist," 385–408, and his *Thomas Starkey and the Commonweal: Humanist Politics and Religion in the reign of Henry VIII* (Cambridge, 1989), pp. 172–87.

[72] Sieben, *Die Katholische Konzilsidee von der Reformation bis zur Aufklärung.*

[73] That ideological warfare began in 1606 with the imposition of an Oath of Allegiance in England and of a papal interdict in Venice. The most complete discussion of the English and French aspects of the controversy is still that of Charles H. McIlwain in the lengthy introductory essay he wrote for his edition of *The Political Works of James I* (Cambridge, Mass., 1918), pp. xxxv–lxxx. J.H.M. Salmon also touches upon those aspects very helpfully in his "Gallicanism and Anglicanism in the age of the Counter Reformation," ch. 2 of his *Renaissance and Revolt: Essays in the intellectual and social history of early modern France* (Cambridge, 1987) pp. 155–88. Salmon also offers a brief discussion of the intricate linkages between France and Venice and Venice and England and sets them in a broader context in "Catholic resistance theory, Ultramontanism, and the royalist response, 1580–1620," in Burns and Goldie eds., *The Cambridge History of Political Thought 1450–1700*, 219–53. I know of no full account of the complete controversy in its Venetian, French and English dimensions as it played out in the years between 1606 and 1620. I draw in what follows on Francis Oakley, "Constance, Basel, and the Two Pisas: The Conciliarist Legacy in Sixteenth- and Seventeenth-Century England," *Annuarium Historiae Conciliorum*, XXVI (No. 1, 1994), 1–32.

subsequent attempt of the Estates-General to impose on churchmen, royal officials and others an oath which its opponents portrayed as modelled on the earlier English oath of allegiance. Enough is known about this period of ideological turbulence to make it clear that it led to enhanced access to, increased circulation of, and renewed acquaintance with the history of the fifteenth-century councils and the writings of conciliarist authors. Here it must suffice to note that it was in the context of these events that Edmond Richer, Syndic of the Sorbonne, published in 1606 his important new edition of the works of Jean Gerson, which made conveniently available, not only Gerson's own conciliarist tracts, but also the most important of Pierre d'Ailly's, along with those of their sixteenth-century successors, Mair and Almain.[74] Only five years after the appearance of Richer's edition, moreover, and as the controversy over the indirect power continued to unfold, the Calvinist author Melchior Goldast published the first volume of his enormous three-volume *Monarchia S. Romani Imperii*, which included, along with William of Ockham's *Dialogus* and a host of other works, John of Paris's proto-conciliarist *Tractatus de regia potestate et papali* (1302), several of Gerson's, Gregor Heimburg's, Matthias Doering's, Philippus Decius's and Jacques Almain's conciliar tracts, Richer's *De ecclesiastica et politica potestate* (1611)—with its own reaffirmation of conciliar theory, Latin versions of several Venetian efforts to vindicate the republic against papal condemnation, including Paolo Sarpi's *Considerazioni sopra le censure della santità di papa Paulo V contra la Serenissima Republica di Venetia* (1606) and the *Trattato del Interdetto della Santità di Paolo V*. This last work, signed by seven prominent Venetian clerics (Sarpi included) but apparently written *in toto* by Sarpi himself, characteristically invoked the authority of the Councils of Constance and Basel and the conciliarist writings of Gerson, Almain and Mair.[75] In the early sixteenth century, both of

---

[74] See Edmond Richer ed., *Joannis Gersonii . . . Opera* (2 vols., Paris, 1606), II, 675–934.

[75] Fra Paolo Sarpi, *Trattato dell'interdetto della santità di papa Paolo V*, in his *Opere* (9 vols., Bari, 1931–65), VI, *Istoria dell'interdetto e altri scritti edit e inediti*, ed. M.D. Busnelli and Giovanni Gambarin, 3 pts, III, 1–41; see esp. 4, 15–18, 21–23, 27, 30–33. This reliance on conciliarist authors and the concomitant willingness to invoke the authority of Constance and Basel were characteristic of most of Sarpi's writings on the interdict: see, e.g., *Scrittura sopra la forza e validità della scommunica giusta ed ingiusta, e sopra li remedii "de iure" e "de facto" da usare contro le censure ingiuste*, ibid., II, 28, 32–33; *Scrittura intorno l'appelazione al concilio o altro da farsi per mortificare gli atti del pontifice*, ibid., 82–85; *Trattato e resoluzioni sopra la validità delle scommuniche di Giovanni Gersone*,

these men had insisted that ever since the Council of Constance (and in this unlike the Thomists) the theologians of Paris and France had commonly and continuously taught the jurisdictional superiority of council to pope and its concomitant prerogative of limiting the pope's power and submitting him to its own judgment.[76] In 1606 Paolo Sarpi, having evoked Mair's authority to the same effect, argued with reference to the conciliarist position (and in the teeth of Cardinal Bellarmine's papalist denials) that "an opinion which hath the consent of as many, if not a greater number of Universities, Countries and Kingdoms, cannot be said to be mayntained without reason and authoritie nor yet audaciously."[77]

The opinion in question, of course, and one which Richer also defended with gusto and at length in his own contemporaneous response to Bellarmine's criticism of Gerson, was that of the superiority of council to pope. The above passage is quoted from the English translation of Sarpi's *Apologia* which was printed in London within a year of its original publication in Italian.[78] And that fact may serve to focus attention on the somewhat more novel point that the England of the (later) sixteenth and seventeenth centuries, however Protestant, does not appear to have been much less acquainted with conciliar theory and the history of conciliar practice than were the Catholic countries of the Continent.[79]

In the fifteenth century, it is true, England had produced no conciliar theorists of note and English prelates had not played a leading

---

teologo e cancelliero parisino, cognominato il dottore cristianissimo, ibid., 171–84; *Apologia per le opposizioni fatti dall'illustrissimo e reverendissimo signor cardinale Bellarmino alli trattati e resoluzioni di Giovanni Gersone sopra la validità delle scommuniche, ibid.*, III, 43–189; [*Lettere agli inquisitori in Roma*], *ibid.*, 190, 194; *Scrittura in difesa delle opere scritte a favore della serenissima republica nella controversia col sommo pontifice, ibid.*, 236, 255.

[76] John Mair, *Disputatio de auctoritate concilii supra pontificem maximum*, in Jean Gerson, *Opera omnia*, ed. Louis Ellies Dupin (5 vols., Antwerp, 1706), II, 1132, cf. 1144; Jacques Almain, *Expositio circa decisiones Magistri Guilelmi Occam super potestate ecclesiastica et laica*, in Dupin, II, 1070.

[77] Sarpi, *Apologia per le oppositioni fatte dall'illustrissime e reverendissimo signor cardinale Bellarminio alli trattati e resolutioni di Giovanni Gersone*, ed. Busnelli and Gambarin, III, 118. Sarpi devotes no less than a fifth of this work (79–80, 115–54) to a rebuttal of Bellarmine's assertion of the superiority of pope to council.

[78] Under the title *An Apology or Apologeticall Answere, Made by Father Paule a Venetian . . . unto the Exceptions and objections of Cardinall Bellarmine against certain Treatises and Resolutions of John Gerson* (London, 1607). See pp. 64–65.

[79] I base this claim on Oakley, "Constance, Basel, and the Two Pisas" to which reference may be made for the complete argument and the full range of supporting documentation.

role at either Constance or Basel. It is readily understandable, as a
result, that little attention has been paid to the conciliarist legacy to
the Tudor and Stuart period. But two developments served to fam-
iliarize generations of English people even prior to the Oath of Allegiance controversy with the broad outlines of the conciliar experience
and, in the case of a learned Anglican controversialist like Matthew
Sutcliffe (1550?–1629) with a great deal more.[80] First, in the early
1530s, Henry VIII's diplomatic flirtation with conciliarist ideas during the complex negotiations with Rome concerning the marriage
question. Secondly, in the latter half of the century, the inclusion of
materials on the history and ecclesiology of the fifteenth-century councils in such widely-disseminated works as Foxe's *Book of Martyrs* (1563)
and Thomas Bilson's *The True Difference betwene Christian Subjection and
Unchristian Rebellion* (1583).[81] But it was the protracted Oath of Allegiance
controversy, along with its Venetian and French counterparts which
progressively converged on it, that had the effect of making people
in England for much of the seventeenth century better acquainted
with conciliar history and the writings of the conciliarists than at
any previous time—the fifteenth century, I would judge, not excluded.

That fact is clearly reflected in the degree to which the English
and Scottish writers, Protestant no less than Catholic, who for one
reason or another contributed to the controversy made the evocation
of the conciliarist tradition their own. In this James I himself, who
cites John of Paris and the conciliarist writings of Gerson, Mair and

---

[80] A learned churchman who disposed of an impressive degree of scholastic and
canonistic erudition, Sutcliffe showed a marked degree of familiarity with the writings of such prominent conciliarists as Pierre d'Ailly, Jean Gerson, Francesco Zabarella,
Nicholas of Cusa, Panormitanus, Aeneas Sylvius Piccolomini and Jacques Almain—
see Oakley, "Constance, Basel and the Two Pisas," 15–17.

[81] For a succinct account of Henry's conciliar diplomacy, see now Becker, *Die
Appellation vom Papst an ein allgemeines Konzil*, pp. 264–69. The basic studies are P.A.
Sawada, "The Abortive Council of Mantua and Henry VIII," *Academia* (Nanzan
Univ., Nagoya, Japan), XXVII (1960), 1–15; *idem*, "Two Anonymous Tudor Treatises
on the General Council," *Journal of Ecclesiastical History*, XII (1961), 197–214; *idem*,
"Das Imperium Heinrichs VIII, und die erste Phase seiner Konzilspolitik," in Irwin
Iserloh ed., *Reformata Reformanda: Festgabe für Hubert Jedin* (2 vols., Münster, 1965), I,
476–507. Cf. Franklin Le Van Baumer, *The Early Tudor Theory of Kingship* (New
Haven and London, 1940), pp. 49–56; J.J. Scarisbrick, *Henry VIII* (Berkeley and
Los Angeles, 1963), pp. 261–64, 293, 319, 390–91. For the second development,
see John Foxe, *Actes and Monuments of these Latter and Perilous Dayes, Touching Matters
of the Church*, ed. Stephen Reed Cattley (8 vols., London, 1841), III, 416–23 (for
Constance), 605–700 (for Basel). This edition reproduces the contents of the first
English edition of 1563. Thomas Bilson, *The True Difference between Christian Subjection
and Unchristian Rebellion* (Oxford, 1585), esp. pp. 85–94, 270–73, 310–11.

Almain (alluding also to the deposition of John XXIII at Constance and the attempted deposition of Julius II in 1511 at Pisa), was no exception.[82] In his eagerness to prove that those theologians, Catholic though they were, had denied to the pope any temporal authority over kings and any right to depose them, he betrayed a certain insensitivity to their broader constitutionalist proclivities. That insensitivity was not missed by his opponent, Jacques Davy, Cardinal du Perron, who was quick to point out that even the conciliarist theologians whose authority James had invoked still believed the pope to retain the right to *condemn* kings who were guilty of heresy, and denied him the right of *deposition* simply because that right belonged to "the whole body of the Realme."[83] In so doing, du Perron emphasized the importance of Richer's recent edition of Gerson for its having gathered together and reprinted the pertinent works of these theologians. That edition, certainly, was clearly the source of many of the references to conciliarist writings made by English contributors to the oath of Allegiance controversy, and was presumably the edition which James I himself used and presented in 1612 to the university library at St. Andrews.[84] On occasion, it is also possible to identify other routes

---

[82] See James I, *A Premonition to all Most Mightie Monarches, Kings, Free Princes, and States of Christendome*, and his *A Remonstrance for the Right of Kings, and the Independence of their Crownes, Against an Oration of the Most Illustrious Cardinal of Perron*, in Charles H. McIlwain ed., *The Political Works of James I* (Cambridge, Mass., 1918), pp. 119–20, 181, 198, 202–6, 263–64.

[83] Jacques Davy, Cardinal du Perron, *An Oration made on the Part of the Lordes Spirituale in the Chamber of the Third Estate, Translated into English* (St. Omer, 1616), pp. 47–49, 59 and 63. James could bluster that Perron had misrepresented the views of these men. But one of his own quotations from the works of Mair inadvertently revealed that Mair himself was far from denying the right of the people to depose their king—see his *A Remonstrance for the Right of Kings*, in McIlwain ed., *The Political Works of James I*, p. 202. For Mair's own words, see his *Disputatio de statu et potestate ecclesiae*, in Dupin, II, 1128–29. And this point appears not to have been missed later on by the parliamentarian William Prynne, who, defending the right of subjects to resist tyranny, and citing the same work of Mair's, commented that: "lest any should think that none but Puritanes maintained this opinion, K. James himself in his Answer to Cardinal *Perron* justifieth the *French Protestants* taking up *Defensive Arms in France*"—see William Prynne, *The Soveraigne Power of Parliaments and Kingdoms* (London, 1643), pp. 144(2)–45.

[84] Some authors explicitly specify Richer's edition as their source—see, e.g., George Blackwell, *A Large Examination taken at Lambeth: of M. George Blackwell Made Archpriest of England by Pope Clement 8* (London, 1607), pp. 63, 118; William Warmington, *A Moderate Defense of the Oath of Allegiance* ([n.p.], 1612), p. 88. And the frequent citation by others of the particular excerpt from Mair's *Sentences* which Richer had reprinted (IV *Sent.*, dist. 24, qu. 3) gives a further clue to the impact of this edition. For James's gift to St. Andrews, see Rueger, "Gerson, the Conciliar Movement, and the Right of Resistance," 484.

via which these Jacobean authors were acquiring their knowledge of conciliarist thinking,[85] but the pertinent sources had by their day multiplied to such an extent as to render such exercises in identification redundant.

In one of his discussions of the influence model, Skinner stipulates as a minimal precondition for its invocation the ability to produce evidence to the effect that the person being influenced "really had or could have had access to the works" allegedly doing the influencing.[86] Enough has been said to demonstrate that that precondition represents no formidable challenge in this particular case. The less so, it should now be added, in that the constitutionalist resistance theorists of the sixteenth century, whose authority was also to be invoked in the seventeenth by their English parliamentary successors, provided another (if indirect) mode of access to conciliar theory, along with the example of its application to the world of secular politics. As we shall see,[87] that was clear enough in the case of the Calvinists among those sixteenth-century theorists. And if there is no mention of conciliarism in the tracts of Rossaeus or Boucher, the leading resistance theorists of the French Catholic League, one should recognize that their alignment with Rome gave them every incentive to conceal any indebtedness of that sort if it did, indeed, exist.[88]

---

[85] Thus, for example, John Buckeridge, *De potestate papae in rebus temporalibus . . . adversus Robertum cardinalem Bellarminum* (London, 1614), p. 132, had clearly read d'Ailly's *De reformatione ecclesiae* in the edition which Ortwin Gratius had included in his *Fasisculus rerum expetendarum* (Cologne, 1535), even though, eight years before he wrote, it had been republished in London in *Speculum Ecclesiae Pontificiae Nicolaus Clemangis . . . de corrupto Ecclesiae statu* (London, 1606), pp. 145–92. For the reading of Aeneas Sylvius Piccolomini's account of the proceedings at the Council of Basel via the translation included in Foxe's *Book of Martyrs*, see below, nn. 107 and 108.

[86] Skinner, "More's *Utopia*," 164.

[87] See below, pp. 166–67.

[88] Though that alignment did not prevent Juan de Mariana, on the very eve of the Oath of Allegiance controversy, from evoking the analogy of conciliar superiority in the context of discussing whether or not the commonwealth possessed greater power than did the king. He was careful, however, to insist that he himself was passing no judgment on the rectitude of the canonistic claim. See his *De rege et regis institutione* (Mainz, 1605), Lib. I, cap. 8, pp. 72–74. William Prynne, later on, was quick to pick up on this passage. "See Prynne, *The Soveraigne Power of Parliaments and Kingdoms*, p. 68. By contrast, in the works of William Rainolds (Rossaeus), *De justa reipublicae Christianae in reges impios et haereticos authoritate* (Paris, 1590), and Jean Boucher, *De justa Henrici Tertii abdicatione e Francorum regno* (Lyons, 1591), students of conciliar theory are likely to encounter much that may strike them as familiar. But nothing, nonetheless, on which to build a case for anything more than the existence of interesting parallelisms.

Whatever the case, the silence of those Catholic monarchomachs on that particular matter did not carry much weight with the royalist John Maxwell, Bishop of Tuam, when he came in 1644 to launch a long and powerful attack on those Jesuits and Puritans who, "to depresse Kinges averre, that all power is originally, radically and formally inherent in the People or Communitie, and from thence is derived to the Kinge."[89] That deplorable idea these Puritans ("our Rabbies" as he calls them) did not draw from "the sound Protestants of the Reformed Churches" but from such monarchomachs of the previous century as Boucher, Rossaeus and Hotman who, in turn, "borrowed" it (he charged) from "the polluted cisterns" of "the Sorbonistes, and others of that kinde." And in making that charge, he cites the works of John of Paris, William of Ockham, Marsiglio of Padua, Jean Gerson and Jacques Almain.[90] These were men who, he says,

> to oppose the Pope his infallibilitie in judgement, his unlimited power, and to subject him to a Councell, did dispute themselves almost out of breath, to prove that *potestas spiritualis summa* was by Christ *first* and immediately given *unitati*, or *communitati fidelium* . . . [so that] in the case that the power of the Church was abused to heresie or tyrannie, the Pope was deposable (not onely censurable) by a Councell. This question was acutely disputed before, about, and after the Councell of Constance.[91]

I dwell on Maxwell, more because of his vituperative *esprit* than because there was anything really unusual about his attempt to discredit the notion of popular sovereignty and to undercut the parliamentary advocacy of a right of legitimate resistance against tyranny by linking them damagingly with popery. "Jesuit" had become a useful "snarl-word" long before the end of the Elizabethan era,[92] and the coupling of Jesuit and Puritan as bedfellows in sedition had become a cliché by the time James I himself lent it his royal authority by dubbing Jesuits in 1609 as "nothing but *Puritan-papists*."[93] Even

---

[89] John Maxwell, *Sacro-sancta Regum Majestas: or, The Sacred and Royal Prerogative of Christian Kings* (Oxford, 1644), p. 6; cf. p. 3.

[90] *Ibid.*, pp. 14–16.

[91] *Ibid.*, p. 12.

[92] See Thomas H. Clancy, *Papist Pamphleteers: The Allen-Persons Party and the Political Thought of the Counter-Reformation in England, 1572–1615* (Chicago, 1964), p. 88.

[93] James I, *A Premonition to all most Mightie Monarchies, Kings, Free Princes, and States of Christendome*, in McIlwain ed., *The Political Works of James I*, p. 126.

before the Gunpowder Plot of 1605 the "Romish schooles" had come to be viewed, in Thomas Morton's words, as "seminaries of rebellions."[94] But, as we have seen, the great Europe-wide ideological controversy pivoting on the English Oath of Allegiance dispute helped stimulate a marked revival of interest in conciliar theory and in the dramatic actions taken two centuries earlier by the Councils of Pisa, Constance and Basel. As a result, one begins to encounter expressions of alarm from staunch royalists focused now specifically on the unhappy availability of the conciliar precedent of the trial and deposition of popes to those benighted contemporaries who wished to legitimate a right of resistance against temporal rulers. Thus David Owen, writing in 1610 in a work appropriately entitled *Herod and Pilate Reconciled*, argued that the "politique divines" of the day had "learned their errour of the *power of States-men over Kings*," thereby investing "the people and Nobles with the power over Kings, to dispose of their kingdomes," from such papistical schoolmen as John of Paris, Jacques Almain and Marsiglio of Padua. And he went on to berate the Calvinists, Theodore Beza and Lambert Daneau, for endorsing the idea that "as a generall councill is above the Pope, so the Kingdome or the Peeres of the Land, are above the King."[95]

In committing themselves to that position Beza and Daneau had not stood alone. Indeed, they had been at one with most of the leading Protestant advocates of resistance theory in the latter half of the sixteenth century, from John Ponet, exiled bishop of Winchester,

---

[94] Thomas Morton, *An Exact Discoverie of Romish Doctrine in the Case of Conspiracie and Rebellion* (London, 1605), p. 1; cf. his *A Full Satisfaction concerning a Double Romish Iniquitie; Hainous Rebellion, and More than Heathenish Aequivocation* (London, 1606), p. 107, where he characterizes as "a learning substantially popish" the "seditious doctrine of resisting and deposing Kings."

[95] David Owen, *Herod and Pilate Reconciled* (London, 1610), pp. 43–46, 48, 50–51. He returned to similar themes during the Civil War in his *A Persuasion to Loyalty, or the Subjecte Dutie: Wherein is Proved that Resisting or Deposing of Kings is Utterly Unlawfull* (London, 1642), p. 24. The French version of Beza's *De jure magistratuum (Du Droit des magistrats sur leurs sujets)* is to be found in *Mémoires de l'Estat de France sous Charles IX*, ed. Simon Goulart (3 vols., Meidelbourg, 1576), II, 735–90, esp. 777. (For the question of authorship, see Albert Elkan, *Die Publizistik der Bartholomäusnachts und Mornay's "Vindiciae contra tyrannos"* [Heidelberg, 1905] 60–123.) Lambert Daneau was certainly well aware of the conciliarist claims advanced by the Council of Constance and its vindication of those claims via the judgment and deposition of popes—see his *Ad Roberti Bellarmini disputationes theologicas* (Geneva, 1596), pp. 330–31, 343, and 673. But I have been unable to find the passage to which Prynne refers in Daneau's *Politices Christianae Libri Septem* (Geneva, 1596) or in the other writings of his to which I have had access.

writing in 1556 during the reign of Mary Tudor, to George Buchanan writing in 1567, to the authors of the *Vindiciae contra tyrannos* and the *Discours politique* who produced their statements during the French Religious Wars in the wake of the massacre of St. Bartholomew's Day.[96] All of these men—Ponet, Buchanan and DuPlessis Mornay at considerable length—had adduced conciliar theory and practice in order to argue (in the words of the *Vindiciae*) that if the general council can depose the pope, who regards himself "as much in dignity above the Emperor as the Sun is above the Moon," then "who will make any doubt or question, that the general Assembly of the Estates of any Kingdom, who are the representative body thereof, may not only degrade and disthronize a Tyrant, but also disthronize and depose a King, whose weakness and folly is hurtful or pernicious to the State."[97]

It is not surprising, then, that four years after the appearance of Owen's book, and in the process of writing against Cardinal Bellarmine an enormous treatise on the power of the pope in matters temporal (one punctuated with quotations from such proto-conciliarists or conciliarists as John of Paris, Ockham, Pierre d'Ailly, Gerson, Dietrich of Niem, Zabarella, Nicholas of Cusa, Panormitanus, Aeneas Sylvius Piccolomini, Almain and John Mair)—it is not surprising that John

---

[96] A facsimile edition of Ponet's *Shorte Treatise of Politicke Power* is printed in Winthrop S. Hudson, *John Ponet (1516?–1556): Advocate of Limited Monarchy* (Chicago, 1942)—see pp. [102]–[106]; cf. p. [60]. George Buchanan, *De jure regni apud Scotos*, in his *Opera omnia* ed. Thomas Ruddiman (2 vols., Edinburgh, 1715), I, 8, 30, 36. As he himself admitted in 1550, when he was in the hands of the Lisbon Inquisition, he had been in his earlier Catholic days an adherent to the Conciliar position—see Aitken, *The Trial of George Buchanan before the Lisbon Inquisition*, pp. 22–25. Junius Brutus, [i.e. Philippe du Plessis Mornay], *Vindiciae contra tyrannos* (Basel, 1580), pp. 173–74. Anon., *Discours politiques des diverses puissances establies de Dieu au monde*, in *Mémoires de l'Estat de France sous Charles IX*, ed. Goulart, 2nd edn. (3 vols., Meidelbourg, 1579), III, fols. 147^b–213^b (at fols. 209^b–210^b).

[97] I cite this passage from a seventeenth-century English translation—*Vindiciae contra tyrannos . . . Being a Treatise Written in Latin and French by Junius Brutus and Translated Out of Both into English* (London, 1689), p. 142. For a more extensive discussion of this sixteenth-century phase in the influence of conciliarist views on Calvinist resistance theory, see Oakley, "On the Road from Constance to 1688." In that article I now believe that I overstated somewhat Buchanan's indebtedness to Mair, perhaps also the importance of the pupil-teacher relationship. As J.H. Burns made clear a year later (1963), conciliar ideas were prevalent in Scotland even prior to Mair's return from Paris—see his "The Conciliarist Tradition in Scotland." For a carefully nuanced analysis of Mair's political views, see J.H. Burns. "*Politia regalis et optima*: The Political Ideas of John Mair," *History of Political Thought*, II (No. 1, 1981), 31–61.

Buckeridge, Bishop of Ely, felt it necessary to challenge the very pertinence of the conciliar analogy by insisting that according to "many
theologians of great name . . . the ecumenical council is said to have
greater authority over a pope than the people is said to have over a
prince" (my emphasis). For whereas the pope's position is founded
in grace, the king's is founded in nature. And whereas the pope can
be called before a tribunal in which he can "without doubt" be deposed, "no one," the people being inferior to him, "can judge, pun-
ish or depose a king."[98]

Thirty years later, during the first Civil War, John Bramhall, subsequently Archbishop of Armagh, reacting as had Owen to Beza's
invocation of the conciliar analogy, made a similar attempt to neutralize its force by conceding the council's power of deposition while
at the same time noting that it pertained to an elected rather than
an hereditary ruler and that it was "grounded in a known [canon]
law." "The king's crown," he insisted, "sits closer, the Council's
power is greater, the like law is wanting."[99] And around the same
time another royalist, Henry Ferne, Bishop of Chester, accusing his
parliamentary opponents of Jesuitical practice and of borrowing their
arguments from "the *Romane* Schools," derided them for harboring
silent thoughts of parliamentary infallibility and for being willing to
attribute a binding force to the decrees of a parliament acting in
the absence of the king on the grounds that "*[s]uch a power of binding ha's a generall Councell* [of the Church] *to it's decisions, and why should
a Civill Generall Councell of England* [i.e. the parliament] *have lesse power
in it.*"[100]

But such royalist counter-attacks were launched in vain. Even after
the Oath of Allegiance controversy had died down, familiarity with
the conciliarist literature and with the actions of the fifteenth century

---

[98] Buckeridge, *De potestate papae in rebus temporalibus*, pp. 675–76 (citing William
Barclay); cf. pp. 677–86.

[99] John Bramhall, *Serpent-Salve* (1643), in A.W.H. ed., *The Works of the Most Reverend
Father in God, John Bramhall, D.D.* (5 vols., Oxford, 1842–45), III, 316. For citations
of Gerson's *De auferabilitate papae*, *De unitate ecclesiastica*, and *Regulae morales*, see *A Just
Vindication of the Church of England*, ibid., 251, 256; *Schism Guarded, and Beaten Back upon
the Right Owners*, ibid., II, 610.

[100] Henry Ferne, *The Resolving of Conscience upon this Question: Whether upon such a
Supposition or Case, as is Now Usually Made . . . Subjects may Take up Arms and Resist?*
(2nd ed., Oxford, 1643), sig. A 3; *idem, Conscience Satisfied: That There is no Warrant
for the Arms now Taken up by Subjects* (Oxford, 1643), pp. 38–39, where he is replying
to Charles Herle, *A Fuller Answer to a Treatise Written by Doctor Ferne entitled The Resolving
of Conscience . . .* (London, 1682), p. 18.

councils in judging and deposing popes was such that when in April/
May 1628 "parliamentary proceedings came [for the first time in that
era] to be dominated by a contest between King and Commons about
the nature and limits of supreme authority," it was natural for Sir
Dudley Digges (the elder) to reach in debate for a comparison between
their own concerns and that of their conciliar predecessors. Just as
the Fathers assembled at the Council of Basel, he said, had debated
"whether the Pope be above the church or the church above the
Pope, so now is there a doubt whether the law be above the King
or the King above the law."[101] If the successive editions of Foxe's
Book of Martyrs, with its lengthy extracts from Aeneas Sylvius Piccolomini's *De gestis concilii Basiliensis Commentariorum Libri II* can only have
reinforced that familiarity,[102] the English translations of the *Vindiciae*
(which appeared in 1622, 1631, 1648 and 1689), and re-issues of Ponet's
Shorte Treatise of Politicke Power (which appeared in the critical years
of 1639 and 1642) served to draw attention to the pertinence of the
conciliar precedent to the constitutional dilemma with which the mid-
century parliamentarians were now confronted.[103] So, too, did the continued circulation of Buchanan's *De jure regni apud Scotos*, the persistent
notoriety of which is evidenced by its targetting for government condemnation in 1584, 1660, 1664 and 1688 and by its inclusion among
the works condemned by the University of Oxford in 1683.[104]

Thus William Prynne, who made extensive use of the arguments of
Ponet, the *Vindiciae*, Buchanan and the Scottish conciliarist, John Mair,
repeatedly evoked the example of conciliar jurisdictional superiority
set by the Councils of Pisa, Constance and Basel and even by the
conciliabulum of Pisa in 1511.[105] And he also cited at length Aeneas

---

[101] See Conrad Russell, *Parliaments and English Politics: 1621–1629* (Oxford, 1979),
p. 354. For the passage in question, see Robert C. Johnson *et al.* eds., *Commons
Debates 1628* (6 vols., New Haven and London, 1977–83), III, 102 (26 April, 1628).
The editors conclude that "the discourse of the Council of Basel" which Digges
refers to was Aeneas Sylvius Piccolomini's *De gestis concilii Basiliensis commentariorum,
libri II*, and they refer us (not inappropriately) to the latter's rendition of a speech
delivered in 1431 by the Bishop of Burgos. I would append the speculation that
Digges may have been familiar with the *De gestis* via the lengthy translated extract
John Foxe had seen fit to fold into his *Book of Martyrs*.

[102] See above, n. 81.

[103] See Harold J. Laski ed., *A Defence of Liberty Against Tyrants: A translation of the
Vindiciae contra Tyrannos by Junius Brutus* (London, 1924), Introduction, pp. 59–60;
Hudson, *John Ponet (1516?–1556), Advocate of Limited Monarchy*, pp. 209–10.

[104] See Oakley, "From Constance to 1688," 11 and n. 50.

[105] Prynne, *The Soveraigne Power of Parliaments and Kingdoms*, pp. 5–7, 9, 20, 23, 31,
68, 73, 122, 136, 144–45; *ibid.*, *Appendix*, pp. 101, 100–12, 161.

Sylvius's rendition of a speech delivered in 1431 during the debates at Basel. In that speech the Bishop of Burgos, ambassador of the King of Castile, in his attempt to make the case for the superiority of council to pope had appealed to a secular analogy which he clearly assumed would strike his listeners as obvious. "The Pope," he said

> is in the Church as a King is in his Kingdome, and for a King to be of more authority than his Kingdome, it were too absurd. Ergo. Neither ought the Pope to be above the Church.... And like as oftentimes Kings, which doe wickedly governe the commonwealthe and expresse cruelty, are deprived of their Kingdoms; even so it is not to be doubted but that the Bishop of Rome may be deposed by the Church, that is to say, by the generall Councell....[106]

The English translation of the speech which Prynne is citing is the contemporary one printed in Foxe's *Book of Martyrs*,[107] and its appeal to English parliamentarians (at a time when belief in the subordination of king to kingdom had long since lost its status as a simple matter of commonsense) is reflected in the fact that the same lengthy quotation drawn from the same source had been prominently featured a year earlier in William Bridge's rebuttal of one of Henry Ferne's royalist tracts. Bridge also made considerable use of the conciliarist writings of Jacques Almain, and the latter's authority is further evoked, along with that of Ockham, Gerson and Mair, in Samuel Rutherford's *Lex, Rex*, a work written in 1644 by way of response to Maxwell's, *Sacro-sancta Regum Majestas*.[108]

Clearly, then, Figgis was correct in his claim that conciliar theory exerted a demonstrable influence upon the constitutional and resistance theorists of the sixteenth and seventeenth centuries. If, after the onset of the Reformation, the Catholics among them were rarely explicit enough on the matter to warrant anything more than the cautious noting of parallels and similarities, with the Protestants we are on a firmer ground. Encouraged by the frequency of direct citation

---

[106] *Ibid.*, p. 6.

[107] Foxe, *Actes and Monuments*, ed. Cattley, III, 611–12. The Cattley edition reproduces the first English edition (1563). In some later editions the number of pages devoted to Basel was reduced, but this speech was still included. For the original, see Aeneas Sylvius Piccolomini, *De gestis concilii Basiliensis commentariorum libri II*, ed. and trans. Denys Hay and W.K. Smith (Oxford, 1967), pp. 32–33.

[108] William Bridge, *The Wounded Conscience Cured, the Weak One Strengthened and the Doubting Satisfied by Way of Answer to Doctor Ferne* (London, 1642), pp. 2, 7–8; also his *The Truths of the Times Vindicated* (London, 1643), pp. 2–7, 45; Samuel Rutherford, *Lex, Rex: The Law and the Prince* (London, 1644), pp. 50, 418, 449.

of conciliar authors or the conciliar experience, and guided by the corroboration of independent (if frequently hostile) contemporary witnesses, the historian has in this case no reason whatsoever to betray any squeamishness about invoking the influence model. As Skinner rightly observed in relation to one strand in the sixteenth-century phase of the story, "when the Calvinist George Buchanan stated for the first time on behalf of the Reformed Churches a fully secularized and populist theory of political resistance, he was largely restating a position already attained by the Catholic John Mair in his teaching at the Sorbonne over half a century before."[109] And as Zofia Rueger put it in relation specifically to seventeenth-century England, "the conciliar precedent was deemed of sufficient importance and relevance to be invoked frequently enough to force the Royalist writers into a polemic," forming, as a result, "a distinct strand of the controversy over the right of resistance in the years, 1642–1644."[110]

If, then, it may conceivably be stating the case a little too ebulliently to claim, as did Laski, that "the road from Constance to 1688 was a direct one,"[111] one can speak, with some confidence at least of a path from Constance to 1644, and probably, in fact, for some way beyond. Scholars will doubtless disagree about how substantial in individual cases this conciliar legacy was,[112] but they will certainly not be warranted in ignoring it, still less in questioning its existence. At the same time, it should be noted that at least in this particular test case Condren's recommended term "use"[113] catches what was going on rather more effectively than the vaguer term "influence." And it may have the added advantage of prompting us, when we are inclined to claim that A was "influenced" by B or "borrowed" from B, to go on (as Collingwood recommended) and ask ourselves "what there was in A that laid itself open to B's influence, or what there was in A that made it capable of borrowing from B."[114] In

---

[109] Skinner, "The Origins of the Calvinist Theory of Revolution," 325.

[110] Rueger, "Gerson, the Conciliar Movement, and the Right of Resistance," 486.

[111] Laski, "Political Theory in the Later Middle Ages," 838.

[112] Thus, for example, Julian Franklin, in his review of Skinner's *Foundations of Modern Political Thought* (*Political Theory*, VII [No. 4, 1979], 558), argues that "the specific influence" of the conciliarists on the ideas of Beza and DuPlessis Mornay was "only marginal."

[113] See above, nn. 11 and 12.

[114] These are the questions Collingwood insists (*The Idea of Nature*, p. 128) must be asked if we are to avoid the practice of "a frivolous and superficial type of history." Claudio Guillén appears to have had something similar in mind when he

effect, it may encourage us not to rest on a simple assertion that influence has occurred, but to go on to ask the further and more probing "so what" question, and, as a result, to give reasons for our belief that the fact of influence is, in a given instance, noteworthy, significant, possessed of a measure of explanatory power. And that brings us, of course, to Figgis's third and most important influence claim, which concerned the very status and significance of conciliar theory in the history of political thought.

IV

In this connection, Figgis claimed, it will be recalled, that conciliar theory exerted the subsequent influence it did (or, translated into Condren's terminology of usage, lent itself to the subsequent use it received) precisely because of its intrinsic nature, because of the universality and force with which it advanced what was not only an ecclesiological option but, beyond that, a political theory. In this connection, too, notice should be taken of some pertinent reservations which historians have expressed (though not necessarily with explicit reference to Figgis) about the failure of the conciliarists to translate theory into practice, about the coherence and universality of their theoretical position itself, and about the degree to which the early-modern constitutionalists who appealed to it in support of their own claims did so selectively and without an historically accurate understanding of the position itself.

Thus, thirty years ago, while conceding that conciliarism was "indubitably" a "political doctrine," that it was a "ruthless" application of what he called "the ascending theory of government" (that is, popular sovereignty) to the one body "which at first sight would have seemed immune" to it, Walter Ullmann expressed grave doubts about the degree to which the conciliarists had really acted on their principles. By their deeds, he implied, ye shall know them. The old Romano-canonical principle "What touches all, must be approved by all" was

---

properly insisted that "to ascertain an *influence* is to make a value judgment, not to measure a fact. The critic is obliged to evaluate the function or the scope of the effect of A in the making of B, for he is not listing the total amount of these effects, which are legion, but ordering them. Thus 'influence' and 'significant influence' are practically synonymous." See Guillén, "The Aesthetics of Literary Influence," pp. 38–39.

a persuasive political slogan, but one missed its appearance in practice. Constance and Basel were "as heretofore" merely "ecclesiastical assemblies" dominated, moreover, by the higher clergy. "The lower clergy and the educated layman," he argues, "were . . . knocking at the gate, and were refused entry."

> Laymen indeed could submit memoranda, reports, make speeches and take part in the council's debates, but they were not allowed to vote except in so far as they were delegates of Kings who were not of course merely laymen; in so far the old theocratic-descending point of view was applied once again.[115]

Or as J.B. Morrall had put it when expressing similar sentiments a few years earlier, the early fifteenth-century conciliar thinkers "were all strict believers in clerical monopoly of church government," and the conciliar theory itself was "still inseparably wedded to the orthodox hierarchical conception of authority as coming from above rather than below." As a result, "all the ingenuity of thinkers even of Gerson's calibre could not give the representative principle, based essentially on delegation from below, its full expression."[116]

It would be easy enough to take exception to this assessment of the fifteenth-century councils. At Basel, voting rights were extended in unprecedented degree to members of the lower clergy and it is implausible to dismiss the grant of a vote to lay ambassadors simply as an acknowledgment of the allegedly clerical status of their royal or princely masters. But Ullmann's remarks and those of Morrall were addressed to the theoretical formulations of the conciliarists and not merely to their alleged failure to translate theory into practice. That lag in practice, they implied, was but the reflection of the internal incoherence of the theory itself. The conciliarists were unable fully to escape the gravitational attraction of "the old theocratic-descending point of view." What they did, Ullmann claimed, "was

---

[115] Walter Ullmann, *Principles of Government and Politics in the Middle Ages* (2nd ed., London, 1966), pp. 288–315; *idem., A History of Political Thought in the Middle Ages* (Harmondsworth, Middlx., 1965), pp. 219–25, 313–14. For an earlier and fuller analysis of these and J.B. Morrall's affiliated claims, though not of those advanced later by J.P. Canning and Cary J. Nederman, see Oakley, "Figgis, Constance and the Divines of Paris," 376–86. For the background to Ullman's treatment of conciliar thinking in particular and medieval constitutionalism in general, see Francis Oakley, "Celestial Hierarchies Revisited: Walter Ullmann's Vision of Medieval Politics," *Past and Present*, LX (1973), 3–48. See above, ch. 2.

[116] J.B. Morrall, *Political Thought in Medieval Times* (New York, 1962), pp. 126–27.

to refurbish the old episcopalist system under the cover of a progressive movement: stripped of its inessential paraphernalia, conciliarism was a late-medieval revival of episcopalism."[117] That being so, and given what Morrall called "the ambiguity inherent in the whole conciliar position,"[118] its place likewise in the history of political thought can only be an ambiguous one. Nor should the eagerness of the early-modern constitutionalists and resistance theorists to evoke the conciliar precedent encourage us to overlook that fact. Conciliarist ideas may well have influenced such theorists but the latter, Ullmann insisted, did not swallow their conciliarism whole. Instead, they selected from among the conciliar materials handed down to them and chose to emphasize "only one strand of conciliarist thought."[119] And even then, if a forceful argument recently advanced by Cary J. Nederman is correct, they read those selected materials anachronistically, rein-terpreting them "selectively and in accordance with their own par-ticular problems and assumptions."[120]

The issues these criticisms raise are exceedingly intricate. As they clearly impinge directly on Figgis's third influence claim, they render the assessment of its validity a rather more complicated affair than that of the two preceding. Complex and taxing, it may be, but not impossible. And I would suggest that it can best be approached by posing four questions.

First, did the restriction on voting rights at the fifteenth-century councils really witness to some fundamental ambiguity in conciliar theory itself, signalling that what the conciliarists were engaged in was nothing more, in essence, than a "revival of episcopalism?" Secondly, what aspects of conciliar theorizing and practice were the seventeenth-century parliamentarians or, for that matter, their sixteenth-century

---

[117] Ullmann, *Principles of Government*, p. 314; cf. *idem, History of Political Thought*, pp. 223–25.

[118] Morrall, *Political Thought in Medieval Times*, p. 128.

[119] Quoting here Ullmann's review of Oakley, *The Political Thought of Pierre d'Ailly*, in *Renaissance News*, XVIII (No. 4, 1965), 305–7.

[120] An allegation made with specific reference to the use made of Gerson's ideas but as part of a sweeping dismissal of the pertinence to the shaping of early-modern constitutionalism of conciliar theory in particular and medieval ecclesiology in general. See Cary J. Nederman, "Conciliarism and Constitutionalism: Jean Gerson and Medieval Political Thought," *History of European Ideas*, XII (No. 3, 1990), 189–209 (at 189–92). For a rebuttal, see Francis Oakley, "Nederman, Gerson, Conciliar Theory and Constitutionalism: *Sed Contra*," *History of Political Thought*, XVI (No. 1, 1995), 1–19.

monarchomach predecessors invoking? Thirdly, why was it, after all, if the conciliar precedent was unhelpfully ambiguous, that they insisted on flourishing it, knowing (as they had to) that it could expose them also to the damaging charge of crypto-popery? Fourthly, in evoking the conciliar experience and exploiting the ideas of the conciliarists was their understanding historically accurate, or were they reading those theorists anachronistically, reinterpreting their thinking "selectively" through the distorting lens interposed by their own later "problems and assumptions?" I will address each of these questions in turn.

First, it should be noted that conciliar theory possessed no monolithic unity.[121] It is embedded in a vast body of writing produced under differing circumstances (political and diplomatic as well as strictly ecclesiastical), across a period stretching from the early-fourteenth to the mid-sixteenth centuries, by authors representing several different vocations (theologian, canonist, curial official) and, when they made their particular conciliarist pronouncements, serving in differing capacities (cardinals, bishops, representatives of princes, kings, universities and religious orders). Even if we limit ourselves to the Parisian conciliarists on whom Skinner concentrates and whose names crop up so frequently in the works of the seventeenth-century English controversialists, we will encounter important shades of difference in their respective positions. The matter of voting rights affords a good illustration of that fact. Thus whereas Mair does not discuss voting rights and makes no mention of lay representation in general councils,[122] d'Ailly, Gerson and Almain do both. But while Gerson insists that the right to vote be enjoyed by the lower clergy as well as by the bishops and that no member of the faithful be refused a hearing, he is willing to see the laity restricted to a merely consultative or advisory capacity—though it is important to note that he sees nothing permanent or necessary about such a restriction.[123] Almain

---

[121] A point emphasized much of late by Guiseppe Alberigo, *Chiesa conciliare: Identità e significato del conciliarismo* (Brescia, 1981), esp. p. 17, and Fasolt, *Council and Hierarchy*, esp. pp. 318–19.

[122] He defines a general council as follows: "A council ... is a congregation [of representatives] drawn from every hierarchical rank whose concern it is, summoned by those to whom that duty pertains, to deal according to the common intention with matters concerning the general welfare of Christendom" ("Concilium ... est congregatio ex omni statu hierarchico, quorum interest, convocata ab iis quibus incumbit, ad tractandum communi intentione, de utilitate publica Christiana") Mair, *Disputatio de auctoritate concilii*, Dupin, II, 1132.

[123] Just as in some periods, he says, prelates have been elected by the whole people

follows him faithfully in this,[124] but d'Ailly is a good deal more forth-coming. Though the unlearned and those of the lowest ranks are not specifically summoned to the council, no Catholic, he insists, should be excluded. Nor should kings, princes, or their representatives be denied a vote, any more than should doctors of theology or of canon or civil law, for they are all men with authority over the people.[125]

The selective procedures suggested here are by no means demo-cratic, but it would surely be anachronistic to expect them to be so. If that is what Morrall means when he speaks of giving the repre-sentative principle its "full expression" (and his comparison with the make-up of the House of Commons prior to the Great Reform Bill of 1832 suggests that it is),[126] then the conciliar theorists undoubt-edly fall short of the mark. But then, so too, of course, would the Estates in sixteenth-century France and the parliament in seven-teenth-century England. As d'Ailly put it, "what touches all must be approved by all, or at least by many and the more notable ones."[127] An aristocratic principle of selection is clearly at work, but the impor-tant thing to recognize is that it is not predicated upon the posses-sion of hierarchical powers of a sacerdotal nature. That is the factor fundamental to any episcopalist position, but clearly not the one d'Ailly has in mind, for he pointedly insists that doctors of theology

---

and clergy and in others by the clergy alone, similarly the council, if it so desires, is at liberty to extend or restrict the vote in accordance with the needs of the times: Jean Gerson, *De potestate ecclesiastica, ibid.*, 250; cf. his *Sermo: "Ambulate dum lucem habetis," ibid.*, 973.

[124] Jacques Almain, *Tractatus de auctoritate ecclesiae*, Dupin, II, 1011–12, *idem, Expositio . . . de potestate ecclesiastica et laica, ibid.*, 1067, and *idem, Quaestio resumptiva . . . de dominio naturali, civili et ecclesiastico, ibid.*, 973.

[125] Pierre d'Ailly, *Oratio de officio imperatoris*, Dupin, II, 921, and *Disputatio de jure suffragii quibus competat*, in Herman von der Hardt ed., *Rerum concilii oecumenici Constantiensis* (6 vols., Leipzig, 1697), II, 225–27; cf. d'Ailly, *Tractatus de ecclesiastica potestate*, Dupin, II, 941. See d'Ailly, *Tractatus de materia concilii generalis*, ed. Oakley, in *The Political Thought of Pierre d'Ailly*, Appendix III, pp. 244–345 (at 268, 272–73), and cf. my comment, *ibid.*, pp. 152–54.

[126] See Morrall, *Political Thought in Medieval Times*, pp. 128–29, where he com-ments that for Gerson "the presence of the laity is not necessary for they are rep-resented in the Council by the clergy; the argument is reminiscent of the theory of 'virtual' representation in the pre-1832 British House of Commons as put for-ward by those who opposed the reform of that institution." For a succinct analy-sis of the complex notion of representation involved in conciliar thinking, see Brian Tierney, "The Idea of Representation in the Medieval Councils of the West", *Concilium*, XIX (1983), 25–30.

[127] Pierre d'Ailly, *Additio circa tertiam viam supratactam*, in Franz Ehrle ed., *Martin de Alpartils Chronica Actitatorum* (Paderborn, 1906), p. 506.

or of either of the two laws have greater authority over the Christian people and, therefore, a better claim to the vote than ignorant or merely titular bishops or archbishops.[128]

Secondly, and as we have argued, during the late-sixteenth and much of the seventeenth century English people had become better acquainted with the history of the fifteenth-century councils and the writings of the conciliarists than at *any* previous time—the fifteenth century not excluded. And they evoked that history and/or those writings for a variety of purposes: to document from unimpeachably Catholic testimonies the obvious corruption of the old Church and the concomitant need for reform (thus Sir John Hayward and Richard Field); or triumphantly to underscore the obvious contradictions and instability manifest in the Catholic doctrinal tradition (thus Bilson, Sutcliffe); or to debunk the notion that a pontiff who was himself capable of heresy and subject to judgment and deposition could plausibly lay claim to a power to judge kings and declare them deposed (thus Sheldon and James I himself); or, yet again—and this time with a degree of genuine sympathy on the part of those of Calvinist as well as those of Catholic commitment—to help make the case for an ecclesiology of episcopalist or conciliar inclination, or, alternatively, to strengthen the argument for a non-episcopal and synodal form of church government (thus William Warmington, Robert Widdrington, Marc Antonio de Dominis, Robert Parker and Samuel Rutherford).[129] With the exception, however, of Samuel Rutherford, whose ecclesiological sympathies were of distinctly conciliar bent,[130] the parliamentarians showed little interest in such ideological maneuvers. Nor, perhaps more surprisingly, did they seek to exploit the quasi-oligarchic strand (with its evocation of the idea of mixed government) that had been present already in the ecclesiology of John of Paris, had found some resonance in Gerson's conciliar thought, and had been a prominent feature of the conciliarism of d'Ailly, Zabarella and Nicholas of Cusa.[131] Instead, they focused almost exclusively on the precedent established by the central conciliar assertion

---

[128] D'Ailly, *Disputatio de jure suffragii quibus competat*, in von der Hardt ed., *Rerum concilii oecumenici*, II, 225–27.

[129] For a fuller discussion, along with references to the pertinent works of these authors, see Oakley, "Constance, Basel, and the Two Pisas," 30–31.

[130] Samuel Rutherford, *The Due right of Presbyters, or, A Peacable Plea for the Government of the Church of Scotland* (London, 1644), pp. 332–33, 336–37, 340–43.

[131] For which, see the analysis in Oakley, *Coucil over Pope?*, pp. 61–67.

of the ultimate jurisdictional superiority to the pope of the general council acting as representative of the universal church, and on the historic vindication of that superiority by the conciliar judgment and deposition of popes at Pisa, Constance and Basel.[132] And that fact, that selectivity, speaks to our third question.

Neither the English, French and Scottish resistance theorists of the sixteenth century nor the English parliamentarians of the seventeenth appear to have found anything at all ambiguous about the central strand of conciliar thinking upon which they placed so much emphasis. Nor did the French Huguenots appear to have lost any sleep over their indebtedness to scholastic predecessors for their revolutionary ideas. Quite the contrary, in fact. If Skinner is correct, they may even have seen it as a distinct advantage. For it helped them in their attempt "to neutralize as far as possible the hostile Catholic majority by showing them the extent to which revolutionary political actions could be legitimated in terms of impeccably Catholic beliefs."[133] That was far from being the case, of course, with their seventeenth-century English successors. "In Stuart England there was much political capital to be made from convicting one's opponents of popery,"[134] and the sensitivity of the parliamentarians to the charge of crypto-popery and even more of Jesuitry is reflected in their anxious attempts to deflect its force. In relation to the despised doctrine of popular sovereignty Maxwell had charged that "Puritan and Jesuite in this, not only consent and concurre, but like *Herod* and *Pilate* are reconciled to crucify the Lord's anointed."[135] To that Rutherford hotly (if not very effectively) retorted that Maxwell, having taken "unlearned paines, to prove that Gerson, Occam, Jac[obus] de Almaine, Parisian Doctors maintained these same grounds anent the peoples power over Kings in the case of Tyranny [as did the Jesuits]," had by so doing given "himselfe the lye" and inadvertently demonstrated that

---

[132] Cf. Rueger, "Gerson, the Conciliar Movement, and the Right of Resistance," 483: "[T]he conciliar assertion of supremacy and the conciliar deposition of the Pope appeared to offer a unique example of a seemingly successful application of this universal medieval principle [i.e. the right of resistance to a ruler turned tyrant] to the only form of medieval monarchy which was founded exclusively on divine right and excluded the idea of consent — the Papacy. At least this is what to Buchanan seemed to be the chief lesson of the Conciliar Movement."

[133] Skinner, "The Origins of the Calvinist Theory of Revolution," 325.

[134] Johan Sommerville, *Politics and Ideology in England: 1603–1640* (London, 1986), p. 46.

[135] Maxwell, *Sacro-sancta Regum Majestas*, p. 3.

"we have not this Doctrine from Jesuites."[136] But if not from Jesuits, clearly still from papists. And that charge Bridge was forced to shrug off with the rejoinder that "Reason is good wherever we finde it; neither would *Abraham* refuse the use of the Well because Abimalech's men had used it, no more will we refuse good reason, because Papists have used it."[137] A reasonably robust stance, and it prompts me to ask whereof that "good reason" consisted.

In this connection, it is important to emphasize the degree to which the seventeenth-century opponents of absolutism in England confronted a new orthodoxy that had begun to establish itself, especially among Anglican churchmen, long before the end of the Elizabethan era. Johan Sommerville has argued that when Richard Hooker in the 1590s had evoked the commonplace idea that the royal authority flowed by natural law from the consent of the realm, "such ideas were [in fact] already . . . going out of vogue among the higher clergy."[138] A new "divine-right" orthodoxy had begun to develop which, despite that perhaps misleading label, continued the practice of grounding governmental authority in the natural law rather than in the revealed word of God.[139] At the same time, however, it inserted a sharp distinction between the *power* of the king, which was seen to be derived solely and directly from God, and his *title*, which might derive from designation by the people. In framing this type of designation theory, Anglican divines had not hesitated to adduce by way of analogy the fact the pope claimed to hold his power immediately from God alone, even though as an individual he owed his title to a human electoral process. Thus William Barret in 1612, John Buckeridge in 1614, Robert Bolton in 1639—this last insisting against Bellarmine's derivation of royal authority from the community that

> the question is not by what meanes, whether by hereditary succession or election, or any other humane forme, a Prince comes into his king-dome, but whether by the ordinance of GOD we ought to obey him when he is established. . . . [T]he Pope is hoisted into his chaire of pestilence, by the election of the Cardinals or worse meanes, and yet that hinders not our adversaries from holding it a divine ordinance.[140]

---

[136] Rutherford, *Lex Rex*, p. 418.
[137] Bridge, *The Truths of the Times Vindicated*, p. 49.
[138] Sommerville, *Politics and Ideology in England: 1603–1640*, p. 3.
[139] *Ibid.*, p. 12.
[140] W. Barret, *Jus Regis, seu De absoluto et independenti secularium principum dominio et*

This being so, and the opponents of the new orthodoxy in the period leading up to the Civil War having lost, in effect, the ideological initiative, many hesitated to claim in theory for a parliament increasingly bypassed in practice any unambiguous right of resistance to the king, let alone a right of deposition.[141] Only the more robust among those opponents were willing to push forward into what had now, in the past half century, become more radical territory and to invoke against the king the inherent power of the community as wielded through its representatives in parliament. And when they did, secular "parliamentary theory in the later Middle Ages not having kept abreast of practice" and "ecclesiastical conciliarism . . . [having] . . . provided a general theory of constitutions for use by aspiring parliamentarians," it is understandable, as Antony Black has recently asserted, that some among them should "look back . . . on conciliarism as the closest historical precedent for what they were trying to do."[142] But that brings us to our fourth and final question: were these parliamentarians (and their sixteenth-century predecessors), as Figgis believed, correct in their judgment about that precedent? Or were they guilty, in effect, of understanding history anachronistically? And, if the latter, we of course as historians should know better than to indulge their distorted readings.

Given the range and complexity of the vast ocean of literature that it is customary to label as conciliarist, the question may appear more formidable than it in fact is. Central, after all, to the pertinence and force of the conciliar analogy when evoked by constitutionalists, parliamentarians and advocates of legitimate resistance against kings turned tyrant was the assumption that the Church was, as Figgis put

---

obsequio eis debito (Basel, 1612), p. 28; Buckeridge, *De potestate papae*, p. 291; Robert Bolton, *Two Sermons Preached at Northampton at Two Severall Assises There* (London, 1639), sermon 1, p. 16. For a Catholic endorsement of that view, see R. Sheldon, *Certain General Reasons, Proving the Lawfulnesse of the Oath of Allegiance* (London, 1611), pp. 11–12.

[141] See Julian H. Franklin, *John Locke and the Theory of Sovereignty: Mixed Monarchy and the Right of Resistance in the Political Thought of the English Revolution* (Cambridge, 1978), ch. 2, pp. 22–49. Such, indeed, was the hesitancy and confusion in the thinking of the parliamentary leaders on this score that, when the Civil War finally broke out, "they claimed to be fighting for the corporate whole of king-and-parliament against the erring person of Charles"—thus Brian Tierney, *Religion, Law, and the Growth of Constitutional Thought: 1150–1650* (Cambridge, 1982), p. 83.

[142] Or again, "The poverty of theory about secular parliaments contrasts with the wealth of ideas about the representative or constitutional role of councils in the late medieval church"—see Black, *Political Thought in Europe: 1250–1450*, pp. 166, 169, 178. His whole chapter on parliamentary representation (pp. 162–85) is excellent.

it, "one of a class, political societies," and that as a political community it possessed by natural law the ultimate right (as, for that matter, did any natural body) to gather up its resources and exert its inherent power to prevent its own ruin.[143] And although, as we have just seen, they themselves could not on occasion resist the temptation to deploy the papal analogy for their own purposes, central to the response of the royalists was the insistence that the ecclesiastical analogy was invalid, because the papal monarchy was founded in grace not in nature, because it was elective not hereditary, and/or because the general council by virtue of a known canon law possessed a greater authority over a pope than did the estates of any realm over their king.

Now it should be noted that this ideological stand-off is the mirror-image of one that had occurred already during the conciliar epoch itself. Embedded in the conciliarist literature are countless examples and analogies drawn this time from the political arrangements of the *secular* world,[144] invoked, of course, to help elaborate the case for the supreme authority of the general council within the Church. The much-cited speech of the Bishop of Burgos at Basel in 1431 simply represents a particularly striking example, and it should be noted that this conciliarist willingness to rely on secular analogies endured right down to the seventeenth century. Thus Major and Almain in the early-sixteenth century, who came close to treating the ecclesiastical and secular polities univocally; thus Sir Thomas More in the 1530s, when he argued that "counsayles do represent the whole chyrch . . . as a parliament representeth ye hole realme;" thus Paolo Sarpi in 1606, when, defending against Bellarmine's aspersions the orthodoxy of Gerson's conciliarist commitments (and following up on other secular political analogies), he noted that it did not follow from God's having "placed a King to governe a Kingdome"

---

[143] See, for example, Bridge, *The Wounded Conscience Cured*, p. 46.

[144] For some representative passages from the Parisian conciliarists see Jean Gerson, *Tractatus de unitate ecclesiae*, in Gerson, *Opera Omnia*, ed. Dupin, II, 114–15; *idem, Sermo: "Prosperum iter faciet"*, ibid., 279; *idem, De auferabilitate . . . papae*, ibid., 216; *idem, De potestate eccelesiastica*, ibid., 240, 253–55; Almain, *Quaestio resumptiva . . . de dominio naturali, civili et ecclesiastico*, ibid., 970, *idem*, Expositio *circa decisiones Magistri Guillielmi Occam . . . de potestate ecclesiastica et laica*, ibid., 1024, 1075–76, 1107, *idem*, Tractatus *de auctoritate ecclesiae*, ibid., 991, 1009. For John Mair, see Oakley, "From Constance to 1688," 13–19, for Pierre d'Ailly, *idem, The Political Thought of Pierre d'Ailly*, esp. pp. 52–54; for the conciliarists of Basel, see Antony Black, *Monarchy and Community: Political Ideas in the Later Conciliar Controversy: 1430–1450* (Cambridge, 1970), Part I, pp. 7–52.

that that king "is superior to his whol kingdom assembled together."[145]

Moreover, and as I have argued elsewhere,[146] the conciliarists who had pursued that line of march had usually focused their attention also upon the sector wherein ecclesiastical power is at its closest, in quality if not in purpose, to secular governmental authority. When they spoke of the Church as the *corpus Christi* or *corpus Christi mysticum*, those expressions had lost for them the rich sacramental associations present in the earlier Patristic usage and had acquired in their place corporative and political associations. Instead of the parallel being drawn with the sacramental Body of Christ and *corpus mysticum* being taken to denote the incorporation of the faithful with Christ in a mysterious community of salvation, the analogy was drawn now from natural bodies or bodies in general and the expression taken to denote a "moral and political [as opposed to real or physical] body." Further than that, of the traditional categories of ecclesiastical power, it was not the power of order (*potestas ordinis*), the truly sacerdotal power, on which these conciliarists laid their stress. That power, they said, pertained quintessentially to the Eucharist, which they designated not as the mystical but as the "true body of Christ" (*corpus Christi verum*). Their own concern lay rather with jurisdiction (*potestas jurisdictionis*), for that was the power that pertained to the *corpus Christi mysticum*, and especially with its public, coercive and unambiguously nonsacramental and *political* subdivision—the *potestas jurisdictionis in foro externo*, which d'Ailly referred to simply as "the governmental power" (*potestas regiminis*).[147] That was the modality of ecclesiastical power they had in mind when they made their case for the superiority of council over pope. And they grounded that case not simply in Scripture, or church history, or ecclesiastical custom, or canon law (though of course they did all of those things), not simply, that is, in the rights, privileges, customs, and laws proper to the *communitas fidelium*, but also in the mandates of the natural law itself, the law that pertained to the community of mankind.

---

[145] Sir Thomas More, *The Confutation of Tyndale's Answer* in *The Complete Works of St. Thomas More*, ed. Louis A. Schuster *et al.* (20 vols., New Haven, 1963–87), VIII, Part 1, 146/15–21; cf. Brian Gogan, *The Common Corps of Christendom: Ecclesiological Themes in the Writings of Sir Thomas More* (Leiden, 1982), pp. 290–99. Sarpi, *Apologia per le opposizioni fatte dall'illustrissimo e reverendissimo signor cardinale Bellarminio*, ed. Busnelli and Gambarin, III, 128–29. I cite the English version, *Apology or Apologeticall Answere*, pp. 74–75.

[146] Oakley, "Figgis, Constance, and the Divines of Paris," 368–86.

[147] Pierre d'Ailly, *Utrum Petri ecclesia lege reguletur*, in Dupin, I, 667–68.

So far, so good. But, then, not all conciliarists framed their case in this way. A.J. Black, Joachim Stieber, and, more recently, J.H. Burns have all stressed the complex interaction of ideology and diplomacy that led in the 1430s and 1440s to a vigorous papal counteroffensive involving the damaging portrayal of the Baselian conciliarist ecclesiology, and especially the version advocated by John of Segovia, as "constituting a subversive, even revolutionary challenge to the very principle of monarchical authority . . . in the temporal as well as in the spiritual realm." And, further than that, a counteroffensive "propagated, not only in the context of theoretical discussion, but also, and even more vigorously, in serious and energetic diplomatic efforts to establish a monarchical alliance with temporal rulers against the radical attack."[148] Somewhat less emphasis has been placed, however, on the degree to which, partly in response to that counteroffensive and in an attempt to deflect the charge that the so-called "democratic" ideas of the conciliarists posed a threat to every form of monarchy, some of those conciliarists (Panormitanus, Andrew of Escobar, Thomas Strempinski and, above all, John of Segovia) were led to frame their conciliar theories in such a way as to render them *less* relevant, or even *irrelevant*, to matters political. And in this they were followed in part by such early-sixteenth century conciliar thinkers as Pierre Cordier in Paris and Giovanni Gozzadini in Italy.[149]

Indicative of this doctrinal shift is the fact that appeals to natural law, though not entirely lacking, play a less crucial role in the arguments of these Baselian conciliarists than in those of their predecessors and pertain often to issues of merely tributary nature. Similarly, the crucial distinction between the powers of order and jurisdiction is less insistently and less effectively evoked, even in contexts where it would have helped clarify and advance the line of argument. The terms *corpus mysticum* and *corpus politicum*, instead of being used in the earlier conciliarist fashion as synonyms, are contrasted and employed in such a way as to distinguish the universal Church from all other communities in precisely those dimensions most relevant to the strict conciliar theory and to set it apart from political societies in

---

[148] Burns, *Lordship, Kingship and Empire*, p. 9; cf. Black, *Monarchy and Community*, esp. ch. 3, pp. 85–129, and *idem, Council and Commune: The Conciliar Movement and the Fifteenth-Century Heritage* (London, 1979).

[149] I draw here and in what follows on the line of argument developed in my "Natural Law, the *Corpus Mysticum*, and Consent," to which reference may be made for the pertinent texts and for some extracts from the unprinted manuscripts.

general. And the distinction now drawn between the Church as a "mystical" and as a "political" body is aligned with the familiar distinction between the whole membership of the universal Church considered "collectively" and "distributively"—that is, as a single, corporate body and as a mere aggregation of individuals (*omnes ut universitas/ omnes ut singuli*).

Thus, in formulations like that of John of Segovia (Black describes them as constituting "the essence of Baslean Conciliarism"),[150] the Church assembled in general council was identified with the *corpus mysticum* and papal sovereignty seen in contrast as pertaining "to a somewhat lower, merely 'political' order of things."[151] Parallels between Church and secular polity were to be admitted as valid only insofar as the Church was itself regarded as a *corpus politicum*, a collection of particular churches and individual members ruled in accordance with human judgment and reason, the governance of which, like the governance of any kingdom, God assists by a "general" rather than a "special influence." But the Church congregated in a general council was to be regarded rather as a *corpus mysticum* animated and protected by divine grace and not dependent on a merely natural judgment. As a result, it was precisely to the Church as a mystical body directed by the Holy Spirit, as a unique community in which Christ ruled by a special and not merely general influence, that the Baselian arguments for the superiority of council to pope pertained.[152] Their relevance, then, to the mundane realm of secular principalities and powers was understandably remote and had properly to be perceived as such. And had the later constitutionalists and advocates of legitimate resistance to kings turned tyrant relied on these arguments they would, indeed, have been forced to place their emphasis on what was only one facet of a complex and perhaps ambiguous position.

Whether, in invoking the conciliar analogy, they were or were not guilty of an anachronistic reading of the conciliar past depends, then,

---

[150] Black, *Monarchy and Community*, p. 14.

[151] Thus A.J. Black speaking with specific reference to the formulation of Heimerich van de Velde (= de Campo, d. 1460), in his "The Realist Ecclesiology of Heimerich van de Velde," in Edmond J.M. van Eijl ed., *Facultas S. Theologiae Lovanensis, 1432–1797: bijdragen tot haar geschiedenis* (Louvain, 1977), 273–91.

[152] See, esp., John of Segovia's speech at Mainz in 1441, *Deutsche Reichstagsakten, Aeltere Reihe*, ed. H. Weigel *et al.* (17 vols., Gotha-Stuttgart, 1898–1939), XV, 648–759 (at 682–83). For a discussion of this and of related texts, see Black, *Monarchy and Community*, pp. 14–15, 45–47, and 109–12.

on the particular past they have in mind—on the specific strain of conciliarism that informs their understanding of the fifteenth-century conciliar experience. With the monarchomachs of the sixteenth century, who refrained from citing individual conciliar thinkers, the question is not readily susceptible of answer—though his teacher, John Mair, had clearly had a hand in shaping Buchanan's political thinking and *may* have had some impact also on that of Ponet.[153] But with their seventeenth-century English successors we are on much firmer ground. The range of proto-conciliarist and conciliarist literature cited by the English writers of the late-sixteenth and seventeenth centuries is admittedly quite broad. Despite Foxe's inclusion, via his translation of Aeneas Sylvius Piccolomini, of one of John of Segovia's speeches in his *Book of Martyrs*, I do not believe I have come across a single reference to Segovia in the seventeenth-century writers, and references to Marsiglio of Padua, though by no means lacking, do not appear with great frequency. One hears much more of Aeneas Sylvius, Dietrich of Niem, William of Ockham, Nicholas of Cusa, Panormitanus, and Francesco Zabarella. But it is the members of the "School of Sorbonne" who top the list, from John of Paris, via d'Ailly and Gerson, to Almain and Mair. It is almost exclusively from these latter conciliarists, the so-called "Sorbonnists" or "divines of Paris," whose works Richer had recently made conveniently available, that the mid-century parliamentarians are accused by their royalist opponents of having drawn their benighted ideas. And it is upon the authority of those particular conciliarists that they themselves do in fact rely.

That being so, there was nothing anachronistic about their conviction that the fifteenth-century conciliar experience represented a valuable historical precedent that could help advance the case for legitimate resistance that they themselves were struggling to make. The questions which Collingwood viewed it as essential to answer if assertions of historical influence were to reach beyond the superficial pose, in this case, no insurmountable obstacle. Figgis was correct, after all, in his claim that the Parisian conciliarists had given a notably universal expression to the principles underlying the medieval constitutional tradition, and that that notably universal expression was destined to take on a heightened significance in a later era when absolute or quasi-absolute monarchy was coming to be regarded as

---

[153] See Oakley, "From Constance to 1688," 11–31; Hudson, *John Ponet (1516?–1556) Advocate of Limited Monarchy*, pp. 171–72.

the only civilized form of government, when representative assemblies in much of Europe had entered upon a period of decline, and when such traditional medieval limitations on monarchical power were coming to be dismissed as "inefficient clogs upon the wheels of government, not merely wrong but stupid."[154] As John Ponet himself had pointed out "by this lawe [of nature] and argumentes of the Cannonistes and example of deprivacion of a Pope are all clokes (wherewith Popes, bishoppes, priests, Kaisers and Kinges use to defend their iniquity) utterly taken away."[155]

V

Whatever its original intent, the phrase "epistemological hypochondria" (and I believe we owe it to Ernest Gellner) serves well to catch the mood of uneasiness, hesitancy, cognitive timidity even, characteristic of so much of our contemporary intellectual discourse, as also our concomitant unwillingness as we go about our intellectual endeavors even "faintly to trust the larger hope." As a subfield of one of the most central of humanistic disciplines, history of ideas has not proved immune to this general syndrome. In its more traditional forms at least, it has been dismissed as "shopsoiled" and "simpleminded,"[156] derided as "a kind of paper chase of ideas back through the ages . . . usually ending up with Aristotle and Plato,"[157] and, in what has been (improperly) represented as constituting its Lovejovian variant, condemned as resting "on a fundamental philosophical mistake."[158] In comparison with such eye-catching frontal assaults, the

---

[154] Figgis, *Political Thought from Gerson to Grotius*, pp. 60–61.

[155] Ponet, *A Shorte Treatise of Politicke Power*, in Hudson, pp. [104]–[105].

[156] Thus Michel Foucault, *Les mots et les choses* (Paris, 1966), translated as *The Order of Things* (New York, 1970), p. 275, and *idem, L'Archaeologie du Savoir* (Paris, 1969), translated by A.M. Sheridan as *The Archeology of Knowledge* (New York, 1972), pp. 138–39.

[157] Thus Lawrence Stone, *The Past and the Present* (Boston, 1981), pp. 85–86.

[158] Thus Skinner, "Meaning and Understanding in the History of Ideas," in Tully ed., *Meaning and Context*, 54–55, having previously said: "My concern here . . . is not empirical but conceptual: not to insist that such [Lovejovian] histories can sometimes go wrong, but that they can never go right." Viewing this assessment as based on a full-scale misunderstanding of Arthur O. Lovejoy's distinctive historical project, I have entered a sharp dissent to Skinner's claims. See Francis Oakley, *Omnipotence, Covenant, and Order: An Excursion in the History of Ideas from Abelard to Leibniz* (Ithaca and London, 1984), pp. 27–40.

nagging worries expressed in the past few years about the use of the influence model in the history of political thought amount to no more than desultory skirmishes on the margins of the far-flung battleground of cognition. And they are less likely, I would predict, to eventuate in any full-scale abandonment of the approach itself than to induce a helpful intensification of the historian's methodological self-consciousness in pursuing it. When, as in the case study concluded above, the preconditions which Skinner and Herméren properly stipulate can indeed be met and adequate response made to the further questions which Collingwood had earlier posed, then the currently prevalent (and usually unexamined) squeamishness about the use of the influence model should be easy enough to overcome. On this matter, it is long since time for historians to eschew cumbersome and uneasy circumlocutions (they fool nobody anyway), and to liberate the word "influence" itself from the veritable embarrassment of quotation marks that has come to surround it. However sloppily the influence concept may conceivably have been invoked in the past, it has (as it always has had) an important and probably indispensable role to play in the history of ideas. It should be permitted to play it.

CHAPTER SIX

COMPLEXITIES OF CONTEXT: GERSON, BELLARMINE, SARPI, RICHER AND THE VENETIAN INTERDICT OF 1606–1607

> You Papists, though your brawles be endlesse one with another, Canonists against Schoole-men; Franciscans against Dominicks; Nominals against Reals; *Thomas* against *Lumbard; Scotus* against *Thomas; Occam* against *Scotus; Alliacensis* against *Occam; Peter Scot* against *Catharine; Catharine* against *Caietan; Caietan* against *Pighius*; Jesuites against Priests, and Priests against Jesuits: yet forsooth these dogs and cats are all of one Cage, they are all members of the Romish Church.
>
> William Middleton, *Papisto-Mastix or the Protestants Religion defended* (London, 1606)

In this oddly engaging and coincidentally timely effusion, Middleton was concerned, of course, to identify, postulate or construct a unifying context of deplorably shared commitment within which the conflicting views and activities of a seemingly disparate array of historical agents could properly be understood. And in this, had not the practitioners of what is sometimes referred to as "the new history of political thought" themselves proscribed the use of the word in that way, Middleton might well have been said to have "anticipated" their own later preoccupation with contextualization.[1] In focusing our attention over the past quarter of century and more on the

---

[1] See Quentin Skinner, "Meaning and Understanding in the History of Ideas," *History and Theory*, VIII (1969), 3–53; reprinted in James Tully ed., *Meaning and Context: Quentin Skinner and his Critics* (Cambridge, 1988), pp. 29–67, at p. 35 where he derides the practice of "pointing out earlier 'anticipations' of later doctrines" as a kind of "historical absurdity." Fair enough, so long as one steers clear of an excessive degree of literalism likely to deprive one of an eminently useful piece of shorthand which, in the constructing of historical narratives, it would be cumbersome to do without. (As Skinner himself appears, willy-nilly, to have discovered—see David Boucher, "On Schlar's and Franklin's Reviews of Skinner," *Political Theory*, VIII [No. 3, 1980], 406–408—speaking of Skinner's *Foundations of Modern Political Thought* [2 vols., Cambridge, 1978]: "In searching for the origins of the modern

difficulty of wresting genuinely *historical* meanings from the texts handed down to us from the past, these particular representatives of the linguistic turn in the study of the history of ideas have persistently emphasized the importance of reading such texts in their historical (and especially linguistic and ideological) contexts.[2] Straightforward enough, it might seem, but it is one of the intriguing and fruitful byproducts of this approach that it has served also to draw to our (perhaps reluctant) attention the less obvious difficulties and complexities attaching to the very notion of context itself.[3] It is with this latter issue that I shall be concerned in what follows.

Dominick LaCapra has well reminded us that if, in pursuit of the interpretation of texts, we wish to address the matter of context, we must begin by recognizing that "contexts of interpretation are at least threefold: those of writing, reception, and critical reading."[4] Even if, endorsing the preoccupation with authorial intentionality characteristic of the "new historians," we concentrate on the first of those contexts, the picture is complex enough. And not least of all because such contexts "are encountered through the 'medium' of specific texts or practices, and they must [themselves] be reconstituted on the basis of textual evidence."[5] In one of the earliest (and

conception of the state, . . . Skinner is constantly looking for signs in earlier works of later doctrines as if they are somehow immanent. [But] instead of using the language of 'anticipations' he favors that of 'hints'").

[2] Skinner's principal expositions of his position are helpfully reprinted (along with those of some of his critics and his own lengthy reply to those critics) in Tully ed., *Meaning and Context: Quentin Skinner and his Critics.* Cf. for related (though by no means identical) approaches, John Dunn, "The Identity of the History of Ideas," *Philosophy,* XLIII (April, 1968), 85–104. J.G.A. Pocock, *Politics, Language and Time: Essays on Political Thought and History* (New York, 1971), pp. 3–41. For history and "the linguistic" turn in general, see John E. Toews, "Intellectual History after the Linguistic Turn: The Autonomy of Meaning and the Irreducibility of Experience," *American Historical Review,* XCII (Oct., 1987), 879–907, and Dominick LaCapra, "History, Language, and Reading: Waiting for Crillon," *ibid.,* C (June, 1995), 799–828.

[3] A point, it should be noted, now readily conceded by Skinner himself. See his "A reply to my critics," in Tully ed., *Meaning and Context,* pp. 274–83. Cf. David Boucher, *Texts in Context: Revisionist Methods for Studying the History of Ideas* (Dordrecht, 1985), esp. pp. 214–218, 253–56.

[4] Dominick LaCapra, *History and Criticism* (Ithaca and London, 1985), pp. 127–28. He describes the context of writing as including "the intentions of the author as well as more immediate biographical, sociocultural, and political situations with their ideologies and discourses," as well as "discursive institutions such as traditions and genres."

[5] LaCapra, *History and Criticism,* p. 128, where he properly notes that "the difficulties in the process of inferentially reconstructing contexts on the basis of texts (in the large sense) are often obscured or repressed, especially when one is convinced that

most anguished) of critical responses to the type of linguistic and ideological contextualism proposed by Quentin Skinner, Parekh and Berki felt it necessary to insist that "context is not something obvious and given," but something that "has to be constructed, indeed, created by the commentator."[6] Reaffirming that point a decade later, David Boucher noted further that "the scale of [contextual] construction depends upon the historian and the lengths to which he is prepared to go in order to relate what may on the surface seem disparate utterances."[7] And he did so having confessed, in the course of commenting on a whole series of "new histories" of political thought inspired by Skinner's approach, that he simply could not "elicit any agreement from the literature on what a context actually is and how it is related to the texts."[8]

A gloomy confession, it may be, but it is one well-adapted to the role for which I wish to press it into service. Namely, that of setting the historiographic stage for the introduction of the very particular contextual tangle on which I propose in this essay to focus and which may serve, I believe, as a good illustration of the degree

---

a context or set of contexts must be a determinative force with full explanatory power." For a similar emphasis on the textual mediation of contexts, see also Charles Bernheimer, "The Anxieties of Comparison," in Bernheimer ed., *Comparative Literature in the Age of Multiculturalism* (Baltimore and London, 1995), p. 16, where commenting on apprehensions "that the positivities of context [might] be used to resolve the ambiguities of text," he observes that "contexts can be just as ambiguous as texts, from which given that contexts are to a large extent textually mediated their difference is not clearcut.

[6] Bhikhu Parekh and R.N. Berki, "The History of Ideas: A Critique of Quentin Skinner's Methodology," *Journal of the History of Ideas*, XXIV (No. 2, 1973), 163–84 (at 182).

[7] David Boucher, "New Histories of Political Thought for Old," *Political Studies*, XXXI (No. 1, 1983), 112–21 (at 117–8).

[8] He continues (117): "The methodology purports to offer a new type of contextualism. . . . Ideas form the context for ideas; therefore this form of contextualism also embodies a considerable measure of textualism. That is, the apparent meanings of texts, gleaned without knowing the intentions they embody are juxtaposed to construct the linguistic framework in terms of which the intentions of one or two prominent thinkers are inferred. But that leaves a lot of room for maneuver." Cf. Boucher, *Texts in Context*, pp. 255–56. For a critique of the efficacy of Skinner's form of contextualism when applied to the particular case of Hobbes, see Preston King, "The Theory of Context and the Case of Hobbes," in Preston King ed., *The History of Ideas: An Introduction to Method* (London, 1983), pp. 285–315. And for a more recent and full-scale onslaught on both what he calls the "hard linguistic contextualism" of Pocock and the "soft linguistic contextualism" of Skinner, see Mark Bevir's stimulating article, "The Errors of Linguistic Contextualism," *History and Theory*, XXXI (1992), 276–98.

to which the contexts we construct in our efforts to interpret historical texts determine what we see or (perhaps, more important) what we *fail to see* or to regard as noteworthy in those texts.

I

Although our own effort at contextualization will draw us back insistently as far as the fifteenth century, that effort is rendered somewhat problematic in that our story actually begins in Venice towards the end of April, 1606. But it does so with the anonymous publication, supposedly in Paris though in Italian translation, of two short treatises directed against the abuse of the power of ecclesiastical censure that were written almost two centuries previously by the great French theologian, Jean Gerson (1363–1429).[9] Their republication in the vernacular was the work of Paolo Sarpi (1552–1623), best remembered today as the great, acerbic historian of the Council of Trent but serving, at that time, in the official capacity of legal and theological adviser to the Venetian Republic. It was a move that constituted the opening shot in the great war of words and battle of the books occasioned by Pope Paul V's excommunication of the Venetian Doge and Senate and by his imposition of an interdict on all Venetian-ruled territories. Those censures, bruited already in 1605, had come to seem inevitable by mid-April, 1606, were to go formally into effect in May of that year, and were to remain in force until April, 1607.[10] For the Venetian Republic the experience of

---

[9] The tracts in question date to the Spring of 1418, either to the very last days of the Council of Constance or to the weeks immediately after its dissolution. They are entitled: *Resolutio circa materiam excommunicationum et irregularitatum* and *De sententia pastoris semper tenenda* and are printed in Palemon Glorieux ed., *Jean Gerson: Oeuvres complètes* (10 vols., Paris, 1960–73), VI, 291–96. The Italian translations were printed (along with a prefatory statement) at Venice (though supposedly in Paris) as: *Trattato e resoluzione sopra la validità delle scommoniche di Giovanni Gersono Teologo e Cancelliero Parisino, cognominato il dottore Cristianissimo tradotto dalla lingua latina nella volgare con ogni fedeltà. In opusculi due.* I cite from the edition included in Fra Paolo Sarpi, *Opere* (9 vols., Bari, 1931–65), VI, *Istoria dell'Interdetto e altri scritti editi e inediti* ed. M.D. Busnelli and Giovanni Gambarin, 3 pts., II, 171–84.

[10] The story of the Interdict has often been told, with the fullest and most helpful recent account being that of William J. Bouwsma, *Venice and the Defense of Republican Liberty: Renaissance Values in the Age of the Counter Reformation* (Berkeley and Los Angeles, 1968), esp. pp. 359–482. For good shorter recent accounts, see Frederick C. Lane, *Venice: A Maritime Republic* (Baltimore and London, 1973), pp. 481–96, and Luigi

interdict was itself no novelty. In 1509, less than a century earlier
and for the second time in little more than twenty-five years, the
papacy had resorted to the same tactic. On both earlier occasions
it had done so primarily in pursuit of its diplomatic, military and
territorial objectives in Italy.[11] In the 1605–1607 crisis the precipi-
tating factors were rather different. But if they were clear enough—
the Senate's passage in 1602, 1603 and 1605 of laws controlling the
construction of new churches, prohibiting the ecclesiastical resump-
tion of land leased to laymen, and limiting the alienation of land by
laymen to the Church[12]—the significance one attaches to those factors will very much depend on the particular historical context in
which one has chosen to understand the crisis as a whole. Not only,
that is, the politics of the interdict itself, but also the great ideological battle to which it gave rise.

In the historiography of the interdict the contexts evoked have
been multiple: the long and proud history of the *Serenissima Repubblica*
itself;[13] the history of the resurgent Counter Reformation papacy;[14]
more precisely, the situation "of the Venetian Church in the post-
Tridentine era as compared with the situation of the Church in other

---

Salvatorelli, "Venezia, Paolo V, e fra Paolo Sarpi," in Vittore Branca ed., *Storia
della Civiltà Veneziana* (3 vols., Florence, 1979), III, 23–36. Cf. A.D. Wright, "Why
the Venetian Interdict?" *English Historical Review*, LXXXIX (July, 1974), 536–550.
Among the many earlier accounts, reference should be made to Ludwig von Pastor,
The History of the Popes from the Close of the Middle Ages, trans. Ernest Graf *et al.*, (40
vols., London, 1899–1953), XXV, 111–216, and to Antonio Battistella, *La Repubblica
di Venezia ne'suoi undici secolo di storia* (Venice, 1921), pp. 613–43. For a standard bibliography of primary sources and the earlier scholarly literature, see the introduction to Carlo de Magistris, ed., *Carlo Emmanuele I e la contesa fra la Repubblica Veneta
e Paolo V (1605–1607): documenti* (Venice, 1906), pp. xxv–lii.
    [11] Bouwsma, *Venice and the Defense of Republican Liberty*, p. 99, though in the case
of the 1505 interdict Julius II had also specified as a secondary grievance the
Republic's resistance to the papal right to dispose of benefices in Venice.
    [12] Bouwsma, *Venice and the Defense of Republican Liberty*, pp. 344–47; Federico Chabod,
La Politica di Paolo Sarpi (Venice and Rome, 1962), pp. 50–53. Note that the laws
of 1603 and 1605 merely involved the extension to the *terraferma* or mainland territories of regulations long since enforced within the city of Venice itself.
    [13] Thus Battistella, *La Repubblica di Venezia*, pp. 613–43; Lane, *Venice*, pp. 481–96;
Salvatorelli, "Venezia, Paolo V, e fra Paolo Sarpi," 23–36; Gaetano Cozzi, *Il Doge
Nicolo Contarini: Ricerche sul Patriziato Veneziano agli inizi del seicento* (Venice, 1958), pp.
93–147.
    [14] Thus (classically) Pastor, *The History of the Popes*, XXV, 111–216, and, more
recently (and more generally), Aldo Stella, *Chiesa e Stato nelle relazioni dei nunzi pontifici
a Venezia. Ricerche sul giurisdizianalismo veneziano del XVI and XVIII secolo*: Studi e Testi,
No. 235 (Vatican City, 1964), esp. pp. 65–83, 98–101.

parts of Europe at that time;"[15] the biography of that great Venetian historian and propagandist, Paolo Sarpi, in the shaping of whose life the experience of the interdict was determinative;[16] the biography, again, of his most powerful opponent, the great controversialist theologian, Robert, Cardinal Bellarmine (1542–1621), in whose life, on the other hand, it was but an aggravating episode;[17] or, more broadly now, and focussing on the ideological aspect of the crisis, what has been described as "the antithesis between the political and cultural achievement of the Italian Renaissance and the ideals of medieval Catholicism . . . reinvigorated by the Counter Reformation;"[18] or, again, the great Europe-wide ideological strife concerning the doctrine of the *indirect power* of the pope in matters temporal—a doctrine refurbished by Francisco de Vitoria (d. 1546) and transformed into a commonplace by Bellarmine.[19] That enormous outburst of ideological energy, a fully integrated history of which has still to be written, was generated in 1606 by the flourishing of that indirect power in relation not only to Venice but also to England and France. In England, in the wake of the Gunpowder Plot, it led to the imposition of an oath of allegiance on English Catholics, and in France it eventuated, in the wake of the murder of Henri IV in 1610 by a Catholic assassin, in the attempt of the Estates General to impose a similar oath on French office-holders. The ideological strife that followed lasted from 1606 to the early 1620s, generating an enormous body of controversialist literature (some of it contributed by James I of England himself) and coming, particular Venetian and

---

[15] Thus Wright, "Why the Venetian Interdict?" 534–50 (at 534).

[16] Thus Chabod, *La Politica di Paolo Sarpi*, pp. 43–103; Vincenzo M. Buffon, *Chiesa di Cristo e Chiesa romana nelle opere e nelle lettere di fra Paolo Sarpi* (Louvain, 1941), esp. pp. 97–103; Boris Ulianich "Conziderazioni e documenti per una ecclesiologia di Paolo Sarpi," in Irwin Iserloh and Peter Manns eds., *Festgabe Joseph Lortz* (2 vols., Baden-Baden, 1958), II, 363–444; *idem*, the long introduction to his edition, Paolo Sarpi, *Lettere ai Gallicani* (Wiesbaden, 1961), pp. xiii–cxlv; David Wootton, *Paolo Sarpi: Between Renaissance and Enlightenment* (Cambridge, 1983), pp. 46–68. Cf. Giovanni Gambarin, "Il Sarpi alla luce di studi recenti," *Archivo veneto*, Ser. 5, *L-LI* (1959), 78–105.

[17] James Broderick, *Robert Bellarmine: Saint and Scholar* (Westminster, Maryland, 1961), esp. pp. 241–63; cf. John Courtney Murray, S.J., "St. Robert Bellarmine on the Indirect Power," *Theological Studies*, IX (Dec., 1948), 491–535.

[18] Bouwsma, *Venice and the Defense of Republican Liberty*, p. 417.

[19] Francisco de Vitoria, *Political Writings*, ed. Anthony Pagden and Jeremy Lawrence (Cambridge, 1991), pp. 45–108 (and esp. 82–101); cf. Murray, "St. Robert Bellarmine on the Indirect Power."

French issues notwithstanding, to converge progressively on the English Oath of Allegiance controversy.[20] And while this, I believe, is the broader context in which the meaning and historical significance of the polemical exchanges that accompanied the Venetian crisis can most fruitfully be assessed, I also believe that their significance will not fully be disclosed unless one reads the particular group of writings (by Bellarmine, Sarpi and Richer) stimulated by the republication of the Gerson tracts in the context also of the long tradition of conciliarist thinking which had persisted on into the centuries after the dissolution in 1449 of the Council of Basel.

The grounds for such a belief are not likely, I realize, to be immediately obvious. In his recent and very useful history of Catholic conciliar ideas from the age of Reformation to the Enlightenment, Hermann Josef Sieben makes no mention, after all, of the publicistic literature associated with the Oath of Allegiance controversy in general or the Venetian interdict in particular.[21] His silence on the matter, moreover, almost certainly reflects the fact that historical treatments of the Venetian crisis themselves acknowledge in only glancing fashion the pertinence of the conciliarist tradition. And that is true, not only of the general accounts, from those of Pastor and Battistelli to those of Salvatorelli and Bouwsma,[22] but also of works devoted to

---

[20] For the Franco-Venetian aspect of the controversy, see Ulianich's introduction to Paolo Sarpi, *Lettere ai Gallicani*, esp. pp. xix–xxxvii, and William J. Bouwsma, "Gallicanism and the Nature of Christendom," in Anthony Molho and John A. Tedeschi eds., *Renaissance Studies in Honor of Hans Baron* (Decatur, Illinois, 1971), pp. 809–30. For the Franco-English aspect, Charles H. McIlwain ed., *The Political Works of James I* (Cambridge, Mass., 1918), esp. pp. lxv–lxx, John Bossy, "Henry IV, the Appellants and the Jesuits," *Recusant History*, VIII (1965), 80–112, and J.H.M. Salmon's fine essay, "Gallicanism and Anglicanism in the age of the Counter Reformation," ch. 7 of his *Renaissance and Revolt: Essays in the intellectual and social history of early modern France* (Cambridge, 1987), pp. 155–88. And for the Venetian-English connection, G. Cozzi, "Fra Paolo Sarpi, L'Anglicanesimo e la Historia del Concilio Tridentino," *Rivista storica Italiana*, LXIII (1956), 556–619. Cf. Chabod, *La Politica di Paolo Sarpi*. All of these intricate linkages are judiciously assessed and set in their broader context by J.H.M. Salman, "Catholic resistance theory, Ultramontanism, and the royalist response, 1580–1620," in J.H. Burns and Mark Goldie eds., *The Cambridge History of Political Thought 1450–1700* (Cambridge, 1991), pp. 247–53.

[21] Hermann Josef Sieben, *Die Katholische Konzilsidee von der Reformation bis zur Aufklärung* (Paderborn, 1988).

[22] Though Bouwsma is perhaps more alert than most to the pertinence of the conciliarist tradition. See his "Gallicanism and the Nature of Christendom," 805–30, and his *Venice and the Defense of Republican Liberty*.

Paolo Sarpi, to the propagandistic role he played during the crisis, to his religious ideas in general and his ecclesiology in particular.[23]

Given the portrayal of the fate of the conciliar movement and conciliar theory in the years after the dissolution of Basel which, by the mid-twentieth century, had long since become canonical, this state of affairs should occasion little surprise. It was, after all, during a wholly extraordinary period in the life of the Latin Church that conciliar theory had flourished. Though we now know its origins to have been located in a more distant past,[24] it was the disputed papal election of 1378, the subsequent protracted schism with rival lines of claimants competing obdurately for the papal office, and the dismal failure of repeated attempts to put an end to the scandal that had ensured its growth to prominence in the early-fifteenth century. As conciliarist ideas crystallized in the thinking of the leading conciliar theorists at the Council of Constance (1414–18)—Pierre d'Ally (d. 1420), Jean Gerson and Francesco Zabarella (d. 1417), and in that of Nicholas of Cusa (d. 1464) at the Council of Basel-Ferrara-Florence (1431–49)—they coalesced into three affiliated clusters or strands. The first involved the demand for reform of the Church in head and members and the belief (ratified at Constance in 1417 in the decree *Frequens*) that that reform could best be achieved and consolidated through the regular assembly of general councils. The second envisaged the constitution of the Church in quasi-oligarchic terms, its government ordinarily in the hands of the Roman curia, the pope being limited in the exercise of his power by that of the cardinals, with whose "advice, consent, direction and remembrance" he had to rule.[25] The third strand, which may be referred to as "the strict conciliar theory" (and which the Council of Constance

---

[23] Thus Wootton, *Paolo Sarpi*, pp. 45–76; Chabod, *La Politica di Paolo Sarpi*, pp. 43–103; Buffon, *Chiesa di Cristo e Chiesa Romana*, pp. 102–3; Luigi Salvatorelli, "Le idee religiose di Fra Paolo Sarpi," in *Atti della Accademia Nazionale dei Lincei*. Anno CCCCLI, Serie 8, Classe di Scienze morali, storiche e filologiche, Memorie, V (1954), 311–60 (at 330); Ulianich, "Considerazioni e documenti per una ecclesiologia di Paolo Sarpi," 303–444. Ulianich pays somewhat greater attention to the persistence of conciliarist ideas (at least in France) in his subsequent introduction to his edition of Paolo Sarpi, *Lettere ai Gallicani*, pp. xiii–cxlv.

[24] See Brian Tierney, *Foundations of the Conciliar Theory: The Contribution of the Medieval Communists from Gratian to the Great Schism* (Cambridge, 1955).

[25] The words are taken from the alleged *professio fidei* of Boniface VIII. See S. Baluzius and J. Mansi eds., *Miscellanea* (7 vols., Lucca, 1761–64), III, 418.

at its fifth general session endorsed in 1415 in the historic superiority decree *Haec sancta synodus/Sacrosancta*), involved the assertion that
the pope, however divinely-instituted his office, was not an absolute
monarch but in some sense a constitutional ruler; that he possessed
a merely ministerial authority delegated to him by the community
of the faithful for the good of the Church; that that community had
not exhausted its inherent authority in the mere act of electing its
ruler but had retained whatever residual authority was necessary to
prevent its own subversion or ruin; that it could exercise that authority via its representatives assembled in a general council, could do
so in certain critical cases even against the wishes of the pope, and,
in such cases, could proceed if need be to judge, chastise, and even
depose that pope.

With the triumph of Pope Eugenius IV over the Council of Basel,
these three strands, however, had come to be teased apart. Thus,
while the quasi-oligarchic tradition certainly endured beyond that
event, it did so not among the defenders of the strict conciliar theory but at the Roman *curia* itself and in the writings, for example
of the great high papalist, Juan de Torquemada (d. 1468). Similarly,
as the fifteenth century wore on, those who believed that the necessary reform in head and members could be achieved only by means
of general councils increasingly recoiled from advocacy of the strict
conciliar theory. Hence, when in 1511 Louis XII of France, in the
teeth of papal opposition but with the help of several dissident cardinals, succeeded in securing the assembly of a general council at
Pisa, the majority of those churchmen most committed to reform
dashed his hopes by choosing to align themselves with the Fifth Lateran Council (1512–17), which Pope Julius II had convoked by way
of retaliation.

Thus, as recently as a quarter of a century ago, both in his contribution to Fliche and Martin's authoritative *Histoire de l'Église* and
elsewhere, Paul Ourliac could depict the year 1440 as a great ecclesiastical and ecclesiological turning point, after which theologians and
canonists alike had turned energetically to the "constructive" task of
vindicating the papal monarchy.[26] From that historiographic point

---

[26] See Ourliac in E. Delaruelle, E.-P. Labande and P. Ourliac, *L'Église au temps
du Grand Schisme et de la crise conciliare (1378–1449)*, in A. Fliche and V. Martin eds.,
Histoire de l'Église, (21 vols., Paris, 1946–1964), XIV, 285; cf. Paul Ourliac and Henri
Gilles, "La problématique de l'époque: les sources," in Gabriel le Bras ed., *Histoire
du Droit et des Institutions de l'Église en Occident* (18 vols., Paris, 1956–86), XIII, 1, 51.

of view, which had long since established itself as the dominant one, the strict conciliar theory was interpreted as an extreme position with little or no basis in the orthodox doctrinal tradition and with suspect origins in the anti-papal speculations of those fourteenth-century radicals, William of Ockham and Marsiglio of Padua. Already thrust into the shadows by the promulgation in 1439 at the Council of Florence of the decree *Laetentur coeli* (which concluded with a definition of the Roman primacy), it was portrayed as having been proscribed in 1460 by Pius II's bull *Execrabilis* (forbidding appeals from the pope to a future general council), and as having been labelled clearly as a heterodox opinion in 1516 by the Fifth Lateran Council's decree *Paster aeternus*. If it was conceded to have enjoyed a continuing half-life in France among the Gallican jurists and theologians, that fact was itself viewed as constituting something of an historical aberration and one destined in the fullness of time to be obliterated.

But history, of course, tends usually to be written by the victors. The view of the conciliar movement and of conciliar theory described above, and dominant for the past century and more down at least to the time of the Second Vatican Council, constitutes no exception to that rule.[27] That view can be traced back to the historical arguments Juan de Torquemada had developed to defend the papal cause during the Council of Basel and had later incorporated in his enormously influential *Summa de Ecclesia* (*ca.* 1453). Those arguments, further refined in the early sixteenth century by Thomas de Vio, Cardinal Cajetan (d. 1534), were put in canonical form a century later by that great "administrator of doctrine".[28] Robert, Cardinal Bellarmine. Though contested for centuries by writers of Gallican sympathies, they succeeded finally in sweeping the historiographic field in the wake of the political, ecclesiastical and theological developments which culminated in 1870 with the First Vatican Council's triumphant definition of papal primacy and infallibility.

The years since the Second World War, however (and certainly since the publication in 1949 of the first volume of Hubert Jedin's

---

[27] On which, see Thomas M. Izbicki, "Papalist Reaction to the Council of Constance: Juan de Torquemada to the Present," *Church History*, LV (No. 1, 1986), 7–20.

[28] Bouwsma, *Venice and the Defense of Republican Liberty*, p. 297, is responsible for this felicitous designation.

fine *History of the Council of Trent*,[29] have witnessed a marked revival
of scholarly interest in the history of the conciliar movement and in
the career of conciliar thinking during the centuries subsequent to
the ending of Basel.[30] As a result, though it has yet to be fully assimilated into late-medieval and early-modern historiography in general
(and is certainly not reflected in the literature devoted to Venice),
there has been a significant shift in the way in which scholars have
come to view the nature, origins and ultimate fate of conciliar thinking. It is now recognized that conciliar theory long predated both
the Great Schism itself as well as the writings of Ockham and
Marsiglio, and that it had well-articulated roots in the teaching of
the twelfth and thirteenth-century canon lawyers.[31] Similarly, and
more to our point, it has also come to be recognized that its demise
was by no means as rapid as it long was customary to suppose. In
its own day, it turns out, *Execrabilis* was viewed less as an authoritative pronouncement than as a statement of the views of one particular faction. The subsequent and repeated papal condemnations
of the appeal to a future general council themselves witness eloquently to the fact that the decree's proscriptions were widely ignored
right on into the sixteenth century. It now seems clear, again, and
as the Gallicans had long ago insisted,[32] that the crucial phases of
the 1516 decree *Pastor aeternus* are simply too restricted in meaning
to constitute any unambiguous condemnation of the strict conciliar

---

[29] Hubert Jedin, *A History of the Council of Trent*, trans. Ernest Graf (2 vols., London
and Edinburgh, 1957–6), I, 1–165. The first volume of the original *Geschichte des
Konzils von Trient* was published at Freiburg in 1949.

[30] The body of pertinent scholarly literature is now enormous. For useful reviews
of that literature down to 1981, see Hans Schneider, *Der Konziliarismus als Problem
der neueren Katholischen Theologie* (Berlin and New York, 1976); Remigius Bäumer, "Die
Erforschung des Konziliarismus," in Bäumer ed., *Die Entwicklung des Konziliarismus:
Werden und Nachwirken der konziliaren Idee* (Darmstadt, 1976), 3–50; Giuseppe Alberigo,
"Il movimento conciliare (xiv–xv sec.) nella ricerca storica ricente," *Studi medievali*,
XIX (1978), 913–50; *idem, Chiesa conciliare: Identità e significato del conciliarismo* (Brescia,
1981), pp. 340–54; Francis Oakley, "Natural Law, the *Corpus Mysticum*, and Consent
in Conciliar Thought from John of Paris to Matthias Ugonius," *Speculum*, LVI (1981),
786–910. Among subsequent contributions to the field special note should be taken
of Hans-Jürgen Becker, *Die Appellation vom Papst an ein Allgemeines Konzil. Historisches
Entwicklung und Kanonistische Diskussion im späten Mittelalter und der frühen Neuzeit* (Vienna,
1988), and Sieben, *Die Katholische Konzilsidee von der Reformation bis sur Aufklärung*.

[31] This is largely the achievement of Brian Tierney, see above n. 24.

[32] For a classic statement, see Jacques-Benigne Bossuet, *Defensio Declarationis Conventus
Cleri Gallicani de ecclesiastica potestate*, Bk. IV, ch. 18, in *Oeuvres Complètes de Bossuet* (12
vols., Paris, 1836), IX, 312–13.

theory.[33] It is also clear that that theory endured through the late-fifteenth and sixteenth centuries, not only in France but also in Germany, Scotland and Poland, and, perhaps more surprisingly, in England and in Italy itself—where, in Venetian territory for example, it continued to be championed at the University of Padua.[34] Indeed, without the persistence of such ecclesiological tensions into the Age of Reformation, it would be hard to explain the failure of the churchmen assembled at the Council of Trent,[35] and despite the challenges handed down by the novel Protestant ecclesiologies of the day, to promulgate any decree on the nature of the Christian Chruch. And if we recognize that fact, then the idea of undertaking a re-reading both of Gerson's tracts on excommunication and of the responses they stimulated in the context of the ongoing history of conciliar thinking should properly seem less obviously quixotic.

II

When one sets out to undertake such a reading, however, the first thing that strikes one is the degree to which these particular Gersonian tracts focus on ecclesiastical authority in general rather than on the papal office in particular or on the relationship of conciliar authority

---

[33] See Francis Oakley, "Conciliarism at the Fifth Lateran Council?" *Church History*, XLI (1972), 452–63.

[34] See Francis Oakley, "Constance, Basel, and the Two Pisas: The Conciliarist Legacy in Sixteenth- and Seventeenth-Century England," *Annuarium Historiae Conciliorum*, XXVI (1994), 87–118, in which I venture the claim that "people in England for much of the seventeenth century [were] better acquainted with conciliar history and the writings of the conciliarists than at any time preceding—the fifteenth century itself not excluded." One of the surprising conciliarist survivals in Italy was the presence of more than one conciliarist at the court of Pope Julius II himself. See Hubert Jedin, "Giovanni Gozzadini, ein Konziliarist am Hofe Julius II," in Jedin, *Kirche des Glaubens, Kirche der Geschichte: Ausgewählte Aufsätze und Vorträge* (2 vols., Freiburg, 1966), II, 17–74; Nelson Minnich, "Girolamo Massaino: Another Conciliarist at the Papal Court, Julius II to Adrian VI," in Nelson H. Minnich *et al.*, *Studies in Catholic History in Honor of John Tracy Ellis* (Wilmington, DE, 1985), 520–65. For other Italian exponents of conciliarist ideas in the mid-sixteenth century at Padua and elsewhere, see Thomas P. Mayer, "Marco Mantova, a Bronze Age Conciliarist," *Annuarium Historiae Conciliorum*, XIV (1984), 385–408, and his *Thomas Starkey and the Commonweal: Humanist Politics and Religion in the Reign of Henry VIII* (Cambridge, 1989), pp. 172–87.

[35] Among whom, as Sarpi claimed, apprehension about the potential recrudescence of conciliar ideas was widespread—See Paolo Sarpi, *The History of the Council of Trent*, trans. Nathaniel Brent (London, 1676), Bk. II, 216; V, 473; VI, 482–83, 529.

to papal. The second of the tracts, *Esamine di quell' asserzione: Sententia pastoris, etiam injusta, timenda est*,[36] though it refers glancingly to the Council of Constance, makes no reference at all to the relative jurisdictional standing of council and pope. And if the first does so in its eighth *considerazione*—and does so, indeed, quite forcefully, it still devotes no more than a single, one hundred and fifty word paragraph (about a tenth of the whole text)[37] to the matter. That this should be so is not altogether surprising, given the fact that both tracts postdate the election of a pope of undoubted legitimacy and the ending, therefore, of the long agony of the Great Schism. They were written, in effect, in April, 1418, either during the very last days of the Council of Constance or in the days immediately after its dissolution.[38] It has been claimed that the idea of translating them was suggested to Sarpi by the prominent Gallican theologian, Edmond Richer (1559–1631), future Syndic of the Sorbonne (1608–12), who was working hard to wean his Parisian colleagues from their growing ultramontane sympathies and to reattach them to a form of theological as well as political Gallicanism. And Richer was unquestionably a person of conciliarist sympathies. His *De ecclesiastica et politica potestate*, a highly controversial work which he was to publish in 1611, was among other things distinguished by its approving evocation of the superiority decrees of Constance and Basel and of the conciliarist reading of Nicholas of Cusa, Gerson and the "other Parisian Doctors."[39]

But if Paola Sarpi had long been interested in such Gallican commitments and had been in correspondence with leading Gallican authors since 1604, Ulianich, in his careful study of Sarpi's relations

[36] Printed in Busnelli and Gambarin, II, 180–84 (at 183). See above, note 9.

[37] *Resoluzione circa la materia delle scommuniche ed irregolarita*, in Busnelli and Gambarin, II, 175–79 (at 177–78). Of the twelve *considerazioni* only 8 to 12 focus specifically on the pope's exercise of his authority.

[38] See Jean Gerson, *Oeuvres complètes*, ed. Glorieux, I, "Essai biographique," 133.

[39] The work was repeatedly republished, and in French as well as Latin. See the Latin edition printed in Melchior Goldast ed., *Monarchia S. Romani Imperii* (3 vols., Frankfurt, 1611–14), III, 797–806 (at 800–802, 804–805). For an analysis of the work and an account of its publishing history, see E. Puyol, *Edmond Richer: Étude historique et critique sur la Rénovation du Gallicanisme au commencement du xviie siècle* (2 vols., Paris, 1876), I, 212–71, II, 423–24. For the general background, see Aimé-Georges Martimort, *Le Gallicanisme de Bossuet* (Paris, 1953), pp. 13–20; Bouwsma, "Gallicanism and the Nature of Christendom," 809–30; Salmon, *Renaissance and Revolt*, p. 188. Puyol, *Edmond Richer*, is still the standard biography; for a more recent biographical sketch, see J. Carreyre in *Dictionnaire de théologie catholique* (17 vols., Paris, 1909–72), XIII, 2, 2698–2702 s.v. "Richer, Edmond."

with the Gallicans, finds no evidence at all to back the claim that Richer had any involvement in the republication of the Gerson tracts.[40] Even if he had had such an involvement, and had Sarpi at this point actually wanted to evoke against Paul V the spectre of conciliarism, there were certainly other works of Gerson that would have served his purpose far better than the two he actually chose to translate. Also dating to the period immediately after the Council of Constance, for example, was the *An liceat in causis fidei a Papa appellare*,[41] a succinct piece whose defense of the legitimacy of appeals from pope to general council would certainly have been directly pertinent to the situation in which Venice now found itself.

During the interdicts of 1482 and 1509, it should be noted, the Republic had appealed from the judgment of the pope to that of a future general council, and though it was not formally to adopt that tactic in the 1606–1607 crisis, Sarpi, in his official capacity as legal and theological adviser was far from ruling it out.[42] On January 28, 1606, it is true, in his first public consultation immediately prior to his appointment to office (and in the wake of an earlier private consultation in which he had suggested the advisability of an attempt at accommodation),[43] he had advised that the appeal to a council

---

[40] See Paolo Sarpi, *Lettere ai Gallicani*, ed. Ulianich, p. 127, where, in a letter to Jacques Gillot, Sarpi noted that he had been interested in Gallicanism for some twenty years now; cf. Ulianich's lengthy introduction, xiii–cxliii (at xxii). See also Bouwsma, *Venice and the Defense of Republican Liberty*, p. 236; Salvatorelli, "Venezia, Paolo V, e fra Paolo Sarpi." 28.

[41] Text in Jean Gerson, *Oeuvres complètes*, ed. Glorieux, VI, 282–90. The tract was occasioned by the decision of the Polish delegates at Constance (in response to Martin V's unwillingness to condemn the Teutonic knight, John of Falkenberg, for his advocacy of tyrannicide) to appeal to the next general council. Though the surviving evidence is scanty, it seems that, by way of reaction, the pope had had read in consistory on March 10, 1618, the sketch of a proposed bull denying the legitimacy of such an appeal. Gerson wrote, then, to defend that right and the commitment to the ecclesiological principle in which it was grounded—namely that of the superiority of council to pope. In the event, Martin V refrained from promulgating the putative bull. For the incident and its outcome, see Remigius Bäumer, "Das Verbot der Konzilsappellation Martins V in Konstanz, in A. Franzen and W. Müller, *Das Konzil von Konstanz; Beiträge zu seiner Geschichte und Theologie*" (Freiburg, 1964), pp. 187–213; Paul de Vooght, *Les pouvoirs du Concile et l'autorité du Pope au Concile de Constance* (Paris, 1965), pp. 73–76; Alberigo, *Chiesa conciliare*, pp. 233–37.

[42] Chabod, *La Politica di Paolo Sarpi*, pp. 70–71; Salvatorelli, "Venezia, Paolo V, e fra Paolo Sarpi," 27—arguing here against Pastor's claim (*History of the Popes*, XXV, 123–34) that Sarpi was responsible for instigating at this time a hardening in the position the Senate had adopted vis-à-vis the pope.

[43] Salvatarelli, "Venezia, Paolo V, e fra Paolo Sarpi," 27.

was at that time inopportune. Nothing, he had argued, could be more odious to the pope than such a move. It would call into question his very authority, placing it below that of the council and recalling to mind the indignities Eugenius IV had endured at Basel as well as the dangers that had still threatened even at Trent. But if such an appeal, therefore, was to be viewed as a weapon of last resort, it was still (as in his own day Gerson had also insisted), a perfectly legitimate response *di ragione* to a papal abuse of power and one with a long history of use by princes and ecclesiastics alike.[44] Towards the end of April then, when Sarpi returned to the issue in a further advisory to the Doge and Senate after the interdict had actually been imposed, he once more defended the legitimacy of appealing to a future council. And he also concluded that if the Republic were now to deem it helpful to resort to such an appeal, it should not allow itself to be deflected from that course either by previous papal prohibitions or by assertions of the superiority of pope to council.[45]

That being the case, it is perhaps the more striking that the tracts of Gerson he actually chose to translate at this very time were so little concerned with the issue and were so much more generally focused on the abuse of the power of excommunication. That had long been something of a standard *topos* in the literature of ecclesiastical reform.[46] As Sarpi himself was careful to point out in his preface to the translation, it had recently found a clear reflection in the Tridentine canon decreeing that the penalty of excommunication be imposed only with moderation and circumspection.[47] And that sen-

---

[44] See Sarpi, *Scrittura sopra la forza e validità della scommunica giusta e ingiusta e sopra li remedii "de jure" e "de facto" da usare contro le censure ingiuste*, in Busnelli and Gambarin, II, 29–40 (at 33–34). Cf. Chabod, *La Politica di Paolo Sarpi*, pp. 70–71; Salvatorelli, "Venezia Paolo V, e fra Paolo Sarpi," 27–28.

[45] Sarpi, *Scrittura intorno l'appelazione al concilio o altro da farsi per mortificare gli atti del pontifice*, in Busnelli and Gambarin, II, 74–85 (esp. 85). Cf. Chabod, *La Politica di Paolo Sarpi*, pp. 80–82.

[46] See, for example, the typical condemnation in the *Tractatus de materia concilii generalis*, which Pierre d'Ailly, Gerson's mentor, wrote in 1402/3 when he was Bishop of Cambrai—edited by Francis Oakley, *The Political Thought of Pierre d'Ailly: The Voluntarist Tradition* (New Haven and London, 1964), App. III, pp. 244–342 (at 325–26).

[47] *Canones et Decreta Sacrosancti Oecumenici et Generalis Concilii Tridentini sub Paulo III, Julio III, Pio IV Pontificibus Max. Celebrati*, ed. J. LePlat (Antwerp, 1779), Sess. 25, De Reform., c. 3, pp. 301–302. Sarpi, "Al pio e religiose lettore," *Trattato e resoluzione sopra la validità delle scommuniche di Giovanni Gersone*, in Busnelli and Gambarin, II, 173.

timent was clearly shared by Bellarmine himself. Though in his reply to the first tract Bellarmine labored mighily to disagree with Gerson (to the extent, indeed, of misrepresenting at one point what the latter had actually said),[48] he was clearly in accord with the substance of more than half of the twelve *considerazioni* that made up the work.

Why, then, the promptness and vehemence of his reply to it? Two things in particular, and both resonate to the fear that conciliarism was still a present threat and something that called for unremitting viligance on the part of the Church. First, Bellarmine's outraged sense that the purpose of disseminating in the vernacular Gerson's exaggeratedly negative view of the papacy of his own unquestionably troubled era was that of encouraging among contemporary Venetians the fallacious sense that the papacy of their own day was no better.[49] Second, his disapproval of the choice of a "suspect author" like Gerson to speak to this sensitive matter of the force of excommunication when there was no lack, after all, of "safer" authorities to invoke—people such as Saints Thomas, Bonaventure or Antonino.[50] Gerson, he says, may doubtless have been a scholar "of great knowledge and piety," but his views on the matter of the papal authority were of "no moment whatsoever." On that issue, the problem with Gerson was that "the unhappiness" of the times through which he had lived—the protracted nature of the schism and the hope of ending it through the agency of a general council—had conspired to lead him improperly to downplay the authority of the pope and to aggrandize that of the council. As a result, he had fallen into "manifest error contrary to the Sacred Scripture and to the common teaching of the theologians who lived both before and after those times."[51] That "most grave and manifest error" Bellarmine saw

---

[48] As Sarpi was quick to point out, and as Bellarmine in a later tract was ruefully to concede. See Sarpi, *Apologia per le oppozioni fatte dall' illustrissimo e reverendissimo Signor Cardinale Bellarminio alli' Trattati e risoluzioni di Giovanni Gersone sopra la validità delle scommuniche*, in Busnelli and Gambarin, III, 43–189 (at 116-7); cf. Robert, Cardinal Bellarmine. *Risposta alle oppositioni di Fra Paolo Servita contra la scrittura de Cardinale Bellarmino*—printed with continuous pagination (and after the tract of the title) in *Risposta di Card. Bellarmino al Trattato de i sette Theologi di Venetia sopra l'interdetto della Santità di Nostro Signore Papa Paolo Quinto* (Rome, 1606), pp. 73–139 (at 109).

[49] Bellarmine, *Risposta alle oppositioni di Fra Paolo Servita contra la Scrittura de Cardinale Bellarmino*, p. 118. Cf. *Risposta de Card. Bellarmino, ad un libretto intitulato Trattato, e resolutione sopra la validità de la scommuniche di Gio. Gersono* (Rome, 1606) p. 77

[50] *Risposta . . . ad un libretto intitulato Trattato e resolutione sopra la validità de la scommuniche*, pp. 64–65.

[51] *Ibid.*, pp. 64–65.

as being encapsulated so poisonously in the eighth consideration of Gerson's first tract that he viewed the translator who put it forward as pertinent to the present Venetian situation as having revealed himself, by so doing, to be "something less than Catholic" (*Si dimostra poco Catholico*).[52] On this consideration, then, he spent most of his time, and against it he levelled his heaviest artillery.[53]

In Bellarmine's eyes, Gerson's greatest offence in the brief paragraph in question was that of having insisted that the Council of Constance had pronounced it to be heretical to deny the right of an appeal from pope to council. That claim Bellarmine not unreasonably inflated into the assertion that Constance had declared it "to be heresy to deny the superiority of the council to the pope," and he then went on to attack it on three grounds.[54] First, that despite having read and re-read that council's proceedings, he himself had been unable to track down any such declaration. Second, that the superiority decree of Constance's fourth session (the first

---

[52] *Ibid.*, p. 71.

[53] As we shall see, the precise wording of this eighth consideration turns out to be important, and it may be helpful to reproduce here both the Italian and original Latin versions. As follows. For the Italian, see Busnelli and Gambarin, II, 177–78: "CONSIDERAZIONE VIII. Porta più pericolo lo sprezzo delle chiavi verso la persona del summo pontefice che verso l'inferiore, perché dagli abusi degl' inferiori è aperto il ricorso al papa per il beneficio dell'appellazione. E se alcun dica che parimente si può appellare dal papa al concilio generale, dicevano altre volte, inanzi il concilio generale pisano e costanziense, che questo non era in alcun modo lecito; ed allegavano le sue ragioni a favor loro, molto chiare, per quanto loro pareva. Ma nondimeno al presente costantemente si afferma che il negare la superiorità del concilio sopra il papa sia eresia, condannata per constituzione espressissima e praticata nel detto concilio di Costanza, si come altrove più diffusamente è stato mostrato: per il che si risponde altramente, cioè che non si può né debbe celebrar cosi facilmente e per leggier causa un concilio per udir le appellazioni (dove anco fusse lecito appellarsi), si come facilmente si ha ricorso al papa." And the Latin text (Gerson, *Oeuvres complètes*, ed. Glorieux, VI, 295): "Consideratio octava. Contemptus clavium plus habet periculi erga personam Summi Pontificis quam erga inferiores, quoniam ab abusibus inferioribus patet recursus ad papam per appelationis subsidium. Et si dicatur quod ita potest a papa fieri appellatio ad concilium generale, dixerunt olim ante concilium generale Pisanum et Constantiense quod hoc nullo modo licebat; et allegant jura sua pro se valde, sicut eis videtur, expressa. Sed constanter nunc asseritur quod est haeresis damnata per constitutionem expressissimam et practicatam in concilio praedicto Constantiensi, prout alibi diffusius est ostensum. Respondetur igitur aliter quod non pro levibus causis ubi etiam liceret, potest aut debet pro appellationibus prosequendis passim concilium celebrari sicut habet recursus ad papam."

[54] For what follows see Bellarmine, *Risposta de Card. Bellarmino ad un libretto intitulato Trattato, e resoluzione sopra la validità de le scommuniche di Gio. Gersone*, pp. 72–77.

version of *Haec sancta synodus*)[55] was not to be read as applicable to any pope whatsoever and certainly not to any canonically-elected pope universally held to be legitimate. Instead, it was to be viewed as applicable only to the three dubious claimants of that day, over whom the universal Church and the council representing it could unquestionably exercise authority and from whom it could legitimately demand obedience. Third, that the decree in question, dating as it did to a time when there was no unquestioned pope and lacking the subsequent legitimating approbation of Martin V, had no pertinence to anything but the remediation of the Great Schism itself. As a result, Pius II, Julius II (and subsequent popes in their reissues of the bull *In coena domini*) had imposed a sentence of excommunication on anyone appealing from pope to general council. Reason and the teaching of the Scriptures both served to underline the "manifestly erroneous" nature of Gerson's position. So, too, did the general councils of the Church. The Fifth Lateran Council in 1516, for example, had expressly affirmed that the pope is above any council whatsoever. In any case (and this asserted by way of triumphant conclusion), "the Holy Church is not like the Republic of Venice which can be said to be . . . above the prince." "Nor is it like a worldly kingdom," where the power of the monarch is derived from the people. Instead it is "a most perfect kingdom and an absolute monarchy, which depends not on the people . . . but on the divine will alone."[56]

In the absence of a tradition of conciliarist thinking that he thought to be of continuing vitality and capable still of constituting a potent threat to papal authority, it would be hard to explain the forcefulness of Bellarmine's response, or the fact that he devoted a full third of his critique of Gerson's first tract to a refutation of the strict conciliar theory. And it would be similarly difficult to explain his willingness to dismiss some of the reasoning of Gerson's second tract on the mistaken ground that it, too, presupposed the principle of the superiority of council to pope.[57] Such was his preoccupation (obsession even) with the ever present danger posed by that conciliarist principle that he misunderstood what Gerson was actually saying

---

[55] See below, note 69.
[56] Bellarmine, *Risposta de Card. Bellarmino ad un libretto . . . di Gio. Gersone*, p. 76.
[57] *Ibid.*, 80–84.

in the eighth consideration of the first tract and (instinctively, it seems) took him to be speaking, not of the heightened danger attaching to contempt for the power of the keys when that contempt was directed *toward* the person of the pope, but rather when it sprang from the abuse of that power *by* the pope.[58]

Noting later on, in turn, in his own reply to Bellarmine's *Risposta*, that this eighth consideration of Gerson's was in fact "*in favor of* the Apostolic See," (italics mine) Sarpi wryly commented that if one were to ignore the claim about conciliar superiority (which Gerson had advanced only incidentally), there would be nothing in the consideration worthy of reprehension even from Bellarmine's own point of view. But from that latter point of view, of course, what was merely incidental to Gerson and to Sarpi was, in effect, the truly central issue. And by devoting disproportionate attention to it, Bellarmine in fact succeeded in promoting what it had clearly been his intention to deflect. Nothing less than the clear insertion of the old conciliarist claim into the growing body of publicistic literature now being generated by the imposition of the interdict upon Venice, and by that republic's efforts to defend itself and to rally support for its cause in the capitals of Europe—most notably in Paris and London.

The connection with France was particularly important. It went beyond Sarpi's own long-standing interest in the Gallican Church, in which, he confessed later on to the Huguenot Jérôme Groslot de l'Isle, alone among the churches owing allegiance to Rome could still be detected "some vestiges of the ancient liberty."[59] During the crisis of the interdict Venice had appropriated some 2,000 *scudi* to encourage French writers to enter the lists in defense of the Republic, and Pietro Priuli, the Venetian ambassador to Paris, was urged to secure such help from theologians of the Sorbonne.[60] Given the growth of ultramontane sympathies among them, it is not surprising that he had less success with that group than he did with the Gallican jurisconsults. Among the latter, Jacques Leschassier and Louis Servin both wrote in support of the Venetian cause and, by

---

[58] He himself later conceded that he had misread Gerson on this point. See above, note 49.

[59] See Fra Paolo Sarpi, *Lettere ai Protestanti*, ed. M.D. Busnelli (2 vols., Bari, 1931), I, 36–13 September 1608. Cf. Ulianich ed., *Lettere ai Gallicani*, p. cxliv.

[60] For this whole effort see the introduction to Ulianich ed., *Lettere ai Gallicani*, pp. xxii–xxxvii; Bouwsma, *Venice and the Defense of Republican Liberty*, pp. 397–404.

so doing, suggested an alignment of Gallican and Venetian interests in opposition to the papacy.[61]

In September, 1606, moreover, Priuli was able to forward to Venice a list of older theological writings whose republication might help the Venetian cause. It had been drawn up for him, he said, by "one of the leading and oldest doctors" of the Sorbonne, and it included works by such conciliarists or protoconciliarist authors as John of Paris, William of Ockham, Pierre d'Ailly, Jacques Almain, John Mair, and Philippus Decius.[62] Priuli may also have been responsible for inducing Edmond Richer to produce in 1606 his influential edition of the works of Gerson. That edition included also some of the conciliar tracts of d'Ailly, Almain and Mair, and Cardinal du Perron, in his famous *Oration* of 1616 to the Third Estate, later identified it as the source to which "the Maisters of the Kinges retinue of the Parliament of Paris do remit and refer their Readers, to understand what be the batteries and strongest defences of the Jurisdiction Spiritual and temporal [i.e. against the Pope]."[63] Despite Henri IV's policy of strict neutrality vis-à-vis the Venetian affair, Priuli succeeded further in having one of Sarpi's most important public defences of the Venetian position—the *Considerazioni sopra le censure della santità di papa Paulo V contra La Serenissima Republica di Venetia* (1606)—translated into French and republished in Paris.[64] And Ulianich concludes that the "principalissimo Theologo" whom Priuli claimed finally in January 1607 to have induced to write in support of Venice was none other than Richer himself, and that the work in question was the short *Apologia pro Ecclesiae et Concilii auctoritate*,

---

[61] For the sympathies of the Sorbonne theologians, see Martimort, *Le Gallicanisme de Bossuet*, pp. 17–56; cf. Bouwsma, *Venice and the Defense of Republican Liberty*, p. 399; Wootton, *Paolo Sarpi*, p. 50. Leschassier contributed the *Consultatio Parisii cujusdam de controversia inter sanctitatem Pauli V et Serenis. Rempublicam Venetam, ad virum clariss. Venetum* (Paris, 1606), and Servin the *Pro libertate status et reipublicae Venetorum Gallofranci ad Philenetum epistola* (Paris, 1607). Melchior Goldast later made the first of these tracts (along with other Gallican writings, and tracts in support of Venice) readily available in his *Monarchia S. Romani Imperii*, vol. III.

[62] See Ulianich ed., *Lettere ai Gallicani*, pp. xxvi–xxvii.

[63] I quote from the contemporary English translation of Jacques Davy, Cardinal du Perron, *An Oration made on the Part of the Lordes Spirituall in the Chamber of the Third Estate* (St. Omer, 1616), pp. 49–50; cf. pp. 121–22.

[64] See Ulianich ed., *Lettere ai Gallicani*, p. xxviii; Bouwsma, "Gallicanism and the Nature of Christendom," 828–30. Chabod, *La Politica di Paolo Sarpi*, p. 97, dates the *Considerazioni* to no earlier than the end of April, 1606. Printed in Gambarin, II, 185–254.

adversus Joannis Gersonii doctoris christianissimi obtrectatores, which, without publisher or place of publication indicated, was first printed in Italy in 1607.[65]

In that work Richer pursues a line of march that witnesses eloquently to the damage Bellarmine had done to his own papalist cause by his disproportionate focus on the conciliarist element in Gerson's tracts on excommunication. As we have seen, Gerson had devoted no more than a brief paragraph to that matter. Bellarmine, however, had belabored it for some seven long pages. And Richer, writing by way of rebuttal to Bellarmine's representation of Gerson's doctrine as temerarious and evocative of contemporary heretical opinions, was now moved to devote the bulk of his *Apologia* to the Church's constitution in general and the central role of general councils in particular, turning only in the last three pages of a forty-eight page discourse to the issue of the abuse of the power of the keys which had, in fact, been Gerson's chosen subject. If Bellarmine, he argued, was right in his imputation of heterodoxy to Gerson's teaching, what then, are we to make of the similar teaching of those great cardinals, Pierre d'Ailly, Francesco Zabarella and Nicholas of Cusa—or, for that matter, the cognate views of such conciliarists as Panormitanus, Jacques Almain, John Mair and Philippus Decius? And what, indeed, of the Gallican church itself, which "has always received and defended the teaching of Gerson as Catholic and orthodox."[66] If people like Cajetan or Bellarmine were permitted to impute doctrinal deviancy to that teaching, were Almain, Mair or, in these latter days, Paolo Sarpi himself, not to be permitted to rise in its defence (3)?

In the pages that follow this introductory flourish Richer, then, sets forth some fifty-three *axiomata* designed to demonstrate that Gerson's teaching was "altogether in conformity with natural, divine and canon law."[67] In so doing, he is led—in sweeping fashion, and

---

[65] Ulianich ed., *Lettere ai Gallicani*, p. xxix. Though the work was republished later on in the seventeenth century, this first edition (published in Italy and marred by mistakes) does not appear to have enjoyed a wide circulation. I used the copy in the British Library and there appear to be no copies in any North American library. For the background to the work and a publishing history, see Puyol, *Edmond Richer: Étude historique et critique*, I, 97–101; II, 422.

[66] Richer, *Apologia pro Ecclesiae et Concilii auctoritate*, p. 3, ending: "Quis [eveniet] denique toti Ecclesiae Gallicanae, quae Gersonii doctrinam pro Cattolica et Orthodoxa semper imbibit atque propagavit." In what follows, the numbers in parentheses will refer to the pagination of Richer's work.

[67] Richer, *Apologia pro Ecclesiae et Concilii auctoritate*, p. 10: ". . . Gersonii doctrinam legi divinae, naturali, et canonicae penitus conformam esse demonstrare aggrediamur."

with multiple invocations of the conciliarist views of d'Ailly, Gerson, Almain, Mair and the *doctores Parisienses* in general—to insist, among other things, on the fact that absolute or despotic monarchy is repugnant to natural and divine law (14), that the best political regimen is monarchy tempered by aristocracy (15), that the universal Church, therefore, is a monarchical polity, instituted by Christ for a supernatural end, and, via the agency of the ecumenical council, tempered in its makeup by an aristocratic component (20). Its monarch and "essential head" being Christ himself, Peter and his papal successors are no more than "mutable," "secondary," and "accidental" heads (22). As a result, and if need be, the general council, which represents the universal Catholic Church and has its power immediately from Christ, is capable of assembling itself without and even in opposition to the pope (31), of performing every act of jurisdiction that he can (33),[68] and, beyond that, being "superior to the pontiff in infallibility and authority," can act as it did at Constance in the case of Pope John XXIII to curb the pope's abuse of his authority (35–36).

Thus, the existence of a right of appeal from pope to general council is not to be gainsaid (35). Nor, given Bellarmine's own earlier admission that the conciliar status of the *fifth* Lateran Council had remained in dispute among Catholics "down to this day," was he warranted in brandishing its decree of 1516 in order to demonstrate the validity of his counter claim that the pope was superior to the council (39). Nor, again, was that same Bellarmine correct in his claim that the Constance superiority decree *Haec sancta synodus* was applicable only to Constance itself and to the particular conditions of schism then prevailing. Had he read the final version of that decree approved at the *fifth* general session of Constance (and not simply the earlier version concurred in at the fourth), he would have seen that it applied to *any* general council whatsoever (11), and not simply to pontiffs of dubious legitimacy but to those whose titles were wholly uncontested (38–39).[69] Hence, and *pace* Bellarmine's argu-

---

[68] Though it cannot administer the sacraments or preach, acts which presuppose individual human agency. Richer is distinguishing here, and in traditional canonistic and theological fashion, between the *potestas ordinis*, the sacramental power conferred on clerics by ordination, and the *potestas jurisdictionis*, or power of governance or administration, which does not presuppose for its exercise priestly ordination.

[69] And here Richer cites the crucial phrases of the final version of *Haec sancta*. For the formation of the decree and the differing texts approved at the fourth and

ment to the contrary, the rectitude of the claim that Gerson advanced
in the eighth consideration of his first tract on excommunication to
the effect that the Council of Constance had dubbed it heretical to
deny the superiority of council to pope.[70]

And so on. In the sweep and the insistence of its affirmation of
the strict conciliar theory, Richer's *Apologia* is, if anything, more
focused and forceful than his subsequent *De ecclesiastica et politica potestate* (1611), the notorious work that proved to be too radical for the
taste of his colleagues on the Paris theology faculty and led to his
dismissal from the position of Syndic of the Sorbonne.[71] In comparison, indeed, Sarpi's own (and earlier) reply to Bellarmine's critique of Gerson, a much lengthier work than Richer's and published
in September, 1606, is at once more comprehensive, more cautious
and more measured.[72] Nonetheless, in that about a quarter of it is
devoted to matters conciliar and especially to a long rebuttal of
Bellarmine's attack on Gerson's eighth consideration, it clearly continued the process that Bellarmine had hoped to derail but had
unwittingly succeeded in fueling—namely that of drawing to the
attention of a new generation of Europeans the enduring presence
in the Church of a strong tradition of conciliarist thinking. Similarly,
that of acquainting contemporaries with its nature and history and
the degree to which it was grounded in modalities of Catholic ecclesiological thinking dating back to a very distant past.

In the course of the lengthy and sometimes convoluted arguments
with which he buttressed that effort, Sarpi understandably touched

---

fifth general sessions of the council, see the careful discussion in Alberigo. *Chiesa
conciliare*, pp. 165–86. The actual texts are printed side by side on pp. 168–73.

[70] Richer, *Apologia pro Ecclesiae et Concilii auctoritate*, p. 11. Here, having discussed
the fourth and fifth sessions of Constance and the decree *Haec sancta synodus*, Richer
concludes: "Ex his principiis, directe, evidenter, et necessario concludit Gersonius
decretum istud fide Catholica, credi oportere, et propterea haeresim esse per Concilium
Constantiense damnatam, asserere Papa non subesse judicio correctivo Concilii universalis. Ut quid ergo Cardinalis Bellarminus, in examine considerationis octavae
tractatus Gersonii, confidenter asserit, Concilium Constantiense nullibi declarasse
haeresim esse negare superioritatem Concilii supra Papam? An non obsecro haeresis est decretis Conciliorum universalium, et Ecclesiae auctoritati pertinaciter resistere?"

[71] Puyol, *Edmond Richer: Étude historique et critique*, I, 329–66; cf. Martimort, *Le
Gallicanisme de Bossuet*, pp. 53–55.

[72] Sarpi, *Apologia per le opposizioni fatte dall' illustrissimo e reverendissimo Signor cardinale
Bellarminio alli Trattati e Risoluzioni di Giovanni Gersone sopra la validità della scommuniche.*
In the Busnelli and Gambarin edition (III, 43–189), it runs to some 146 pages,
about 44 of them devoted to the conciliar issue. For the dating of the work, see
Busnelli and Gambarin, III, 284.

upon many of the same issues as Richer was to do. Thus, he "antic-ipated" Richer's needling of Bellarmine by reminding the latter that there was little point in his flourishing the authority of the *Fifth Lateran Council* to demonstrate the superiority of pope to council when he himself had earlier conceded that the ecumenicity of that particular council was still a matter of dispute among Catholics.[73] And he went beyond Richer in the range and richness of his his-torical argument, which traversed the centuries from the apostolic era and the general councils of antiquity down to that of Constance and Basel, the *conciliabulum* of Pisa (1510–11) and the Fifth Lateran Council, not omitting a tart reminder to Bellarmine that his dis-missal of the contemporary pertinence of Gerson's arguments (on the grounds that he had been writing during a time of schism when there were three claimants to the papal office) hardly held much water in view of the fact that Gerson had written the two works in question after Martin V had been accepted as the sole legitimate pope and after the Council of Constance was over.[74]

Nevertheless, there was nothing particularly complicated about Sarpi's basic tactical move in this work of his, which was simple enough and, in effect, two-pronged. First, he insisted that the argu-ments which Bellarmine had directed against Gerson's conciliarist commitments had already been assessed and rebutted, either by Gerson himself or by such subsequent and like-minded thinkers as Almain and Mair.[75] If he (Sarpi) was now reproducing some of those rebuttals (and he certainly was), it was not to affirm the truth of Gerson's position but "solely to show that the question needs to be treated on more solid grounds, and that writers as outstanding in learning and piety [as were these conciliarists] were not so easily to be condemned."[76] Second, he also insisted not that Gerson was nec-essarily right in his affirmation of the jurisdictional superiority of

---

[73] Sarpi, *Apologia*, in Busnelli and Gambarin, III, 135, 146–49.

[74] Sarpi, *Apologia*, in Busnelli and Gambarin, III, 171–73. He is commenting here on Bellarmine's response to the twelfth consideration of Gerson's first tract—see Bellarmine, *Risposta . . . ad un libretto . . . sopra la validità de le scommuniche di Gio. Gersone*, p. 80.

[75] Sarpi, *Apologia*, in Busnelli and Gambarin, III, 120.

[76] *Ibid.*: "Io non voglio affermare che l'opinione di Gerson sia la vera, né appor-tar la sua dottrina e ragioni in questa *Apologia* . . . E io qui partarò alcune di esse risoluzioni, non per diffinir cosa alcuna, ma solo per mostrar che bisogna trattar di questa questione non più sodi fondamenti, e non dannare con tanta facilità gli scrittori di eccelente santità e dottrina."

council to pope, but rather that Bellarmine was certainly wrong in his stubborn refusal to acknowledge what such theologians as John Mair, Martinus Navarro, Juan de Mariana and Melchior Cano had persistently underlined—namely that the question of the relationship of pope to council had continued to be a matter of controversy, so that "while in Rome it is not permitted to hold the doctrine of Panormitanus which maintained the superiority of the council, neither does the University of Paris tolerate the upholding of the contrary position."[77] For surely "an opinion which enjoys the concurrence of as many famous scholars as may have held to the contrary, and which has the support of an equal, if not greater, number of universities, regions and kingdoms, can hardly be said to be proposed without reason or authority, still less audaciously."[78]

A quick comparison with the *Trattato del Interdetto del Santità di Papa Paulo V*, also published in 1606 after the Gerson translations but prior to his *Apologia*, reveals the degree to which the vehemence and particular focus of Bellarmine's attack on Gerson had nudged Sarpi further to explore the propagandistic value of emphasizing the pertinence to the present Venetian discontents of both the conciliarist tradition and the history of the late-medieval general councils.[79] In the *Trattato*, it is true, he had also been at pains to insist that the old question of the superiority of council to pope (or vice versa) had "not yet been decided but remains in doubt in the Church of God." In support of that position he had also invoked (as he would later on in the *Apologia*) the witness of John Mair as well as the fact that Bellarmine himself had conceded the ecumenical status of the Fifth Lateran Council still to be in dispute among Catholics.[80] But he had done so very much by way of conclusion to an examination of the limits of the obedience owed to the orders of an ecclesiastical superior, of the notion that not even the pope's powers were unlimited and absolute, of the possibility that popes were capable of being wrong in particular legal judgments, and that they were, indeed, able

---

[77] Sarpi, *Apologia*, in Busnelli and Gambarin, III, 117–118.
[78] *Ibid.*: "Ma una opinione che ha tanti e tanto celebri dottori quanto ne ha la sua contraria, e che è seguita da ugual, se non maggiore numero di università e regioni e regni, non si può dire asserita senza ragione e autorità né meno audacemente."
[79] Though signed by seven Venetian churchmen, the *Trattato del' Interdetto* was, in fact, Sarpi's work. It is printed in Busnelli and Gambarin, III, 3–41.
[80] Sarpi, *Trattato del' Interdetto*, in Busnelli and Gambarin, III, 17–18.

to fall into heresy.[81] What had been in the *Trattato* very much the conclusion of a line of reasoning became, in the *Apologia*, nothing less than the premise or point of departure for the lengthy exploration of conciliar history and conciliarist claims which we have just discussed.

None of which was destined, of course, to bring much cheer to Bellarmine, who felt compelled to return (somewhat wearily) to the fray with responses both to the *Trattato* and to the *Apologia*.[82] These two responses coincide somewhat in tone (testy and legislative) as also in content. Thus, in response to Sarpi's *Apologia* he tried to neutralize the latter's claim that Gerson's tracts on excommunication postdated the ending both of the schism and of Constance by first asserting (without any supporting evidence whatsoever) that they were "most probably" written before the election of Martin V, when there was no true pope but only three rival claimants to the papacy. And to that assertion he appended the nervous "back-up" argument that, even if the tracts were indeed written after the council was over, it was important to remember that the Avignonese pontiff, Benedict XIII, had refused to abandon his claim to the papacy so that there were still two contenders for the papal office.[83] In the response to the *Trattato*, moreover, denying that there was any doubt among Catholics about the superiority of pope to council, he likewise insisted that that truth was "taught and defended" in all the schools of Catholic theology, even "in France itself."[84] And in both *Risposte* he struggled mightily to rebut Sarpi's accusations of inconsistency in what he had had to say about the teaching of the Fifth Lateran Council concerning the relationship of pope to council.[85] In any case, he added, to dare to set the teaching of Constance and Basel against that of the Fifth Lateran Council and to suggest that legitimate general councils could actually disagree one with another smacked of

---

[81] *Trattato del' Interdetto*, in Busnelli and Gambarin, III, esp. 3–17.

[82] Both responses are printed in a single volume bearing the title: *Riposta de Card. Bellarmino al Trattato de i sette Theologi di Venetia sopra l'interdetto della Santità di Nostro Signore Papa Paolo Quinto* (Rome, 1606). But the response to the *Trattato* actually occupies only the first seventy-two pages of a continuously paginated volume and is followed (pp. 73–139) by a reply to Sarpi's *Apologia* which bears the title: *Risposta alle oppositioni di Fra Paulo Servita contra la scrittura de Cardinale Bellarmino*.

[83] *Risposta alle oppositioni di Fra Paulo Sarpi Servita contra la scrittura di Cardinale Bellarmino*, pp. 127–28.

[84] *Risposta de Card. Bellarmino al Trattato de i setti theologi di Venetia*, p. 27.

[85] *Ibid.*, p. 29; also *Risposta alle oppositioni di Fra Paulo Servita*, p. 114.

nothing less than "the reasoning of heretics." If those who toyed with such noxious ideas were "truly Catholic teachers," then they would finally recognize where true legitimacy resided and realize that both Constance and Basel were of dubious legitimacy at the moment when they issued their superiority decrees. For (triumphantly now) "legitimate councils do not contradict one another, and that [council] alone is legitimate which has asserted the authority of the pope to be superior to all the councils."[86]

III

On this note of elegant circularity (the appeal of which to theologians continued with unabated force down into the second half of our own century),[87] the exchange among Bellarmine, Richer and Sarpi stimulated by Gerson's glancing evocation of the superiority of council to pope drew, at long last, to a close. In that it had served to focus so very much attention on the late medieval councils and the ecclesiology of the conciliarist authors, it seems fair to conclude that it had not had the effect that Bellarmine must have desired. Quite the opposite, in fact, and not only in Italy itself. If Richer's *Apologia* did not enjoy a wide circulation, within three years of its publication his later *De ecclesiastica et politica potestate* certainly did, and, along with it, the Latin texts of the other protoconciliarist, conciliarist, Gallican and Venetian writings (the *Trattato* included) that Melchior Goldast was also to include in his influential collection, the *Monarchia S. Romani Imperii* (1611–14).[88] And within a year of its first publication in Italian, an English translation of Sarpi's *Apologia* (as

---

[86] *Risposta del Card. Bellarmino al Trattato de i setti theologi di Venetia*, pp. 22–28, concluding with the words: "Et cosi non sono tra se contrarii, li Concilii legittimi, et quello solo è legittimo che affermo l'autorità del Papa essere superiore à tutti li Concilii."

[87] For a latter-day commitment to much the same point of view, see the alarm raised in 1964 by the distinguished historian of the Council of Florence, Joseph Gill, in his "The Fifth Session of the Council of Constance," *The Heythrop Journal*, V (1964), 131–43, and in his "Il decreto *Haec sancta synodus* del concilio di Costanza," *Rivista di storia della Chiesa in Italia*, XII (1967), 23–30. And for the enduring impact on Catholic ecclesiological thinking of the line of argument pioneered by Torquemada and developed further by Cajetan and Bellarmine, see Izbicki, "Papalist Reaction to the Council of Constance: Juan de Torquemada to the Present," 7–20.

[88] Goldast, *Monarchia S. Romani Imperii*, III, 178–385, 405–564, 762–73, 797–806 (Richer's tract).

also of his *Considerazioni*) was published in London, where its long conciliar section can only have encouraged the already established tendency among English contributors to the Oaths of Allegiance controversy to mine for their own purposes the arguments elaborated in the conciliarist literature.[89]

That this particular feature of the ideological warfare of the day should have escaped the attention of historians to the degree that it has speaks directly to the issue that served as our point of departure. In urging upon us the importance, if we wish to wrest genuinely historical meanings from the texts that come down to us from the past, of placing those texts in the linguistic and ideological context which helped frame them, Quentin Skinner was largely concerned with the threat of anachronism. He was intent upon precluding or reducing the possibility of our attributing meanings to such texts that might make perfectly good sense in the present but could hardly have been available to the author in his own day.[90] That concern, of course, is a perfectly justifiable one, but it is important that it be complemented by a comparable sensitivity to the danger of our misreading the contexts to which we have turned in our effort to comprehend the text. That parallel danger is at least as threatening because of the degree to which contexts are themselves textually mediated. And it is the more threatening given the range of choice open to us in the selection or construction of those contexts, as well as the degree to which we have to depend, as we go about that task of selection or construction, on historiographic traditions which will certainly be marked by their own flaws, which may well incorporate their own anachronisms, and which will not themselves be wholly unburdened with a measure of ideological freight.

The apparent failure of historians to perceive the centrality of the conciliarist issue to the polemical exchange occasioned by the sharpness of Bellarmine's critique of Gerson speaks to this point. As late as 1818 the English historian, Henry Hallam, could describe the Constance decrees *Haec sancta* and *Frequens* as "the great pillars of that moderate theory with respect to papal authority which [not only] distinguished the Gallican Church, . . . [but] is embraced by

---

[89] See Oakley, "Constance, Basel, and the two Pisas: The Conciliarist Legacy in Sixteenth- and Seventeenth-Century England."

[90] Skinner, "Meaning and Understanding in the history of ideas," in Tully ed., *Meaning and Context: Quentin Skinner and his Critics*, pp. 29–67.

almost all laymen and the major part of ecclesiastics on this side of the Alps."[91] Had *that* historiographic viewpoint set the context in which historians read Bellarmine's contributions to the Venetian war of words, then the vehemence of his reaction to the republication of Gerson's tracts and his extreme sensitivity as a loyal papalist to even an oblique evocation of the conciliarist ecclesiology would have been more readily understandable and more appropriately handled. But that historiographic viewpoint did not in fact set the interpretative context. By the end of the nineteenth century, what Hallam had seen as a live ecclesiological option embraced by most northern European Catholics had been consigned, by an ecclesiastical version of "the politics of oblivion,"[92] to the junk heap, if not of history, at least of historiography. Right down to the postwar years and the era of Vatican II, the historiographic tradition which shaped our picture of the conciliar movement and the fate of conciliar ideas after the ending of the Council of Basel was in some measure a reflection of, or, at least, unwittingly complicit with, that particular manifestation of the politics of oblivion.

A situation complex enough, no doubt, but the more complex, so far as it helped frame the interpretative context for our modern understanding of the Venetian battle of the books, in that it was fraught with irony. For if the historiographic tradition in question had its roots in Juan de Torquemada's efforts to vindicate the papal cause during Eugenius IV's darkest days at the Council of Basel, it was a tradition that had been put in canonical form by none other than Bellarmine himself. And it was, or so I would argue, the very triumph of Bellarmine's own portrayal of the heterodox nature and early demise of conciliarism that has stood in the way of our grasping the historical significance of his sharp attack on Gerson's tracts and of the intriguing polemical exchange to which that attack gave rise.

---

[91] Henry Hallam, *View of the State of Europe during the Middle Ages* (3 vols., London, 1901), III, 243 and 265. The work was first published in 1818.

[92] Thus in 1908 the editors of *The Catholic Encyclopedia* did not even deem it necessary to include in that work an article on conciliarism. The subject was given some attention under the heading of "Gallicanism," but the author of that article made the prevailing sentiment of his day quite clear. See A. Degart, in *The Catholic Encyclopedia* VI, 355, s.v. "Gallicanism": "Stricken to death, as a free opinion, by the Council of the Vatican, [theological] Gallicanism could survive only as a heresy; the Old Catholics have endeavored to keep it alive under this form. Judged by the paucity of the adherents whom they have recruited—daily becoming fewer in Germany and Switzerland, it seems very evident that the historical evolution of these ideas has reached its completion."

CHAPTER SEVEN

LOCKE, NATURAL LAW, AND GOD: AGAIN

Of the many *questiones disputatae* roiling the fast-moving waters of Locke scholarship, few have evinced a more persistent capacity to stimulate disagreement than the matter of his natural-law teaching—its status, significance, coherence, consistency. Almost half a century after Von Leyden made readily available in a printed edition the early *Essays on the Law of Nature*, sharply-conflicting assessments of that teaching continue to appear.[1] Since Curtis and Lamprecht focused attention on it in the first modern analyses of Locke's moral philosophy, debate over the nature of that teaching has been stubborn in its persistence. As a result, one is sorely tempted to indulge the gloomy conclusion that we are no closer to agreement now than we were in 1918 when Lamprecht framed his lucid and still valuable analysis.[2]

That temptation, however, is not one to which we should too readily yield. With the benefit of hindsight it is possible now to see that the publication of Von Leyden's edition (making available important materials from the Lovelace collection to which most earlier scholars had not had access) was indeed a turning-point in our understanding of the central position Locke's natural-law teaching occupied in his thought as a whole. Writing prior to that event, and without access to the Lovelace materials, Leo Strauss had found it possible to conclude that Locke "cannot have recognized any law of nature in the proper sense of the term." Less forgivably, even after

---

[1] John Locke, *Essays on the Law of Nature*, ed. and trans. W. Von Leyden Oxford, 1954); cf. the more recent translation of these essays in John Locke, *Questions concerning the Law of Nature*, ed. and trans. Robert Horwitz, Jenny Strauss Clay, and Diskin Clay (Ithaca and London, 1990). The conflicting interpretations are those of David E. Soles, "Intellectualism and Natural Law in Locke's *Second Treatise*," *History of Political Thought*, VIII (No. 1, 1987), 63–81, and W. Randall Ward, "Divine Will, Natural Law and the Voluntarism/Intellectualism Debate in Locke," *ibid.*, XVI (No. 2, 1995), 208–18.

[2] Sterling P. Lamprecht, *The Moral and Political Philosophy of John Locke* (New York, 1918). The only previous monograph on Locke's ethics was that of Mattoon Monroe Curtis, *An Outline of Locke's Ethical Philosophy* (Leipzig, 1890).

examining the Lovelace materials and in the teeth of the textual evidence, he still stubbornly wondered if Locke did not really "intend to follow the lead given by Hobbes and to replace the traditional natural-law teaching by a moral teaching which is grounded in the desire or instinct for self-preservation."[3] In 1960, Richard Cox blithely endorsed much the same point of view and, as late as 1967, Philip Abrams could indicate his own inclination to prefer it to the position staked out by Von Leyden.[4] But while it is rare for major interpretations ever to be superseded in any definitive fashion, Strauss's viewpoint on this particular issue appears to have been at least as effectively sidelined in the subsequent scholarship as has the very different case argued in the same era by C.B. McPherson.[5]

---

[3] Leo Strauss, *Natural Right and History* (Chicago, 1953), pp. 202–51 (at 220); *idem*, "Locke's Doctrine of Natural Law," in Strauss, *What is Political Philosophy? and other Studies* (Glencoe, IL., 1959), pp. 197–220 (esp. pp. 204, 206, 214–15).

[4] Richard H. Cox, *Locke on War and Peace* (Oxford, 1960), pp. 45–105 at 88–89; Philip Abrams ed., *John Locke: Two Tracts on Government* (Cambridge, 1967), Introduction, p. 108 n. 12.

[5] C.B. MacPherson, *The Political Theory of Possessive Individualism: Hobbes to Locke* (Oxford, 1962). The body of scholarly literature addressing the natural-law issue in Locke has now become quite extensive. In addition to the works already cited, see J.W. Gough, *John Locke's Political Philosophy* (Oxford, 1950, 1956), ch. 1; John T. Noonan, Jr., "The Protestant Philosophy of John Locke," in *Philosophical Studies in Honor of . . . Ignatius Smith, O.P.*, ed. J.K. Ryan (Westminster, MD, 1952), pp. 92–126; John Wild, *Plato's Modern Enemies and the Theory of Natural Law* (Chicago, 1953), pp. 127–32; W. von Leyden, "John Locke and Natural Law," *Philosophy*, XXXI (1956), 23–35; John W. Yolton, "Locke on the Law of Nature," *The Philosophical Review*, LXVII (1958), 477–98; Charles H. Monson, "Locke and his Interpreters," *Political Studies*, VI (1958), 120–26; A.P. Brogan, "John Locke and Utilitarianism," *Ethics*, LXIX (1959), 90–91; Raymond Polin, *La politique morale de John Locke* (Paris, 1960), pp. 95–128; Raghuveer Singh, "John Locke and the Theory of Natural Law," *Political Studies*, IX (1961), 105–18; Martin Seliger, "Locke's Natural Law and the Foundation of Politics," *Journal of the History of Ideas*, XXIV (1963), 337–54; Michael Bertram Crowe, "Intellect and Will in John Locke's Conception of the Natural Law," in *Atti del XII Congresso Internazionale di Filosofia, Venezia, 12–18 Settembre 1958* (Florence, 1961), 129–34; James W. Byrne, "The Basis of Natural Law in Locke's Philosophy," *Catholic Lawyer*, X (1964), 55–63; Francis Oakley and Elliot W. Urdang, "Locke, Natural Law, and God," *Natural Law Forum*, XI (1966), 92–109; John Dunn, *The Political Thought of John Locke* (Cambridge, 1969), pp. 187–99, and his *Locke* (Oxford, 1984), esp. pp. 30–31, 58–62; Hans Aarsleff, "The State of Nature and the nature of man in Locke," in *John Locke: Problems and Perspectives*, ed. John W. Yolton (Cambridge, 1969), pp. 99–136; A.W. Sparkes, "Trust and Teleology: Locke's Politics and his Doctrine of Creation," *Canadian Journal of Philosophy*, III (1973), 263–73; James O. Hancey, "John Locke and the Law of Nature," *Political Theory*, IV (1976), 439–55; Merwyn S. Johnson, *Locke on Freedom* (Austin, 1978), pp. 26–41; S.B. Drury, "John Locke, Natural Law and Innate Ideas," *Dialogue*, XIX (1980), 531–45; James Tully, *A Discourse on Property: John Locke and his adversaries* (Cambridge, 1980), pp. 34–50, and his "Governing conduct: Locke on the reform of thought

In that subsequent vein of commentary many issues pertaining to Locke's natural-law teaching have been addressed, but two may be singled out as having been dwelt upon with the greatest degree of insistence. First, the matter of the relationship between the intellectualist/rationalist and voluntarist aspects of that teaching, which, during Locke's own lifetime, had already drawn acerbic commentary from Thomas Burnet. On those aspects, early in the present century, Lamprecht had focussed renewed attention, arguing that Locke "vacillated between two theories of the relation of God's will to the moral law," according to one of which (the intellectualist) "things are commanded or forbidden by God because they are right or wrong," while, according to the other (the voluntarist) "they are right or wrong because God commands or forbids them."[6] Second, the matter of the relationship between Locke's intellectualism *and* voluntarism, on the one hand, and, on the other, the element of hedonism which became increasingly prominent in his thinking from the late 1670s onward. With the second I will not be concerned

---

and behavior," first published in 1988 and reprinted in Tully, *An Approach to Political Philosophy, Locke in Contexts* (Cambridge, 1993), pp. 179–241; G.A.J. Rogers, "Locke, Law and the Laws of Nature," in *John Locke: Symposium Wolfenbuttel 1979*, ed. Reinhardt Brandt (Berlin and New York, 1981), pp. 146–62; John Colman, *John Locke's Moral Philosophy* (Edinburgh, 1983); David Wootton, "John Locke: Socinian or natural law theorist," in James E. Crimmins ed., *Religion, Secularization and Political Thought from Thomas Hobbes to J.S. Mill* (London and New York, 1989), pp. 39–67; Horowitz, Introduction to John Locke, *Questions concerning the Law of Nature*, ed. Horowitz *et al.*, pp. 1–28, 45–62; Stephen Buckle, *Natural Law and the Theory of Property: Grotius to Hume* (Oxford, 1991), pp. 125–90; Michael Ayers, *Locke* (2 vols., London and New York, 1991), II, Part 2, "God, Nature, and the Law of Nature," 129–62; J.B. Schneewind, "Locke's moral philosophy," in *The Cambridge Companion to Locke*, ed. Vere Chappell (Cambridge, 1994), 129–225; Ian Harris, *The Mind of John Locke: A Study of political theory in its intellectual setting* (Cambridge, 1994), pp. 78–106; Stephen Darwell, *The British Moralists and the Internal "Ought": 1660–1740* (Cambridge, 1995), pp. 23–52, 149–75. The quickening since the 1950s in Locke scholarship in general is dramatically evident in Roland Hall and Roger Woolhouse, *80 Years of Locke Scholarship: A Bibliographical Guide* (Edinburgh, 1983), which takes the story down to 1981. For a helpful collection of many of the crucial journal articles, see Richard Ashcraft ed. *John Locke: Critical Assessments* (4 vols., London and New York, 1991). In the second volume, 1–129 he reprints the articles of Von Leyden, Yolton, Seliger, Byrne, Oakley and Urdang, Sparkes and Drury listed above.

[6] Thomas Burnet, *[First] Remarks Upon an Essay Concerning Human Understanding, in a Letter Addressed to the Author* (London, 1697), p. 6, where he needles Locke by asking him to clarify his position on the issue: "You seem to resolve all into the Will and Power of the Law-Maker: But has the Will of the Law-Maker no Rule to go by? And is not that which is a Rule to his Will, a Rule also to Ours, and indeed the Original Rule?"; Lamprecht, *The Moral and Political Philosophy of John Locke*, pp. 105–8.

here. Although some have portrayed the relationship in questions as a tension-ridden one,[7] Locke himself clearly did not think it was, firmly distinguishing between moral obligation and psychological motivation, between moral rectitude "in itself" and the "good" constituted by the pleasure and pain which "either accompanies [the moral or immoral] action or is looked on as a consequence of it." Hence "the punishments and rewards which God has annexed to moral rectitude or pravity as proper motives to the will" and the relationship of which to moral rectitude is one of complementarity rather than competition.[8] And the scholarship of the past quarter of a century has been marked by something of a burgeoning consensus to the effect that, in so arguing, Locke was not completely deluding himself.[9]

If it would be redundant, then, to dwell further on this latter issue, that is by no means the case with the prior matter of the relationship between the intellectualist and voluntarist strands in Locke's thinking. Here, although our understanding of his natural-law teaching has undoubtedly been advanced by the work of the past several decades, the progress made has been piecemeal rather than systematic, the territory legitimately won has not really been consolidated into any viable scholarly consensus, later contributors to the debate have not always paid adequate attention to (or even been aware of) the arguments of their predecessors, and, as a result, in the more recent contributions a regrettable degree of intellectual slippage has sometimes been evident.[10] It is to this particular issue, then, that I propose now to return. And in so doing I will take as my point of

---

[7] E.g., Richard I. Aaron, *John Locke* (2nd ed., Oxford, 1955), p. 257; Von Leyden, introduction to his edition of the *Essays on the Law of Nature*, pp. 71–73; Mabbott, *John Locke*, pp. 112–28.

[8] See especially his note on *Voluntas* (1693), Ms. Locke c. 28, fol. 114v, printed in Von Leyden ed., *Essays on the Law of Nature*, pp. 22–23.

[9] Thus Hans Aarsleff, "The State of Nature and the nature of man in Locke," and his "Some observations on recent Locke scholarship," both in Yolton ed., *John Locke: Problems and Perspectives*, 99–136, 262–71 (at 127, 262–63); Tully, *A Discourse on Property*, p. 43; *idem*, "Governing conduct," esp. pp. 201–208; Colman, *John Locke's Moral Philosophy*, esp. pp. 68–69, 235–36; Buckle, *Natural Law and the Theory of Property*, pp. 129–30, 146; Ward, "Divine Will, Natural Law and the Voluntarism/Intellectualism Debate in Locke," 213–16.

[10] Thus, for example, in 1976 Hancey, "John Locke and the Law of Nature," could still speak (441, 447–48) of *"the Traditional conception of the Law of Nature"* (italics mine) as if that tradition was a unified one, and in 1995 Ward, "Divine Will, Natural Law and the Voluntarism/Intellectualism Debate in Locke," could write as if the voluntarism involved in the debate in question was limited to the matter of the *binding force* of the natural law and did not extend to its content.

departure the shifting context and focus of the discussion surrounding it since the mid-1960s when, moved especially by the confusions we felt Strauss and Singh had sponsored, Elliot Urdang and I transgressed the traditional confines of medieval studies in order to insert ourselves into what was a quintessentially early-modern debate.[11]

When we did so, the question which preoccupied most scholars attempting to assess the intellectualist and voluntarist strands in Locke's thinking appeared to be that of deciding whether (as with Strauss, Cox, Wild and Byrne)[12] he was simply to be read out of "the classical and Christian natural-law tradition" or as with Singh (Curtis *redivivus?*), securely reinstated within it.[13] That being so, and coming at the issue as we did from the direction, not of subsequent but of antecedent intellectual developments, we were at pains to stress two things. First, that it was simply improper to speak of any *single* "classical and Christian" or even "medieval" natural-law tradition which could then be contrasted with a "modern" notion of natural law. On the contrary, in the later Middle Ages and persisting on into the sixteenth and seventeenth centuries there had been two main traditions of natural-law thinking. One of them was grounded in one or other form of ontological essentialism (or "realism," to use the medieval term). The other was grounded in the type of theological voluntarism characteristic of William of Ockham (d. 1349) and of his fourteenth- and fifteenth-century nominalist successors. Second, that the failure to appreciate that fact (or fully to understand what it entailed) had had the effect of impeding our understanding of Locke's own natural-law thinking, which, we argued, could be most accurately understood as a pretty faithful continuation of the late-medieval voluntarist tradition.

[11] Oakley and Urdang, "Locke, Natural Law, and God."

[12] Strauss, *Natural Right and History*, pp. 202–57, *idem*, "Locke's Doctrine of Natural Law," 197–220; Cox, *Locke on War and Peace*, pp. 88–89; Wild, *Plato's Modern Enemies and the Theory of Natural Law*, pp. 127–32; Byrne "The Basis of Natural Law in Locke's Philosophy," esp. 58–60. Note that even Colman, in his most impressive *John Locke's Moral Philosophy*, can speak (pp. 238 and 240) of "the classical natural law tradition" and "the classical natural law conception" and (p. 240) can say that Locke "could not be considered a natural law theorist if he maintained that the content of morality was . imposed by God upon man. . . ."

[13] Singh, "John Locke and the Theory of Natural Law," esp. 111–12. Or, earlier on, Curtis, *An Outline of Locke's Ethical Philosophy*, p. 61: ". . . [W]e may suppose that Locke's views on natural law were in general accord with those of Tully [i.e., Cicero]. And this we find to be the case. . . ." Or, later, Hancey, "John Locke and the Law of Nature," 447–48.

In so arguing, we harbored no illusion that we were the first commentators on Locke to be aware of the fact that the medieval natural-law tradition had by no means been a homogeneous one.[14] Nor, for that matter, were we to be the last.[15] Among the earlier commentators, Curtis, Lamprecht, Gough, Von Leyden and Singh, for example, were all of them aware of the intellectualist-voluntarist split in that tradition. Unfortunately, however, most of them appear to have depended for their understanding of the issue upon one of the most frequently cited of Otto Gierke's lengthy footnotes.[16] And though he did not acknowledge the fact, Gierke had based his analysis of the scholastic authors he cites in that note, not (or so I would judge) on his own independent analysis of their texts, but rather on the somewhat tendentious characterization of their views to be found in the *De Legibus ac Deo Legislatore* of Francisco Suarez (d. 1617). In that summation, Suarez had contrived to assimilate Aquinas's much more intellectualistic position to his own more juridical one, improperly ascribing thereby to the earlier Thomists the distinctly Suarezian teaching that the binding force of the natural law, though not its content, was to be ascribed to its legislation by the divine will.[17] As a result, Gough, Von Leyden and Singh, in attempting to assess the precise balance of intellectualist and voluntarist elements in Locke's thinking and to appraise it in the light of earlier scholastic views, were operating perforce with a distorted understanding of those views.

---

[14] Gough, *John Locke's Political Philosophy*, p. 4; Von Leyden, *John Locke: Essays*, pp. 51–60; Singh, "John Locke and the Theory of Natural Law," 110–12.

[15] See Drury (1980), "John Locke: Natural Law and Innate Ideas," 542; Tully, *A Dicourse on Property* (1980), pp. 40–41, and his "Governing Conduct," (1988), pp. 201–6; Colman, *John Locke's Moral Philosophy* (1983), p. 240; Ayers, *Locke* (1991), II, 131–34.

[16] See Otto Gierke, *Political Theories of the Middle Ages*, ed. and trans. F.W. Maitland (Cambridge, 1900), pp. 172–73, n. 256, where he explains, helpfully enough, that "The older [scholastic] view, which is more especially that of the Realists, explained the *Lex Naturalis* as an intellectual act independent of Will—as a mere *lex indicativa* in which God was not lawgiver but a teacher working by means of Reason—in short, as the dictate of Reason as to what is right, grounded in the Being of God but unalterable even by him. . . . The opposite position, proceeding from pure Nominalism, saw in the Law of Nature a mere divine Command, which was right and binding because God was the Lawgiver."

[17] Compare Gierke, *Political Theories of the Middle Ages*, pp. 172–73, n. 256, with Francisco Suarez, *De Legibus ac Deo Legislatore* (Coimbra, 1612), Lib. II, c. 6, reproduced in James Scott Brown ed., *The Classics of International Law: Selection from Three Works of Francisco Suarez, S.J.*, (2 vols., Oxford, 1944), I, 119–29 (English translation at II, 187–208). Cf. Oakley and Urdang, "Locke, Natural Law and God," 99–100.

All of this we pointed out in 1966, but so far as I have been able to ascertain, we did so to little or no effect.[18] Many of the subsequent commentators address the issue with only the most glancing of references to the scholastic past[19] or with really none at all, attempting instead to come to terms with Locke's seemingly conflicting statements in no broader a context than that provided by his own *oeuvre* taken as a whole or, at most, that constituted by the writings of his seventeenth-century contemporaries.[20] Others, properly recognizing the pertinence of scholastic antecedents, bring to their interpretative effort, nonetheless, a somewhat wavering understanding of the nature of the voluntarist tradition.[21] And none, to my knowledge, has attempted to bring into a meaningful configuration the newer perspectives generated by the advances evident both in recent Locke

---

[18] Our article appears to have attracted no attention at all until 1983, when it was listed in Hall and Woolhouse, *80 Years of Locke Scholarship*. And even then, it appears to have had no impact on the continuing discussion of the relationship between the intellectualistic and voluntaristic strands in Locke's natural law teaching until 1988, when James Tully, citing it and the earlier works of mine on which it built, concluded that it had "put past doubt" the fact that Locke considered "both the obligation and the content of natural law" to be "derived from god's will"— see his "Governing conduct," 206 n. 104, and 202–3, nn. 93 and 95. Cf James Tully, "Locke," in J.H. Burns and Mark Goldie eds., *The Cambridge History of Political Thought: 1450–1700* (Cambridge, 1991), 625. In 1991 Ashcraft reprinted the (Oakley-Urdang) article in his *John Locke: Critical Assessments*, II, 63–83.

[19] Thus, for example, Abrams, *John Locke: Two Tracts on Government*, pp. 80–81, where he, too, relies (as did Colman later on) on what he calls "Gierke's famous analysis of medieval theories of law" (i.e., the footnote); cf. Colman, *John Locke's Moral Philosophy*, p. 269, n. 6. See also Dunn, *The Political Thought of John Locke*, and his *Locke*; Hancey, "John Locke and the Law of Nature;" A.W. Sparkes, "Trust and Teleology, Locke's Politics and his Doctrine of Creation;" Drury, "John Locke: Natural Law and Innate Ideas;" Darwall, *The British Moralist and the Internal "Ought": 1640–1740*.

[20] Thus Parry, *John Locke*; Soles, "Intellectualism and Natural Law in Locke's *Second Treatise*;" Harris, *The Mind of John Locke*; Ward, "Divine Will, Natural Law and the Voluntarism/Intellectualism Debate in Locke;" Horwitz, Introduction to John Locke, *Questions concering the Law of Nature*, Horwitz *et al.*, esp. pp. 10–28.

[21] That is in some measure true even of the fine analysis of Tully, *A Discourse on Property*, p. 41, where he incorrectly asserts that the Ockhamists believed "natural laws" to be "imperatives *accepted on faith*" (italics mine), and of Ayers, *Locke*, II, 190 and 196, where running together the orders of creation and redemption and perhaps unconscious of the fact that the late-medieval preoccupation with the implications of the divine omnipotence had found expression in more than one particular theology of justification, he appears incorrectly to assume that what he calls a "strong, seriously meant voluntarism" must necessarily go hand in glove with a staunchly Calvinistic doctrinc of election. In any case, theories of natural law pertain to the realm, not of *revealed* or *dogmatic theology*, but to that of *natural theology*. On all of which, see the brief discussion in Francis Oakley, *The Western Church in the Later Middle Ages* (Ithaca and London, 1979), pp. 133–48.

scholarship and in our knowledge and understanding of the nominalist thinkers of the fourteenth and fifteenth centuries.

In this essay, then, it is my purpose to try to remedy this last defect. So far as our understanding of Locke's natural-law teaching is concerned, scholarly developments in both fields manifest a happy degree of intellectual convergence that it is now time to explore, turning first to the Lockean texts themselves, and then to the pertinent scholarship. The texts—including those that most stubbornly resist interpretation—remain, of course, the same. But how we should look at them has in significant measure been changed by the scholarly advances of the past quarter-century.

I

Although Curtis and Singh contrived to stitch together from disparate statements strewn across Locke's works what they took to be a consistently intellectualist theory of natural law, few today, I suspect, would be inclined to challenge the claim that it is, rather, the voluntarist strand that figures most prominently and most persistently in his texts taken as a whole. Certainly, it is the strand that is interwoven throughout his thinking. It emerges in the second of his early *Tracts on Government* (1660–62) and in his *Commonplace Book* (1661), occupies a prominent place in his *Essays on the Law of Nature* (1660–64), continues on through the *First* and *Second Treatises of Government* (1689–90), the *Essay Concerning Human Understanding* (1690) and the paper *Of Ethics in General* (containing material Locke withheld from the *Essay* when he published it), and is still present in *The Reasonableness of Christianity* published in the last decade of his life.[22] It is to the divine will that these texts trace the natural law no less than the divine (positive) law, distinguishing the former from the latter by virtue of the fact that God makes it known to us, not by divine rev-

---

[22] Abrams ed., *John Locke: Two Tracts on Government*, pp. 220–22; Von Leyden ed., *Essays on the Law of Nature*, esp. Essays I, IV and VI, pp. 111–13, 151, 185–87; *First Treatise of Government* §§ 86 and 166, *Second Treatise of Government* § 135, ed. Peter Laslett, *John Locke: Two Treatises of Government* (Cambridge, 1988), pp 205, 261–62, 358; *An Essay Concerning Human Understanding*, I, ii, §§ 6, 12 and 18, II, xxviii, §§ 5 and 8, ed. Peter H. Nidditch (Oxford, 1975), pp. 351–52; *Of Ethics in General*, printed in Lord King, *The Life of John Locke*, new ed. (2 vols., London, 1830), II, 130–31, 133; *The Reasonableness of Christianity*, in *The Works of John Locke* 10th ed. (10 vols., London, 1801), VII, 144.

elation, but by the light of nature.[23] To the fact that it is, indeed, a disclosure of that divine will (which binds "of itself and by its intrinsic force") natural law owes its obligatory force, for it is "the decree of a superior will, wherein the formal cause of a law appears to consist."[24] Further than that, it is from the declaration of the same omnipotent will, which "delimits the obligation and the ground of our obedience," that the very nature and content of the natural law's precepts and prohibitions derive.[25] If Locke does not hesitate himself to refer to that law as the "law of Reason" or to equate it with "Reason, the common Rule and Measure God hath given to Mankind" or implanted in us,[26] he is at the same time careful to insist, defining natural law again as the "decree of the divine will," that it is

> less correctly termed by some people the dictate of reason [*dictatum rationis*] since reason does not so much establish and pronounce this law of nature as search for it and discover it as a law enacted by a superior power and implanted in our hearts. Neither is reason so much the maker of that law as its interpreter, unless, violating the dignity of the supreme legislator, we wish to make reason responsible for that received law which it merely investigates; nor indeed can reason give us laws, since it is only a faculty of our mind and part of us.[27]

If such, then, were the only "intellectualist" texts with which Locke confronts the would-be interpreter of his natural-law thinking, his credentials as a thorough-going voluntarist could hardly have been drawn seriously into question. But they are not, of course, the only such texts and problems begin to emerge as soon as the interpretative action moves from the human side of the equation to the divine.[28]

---

[23] "Second Tract on Government," in Abrams ed., *John Locke: Two Tracts on Government*, p. 222; Von Leyden ed., *Essays on the Law of Nature*, Essay II, pp. 132–33, Essay VI, pp. 186–87.

[24] Von Leyden ed., *Essays on the Law of Nature*, Essay VI, pp. 186–87, Essay I, pp. 110–13. Cf. Locke's *Common-Place Book*, in King, *Life of John Locke*, II, 94.

[25] Von Leyden ed., *Essays on the Law of Nature*, Essay VI, pp. 185–87.

[26] *Second Treatise of Government*, §§ 6, 10–11, 56; ed. Laslett, pp. 271, 273–74, 305.

[27] Von Leyden, ed., *Essays on the Laws of Nature*, Essay I, pp. 110–11, where Locke has just defined natural law as "the decree of the divine will discernible by the light of nature and indicating what is and what is not in conformity with rational nature, and for this very reason commanding or prohibiting." Cf. Essay VII, pp. 198–99, where he speaks again of the conformity or harmony between natural law and man's rational nature.

[28] In contrast to the position we took in 1966 (see Oakley and Urdang, 96), I would now judge that it is only when Locke addresses the divine side of the question and evokes (if only indirectly and by implications) the old question of the primacy of will or reason in God that such problems do emerge.

For it is at that point that some of Locke's own statements signal
the pertinence of the question that Thomas Burnet put to him so
forcefully after the publication of the *Essay Concerning Human Understanding*,
but to which Locke vouchsafed no clear reply. If moral good and
evil are grounded in the precepts of the divine law, what then, Burnet
asked, is the ultimate ground of that law itself? Can it really be "the
Arbitrary Will of God" rather than "the intrinsick Nature of the
Things themselves?" Locke, he charged, seemed "to resolve all into
the Will and Power of the Law-Maker. But, then, has the Will of
the Law-Maker no Rule to go by? And is not that which is a Rule
to *his* Will, a Rule also to Ours and indeed the Original Rule?"[29]

The question was a good one, and it is a fact that scattered across
Locke's works are remarks which could conceivably be read to suggest that God's will was indeed subject to some such "Original Rule."
He more than once spoke, after all, of natural law as being an "eternal law" and insisted that its obligations were "so great, and so
strong," that in the case at least of "*Grants, Promises* and *Oaths*"
". . . *Omnipotency* itself can be tyed by them."[30] "That unlimited power,"
or so he says elsewhere, "cannot be an excellency without it be regulated by wisdom and goodness."[31] Indeed, "we might say that God
himself *cannot* choose what is not good; the freedom of the Almighty
hinders not his being determined by what is best."[32] The "eternal
law of right" being "holy, just and good," it is not open to abrogation or repeal "whilst God is an holy, just, and righteous God."[33]
For "this law does not depend on an unstable and dangerous will,
but on the eternal order of things." It is "a fixed and permanent
rule of morals," proclaimed by reason and "firmly rooted in the soil
of human nature." Only if human nature itself were to be changed
could it be "altered or annulled."[34]

So presented, such texts would certainly appear to suggest the
need to insert some sort of rationalistic qualification into what has
otherwise to be acknowledged as the controlling voluntarism of Locke's

---

[29] Thomas Burnet, [*First*] *Remarks Upon an Essay Concerning Human Understanding in
a Letter Addressed to the Author* (London 1697), p. 6.
[30] *Second Treatise of Government*, § 195, ed. Laslett, pp. 395–96. Cf. *First Treatise of
Government*, § 6, *ibid.*, p. 144, where he refers to "Promises and Oaths, which tye
the infinite Deity."
[31] King, *Life of John Locke*, I, 228 (entry under Sunday, August 7, 1681).
[32] *Essay Concerning Human Understanding*, II, xxi § 49, ed. Nidditch, p. 265.
[33] *The Reasonableness of Christianity*, in *The Works of John Locke*, VII, 111–12.
[34] Von Leyden ed., *Essays on the Law of Nature*, Essay VII, pp. 198–99.

natural law thinking. And that is, in effect, precisely what scholars like Lamprecht and Von Leyden have long insisted. But the fleeting and fragmentary nature of the statements involved, as well as Locke's manifest uneasiness with any probing discussion of the divine nature,[35] suggest the wisdom of refraining from conceding the point until the texts in question have been appraised more fully, and in a threefold context. First, that provided by the works in which they themselves appear. Second, and more broadly, that constituted by Locke's thinking taken as a whole (theological as well as ethical, ontological as well as epistemological) and by the intellectual currents prevailing in his lifetime. Third, and most challenging of all, that provided by the long and tense history of Christian attempts to harmonize, and in moral philosophy as well as ontology, the conflicting implications flowing from the disparate notions of the divine embedded in the biblical and Greek philosophical patterns of thought. It is to an exploration of that threefold context that I propose now to turn, beginning with the last and most general and ending with the first and most particular.

II

There can be few developments in the history of philosophy more tangled and complex than the movement of ideas in late antiquity that had culminated by the fourth century C.E. in the Neoplatonic patterns of thought encountered by St. Augustine in what he was wont to call "the books of the Platonists."[36] Among other things, this movement had involved a persistent tendency to understand the mysterious Demiurgos of Plato's *Timaeus* not as a mythic symbol but literally as a World-Maker, to conflate him with the Transcendent Unmoved Mover of Aristotle's *Metaphysics*—the final and highest good whom he himself call "god"—and to treat Plato's eternally subsistent Ideas or Forms not as independent entities but as thoughts or ideas *in the mind* of the supreme God resulting from that conflation. Thus emerged the notion of a transcendent God, at once the Highest

---

[35] I am referring to his *Examination of Malebranche's Opinion of Seeing All Things in God* and the related *Remarks Upon Some of Mr. Norris's Books*, works in which Locke is forced, of necessity, to direct some attention to Malebranche's discussion of the divine ideas. On which, see Oakley and Urdang, 107–9.

[36] E.g. *Confessiones*, VII, 9, 20, 21.

Good to which all things aspire, the First Cause to which all things owe their being, the Supreme Reason from which all things derive their order and intelligibility, and, increasingly (for Neoplatonism was no less a path of salvation than a philosophy), the object of a lively devotional sentiment.

In light of this development, it is easy enough to comprehend how St. Augustine, following the trail blazed by Philo Judaeus and later broadened by the Greek Fathers of the Church, was able to engineer in a fashion that proved to be definitive for Latin Christian philosophy the further conflation of the Neoplatonic God—the God of the philosophers, as it were, in its final and most developed version—with the biblical God of Abraham, Isaac and Jacob, the personal God of power and might who not only transcends the universe but also created it out of nothing. In so doing, by agreeing with Philo, the Neoplatonists and many of his Christian predecessors that the creative act was indeed an intelligent one guided by Ideas of the Platonic mould but ideas located now in the divine mind, he responded to the Greek concern to vindicate philosophically the order and intelligibility of the universe. By virtue of his authority, then, he secured for the doctrine of the divine Ideas an enduring place in Christian philosophy and theology.

That very doctrine witnesses, however, to the severe internal tensions that Augustine's synthesis involved. In the historic encounter between the Greek philosophical tradition and religious views of biblical provenance, the great stumbling block had been (and necessarily remained) the difficulty of reconciling the personal and transcendent biblical God of power and might, upon whose will the very existence of the universe was contingent, with the characteristically Greek intuition of the divine as limited and innerworldly and of the universe as necessary and eternal—or, to put it somewhat differently, with the persistent tendency of the Greek philosophers to identify the divine with the immanent and necessary rational order of an eternal cosmos.[37] Those tensions mounted in the course of the twelfth and thirteenth centuries, when Augustine's treaty had, as it were, to be renegotiated and a far more difficult accommodation reached with full-scale philosophical systems of Arab-Aristotelian amalgam.

---

[37] For a discussion of this point and its implications, I venture to refer to the essays gathered together in Daniel O'Connor and Francis Oakley eds., *Creation: The Impact of an Idea* (New York, 1969).

Asserting not only the eternity of the world but also its necessity, those systems confronted Christian scholastic thinkers with the picture of a determined world in which everything had to be what it was and which permitted no room for the play of free will in either man or God. And not even the subtle philosophical and theological diplomacy of an Aquinas proved capable of convincing his more conservative contemporaries that such an accommodation was truly possible without the abandonment or radical modification of beliefs so fundamental to Christianity as to be non-negotiable. Edging beyond the hallowed "negative way" of attempting to come to terms with the divine nature,[38] Aquinas argued that by extrapolating from our human knowledge of created things and by recourse to an analogical use of terms, it was possible without equivocation to predicate of God such positive attributes as intelligence, wisdom and goodness. Bolder in his rationalism than many of his more conservative contemporaries, he set out, by blending Aristotelian and Augustinian notions (including the doctrine of the divine ideas), to demonstrate that God's creative act was not only a free but also a rational one, thus vindicating the order, rationality and intelligibility of the universe. Assuming the primacy of reason over will not only in man but in God, he regarded what in later parlance would be called the (moral) natural law and the (physical) laws of nature in comparatively "Greek" fashion as both of them the external manifestations of an indwelling and immanent reason. Thus he spoke of an "eternal law" that orders to their appropriate ends all created beings, irrational no less than rational, and defined that law as "nothing other than the idea of the divine wisdom insofar as it directs all acts and movements" and governs "the whole community of the universe."[39]

It was the advantage of this way of looking at things that it enabled one to regard the whole of being, the realm of nature no less than that of man, as in its own fashion subject to the norms of the same

---

[38] The way pursued by such influential Christian thinkers as the anonymous author whom we know as Dionysius the Areopagite and his ninth-century translator, John Eriugena, as also by such Jewish thinkers as Avicebron (d. *ca.* 1058) and Maimonides (d. 1204). In accordance with that approach to the knowledge of the divine, we cannot aspire to know what God *is.* The best we can hope to do is to struggle through to a knowledge of what he is *not.* There is a lucid account of the degree to which Aquinas edged beyond that position and of what his doctrine of analogy involved in Brian Davies, *The Thought of Thomas Aquinas* (Oxford, 1993), pp. 58–97.

[39] *Summa theologiae*, Ia IIae, qu. 91, art. 1 and 2; qu. 93, art. 1.

eternal law. The correlative disadvantage, however, was that that subjection to law could arguably be taken to extend to God himself, thus threatening his freedom and omnipotence. For the eternal law is nothing other than one aspect of the divine reason itself, and in God reason is prior to will. It would appear, therefore, that the old discord between Greek and biblical notions of the divine, far from being resolved in the new accommodations spawned by the theology of the schools, was simply transposed into another key, reappearing at the level, as it were, of the divine psychology. And with Aquinas's doctrine of eternal law, the tensions involved had for some not only survived but been intensified to breaking point.

During the century following his death in 1274, then, many of the rationalistic commitments characteristic of Aquinas and of those who trod in his footsteps were called into question—among them the priority accorded to the divine intellect over the divine will and the confidence in the capacity of analogical reasoning to cast a conceptual net really capable of encompassing in a meaningful commonality of discourse the natures of both God and man and bridging the gulf dividing the infinite from the finite.[40] The inclination now was to take the divine omnipotence as the fundamental principle, to accord to the divine will the primacy in God's workings *ad extra*, and to understand the order of the created world (both the moral order governing human behavior and the natural order governing the behavior of irrational beings) no longer as a participation in a divine reason that is in some measure transparent to the human intellect, but rather as the deliverance of an inscrutable divine will. The hallowed doctrine of the divine ideas came now under challenge,[41] and with it the epistemological realism and the whole metaphysics of essences in which it was embedded, as well as the affiliated understanding of the universe as an intelligible organism penetrable by *a*

---

[40] For a detailed and carefully nuanced discussion of the issues embedded in this shift, see Marilyn McCord Adams, *William Ockham* (2 vols., Notre Dame, Ind., 1987), II, 903–1010.

[41] Though respect for the authority of St. Augustine softened the impact of this challenge. Thus William of Ockham was careful to retain the *language* of the traditional doctrine even while emptying it of its traditional content. If we are to speak of the divine ideas we must remember that we are speaking, not of any universal ideas, but merely of the ideas which God has of actual or possible individual creatures. See William of Ockham, *Scriptum in librum primum Sententiarum (Ordinatio)*, I, dist. 35, qu. 5, esp. art. 3; ed. G.I. Etzkorn and F.E. Kelley (New York, 1979), 485–507. The whole question is devoted to the matter.

priori reasoning precisely because it was itself ordered and sustained by an indwelling and immanent reason. The tendency, therefore, was to set God over against the world he had created and which was constantly dependent upon him, to view it now as an aggregate of particular entities linked solely by external relations, comprehensible (and, if God so chose, capable of existing) each in isolation from the others, and, as a result, open to investigation only by some form of empirical endeavor.

With its characteristic linkage of an emphasis on the divine omnipotence and a concomitant understanding of the natural law as imposed by the divine will with a commitment to ontological particularism, epistemological "nominalism" and a species of methodological empiricism, this tendency became dominant among the scholastic thinkers affiliated with the late-medieval nominalist school. Despite its diversity, that school still drew its basic inspiration from the philosophical and theological writings of William of Ockham (d. 1349). In relation especially to ethical and legal issues, its guiding principles found a particularly powerful and influential expression in the thinking of Pierre d'Ailly (d. 1420).[42] And moved in this, it may be surmised, by Suarez's listing of the leading late-medieval voluntarists, it was at both of these men, along with Andreas de Novo Castro (b. *ca.* 1340), that Ralph Cudworth, the Cambridge Platonist and a contemporary of Locke's, pointed an accusing finger when he signaled his alarm about the re-emergence in his own day of the voluntarist ethic "promoted and advanced by such as think nothing so essential to the Deity as uncontrollable power and arbitrary will," and teaching "that there is no act evil but as it is prohibited by God, and which cannot be made good if it be commended by God. And so on the other hand as to good."[43]

---

[42] For a fuller discussion of their views, see Francis Oakley, "Medieval Theories of Natural Law: William of Ockham and the Significance of the Voluntarist Tradition," *Natural Law Forum*, VI (1961), 65–83; Arthur S. McGrade, *The Political Thought of William of Ockham: Personal and Institutional Principles* (Cambridge, 1974), pp. 173–96; Oakley, *The Political Thought of Pierre d'Ailly: The Voluntarist Tradition* (New Haven and London, 1964), pp. 163–97. D'Ailly's discussion in his *Sentences* of the nature and grounding of law and of its various modalities is extensive enough as to constitute almost a "treatise on law" in its own right.

[43] Ralph Cudworth, *Treatise Concerning Eternal and Immutable Morality*, Bk. I, chs. 1 and 3; in Cudworth, *The True Intellectual System of the Universe*, ed. Thomas Bird (2 vols., New York, 1838), II, esp. 369–71. Interestingly enough, he links the remergence in his own day of ethical voluntarism with the revival of "the physiological hypotheses of Democritus and Epicurus" (i.e. forms of atomism) and with their

The bluntness of that accusation notwithstanding, it should be noted that it would be easy enough in the cases of both Ockham and d'Ailly, by adopting an interpretative stance akin to that used by Singh in his approach to Locke, by responding disproportionately to their more practical evocations of the authority of natural law, and by focussing too exclusively on texts that appear to smack of intellectualism, to conclude (as Shepard, Lewis and Sabine did) that "Occam [and, *we* may add, d'Ailly] held to the time-honored ancient and medieval tradition of eternal, immutable principles of nature discoverable by the use of reason."[44] Thus, it is indeed the case that, according to d'Ailly, morally correct action is nothing other than action in conformity with "the dictates of reason" and "the light of natural reason."[45] And, according to Ockham, that no act is "perfectly virtuous unless it is elicited in conformity with right reason"—indeed, beyond that, unless "the will through that act wishes that which is dictated by right reason because it is dictated by right reason."[46] And to follow the dictate of right reason is nothing other than to obey the natural law, which he describes as "absolute," "immutable, and admitting of no dispensation."[47]

Such formulations, however, serve only to mislead if one misses

---

successful application "to the solving of some of the phenomenon of the visible world" (i.e. contemporary scientific endeavor). Cf. Suarez, *De Legibus ac Deo Legislatore*, Lib. II, c. 6 (ed. Brown, I, 121), where, along with Jean Gerson, he, too, lists Ockham, d'Ailly and Novocastro as the representative exponents of the voluntarist position.

[44] Max A. Shepard, "William of Occam and the Higher Law," *American Political Science Review*, XXVI (1932), 1005–23, and XXVII (1933), 24–38, where he adds that "no really essential difference exists between Occam and Aquinas on this point, and that it is on the whole erroneous to extend the nominalistic-realistic schism to embrace their respective theories of natural law." These articles and their findings are commended by Ewart Lewis, *Medieval Political Ideas* (2 vols., London, 1954), I, 334 n. 32, and George H. Sabine, *A History of Political Theory* (rev. ed. New York, 1958), p. 306.

[45] Pierre d'Ailly, *Questiones super I, III et IV Sententiarum* (Nicolaus Wolff: Lyons, 1500), I, qu. 2, art. 2, M, f. 62v: ". . . [P]er recte agere moraliter nihil aliud intelligo nisi agere conformiter dictaminis rationis." *Ibid., Princ in I Sent.*, L, ff. 23v–24v: ". . . prima principia moralia solum per sinderism et lumen rationis habita."

[46] Ockham, *Super quatuor libros Sententiarum*, (Jean Trechsel: Lyons, 1495), III, 12 CCC: ". . . nullum actus est perfecte virtuosus nisi voluntas per illum actum velit dictatum a recta ratione propter hoc quod est dictatus a recta ratione."

[47] Ockham, *Dialogue*, I, vi, cap. 100; printed in Melchior Goldast ed., *Monarchia S. Romani Imperii* (3 vols., Frankfurt, 1611–14), II, 629, l. 45: ". . . utens naturali dictamine rationis, hoc est utens jure naturali," cf. *Dialogus* III, ii, I, cap. 10 (*ibid.*, II, 878, lines 27–31, and III, ii, III, cap. 6 (*ibid.*, 932, line 65): ". . . quia jure naturale est immutabile primo modo et invariabile et indispensable."

the fact that they are subject in the thinking of both men to a very important qualification. That qualification, which they signal by the employment of such expressions as "according to the laws ordained and instituted by God," "given the divine ordination," "by the ordained law," "by the natural or naturally ordained power,"[48] reflects the insertion into their discussions of the moral order (as also, for that matter, the order of physical nature and the order of salvation) of a crucial scholastic distinction that enjoyed an extraordinarily persistent career from the beginning of the thirteenth century right down to the early years at least of the eighteenth. The distinction in question was that between God's power understood as absolute and as ordained (*potentia dei absoluta et ordinata*), and it was deployed in an effort to vindicate the freedom and omnipotence of God while at the same time affirming the stability of the particular order he has freely chosen to institute.[49] In the wake of the particular formulation it received at the hands of Duns Scotus (d. 1308), that distinction came to be understood by some (not least among them d'Ailly and Suarez) as envisioning the possibility that God's absolute power, by virtue of which he can do anything that does not involve a formal contradiction, is a potentially active power whereby he can contravene (and *has* actually contravened) the laws—moral, natural, salvational—which he has by his ordained power in fact established.[50]

---

[48] Thus William of Ockham, *Quodlibeta septem*, Quodl. VI, qu. 1, art. 1; ed. Joseph C. Wey (New York, 1980), 586; *idem, Scriptum in librum primum Sententiarum (Ordinatio)*, Prol., qu. 7; ed. Gedeon Gál and Stephen Brown (New York, 1967), 187, 197, 202, 205; *De libertate creaturae rationalis*, in Jean Gerson, *Opera omnia*, ed. Louis Ellies Dupis (6 vols., Antwerp, 1706), I, 632; *idem, De Trinitate*, in Dupin, I, 619; *idem, Sent.* I, art. 2 JJ, f. 96r; and *Sent.* IV, qu. 1, art 2 J, f. 188v.

[49] Since the 1960s this distinction has become the subject of a voluminous scholarly literature. Of recent years at least four books have made it the exclusive focus of their concern—see Francis Oakley, *Omnipotence, Covenant, and Order: An Excursion in the History of Ideas from Abelard to Leibniz* (Ithaca and London, 1984); Eugenio Randi, *Il sovrano e l'orologiaio: Due immagini di Dio nel dibattito sulla "potentia absoluta" fra XIII e XIV secolo* (Florence, 1987); William J. Courtenay, *Capacity and Volition: A History of the Distinction of Absolute and Ordained Power* (Bergamo, 1989); Lawrence Moonan, *Divine Power: The Medieval Power Distinction up to its Adoption by Albert, Bonaventure, and Aquinas* (Oxford, 1994), this last now providing the best account of the emergence of the distinction in the early-thirteenth century. There is a good, recent synoptic account in Gijsbert van der Brink, *Almighty God: A Study of the Doctrine of Divine Omnipotence* (Kampen, 1993), pp. 68–92. For an instance of the use of the distinction as late as the early-eighteenth century, see Samuel Willard, *A Compleat Body of Divinity* (Boston, 1726), qu. 4, sermon XXII, p. 70, col. 2, the terms used being "unlimited and absolute Power" and "ordinate Power."

[50] For this development (which is not really germane to Locke's thinking) reference

But it is now generally accepted that in its inception, and as formulated by such thinkers as Aquinas, the distinction did not involve any understanding of the absolute power as a presently active one. Instead, it was taken to refer to God's ability in principle to do many things that he does not in fact choose to do. It referred, that is,

> to the total possibilities *initially* open to God, some of which were realized by creating the established order . . . [with] . . . the unrealized possibilities . . . now only hypothetically possible. Viewed another way, the *potentia absoluta* is God's power considered absolutely, . . . without taking into account the order established by God. Potentia ordinata, on the other hand, is the total ordained will of God, the complete plan of God for his creation.[51]

And that is the meaning later attached to it, and with admirable concision, in the theological textbook that enjoyed so wide a circulation in Locke's own lifetime—*The Marrow of Sacred Divinity* by William Ames.[52]

Whether the earlier or the later meaning was attached to it, the pertinence of the distinction to the status of the divinely-established order is not in doubt. Its impact was such as to underline the contingency of that entire order while at the same time affirming its *de facto* stability. And that impact was two-fold precisely because it inserted, side by side with the Old Testament vision of Jahweh as

---

may be made to Oakley, *Omnipotence, Covenant, and Order*, pp. 52–59. In 1961 and 1966, I took this later usage to reflect the controlling meaning of the distinction throughout its history and attributed it (incorrectly), therefore, to Ockham. See Oakley, "Medieval Theories of Nature Law," 71–72; *idem*, "Christian Theology and the Newtonian Science: The Rise of the Concept of the Laws of Nature," *Church History*, XXX (1961), 435–57 (at 439–40, 443–44); Oakley and Urdang, "Locke, Natural Law and God," 101–102. Although there are some "Scotistic" hesitations in Ockham, his usage of the distinction is by and large aligned with Aquinas's "classic" version. For which, see Courtenay, *Capacity and Volition*, pp. 119–23, and Adams, *William Ockham*, II, 1186–1207 (a detailed analysis more sensitive to the Scotistic elements in Ockham's usage than is Courtenay's).

[51] Thus William J. Courtenay, "Nominalism and Late Medieval Religion," in *The Pursuit of Holiness in Late Medieval and Renaissance Religion*, ed. Charles Trinkaus and Heiko A. Oberman (Leiden, 1974), 39.

[52] William Ames, *The Marrow of Sacred Divinity*, Bk. I, ch. 6, §§ 16–20, in John D. Eusden ed., *The Marrow of Theology* (Boston, 1968), 93: "The absolute power is that by which God is able to do all things possible though they may never be done," while "the ordained power is that by which he not only can do what he wills but does actually do what he wills." First published as *Medulla theologica* in Amsterdam in 1623, the book went through twelve reprintings in the Latin edition, a Dutch translation (1656), and, between 1638 and 1643, three printings of the English translation—see Eusden pp. 1–3.

a God of power and might, another fundamentally biblical theme—
that of God's covenant and promise. The only force capable of binding omnipotence without thereby denying it is, after all, the omnipotent
will itself. Conversely, if that will were somehow incapable of binding itself it could hardly be regarded as truly omnipotent. While God
cannot be said to be bound by the canons of any merely human
reason or justice, he is certainly capable by his own free decision of
binding himself to follow a certain pattern in dealing with his creation, just as an absolute monarch can similarly bind himself in his
dealings with his subjects. Nor is that analogy an improper or misleading one. It is a commonplace in the medieval texts themselves.[53]
Thus the biblical God who knows, of course, no absolute necessity
has freely chosen to bind himself by a hypothetical necessity (*necessitas ex suppositione; necessitas consequentiae,* what Chaucer accurately designates in the *Nun's Priest's Tale* as a "necessitee condicionel")—an
"unfailing necessity appropriate to God," as one nominalist theologian put it, "because of his promise, that is, his covenant, or established law [*ex promisso suo et pacto sive statuta*]."[54]

The impress of this "convenantal" way of thinking is evident in
what Ockham and d'Ailly have to say on a broad array of issues,
from the order of (physical) nature, via that of salvation, to that of
the moral life. Thus, for Ockham, "evil is nothing other than the
doing of something opposite to that which one is obliged to do,"
and it is God, free himself from all obligation, whose will is the
source of that obligation.[55] Robbery, adultery, hate of God even—

---

[53] There is a good example in one of the sermons preached by the late-medieval
scholastic, Gabriel Biel. See his "On the Circumcision of the Lord" (*ca.* 1460), translated in Heiko A. Oberman ed., *Forerunners of the Reformation: The Shape of Late Medieval
Thought* (New York, 1966), 165–76. For instances of the use of the royal/papal analogy to illuminate the *potentia dei absoluta/ordinata* distinction, and the use, in turn, of
that distinction by canon, civil, and early-modern prerogative lawyers to illuminate
the nature of imperial, royal and papal power, see Francis Oakley, "Jacobean
Political Theology: The Absolute and Ordinary Powers of the King," *Journal of the
History of Ideas,* XXIX (No. 3, 1968), 323–46 (see below, ch. 8), and *idem, Omnipotence,
Covenant, and Order,* pp. 55–56, 92–118.
[54] Robert Holcot, *Super libros Sapientiae* (Hagenau, 1494), lect. 145B; I cite the
translation in Oberman ed., *Forerunners of the Reformation,* 149. Cf. Geoffrey Chaucer,
The Nonne Preestes Tale, in *The Canterbury Tales* (Oxford and London, 1906), p. 259.
For the convenantal theme in late medieval theology in general, see Berndt Hamm,
Promissio, Pactum, Ordinatio: Freiheit und Selbstbindung Gottes in der scholastischen Gnadenlehre
(Tübingen, 1977).
[55] William of Ockham, *Questiones in librum secundum Sententiarum (Reportatio),* qu. 3–4;
ed. Gedeon Gál and Rega Wood (New York, 1981), 59.

all such vices could be stripped of their evil and rendered meritorious if they were to "agree with the divine precept just as now *de
facto* [i.e., *de communi lege*, by God's ordained power] their opposites
agree with the divine precept."[56] If such a possibility would appear
to contradict Ockham's emphasis on right reason, it has to be recognized that there is nothing final about right reason, which he
clearly subordinates to the divine will. Only "by the very *fact that the
divine will wishes it*," he says, does "right reason dictate what is to be
willed."[57] Only "in the presently prevailing order" (that established
by God's ordained power) is an act's conformity with right reason
a necessary condition for its being "perfectly" or "intrinsically and
necessarily virtuous."[58] Only in that presently prevailing order, then,
is it possible to speak of the natural law as being absolute, immutable
and admitting of no dispensation.

Similarly d'Ailly, though at somewhat greater length. While he
insists that "in God it is the same to will and to understand"[59] and
that the divine will and intellect can be distinguished neither really
nor formally, he also insists that to say that we can distinguish by
reason between the divine will and intellect can be regarded, though
not literally true, as the abbreviated expression of something true.
For "these terms [will and intellect], standing for the same thing,
have diverse and distinct ideas [*rationes*] corresponding to them in
the [human] mind."[60] To speak as he does, then, of the divine will
as the first "uncreated" or "eternal" law or as "the first law in the
genus of obligatory law (just as it is "the first cause in the genus of
efficient causes")[61] is simply, he says, to echo "the way of speaking
of the saints and of the learned." And, in accordance with that way

---

[56] Ockham, *Reportatio*, II, qu. 15; ed. Gál and Wood, 352: ". . . dico quod licet
odium dei, furari, adulterari et similia habeant malam circumstantiam annexam et
similia de communi lege quatenus fiunt ab aliquo qui ex praecepto divino obli-
gatur ad contrarium: sed quantum ad omne absolutum in illis actibus possunt fieri
a deo sine omni circumstantia mala annexa. Et etiam meritorie possunt fieri a via-
tore si caderent sub praecepto divino, sicut nunc de facto eorum opposita cadunt
sub praecepto."

[57] Ockham, *Ordinatio*, I, dist. 41, qu. unica; ed. Etzkorn and Kelley, 610: ". . . Sed
eo ipso quod voluntas divina hoc vult, ratio recto dictat quod est volendum."

[58] Ockham, *Sent.* III, 12 CCC. The qualifying phrases are "stante ordinatione
quae nunc est" and "stante ordinatio divina."

[59] D'Ailly, *Princ in I Sent.*, R. f. 26r: ". . . cum in deo sit idem esse velle et intel-
ligere." Cf. *Princ. in II Sent.*, F, f. 28(B)r.

[60] D'Ailly, *Sent.* I, qu. 6, art. 2, L, f. 97 r.

[61] See, e.g., D'Ailly, *Princ. in I Sent.*, D, f. 21r, and J, f. 23r; *Princ. in II Sent.*, J,
f. 29r.

of speaking, it is more appropriate to regard the divine will than the divine intellect as obligating law, since the divine will is the effective cause of things, whereas the divine intellect is not, in that whatever that will decrees actually comes to pass, but not whatever that intellect comprehends.[62] That obstacle disposed of, then, and attaching obligation solely to precepts and prohibitions and not to such ancillary signs of the divine will as counsel or permission,[63] d'Ailly distinguishes from the divine will (which is itself the first obligatory law) those created laws, divine and natural, which are the signs by which the dispositions of that obligating will are made known to us. And what distinguishes the natural law from the divine law is the fact that whereas in the case of the latter the signs which make known the divine will are "supernatural and supernaturally given" and contained, either "explicitly or implicitly . . . in the Divine Scriptures," in the case of the former those signs, either directly or via subsequent investigation "by the light of natural reason," are "naturally possessed."[64]

Presupposed throughout this discussion of the moral order (no less than in his parallel discussion of the natural order and its physical laws) is the crucial and familiar distinction between God's power as absolute and ordained. If in the natural order presently prevailing "every secondary cause . . . produces its effect *ex natura rei*," we must never forget that that secondary cause is itself a cause not because of the nature of things but "solely because of the will of God," who, in choosing *de potentia ordinata* to limit himself to producing some natural effect by means of a secondary cause, "not only produces that effect, but also makes the secondary cause to be the cause of that effect."[65] Being himself "the first cause in the genus of efficient causes," he could of his absolute power produce that effect directly and without recourse to any secondary cause. Just as, for example, and there being no contradiction involved, he could produce in us an intuition

---

[62] D'Ailly, *Princ. in II Sent.*, G, f. 28[B]v.

[63] D'Ailly, *Utrum Petri Ecclesia lege reguletur*, in Dupin, I, 663.

[64] D'Ailly, *Princ. in I Sent.*, K–L, ff. 23v–24r; *Tractatus de ecclesiastica potestate*, in Dupin, II, 930.

[65] D'Ailly, *Sent.* IV, qu. 1, art. 1, E, f. 185r: "Prima [propositio] est quod quandocumque deus facit aliquem effectum mediante causa secunda, ipse non solum facit illum effectum, sed etiam facit causam secundam esse causam illius effectus"; *ibid.*, F, f. 185v: "Sequitur octava propositio quod licet omnis causa secunda proprie dicta causet effectum ex natura rei, tamen quod ipsa sit causa proprie dicta non est ex natura rei quia solum ex voluntate dei."

of a non-existing object.[66] And being similarly "the first obligating law in the genus of obligating law," he could likewise by the absolute power oblige a rational creature directly by himself and without recourse to the sort of created law via which, of his ordained power, he limits himself in imposing such an obligation.[67] Indeed, the prescriptions of such created laws being radically contingent, he could *de potentia absoluta* make it meritorious to hate God, since he can do anything that does not involve a contradiction, and since acts are good and just or bad and unjust not of their own intrinsic nature or essence but simply because God has enjoined or forbidden them.[68]

III

If, then, one is properly to understand what the late-medieval nominalist (or voluntarist) theologians have to say about the natural law and the moral order (no less than what they have to say about physical law and the natural order or, for that matter, about justification, the sacraments, and the order of salvation), it is necessary to recognize the crucial role played in their thinking by the distinction between God's power as absolute and ordained. Or, put differently, by the dialectic of omnipotence and covenant.[69] Elsewhere I have argued that the same covenantal tradition is similarly the appropriate context in which to attempt an understanding of the physicotheological views espoused in Locke's own lifetime by such luminaries of the new scientific thinking as Walter Charleton, Robert Boyle and Sir Isaac Newton himself.[70] Margaret Osler has recently (and forcefully) argued a similar case in relation to Pierre Gassendi,

---

[66] D'Ailly, *Princ. in I Sent.*, K, f. 23v; *Sent.* I, qu. 3, art. 1, M, f. 72v.

[67] D'Ailly, *Princ. in I Sent.*, K, f. 23v.

[68] D'Ailly, *Princ. in I Sent.*, H, f. 22v; *Sent.* I, qu. 14, art. 3, T–U, f. 174v, Andreas de Novo Castro, *Primum scriptum Sententiarum* (Paris, 1514), Dist. 48, qu. 1 and 2, fols. 251r–262r, though he does not develop any fully-fledged theory of natural law, does commit himself (as Cudworth suggests) to an ethical voluntarism aligned with that of Ockham and d'Ailly and supported by a similar invocation of the dialectic of the *potentia dei absoluta/ordinata*. For a useful brief discussion, see Leonard A. Kennedy, "Andrew of Novo Castro, O.F.M. and the Moral Law," *Franciscan Studies*, XLVIII (1988), 28–39.

[69] These interconnections are all discussed in Oakley, *Omnipotence, Covenant, and Order.*

[70] See Oakley, "Christian Theology and the Newtonian Science," and *idem, Omnipotence, Covenant, and Order,* pp. 67–92.

and it should be recalled that Cudworth linked the reemergence in his day of theological and ethical voluntarism with the contemporaneous revival of the type of Epicureanism which Gassendi and Charleton espoused.[71] The intimacy of Locke's intellectual affiliations with both Boyle and Gassendi having long been remarked,[72] it will be my purpose now to urge the pertinence of that same convenantal context to the attempt to resolve the difficulties in Locke's natural-law thinking. If much of the commentary focused on that topic does little to encourage such an interpretative approach, its promise is signalled indirectly, nonetheless, by some recent studies concerned with his ontology, epistemology, natural and moral philosophy.[73]

Thus while conceding that Locke clearly "disliked the language" and methods of the scholastics, Milton has insisted that he "continued to be concerned with their problems," that he worked "perhaps unconsciously" within the late-medieval nominalist tradition and not against it, and that "neither this fact nor its consequences have been adequately understood."[74] Among those consequences were the conclusions that Locke no less than Ockham or d'Ailly appears to have drawn from the preoccupation with the divine omnipotence that he shared with them—a particularist ontology, a nominalist epistemology, and a commitment to a form of empirical induction. Against Norris's claim that universal natures exist in the ideas of God, Locke

---

[71] Margaret J. Osler, *Divine Will and the Mechanical Philosophy: Gassendi and Descartes on Contingency and Necessity in the Created World* (Oxford, 1994). She aligns Boyle, Charleton and Newton with the distinctive "style of science" characteristic of Gassendi and reflective of the "epistemological and metaphysical assumptions" linked with the late-medieval nominalist or voluntarist theology. "[T]heological language . . . [may have] . . . dropped out of scientific discourse," she concludes (p. 236), but "contemporary styles of science are historically linked to the dialectic of the absolute and ordained powers of God." Cf. Cudworth, *Treatise Concerning Immutable Morality*, Bk. I, chs. 1–3, in Cudworth, *The True Intellectual System of the Universe*, II, 367–83.

[72] Reference may be made back to Richard J. Aaron, *John Locke* (2nd ed., Oxford, 1955), pp. 8–14, who concludes that if Locke "is to be grouped with any European group we must follow Leibniz in grouping him with the Gassendists." Cf. Thomas M. Lennon, "The Epicurean new way of ideas: Gassendi, Locke, and Berkeley," in *Atoms, pneuma, and tranquillity: Epicurean and Stoic themes in European Thought*, ed. Margaret J. Osler (Cambridge, 1991), 259–71.

[73] See John R. Milton, "John Locke and the Nominalist Tradition," in Brandt, 127–45; G.A.J. Rogers, "Locke, Law and the Laws of Nature," *ibid.*, 146–62; Tully, "Governing Conduct," esp. pp. 179–225; Ayers, *Locke*, II (Ontology), and esp. Part 2: "God, Nature and the Laws of Nature," 131–202; J.B. Schneewind, "Locke's moral philosophy," in Vere Chappell ed., *The Cambridge Companion to Locke* (Cambridge, 1994), 199–225.

[74] Milton, "John Locke and the Nominalist Tradition," 128–29.

insisted therefore that, not simply created things, but "whatever exists, *whether in God or out of God*, is singular" (italics mine), so, that the universality of ideas "consists . . . only in representation, abstracting from particulars."[75] God being able to do whatever does not involve a contradiction (a point Locke emphasizes especially in relation to natural phenomena),[76] and our knowledge of the contingent particularities of the created world thus depending, as it must, upon inductive generalization, of that world we can have no certain *knowledge*, only (in his terms) "judgment" or "opinion." Such natural phenomena as the laws governing matter and motion, though they have a "constant and regular connexion, in the ordinary course of Things," lack the absolute necessity that pertains to mathematical propositions and have to be attributed "to nothing else, but the arbitrary Determination of that All-wise Agent, who has made them to be, and to operate as they do, in a way wholly above our weak Understandings to conceive" so that "we cannot but ascribe them to the arbitrary Will and good Pleasure of the Wise Architect."[77]

All of which Rogers, whose concern, unlike Milton's, is not with Locke's nominalism but with his moral teaching, claims nonetheless to be directly pertinent to that moral teaching. Arguing that "it is probably impossible to overestimate the primacy of Locke's theism for his whole account of the natural and moral order," he insists that "only through an awareness of the interactions between epistemological, moral and theological viewpoints can we approach a proper understanding" of what he has to say about natural law.[78] There is, in effect, a "symmetry," at once both epistemological and ontological, "between Locke's moral theory and his philosophy of science," between his notions of natural law in the moral order and

---

[75] *Remarks upon some of Mr. Norris's Books*, §§ 20, 21, 4; in *The Works of John Locke*, X, 251, 257. Cf. *Essay Concerning Human Understanding*, III, iii, § 1, ed. Nidditch, p. 409; "All Things that exist being Particulars . . ." Elsewhere it should be noted, Locke does seem to wobble a bit on this issue. See below pp. 245–46, and notes 96 and 97.

[76] *Essay Concerning Human Understanding*, IV, iii, § 6, and II, xiii, §§ 21–23, ed. Nidditch, pp. 541 and 176–78; *Journal*, entry for 9 July, 1676, Ms. Locke, f. 1, pp. 313–4, printed in Von Leyden ed., *Essays on the Law of Nature*, p. 259; *Remarks upon some of Mr. Norris's Books*, § 10; *The Works of John Locke*, X, 253. Cf. the pertinent remarks of Ayers, *Locke*, II, 150–53.

[77] *Essay Concerning Human Understanding*, IV, iii, §§ 28–29, ed. Nidditch, pp. 559–60. Cf. Milton, "John Locke and the Nominalist Tradition," 135–41; Ayers, *Locke*, II, 150–53; Rogers, "Locke, Law and the Laws of Nature," 153.

[78] Rogers, "Locke, Law and the Laws of Nature," 156, 147.

laws of nature in the physical world. For the two were "intimately connected," sharing, as it were, a "common ancestry in the question of the relation between God and his universe."[79] Both were grounded in the divine will. Both, therefore, were radically contingent. In both cases, accordingly, whatever stability was manifest in "the ordinary course of things," there could be for Locke no question of their prescriptions or uniformities possessing any sort of absolute or unconditional necessity. At the same time the laws, both moral and physical, that God has chosen to ordain are more than fleeting contingencies. They are, indeed, *laws*, and they guarantee or reflect the existence of an order in that they possess a conditional or hypothetical necessity,[80] or, to evoke a happy formulation recently contributed by Michael Ayers and in relation to both the natural and the moral order:

> The necessity of the law is *hypothetical but hard* [italics mine]: God was free to will what laws he liked in that he was free to create what things he liked, but in creating free and rational beings capable of pleasure and pain he ipso facto willed a certain law for those beings; just as, in choosing to create matter, he chose certain necessary laws of motion.[81]

This position is clearly in harmony with d'Ailly's insistence that while it is the divine will that makes natural causes to be *causes*, they produce their effects, nonetheless, *ex natura rei*. And it is equally in harmony with Ockham's earlier insistence that while it is the divine will that is the source of obligatory moral precepts, nonetheless, in the divinely-ordained moral economy presently prevailing, our right reason dictates to us what it is that we must do if we are to act virtuously.[82] And that degree of harmony is such as to confirm the wisdom of keeping in mind, when one approaches the more troublesome of Locke's natural law texts, that dialectic of omnipotence and covenant in the absence of which the natural-law thinking of Ockham and d'Ailly would itself be open to accusations of incoherence no less worrying than those levied against Locke.

Though, in company, for that matter, with Hobbes, Locke does

---

[79] Thus Rogers, *ibid.*, 154, 147; similarly Ayers, *Locke*, II, 131–32.
[80] Rogers, "Locke, Law and the Laws of Nature," esp. 159–60; Ayers, *Locke*, II, 163, 189–90.
[81] Ayers, *Locke*, II, 189–90.
[82] See above, pp. 235–36.

appear to have been aware of the related scholastic distinction between
what was sometimes referred to as the secret and revealed will of
God (*voluntas dei beneplaciti et signi*),[83] he never to my knowledge explicitly invoked the absolute/ordained power distinction. But the currency
of that latter distinction in his own day was so widespread among
Catholics and Protestants alike as to suggest the likelihood of his
being familiar with it.[84] Certainly, it would appear to be implicit in
the language he used in the seventh of his *Essays on the Law of Nature*
and in the very passage which must necessarily serve as the crux of
any argument that attempts (as with Leyden) to prove that Locke
wavered inconsistently between a voluntarist and intellectualist position. Or *a fortiori* of any argument that attempts (as with Singh) to
establish in the teeth of all Locke's unambiguously voluntaristic statements that his natural-law teaching was *au fond* an intellectualist one.

   In that seventh essay it is his purpose to respond to the objection
that, given the degree to which men and nations differ about "the
law of nature and the ground of their duty" (some even lacking any
sense at all of law or moral rectitude), one has to conclude either
that there is no natural law whatsoever or that its binding force is
by no means universal. In the teeth of that objection Locke is at
pains to insist that the binding force of natural law is not only universal but also perpetual.[85] In connection with our present concern,
however, what is most striking about the argument he advances in
support of that contention is not what it says, but what it does *not*
say. The strongest and most obvious card he could have played
would have been to ground the universality and perpetuity of the
natural law in the very being of its divine author. But that he con-
spicuously fails to do. Instead, he grounds it in the nature of man.
"The bonds of this law," he says, are perpetual and coeval with the

---

[83] A distinction somewhat narrower than the absolute/ordained power distinction and one that dated back to the twelfth century. See the comment of Ian Harris
on the matter in his *The Mind of John Locke: A study of political theory in its intellectual
setting* (Cambridge, 1994), pp. 316 and 390–91 n. 69. The text to which Harris
refers is in Von Leyden, *Essays on the Law of Nature*, Essay IV, fol. 60, p. 156. For
Hobbes's usage, see *The Question Concerning Liberty, Necessity and Chance Clearly Stated
and Debated Between Dr. Bramhall, Bishop of Derry, and Thomas Hobbes of Malmesbury*
(London, 1656), pp. 10–11, 78–79.

[84] For the early-modern usage of the distinction, see Oakley, "Christian Theology
and the Newtonian Science;" *idem*, "Jacobean Political Theology" (see below, ch. 8);
idem, Omnipotence, Covenant and Order. I return to the issue in a forthcoming article
(see below, ch. 9).

[85] Essay VII, in Von Leyden ed., *Essays on the Law of Nature*, pp. 190–93.

human race, beginning with it and perishing with it at the same time."[86] Asserting thus the existence of a "harmony" (*convenientia*) between natural law and man's rational nature, he goes on then to elucidate that claim by asserting (and as we have seen) that natural law does not "depend on an unstable and changeable will, but on the eternal order of things." For "certain essential features of things are immutable, and certain duties arise out of necessity and cannot be other than they are."[87]

If one isolated that last statement and ignored Locke's earlier alignment of the perpetuity and binding force of natural law with the historical existence of the human species, it would be easy enough to take him to be making more sweeping claims than he actually is. But thus far, in fact, his position would appear to be aligned more or less with that taken by Ockham when he spoke of natural law as being absolute, immutable, and admitting of no dispensation. As with Ockham (or for that matter, with d'Ailly), what could well be taken to be a sweepingly intellectualistic statement[88] is subject to a crucial qualification. As with them, too, that qualification extends to the natural no less than the moral order. The necessity he has in mind, Locke goes on to make clear, is not an absolute but rather a contingent or conditional necessity, one that depends on the particular choice that God has made, one that reflects, therefore, the balancing of omnipotence with covenant or promise. "God *could have created* men," he points out, "such that they would be without eyes and not need them." But he did not choose so to act. As a result, "so long as they [men] use their eyes and want to open them, and so long as the sun shines, they must of necessity come to know the alternations of day and night, be aware of the differences of colors," and so on.[89] Similarly, "*since man has been made such as he is*, equipped with reason and his other faculties and destined for this mode of life, there necessarily results from his inborn constitution some definite duties for him, which cannot be other than they are." If "this natural duty *will never be abolished*," it is not simply because (being subject to it) "human beings cannot alter this law," but also

---

[86] *Ibid.*, pp. 192–93.

[87] *Ibid.*, pp. 198–99.

[88] And, in fact, has been. See Singh, "John Locke and the Theory of Natural Law," 112.

[89] Essay VII, in Von Leyden ed., *Essays on the Law of Nature*, pp. 200–201 (italics mine).

because God certainly *would not wish to do so*. For since, according to His infinite and eternal wisdom, He has made man such that these duties of his necessarily follow from his very nature, He surely will not alter what has been made and create a new race of men, who would have another law and moral rule, seeing that natural law stands and falls together with the nature of man as it is at present.[90]

With this passage, understood thus as emphasizing the ultimate dependence on the divine will of the presently-ordained moral order, should also be aligned, I would argue, the interpretation of the difficult passage in *The Reasonableness of Christianity* to which we drew attention earlier and which has helped fuel the arguments of those who have urged the insertion of some sort of rationalistic qualification into Locke's overarching voluntarism.[91] In that passage, it will be recalled, and in the context of a discussion of the order of salvation, Locke had spoken of "that eternal law of right, which is holy, just, and good," as not being subject to abrogation or repeal "whilst God is an holy, just, and righteous God, and man a rational creature." And he had gone on immediately to add that

> the duties of that law, arising from the constitution of his very nature, are of eternal obligation; nor can it be taken away or dispensed with, without changing the nature of things, overturning the measures of right and wrong, and thereby introducing and authorizing irregularity, confusion, and disorder in the world.[92]

As in the seventh *Essay*, the "nature" being referred to here is clearly not the nature of God, but that of man as, by divine choice, he is presently constituted. Just as, in the world of nature and because it would involve no contradiction, God *could* in the absoluteness of his power, and by one of those "extraordinary effects [that] . . . we call miracles," "put out of its ordinary course some phenomenon of this great world" or even "create another world separate wholly from this,"[93] so, too, by changing human nature itself, could he abrogate the natural law as it is presently constituted. But "could" is not the

---

[90] *Essay VII*, in Von Leyden ed., *Essays on the Law of Nature*, pp. 198–201 (italics mine).

[91] See above, p. 226, and note 33.

[92] *The Reasonableness of Christianity*, in *The Works of John Locke*, VII, 111–12.

[93] See *Journal*, entry for 9 July, 1676, Ms. Locke, fol. 1, pp. 313–4, printed in Von Leyden, *Essays on the Law of Nature*, p. 259. Similarly, the entry under Sunday, 18 September, 1681, printed in King, *Life of John Locke*, II, 232–34, where he is discussing miracles.

same as "will." No contradiction, after all, is involved in omnipotency's choosing to bind itself. God is, indeed, a "holy, just and righteous God," and as in the *Two Treatises* Locke twice reminds those who seek to emancipate princes from the bonds of the law, God, his freedom and greatness notwithstanding, condescends to "tye Himself with oaths and promises."[94]

IV

This "convenantal" reading of Locke's natural law thinking draws sustenance, then, not only from our contemporary understanding of such pertinent late-medieval thinkers as Ockham and d'Ailly, but also from the current inclination at least of some Locke scholars to take more seriously than heretofore the need to probe his unexpected indebtedness to the scholastic past, to stress accordingly the interconnectedness among his theological, ontological and epistemological commitments, and, as a result, between his natural and moral philosophizing. So far as his natural-law thinking is concerned, the Locke who emerges is unquestionably and unqualifiedly a voluntarist. But he is a voluntarist of the late-medieval stamp whose emphasis on the divine omnipotence is so modulated as to accommodate a firm commitment to the existence of an order—natural, moral, salvational—seemingly intellectualistic in nature but actually grounded in the divine will, choice, promise and covenant. Not an emphasis on omnipotence, that is to say (and as the Third Earl of Shaftesbury appears to have suspected), that involves any divinely subversive, Cartesian transcendence of the principle of non-contradiction itself.[95]

Some difficulties of course remain. They are not, I would judge, substantial enough to constitute any formidable impediment to the acceptance of the interpretation advanced in this essay. But as they

---

[94] *First Treatise of Government*, § 6, *Second Treatise*, § 195; ed. Laslett, pp. 144, 395–96. The focus in these texts is, in fact, the subjection of *princes* to the law. God is no more than glancingly involved by way of a comparison intended to drive home a political point. The covenantal reading of these fleeting allusions is mine.

[95] Shaftesbury appears simply to have assumed that the grounding of the distinction between good and evil in the determination of the divine will necessarily involved or presupposed a further commitment to the view that "if each part of a Contradiction were affirm'd for Truth by the Supreme Power, they would consequently become *true.*"—*An Inquiry concerning Virtue, or Merit*, Bk. I, part 3, § 2, in *Characteristicks of Men, Manners, Opinions, Times* (3 vols., London, 1711), II, 50.

may well suffice for some to generate an undertow of interpretative unease, I should like, by way of conclusion, to emphasize the degree to which they stem from the reticence and incompleteness of Locke's theologizing and from his seemingly instinctive impatience with any attempt to discuss the divine psychology.

First, it should be conceded that nothing has been said by way of affirming Locke's nominalism that can do anything more than *isolate* the passage in the *Essay concerning Human Understanding* in which, while insisting that our human reason can reach only to a knowledge of the "nominal essences" of substances, he acknowledges that the knowledge of their "real essences" is possessed certainly by God, perhaps also by angels.[96] Fraser interpreted that text as implying that "the 'real essences' incognisable at the side point of view of a finite intelligence, are fully known only at the Divine centre, or in Platonic language in the Divine Ideas," and, on its basis, Lovejoy even went so far as to venture the claim that "in his epistemology he [Locke] was essentially a Platonist."[97] If the latter claim is clearly idiosyncratic, the former is at least arguable, though arguable, it should be noted, only in relation to this particular text. Elsewhere, after all, Locke is insistent upon the form of nominalist particularism that would appear to be his controlling teaching.[98] Second, he is far from diffident about ascribing to God the attributes of wisdom and goodness. If the same can be said also of his late-medieval nominalist predecessors, they were unlike him in having discussed in depth and with no little precision what exactly was involved in predicating such recognizably human attributes of a transcendent divinity.[99] They were

---

[96] *Essay Concerning Human Understanding*, III, vi, §§ 2–3, ed. Nidditch, pp. 439–40.

[97] See Alexander Campbell Fraser's edition of the *Essay Concerning Human Understanding* (2 vols., Oxford, 1896), II, 58 n. 1. Arthur O. Lovejoy, *The Great Chain of Being* (New York, 1961), p. 360 n. 2 (cf. pp. 228–29); Singh, "John Locke and the Theory of Natural Law," 111, makes much of Lovejoy's claim in his own, rather strained, effort to make something of an epistemological Realist of Locke. For a response, see Oakley and Urdang, "Locke, Natural Law, and God," 106 n. 78.

[98] *Remarks upon some of Mr. Norris's Books*, § 4, in *The Works of John Locke*, X, 251, where, in the general context of responding to Norris's discussion of the divine ideas and in specific response to his claim that "all created things are individuals," Locke asks, "Are not all things that exist individuals? If so, then say not, all created, but all existing things are individuals; and if so, then the having of any general idea proves not that we have all objects present to our minds. But this is for want of considering wherein universality consists, which is only in representation, abstracting from particulars." Cf. *ibid.*, §§ 11–12, 20–21, pp. 253–54, 256–57, concluding with the statement: "Whatever exists, whether in God or out of God, is singular."

[99] For a detailed discussion of Ockham's position on the matter, see Adams,

not prone, certainly, to slipping startlingly, as does Locke on one occasion, into speculating that "God himself cannot choose what is not good" and that "the freedom of the Almighty hinders not his being determined by what is best."[100] But that speculation hinges on an acknowledgment of the perfection of the divine being. And it is preceded, it should be noted, by the cautious qualification that one might risk such a statement only "if it was fit for such poor finite creatures as we are to pronounce what infinite wisdom and good-ness could do."[101] That qualification is in direct continuity with the age-old and rueful preoccupation on the part of Christian theolo-gians (pre-scholastic, scholastic, and post-scholastic alike) with the stringency of the limits that hem in our ability to make cognitively meaningful statements about the ineffable God.[102] And it is char-acteristic also of Locke's theological temperament. "To say that we partake in the knowledge of God or consult his understanding," he insists,

> is what I cannot conceive for true. God has given me an understanding of my own; and I should think it presumptuous in me to suppose I apprehended anything by God's understanding, saw with his eyes, or shared of his knowledge. I think it more possible for me to see with other men's eyes, and understand with another man's understanding, than with Gods; *there being some proportion between mine and another man's understanding, but none between mine and God's* (italics mine).[103]

William Ockham, II, 903–60 (a lengthy chapter devoted to "Divine Simplicity, Divine Attributes, and the Meaning of Divine Names").

[100] *Essay Concerning Human Understanding*, II, xxi, § 49, ed. Nidditch, p. 265. Cf. the entry for 7 August, 1681, in King, *Life of John Locke*, II, 228: "But yet that unlimited power cannot be an excellency without it be regulated by wisdom and goodness, for since God is eternal and perfect in his own being he cannot make use of that power to change his own being into a better or another state; and there-fore all the exercise of that power must be in and upon his creatures, which can-not but be employed but for their good and benefit, [as much as the order and perfection of the whole can allow each individual in its particular rank and station]."

[101] *Essay Concerning Human Understanding*, II, xxi, § 49, ed. Nidditch, p. 265.

[102] A point on which A.P. Martinich has recently (and properly) insisted upon in relation also to Hobbes—see his *The Two Gods of Leviathan: Thomas Hobbes on Religion and Politics* (Cambridge 1992), pp. 185–203.

[103] *Examination of P. Malebranche's Opinion of Seeing all things in God*, § 52; in *The Works of John Locke*, IX, 251. Cf. *Some Thoughts Concerning Education*, § 136, printed in James L. Axtell ed., *The Educational Writings of John Locke* (Cambridge, 1968), p. 242: ". . . I think it would be better if Men generally rested in such an Idea of *God*, without being too Curious in their Notions about a Being, which all must acknowledge incomprehensible; . . . And I am apt to think, the keeping children constantly Morning and Evening to acts of Devotion to God, as to their Maker,

Hence his dismissive conclusion, when finally he was forced to focus on Norris's and Malebranche's discussion of the divine ideas, that it was only "those who would not be thought ignorant of anything to attain it, make God like themselves." Were not that the case, he adds, "they could not talk as they do, of the mind of God, and the ideas in the mind of God, exhibitive of all the whole possibility of being."[104]

Preserver and Benefactor, . . . will be of much more use to them in Religion, Knowledge and Vertue, than to distract their Thoughts with curious Enquiries into his inscrutable Essence and Being."

[104] *Remarks Upon Some of Mr. Norris's Books*, § 11, in *The Works of John Locke*, X, 253. Cf. *Examination of P. Malebranche's Opinion*, § 52, *ibid.*, IX, 253.

CHAPTER EIGHT

JACOBEAN POLITICAL THEOLOGY: HOLDSWORTH, MCILWAIN, AND THE ABSOLUTE AND ORDINARY POWERS OF THE KING

It is in the great constitutional conflicts between the Stuart kings and their opponents and critics that much of the enduring universal significance as well as the the historical drama of early-modern English history lies. In a century scarred by a savage and epic struggle for national survival, generations of English schoolboys continue to cut their historiographic teeth on the chivalrous joustings of Cavalier and Roundhead, and one would like to think that this reflects something more than an ironic national predilection for thc mock-heroic or some sure pedagogic instinct for the peripheral. Interest has turned increasingly from the great clash of hostile armies to that of competing political and constitutional theories which both presaged and accompanied it. And with this shift of emphasis has come a greater willingness to extend the courtesy of sympathetic examination to "those murky discussions about emergency powers and the King's different persons which tried to justify Stuart despotism."[1] Among these discussions, the judgment delivered in 1606 by Chief Baron Fleming in Bate's Case stands out as being of critical importance.[2] At its heart lay the crucial remarks which Fleming made about the "absolute" and "ordinary" powers of the King, and this important distinction has yet to receive the close scrutiny it deserves. The purpose of this essay is to focus attention upon it, to trace the history of its development and diffusion, and to attempt to comprehend its meaning. But first, the distinction itself and the modest body of secondary literature concerned with it.

---

[1] Geoffrey R. Elton, *England under the Tudors* (London and New York, 1960), p. 403.
[2] Thus John W. Allen, *English Political Thought 1603–1660* (London, 1938), p. 8, describes it as "a first halting step towards the formulation of a theory of 'absolute' prerogative such as would cover and justify all the positive claims made and disputed down to 1640."

Fleming was by no means the only lawyer involved in the great Stuart state trials to make use of the twin categories "absolute" and "ordinary" when discussing the royal power; they crop up again in the Post-Nati case (1608),[3] Darnel's case (1627),[4] and the Ship-Money case (1637).[5] His formulation, however, is the one that has most often engaged the attention of modern historians, and it is certainly the most complete. "To the King," he said,

> is committed the government of the realm and his people; and Bracton saith, that for his discharge of his office, God had given him power, the act of government, and the power to govern. The Kings power is double, ordinary and absolute, and they have several lawes and ends. That of the ordinary is for the profit of particular subjects, for the execution of civil justice, the determining of meum; and this exercised by equitie and justice in ordinary courts, and by the civilians is nominated *jus privatum* and with us, common law; and these laws cannot be changed, without parliament: and although that their form and course may be changed, and interrupted, yet they can never be changed in substance. The absolute power of the King is not that which is converted or executed to private use, to the benefit of any particular person, but is only that which is applied to the general benefit of the people and is *salus populi*; as the people is the body, and the King the head; and this power is guided by the rules, which direct only at common law, and is most properly named Pollicy and Government; and as the constitution of this body varieth with the time, so varieth this absolute law, according to the wisdome of the King, for the common good.[6]

This statement of Fleming's would seem to suggest that the distinction between the absolute and ordinary powers was cognate to or partially aligned with other and better-known classifications of the royal power.[7] But even if we ignored the existence of such concordances we would still find that before Fleming's judgment focused public attention upon it, the distinction had a history (or pre-history) in England stretching back at least to the fifteenth century.

---

[3] In Bacon's speech; see T.B. Howell, *A Complete Collection of State Trials* (33 vols., London, 1816–26), II, 580.

[4] In a speech of Attorney-General Heath; see Howell, *State Trials*, III, 35–37.

[5] In the argument of Attorney-General Banks; see Howell, *State Trials*, III, 1016.

[6] Howell, *State Trials*, II, 389.

[7] Into *gubernaculum* and *jurisdictio*, "regal" and "political" powers, indisputable and disputable, inseparable and separable, indelegable and delegable prerogatives. See Charles H. McIlwain, *Constitutionalism: Ancient and Modern* (rev. ed., Ithaca, N.Y., 1947), p. 125. Margaret Atwood Judson, *The Crisis of the Constitution: An Essay in constitutional and political thought in England 1603–1645* (New Brunswick, N.J., 1949),

It appeared in the Year Book for 1469 as *potentia ordinata et absoluta*, being applied there, however, to the difference between the legal powers wielded by the Court of Chancery and those wielded by the Common Law Courts.[8] It appeared in 1539, in a work published by Rycharde Taverner, one of Thomas Cromwell's men,[9] in 1551, in a report of Daniel Barbaro, the Venetian Ambassador,[10] and, towards the end of the century, in an introductory outline for a *Treatise on the King's Prerogative* started but not completed by Sir John Doderidge (future Justice of the King's Bench).[11] Lambarde, another common lawyer, made extensive use of the same distinction in his *Archeion*, a treatise written at about the same time but printed only in 1635,[12] and it cropped up again, very early in James I's reign, in a work by Albericus Gentilis, the Professor of Civil Law at Oxford.[13]

It was during James' reign, indeed, that it seems to have come into its own. In the same year as Bate's case, Edward Forset again made use of it,[14] and in 1607, employing words that were later to cause an uproar, Sir James Cowell, Professor of Civil Law at Cambridge, described the King as "*supra legem* by his absolute Power" and defined the royal prerogative as "that special Power, Pre-eminence, or Privilege which the King hath over and above other Persons, and above the ordinary course of the Common Law."[15]

Other formulations of varying degrees of precision are to be found in Bacon's writings, in the Acts of the Privy Council, in the records of Parlimentary debates,[16] and in several of the speeches of James I

---

p. 112. Francis D. Wormuth, *The Royal Prerogative 1603–1649: A Study in English Political and Constitutional Ideas* (Ithaca, N.Y., 1939), pp. 55–60.

  [8] YB 9 Edward IV, Trin. 9; ed. as *Les Reports des Cases en Ley du Roy Edward le Quart* (London, 1680).

  [9] Rycharde Taverner, *The garden of Wysedome* (London, 1539), Bk. I, sig. Di r–v.

  [10] "Report of Daniel Barbaro . . . of his legation in England, delivered in the Senate, May, 1551"; *Calendar of State Papers: Venetian*, ed. Rawden Brown (6 vols., London, 1864), V. 341–42.

  [11] "Treatise on the King's Prerogative," Harleian Ms 5220, Brit. Mus. ff. 9v–10v.

  [12] William Lambarde, *Archeion or, a Discourse upon the High Courts of Justice in England*, ed. Charles H. McIlwain and Paul L. Ward (Cambridge, Mass., 1957), pp. 39–40, 48–49, 61–63, 66–68.

  [13] Albericus Gentilis, *Regales Disputationes Tres* (London, 1605), Disp. I, 10–11.

  [14] Edward Forset, *A Comparative Discourse of the Bodies Natural and Politique* (London, 1606), pp. 20–21.

  [15] Dr. James Cowell, *A Law Dictionary or Interpreter of Words and Terms used either in the Common or Statute Laws* (London, 1727), s.v. "King" and "Prerogative."

  [16] See the speeches of Martyn and Hobart, in *Parliamentary Debates in 1610*, ed. S.R. Gardiner, Camden Society, LXXXI (London, 1861), pp. 89, 119–20; Bacon's "A View of the Differences in question betwixt the King's Bench and the Council

himself.[17] The most forthright reiteration of the distinction, however, is to be found, not in James's writings, but in a work written towards the end of his reign (though published much later) by Davies, Attorney-General for Ireland. "By the positive law," he said,

> the King himself was pleased to limit and stint his absolute power, and to tye himself to the ordinary rules of the Law . . . [but we should not forget that he continues to] . . . exercise a double power *viz.* an absolute power, or *Merum Imperium*, when he doth use Prerogatives onely, which is not bound by the positive law; and an ordinary power of Jurisdiction, which doth cooperate with the law.[18]

Clearly, then, an important distinction, and one widespread and persistent enough to merit close attention. But where did it come from? What did it mean? The problem of origins has elicited an extremely limp response.[19] So too, the problem of interpretation, for the distinguishing feature of much of the scholarly comment has been its vagueness. "Absolute" and "ordinary," as used by the sixteenth and seventeenth-century lawyers were, we are told, "unresolved terms."[20] Their use by Fleming was "mysterious."[21] His judgment was "a fumbling and tentative expression of a quite indefinite theory,"[22] or, again, "difficult to understand . . . as an exposition of law."[23]

Despite this undertow or scholarly diffidence, however, two theories concerning the question of origins have established themselves and around them much of the subsequent discussion has eddied.

---

in the Marches," in James Spedding ed., *The Letters and Life of Francis Bacon* (7 vols., London, 1861–72), III, 371; *Acts of the Privy Council of England 1613–14* (London, 1921), p. 214; speech of Sir Benjamin Rudyard in the Parliament, 28 April, 1628, in Howell, *State Trials*, III, 173.

[17] See Charles H. McIlwain, ed., *The Political Works of James I* (Cambridge, Mass., 1918), pp. 307–10, for his speech to both Houses in 1610. See also his speech of 1616 in the Star-Chamber, *ibid.*, 333, and his remarks in the case of *Commendams*— *Acts of the Privy Council of England, 1615–16* (London, 1925), pp. 601–602.

[18] Sir John Davies, *The Question concerning Impositions, Tonnage, Poundage . . . fully stated and argued from Reason, Law and Policy* (London, 1656), pp. 30–31.

[19] Thus even those works which mention the distinction often have little or nothing at all to suggest about its source or sources—see Allen, *English Political Thought: 1603–1660*; Wormuth, *the Royal Prerogatives*; George L. Mosse, *The Struggle for Sovereignty in England from the Reign of Queen Elizabeth to the Petition of Right* (East Lansing, Mich., 1950); Elton, *England under the Tudors*; Sir David Lindsay Keir, *The Constitutional History of Modern Britain since 1945* (7th ed., London, 1964).

[20] Elton, *England under the Tudors*, pp. 402–403.

[21] R.F.V. Heuston, *Essays in Constitutional Law* (2nd ed., London, 1964), p. 62.

[22] Allen, *English Political Thought: 1603–1660*, p. 16.

[23] Frederic W. Maitland, *The Constitutional History of England* (Cambridge, 1920), p. 258.

The first of these theories was advanced by Holdsworth—who seems also to have been the first to devote much attention to the general issue. He regarded the Stuart distinction between the "absolute" and "ordinary" powers of the King as a transposition into a new key of the cognate distinction which, as we have seen, was used in the fifteenth century to denote the disparate legal powers wielded by the Court of Chancery and the common law courts. The Tudor lawyers, he said, simply "borrowed" the terms and endowed them with a new meaning in order to give "legal expression to the constitutional position of a King who was the head and representative of the state, and yet not possessed of uncontrolled power within it." On the source of the fifteenth-century usage itself he had, however, nothing to say.[24]

Nor did McIlwain, who advanced the second theory. In fact, he made no reference at all to the occurrence of the distinction in the Year Book of 1469, but noted instead the clear statement of the distinction made in 1605 by the civilian, Gentilis, and also the similar formulation (to which Gentilis refers) in one of the commentaries of the great fourteenth-century jurist, Baldus de Ubaldis. He noted, too, that this distinction of Baldus' between a *potestas ordinaria* and a *potestas absoluta* "seems to be about the same" as the one which Bracton had drawn a century earlier between *gubernaculum* and *jurisdictio*. And this distinction of Bracton's he regarded, in turn, as "nothing but a commonplace of late-thirteenth century European political theory" and as lying at the heart of medieval constitutionalism.[25]

Plucknett follows Holdsworth on this matter of origins,[26] but the greater part of the scanty literature on the subject has reflected the influence of McIlwain's approach.[27] The same, by and large, is true of discussion concerning the meaning of the distinction. It was Holdsworth's contention that when the Tudor lawyers "borrowed" the terms *absolute* and *ordinary* and applied them to the royal power, they did so to distinguish "between the doing of such acts as to

---

[24] William S. Holdsworth, *A History of English Law* (13 vols., London, 1922–52), IV, 202, 206; cf. II, 596–597.

[25] McIlwain, *Constitutionalism: Ancient and Modern*, pp. 77ff., 86ff., 92, 123ff., 166–67.

[26] Theodore F.T. Plucknett, *A Concise History of the Common Law* (5th ed., London, 1956), pp. 193–95.

[27] Thus Judson, *Crisis of the Constitution*, esp., pp. 25 and 111ff.; Francis D. Wormuth, *The Origins of Modern Constitutionalism* (New York, 1949), pp. 34–40; Heuston, *Essays in Constitutional Law*, p. 62; and, perhaps, Elton, *England under the Tudors*, pp. 402–3.

which he had an unfettered discretion, and the doing of such acts, such as the issue of proclamations, the making of grants, or the seizure of property, for which the law had prescribed conditions." This use of the term *absolute* did not mean that the King "was freed generally from legal restraint; but merely that as to the particular act to which the adjective was applied he had a free discretion as to the question whether he would do it at all, or if he wished to do it, as to how he would do it." The term tended, however, to give "countenance to the idea that the King had a large and indefinite reserve of power which he could on occasion use for the benefit of the state," or that he had "inseparably attached to his person, a general absolute prerogative to act as he pleased."[28] It is hardly surprising, then, that under James I a "new twist" was given to the distinction between the absolute and ordinary powers, and this became "the corner stone" of a "new royalist theory." This theory "instead of saying . . . that the King had certain absolute prerogatives (such as the right to make war) which could not be questioned by Parliament or the courts, and certain ordinary or private prerogatives which could be so questioned, . . . laid down that he had an overriding absolute prerogative to deal with matters of state," no exercise of which was open to question. And Holdsworth cites the judgment of Fleming in Bate's case as an illustration of this theory.[29]

McIlwain, on the other hand, saw a much higher degree of continuity in English constitutional history.[30] For him, the distinction between the absolute and ordinary powers was just another way of stating Bracton's "familiar" distinction between *gubernaculum* and *jurisdictio*, a distinction which is the key to the English, indeed, to the whole medieval constitutional tradition. By *gubernaculum*, according to McIlwain, Bracton meant the government of the kingdom, which pertained to the King alone and in which there were no bounds to his discretion. This was the realm of the later absolute power. By *jurisdiction*, on the other hand, he meant "those prescriptive rights of tenants or subjects which are wholly outside and beyond the legitimate bounds of the royal administration." This was the realm of the later ordinary power. The King swore to maintain these rights and they formed "a negative, legal limit" to his government. Fortescue

---

[28] Holdsworth, *History of English Law*, IV, 206–207.
[29] Holdsworth, *History of English Law*, VI, 20–22.
[30] McIlwain, *Constitutionalism: Ancient and Modern*, pp. 67–130.

was thinking in the same terms, and not in terms of mixed monarchy, when he described England as a *regimen politicum et regale*, and what both men had in mind was a constitution in which there was a "parallelism" between government and *jurisdictio*, a monarchy that was absolute, but absolute only "within certain definite limits established by law."

This way of thinking, McIlwain went on to claim, persisted into the seventeenth century, but under James I a tension arose between *gubernaculum* (or the absolute power) and *jurisdictio* (or the ordinary), the parallelism began to break down, and the supremacy of one over the other was asserted. The trouble was that whereas "precedent clearly recognized the power of the King as absolute in government" it "provided no adequate check for an abuse or undue extension of the King's discretionary power beyond its legitimate sphere." And in face of what was a perfectly legal but what seemed to them an undue extension of the absolute power, the opponents of the early Stuarts began to rely exclusively "on the precedents of the ancient *jurisdictio*" and to try to impose a "new and unprecedented" legal and political control over that absolute power or *gubernaculum*.

The brief remarks which Maitland, Allen, Carlyle, Plucknett and Keir made about the absolute and ordinary powers would suggest that they inclined towards an interpretation of their meaning at least cognate to that of Holdsworth.[31] Since the publication in 1940 of McIlwain's work, however, such discussion of the issue as there has been has proceeded almost wholly in his terms and within the framework of his theory.[32] To have been able to impose his problematic on the whole debate is a tribute both to his synthetic powers and to the sustained force of his argument, but it remains to be seen if another look at the source of the distinction will confirm this trend towards consensus. For it is clear that the question of origins and that of interpretation are intimately related, and it is now time to insist that the full story of the source of the distinction has yet to be told.

---

[31] Maitland, *Constitutional History of England*, pp. 258–59; Allen, *English Political Thought: 1603–1660*, pp. 8, 16–17; Carlyle, *History of Medieval Political Theory*, VI, 20, 452–53; Plucknett, *Concise History of the Common Law*, pp. 193–97; Keir, *Constitutional History of Modern Britain*, pp. 152–53.

[32] Judson, *Crisis of the Constitution*, pp. 25ff., 111ff.; Heuston, *Essays in Constitutional Law*, pp. 61–62; Wormuth, *Origins of Modern Constitutionalism*, pp. 34–39; perhaps also Mosse, *Struggle for Sovereignty in England*, esp. pp. 50–51, 76–78, 81–84.

Though McIlwain and those who follow him regard the distinction between the absolute and ordinary power as simply another way of stating a distinction fundamental to a medieval constitutional tradition that was the perquisite of no one single country, their arguments, nevertheless, are curiously insular in scope and turn almost exclusively on the English experience. And yet it was not uncommon for French royal theorists, at least from the sixteenth century onwards, to distinguish between those acts which the King did of his "absolute power" and those which he did of his "ordinary," "civil" or "regulated" power.[33] Thus Gentillet and Chasseneuz made full use of the distinction,[34] and Bodin himself spoke of the prince as being able by his "absolute power" to "derogate from the ordinary right"—though not from the laws of God and of nature.[35]

Gentillet, Chasseneuz and Bodin were all of them students of the Roman law. So too were Gentilis and Cowell in England and the expatriate Scot, William Barclay[36]—all of whom made use of the distinction. It should not surprise us, then, that W.F. Church should attribute its diffusion in France to the influence of the French "Romanists," who, while they believed "that the submission of the prince to law was purely voluntary... nevertheless held that he ought to abide by the principles which it contained."[37] This claim

---

[33] See François Oliver-Martin, *Histoire du droit français des origines à la Revolution* (Paris, 1948), pp. 342, 520–21; Georges Weill, *Les théories sur le pouvoir royal en France pendant les guerres de religion* (Paris, 1891), p. 153; William F. Church, *Constitutional Thought in Sixteenth-Century France: A Study in the Evolution of Ideas* (Cambridge, Mass., 1941), pp. 63–65, 141–42; A. Lemaire, *Les lois fundamentales de la monarchie française* (Paris, 1907), p. 103.

[34] Innocent Gentillet (d. 1595), *Discours sur les moyens de bien gouverner... contra Nicolas Machiavel Florentin* (Paris, 1576), pp. 47–48, 60–61; cf. the English translation by Simon Patricke, *A Discourse upon the Meanes of Well Governing and Maintaining in Good Peace, A Kingdome, or other Principalitie... against Nicholas Machiavell the Florentine* (London, 1602), pp. 19, 27. Barthelemi de Chasseneuz, *Consilia* (Lyons, 1588), 168b col. 2; cited in Church, *Constitutional Thought in Sixteenth-Century France*, p. 64, note 59. (He uses the terms *potestas absoluta/ordinaria*). The validity of the distinction was denied by Lambert Daneau—an indication, perhaps of the extent to which it was current. See his *Ethices christianae liber secundus* (1577), in the *Opuscula* (Geneva, 1643), p. 129; cited in Weill, *Les théories sur le poivoir royal en France*, p. 153.

[35] Jean Bodin, *Les six livres de la république*, Bk. I, ch. 8 (Paris, 1580), pp. 133 and 156; cf. the English translation by Richard Knolles, *The Six Bookes of a Commonweale* (London, 1606), pp. 92 and 108–109. (Now available in a facsimile reprint edited with an introduction by Kenneth Douglas McRae [Cambridge, Mass., 1962]).

[36] William Barclay, *De regno et regale potestate adversus Buchananum, Brutum, Boucherium, et reliquos Monarchomachos* (Paris, 1600), Bk. IV, ch. 19, p. 308. For Gentilis and Cowell, see above, notes 13 and 15.

[37] Church, *Constitutional Thought in Sixteenth-Century France*, pp. 63–64.

draws added strength from the fact that Gentillet and Bodin, like Baldus before them, link the distinction with the famous law of the Emperor Theodosius usually referred to as the *lex digna*:

> It is a saying worthy of the majesty of the ruler that the prince should profess himself to be bound to the laws. So much does our authority depend upon the authority of the law. And in fact it is nobler for the emperor to submit the principate to the laws.[38]

Baldus had introduced the terms *absolute* and *ordinary* in his gloss on this particular law in an attempt to make it clear that the prince was bound to live according to the laws not "out of necessity, but out of benevolence," and his interpetation is cited by Bodin and Gentilis—both of them usually included, like him, within the ranks of the post-glossators.[39]

But despite a marked increase of interest in the thought of the medieval civilians, current scholarly discussions make little or no mention of the distinction between the absolute and ordinary powers and one gets the impression that it cannot have bulked very large in civilian political theorizing.[40] This impression is strengthened by the fact that when Bodin makes use of it he feels it necessary to cite the authority of Pope Innocent IV—one of the most distinguished of medieval canonists—and to append the comment that by "the

---

[38] C. 1, 14, 4; in *Corpus Juris Civilis*, ed., Paulus Krueger, Theodor Mommsen and Rudolfus Schoell (3 vols., Berlin, 1899–1902), II, 68. For a discussion of the text itself and some disagreement about the best way to translate the last line, see Fritz Schulz, "Bracton on Kingship," *English Historical Review*, LX (May, 1945), 160–61, and Ernst H. Kantorowicz, *The King's Two Bodies: A Study in Medieval Political Theology* (Princeton, 1957), pp. 104ff. I have preferred to follow Schulz's version of the line in question.

[39] Baldus de Ubaldis, *Commentaria super Codice* (Lyons, 1545), *ad* C. 1, 14, 4, fol. 55; Gentillet, *Discours sur les moyens de bien gouverner*, pp. 60–61 (English ed., p. 27); Bodin, *Six livres de la république*, Bk. I, ch. 8, p. 145 (English ed., p. 103); Gentilis, *Regales Disputationes Tres*, Disp. I, 10–11. For a useful, brief discussion of the post-glossators, see M.H. Keen, "The Political Thought of the Fourteenth-Century Civilians," in *Trends in Medieval Political Thought*, ed. Beryl Smalley (Oxford, 1965), pp. 105–126.

[40] For example, there is no discussion of the distinction in Gaines Post's lengthy and far-reaching studies of the impact of Roman law on the European tradition— see his *Studies in Medieval Legal Thought: Public Law and the State 1100–1327* (Princeton, 1964). Note, too, that the post-glossators Bartolus of Sassoferato and Cynus of Pistoia both comment on the *lex digna* in a fashion quite in harmony with that of Baldus but without employing his terminology of the two powers. See Bartolus, *Aurea Lectura . . . super prima parte Codicis* (Venice, 1492), fol. 36; Cynus, *Lectura . . . super aurea volumine Codicis* (Venice, 1493), fol. b 8v.

ordinary right" he himself understands Innocent to have meant the
"laws of his country."[41]

This reference to Innocent IV is a significant one. Despite Bodin,
Innocent himself does not seem to have employed the precise terms
"absolute" and "ordinary," but he came quite close to so doing and
the distinction occurs in the canonists glosses long before the time
of Baldus, who, as commentator on both laws, may well have transferred it from the canon law into his Commentary on the *Codex
Justinianus*.[42] Certainly, the canonistic usage of the distinction seems
to have been more common than the civilian. It occurs in the glosses
of Hostiensis (d. 1271), Johannes Andreae (d. 1348) and Henricus de
Bouhic (d. *ca.* 1350)[43] it was employed by other jurists[44] and by a
series of publicists;[45] it was known well-enough in the late-fifteenth
century for the French lawyers to employ it in their defense of the
Gallican liberties against papal encroachment.[46]

---

[41] *Six livres de la république*, I, 8, p. 133, Bodin's explication of the ordinary law
appears, not in the French version, but in the Latin and in the English translation
(which is based on the Latin as well as the French). Thus, *De republica: Libri sex*
(Ursellis, 1601), p. 135, reads: "... qui ordinario juri (id est, ut ego interpretor,
patriis legibus) derogare potest." (Cf. English ed., p. 92). In the text to which Bodin
refers, Innocent does not speak of the absolute and ordinary powers as such but
does note the contrast between the *jus commune* of the Church and mandates springing from the *plenitudo potestatis* of the pope. See Innocent IV, *Apparatus super libros
decretalium* (Venice, 1481), *ad* X, 1, 6, 20 *in v.* ordinationem (no foliation).

[42] Baldus certainly seems to have been familiar with the canonistic usage—see
his gloss *ad* X, 2, 26, 13 *in v.* omnia jura (*Commentaria super decretalibus* [Lyons, 1521],
fol. 247v), where he applies the distinction to the papal authority. I would like to
express my gratitude to Professor Gerard E. Caspary of Smith College for his kind-
ness in drawing my attention to this and to several of the other canonistic texts
cited below.

[43] Hostiensis (Henricus de Segusio), *Lectura in Quinque Decretalium Gregorianarum Libros*
(Paris, 1512), *ad* X, 5, 31, 8 *in v.* Ita and *ad* X, 3, 35, 6 *in v.* nec summas Pontifex,
fols. LXXIr and CXXXr; Johannes Andreae, *In tertium Decretalium librum Novella
Commentaria* (Venice, 1581), *ad* X, 3, 35, 6, fol. 179v, § 28; Henricus de Bouhic,
Opus praeclarissimum distinctionum ... super quinque libros decretalium (Venice, 1576), *ad* X,
5, 31, 8, X, 1, 21, 1 and X, 1, 31, 2, fols. Iv r, xlviii r, and lxix v.

[44] See Edward Winkelmann (ed.), *Acta Imperii Inedita* (2 vols., Innsbruck, 1885),
II, 843 (No. 1182); cf. Albert Hauck, *Kirchengeschichte Deutschlands* (6 vols., Leipzig,
1911–35), V 2, 638. Also *Tractatus alter de Cardinalibus*, qu. 45; in Franciscus Zilletus
(ed.), *Tractatus Illustrium in utraque ... juris facultate Jurisconsultorum* (Venice, 1584), fol.
61v. For the dating of this work, see Hubert Jedin, *A History of the Council of Trent*,
trans. Ernest Graf (2 vols., London, 1957–61), I, 81.

[45] For these, see Michael J. Wilks, *The Problem of Sovereignty in the Later Middle Ages*
(Cambridge, 1963), pp. 291 note 2, 294ff., 311, 319 note 5, 349ff. Also, J.G. Sykes,
"John de Pouilli and Peter de la Palu," *English Historical Review*, XLIX (April, 1934),
237.

[46] See Augustin Renaudet, *Préréforme et Humanisme à Paris pendant les premières guerres*

A careful and systematic checking of the elaborate network of cross-reference which pierce the jungle of glosses on the two laws would, no doubt, reveal additional instances of its use by canonists and civilians alike. But the texts already cited should themselves suffice to establish the fact that the absolute and ordained or ordinary powers (Hostiensis uses the two latter terms interchangeably) enjoyed a career in the canonistic literature dating back well into the thirteenth century, and in the civilian literature dating back at least to the mid-fourteenth century. Few scholars today are likely to be surprised at the close correspondence between the two laws on this matter, or, indeed, between the two laws, on the one hand, and the arguments of the Romanizing French jurists of the sixteenth century on the other. Pope Emperor, French King—the parallels between their positions are obvious and the jurists themselves constantly insist upon them.[47] But Hostiensis, in one of his allusions to the absolute and ordained powers, reveals the existence of yet another parallelism, one which may well, perhaps, be more surprising, but which is, in fact, the most important one of all.

The parallel he draws is one between the powers of the Pope and the powers of God.[48] In this, as in other things, Johannes Andreae follows his lead,[49] but the most extensive (and by far the most illuminating) elaboration of this parallelism is the work, not of a canonist, but of the theologian and publicist, Aegidius Romanus. It is in the third book of his *De ecclesiastica potestate*, which he wrote in 1301, that Aegidius distinguishes between the *potestas absoluta* and the *potestas regulata* of the pope. Although by the former, he says, the pope is "without halter and bit," nevertheless he himself ought to regulate his own actions. Thus, although he is above all positive laws it is fitting that he should govern the Church by his *potestas regulata*—that is, in accordance with "the common law" taking in this "an example from

---

d'Italie: 1494–1517 (Paris, 1916), pp. 201–202 and esp. 202, note 3, for the important speech of the royal advocate Lemaistre in February 1487/8.

[47] Thus, in the texts cited above (notes 41 and 43), Bodin uses the papal analogy when speaking of the French King, Johannes Andreae, Hostiensis and Henricus de Bouhic use the analogy of the prince when talking about the pope, and nearly all of them—canonists, civilians, sixteenth-century French lawyers—cite the *lex digna* to bolster their arguments.

[48] *Lectura in Quinque Decretalium, ad* X, 3, 35, 6, fol. CXXXr, where he cites St. Jerome on the problem: "Cum deus omnia possit hoc solum non potest: suscitare virginem post ruinam." (See below, n. 52).

[49] *In tertium Decretalium librum Novella Commentaria, ad* X, 3, 35, 6, fol. 179v.

God himself, whose vicar he is."[50] And, for this point, Aegidius refers us back to the lengthy discussion of the parallel which is to be found earlier on in the tract.

There (and in a later passage) he notes in the operation both of God's government of the natural world and of the pope's government of the Church a double modality. The first is that which is in accordance with "the common law," or "the common course," or "the common course of nature." The second, that which results from an exercise of the *plenitudo potestatis* or of "the special providence of God," or is in accordance with the "special" law. In the first (and more normal) mode God does not interfere with the operation of the secondary causes which reflect, after all, the laws which he himself has given to nature. Nor does the pope fail to respect the common laws of the Church or to rule within the terms of their provisions. In God and the pope, however, there resides a plenitude of power by which they can do directly, without the intermediary of secondary causality, whatsoever they can do indirectly by means of secondary causes. Thus, for some special reason, God can act "aside from" (*praeter*) the common laws of nature and perform a miracle—as, for example, when he enabled Mishach, Shadrach and Abednego to emerge unscathed from the flames of Nebuchadnezzar's fiery furnace (Daniel, iii, 20ff.). Similarly, for a comparably special reason, the pope can act "aside from" the laws of the Church and himself perform a function which is commonly the task of a secondary agent, since, in the government of the Church, he too possesses a plenitude of power and can do without a second cause whatever he normally does by means of one. In other words—though Aegidius does not quite use them—the Pope, by an exercise of his absolute power, can perform a "papal miracle."[51]

But papal miracle or no, there was not, at the time, anything very novel about this—except, perhaps, the length to which Aegidius takes the parellelism. When Hostiensis had drawn the same parallel a few years earlier he had referred to a celebrated remark of St. Jerome concerning the omnipotence of God, and though he seems to have

---

[50] *Aegidius Romanus: De ecclesiastica potestate*, ed. Richard Scholz (Weimar, 1929), Bk. IV, ch. 7, pp. 181–82.

[51] This summary draws on both passages—see *De ecclesiastica potestate*, Bk. III, chs. 2, 3, and 9, pp. 149–59, 190–95. For the references to Daniel 3, 20ff., see pp. 158 and 192.

been acquainted with this remark through the medium of Gratian's *Decretum*, his use of the parallel at all is probably a reflection of the profound and enduring scholastic concern with the whole question of divine omnipotence.[52] Even before the rise of scholasticism, St. Peter Damian (d. 1072) had devoted a complete tract to the problem and had asserted that God, being omnipotent, can act in a manner "contrary to the common order of nature" or "the custom of nature"— as he did, indeed, when he saved the three youths from Nebuchadnezzar's fiery furnace—for he who gave "the law and order to nature" can hardly be subject to its laws.[53] The same issue was taken up again in the next century by Hugh of St. Victor (d. 1141), Peter Abelard (d. 1142), and Peter Lombard (d. 1160),[54] and its inclusion in Lombard's *Liber sententiarum*, which was to become *the* theological textbook of the Middle Ages, meant that the attention of all subsequent medieval theologians was focused on it.

Though Abelard clearly distinguished a province for the ordained will of God, Albert the Great, Aquinas's famous master, was one of the first scholastics to have used the precise distinction between the *potentia absoluta* and *potentia ordinata*.[55] Aquinas, Scotus and Ockham did likewise—Scotus and Ockham discussing the meaning of the distinction in some detail.[56] And with the dominance of the Ockhamist

---

[52] Jerome, *Epistola and Eustochium* (*De custodia virginitatis*), in Jacques Paul Migne, *Patrologiae Cursus Completus*... series latina (221 vols., Paris, 1844ff.), 22, 397–8 (Hereafter cited as PL). Gratian included the relevant passage as C. 32, q. 5, c. 11, Aemilius Friedberg (ed.), *Corpus Juris Canonici* (2 vols., Leipzig, 1879–81), I, 1135.

[53] *De divina omnipotentia*, esp. chs. 1, 10 and 11; the citations are from chs. 10 and 11; in PL 145, 610D–614C. He cites the remarks of St. Jerome early in the tract and discusses them at come length (596ff.).

[54] Hugh of St. Victor, *De sacramentis christianae fidei*, Bk. I, part 2, ch. 22, in PL 176, 214–16; *Summa sententiarum*. Tract, I, ch. 14 in *ibid.*, 68–70. Abelard, *Introductio ad theologiam*, Bk. III, ch. 4 in PL 178, esp. 1092; cf. his *Sic et Non*, in PL 178, 1393ff., where he, too, cites St. Jerome. Lombard, *Sent.*, I, dist. 42, s5, in PL 192, 636.

[55] Abelard, *Introductio ad theologiam*, Bk. III, ch. 4, in PL 178, 1092; Albertus Magnus (1193–1280), *Super quatuor libros Sententiarum*, I, dist. 42, art. 6, and dist. 43, art. 3; also *Summa Theologiae*, Part I, Tract XIX, qu. 78, *membrum* 2, both in *Opera Omnia*, ed. Auguste Borgnet (36 vols., Paris, 1890–99), XXVI, 362–66, 381, and XXXI, 832–34. It should be noted that the authenticity of the *Summa* is in dispute among scholars. Cf. Ernst Borchert, *Der Einfluss des Nominalismus auf die Christologie der Spätscholastik* (Münster i.W., 1946), pp. 48–50.

[56] Thomas Aquinas, *Summa Theologiae*, Ia pars, qu. 25, art. 5; cf. qu. 19, art. 3 (he uses the term "potentia *ordinaria*"). John Duns Scotus, *In quatuor libros Sententiarum*, I, dist, 44, qu. *unica* (2 vols., Antwerp, 1620), I, 443–44. William of Ockham, *Opus nonaginta dierum*, ch. 95, in Hilary S. Offler ed., *Guillelmi de Ockham: Opera Politica* (3 vols., Manchester, 1940–63), II, 718ff.; cf. his *Tractatus contra Benedictum* Bk. III, ch. 3, in *Opera Politica*, III, 230–34; also his *Quodlibeta septem una cum tractatu de sacramento*

and "nominalist" theology at so many universities in the fourteenth and fifteenth centuries the distinction began to play a very important role in theological discussions. Whether or not the theological usage preceded the canonistic is a moot point. But Albert the Great implied that the theological usage was already customary in his own day,[57] and the distinction certainly seems to bulk larger in the theological literature and to play a more crucial role. In any case, the theological, canonistic, civilian, and French usage are all intimately interrelated. If, in the texts already cited, Hostiensis, Joannes Andreae, and Aegidius Romanus can draw our attention to the theological parallel, Duns Scotus, Ockham, Pierre d'Ailly, Altenstaig and the Scottish scholastic, John Major (d. 1550), can reciprocate by citing the canonistic or general juristic analogy.[58] This being so, it is surely improper to suppose that those English references to the absolute and ordinary powers of the King which we listed earlier on can be fully understood if taken in isolation from the other juristic and from the theological parallels. In these matters, as in others, Tudor and Stuart England was much less immune to changes in the intellectual temperature and pressure of continental Europe than we tend often to suppose.

The relevance of the French experience to the English political scene was well understood in the sixteenth and early-seventeenth centuries, and it is hard to believe that the French use of the distinction between the absolute and ordinary powers went unnoticed in England.[59] Moreover, even if it did, the works of Gentilis and

---

altaris (Strasbourg, 1491), Quodl, VI, qu. 1, fol. 91r, and his *Quaestiones in IV libros Sententiarum* (Lyons, 1495), Prologus, qu. 1 E. Cf. the lengthy discussion of the two powers in Altenstaig, *Vocabularius Theologie completens vocabularium descriptiones, diffinitiones et significatus ad theologiam utilium* (Hagenau, 1517), fols. CLXXVr and CXCVIIr. It is only recently that the importance of the distinction for late-medieval theology has been fully recognized and properly understood—see especially Heiko A. Oberman, *The Harvest of Medieval Theology: Gabriel Biel and Late Medieval Nominalism* (Cambridge, Mass., 1963), pp. 30–56. For the prenominalist usage, see Borchert, *Der Einfluss des Nominalismus*, pp. 46–60.

[57] "Ad hoc *dici consuevit*, quod potentia Dei potest accipi absolute, et potest accipi ut disposita et ordinata secundum rationem scientiae et voluntatis" etc. (Italics mine) – in *Summa Theologiae*, I, Tract. 19, qu. 78, *membrum* 2, in *Opera omnia*, XXXI, 832.

[58] For Scotus and Altenstaig, see the texts cited above, notes 56 and 57. Ockham, *Quodlibeta*, VI, qu. 6, fol. 91r; Pierre d'Ailly, *Quaestiones super I, III et IV Sententiarum* (Lyons, 1500), I, qu. 9, art. 2 M, fol. 120r; John Major, *In primum Sententiarum* (Paris, 1510), I, dist. 44. qu. 1, fol. ci v.

[59] The period witnessed a vertiable flood of translations of French political literature into English. See J.H.M. Salmon, *The French Religious Wars in English Political*

Cowell (which appeared in 1605 and 1607, respectively) drew attention to the related civilian usage, and Sir John Davies, at least, must surely have been acquainted with it for he refers to Baldus several times and cites the *lex digna* when drawing the distinction.[60]

I know of no evidence to suggest that Englishmen of the seventeenth century were familiar with the canonistic version, but it was clearly not unknown in the sixteenth, for in 1528 Henry VIII himself noted that although a dispensation "to proceed to a second marriage" was "a thing that the Pope perhaps cannot do in accordance with the divine and human laws already written, *using his ordinary power*," he might possibly be able to do it "*of his mere and absolute power*, as a thing in which he may dispense above the law."[61]

It is not, however, the influence of the canonistic, civilian or French usage which is most clearly evident in the English references to the distinction but that of the theological. This is hardly surprising since it was a usage unembarrassed by association with alien legal systems and one familiar to anybody well-acquainted with Protestant theological literature on the continent or in England. Luther himself chose to brand the distinction as the work of "sophists" but he used it nonetheless, and it passed into the Protestant theological heritage at large, being disseminated in England by such widely-read theological manuals as those of William Perkins and William Ames.[62]

Thought (Oxford, 1959), esp. pp. 2ff. and Appendix A, pp. 171–80. See also George L. Mosse, "The Influence of Jean Bodin's *Republique* on English Political Thought," *Medievalia et Humanistica*, V (July, 1948), 73–83 and the works cited by Salmon, pp. 2–3, note 4. Note that Gentillet's whole discussion of the two powers of the King, "absolute" and "civil" was intended as an elucidation of Philippe de Commines' claim that the Prince could not tax his subjects without their grant and consent—a claim cited later on, after all, by none other than Chief Justice Coke. See Gentillet, *Discourse upon the Meanes of Wel Governing*, pp. 19 and 28 (French ed., pp. 47 and 62); cf. *Mémoires de Philippe de Commynes*, ed. R. Chantelauze (Paris, 1881), Bk. V, ch. 19, p. 398; Sir Edward Coke, *The Fourth Part of the Institute of the Laws of England* (London, 1797), ch. 1, p. 28.

[60] Davies, *The Question concerning Impositions*, pp. 6 and 30.

[61] "Instructions to Sir Francis Bryan and Peter Vannes, sent to the Court of Rome," in John S. Brewer *et al.* eds., *Letters and Papers, Foreign and Domestic, of the reign of Henry VIII* (22 vols., London, 1862–1932), IV, Part 2, 2158 (No. 4977); cited in Franklin L. Baumer, *The Early Tudor Theory of Kingship* (New Haven, 1940), p. 137 note 44. (Italics mine).

[62] Martin Luther, "*Vorlesungen über 1 Mose*," ch. 19, 14–20, ch. 20, 2, in *D. Martin Luthers Werke* (69 vols., Weimar, 1887–1963) XLIII, 71–82, 106. (Note that Luther uses the expressions *potestas ordinaria* and *potestas ordinata* interchangeably). For a discussion of the meaning which Luther ascribed to these terms, see John Dillenberger, *God Hidden and Revealed* (Philadelphia, 1953) esp. pp. 43ff., 139ff. William Perkins,

There, indeed, along with the closely related distinction between the extraordinary and ordinary providence of God, it became so common that Robert Boyle was later to use it to reconcile the Christian belief in the possibility of the miraculous with the scientific insistence on the uniformity of nature. Thus, by his "absolute or supernatural power," he said, God interfered with "the ordinary and settled course of nature" (the product of His "ordinary providence") and saved Mishach, Shadrach and Abednego from destruction in Nebuchadnezzar's fiery furnace.[63] By now, surely, a familiar illustration of a familiar distinction to illustrate a familiar point![64]

Given this degree of continuity on the theological level it should come as no surprise to read the Earl of Strafford's statement in 1641 that "the prerogative must be used, as God doth his omnipotency, at extraordinary occasions":[65] or Sir John Davies' argument that in limiting and stinting "his absolute power" and tying "himself to the ordinary rules of the Law, in common and ordinary cases" the King "doth imitate the Divine Majesty, which in the Government of the world doth suffer things for the most part to passe according to the order and course of Nature, yet many times doth show his extraordinary power in working miracles above Nature."[66] Nor should we

---

A. Golden Chaine or the Description of Theologie, in *The Workes of that Famous and Worthie Minister of Christ in the University of Cambridge, M.W. Perkins* (3 vols., Cambridge, 1608–31), I, 13, 32, and his *A Godly and Learned Exposition,* in *Workes,* III, 233–34. William Ames, *The Marrow of Sacred Divinity* (London, 1642), Bk. I, ch. 6, pp. 18–20. Many other references could be given. For some of these and for a discussion of the role of the absolute and ordained powers in seventeenth-century theological and scientific thinking, see Francis Oakley, "Christian Theology and the Newtonian Science: The Rise of the concept of the Laws of Nature," *Church History,* XXX (No. 4., 1961), 445ff.

[63] *Some Considerations about the Reconciliableness of Reason and Religion,* in *The Works of the Honourable Robert Boyle,* ed. Thomas Birch (6 vols. London, 1772), IV, 161–62, and *A Disquisition about the Final Causes of Natural Things,* in *Works,* V, 412–14; cf. his *A Free Inquiry inot the Vulgarly received notion of Nature,* in *Works,* V, 162, 197–98, 211, 216.

[64] This same illustration from Daniel had been used to illustrate this same (or a similar) point, not only by Damiani and Aegidius Romanus (see above, notes 51 and 53, but also by Ockham, d'Ailly, John Major, and probably by many other medieval scholastics. Luther, Melanchthon and many seventeenth-century theologians followed suit. For the texts, see Oakley, "Christian Theology and the Newtonian Science," 449 and 456 note 104.

[65] Made when he was defending himself before the Lords and insisting that the King must have a prerogative or emergency power since "there must be a prerogative if there must be extraordinary occasions"—*Calendar of State Papers, Domestic Series, 1640–41* (London, 1882), p. 542; cf. Judson, *The Crisis of the Constitution,* p. 147.

[66] *The Question concerning Impositions,* pp. 30–32. For a comparable passage, see Forset, *A Comparative Discourse,* pp. 20–21.

be tempted to dismiss as a mere baroque affectation the numerous and comparable parallels which James I drew between the position of God in the universe and his own position in the Kingdom. Speaking in the Star Chamber in 1616, and distinguishing his "absolute" from his "private" prerogative, James said:

It is Atheisme and blasphemie to dispute what God can doe: good Christians content themselves with is will revealed in his word. So it is presumption and high contempt in a subject, to dispute what a King can doe, or say that a King cannot doe this, or that; but rest in that which is the King's revealed will in his Law.[67]

There is every reason to think that he meant precisely what he said. W.H. Greenleaf has recently insisted on the importance of the "argument by correspondence" or analogy in James's political thinking,[68] and it may now be suggested that if we are to understand James at all, we must be prepared to take his definition of "political blasphemy" at least as seriously as we take Aegidius Romanus's explication of the "papal miracle." For what is certainly involved here—and only a little less certainly in the general English usage of the distinction between the absolute and ordinary powers of the King—is a piece of what the late Ernst Kantorowicz like to call "political theology."[69]

So much for the question of origins. It must now be asked what light these findings shed on the related question of meaning. Surely not a little. We have seen that many of those Englishmen who used the distinction thought the theological analogy relevant and illuminating. We have seen, too, that the whole purpose of the theological usage was to emphasize the omnipotence of God, who can do anything that does not involve a contradiction, and to prelude the possibility of denying him, as Charleton put it in 1652, "a *reserved power*, or infringing, or altering any one of those laws, which [he] Himself ordained, and enacted, and chaining up his armes in the adamantine fetters of Destiny."[70] As a scientist, Charleton was talking,

---

[67] In McIlwain ed., *The Political Works of James I*, pp. 333–34; cf. his "Speech to the Lords and Commons . . . xxi March, 1609," *ibid.*, esp. pp. 309–10. The whole speech is highly theological in content.

[68] W.H. Greenleaf, "James I and the Divine Right of Kings," *Political Studies*, V (No. 1, 1957), 36ff.; see also now his *Order, Empiricism and Politics: Two Traditions of English Political Thought 1500–1700* (Oxford, 1964), chs. 1–3.

[69] See esp. his *The King's Two Bodies: A Study in Medieval Political Theology* (Princeton, N.J., 1957).

[70] Walter Charleton (d. 1707), member of the Royal Society, *The Darkness of Atheism dispelled by the Light of Nature: a physico-theologicall Treatise* (London, 1652), p. 329.

of course, about those natural laws which God imposed upon the
material world when he created it—as also were all of those who
illustrated the operation of the absolute as opposed to the ordained
power by citing the miraculous deliverance of the three youths from
Nebuchadnezzar's furnace. But most of them were also interested in
the operation of God's power in the moral order and the economy
of salvation. And there, too, they emphasized that though God normally condescends to limit himself and, by his ordained power, to
operate in accordance with "the common law" which he has established, nevertheless he could, by his absolute power, act "aside from
or contrary to that law" (*praeter illam legem vel contra eam*).[71] Just as the
pope, Ockham said, can do something "absolutely" which he cannot
do in accordance with the law.[72] Or again, as John Major and others
said, just as a King can do many things *de facto* which he cannot
do *de jure*.[73]

The very use by theologians of these political analogies points, of
course, in the direction of the juristic usage and suggests that its
meaning was very similar. That the main thrust of the canonistic
usage is the same as the theological is brought home most forcefully
by the fact that on one of the occasions when the distinction was
invoked *against* the pope (in an attempt to limit burdensome papal
fiscal demands) the authors of the appeal in question admitted,
nonetheless, that

> by his plenitude of power (which power is infinite) the same lord our
> pope can act above and against the law [*jus*], especially those laws
> which are of positive justice, and can dispense and derogate from them
> or abrogate them.[74]

Although this involves a negative assessment of the normal range of
papal power, not even Aegidius Romanus himself conceived the
absolute power of the pope in more far-reaching terms.

Some of the civilians expressed comparable sentiments about the

---

[71] This particular formulation is that of Duns Scotus, *In Quatuor libros Sententiarum*,
I, dist. 44, qu. 1, 443.
[72] *Quodlibeta*, VI, qu. 1, fol. 91r.
[73] Major, *In primum Sententiarum*, dist. 44, qu. 1, fol. ci v; cf. Scotus, *In Quatuor
libros Sententiarum*, I, dist. 44, qu. 1, 443; Altenstaig, *Vocabularius Theologie*, fol. CXCVIIr.
The civilian Cynus of Pistoia also made use of this particular formula (which Scotus
attributed to the jurists)—see the text cited in R.W. and A.J. Carlyle, *A History of
Medieval Political Theory in the West* (6 vols., Edinburgh and London 1903–36, VI, 16.
[74] Winkelmann, *Acta Imperli Inedita*, II, 843 (No. 1182).

absolute power of the prince,[75] but it would be improper to ignore the extent to which the sharp edges of the distinction were blunted when it descended from the purity of the theological sphere and plunged into the density of the juristic atmosphere. The absolute power of God, curtailed only by the principle of non-contradiction, transcended all laws—physical, natural or divine. The absolute power of the pope, however, was conceived usually to transcend only human positive law, and the absolute power of the prince, though it too, transcended positive law, was not in the eyes of most civilians superior to the binding force of contracts made with his subjects.[76] The complexity and tenacity of the native legal traditions through which the distinction had to pierce as it made its way into French and English juristic and political thinking did something to further this process of modification—so much so, indeed, that there are occasions on which the outlines of the distinction become blurred and the precise meaning accorded to it hard to grasp. Its "absolutist" tone, however, was clearly not lost on Daneau, who promptly denied its validity. Nor was it lost on Chasseneuz, Gentillet or Bodin. All agreed, along with their canonist and civilian predecessors, that the King was subject to natural and divine law. All agreed that he must normally by assumed to operate in accordance with his ordinary, civil or regulated power—that is, within the limits imposed (or self-imposed) by the established law. All agreed, too, that of his absolute power he was superior to the positive law and could dispense with it.[77] But not even the most "Romanizing" of these jurists felt free to abandon the traditional doctrine that the King was limited by the two great, undeniable, fundamental laws of the realm: the Salic law and the prohibition against alienating the royal domain.[78]

Such a hesitation undoubtedly comported ill with their emphasis on the absolute power of the King and certainly introduced a further element of fuzziness that was absent from the theological usage of

[75] Baldus, *Commentaria super Codice*, ad C. 1, 14, 4, fol. 552, Jason de Mayno (see Carlyle, *History of Medieval Political Theory*, VI, 149 and note 2 where he cites the text), and William Barclay *De regno et regali potestate* (Paris, 1660), Bk. III, ch. 14, p. 193; cited in Carlyle, *History of Medieval Political Theory*, VI, 448 note 1.

[76] See Carlyle, *History of Medieval Political Theory*, VI, 16, 19ff., 154ff. The tendency was to ground the binding force of contracts not in the positive law but in the *jus gentium* or the natural law.

[77] See the texts cited above, notes 33–35.

[78] See the discussion in Church, *Constitutional Thought in Sixteenth-Century France*, pp. 49, 81.

the distinction.[79] There is a comparable lack of coherence is some of the English appeals to the distinction, though it is not to be ascribed to anything akin to the French doctine of fundamental law.[80] Thus, the remarks of Sir John Doderidge about the "absolute" and "ordinate" powers of the King are too brief and incomplete to convey any precise meaning. The same is only a little less true of the elliptic formulations ascribed to Chief Justice Coke,[81] and even James I, who cited the theological analogy at length, was not wholly consistent nor fully clear on the matter.[82]

Despite these confusing formulations, however, the traditionally "absolutist" implications of the distinction were certainly recognized in England, not only by those who denied its validity but also by most of those who cited it with approval. In 1539 Taverner mentioned with sorrow those who gave to the prince "an ordinarye power, and an absolute power, whereof the one can do what the lawes, pactes, and leagues demaunde, the other whatsoever it lusteth," and, linking this with the Romanist maxim *quod principi placuit legis habet vigorem*, wrote "wolde God the eares of chrystian rulers were not tykled wyth lyke tales, and yf they be that they wold with lyke severitie reject them."[83] In 1628 Sir Benjamin Rudyard, deploring the ravages wrought in the name of "Reason of State," but unwilling

---

[79] That this was realized at the time is reflected, perhaps, in the attempt made to justify these limitations on the royal power by postulating something akin to a divine fundamental law governing the operations of God. See Jehan Savaron (d. 1622), *De la souveraineté du Roy et que sa Majesté ne la peut souzmettre à qui que ce soit, ny aliener son Domaine à perpetuité* (Paris, 1620), pp. 4–5: "... Ce n'est pas affoiblir vostre puissance souveraine, de dire que V[ostre] M[ajesté] ne la peut sousmettre ny ceder a personne, ains c'est la luy reserver entière et incommunicable. La puissance de Dieu n'est point jugee moindre pour ce qu'il ne peut pecher, ny mal faire, mais est d'autant plus perfectionée."

[80] For the whole tangled dispute about the existence and nature of fundamental law in England, see J.W. Gough, *Fundamental Law in English Constitutional History* (Oxford, 1961), esp. chs. 3 and 4.

[81] At least by indirection, Coke would seem to have been making the uncharacteristic suggestion that the absolute power was neither disputable nor bounded by law. See *Pym's Diary* for his reported statement in Parliament on February 19, 1621—Wallace Notestein, Frances Helen Relf and Hartley Simpson eds., *Commons Debates 1621* (7 vols., New Haven, 1935), IV, 79. See also *The Anonymous Journal*, in *ibid.*, II, 193. Wormuth, *The Royal Prerogative*, p. 56, says that Coke found the distinction in the common law.

[82] McIlwain, *Political Works of James I*, pp. 309–310. Another unclear use of the distinction occurs in Bacon's argument in the Post-Nati Case—see Howell, *State Trials*, II, 580; cf. Mosse, *Struggle for Sovereignty in England*, pp. 74ff.

[83] *The garden of wysedome*, Bk. I, sig. Di r–v.

to deny that "the King ought to have a trust left and deposited in him" (for "extraordinary cases must happen") felt is necessary to try to turn the theological tables on the defenders of the absolute power by pointing out that

> God himself has constituted a general law of nature to govern the ordinary course of things, he hath made no law for miracles; yet there is in this observation of them, that they are rather "praeter naturam" than "contra naturam" and always "propter bonos fines" for King's Prerogatives are rather besides the law, than against it.[84]

If such an argument lacks the power to convince it is because it proceeds a little too much in terms of the mental world from which the distinction itself drew its original sustenance. Gentilis, Cowell, Forset, Davies speak in similar terms. For them the absolute power or prerogative of the King, like that of God, clearly transcended the ordinary. There was no question simply of two coordinate or parallel powers, each restricted to its own proper sphere. The absolute power not only "admitteth no questioning disputes" (Forset), but is also an "unlimited power," one "not bound by the positive law" (Davies), one "above the ordinary course of the common law" (Cowell). Indeed, at least according to Gentilis, it is so absolute that the King could take away the lawful right of one of his subjects "even without cause."[85]

The formulations of the common lawyers who pressed the distinction into service in the great Stuart state trials are a good deal less precise and a good deal less clear but their main thrust is undoubtedly similar and they should surely be viewed in the same broad context. Thus, for Fleming, the common law which *controls* the exercise of the ordinary power is at the most a mere *vis directiva* when it comes to the absolute power, which, in any case, has its own "absolute law" and one that "varieth ... according to the wisdom of the King for the common good."[86] Similarly, for Heath, there can

---

[84] In a speech in Parliament, April, 1628; in Howell, *State Trials*, III, 173–74.

[85] See the texts cited above, notes 13, 14, 15 and 18. Note, however, that none of these men suggested that the King was not subject to the divine and natural laws, and Gentilis, like most of the late-medieval civilians and like Bodin, did believe that the King was bound by his contracts—see *Regales Disputationes Tres*, Disp. I, 17–18.

[86] Howell, *State Trials*, II, 389; see the text quoted for footnote 6 above. Cf. Thomas Aquinas, *Summa Theologiae*, Ia Iae, qu. 96, art. 5, ad 3um, where he interprets the Romanist maxim *princeps legibus solutus est* to mean that the ruler is above

be no question of disputing the legality of that which the King commands of his absolute power, for though he "hath rules to govern himself by" he is not subordinated to them in the same way as are his subjets, since, unlike them, he is "the head of the same fountain of justice."[87] Bacon asserts that although some of the King's prerogatives can be disputed in "his ordinary courts of Justice," he possesses also another prerogative, "free jurisdiction," or "sovereign power" which is not held "mediately from the law, but immediately from God." By this power he can *pro bono publico* "temper, change, and control" the common law and "mitigate" or "suspend" acts of Parliament. "And this inherent power of his and what participateth thereof, is therefore exempt from controlment by any Court of Law."[88]

Now Bacon made this point to rebut charges that the King did not have the power by law to set up a prerogative court judging in accordance with equity. He was seeking to contrast that power of the King "which is delegate to his ordinary judges in Chancery or Common Law" with that "inherent power" which he "exerciseth by his Councils." These Councils "are not delegations of power, but assistances thereof inherent in himself," and because of this "the Council Table judgeth matters in equity when they are referred to them"[89] Bacon's purpose here is noteworthy because it reveals the link between the doctrine of the absolute and ordinary powers and the growing tendency of the royal council to rely in cases concerning "the state of the Commonwealth" upon its "high and pre-eminent power," to stress the existence of extraordinary was well as ordinary rules of judicial procedure, to consider that it was free to dispense not only with the ordinary rules of procedure but also the ordinary rules of law, and, if necessary, "to make the ordinary law yield to what it considered to be state necessity."[90] And herein lies the relevance

---

the law with repect to its constrainting force (*vis coactiva*) but not with respect to its directive force (*vis directiva*), and where he cites the *lex digna* in support of this latter contention that the ruler should voluntarily submit himself to the direction of the law.

[87] In Darnel's Case, Howell, *State Trials*, III, 35–37. The point he makes is analogous to one made by Scotus (*In Quatuor libros Sententiarum*, I, dist. 44, qu. 1, 443).

[88] In his *View of the Differences in question betwixt the King's bench and the Council in the Marches*, in Spedding ed., *Letters and Life of Francis Bacon*, III, 371–74.

[89] *Ibid.* Though Bacon did admit that the Chancellor wielded an "absolute" as well as an "ordinary" power. See below, n. 91.

[90] These developments are discussed by Holdsworth, *History of English Law*, IV, 86–87 and V, 186–87, but he does not link them to his discussion of the absolute

of those formulations of the distinction to be found in Lambarde's *Archeion*. For he speaks of a "law absolute and ordinarie," of the wielding by King and council of an "irregular and uncontroulable authority," and points out, in connection with the Court of Star Chamber, that

> Albeit, here within this Realme of *England*, the most part of *Causes* in complaint are and ought to be referred to the ordinarie processe and solemne handling of *Common Law*, and regular distribution of Justice; yet have there always arisen, and there will continually, from time to time, grow some rare matters, meet (for just reason) to be reserved to a higher hand, and to be left to the aide of absolute *Power*, and irregular Authoritie.[91]

Towards the end of *Constitutionalism: Ancient and Modern*, McIlwain comments that "in it all there is no period more important than that of the early Stuart Kings of England, and none more in need of a discriminating reconstruction—and a reconstruction, I may add, which will take proper account of earlier precedent as well as contemporary conditions."[92] Our own findings show that those "earlier precedents" must include, not only the English but also the continental, and those "contemporary conditions," not only the much-analyzed phenomena of legal and political life but also that whole mental climate, so alien to us today, which made of the theological analogy a powerful and important weapon in the arsenal of legal

---

and ordinary powers of the King. He points out that it was "laid down in Star Chamber that 'exorbitante offences are not subjects to an ordinaryre course of law.'" He points out, too, (*History of English Law*, V, 173ff.) that the distinction between ordinary and extraordinary rules of procedure had become common in France during the fourteenth and fifteenth centuries.

[91] Lambarde, *Archeion*, ed. McIlwain and Ward, pp. 61, 66 and 48. Lambarde also draws a further distinction concerning the double jurisdiction of the Chancellor ("the one, of *Common Law*; the other, or *Equitie*; that first being limitted in power, and his latter being meere, absolute, and infinite") for the King had committed to his Chancellor "his owne Regall, absolute, and extraordinarie preheminence of *Jurisdiction* in *Civill* Causes, as well for amendment as for supply of the *Common Law*" (*Archeion*, pp. 32 and 39). Cf. Coke, *Fourth Part of the Institutes*, ch. 8, p. 79, where he draws the same distinction concerning Chancery. This is clearly in the lineage of the similar distinction which appears in the Year Book for 1469 (see above, note 8). Plucknett, *Concise History of the Common Law*, pp. 193–95, says that Bacon "must surely have been thinking of this passage" when he hailed James I's vindication of Chancery" as the court of the King's 'absolute power.'" He also says that "there is a world of difference between their meaning in 1469 and the use Bacon made of them in 1616" but it may now be argued that Bacon was being perhaps a little less anachronistic than Plucknett suggests.

[92] *Constitutionalism: Ancient and Modern*, p. 130.

and political dialectic. The distinction between the absolute and ordinary powers of the King was essentially a piece of political theology, and from this fact—so often underlined in the seventeenth-century literature itself—it drew much of its authority and its power to convince. Its history was longer, richer, more dense and more intricate than has heretofore been supposed, and it is against the background of this long history that the English appeals to the distinction should be viewed. If this is done, they (or the majority of them) will be seen to have postulated the existence, not of two parallel or coordinate powers each confined by law to its own proper sphere, but rather of two powers, one of which was in essence superior to the other, and which in time of necessity or for reason of state could transcend the other and encroach upon its domain.

It would seem, then, that Holdsworth, whose views on the subject have not attracted much support, was on the right track in his general assessment of the meaning of the distinction. His further assertion that its use tended to give "countenance to the idea that the King had a large and indefinite reserve of power which he could on occasion use for the benefit of the state"[93] is somewhat less persuasive, but only because it puts the cart before the horse. We now know that from the twelfth-century onwards, Kings and popes had appealed with mounting frequency to the public utility, to the "state of the realm" (*status regni*), or to the "state of the Church" (*status ecclesiae*), and by so doing had demanded of their subjects "a sacrifice of private rights and of the law that protected them."[94] We know, too, that it had become increasingly common practice among the glossators on both laws to cite the principle of the common welfare or public utility in order to justify the exercise by Kings and popes of a prerogative that made them "superior, in an emergency or necessity, to the private law and private rights."[95] And, in fact, those medievals who drew the distinction between the two powers of King or pope repeatedly insisted (as did Fleming later on) that the absolute power was to be employed and the normal course of the common law superseded, not arbitrarily and "without cause," but only "for reasonable cause" or "great and necessary cause," or "great, just and

---

[93] *History of English Law*, IV, 206–207.
[94] Post, *Studies in Medieval Legal Thought*, p, 12; the whole of his "Introduction," pp. 3–24, and cf. ch. 5 (pp. 241–309) is immediately relevant.
[95] *Ibid.*, p. 13.

necessary cause," or "for reasonable cause" and "because of the public utility of the church or people."[96] Holdsworth to the contrary, then, it was the *very prevalence* of such ideas, so much more ancient than he imagined, that led English royalists to adopt for their own purposes a well-worn distinction that had already been used in analogous matters for several centuries and to express a cognate point of view.

It follows, of course, that McIlwain's interpretation, which in its day succeeded so well in setting the terms for subsequent discussion of the issue, will no longer hold up. And it falls down because the sixteenth- and seventeenth-century formulations of the distinction cannot be assimilated to his general interpretation of medieval and early-modern constitutionalism. The absolute and ordinary powers of which the seventeenth-century English lawyers and publicists spoke were simply not the same as *gubernaculum* and *jurisdiction*—the parallel powers which McIlwain claimed to find in Bracton—no more, indeed, than were the absolute and ordinary powers mentioned by Baldus or by those other medieval jurists whom McIlwain does not cite.

Nor is this all. Of recent years, McIlwain's magisterial analysis of the development of Western constitutionalism has been subjected to criticism at points other than this. The scholarly concerns of his critics have not been identical; their criticisms have been of a piecemeal nature; but their general drift is similar. In 1960, R.W.K. Hinton rejected the interpretation of Sir John Fortescue's constitutional theory advanced by McIlwain and also by Chrimes. He did so in favor of the view argued earlier on by the Rev. Charles Plummer to the effect that by *dominium politicum et regale* Fortescue had meant to describe "a constitutional or parliamentary government," a mixed monarchy, something akin, in fact, to the form enshrined in nineteenth-century English constitutional theory—and not, therefore, a regime in which a sharp distinction was drawn between *gubernaculum* and *jurisdictio*. "Not until the reigns of James I and Charles I," Hinton added, "do we encounter a widely accepted constitutional theory

---

[96] In order of quotation: *Hostiensis, Lectura in Quinque Decretalium, ad.* X, 3, 35, 6, *in v.* nec summus Pontifex, fol. CXXXr; Aegidius Romanus, *De eccl. pot.*, Bk. III, ch. 9, pp. 192, 194; Johannes Andreae, *In tertium Decretalium librum Novella Commentaria, ad.* X, 3, 35, 6, fol. 179v; Winkelmann, *Acta Imperii Inedita*, II, 843 (No. 1182); Baldus de Ubaldis, *Commentaria super decretalibus, ad.* X, 2, 26, 13 *in v.* omnia jura, fol. 247r.

of the sort Dr. McIlwain ascribed to Fortescue and [Sir Thomas] Smith."[97]

Yet McIlwain did not regard the constitutional position which he had ascribed to Fortescue as a fifteenth-century innovation. It was, rather, the position he had already ascribed to Bracton. Here again, however, his interpretation has been heavily and convincingly criticized and the conclusion firmly drawn that "the distinction between *jurisdiction* and *gubernaculum* . . . seems the product of McIlwain's classificatory acumen rather than Bracton's."[98] But, if this is so, it would also seem that the validity of much of McIlwain's general interpretation of medieval constitutionalism is open to question. It will be recalled that the sharp distinction which he found in Bracton between *gubernaculum* and *jurisdiction* he also alleged to be nothing other than "a commonplace of late thirteenth-century European political theory," and nothing less than the very foundation of medieval constitutionalism.[99] Scholars are now telling us, nevertheless, that it is to be found neither in Bracton nor in Fortescue and we ourselves have seen that it is certainly not to be found in Baldus de Ubaldis. Where then is it to be found? In the Jacobean lawyers—above all, in Sir Edward Coke—Hinton would seem to suggest.[100] Our own findings on the absolute and ordinary powers, however, run counter to this, and the celebrated remarks of Coke which Hinton cites are susceptible of a very different interpretation.[101]

---

[97] R.W.K. Hinton, "English Constitutional Theories from Sir John Fortescue to Sir John Eliot." *English Historical Review*, LXXV (July, 1960), 410–17, 421. Earlier on, however, Hinton had indicated his general agreement with McIlwain's approach—see his "Government and Liberty under James I," *Cambridge Historical Journal*, XI (No. 1, 1953), 48. Cf. Corinne Comstock Weston, "The Theory of Mixed Monarchy under Charles I and After," *English Historical Review*, LXXV (July, 1960), 426.

[98] Ewart Lewis, "King above Law? 'Quod Principi Placuit' in Bracton," *Speculum* XXIX (No. 2, 1964), 266. See also the similar but more detailed criticism of McIlwain on *gubernaculum* in Brian Tierney, "Bracton on Government," *ibid.*, XXXVIII (No. 2, 1963), 295–317, and esp. 306ff. Tierney refers also to the similarly critical analysis to be found in the Göttingen doctoral thesis of Wiebke Fesefeldt: "Englische Staatstheorie des 13 Jahrhunderts: Henry de Bracton und sein Werk." (Since published under the same title [Göttingen, 1962]).

[99] McIlwain, *Constitutionalism: Ancient and Modern*, pp. 77ff.

[100] "English Constitutional Theories from Sir John Fortescue to Sir John Eliot," 421ff.

[101] See the detailed and judicious discussion in Gough, *Fundamental Law in English Constitutional History*, pp. 31ff. In any case, a recent critic has drawn attention to the imprecision of Hinton's (as well as of McIlwain's) categories—see Conrad Russell, "The Theory of Treason in the Trial of Strafford," *English Historical Review*, LXXX (Jan., 1965), 35–37.

It may well, then, be time to admit that McIlwain's forceful interpretation of medieval and early modern constitutionalism—despite (and in part because of) the powerful stimulus it has given to scholarly investigation—can no longer be regarded as fully adequate. No other theory of comparable scope, vigor and force has yet emerged to take its place. But we are not altogether lacking in guidelines. In criticizing McIlwain's analysis of Bracton, Tierney has recently reminded us that since he wrote, studies in medieval public law have begun to make it clear that already in the thirteenth century

> there was a growing area of policy formation where the King (although normally bound by the law) claimed the right to initiate extra-legal actions affecting his subject's rights and liberties, sometimes in association with, sometime independently of, the spokesman for the *universitas* [regni].

They have also made it clear that this development "was intimately linked to the growth of the ideas of the state and the public welfare," ideas which we now know to have generated long before the Renaissance a doctrine of *raison d'état*.[102] During the course of its long history, the distinction between the absolute and ordinary powers linked up with these developments at more than one point, and it may be suggested, by way of conclusion, that it is these developments above all that we ought to keep in mind when we approach the intricate problems of early-modern constitutional history, and especially those "murky" and exasperating discussions of the royal prerogative in England.

---

[102] Tierney, "Bracton on Government," 309–10. See 310 n. 39 for references to the relevant literature and notably to the fundamental studies of Gaines Post, so curiously neglected by students of early-modern English constitutional history.

CHAPTER NINE

"ADAMANTINE FETTERS OF DESTINY:" THE ABSOLUTE AND ORDAINED POWER OF GOD AND KING IN THE SIXTEENTH AND SEVENTEENTH CENTURIES

> ... [W]e must cautiously abandon [that more specious opinion of the *Platonist* and *Stoick*] ... in this, that it ... blasphemously invades the cardinal Prerogative of Divinity, *Omnipotence*, by denying him a reserved power, of infringing, or altering any one of those Laws which [He] Himself ordained, and enacted, and chaining up his armes in the adamantine fetters of Destiny.
>
> Walter Charleton, *The Darknes of Atheism Dispelled by the Light of Nature: A Physico-Theologicall Treatise* (London, 1652)

Of the various attributes characteristically ascribed to God in the Christian tradition—goodness, wisdom, omniscience, omnipotence and the like—, it is omnipotence which of recent years has most persistently been the object of focused attention among philosophers and historians alike. That that should be the case with philosophers working in the Anglo-American analytic tradition is not altogether surprising. While it is doubtless a development few would have predicted half a century ago, the years since then have seen something of a recrudescence of interest in a legislative or divine-command ethic.[1] And had that not itself conspired to make omnipotence an obvious focus of philosophic attention, the deepening contemporaneous preoccupation with modal logic or the logic of possibility would surely have succeeded in so doing. Understood classically as affirming of God the ability to do all things, and connoting a *virtual* capacity for action (as opposed to a power exercised in actuality), omnipotence has proved to be something of a troublesome notion, inviting

---

[1] See e.g., Robert M. Adams, "Divine Command Metaethics Modified Again," *Journal of Religious Ethics*, 7 (No. 1, 1979), 66–79; Janine Marie Itziak ed., *Divine Command Morality: Historical and Contemporary Readings* (New York, 1979); Paul Helms ed., *Divine Command and Morality* (Oxford, 1981); P. Alston, "Some Suggestions for Divine Command Theorists," in *Divine Nature and Human Language: Essays in Philosophical Theology*, ed. P. Alston (Ithaca and London, 1989).

unrestrained speculation about hypothetical divine action and generating a veritable cat's cradle of philosophical conundrums concerning the relationship of God's power to his will, wisdom, goodness and justice.

With these taxing problems medieval theologians and philosophers alike were forced to grapple,[2] and philosophers of our own era have found them no less directly pertinent to their own logical and ethical concerns.[3] In 1955 Mackie inaugurated what was destined to become an ongoing discussion of omnipotence in the philosophical journals,[4] and such philosophers as Kenny and Keane, Cowan and Wolfe, Dummett, Plantinga, Swinburne and Geach have been drawn into the fray. Since then, as a result, the pages of *Mind, Philosophy,*

---

[2] For a good, recent synoptic account (both systematic and historical) see Gijsbert van den Brink, *Almighty God: A Study of the Doctrine of Divine Omnipotence* (Kempen, 1993).

[3] Thus Anthony Kenny, *The God of the Philosophers* (Oxford, 1979), pp. 112–15, points out that in discussing the nature and reach of God's power, Peter Abelard (d. ca. 1142) introduces or reinvents "a number of distinctions which are of great importance in modal logic and the logic of possibility," and that "the dispute between those who, like Abelard and Leibniz, think that God must have chosen the best world, and those who like Aquinas think that God must have chosen a good world but could have chosen another better one, is a reflection within natural theology of a dispute which is familiar to contemporary philosophers in the field of ethics." Or, as James Conant puts it in relation to the scholastic discussions of omnipotence: "Posed here in a theological guise is a version of a question that has continued to haunt philosophy up until the present: do the laws of logic impose a *limit* which we run up against in our thinking?"—"The Search for Logically Alien Thought: Descartes, Kant, Frege, and the *Tractatus*," *Philosophical Topics*, 20 (1991), 115–80 (esp. 115–23).

[4] J. Mackie, "Evil and Omnipotence," *Mind*, 64 (1955), 200–12. The periodical literature ensuing has now become too voluminous to list here—Van den Brink, *Almighty God*, p. 134, notes that between 1955 and 1990 over a hundred journal articles or chapters and sections of books were devoted to problems pivoting on the concept of omnipotence. Many of these are listed in his excellent bibliography (at pp. 276–95). The following should suffice to convey the flavor and philosophical range of the debate: G.B. Keene, "A Simpler Solution to the Paradox of Omnipotence," *Mind*, 69 (1960), 74–78; Bernard Mayo, "Mr. Keene on Omnipotence," *ibid.*, 70 (1961), 249–50; G.B. Keene, "Capacity-Limiting Statements," *ibid.*, 251–52; G. Mavrodes, "New Puzzles Concerning Omnipotence," *Philosophical Review*, 72 (1963), 221–23; Michael Dummett, "Bringing about the Past," *ibid.*, 73 (1964), 338–59; C. Wade Savage, "The Paradox of the Stone," *ibid.*, 76 (1967), 74–79; John Wolfe, "Omnipotence," *Canadian Journal of Philosophy*, 1 (1971), 245–57; P.T. Geach, "Omnipotence," *Philosophy*, 48 (1973), 7–20, and his "An Irrelevance of Omnipotence," *ibid.*, 327–33; Jonathan Harris, "Geach on God's Alleged Ability to do Evil," *ibid.*, 51 (1976), 208–15; Alvin Plantinga, "Possible Worlds," *The Listener* (13 May, 1976), 604–606; M. MacBeath, "Geach on Omnipotence and Virginity," *Philosophy*, 62 (1988), 395–400. For a useful anthology of pertinent medieval and early–modern texts juxtaposed with works of modern philosophical commentary, see Linwood Urban and Douglas N. Walton eds., *The Power of God: Readings on Omnipotence and Evil* (New York, 1978).

Philosophical Review, and even *The Listener* have been punctuated by their efforts to grapple with those venerable questions concerning the divine power that had exercised St. Peter Damiani in the mid-eleventh century, brought Abelard to grief a half-century later, and subsequently led Peter Lombard to devote to them a crucial and influential section of his *Sentences*—whether God of his omnipotence could undo the past, whether he could have made things other than he had, or created a world better than he did, and so on.[5]

While no medievalist can be expected to be anything but gratified by this unexpected testimony to the enduring significance and power of medieval scholastic concerns, those of us interested especially in the intellectual developments of the later-medieval centuries have particular reason to be energized by it. The more so in that the years since Mackie launched this contemporary philosophical debate have also seen an intensification of interest on the part of historians in the ways in which, during these particular centuries, medieval thinkers themselves came to terms with the implications of the divine omnipotence and dealt with the theological and philosophical puzzles characteristically generated by that notion. Unlike the philosophers, whose concerns have been somewhat more broad-ranging, the historians have focused in particular on a quintessentially scholastic distinction which was developed, it has been said, "as a 'yes and no' answer to the question whether God is able to do or arrange things

---

[5] Not excluding St. Jerome's enduringly popular speculation concerning God's inability to restore the virginity of a fallen woman. On which, see Kenny, *The God of the Philosophers,* p. 100, Geach, "Omnipotence," 15, MacBeath, "Geach on Omnipotence and Virginity," 345–400. This had been the comment that had provoked Damiani into making quite extreme claims for the reach of the divine power in his famous disputation (*ca.* 1067) and had led him to speculate about God's ability even to undo the past—i.e. so to act that an actual historical event would not have occurred. See, especially, André Cantin ed., *Pierre Damian: Lettre sur la toute-puissance divine* (Paris, 1972), pp. 385–90, 432, 442–44, 446, 448–50, 472–80. Brief comments in Kenny, *The God of the Philosophers,* pp. 100–102, and Francis Oakley, *Omnipotence, Covenant, and Order: An Excursion in the History of Ideas from Abelard to Leibniz* (Ithaca and London, 1984), pp. 41–46. Lengthier and more recent analysis in Irven Michael Resnick, *Divine Power and Possibility in St. Peter Damiani's De divina omnipotentia* (Leiden and New York, 1992). To such issues Lombard had devoted distinctions 42–44 of the first book of his influential textbook (*ca.* 1158), making them thereby part of the required agenda for subsequent theologians on into the early-modern era. It should be noted that the philosophical significance of omnipotence takes on a somewhat different coloration if one approaches it (as does Michael Gillespie) with the preoccupations characteristic, not of the Anglo-American analytic tradition, but of contemporary continental philosophy. See below, n. 153.

other than he did in creating the orders of nature and grace."[6] The distinction in question is that between God's power understood as absolute and as ordained (*potentia dei absoluta et ordinata*), which the theologians and philosophers of the period deployed as part of their great effort of accommodation between Greek philosophical and biblical notions of the divine, and the historical significance of which the scholarship of the past forty years has served increasingly to vindicate.[7] But while that distinction has been the subject of a very considerable body of historical work (including four books in the past dozen years alone),[8] attention has focused largely on the extent of its usage and the meanings attached to it during the period running from the late-twelfth to the early-fifteenth centuries. So far as our knowledge of its history during subsequent centuries goes, we still in some degree linger in the hunting and gathering stage of scholarship. In what follows, then, after some introductory observations concerning the emergence of the distinction and the meanings attaching to it during the Middle Ages, it will be my purpose to try to trace at least the broad outlines of its career from the late-fifteenth to the early-eighteenth centuries—by whom it was employed, the meanings characteristically attached to it, the significance of its role in the intellectual history of the era. But, first, the medieval phase.

1. *The medieval phase: Formation, currency, use and meaning of the distinction*

Although a widely-used neoscholastic manual of the late-nineteenth century readily acknowledged the distinction between the *potentia dei absoluta et ordinata* to have been something of a commonplace "among

---

[6] The words are those of William J. Courtenay, *Capacity and Volition: A History of the Distinction of Absolute and Ordained Power* (Bergamo, 1990), p. 11.

[7] Of the philosophers who have contributed to the contemporary omnipotence debate only Geach and Harris, to my knowledge, have dwelt at all on this distinction—see Geach, "An Irrelevance of Omnipotence," 328; Harris "Geach on God's Alleged Ability to do Evil," 209.

[8] Oakley, *Omnipotence, Covenant, and Order* (1984); Eugenio Randi, *Il sovrano e l'orologiaio. Due immagini di Dio nel dibattito sulla "potentia absoluta" fra XIII e xiv secolo* (Firenze, 1987); Courtenay, *Capacity and Volition* (1990); Lawrence Moonan, *Divine Power: The Medieval Power Distinction up to its Adoption by Albert, Bonaventure and Aquinas* (Oxford, 1994). The same years saw also the publication of a volume of papers on the subject—Angela Vitesse ed., *Sopra la volta del mondo: onnipotenza e potenza assoluta di Dio tra Medioevo e eta Moderna* (Bergamo, 1986).

the Catholic doctors,"[9] the older generation of historians of medieval philosophy paid little attention to it. So little, indeed, that it would be easy to come away from a reading of De Wulf, Gilson or Copleston on Thomas Aquinas and William of Ockham innocent of any suspicion that the former had invoked the distinction at all (he did so, in fact, on thirty or more occasions)[10] or that it had played so important a role in the latter's thinking.[11] In the 1920s and 1930s, however, scholars with interests in medieval *theology* had already begun the attempt to recover the distinction's history and, with the burgeoning of interest in the matter evident since the late-1950s, the outlines of a reasonably clear (if somewhat conflicted) history have begun to emerge.[12] Two aspects of this picture call for commentary here. First, the story of the distinction's emergence on the theological and philosophical scene, the sort of people who used it and the matters to which they applied it. Second, the shifting meanings they attached to it.

   Though they are not intended to do so, the seemingly whimsical discussions in the recent philosophical literature concerning God's ability to restore her virginity to a woman who has lost it (thereby undoing the past)[13] may serve to direct us back to the point of departure for the medieval debate on the issue of the divine omnipotence.

---

[9] Thus Joseph Kleutgen, *Institutiones Theologicae in usum scholarum: I De ipso dei* (Ratisbon, 1881), pp. 384–86 [Pars I, lib. 1, qu. 3, cap. 4, art 4]. Cf. A. Farges and D. Barbadette, *Cours de philosophie scolastique d'après la pensée d'Aristote et de S. Thomas mise au courant de la science moderne* (2 vols., Paris, 1898), II, 352 [Lib. II, cap. 2, art. 3, § 91B].

[10] For an account of his use of the distinction, see Lawrence Moonan, "St. Thomas Aquinas on Divine Power," *Atti del Congresso Internazionale per il VII centenario di san Tommaso*, 3 (Naples, 1977), 366–407; idem, *Divine Power*, pp. 228–95.

[11] See Maurice de Wulf, *Histoire de la philosophie médiévale*, 6th ed. (3 vols., Paris, 1947), III; Étienne Gilson, *History of Christian Philosophy in the Middle Ages* (New York, 1955); idem, *The Christian Philosophy of St. Thomas Aquinas* (New York, 1956). F.C. Copleston, *Aquinas* (Harmondsworth, Middlx., 1955); idem, *A History of Philosophy* (9 vols., New York, 1943–75), II and III.

[12] For useful discussions of the pertinent historiography, see Courtenay, *Capacity and Volition*, pp. 11–24; Gijsbert van den Brink, "De absolute en geordineerde macht van God. Opmerkingen bij de ontwikkeling van een onderscheid," *Nederlands Theologisch Tijdschrift*, 45 (1991), 204–222. Cf. the remarks of Randi, *Il sovrano e l'orologiaio*, pp. 1–12. Courtenay (pp. 201–207) and Randi (pp. 173–85) both give helpful bibliographies of the (by now) extensive body of scholarly work devoted to the distinction. Van den Brink, *Almighty God*, pp. 276–95, does likewise but his bibliography includes also the theological and philosophical literature concerning omnipotence in general.

[13] See above, note 5.

The debate, in effect, which led first to the development of the absolute/ordained power distinction and then, as the thirteenth century wore on, to its deployment along the battle lines hastily erected by academic theologians in their effort to deflect what they took to be a new threat to Christian orthodoxy posed by a philosophic necessitarianism of Arab-Aristotelian provenance. St. Jerome's letter to Eustochium lauding the grandeur of virginity and expressing to that end his belief that even God, "who can do all things, . . . cannot raise up a virgin after she has fallen" had been taken by some, or so St. Peter Damiani concluded six centuries later, as "an occasion for imputing a lack of power to God."[14] Hence Damiani's famous disputation *De divina omnipotentia* (*ca.* 1067) which inaugurated the anxiously persistent medieval scrutiny of that particular divine attribute. Over the course of the twelfth century, that preoccupation led theologians to distinguish increasingly between capacity and volition, to tease apart, that is, the consideration of what God could do hypothetically and *in abstracto*, given the very absoluteness of his power, and the consideration of what he had chosen and willed to do in actuality. And, during the first three quarters of the thirteenth century, the period that proved to be formative for the distinction, the familiar terms *potentia dei absoluta* came to be used of the former, and *potentia dei ordinata* of the latter.

While signalling his suspicion that there may well have been earlier (though as yet unidentified) instances of its use before 1215, Lawrence Moonan identifies "one of the earliest undeniably recognisable uses of the Power Distinction" as having surfaced around that time in the *Summa theologiae* of Geoffrey of Poitiers (fl. 1215).[15] Geoffrey, like the other early users, was a secular master in the Faculty of Theology at the fledgling University of Paris, and Moonan in tracing the career of the distinction describes it as having entered into the thinking of Dominican and Franciscan theologians alike via

---

[14] Ep. XXII (*Ad Eustochium*), in *Select Letters of St. Jerome*, ed. F.A. Wright (London, 1973), p. 62; Cantin ed., *Pierre Damien: Lettre sur la toute-puissance divine*, p. 406.

[15] Moonan, *Divine Power*, pp. 57–61. This book provides the best, most recent and most detailed account of the distinction's formative phase. The terms Gregory actually uses are *de potentia absoluta* and *de potentia conditionali*. Moonan rejects (pp. 61–63) Courtenay's suggestion that an earlier instance of the distinction's use had occurred in an anonymous commentary on the Pauline epistles dating to around 1200—see William J. Courtenay, "The Dialectic of Omnipotence in the High and Late Middle Ages," in *Divine Omniscience and Omnipotence in Medieval Philosophy*, ed. T. Rudavsky (Dordrecht, 1985), 243–65 (at 247).

the works of such secular masters-turned-friar as Roland of Cremona
(d. 1259), Hugh of St. Cher (d. 1263) and Alexander of Hales (d. 1245),
as having received in mid-century a particularly clear (indeed, classic) formulation at the hands of Albertus Magnus (d. 1280) and
Aquinas (d. 1274), and as having migrated to Oxford via the works
of the Dominican, Robert Kilwardby (d. 1279) and the Franciscans,
Roger Bacon (d. 1292?) and Richard of Cornwall (fl. 1250). The
stage was thus set for the enactment of the somewhat more familiar story of its later use by John Duns Scotus (d. 1308) and his followers, by William of Ockham (d. 1349), and on into the fifteenth
century by the host of thinkers influenced by Ockham whom historians, however imprecisely but for want of a more convenient term,
are still accustomed to calling "nominalists." And among the most
prominent of those figures were Robert Holcot (d. 1349), Adam
Wodeham (d. 1358), and Pierre d'Ailly (d. 1420).

Given the traditional disposition to view the distinction as a quintessentially nominalist gambit and one favored especially by Franciscan
thinkers, it is important to note that the picture which has emerged
from the scholarly labors of the past few years does not support such
a view. It was far from having been a monopoly of the nominalists,
and it enjoyed widespread use among Dominican and secular theologians as well as among their Franciscan confrères. It is important
to note, too, that while it was first invoked by university theologians
in connection with theological issues pertaining to the order of salvation[16] and discussed in specialized academic works addressed to fellow theologians, it speedily found its way into Faculty of Arts circles,
where it assumed a role in connection with issues pertaining to philosophical theology and natural philosophy. By mid-thirteenth century,
moreover, it had also made its way into at least one non-academic
work which was "seized upon eagerly by preachers, littérateurs, and
pious writers" and enjoyed a career of enduring popularity throughout the Middle Ages.[17] By about the same time, the distinction (or,
rather, a version of it) had been introduced into the canon law by
the great canonist Hostiensis (d. 1271). Referring explicitly to the

---

[16] E.g. whether a means for our redemption other than Christ's incarnation,
suffering and death was possible for God—see Moonan, *Divine Power*, pp. 64–66.

[17] The work in question was the *Compendium theologicae veritatis* of the Dominican,
Hugh of Strasbourg (fl. 1265), an uneven digest of potted knowledge which may
have served to transmit a familiarity with the distinction to people who did not
move in university circles. See Moonan, *Divine Power*, pp. 319–26.

theological usage and even to St. Jerome's views on the case of the fallen virgin, Hostiensis used it to elucidate what the pope, in the absoluteness of his *plenitudo potestatis* or absolute power, could do that was not open for him to do when acting in accordance with his merely ordained or ordinary power.[18]

By the time of Aquinas's death in 1274, then, those employing the distinction were already easing it into the familiar role it was to play during the fourteenth century and beyond. And that role extended to matters pertaining to epistemology, philosophical theology, natural philosophy, ethics and civil law, no less than to canon law, sacramental theology and the theology of justification. In that later phase the *potentia dei absoluta* was invoked to assert the possibility of our having intuitions of non-existing objects,[19] to facilitate the scientific pursuit of speculative possibilities pertaining to notions of infinity, the void, and the plurality of worlds,[20] to underline the utter dependence of moral norms on the mandates of the divine will,[21] and, by analogy, to make the point that while the prince (imperial no less

---

[18] I.e., identifying the *potentia absoluta* with the pope's *plenitudo potestatis*, Hostiensis ascribed to the pope the ability in virtue of that absolute power to act, for reason and in extraordinary situations, outside his normal jurisdictional competence or above the law to which, of his ordinary or ordained power (he appears to use the adjectives interchangeably) he has bound himself. See Hostiensis (Henricus de Segusia), *Lectura in Quinque Decretalium Gregorianarum Libros* (Paris, 1512), *ad* X, 5, 31, 8 *in v.* Ita and *ad* X, 3, 35, 6 *in v.* nec summus Pontifex, fols. LXXI r and CXXX r.

[19] See William of Ockham, *Quodl.* VI, qu. 6, in *Quodlibeta septem*, ed. Joseph C. Wey, *Opera theologica* 9 of *Guillelmi de Ockham Opera philosophica et theologica ad fidem codicem manuscriptorum edita* (St. Bonaventure, N.Y., 1980), 604–6; Ockham, *Reportatio* II, qu. 15E, in "The Notitia Intuitiva of Non-Existents According to William of Ockham," ed. Philotheus Boehner, *Traditio*, 1 (1943), 248–50. Cf. Pierre d'Ailly, *Quaestiones super I, III et IV Sententiarum* (Lyons, 1500), I, qu. 3, art. 1, M, fol. 72v, for the same claim. There is a good recent discussion of the issue by John F. Boler, "Intuitive and Abstractive Cognition," in *The Cambridge History of Later Medieval Philosophy*, ed. Norman Kretzmann, Anthony Kenny, and Jan Pinborg (Cambridge, 1982), 460–78.

[20] For the employment of the distinction in relation to these scientific questions, see Annaliese Maier, *Die Vorläufe Galileis im 14. Jahrhundert: Studien zur Naturphilosophie der Spätscholastik* (Rome, 1949), esp. pp. 155–215; Edward Grant, "The Condemnation of 1277, God's Absolute Power, and Physical Thought in the Late Middle Ages," *Viator*, 10 (1970), 211–44; e.g. John E. Murdoch, "Infinity and Continuity," in *The Cambridge History of Later Medieval Philosophy*, ed. Kretzmann *et al.*, 566–69; Amos Funkenstein, *Theology and the Scientific Imagination from the Middle Ages to the Seventeenth Century* (Princeton, 1986), esp. pp. 59–63, 152–79.

[21] By evoking, for example, the possibility of God's being able to render meritorious for mortals the very act of hating God himself. See William of Ockham, *Quaestiones in librum secundum Sententiarum (Reportatio)*, qu. 15; ed. Gedeon Gál and Rega Wood (New York, 1981), p. 352; Pierre d'Ailly, *Sent.* I, qu. 14, art. 3, T–U, fol. 174v.

than papal) should indeed live and discharge his duties in accordance with the law, he was not bound to do so out of necessity. Instead, he did so out of benevolence, that is, by freely choosing so to bind himself in the normal exercise of his power, while, of his absolute power, retaining the prerogative of being able to act above or aside from the law.[22] Similarly, and long before the thirteenth century was over, the distinction had begun to break out from the restricted academic circles in which it had been nurtured and was heading toward the homiletic, humanist, and even vernacular literary settings into which it was later to find its way.[23]

All of this, it may be, clear enough. The plot, however, thickens when one turns to our current understanding of the meanings that medievals attached to the distinction. If omnipotence itself is an ungrateful concept, prolific of confusion, the distinction between the absolute and ordained powers, developed after all in an effort to dispel that confusion, was not without its own problems. In the course of two of his discussions of that distinction Ockham himself took rueful note of the misunderstanding surrounding it and warned of the ease with which anyone who "has not been excellently instructed in logic and

---

[22] For the legal usage, see Francis Oakley, "Jacobean Political Theology: The Absolute and Ordinary Powers of the King," *Journal of the History of Ideas*, 29 (No. 3, 1968), 323–46 (see above, ch. 8); *idem*, "The Hidden and Revealed Wills of James I: More Political Theology," *Studia Gratiana*, 15 (1972), 365–75; *idem, Omnipotence, Covenant, and Order*, pp. 93–118; Michael Wilks, *The Problem of Sovereignty in the Later Middle Ages* (Cambridge, 1964), pp. 294–95, 311, 319, 394–95, 441. J. Marrone, "The Absolute and Ordained Powers of the Pope: A Quodlibetical Question of Henry of Guent," *Medieval Studies*, 35 (1974), 7–27; Eugenio Randi, "La Vergine e il papa. *Potentia Dei absoluta e plenitudo potestatis* papale nel xiv secolo," *History of Political Thought*, 5 (1984), 425–45; *idem, Il sovrano e l'orologiaio*, pp. 33–36, 88–94; J.P. Canning, *The Political Thought of Baldus de Ubaldis* (Cambridge, 1987), pp. 74–76; Kenneth Pennington, *The Prince and the Law: 1200–1600* (Berkeley-Los Angeles-Oxford, 1993), pp. 64–77.

[23] For the homiletic usage see, e.g., Pierre d'Ailly (d. 1420), "Sermo de sancto dominico" and "Sermo de quadruplici adventu domini," in *idem, Tractatus et sermones* (Strassburg, 1491), sig. C4v and t5v–t6r. Charles Trinkaus finds the distinction present in the writings of Coluccio Salutati (d. 1406)—see his *In Our Image and Likeness: Humanity and Divinity in Italian Humanist Thought* (2 vols., London, 1970), I, 51–102, and his "Coluccio Salutati's Critique of Astrology in the Context of his Natural Philosophy," *Speculum*, 64 (No. 1, 1989), 46–68 (at 53–58, 61–62). For its echoes in vernacular writings, see Kathleen M. Ashley, "Divine Power in Chester Cycle and Late Medieval Thought," *Journal of the History of Ideas*, 39 (No. 3, 1978), 387–404, as also the subsequent exchange in vol. 40 (No. 3, 1979), of the same journal: James R. Royse, "Nominalism and Divine Power in the Chester Cycle," 475–76, and Kathleen M. Ashley, "Chester Cycle and Nominalist Thought," 477; Randi, *Il sovrano e l'orologiaio*, pp. 51–53.

theology" could fall into error on the matter.[24] And the extent of the disagreement about the distinction's meaning and purpose that has persisted among twentieth-century commentators witnesses power-fully to the pertinence of that warning. But, if one may be permit-ted to indulge a measure of expository simplification, it is possible to distinguish three successive phases in the way in which modern scholars have understood what its medieval users meant by the dis-tinction, as well as their purpose in invoking it.

During the first of these phases, which extended down into the third quarter of the present century when Irwin Iserloh and Gordon Leff were making their principal contributions, commentators, by dwelling disproportionately on the absolute wing of the *absoluta/ordi-nata* dyad, tended by and large to take a negative view of its impact. They usually understood God's absolute power as a presently-active one with an ever-present potential for cutting across or running counter to the order—natural, moral, salvational—currently estab-lished *de potentia ordinata*. As a result, they inclined to regard the dis-tinction's popularity in the later Middle Ages as a symptom of the incipient collapse of the whole scholastic endeavor to harmonize rea-son and revelation. Ockham in particular and the nominalists in gen-eral were characteristically represented as wielding the distinction with skeptical, even mischievous intent—despite reassurances to the contrary collapsing the ordained into the absolute power, transforming "the entire foundation of . . . [God's] ordained law" into "the most fleeting of contingencies ever liable to be dispensed with," "throw-ing all certainty, morality, and indeed probability into the melting pot," creating a mere "as-if" theology prone to marginalizing the divine assurances revealed to us in the Scriptures and handed down to us by tradition, calling into question even, under the looming shadow of the divine omnipotence, the very necessity of church, priesthood, and sacraments.[25]

---

[24] Ockham, *Opus nonaginta dierum*, cap. 95, in R.F. Bennett and H. Offler eds., *Guillelmi de Ockham: Opera politica* (3 vols., Manchester, 1940–56), II, 728; *Tractatus contra Benedictum*, lib. III, cap. 3, in *ibid.*, III, 234.

[25] See Gordon Leff, *Bradwardine and the Pelagians* (Cambridge, 1957), p. 132, and *idem, Medieval Thought from St. Augustine to Ockham* (Harmondsworth, Middlx., 1958), p. 289; Erwin Iserloh, *Gnade und Eucharistie in der philosophischen Theologie des Wilhelm von Ockham* (Wiesbaden, 1956), pp. 67–79; Werner Dettloff, *Die Entwicklung der Akzeptations- und Verdienstlehre von Duns Scotus bis Luther* (Münster, 1963), pp. 363–65. Leff has since distanced himself from Iserloh's interpretation and has indicated his wish to distinguish the use made of the distinction by Ockham himself from the

Given Ockham's robust insistence that this "common distinction of the theologians," when "sensibly understood, is in harmony with the orthodox faith,"[26] it is not surprising that, as time wore on, and during what I would characterize as the second phase of modern scholarly commentary, such a "sensible" understanding did indeed emerge. As a result, it is now possible to identify, and with a high degree of confidence, what was the original or "classical" meaning possessed by the distinction as it emerged in the early thirteenth century and as it was formulated by such crucial figures as Alexander of Hales, Albertus Magnus and Aquinas. Prominent among the scholars who determined that this was a meaning that persisted on into the fourteenth century were Paul Vignaux (writing already in the 1930s and 1940s), William J. Courtenay (writing in the 1960s and early 1970s) and Lawrence Moonan who, joining the fray in the mid-1970s, coined (in relation to Peter Damiani) the term "Outrageous View," which is sometimes attached to the earlier sense of the distinction as having involved the notion of an all-too-presently-active modality of divine power (the *potentia absoluta*) ever likely to operate in contravention of the order established *de potentia ordinata*.[27]

The classical understanding of the distinction was dominant among theologians down into the final quarter of the thirteenth century. And two related (if separable) features distinguished it from the so-called "Outrageous View." The first was its dialectical character. Neither term of the distinction was understood in isolation from the other. Its impact, therefore, was two-fold. If the invocation of the absolute power served to affirm the freedom of God and the contingency of the entire created order of nature and grace, the juxtaposition with it of the ordained power served at the same time to affirm the *de facto* stability and reliability of that contingent order. And if the impact was two-fold, it was so precisely because the distinction inserted, side by side with a dramatic vindication of the Old Testament vision of Yahweh as a God of might and power, another fundamentally biblical theme concerning God's relationship with his

---

more radical use to which his "followers and successors" put it—see his *William of Ockham: The Metamorphosis of Scholastic Discourse* (Manchester, 1975), esp. pp. 15–16, 450, 470–71.

[26] Ockham, *Tractatus contra Benedictum*, Lib. III, cap. 3, in *Opera politica*, ed. Bennett and Offler, III, 230.

[27] Lawrence Moonan, "Impossibility and Peter Damiani," *Archiv für Geschichte der Philosophie*, 62 (1980), 146–63.

creation—namely, that of his self-commitment, covenant and promise. While the omnipotent God cannot be said to be *bound* by the natural, moral or salvational order he himself has established, he is certainly capable by his own free decision of committing himself by covenant and promise to follow a certain pattern in his dealings with his creation. Just as an absolute monarchy, to evoke the analogy that was so obvious as to have entered theological discourse before the thirteenth century was out and to have resurfaced seven centuries later right at the outset of the contemporary philosophical debate concerning omnipotence—just as an absolute monarch can bind himself in his dealings with his subjects.[28]

The second distinguishing feature of the classical understanding of the distinction concerned especially the meaning attributed to the *potentia dei absoluta*. During the first three-quarters of the thirteenth century its users were not inclined to understand the absolute power as a presently-active one by means of which God intervened in the world to act apart from or to set aside the order established *de potentia ordinata*. Instead, they used the term *potentia absoluta* to denote God's power in itself taken *in abstracto* and without reference to the orders of nature and grace he had actually willed to establish. Thus, if "by his absolute power," as Aquinas put it, "God can do many things other than those he foresaw that he would do and preordained so to do," it remains the case that "nothing can come to be that he has not foreseen and preordained."[29] The absolute power for Aquinas, then, refers to God's ability to do many things that he does not choose to do. Or, put in the temporal terms that Courtenay uses, it refers "to the total possibilities *initially* open to God, some of which were realized by creating the established order." And "the unrealized possibilities are now only hypothetically possible."[30] Similarly, for Ockham, at least in so far as his *controlling* teaching is concerned, Courtenay

---

[28] For this dialectical/covenantal theme, see esp. Heiko A. Oberman, *The Harvest of Medieval Theology: Gabriel Biel and Late Medieval Nominalism* (Cambridge, Mass., 1963), pp. 30–56; William J. Courtenay, *Covenant and Causality in Medieval Thought* (London, 1984); Bernd Hamm, *Promissio, Pactum, Ordinatio: Freiheit und Selbstbindung Gottes in der Scholastischen Gnadenlehre* (Tübingen, 1977); Oakley, *Omnipotence, Covenant, and Order.* For the contemporary instance, see Mackie, "Evil and Omnipotence," 211–12.

[29] *Summa theologiae*, Ia, qu. 25, art. 5; trans. Thomas Gilby, *Summa theologiae*, (59 vols., New York, 1964–76), V, 123.

[30] Thus William J. Courtenay, "Nominalism and Late Medieval Religion," in *The Pursuit of Holiness in Late Medieval and Renaissance Religion*, ed. Charles Trinkaus and Heiko A. Oberman (Leiden, 1974), pp. 29–59 (at 39).

has succeeded in carrying the day in his insistence against the older
school of interpretation that that thinker, too, adhered to the classical understanding of the distinction and did not envision the absolute
power as a presently active one.[31]

That said, the presence of certain hesitations in Ockham's thinking witnesses, not only to the difficulty of keeping the theological
signal securely on frequency (or, at least, securely on the classical
frequency), but also to the gathering strength in his own day of a
very different understanding of the distinction, which, in the third
and current phase of scholarly commentary, has come to attract
growing attention. That different understanding was encouraged especially by the emergence in Hostiensis of the parallel legal/constitu-
tional usage, but also by the willingness of some theologians, evoking
the legal metaphor, to use such formulations as *de lege ordinata* and,
beyond that, to seed their discourse with analogies drawn from the
absolute and ordained power of human sovereigns or even of human
agents in general.[32] In this respect, a considerable importance attaches
to the distinctive and influential formulation which Duns Scotus had
given the distinction towards the end of the thirteenth century—
though it now seems clear that the roots of his more juristic formulation reached back to "the same scholarly generation as the
formulators of the more properly theological definition."[33] Scotus,

---

[31] See Courtenay, "Nominalism and Late Medieval Religion," 37–43; *idem, Capacity
and Volition*, pp. 16–21. Thus, in 1975, Leff was led to distance himself from Iserloh's
interpretation (see above, note 25). Cf. the comment by Eugenio Randi, "Ockham,
John XXII and the Absolute Power of God," *Franciscan Studies*, 46 (1986), 205–16
(esp. 205–6).

[32] For the hesitations in Ockham's thinking, see Oakley, *Omnipotence, Covenant, and
Order*, p. 52; Van den Brink, *Almighty God*, pp. 78–82; Marilyn Adams, *William
Ockham* (2 vols., Notre Dame, Ind., 1987), II, 1186–1207. Thus, for example, Ockham
himself slips into illustrating the distinction by adducing the example of the pope
who, in absolute terms, can do things he cannot do "in accord with the laws he
himself has decreed," thus inadvertently suggesting that God's absolute power, far
from referring solely to the possibilities initially open to God, is a presently active
power working, like the dispensing power of a monarch, to contravene the laws he
has himself established. See Ockham, *Quodl.* VI, qu. 1, in *Quodlibeta septem*, ed. Wey,
585–86. Among the destabilizing (or inevitably complicating) factors were the particular wording of the distinction, the intersection with it of the issue of miracles
(understood as extraordinary actions involving departures from the ordinary course
of things), and, as Courtenay has properly noted, the problems created by the
employment of temporal language. For which, see Courtenay, *Capacity and Volition*,
pp. 77–79; Van den Brink, *Almighty God*, pp. 74–77.

[33] Thus Katherine H. Tachau, "Logic's God and the Natural Order in Late
Medieval Oxford: the Teaching of Robert Holcot," *Annals of Science*, 53 (1996),

however, remains "the theologian in whom the canon-law usage on absolute and ordained power all but replaced the earlier theological tradition, as far as the definition of the distinction is concerned."[34] He distinguished (by analogy not only with kings but with any free agent within whose power the law falls) between the ordained power whereby God acts *de jure*, in accordance with the rightful law he has himself established, and the absolute power whereby *de facto* he can act apart from or against that law. In such a formulation, the absolute power exceeds the ordained and the implication is clear that *potentia dei absoluta*, rather than referring simply to the realm of logical possibility prior to God's ordination of things, is to be construed as a presently active and extraordinary power capable of operating apart from the order established *de potentia ordinata* and prevailing in the ordinary course of things.[35]

Eugenio Randi has shown that this tendency toward an "operationalization" of the absolute power[36] was prevalent among the fourteenth-century disciples of Scotus, and a similar tendency is evident in such "nominalist" figures as Robert Holcot and Adam Wodeham, with

235–67 (at 242), referring specifically to the *Sentences* commentary (1230–39) of Hugh of St. Victor, a *doctor utroque jure*. For this and what follows, see esp. Eugenio Randi, "La Vergine e il papa," 425–45; *idem*, "Ockham, John XXII and the Absolute Power of God," *Franciscan Studies*, 46 (1986), 205–16; *idem*, "A Scotistic Way of Distinguishing Between God's Absolute and Ordained Powers," in *From Ockham to Wyclif*, ed. A. Hudson and M. Wilks (Oxford, 1987), pp. 43–50; *idem*, *Il sovrano e l'orologiaio*, pp. 51–105. Cf. Oakley, *Omnipotence, Covenant, and Order*, pp. 52–59; Van den Brink, *Almighty God*, pp. 78–87; Katherine H. Tachau, "Robert Holcot on Contingency and Divine Deception," in *Filosofia e Teologia nel Trecento: Studi in ricordo di Eugenio Randi*, Jole Agrimi *et al.* (Louvain-la-Neuve, 1994), 157–96; Leonard A. Kennedy, *Peter of Ailly and the Harvest of Fourteenth-Century Theology* (Queenston, 1986), and *idem*, "The Fifteenth Century and Divine Absolute Power," *Vivarium*, 27 (1989), 125–52.

[34] Courtenay, *Capacity and Volition*, pp. 100–101. Note that Courtenay insists that when he employs the distinction in relation to ethics and to grace and justification, Scotus's usage is the classical one favored by such thirteenth-century predecessors as Aquinas. It is in the *definition* of the distinction that he offers in his *Ordinatio* and *Lectura* that Scotus reflects "the tendency to interpret *potentia absoluta* as a type of action rather than a natural sphere of unconditioned possibility." Cf. the careful analysis in Adams, *William Ockham*, II, 1186–98, and the discussion in Van den Brink, *Almighty God*, pp. 78–80.

[35] The two crucial texts are J. Duns Scotus, *Ordinatio*, I, dist. 44, qu. un., in *Opera omnia*, ed. C. Balic (31 vols., Rome, 1950–93), VI, 363–69, and his *Lectura*, I, dist. 44, qu. un., *ibid.*, XVII, 535–36.

[36] The term appears to be Heiko Oberman's and he uses it to denote "the transition from the speculation about what God *could* have done to what he *actually* does 'extra ordinem'."—Oberman, "*Via Antiqua* and *Via Moderna*: Late Medieval Prolegomena to Early Reformation Thought," *Journal of the History of Ideas*, 48 (No. 1, 1987), 23–40 (at 39). See the works of Randi, cited above, n. 33.

the former leaning on the princely analogy and the canonistic usage[37] and the latter edging toward an identification of the absolute power with supernatural, miraculous action.[38] At Oxford in Holcot's day, indeed, the "operationalized" version appears to have represented the more common understanding of the absolute power, and, by 1375–76, then, when Pierre d'Ailly came to comment on Lombard's *Sentences*, that shift in understanding was so far advanced that he felt it necessary, in discussing the distinction, to discriminate between two meanings that could be attached to the ordained power.[39] He began by insisting in classical fashion that the distinction in no way involves the ascription to God of "two powers, one absolute and the other ordained" but merely indicates that God's power can be understood in two ways. Understood as absolute it refers to what "he can do simply and absolutely" limited by nothing except the principle of contradiction itself—understood, that is to say, without keeping in mind the divinely-willed order to which the Scriptures and the uniformities of the natural world bear their respective witness. Understood as ordained, however, the divine power can be taken to denote two very different things. First, and more strictly speaking, it can mean what God can do given the ordination by which he has eternally willed what is to be done. Second, and speaking less narrowly, it can refer to everything that God is able to do by his absolute power provided only that it does not contravene any truth of the ordained law or sacred Scripture. It is this second and broader understanding that d'Ailly himself viewed as the more appropriate one, and it is certainly more consonant with his equation of "the common course of nature" with what is possible by the ordained power, and his con-

---

[37] Courtenay, *Capacity and Volition*, pp. 130–31. Tachau, "Robert Holcot on Contingency and Divine Deception," 171–73, 195–96; *idem*, "Logic's God and Natural Order in Late Medieval Oxford," 255.

[38] Thus Katherine H. Tachau, *Vision and Certitude in the Age of Ockham. Optics, Epistemology, and the Foundation of Semantics, 1250–1345* (Leiden, 1988), pp. 284–88, 294–95, and the texts cited therein. Courtenay, *Capacity and Volition*, pp. 131–32, indicates his own disagreement with Tachau's interpretation of those texts.

[39] Tachau, "Logic's God and the Natural Order in Late Medieval Oxford," 255, notes further that "Holcot tells us that at Oxford in his time, the *usual* understanding, of the dichotomy is not the purportedly 'classical' one." Cf. *idem*. "Robert Holcot on Contingency and Divine Deception," 170–73. The crucial text of D'Ailly's is *Sent*. I, qu. 13, art. 1, C–D, fols. 159r–159v, but it should be understood in the context of d'Ailly's employment of the distinction in the full *corpus* of his writings, not excluding his sermons and his publicistic efforts. For which, I venture to refer to Francis Oakley, *The Political Thought of Pierre d'Ailly: The Voluntarist Tradition* (New Haven and London, 1964), pp. 26–33.

comitant identification of God's absolute power with his extraordinary, supernatural or miraculous action.[40]

Such an understanding of the absolute/ordained power is not, then, to be dismissed as an historiographic fiction generated by some modern misreading of the medieval texts. Nor is it to be bracketed as grounded in a *late-medieval misreading* of the earlier classical theological usage.[41] Even in the early-thirteenth century the intersection with the distinction of the notion of miraculous divine action[42] was already contriving to nudge the understanding of the absolute power in an "operationalizing" direction. By the fourteenth century, as a result, and as Randi correctly insists,[43] we are confronted with two very different understandings of the distinction. Both, as we shall see, persist on into the sixteenth and seventeenth centuries. But so, too, it should be noted, does the dialectical or covenantal view of the relationship of the two powers, and we should not assume that the "non-classical" understanding of the absolute power as a power of extraordinary supernatural or miraculous interposition necessarily entailed, as the older commentators apparently assumed, its evocation for destructive purposes or to further the cause of a debilitating skepticism.[44] And that is to say that the non-classical view of the absolute power as a presently-active one was not necessarily at odds with the covenantal aspect of the classical view. The sixteenth- and seventeenth-century usage of the distinction, to which we may now at last turn, serves to underline that fact.

---

[40] See *Sent.* I, qu. 9, art. 2, M. fol. 120 v; *Sent.* IV, qu. 1, art. 2, J–N, fols. 187r–188r; *Sent.* I, qu. 1, art. 2, JJ, fol. 56r; *De Trinitate*, in Jean Gerson, *Opera omnia*, ed. Louis Ellies Dupin (6 vols., Antwerp, 1706), I, col. 619; *De libertate creaturae rationalis, ibid.*, col. 632; *Tractatus de anima*, cap. 11, pars 4, ed. Olaf Pluta, in his *Die philosophische Psychologie des Peter von Ailly* (Amsterdam, 1987), p. 68 (of the edited text), where what is possible *naturaliter* is contrasted with what may happen *de supernaturali et absoluta potentia Dei*.

[41] Courtenay hewed to the former view in the early 1970s but appears now to incline to the latter. See the interesting historiographic comments in his *Capacity and Volition*, pp. 18–21.

[42] Courtenay, *Capacity and Volition*, pp. 77–79.

[43] Randi, "Ockham, John XXII and the Absolute Power of God," esp. 205–6, 215–16. Similarly Tachau, see n. 39 above.

[44] Though Leonard A. Kennedy would appear to believe that it does. See his *Pierre d'Ailly and the Harvest of Fourteenth-Century Philosophy*, pp. 7–57, 197–203.

2. *Early Modern Usage* (i): *Theology—Scholastic, Lutheran, Reformed*

Of the career of the distinction across the course of the fifteenth
century we have only a rather sketchy sense. A good deal of detailed
research will have to be done before we can claim to have a truly
reliable picture of that particular stretch of history.[45] But we do
know that the distinction was prevalent enough to have found echoes
in the homiletic literature,[46] and its diffusion beyond strictly scholastic theological and philosophical circles is reflected also in the references which both Erasmus and Sir Thomas More made to it in the
early years of the sixteenth century. Thus the latter, speaking against
Tyndale about the order of grace and what he calls the "specyall
prerogatyve" of God's mercy, describes that prerogative as being
exercised by "hys absolute power [which] is neyer bounden vnder
any rule of his ordinary iustyce." And the former, dwelling likewise
in his *Hyperaspites Diatribae* on the individual's spiritual transformation,
hastens to make clear that "I speak of those things which he [God]
does for the most part" and adds: "Always I except the *potentia absoluta* of God by which, suddenly he makes those whom he wishes
different."[47] Just as, for that matter, referring some years earlier in
his *De libero arbitrio* to God's miraculous delivery of Mishach, Shadrach
and Abednego from Nebuchadnezzar's fiery furnace (Daniel 3:13ff.)
he had contrasted that rarely exercised divine ability to disrupt the

---

[45] See the preliminary probings of Kennedy, "The Fifteenth Century and Divine
Absolute Power," 125–52. He concludes (152) that "on the eve of the Reformation
many philosophers and theologians [especially Scotists and nominalists] were making extensive applications of the notion of divine absolute power."

[46] On which, see John W. O'Malley, "Preaching for the Popes," in *The Pursuit
of Holiness in Late Medieval and Renaissance Religion*, ed. Trinkaus and Oberman, pp.
408–40 (at 415); E. Jane Dempsey Douglass, *Justification in Late Medieval Preaching: A
Study of John Geiler of Keisersberg* (Leiden, 1966), pp. 82, 163–65. Geiler appears to
have made use of the idea but not the technical terminology.

[47] Thomas More, *The Confutation of Tyndale's Answer*, 4, in *The Complete Works of
St. Thomas More*, ed. Richard S. Sylvester (8 vols., New Haven, 1963–87), VIII, 1,
569. Desiderius Erasmus, *Opera omnia*, ed. J. Le Clerc (10 vols., Leiden, 1703–6),
X, 1527E: "Semper excipio Dei potentiam absolutam, qua subito facit alios quos
vult. De iis, quae plerumque facit, loquar." My attention was drawn to this passage by Charles Trinkaus, "Erasmus, Augustine, and the Nominalists." *Archiv für
Reformationsgeschichte*, 67 (1976), 5–32, reprinted in *idem, The Scope of Renaissance Humanism*
(Ann Arbor, 1983), 274–301 (at 282 and 295 n. 28). Trinkaus rightly identifies the
passage as an invocation of the *potentia absoluta ordinata* distinction in its second, more
Scotistic, sense, involving the understanding of the *potentia absoluta* as a presently
active power.

natural "effect of secondary causes" with what he called God's "ordained will."[48]

Both men clearly conceived of the *potentia dei absoluta* as a presently active power, and the same Scotistic imprint is evident (though unevenly so) in the manner of the distinction's employment by the scholastic authors in whose writings the Protestant Reformers are most likely to have encountered it. Prominent among them were Gabriel Biel (d. 1495), whose works circulated widely in German university circles of the early sixteenth century and with whose views Luther clearly felt he had to come to terms; John Mair or Major (d. 1551), sometime teacher of the Scots reformer, George Buchanan; Jacques Almain (d. 1515), another of Mair's pupils and one chosen by the Parisian Faculty of Theology in 1512 to defend the conciliarist cause against the attacks of Thomas de Vio, Cardinal Cajetan; and Johannes Altenstaig (d. ca. 1525), whose *Vocabularius Theologiae* (1517), an extremely useful compendium of traditional theological definitions, went through no less than five editions between 1517 and 1619.[49]

Of these four authors, Almain alone fails to offer a definition of

---

[48] Erasmus, *Opera omnia*, IX, 1231E–F. Here Erasmus appears (unwittingly?) to hover on the edge of conflating the *potentia absoluta/ordinata* distinction with an even older, and somewhat narrower, scholastic distinction concerning the divine will which had enjoyed a continuous career from the time of Hugh of St. Victor in the twelfth century. The distinction in question was that between the *voluntas dei beneplaciti* (referred to variously over the centuries as the will of God's good pleasure or his secret, concealed or hidden will) and the *voluntas dei signi*, commonly referred to as his "signifying" or "revealed" will made known to us in the Sacred Scriptures. For similar conflations of the two distinctions in Luther, Hubmaier and James I of England, see below notes 67, 68, 69, 70, and 148.

[49] For discussions of these authors see for Biel, Oberman, *The Harvest of Medieval Theology*; for Mair, J.H. Burns, "*Politia regalis et optima*: The Political Ideas of John Mair," *History of Political Thought*, 2 (1981), 31–61; Francis Oakley, "On the Road from Constance to 1688: The Political Thought of John Major," *Journal of British Studies*, 2 (1962), 1–31; for Almain, Olivier de la Brosse, *Le Pape et le Concile: La comparaison de leurs pouvoirs à la veille de la Réforme* (Paris, 1965); Francis Oakley, "Conciliarism in the Sixteenth Century: Jacques Almain Again," *Archiv für Reformationsgeschichte*, 68 (1977), 111–32; For Altenstaig, Friedrich Zoepfl, *Johannes Altenstaig: Ein Gelehrtenleben aus der Zeit des Humanismus und der Reformation* (Münster: i. W., 1918), esp. pp. 56–58 for the publishing history of the *Vocabularius*. Given the closeness of his relationship to the young Luther, reference should be made also to Johannes von Staupitz (d. 1524) who, using *de possibili* and *de lege* as terms equivalent to *potentia absoluta/ordinata*, discussed in convenantal terms (and, it may be, under Scotist influence) the structures of justice which, of his ordained power, God had established. For which, see David C. Steinmetz, *Misericordia Dei: The Theology of Johannes von Staupitz in its Late Medieval Setting* (Leiden, 1968), pp. 44–56.

the distinction, but that does not preclude his invoking it with some frequency, primarily in relation to the theology of justification. The language he uses, moreover, suggests that he at least leaned towards an "operationalized" understanding of the absolute power. That is to say, he contrasts what is possible *de potentia dei absoluta* (or "simply, by the absolute law," or, again, "by the mercy of God and apart from the laws") with what happens "regularly and by the ordained power," or "by the common law," or "the law decreed by God," or "according to the common course of the law" and "excluding a miracle."[50] And, in another setting, he also reveals his familiarity with the congruent (if only analogous) canonistic application of the distinction to the power of the pope.[51]

As for the others, though the definitions they offer are traditional enough and doubtless susceptible of being read as an affirmation of the classical understanding of the distinction (Courtenay, certainly, has read Biel in this way),[52] Biel and Mair both employ language and cite parallels that point in the direction of a conception of the absolute power as a presently active one,. Thus, having described the *potentia dei ordinata* as "that which is in conformity with the ordained law made known to us through the scriptures or revelation," Mair adduces by way of parallel the ability of a king to do many things *de facto* which he cannot do *de jure scripto*. And Biel's examples are such as to lead Oberman to the conclusion that they involve instances in which "the realm of the *potentia absoluta* breaks into that of the *potentia ordinata*" thus underlining the fact that for him "the realm of the *potentia absoluta* is not merely hypothetical and the sum of all uncontradictory possibilities."[53] With Altenstaig, moreover, who,

---

[50] Jacques Almain, *De penitentia*, fols. 3r, 5v, 6v, 13r, 23v; *idem, Moralia*, fols. 16v, 33r–v, 38v–39r, 42v–43r, 45v, 51r, 73v, 74v—both printed (though with individual pagination) in *Aurea clarissimi et acutissimi doctoris theologi Magistri Jacobi Almain Senonensis Opuscula* (Paris, 1518). Cf. *Embammata phisicalia Magistri Jacobi Almain Senonensis* (Paris, 1506), fol. 76v.

[51] Almain, *Quaestio resumptiva ... de dominio naturalis*, in Gerson. *Opera omnia*, ed. Dupin, II, 968A, and *Expositio ... super potestate ecclesiastica et laica, ibid.*, 1091C–D, 1094A.

[52] Courtenay, *Capacity and Volition*, p. 180: "[Biel's] definition appears in line with Thomas, Ockham and Rimini. In that regard, Biel was more traditional in his usage than many late fourteenth century authors."

[53] Thus John Mair, *In primum Sententiarum* (Paris, 1510), dist. 44, qu. un., fol. c. iv: "Potentia absoluta dei se extendit ad illa que non implicant [contradictionem] ... Alia est potentia dei ordinata et est illa que est conformis legi ordinate que nobis constat per scripturam vel revelationem; non quod sunt due potentie in deo realiter

under the headings "Potentia dei" and "Ordinatum," chooses to echo the definitions given earlier on by Scotus and d'Ailly, the sympathy with the Scotistic or "juristic" understanding of the distinction is clear.[54]

So far as the scholastic tradition is concerned, then, the distinction was well-placed in the early-sixteenth century to ensure a continuing presence in the intellectual discourse of the day. And while, if so disposed, one could probably (though with varying degrees of strain) elicit from the definitions given the original, classical understanding that had prevailed during much of the thirteenth century, the authorities cited, the language used and the parallels drawn reflect, nonetheless, an unmistakable tilt toward the later conception of the *potentia absoluta* as a presently active power of extraordinary interposition. That tilt is evident in the gradual adoption of the terms "extraordinary" and "ordinary" as synonyms for the older "absolute" and "ordained." And it appears to have been characteristic of the Catholic scholastic tradition throughout the sixteenth and seventeenth centuries, and continued on, indeed, into the neoscholastic manuals of the nineteenth and twentieth centuries.

Three examples must suffice to illustrate the scholastic understanding of the distinction in this period, examples drawn both from the older tradition of commentary on Lombard's *Sentences* and from the newer mode of Thomistic philosophical commentary pioneered by Cajetan and Francisco de Vitoria (d. 1546) and followed especially by the *Conimbricenses* (the Jesuit commentators at the University of Coimbra in Portugal) and by those teaching at Alcala and Salamanca in Spain.

The first example is drawn from a series of lectures on the first book of Lombard's *Sentences* delivered in 1542 to students at Ingolstadt by none other than the anti-Lutheran polemicist, John Eck (d. 1543). For the distinction of these lectures one can claim nothing and, given the fact that they were first published in 1976,[55] for their influence even less. Their interest, rather, lies in the fact that they can be presumed

---

distincte, sed deus propter duplicem modum agendi quem habet vel habere possit duabus nominibus vocatur, sicut dicimus multa potest rex de facto que non potest de jure scripto." Gabriel Biel, *Super quattuor libros Sententiarum* (Lyons, 1519), I, dist. 17, qu. 1, [art. 3], and IV, dist. 1, qu. 1 art. 3H. The Biel texts are cited and discussed in Oberman, *The Harvest of Medieval Theology*, pp. 45–46.

[54] Johannes Altenstaig, *Vocabularius Theologie complectens vocabulorum descriptiones, diffinitiones, et significatus ad theologiam utilium* (Hagenau, 1517), fols. cxcvii r and clxxv r.

[55] Edited with an introduction by Walter L. Moore, Jr., *In Primum Librum Sententiarum Annotatiunculae D. Johanne Eckio Praelectore* (Leiden, 1976).

to reflect all too faithfully the scholastic clichés of the day. Thus, commenting on Lombard's forty-second, forty-third and forty-fourth distinctions focusing on those questions concerning the divine power that had exercised Damiani and led Abelard into the theological doldrums, Eck evoked once more St. Jerome's opinion concerning the fallen virgin and cited the divine delivery of the three youths from the flames of the Babylonian furnace. The latter event, it should be noted, adduced explicitly to document an actual, historically-attested exercise by God of that absolute power by virtue of which he can do anything that does not involve a contradiction. By virtue of that power, accordingly, he can act apart from "the common law," "common course," or "common rule which he put into things, [and] which, of his ordained power, he normally observes."[56] Because he was still using the traditional terminology and because he worried (in equally traditionalist fashion) that the contrast of absolute and ordained might improperly be taken to suggest that God by his absolute power might act in a disorderly way, Eck made the further point that the divinely-imposed order was of two kinds, a "general" one and a "special." That fire burns and consumes what it touches pertains to the "general ordained power." But when, by God's absolute power, the three youth's were not consumed by the flames of Nebuchadnezzar's furnace, that happy outcome may be said to have occurred by "God's special ordained power," since "God had foreseen it from all eternity."[57]

A considerable interest attaches to this last formulation and it warrants more extended commentary. In analyzing the uneasy rela-

---

[56] Eck, *In Primum Librum Sententiarum*, dist. 42, ed. Moore, 122–26. Cf. dist. 43 and 44, *ibid*, pp. 127–28. The crucial passage (at 123) is worth citing: ". . . [Duplex est potentia Dei: ordinata una, altera absoluta. Potentia Dei ordinata est qua ipse cooperetur creaturis secundum legem communem quam ipsis indidit. . . . Potentia dei absoluta est quae non concernit illam regulam communem quam indidit rebus, sed extendit se ad omne illud quod non includit contradictionem fieri. Verbi gratia, quando ignis comburit vestem est secundum communem cursum et naturam ignis. Sed quod non laesit et consumpsit tres pueros in camino fuit de potentia Dei absoluta. Ita de potentia sua absoluta Deus possit Judam salvare, quia non implicat contradictionem fieri."

[57] *Ibid.*, dist. 42, 123. In his "Catholic Teacher and Anabaptist Pupil: The Relationship between John Eck and Balthasar Hubmaier," *Archiv für Reformationsgeschichte*, 72 (1981), 68–97 (at 81–83). Walter L. Moore, Jr. draws attention to the comparable use Eck made of the power distinction in his *Chrysopassus* and concludes that here, too, Eck envisages the *potentia absoluta* as functioning "not merely in the realm of *unrealized* possibility" but as "a power according to which God at times acts in contravention of his ordained power."

tionship in some of the pertinent medieval texts between discussions of God's miraculous activity and the *potentia dei absoluta/ordinata* distinction as it emerged in the late-twelfth and early thirteenth centuries, Courtenay has insisted that miracles *could not* properly be taken to be instances of an exercise of the absolute power because that term referred, not to a mode of divine activity, but to the hypothetical realm of all that was *in abstracto* logically possible for God to do. As the ordained power referred, in contrast, to the totality of what God, from that broader realm of possibilities, had actually chosen to come about, miraculous happenings had accordingly to be understood as falling within the realm of the *potentia ordinata*. "Miracles," being "temporary suspensions of the very laws God had established,... what was probably needed," he adds,

> was further discussion of some distinction within *potentia ordinata* between the total ordained will of God (divine providence or *lex aeternalis*) and specific laws now in effect (*lex ut nunc*), which have been suspended or altered from time to time. Without such a discussion, the foreordained but miraculous activity of God had the potentiality of floating free from *potentia ordinata* and compromising the non-action status of *potentia absoluta*.[58]

That, of course, would have been one way of resolving the issue. But if Eck's formulation does indeed introduce into the realm of the *potentia ordinata* Courtenay's wished-for distinction, we should not miss the fact that that move does not lead Eck himself to abandon the view that miracles constitute an actual exercise of the *potentia dei absoluta*. As a result, a curious reversal is embedded in his thinking. Whereas, in the classical version of the distinction, the realm of the *potentia ordinata* (representing as it does what God has actually chosen to effect from among the totality of possibilities initially open to him) can be said to fall "entirely *within* that of *potentia absoluta*,"[59] with Eck, on the other hand, the *potentia absoluta*, defined now more narrowly as the realm of God's extraordinary action, falls within the realm of the *potentia ordinata*. Within that realm it is contrasted as an exercise of God's special ordained power with the workings of that general ordained power evident in the ordinary course of things. And, as we shall see, this appears to be what many sixteenth- and

---

[58] Courtenay, *Capacity and Volition*, pp. 18–19, 69, 73, 77–78. The words cited appear at p. 78.
[59] *Ibid.*, p. 19.

seventeenth-century authors had in mind when they distinguished
between the "absolute" and "*ordinary*" power, or, more clearly, between
the "*extraordinary*" and "*ordinary* providence" of God. Indeed, if I were
to be permitted a moment of helpful expository anachronism, I would
probably be tempted to say that Eck's intriguing formulation witnessed the ongoing process by which the original distinction was
reshaped until it coincided with that later and enduringly popular
distinction concerning the working of divine providence.

Not all the early-modern scholastics, however, were quite so clear
on the matter as was Eck. Thus—our second example—discussing
the distinction some forty years later and alluding to the definitions
given by both Aquinas and Scotus, those responsible for the commentary on Aristotle's *Physics* published by the Jesuits at Coimbra
managed, along with a clearly "operationalized" understanding of
the *potentia absoluta*, to evoke some echoes of the classical meaning.
Thus they understood God's "extraordinary or absolute power" to
be his power taken in itself (*simpliciter*) and extending to everything
that does not involve a contradiction. But they contrasted it with
God's "ordinary power" (*potentia ordinaria*), which extends only to the
limited range of possibilities congruent with 'the common and habitual course or order put into things," and viewed it as the power in
virtue of which "God can act apart from the accustomed [natural]
order," which in fact he did when he delivered the three youths
from the Babylonian furnace.[60]

This understanding of the absolute power appears to have been
shared by Francisco Suárez when some twenty years later in his *De
Legibus ac Deo Legislatore*, speaking of the eternal law and citing the
crucial text from Scotus, he contrasted what is possible for God,
using his power to grant dispensations from the established law (*secundum statutam legem*), with what is possible to him "by the ordinary
law, that is, by the law which he has imposed on himself," or again,
"in accordance with his ordained power (*potentia ordinata*).[61] In his

---

[60] *Commentarii Collegii Conimbricensis Societatis Jesu: In octo libros Physicorum Aristotelis
Stagiritae* (Coimbra, 1592), Lib. II, cap. 7, qu. 16, art. 1, pp. 312–13; cf. Lib. VIII,
cap. 10, qu. 3, pp. 823–24.
[61] Francisco Suarez. *Tractatus de legibus ac deo legislatore* (Coimbra, 1612), Lib. II,
cap. 2, 104, col. 1C–D. Though in this particular passage he does not use the term
potentia absoluta to describe the dispensing power in question, he does so a little later
on in chapter 15 when discussing the question "Utrum deus dispensare possit in
lege naturali etiam de absoluta potestate. See *ibid.*, 164, col. 2C—the phrase used
is "secundum potentiam Dei absolutam."

Metaphysical Disputations (1597), moreover, Suárez had dealt with the distinction at somewhat greater lengths and in more explicit fashion. There, referring to Aquinas's definition, he distinguishes between the absolute and *ordinary* power of God, defining the former as that power taken in itself (*secundum se*), absent any determination of the will and setting aside other causes and the nature of things. The latter, however, he describes (d'Ailly fashion) as being understood in more than one way. In the first place, and in the classical manner, it was taken to refer to the power of God as it pertains to the realm of those things in the natural and supernatural orders alike which he has determined will at some time come about. In the second place, however, it was taken to denote the power of God as it operated "in accordance with the common laws and causes which he has established in the universe." This second usage he viewed as the more common one (*magis usitatus*). And in accordance with that usage, he makes it clear that, of his absolute power "or through the intervention of some miracle," God can indeed act *de facto* "aside from" the ordinary power.[62]

Given the weight of Suárez's authority, it is not surprising, then, that the memory of the two ways of understanding the distinction survived on even into the neoscholastic manuals of the past century, so that Kleutgen, for example, is careful to describe both ways, noting that the term *potentia ordinaria* (rather than *ordinata*) is the more appropriate one to use for the second "operationalized" version, which he viewed, moreover, as the version most commonly subscribed to.[63] Suárez's influence also made itself felt beyond the scholastic circles of the Catholic world. Étienne Gilson has described the *Metaphysical Disputations* as the most notable expression of that "deuxième Scholastique" which informed the philosophical instruction Descartes received from his Jesuit teachers of La Flèche, and we know that that same work also exerted a shaping influence on the

---

[62] Francisco Suárez, *Metaphysicarum Disputationum* (2 vols., Mainz, 1600), Disp. XXX, sect. 17, §§ xxxii–xxxiii; Disp. XXXIII, sect. 7; II, 150, col. 1–151, col. 2; 289 col. 1.

[63] Kleutgen, *Institutiones theologicae in usum scholarum*, I, Pars I, lib. 1, qu. 3, cap. 4, art. 4, pp. 384–85. Noting that "apud orthodoxos quoque theologos non una est hujus distinctionis expositio," he describes the second usage as follows: "Complures vero in hunc modum distinguunt: Ordinatae potentiae tribuenda sunt ea, qua Deus operatur secundum modum et legem communem sive naturae sive gratiae . . .; absolutae, quae praeter communem legem operatur. . . . In hac expositione, quae quidem usitatissima est, pro ordinata potentia rectius dicitur ordinaria."

way in which such representatives of Lutheran scholasticism as Johann
Gerhard (d. 1637) and Johann Quenstedt (d. 1688) went about their
own intellectual endeavors in the seventeenth century.[64] By their day,
however, the *potentia dei absoluta/ordinata* distinction had long established a presence in Protestant theology (Luther himself, after all,
had commented on it), and there is no reason to attribute their
employment of the distinction simply to Suárezian influence.

Of course, Luther's own attitude towards the distinction had been
an impatient and ambivalent one. In his *Lectures on Genesis* (1539), it
is true, echoing the second, more Scotistic or juristic view, he contrasted
God's *potestas ordinata* or *ordinaria* (both terms occur in the text) with
his *potestas extraordinaria* "or, as the Scholastics put it, *potestas absoluta.*"
By the former, God condescends to act through secondary causes
and "through his creatures, whom he does not wish to be idle." It
is in accordance, then, with "God's ordained power that water damp-
ens, fire burns, etc." But by the extraordinary interposition of God's
absolute power, "in accordance with which he acted *at that time,*"
Daniel's companions were delivered from the flames of the Babylonian
furnace.[65]

That said, however, the presence of the qualifying phrase dis-
tancing from the present such divine departures from the order established *de potentia ordinata* should not escape our attention. The less
so, in that Luther himself underlines its significance by insisting that
God "no longer wishes to act through his extraordinary or . . . absolute
power," that by it, certainly, he "does not command us to do anything," that it is, instead, "in accordance with the ordained power
that he wishes us to act."[66] And he underlines it again by bringing
the power distinction into connection with the older (and narrower)
distinction between the hidden or secret will (*voluntas beneplaciti*) and

---

[64] Étienne Gilson, *Index scolastico-Cartésien* (2nd ed. rev., Paris, 1979), p. 358.
Robert P. Scharlemann, *Thomas Aquinas and John Gerhard* (New Haven and London,
1964), who comments (p. 15) that "Suarez' *Disputationes* . . . became the model for
Protestant school metaphysics." And again, (p. 17) "Suárez's *Disputationes* became
the prevailing model because it fulfilled the humanistic as well as the ontological
purpose."

[65] Martin Luther, *Vorlesungen über I Mose*, cap. 19, 14–20, cf. cap. 20, 2, in
D. Martin Luthers Werke: Kritische Gesamtausgabe (91 vols., Weimar, 1883–1980), XLIII,
71–82, 106 (italics mine). I quote here from the crucial passage at 71 lines 7ff.,
and cite here and in what follows (though with one or two emendations) the translation in Jaroslav Pelikan ed., *Luther's Works* (55 vols., St. Louis, 1955–86), III,
274–90.

[66] *Ibid.*

the revealed will (*voluntas signi*) of God.[67] Thus he contrasts God's *potentia ordinata* with his "secret" power or will, stipulating that he "does not wish to govern us through his secret will but in accordance with the will which is regulated and revealed by the Word." It is not with the hidden or "naked" (*nudus*) God that we should deal. Instead, "we must reflect on the ordained power, that is, the incarnate Son, for in him are hidden all the treasures of the Godhead (Col. 2:3)."[68]

Although he, in turn, understood very differently what exactly it was that the divine will revealed in Holy Scripture actually taught about the moral capacity of humankind, the Swiss Anabaptist, Balthasar Hubmaier (d. 1528), sometime student of scholastic theology under the mentorship of John Eck, similarly conflated the power distinction with that between God's secret and revealed will. Thus in his *Andere Büchlein* (1527), a work which may have been influenced by and modeled on Erasmus's *De libero arbitrio*,[69] he contrasts God's "hidden" or "secret" will (which, he says, the Schoolmen know as "the absolute power or will") with the "preached" and "revealed power and will." By the former, he says, God "can without any injustice be merciful to whomever he wills or harden the same, save or condemn." By the latter, which in the Scriptures, we must be careful to discriminate from the former, God "wills not to act toward us poor people according to his omnipotence but according to his mercy, as he has sufficiently testified the same to us through his most beloved Son and through all those who point to him in the Old and New Testaments."[70]

---

[67] Note that in his *De servo arbitrio* [*Werke*, XVIII, 719 (cf. 715)] Luther appears fully to conflate the *potentia absoluta/ordinata* distinction within the *voluntas dei beneplaciti/signi* distinction, using the terms *voluntas absoluta* and *voluntas ordinata seu signi*. For the similar conflation in Erasmus, see above, n. 48.

[68] *Vorlesungen über I Mose* in *Werke*, XLIII, 72–73 and 82; *Luther's Works*, ed. Pelikan, III, 276, 289. For a careful and probing comment on these tangled passages, see Oberman, "*Via Antiqua* and *Via Moderna*: Late Medieval Prolegomena to Early Reformation Thought," 30–34; cf. Van den Brink, *Almighty God*, pp. 87–88, and, for an older and somewhat different approach, John Dillenberger, *God Hidden and Revealed* (Philadelphia, 1953).

[69] This case is made especially by Thor Hall, "The possibilities of Erasmian Influence on Denck and Hubmaier in Their Views on the Freedom of the Will," *Mennonite Quarterly Review*, 35 (1961), 149–70. Certainly, Hubmaier is at one with Erasmus in conflating the power distinction with that between the *Voluntas dei beneplaciti et signi*. But, then, so too was Luther. For the link with Eck, see Moore, "Catholic Teacher and Anabaptist Pupil," 68–97—especially 81–85 and 93 for his comparison of the use they both make of the power distinction and his conclusion that "in the use they make [of it] there is common ground."

[70] Balthasar Hubmaier, *Das andere Büchlein von der Freiwilligkeit des Menschen*, pt. III;

During the following decade, however, Calvin was to take a very different and even firmer line on the *potentia dei absoluta*. Reacting sharply, it would seem, against what he took to be the late-medieval exploitation of that notion to explore hypothetical possibilities suggesting an order of salvation very different from that revealed in the Scriptures, and identifying God's power with his will, justice and goodness, he sharply rejected in general the distinction between the "puissance absolue" and "puissance ordinaire," and especially that "doctrine diabolique" or "fiction" (*commentum*) of the absolute power peddled by the "Sophistae" (i.e., scholastics), "docteurs Sorboniques" or papist theologians.[71] One could speculate[72] about whether or not Calvin would have approved of the distinction had he encountered it in its original classical form, but it would be fruitless, I think, to do so. Steinmetz is probably correct in arguing that Calvin, given his unwillingness "to entertain even a hypothetical separation of God's power from his justice," was "not only opposed to the abuse" of the distinction (as one of his successors was to speculate)[73] but "to the distinction as such." For Calvin, he insists,

> Whatever God has done, is doing or plans to do is an expression of his *potentia ordinata*, even if the justice that guides his will is secret and hidden from us. That ordered power is displayed in miracles, providence and predestination.[74]

in *Schriften*, ed. Gunnar Westin and Torsten Bergsten, Quellen und Forschungen zur Reformationsgeschichte, 29 (Heidelberg, 1962), pp. 416–18, Thus of the absolute power he says (p. 416): "Dissen offenbarten gewalt haben die Schülen gehayssen ainenn vollmechtigenn gwalt oder willen Gottes." And of the ordained power (p. 417): "Den offenbartten gwalt und willen Gottes nennen die Schülen ainen ordentlich gwalt und willen." I quote from the translation of the work in H. Wayne Pipkins and John H. Yoder eds., *Balthasar Hubmaier: Theologian of Anabaptism* (Scottsdale, Penn., 1989), pp. 449–91 (at 472–73). Cf. the analysis in David C. Steinmetz, "Scholasticism and Radical Reform: Nominalist Motifs in the Theology of Balthasar Hubmaier," *Mennonite Quarterly Review*, 45 (1971), 123–44 (esp. 130–31).

[71] See *Institutes of the Christian Religion*, III, 23, § 2, and I, 17, § 2; ed. and trans. John T. McNeill and Ford Lewis Battles (2 vols., Philadelphia, 1960), I, 214, and II, 950. Cf. his *De aeterna Dei praedestinatione*, in *Joannis Calvini Opera quae supersunt Omnia*, ed. Wilhelm Baum, Eduard Cunitz and Edward Reuss (59 vols., Brunswick and Berlin, 1863–1900), VIII, 361. And for his rejection of the distinction in so many of his sermons, see Richard Stauffer, *Dieu, la création et la Providence dans la prédication de Calvin* (Berne, 1978), pp. 112–16 and 136–40 (esp. 139–40, nn. 134 and 141).

[72] As does Van den Brink, *Almighty God*, p. 90.

[73] See below, p. 305 and note 82.

[74] David C. Steinmetz, *Calvin in Context* (New York and Oxford, 1995), ch. 3: "Calvin and the Absolute Power of God," pp. 40–52 (at 49–50).

Recognizing, nonetheless, that for Calvin God's preordination of things itself comprehended divine action reaching beyond the fixed order of nature and grace, it seems reasonable to acknowledge the rectitude of the claim that "Calvin in a sense implicitly uses the distinction in its later operationalized interpretation, but then as on a par with the distinction between *providentia ordinaria* and *extraordinaria.*"[75] Later theologians in the Reformed tradition, certainly (and especially the Puritan "federal" theologians in the Netherlands and in Old and New England), found the latter distinction perfectly congenial. Thus, for example, Dudley Fenner (d. 1587) in the first methodical Puritan *summa* of theology;[76] William Perkins (d. 1602); William Ames (d. 1633); John Norton (d. 1663); Increase Mather (d. 1723); Thomas Shepard (d. 1649); Samuel Willard (d. 1707).[77] The distinction was embed-

---

[75] Thus Van den Brink, *Almighty God*, p. 90. The qualification "implicitly" is important. The terms "ordinary" and "extraordinary" do not sit well with the intensity of Calvin's belief in the omnipresence and immediacy of God's providential action. Cf. Heiko A. Oberman, *The Dawn of the Reformation: Essays in Late Medieval and Early Medieval Thought* (Edinburgh, 1986), ch. 10: "The 'Extra' Dimension in the Theology of Calvin," pp. 234–58 (at 255–58), and his "*Via Antiqua* and *Via Moderna*: Late Medieval Prolegomena to Early Reformation Thought," 38–39.

[76] Dudley Fenner, *Sacra theologia sive Veritas* (Geneva, 1589), fol. 18r, where, admittedly, he does not use the *providentia ordinaria/extraordinaria* distinction but, discussing the *gubernatio dei*, distinguishes schematically between the "ordinary" mode of operation in accord with "the common law" God has imposed on his creation and the "extraordinary" by which God "does great things beyond understanding" (Job. 9:10). Similarly, among the earlier Reformers, Ulrich Zwingli, *Ad illustrissimum . . . Principem Philippum, sermonis de providentia dei anamneme* (Zurich, 1530), fol. 63v, where he equates natural action as that which is in accord with the order established in the beginning and miracles with action apart from (*praeter*) that order. Also Philip Melancthon, *Initia Doctrina Physicae* (*ca.* 1549), where, under the headings *De providentia* and *De contingente* and insisting against the Stoics that God is "a most free agent not bound to secondary courses," he notes that we are to understand the term *necessitas physica* (which is "the mode of action ordained in natural causes") to refer to "the order presently established" by God, which he can interrupt as he did when he stopped the action of the fire and delivered the three youths from Nebuchadnezzar's furnace—in *Philippi Melancthonis Opera . . . omnia*, ed., C.G. Bretschneider (29 vols., Halis Saxonum, 1846), XIII, 206–7.

[77] William Perkins, *A Resolution to the Countrey-man*, in *The Workes of That Famous and Worthy Minister of Christ . . . M.W. Perkins* (3 vols., Cambridge, 1608–31), III, 657, where he contrasts the "general providence" whereby God acts via secondary causes in accord with "the usual course and order of nature" and that immediate governance of the world whereby "his providence worketh without means." So "against the course of nature he made . . . the fire not to burn the three children [in the Babylonian furnace]." Cf. Perkins, *An Exposition of the Symbole, Workes* I, 159, and his *A Discourse of the Damned Art of Witchcraft, Workes*, III, 609 (in both cases again citing Dan. 3:23ff.). William Ames, *The Marrow of Sacred Divinity* (London, 1642), Bk. I, ch. 9, esp. pp. 39–41, contrasting "the Ordinary and usuall" providence, "whereby

ded in the Westminster Confession (1647) and, though the terminology employed was not uniform, it endured well into the eighteenth century, being deployed not only by divines but also by laymen of scientific bent.[78]

What significance attaches to the fact that the federal theologians did not associate the *providentia dei ordinaria/extraordinaria* distinction with the terminology of *potentia absoluta/ordinata* is not clear.[79] What is reasonably clear, however, is that Calvin's friends and earliest followers in the Reformed tradition appear to have shared his disapproval of scholastic speculations pivoting on the discrimination of an absolute power from God's ordained power. Thus, while Peter Martyr Vermigli (d. 1562), one of the most influential of the Reformed theologians, did invoke the *potentia absoluta/ordinata* distinction, he was reluctant to explore considerations based on an appeal to the absolute power.[80] And when Lambert Daneau (d. 1595), who had taught for a while with Theodore Beza at the Genevan Academy, adduced the distinction in his commentary on the first book of Lombard's *Sentences* (1580), he did so disapprovingly.[81]

God observeth that order in things which was appointed from the beginning" with the "Extraordinary and unusuall," whereby he operates miraculously "beyond the usuall, and appointed order," as he did when he delivered the three youths from the Babylonian furnace. Ames also aligns the ordinary with God's "mediate" providence and the extraordinary with the "immediate." Similarly, in terminology and exemplification, John Norton, *Orthodox Evangelist* (London, 1654), pp. 103–4, 124. Increase Mather, *The Doctrine of Divine Providence Opened and Applyed* (Boston, 1684), pp. 21–24, 45–47, 53–54; Thomas Shepard, *Three Valuable Pieces viz. Select Cases resolved* (Boston, 1747), pp. 9–10; Samuel Willard, *A Compleat Body of Divinity* (Boston, 1726), pp. 38–39, 136 and 144.

[78] *The Westminster Confession of Faith* (1647), ch. 5; in Philip Schaff, *The Creeds of Christendom* (3 vols., New York, 1877), III, 612–13. For the seventeenth century in general, see Perry Miller, *The New England Mind: The Seventeenth Century* (Boston, 1961), pp. 224–35; Keith Thomas, *Religion and the Decline of Magic* (New York, 1971), pp. 78–96, 109–12. For the eighteenth, David Spadafora, *The Idea of Progress in Eighteenth-Century Britain* (New Haven and London, 1990), pp. 111–14, 121–24, where he cites among others Thomas Burnet (d. 1750), William Whiston (d. 1752), Thomas Broughton (d. 1774), Thomas Hartley (d. 1784), and David Hartley (d. 1757). See also, Georges Gusdorf, "Déclin de la providence," *Studies in Voltaire and the Eighteenth Century*, 153 (1976), 951–99; Henry F. May, "The Decline of Providence," *ibid.*, 154 (1976), 1401–16.

[79] Though see below, pp. 305–6 and nn. 86 and 87, for comment on the fact that, among them, Perkins, Ames, Norton and Willard (but not Fenner, Mather and Shepard) did cite the absolute/ordained distinction elsewhere.

[80] See John P. Donnelly, *Calvinism and Scholasticism in Vermigli's Doctrine of Man and Grace* (Leiden, 1976), pp. 27, 71, 119–20, 167.

[81] Lambert Daneau, *Commentarius triplex in Petri Lombardi ... librum primum Sententiarum*

Nonetheless, before the century was out, Francis Turretino (d. 1628) in Geneva was moved to try to neutralize Calvin's attack on the distinction by arguing that it was really an attack, not on the distinction itself, but on its abuse by late medieval scholastic theologians.[82] And, in the following century, other exponents of the later Reformed theology as well as representatives of what was by then a burgeoning Lutheran scholasticism did not hesitate to make the distinction their own. Thus Amandus Polonus (d. 1610), Johann Alsted (d. 1638) and Johann Heidegger (d. 1698) in the Reformed camp;[83] and, among the Lutherans, Johann Gerhard, Abraham Calovi (d. 1686), and Johann Quenstedt.[84]

Bavinck has claimed that those later Reformed theologians, in deploying the distinction, understood it in the classic fashion favored by Aquinas.[85] The same, certainly, is by and large true of those among the federal theologians—Perkins, Ames, Norton and Willard—who, while evoking the ordinary/extraordinary providence distinction, went on in their analyses of the divine omnipotence to draw attention also (though separately) to the traditional *potentia absoluta/ordinata* distinction. The terms they use are "absolute" as contrasted with "actuall power" (Perkins), or "absolute" as opposed to "ordinate or actuall" (Ames), or "absolute and unlimited" versus ordinate

---

(Geneva, 1580), censura ad dist. 43, 692–94, where he contrasts the *potentia ordinaria et nota* with the *potentia extraordinaria et absoluta.*

[82] Francisco Turretino, *Institutio Theologiae Elencticae* (3 vols., Edinburgh, 1847), I, locus tertius, qu. 21. Having distinguished here (at 221) between the *potentia absoluta* and the *potentia actualis et ordinata*, Turretino goes on: "Si quidam ex nostris Theologis *potentiam absolutam* rejicere videntur, tanquam commentum profanum et detestible, ut Calvin, lib. iii. Insti c. 23, s. 2, hoc intelligunt, non absolute, sed secundum quid, ratione abusus Scholasticorum, qui multa portentosa dogmata inde extruxerunt, quasi absolutae potentiae ratio in eo consisteret, quod Deus possit quicquid a nobis excogitari potest, sive bonum, sive malum, sive contradictorium, sive non; puta quod possit mentire, peccare, quod possit aliquid quod repugnat naturae rerum, etc., hanc potentiam absolutam recte negat Calvinus, quia non esset potentiae et virtutis, sed impotentiae et imperfectionis; sed noluit negare Deum per potentiam absolutam plura posse praestare quam revera praestet per actualem."

[83] For this claim I rely on the account in H. Bavinck, *Gereformeerde Dogmatik* (4 vols., 4th ed., 1928), II, 215–219 and n. 1. The first section of the volume (minus the references) is available in English translation as *The Doctrine of God*, ed. and trans. William Hendriksen (Edinburgh, 1977)—see 241–45. To this useful account my attention was drawn by Van den Brink, *Almighty God*, p. 90 n. 95.

[84] Johannus Gerhard, *Locorum Theologicorum* (9 vols., Geneva, 1639), I, pt. 3, cap. 14, cols. 132–36; Abraham Calovi, *Systema locorum Theologorum* (2 vols., Wittenberg, 1655), II, cap. 10, 486–87; Johannes Andrea Quenstedt, *Theologia Didactico-Polemica, sive Systema Theologicum* (Wittenberg, 1696), pt. 1, cap. 8, pp. 293, 535.

[85] Bavinck, *Gereformeerde Dogmatik*, II, 218–19.

and limited" (Norton and Willard), and they deploy the distinction in a very matter of fact way as something not seeming to call for argument.[86] Thus Willard:

> Divines do from Scripture observe a two-fold Power ascribed to God, viz. 1. An unlimited and absolute Power, by vertue of which he can do all possible things, even such things as he never actually doth.... 2. An ordinate power, which is not a Power different from the former, but the former considered, as God has pleased to set limits or bounds to it by the Decree with respect to his exerting of it in his works of Efficiency.... Not that his Arm was shortened in these respects, but because his purpose, and sometimes his promise has tied his hands; his Will was otherwise and he pursues that in all he doth.[87]

The Lutheran scholastics, on the other hand, though less precise in their formulations of the distinction, inclined somewhat to the later, operationalized understanding of the absolute power. Johann Gerhard, whose particular formulation Friedrich Schleiermacher (d. 1834) appears to have had in mind when he himself rejected the distinction,[88] defined the absolute power (by which God can do many things that he does not in fact choose to do) as the divine power considered apart from such other divine attributes as wisdom and justice. But he contrasts it, nonetheless, with an *ordinary* (not an *ordained*) power, and, at least in so far as that power is aligned with the order which God of his freedom has chosen to establish in nature, Gerhard appears to envisage the possible exercise of a presently-active absolute power by which that order can be changed.[89] Similarly (though somewhat more clearly), Abraham Calovi distinguishes the "absolute" or

---

[86] Perkins, *A Golden Chaine or the Description of Theology*, in *Workes*, I, 13—cf. his *Exposition of the Symbole of the Creed*, ibid., 138–39, and *A godly and learned Exposition . . . upon the 3 first chapters of the Revelation*, ibid., 233–34, where he contrasts God's *potential* and *actuall* power; Ames, *The Marrow of Sacred Divinity*, Bk. I, cap. 6, p. 21, contrasting "the absolute power . . . whereby God is able to doe all things possible though they shall never be" with "the ordinate power . . . whereby he not only can doe that which he will, but also in very deed doth actually doe whatsoever he will;" Norton, *The Orthodox Evangelist*, p. 19; Willard, *A Compleat Body of Divinity*, pp. 68–71.

[87] Willard, *A Compleat Body of Divinity*, p. 70.

[88] See the translated extract from his *The Christian Faith* in Urban and Walton eds., *The Power of God*, pp. 119–27 (at 122–24). Schleiermacher cites Gerhard's *Locorum Theologicorum* several times in the course of his discussion of the various distinctions traditionally invoked to elucidate the divine omnipotence.

[89] Gerhard, *Locorum Theologicorum*, I, pt. 3, cap. 14, cols. 131–36. He adds, however, that insofar as the *potentia ordinaria* is invoked "respectu reliquorum attributorum divinarum, . . . Deus . . . nihil enim agit, quod suae sapientiae, vel justitiae, vel misericordiae, veritati repugnet atque adversetur."

"irregular" (*inordinata*) or "extraordinary" power, which is "outside the order of that power" which God normally exercises, from that "actual" or "ordinary power" which pertains, not to the other divine attributes in harmony with which God must always act, but "to the order established in nature, apart from and against which God is certainly able to act."[90] And even though Quenstedt, as we have seen, deployed elsewhere in his *Theologica Dialectica-Polemica* the distinction between the *providentia ordinaria et extraordinaria*, he also evoked a distinction between the *potentia dei absoluta et ordinaria*. The ordinary power is manifested in "the accustomed governance of the universe" and in "the order established in nature." But by the absolute power God "can do many things that he cannot do by the ordinary."[91]

3. Early Modern Usage (ii) Philosophy and Science

So far as the theologians were concerned, then, Lutheran and Reformed as well as Catholic, and although the terminology employed was subject to the fluctuations already noted, the five-centuries old *potentia dei absoluta/ordinata* distinction exerted a continuing gravitational pull on into the early years, at least, of the eighteenth century. As in the fourteenth and fifteenth centuries, moreover, it continued to be understood in more than one way—both in the original, classical sense and in the more juridical or Scotistic sense involving an operationalization of the absolute power. Furthermore, perhaps as a result of the tension between these two traditional understandings, the intuition central to the second, operationalized meaning was by a salutary clarification captured in the reformulation of the distinction as one between the ordinary and extraordinary providence of God.

No more than in the Middle Ages, however, was the currency of the distinction in this period confined to strictly theological circles or settings. We have already encountered the Coimbran commentators and Suárez deploying it to more generally philosophical ends and, in the seventeenth century, they were by no means alone in so doing.

---

[90] Calovi, *Systema locorum Theologicorum*, II, 486–89. Note esp. 489: "Distinguitur communiter potentia Dei in *absolutam*, qua quicquid esse potest, facere potest: et *ordinariam*, quae respectam habet non ad reliqua Dei attributa, (contra haec enim nihil valet absoluta potentia, quum Deus seipsum ab negare nequeat) sed ad *ordinem in natura institutum praeter et contra quem* agere omnino valet Deus."

[91] Quenstedt, *Theologia Didactico-Polemica*, Pt. I, cap. 8, p. 293.

The diversity of the philosophical currents coursing through the century, the complexity of their interactions one with another, and the reluctance of the more fashionable of thinkers (the so-called *recentiores*) to acknowledge the remotest indebtedness to a discredited scholastic past—all of these things render somewhat premature any attempt to construct a continuous narrative of philosophical or scientific usage. But even if, as Bishop Berkeley (d. 1753) noted at the start of the following century, "the Disputations of the Schoolmen" were to be "blam'd for intricacy triflingness [,] and confusion," he still insisted that it had to "be acknowledg'd that in the main they treated of great and important subjects." And half a century and more earlier, in the course of his intricate exchanges with Hobbes on matters pertaining to liberty and necessity, John Bramhall, Archbishop of Armagh (d. 1663), had deplored the confidence with which

> now-a-days particular men slight all the schoolmen, and philosophers, . . . as if they were not worthy to unloose the shoe-strings of some modern author.[92]

Fashionable condescension notwithstanding, and right from the start of the century, it is easy enough to detect traces of scholastic categories, preoccupations and modes of thought in thinkers as different from one another in philosophic temperament as Francis Bacon (d. 1626), René Descartes (d. 1650), Baruch de Spinoza (d. 1677), Marin Mersenne (d. 1648), Pierre Gassendi (d. 1655), Walter Charleton (d. 1703), Robert Boyle (d. 1691), Thomas Hobbes (d. 1679), John Locke (d. 1704) and Sir Isaac Newton himself (d. 1727). And not least among such traces the old intense engagement with the issue of divine power, capacity and will and the battery of distinctions traditionally deployed in an attempt to understand them. *Necessitas absoluta/necessitas ex suppositione, voluntas dei beneplaciti/signi, potentia dei absoluta/ordinata seu ordinaria*, and/or *providentia extraordinaria/ordinaria*—all of them crop up, especially in the writings of the scientist-philosophers or physico-theologians of the era. And they also generate echoes or, at least, harmonics in such thinkers as Blaise Pascal (d. 1662) and Pierre Malebranche (d. 1702) or, later on, in Berkeley himself and in Christian Wolff (d. 1754).

---

[92] *Workes of George Berkeley, Bishop of Cloyne* (9 vols., London and Edinburgh, 1948–57), I, 55 (from Notebook A); John Bramhall, *A Vindication of True Liberty from Antecedent and Extrinsecal Necessity* (1655), in *The Works of the Most Reverend Father in God, John Bramhall, D.D.*, ed. A.W.H. (5 vols., Oxford, 1842–55), IV, 35.

Thus, writing around 1603, and in this following in the footsteps of Erasmus, Luther, and Hubmaier, Bacon conflates the distinction between God's preached or revealed and secret will (or the will of his good pleasure) with that between his ordinary power and the power by which he can (and does) derogate from that ordinary dispensation.[93] Though the *voluntas dei beneplaciti/signi* distinction is not necessarily foreign to them (Mersenne, Hobbes, Charleton all refer to it),[94] Bacon's conflation of it with the power distinction is not to be found in the works of that "community of thinkers who," as Margaret Osler has claimed, "shared a fairly explicit concern to formulate a mechanical philosophy to provide metaphysical foundations for ... [contemporary] ... developments in natural philosophy," who "knew each other personally and reacted to each other's work," and whose thinking "still bore the mark of ideas that had been forged in medieval debates about the relationship between God's absolute and ordained powers."[95] Prominent among those thinkers were Marin Mersenne, René Descartes, Thomas Hobbes, Pierre Gassendi, and Walter Charleton.

Of this group, and in his treatment of the power distinction, it was Mersenne who hewed to the most traditionalist line. Thus, although in his massive and unfinished commentary on the book of Genesis he contrasted the *potentia absoluta* (or *extraordinaria*) with *potentia ordinaria* rather than *ordinata*, appearing to align the latter with action in accord with the order of nature and the common course of things, he also commended to the reader Aquinas's classical formulation of the distinction in the *Summa theologiae*.[96] Accordingly, he

---

[93] Francis Bacon, *A Confession of Faith*, in *The Works of Francis Bacon*, eds. James Spedding, Robert Leslie Ellis and Douglas Denon Heath (14 vols., London, 1859–74), VII, 220–24.

[94] Marin Mersenne, *Quaestiones celeberrimae in Genesim* (Paris, 1623), cols. 329–30; Thomas Hobbes, *The Quaestions Concerning Liberty, Necessity and Chance Clearly Stated and Debated Between Dr. Bramhall, Bishop of Derry, and Thomas Hobbes of Malmesbury* (London, 1656), pp. 10–11, 78–79; Walter Charleton, *The Darknes of Atheism dispelled by the Light of Nature: a physico-theologicall Treatise* (London, 1652), pp. 353–54; cf. 125–26.

[95] Margaret J. Osler, *Divine will and the mechanical philosophy: Gassendi and Descartes on contingency and necessity in the created world* (Cambridge, 1994), pp. 6 and 154. She continues (at p. 154): "In the seventeenth century, when interest in natural philosophy was rising, these medieval ideas [concerning the divine omnipotence] were transformed into views about the epistemological status of knowledge about the world." Osler advances her argument with specific reference to Descartes and Gassendi but it applies in some measure to the whole group of thinkers to whom she refers.

[96] See above, p. 287 and n. 29.

stressed that while we say that what God has actually willed to do he does by his ordinary power, we must also acknowledge the contingency of that willed course of events. For by his absolute power (which reaches to everything that does not involve a contradiction) God could have chosen to do things other than those he actually preordained to come about, even to the extent of making worlds better than he did.[97]

Descartes' concern to vindicate the divine freedom and omnipotence, however, went much further than that—too far, indeed, to permit him to hedge in the absoluteness of God's power even by so modest a limitation as that constituted by the law of non-contradiction. In common with so many of the scientists of his day, he viewed the laws of nature as imposed on the physical world by God, just as (he says) "a king establishes laws in his kingdom." Unlike those scientists, however, and unlike Mersenne to whom he made the point in two famous letters of 1630, he insisted that God's supreme legislative power extends even to the "eternal truths" of mathematics which he "has established" and which, like the rest of creation, are "entirely dependent" on him. Just as he was free not to create the world, so too (though the very thought defies our merely human comprehension) was he free so to act from all eternity that not all the lines from the center of a circle to its circumference would be equal or that twice four should not make eight.[98]

Having, like Mersenne, been a pupil of teachers at the Jesuit college of La Flèche for whom Suárez's *Metaphysical Disputations* was the *chef d'oeuvre* in metaphysics, and being himself directly acquainted with the philosophical commentaries of the Coimbrans,[99] it is not

---

[97] Mersenne, *Quaestiones celeberrimae in Genesim*, cols. 331–33. For the general background to this work, see Peter Dear, *Mersenne and the Learning of the Schools* (Ithaca and London, 1988), esp. pp. 48–79.

[98] Descartes, Letters to Mersenne, April 15 and May 27, 1630, in *Oeuvres de Descartes*, ed. Charles Adam and Paul Tannery (11 vols., Paris, 1964–74), I, 145, 151–52; also his *Meditationes de prima philosophia*, Resp. ad sextas objectiones, *ibid.*, VII, 436. Cf. his Letter to Mesland, May 2, 1644, in *ibid.*, IV, 118–19. Van den Brink, *Almighty God*, p. 101 n. 30, rightly notes that "at all these places Descartes uses perfect tenses in describing God's power," so that they are instances strictly speaking, not of what God "could make" true, but of "what he could *have made* true."

[99] As Descartes himself acknowledges—see his letter to Mersenne, September 30, 1640, in *Oeuvres de Descartes*, ed. Adam and Tannery, III, 185. Cf. Étienne Gilson, *Index Scholastico-Cartésien* (2nd rev. ed. Paris, 1979), p. iv. For Descartes and the scholastics, see also Roger Ariew, "Descartes and scholasticism: the intellectual background to Descartes' thought," in *The Cambridge Companion to Descartes*, ed. John

surprising that Descartes, too, alludes to the power distinction. The terms he uses are *potentia extraordinaria et ordinaria*, thereby suggesting the notion of a presently active absolute power. Nevertheless, he is adamant in his insistence that if, in the absoluteness of his power, God had indeed created those eternal truths the denial of which would constitute a logical contradiction,[100] he had also created them to be *necessary* and immutable. As a result, they are conserved in perpetuity by the "ordinary concourse" or ordinary power and are not subject, accordingly, to any intrusion by the absolute power.[101] Further than that, he also claims that those eternal truths are imprinted on our minds "just as a king would imprint his laws on the hearts of all his subjects had he power enough to do so." But we should not assume those truths to be changeable by God in the same way as human laws are subject to change by a king. To any such suggestion, he insists, the answer must needs be that

> Yes [he can change them] if his will can change.—But I understand them to be eternal and immutable.—And I judge God likewise [to be eternal and immutable].[102]

So it is, in effect, on grounds not only of God's omnipotence but also of his immutability that Descartes laid the foundations for the *a priori* demonstrative science he wished to vindicate. For him, as Kenny has put it, it is the immutable will of God which lays down

> the laws of nature, which are enshrined in the eternal truths [including] . . . not only the laws of logic and mathematics, but also the law of inertia and other laws of motion . . . [and which] provide the foundation of mechanistic physics. The physics is immutable, because God's will is immutable.[103]

Cottingham (Cambridge, 1992), pp. 58–90, and Dennis Des Chene, *Physiologia: Natural Philosophy in Late Aristotelian and Cartesian Thought* (Ithaca and London, 1996).

[100] Van den Brink, *Almighty God*, p. 96, where he adds that Descartes included under the rubric of eternal truths, not only mathematical truths, but also "fundamental physical intentions" as well as "logical metaphysical and even moral principles."

[101] The passages concerning the extraordinary/ordinary power distinction occur in the *Meditationes de prima philosophia*, Resp. ad sextas objectiones, and in the *Epistola ad. G. Voetium*, in *Oeuvres de Descartes*, ed. Adam and Tannery, VII, 434–35, and VIII 2, 162–68. For the *concursus ordinarius*, see the *Principia philosphiae, ibid.*, VIII 1, 61, and the comment in Des Chene, *Physiologia*, pp. 319–24.

[102] Letter to Mersenne, April 15, 1630, *Oeuvres de Descartes*, ed. Adam and Tannery, VII, 145–46.

[103] Kenny, *The God of the Philosophers*, pp. 16–22 (at 21–22)—a very lucid account. Cf. Edward B. Davis, "God, Man and Nature: The Problem of Creation in Cartesian Thought," *Scottish Journal of Theology*, 44 (1991), 325–48, who comments (347) that:

The bracketing of the absolute or extraordinary power of God which this position involved does not appear, however, to have recommended itself to Pierre Gassendi, with whom (along with other members of their circle and acting at Descartes' request) Mersenne had shared for comment and criticism the manuscript of the *Meditations*.[104] Unlike Descartes' version of the mechanical philosophy, Gassendi's reflects the convergence between a voluntarist theology, a "nominalist" epistemology, and a commitment to empirical methods seen as the only means of access to knowledge in a radically contingent world.[105] Although he refers to the related distinction between absolute necessity and necessity *ex suppositione*, he does not explicitly invoke the power distinction as such. Osler has argued, nonetheless, that the dialectic of the *potentia dei absoluta/ordinata* "provided the conceptual background for his voluntarist theology," and that he was committed to the view that God, who can do anything that does not involve a contradiction, "is free from the laws of nature which he constituted by his own free will." Against Descartes and his created eternal truths he was led, then, to emphasize the contingency of "the course of nature" or "General Order of Causes and Effects" that God has "ordained and instituted from all eternity," as also to insist that

> If some of the natures [of things] are immutable and eternal and could not be otherwise than they are, God would not have existed before them. Otherwise such things would not be natures. . . . The thrice great God is not, as Jupiter of the poets is to the fates, bound by things created by him, but can by virtue of his absolute power [*absoluta sua potentia*] destroy anything that he has created.[106]

"For a demonstrative science of nature to be possible, God's absolute power had to be constrained by God's ordained power." Davis also makes an interesting (if inconclusive) suggestion (345–6) about shared intellectual sympathies between Descartes and the Puritan theologian, William Ames (see above, pp. 305–6). Ames was professor of theology at the University of Franeker in Friesland in 1629 when Descartes was enrolled there. It should be noted that no real scholarly consensus exists on the interpretation of Descartes' teaching on the creation of the eternal truths. The literature on the issue is extensive—see the listing in Osler, *Divine Will and the Mechanical Philosophy*, p. 121 n. 13. I found particularly helpful Osler's own account (pp. 118–52), Van den Brink's *Almighty God*, pp. 95–115 (a good critical and synoptic account), Davis, "The Problem of Creation in Cartesian Thought," and Kenny, *The God of the Philosophers*.

[104] Osler, *Divine Will and the Mechanical Philosophy*, p. 111.

[105] Here, and in what follows, I am dependent on Osler, *Divine Will and the Mechanical Philosophy*—see esp. pp. 34, 53–56, 94, 153–55, 164–65.

[106] Pierre Gassendi, *Disquisitio metaphysica seu dubitationes et instantiae adversus Renatus Cartesii metaphysicam et responsa*, ed. and trans. Bernard Rochat (Paris, 1962), p. 481;

Even clearer, if anything, in his ascription to God of a presently-active absolute power is Walter Charleton, another member of the partially visible, partially invisible "college" linked with Mersenne. Charleton was an Anglican, a royalist, and physician to Charles I. He may have spent some time in the early 1650s in Paris, and he certainly embraced with enthusiasm Gassendi's version of the mechanical philosophy, which he was largely responsible for introducing and popularizing in England.[107] Conscious of the importance of the scholastic heritage[108] and insistent on the overriding omnipotence of God, he affirmed (in medieval fashion) the concomitant possibility that God, whose prerogative it is to know no impossibility, could have created had he so wished a plurality of worlds.[109] That he had chosen not to do, but having, in the world he had actually willed into being, "ordained, enrolled and enacted by the counsel of an infinite Wisdome" the "immutable Tenor, or settled course" which "all things observe," like an "absolute Monarch he has not failed to reserve to himself an absolute superiority, or capacity, at pleasure to infringe, transcend, or pervert" to "the causation of some extraordinary effect" those "ordinary and establisht Laws of Nature." And, as if to dispel any possible doubt remaining, he goes on to say:

> God hath, in times prelapsed, frequently manifested his prerogative of causing effects not only superior but also contradictory to the *ordinary and establish Laws of Nature*, his *ordinary* instrument, when such effects seemed either necessary or expedient to his Providence, and therefore our Conclusion, viz. that his arme is not shortned, and he can doe the like in the future, upon any occasional emergency designed by his *secret counsel*; comes not much short of perfectly Apodictical.[110]

"At non fuit Deus ante naturas [rerum], si illae quidam immutabiles, ac aeternae fuerunt; si aliter, quam sint, esse non potuerunt; . . . Cum vero non, ut Jupiter Poëtarum fatis, ita Deus ter-maximus rebus a se conditis alligetur; sed absoluta sua potentia destruere quicquid condidit, possit." I reproduce Osler's translation of this passage—*Divine Will and Mechanical Philosophy*, p. 1; cf. pp. 153–65.

[107] See Lindsay Sharp, "Walter Charleton's Early Life, 1620–1659, and the Relationship to Natural Philosophy in Mid-Seventeenth Century England," *Annals of Science*, 30 (1973), 311–40; Margaret J. Osler, "Descartes and Charleton on Nature and God," *Journal of the History of Ideas*, 40 (1979), 445–56.

[108] Charleton, *The Darkness of Atheism*, sig. a2r–a3r.

[109] Walter Charleton, *Physiologia-Epicuro-Gassendo-Charletoniana*: or *A Fabrick of Science Natural, Upon the Hypothesis of Atoms* (London, 1654), pp. 11–14. This work comes close at times to being a verbatim English rendering of Gassendi's *Animadversiones in decimum librum Diogenis Laerti* (1649)—see Osler, *Divine Will and Mechanical Philosophy*, p. 195; *idems*. "Descartes and Charleton on Nature and God," 446–47. Cf. Charleton *The Darknes of Atheism*, p. 237.

[110] Charleton, *The Darkness of Atheism*, pp. 70–71 (referring to "a miraculous dis-

As the invocation of the "secret counsel" of God and an affiliated reference to the inscrutability of "the Polity of God" suggest, Charleton is at least inclined to align with God's "concealed will" (which he discusses elsewhere) the absolute power of extraordinary interposition, and with the "revealed will" that "ordinary Providence which sustains the normal course of things."[111] But Hobbes, another member of the Mersenne circle in Paris, though he mentioned the secret and revealed will, betrayed no similar inclination. "The Protestant doctors," he noted, ". . . did use to distinguish between the secret and revealed Will of God; the former they called *voluntas beneplaciti*, which signifieth absolutely his Will, the other *voluntas signi*, that is, the signification of his Will."[112] Hobbes made that acknowledgment in the course of his controversy with Bishop Bramhall over free will and determinism, and Bramhall was quick to note that he was, in fact, "beholding to the Schools" for the distinction and would have done well more generally "to retain the ancient School terms; for want of which his discourse is still ambiguous and confused."[113] Among the terms not retained, it turns out, are *potentia dei absoluta et ordinata*, which Bramhall himself introduces more than once into the exchange, clearly favoring himself the "classical" usage.[114] But if Hobbes does not explicitly invoke that traditional distinction, even where (as in his commentary on his friend Thomas White's *De mundo*) it might have helped forward his argument, he certainly comes close to so doing.[115] For in the third part of *Leviathan* he contrasts mira-

---

pensation" from the laws of nature), 129–30, 136–37, 152, 217. Cf. Charleton, *The Harmony of Natural and Positive Divine Laws* (London, 1682), p. 11.

[111] Charleton, *The Darkness of Atheism*, pp. 125–26 and 353–54 where, speaking of "the Arcana of God's Decrees," he explicitly invokes the distinction between the hidden and revealed wills.

[112] Hobbes, *The Quaestions Concerning Liberty, Necessity and Chance*, pp. 10–11, 78–79.

[113] Bramhall, *Castigations of Mr. Hobbes his last Animadversions in the case Concerning Liberty and Natural Necessity* (1657), in *Works*, IV, 177–506 (at 211, 239).

[114] Bramhall, *Castigations, ibid*, 245, where, speaking of the fallen angels, he says: "God could by his absolute power have kept them in their first estate, yet He would not. By his absolute power, He can do all things which do not imply contradiction or imperfection: but by His ordinate power He cannot change His decrees, or alter what He hath ordained." Cf. *ibid.*, 315, and his *A Vindication of True Liberty from Antecedant and Extrinsecal Necessity* (1655), in *Works*, IV, 3–196 (at 77–78). For Bramhall's controversy with Hobbes, see Samuel I. Mintz, *The Hunting of Leviathan* (Cambridge, 1962), ch. 6, pp. 110–26, and for Hobbes and theology in general, A.P. Martinich, *The Two Gods of Leviathan: Thomas Hobbes on Religion and Politics* (Cambridge, 1992).

[115] Especially in relation to the old question White raised in his "Third Dialogue" as to whether "the existing world is the best of those creatable"—see Thomas

cles, "supernatural works" effected "by the immediate hand of God" with those things that "proceed from nature (which is not the immediate, but the ordinary work of God)" and that reflect *"his operation by the way of nature, ordained in the creation."*[116] And though the precise terms are not used, what is involved here is an evocation of the distinction between the extraordinary and ordinary providence of God.

Among the thinkers of the next generation who were concerned with natural philosophy and had intellectual affiliations with one or more of the Mersenne-Gassendi group, John Locke (and in this like Hobbes) nowhere explicitly invokes the power distinction as such. But it is clearly presupposed (and, in his case, in its classical form) in the argument he advances in one of his early essays on the natural law.[117] In the case, however, of Robert Boyle, "the great father figure of British natural philosophy in his time,"[118] the reliance on the distinction is quite explicit. It is put in terms of overlapping con-

Hobbes, *Thomas White's "De Mundo" Examined*, ed. H.W. Jones (London, 1976), pp. 390–94.

[116] *Leviathan*, III, ch. 37; ed. Michael Oakeshott (Oxford, 1946), 285–91. George Wright, "1688 Appendix to Leviathan," *Interpretation*, 18 (No. 1, 1991), 323–413 (at 347 n. 78) views this as an instance of the *potentia dei absoluta/ordinata* distinction. Martinich, *The Two Gods of Leviathan*, pp. 236–45, points out that this chapter of *Leviathan* contains "two inconsistent discussions of miracles," with the difference between them pivoting on the matter of who can perform them—whether some "extraordinary minister" of God or God himself. I focus here on the second of those alternatives. Hobbes's discussion of miracles and Martinich's interpretation of that discussion together form one of the points at issue between Martinich and a fellow Hobbes specialist—see Edward Carley, "Calvin and Hobbes, or Hobbes as an Orthodox Christian," Aloysius P. Martinich, "On the Proper Interpretation of Hobbes's Philosophy," and Edward Carley, "Reply to Professor Martinich," all in *Journal of the History of Philosophy*, 34 (No. 2, 1996), 257–87.

[117] See Essay VII, in John Locke, *Essays on the Law of Nature*, ed. and trans. W. Von Leyden (Oxford, 1954), esp. pp. 192–93, 198–201. For the point in question, see Francis Oakley and Elliot W. Urdang, "Locke, Natural Law, and God," *Natural Law Forum*, 11 (1966), 92–109 (at 104–105), and Francis Oakley, "Locke, Natural Law, and God—Again," *History of Political Thought*, XVIII (No. 4, 1997), 624–51 (see above, ch. 7).

[118] The words quoted are those of J.E. McGuire, "Boyle's Conception of Nature," *Journal of the History of Ideas*, 33 (No. 4, 1972), 523–42 (at 524). For other discussions emphasizing the theological dimension of Boyle's scientific thinking, see Eugene M. Klaaren, *The Religious Origins of Modern Science* (Grand Rapids, Mich., 1977), Oakley, *Omnipotence, Covenant and Order*, ch. 3, pp. 67–92, 142–51; Margaret J. Osler, "The intellectual sources of Robert Boyle's philosophy of nature," in *Philosophy, science, and religion in England 1640–1700*, eds. Richard Kroll *et al.* (Cambridge, 1992), pp. 178–98; Jan W. Wojcik, "The theological context of Boyle's *Things above Reason*," in *Robert Boyle Reconsidered*, ed. Michael Hunter (Cambridge, 1994), pp. 139–55; Jan W. Wojcik, *Robert Boyle and the Limits of Reason* (Cambridge, 1997). Hunter's "Introduction" to *Robert Boyle Reconsidered*, 1–5, gives a useful overview of the current state of Boyle studies.

trasts between the extraordinary and ordinary providence of God, between God's "absolute or supernatural power," by virtue of which he is "able to do whatever involves no contradiction," and his "ordinary and upholding concourse," between God's exercise of his irresistible power and that "general concourse [by which he] maintained the order of nature"—between, in effect, those "extraordinary interpositions" of God's power by which he can "suspend" or "overrule or control" the "instituted order" or "ordinary and settled course of nature," or "settled laws of nature" established by his will. As, indeed, he actually did when he miraculously delivered the three youths from the natural action of the cruel flames in Nebuchadnezzar's furnace.[119]

Although there appears to be a growing disposition among historians of science to embrace the idea that "the theological framework of *potentia dei absoluta et ordinata* guided Newton and many of his contemporaries when they inquired into the relationship between God and the world,"[120] Newton himself did not explicitly invoke the distinction in any of its forms.[121] Nor did any of the other scientific *virtuosi* give it the prominence which it had received at the hands of Boyle. Among the leading philosophers of the era, it is true, Spinoza clearly acknowledged its currency, understanding the *potentia dei absoluta/*

---

[119] Robert Boyle, *Some Considerations about the Reconcilableness of Reason and Religion*, in *The Works of the Honourable Robert Boyle*, ed. Thomas Birch, new ed. (6 vols., London, 1772), IV, 161–63; *The Excellency of Theology or the Pre-eminence of the Study of Divinity above that of Natural Philosophy*, ibid., 12; *Advices on judging of things said to transcend reason*, ibid., 462–63; *A Disquisition about the Final Causes of Natural Things*, *Works*, V, 412–14; *A Free Inquiry into the Vulgarly received notion of Nature*, ibid., 162–64, 197–98, 211, 216, 213; *The Christian Virtuoso: showing that by being addicted to Experimental Philosophy, a man is rather assisted than indisposed to be a good Christian*, ibid., 520–21. The episode of Nebuchadnezzar's fiery furnace (which Boyle invokes twice in the above-cited texts and again in *Some physico-Theological considerations about the possibility of the resurrection*, *Works*, IV, 201–202) had long been a favorite one invoked (as with Ockham) either to illustrate the contingency of natural or secondary causality or (as with those who viewed the *potentia dei absoluta* as a presently-active power or equated it with God's extraordinary providence) to illustrate an actual intrusion of the absolute power to set aside the natural order established *de potentia ordinata*. It was invoked to serve the latter purpose in the works of Aegidius Romanus, d'Ailly, Biel, Mair, Erasmus, Luther, Eck, Suarez, Perkins, Ames, Preston, Mather, Shepard, Bramhall and Boyle.

[120] Thus B.J.T. Dobbs, *The Janus faces of genius: The role of alchemy in Newton's thought* (Cambridge, 1991), pp. 110–13 (at 110), and the pertinent works cited in nn. 45 and 46; James E. Force, "Newton's God of Dominion," in James E. Force and Richard H. Popkin, *Essays on the Context, Nature and Influence of Isaac Newton's Theology* (Dordrecht, 1990), pp. 75–102.

[121] Though see J.E. McGuire, "Force, Active Principles, and Newton's Invisible Realm," *Ambix*, 15 (No. 3, 1968), 154–208 (at 190–91).

ordinata version in its classical sense, and linking the notion of a presently-active power of divine interposition instead with the *potentia extraordinaria/ordinaria* variant.[122] But given the nature of his metaphysical commitments it can have had little play in his own thinking. Moreover, while there are intriguing questions to be pursued concerning its relationship with cognate distinctions pertaining to the divine power and will that one encounters in the works of such contemporaries and successors as Blaise Pascal, Nicolas Malebranche and Bishop Berkeley, voluntarists all, we can do no more here than simply signal the existence of such questions.[123] What we can and should do, however (as we eavesdrop upon the unfamiliar melodies of the following century), is to take note at least of the powerful echoes of the Scotistic-juristic understanding of the power distinction still to be heard in the *Theologia naturalis* of that great philosophical systemizer, Christian Wolff. For in that work, and in the context of his discussion of divine providence, he invokes related distinctions

---

[122] See his *Principia philosophiae more Geometrico demonstrata, Appendix continens Cogitata metaphysica*, cap. IX *De potentia dei*, §§ 4 and 5; in Benedictus de Spinoza, *Opera quae supersunt omnia*, ed. C.H. Bruder (3 vols., Leipzig, 1843–46), I, 134. Cf. the related passages listed s.v. *Absolutus* and *Potentia* in Emilia G. Boscherini, *Lexicon Spinozianum* (2 vols., The Hague, 1970), I, 5–7, II, 850–55.

[123] See Pascal's discussion of the contrast between God's "volonté absolue" and his "volonté générale et conditionelle"—*Ecrits et fragments de Pascal sur la grace*, in *Oeuvres de Blaise Pascal*, ed. Leon Brunschsvigg *et al.* (14 vols., 1904–1914), XI, 128–44. Similarly, for Malebranche's distinction between God's action by a *volonté générale* and by *volontés particulières*, or between "the ordinary course of [God's] *providence générale*" and a "particular and miraculous providence," see Ginette Dreyfus, *La Volonté selon Malebranche* (Paris, 1955) and Nicolas Malebranche, *Treatise on Nature and Grace*, ed. and trans. Patrick Riley (Oxford, 1992), esp. Riley's fine introduction, (pp. 1–103) which discusses at some length the rich and highly pertinent interchanges on these matters among Antoine Arnaud, Leibniz and Malebranche. For these, see also Donald R. Rutherford, "Natures, Laws, and Miracles: The Roots of Leibniz's Critique of Occasionalism," in *Causation in Early Modern Philosophy: Cartesianism, Occasionalism, and Preestablished Harmony*, ed. Steven Nadler (University Park, Penn., 1993), pp. 136–58, and Steven Nadler, "Choosing a Theodicy: The Leibniz-Malebranche-Arnauld Connection," *Journal of the History of Ideas*, 55 (No. 4, 1994), 573–89. And again, "Nature" being for him nothing but "the Ordinance of the free Will of God" and the "laws of nature or morality" being but "so many decrees of the divine will," Berkeley's discrimination between God's sustenance of "the ordinary course of things" (or his "operations . . . [that are] regular and uniform") and his "interruption" of the "natural course" by a miracle—or, put differently, his choosing to "display his overruling power in producing some appearance out of the ordinary series of things"—see Notebook A in *Works of George Berkeley, Bishop of Cloyne*, ed. A.A. Luce and T.E. Jessup (9 vols., London and Edinburgh, 1948–57), I, 95; *idem, Principles of Human Knowledge, Works*, II, 53–54, 65, 67–68; *Sermon on the Will of God, Works*, VII, 129–30.

between God's "ordinary concourse" (by which he sustains the natural order) and the "extraordinary or miraculous concourse" (by which he acts against it), or, again, between God's "ordinary' or natural and "extraordinary or supernatural" conservation of things.[124]

4. Early-modern usage (iii): Politics and law

Historians of science sympathetic with the "social contextualist" approach to their field,[125] struck in general by the interweaving in the physico-theological arguments of the seventeenth century apologists for science of theological, natural-philosophical and political concerns, and in particular by their explicit invocation of the God-king parallelism, have sometimes been led to make reductive claims to the effect that a particular natural philosophy was actually "generated" with a view to serving social or political ends. Thus James and Margaret Jacob have argued that reforming scientists of conservative

---

[124] Christian Wolff, *Theologia naturalis* (2 vols., Verona, 1779), I, 169–73. The terms used are *concursus dei ordinarius/extraordinarius sive miraculosus; conservatio ordinaria/extraordinaria vero supernaturalis.*

[125] I have particularly in mind the following: James R. Jacob, "The Ideological Origins of Robert Boyle's Natural Philosophy," *Journal of European Studies*, 2 (No. 1, 1972), 1–21; *idem, Robert Boyle and the English Revolution: A Study in Social and Intellectual Change* (New York, 1977); Margaret Jacob, *The Newtonians and the English Revolution: 1689–1720*, new ed. (New York, 1990); James R. and Margaret C. Jacob, "The Anglican Origins of Modern Science: The Metaphysical Foundations of the Whig Constitution," *Isis*, 71 (June, 1980), 251–67; Steven Shapin, "Social Uses of Science," in *The Ferment of Knowledge: Studies in the Historiography of Eighteenth-Century Science*, eds. George S. Rousseau and Roy Porter (Cambridge, 1980), 93–139; *idem,* "Of Gods and Kings: Natural Philosophy and Politics in the Leibniz-Clarke Disputes," *Isis*, 72 (June, 1981), 187–215; *idem,* "Licking Leibniz," *History of Science*, 19 (1981), 298–99. Shapin includes a useful bibliography of works in this genre in his *The Scientific Revolution* (Chicago and London, 1996), pp. 204–5, noting the criticism to which they have been subjected not only by "historians of an 'internalist' disposition" but also by "more sociologically inclined historians." In his *A Social History of Truth: Civility and Science in Seventennth-Century England* (Chicago and London, 1994), he himself takes issue with claims advanced by James R. Jacob at more than one point concerning Boyle. For criticisms of the "social contextualist" approach, see Timothy Shanahan, "God and Nature in the Thought of Robert Boyle," *Journal of the History of Philosophy*, 26 (Oct., 1988), 549–69; Wojcik, *Robert Boyle and the Limits of Reason*, pp. 217–19; Malcolm Oster, "Virtue, providence and political neutralism: Boyle and Interregnum politics," in *Robert Boyle Reconsidered*, ed. Hunter, pp. 18–36, where it is noted (p. 19) that "Jacob's treatment of both Boyle and the Royal Society was open to the charge of being excessively monocausal." In this last work, Hunter offers a balanced (if somewhat negative) appraisal of the contributions of the Jacobses and Shapin.

bent like Boyle and Charleton "*developed* a metaphysics of God and matter that authorized a conservative interpretation of the social hierarchy and answered the radicals by rendering their social views untrue in terms of the conservative metaphysics," so that "a conservative matter theory *was constructed* which outlawed radicalism from the universe."[126] Less implausibly, and with particular reference to the celebrated exchange in 1715–16 between Leibniz and Newton's apologist, Dr. Samuel Clarke, Steven Shapin has seen the God-king parallelism which both men invoked in the course of that exchange as witnessing to the degree to which late seventeenth and early-eighteenth century conceptions of God's attributes and his role in nature functioned in overtly political as well as natural philosophical and theological settings, "For in such settings," he argues, "conflicting conceptions of political and moral order" were "sustained by the invocation of diverging notions of divine and natural order."[127]

It is one of the weaknesses of this approach that it can lead all too readily to the sort of casually reductive claims mentioned above. And that tempts one to insist on the need to measure such "social contextualist" interpretations of philosophical and theological ideas against the longer *philosophical* and *theological* context in which those ideas are embedded.[128] But my purpose here is less to probe the weaknesses of the approach than to call attention to one of its correlative strengths. Namely, the clarity with which it brings into focus the fact that "the cultures of theology, politics, and natural philosophy overlapped because they were connected in legitimations, justifications and criticisms, especially in the use of conceptions of God and nature to comment on political order."[129]

The words are Shapin's and they are written by way of specific commentary on the significance attaching to the God-king paral-

---

[126] Thus Jacob and Jacob, "The Anglican Origins of Modern Science," 252 (italics mine).

[127] I.e., here the explicit emphasis is not on the *generation* of particular views in natural philosophy but on the *use* to which they were put. See Shapin, "Licking Leibniz," 298–99 and his "Of God and Kings," 215. Elsewhere, it is true, Shapin goes much further and speaks of "the natural philosophy of Boyle and the early Royal Society" as having been "generated with a view to . . . social and moral uses"— "History of Science and its Sociological Reconstructions," *History of Science*, 20 (1982), 157–211 (at 182). Cf. the pertinent passages in *The Leibniz-Clarke Correspondence*, ed. H.G. Alexander (Manchester, 1956), pp. 14, 19–20.

[128] See below, pp. 330–31 and nn. 158, 159 and 160.

[129] Shapin, "Of God and Kings," 202.

lelisms that both Clarke and Leibniz invoke in the course of their historic exchange. But if one brings to that exchange some sense of the age-old tradition of theological and philosophical commentary on the divine omnipotence and especially an acquaintance with the five-centuries-old tradition of distinguishing between God's power as absolute and as ordained,[130] two qualifications of Shapin's claim are clearly in order. First, an insistence on the fact that, theologically speaking, there was nothing extraordinary about the God-king parallelisms invoked in that particular exchange, as also on the related fact that such parallelisms were not at home solely in the particular political or constitutional circumstances of the early eighteenth century. Second, a clearer acknowledgment of the fact that the interaction involved between theological and legal/political motifs was by no means unidirectional but rather (and unmistakably) reciprocal. I will address these two points in turn.

First, it is clear that the God-king parallelism has had, over the centuries, a remarkably widespread and enduring appeal. Two and a half centuries after the Clarke-Leibniz exchange, and speaking about "the paradox of Omnipotence" in the very article which put that issue on the agenda of contemporary philosophers working in the Anglo-American analytic tradition, Mackie himself (almost instinctively, it seems) invoked the "parallel Paradox of (legislative) Sovereignty" in an attempt to clarify the point at issue.[131] In so doing, he was unwittingly treading in the footsteps of many a medieval and early-modern author who, long before Clarke and Leibniz initiated their historic correspondence, had done likewise. That that should have been the case with medieval authors who (like Scotus or d'Ailly) favored the juridical or operationalized understanding of the *potentia absoluta* is not, perhaps, too surprising.[132] But such was the obvious appeal of the princely analogy that even Ockham, who hewed to the earlier, classical understanding of the distinction, was led nonetheless to invoke it and to do so in both its papal and regal variants.[133] And a similar pattern is evident in writers of the sixteenth and seventeenth

---

[130] For an attempt to do precisely that, I venture to refer to Oakley, *Omnipotence, Covenant, and Order*, pp. 67–92.

[131] Mackie, "Evil and Omnipotence," 210–12.

[132] Duns Scotus, *Ordinatio*, I, dist. 44, qu. unica, in Balic ed., *Opera omnia* VI, 363–69, *Lectura*, I, dist. 44, qu. unica, *ibid.*, XVII, 535–36; d'Ailly, *Sent.* I, qu. 9, art. 2 M, fol. 120r.

[133] Ockham, *Quodl.* VI, qu. 1, and *Quodl.* VI, qu. 4; ed. Wey, 586 and 598.

centuries as they sought to illustrate the several distinctions between the *potentia dei absoluta et ordinata*, the *voluntas dei beneplaciti et signi*, and the extraordinary and ordinary providence of God. Thus, for example, John Mair, William Perkins, Hugo Grotius, René Descartes, Walter Charleton, Bishop Bramhall and Nehemiah Grew.[134]

But if the invocation of the princely analogy in order to elucidate the working of the divine power was by the eighteenth century something of a cliché, so, too, it should be emphasized, was the invocation of the divine omnipotence in an attempt to clarify the reach of the legal and governmental powers of the human sovereign, whether papal, imperial or royal. Already in the thirteenth century the canonist, Hostiensis, invoking the theological power distinction and flourishing St. Jerome's comment on the sad case of the fallen virgin, had deployed an analogous distinction between the absolute and ordained (or ordinary) power of the pope, attributing thereby to the latter a power of extraordinary interposition to act on occasion apart from or beyond the limits of the law to which he was ordinarily bound.[135] Not long afterwards the theologian and publicist, Aegidius Romanus (d. 1316), elaborated that parallelism repeatedly and at great length. Although by his absolute power, he says, the pope is "without halter and bit," nevertheless he himself ought to regulate his own actions. Thus, although he is above all positive laws, it is fitting that he should govern the church by his "regulated power," that is, in accordance with "the common law," taking in this respect the "example of God himself, whose vicar he is." For God does not normally interfere with the operation of the secondary causes which reflect, after

---

[134] Mair, *In primum Sententiarum* (Paris, 1510), I, dist. 44, qu. 1, fol. ci v; Perkins, *A Treatise of God's free Grace and Man's Free-will*, in *Workes*, I, 704, col. A–B; Hugo Grotius, *De veritate religionis Christianae* (Boston, 1809), Bk. I, § xii, p. 24; Descartes to Mersenne, April 15, 1630, in *Oeuvres des Descartes*, ed. Adam and Tannery, I, 145; Charleton, *The Darknes of Atheism*, pp. 125 and 136; Bramhall, *Castigations of Mr. Hobbes*, in *Works*, IV, 245; Nehemiah Grew, *An Idea of a Phytological History Propounded* (London, 1673), pp. 102–103. Note that the royal analogy readily suggested itself also to those working with the bleak equations of free will and divine election. Se, e.g., Erasmus, *De libero arbitrio*, in *Opera Omnia*, IX, 1241F–1242A; the exchanges between Leibniz, Pierre-Sylvain Régis, Arnauld, Laurent Boursier and Malebranche discussed by Riley in the introduction to his translation of Malebranche's *Treatise on Nature and Grace*, 17–18, 30–36; and Leibniz himself—see his *Essays on the Justice of God and the Freedom of Man in the Origin of Evil*, in G.W. Leibniz, *Theodicy: Essays on the Goodness of God, the Freedom of Man and the Origin of Evil*, ed. Austin Farrer (London, 1951), p. 127.

[135] See above, pp. 282–83, and n. 18.

all, the "common law" with which he governs the universe. In God and the pope alike, however, there resides a plenitude of power by which they can do directly, without the intermediary of secondary causality, whatsoever they can do indirectly by means of them. Thus, for some extraordinary reason, by his "special providence" or "special law," God can act "aside from" the common laws of nature and perform a miracle—as he did in Nebuchadnezzar's fiery furnace. Similarly, for some comparably special reason, the pope can act "aside from" the laws of the church and himself perform a function that is commonly the task of a secondary agent.[136]

In this, the example set by Hostiensis and Aegidius was followed by such canonists as Johannes Andreae (d. 1348), Henricus de Bouhic (d. 1358) and Panormitanus (d. 1445), as also by such theologians as Jacques Almain. It was followed also by the great jurist Baldus de Ubaldis (d. 1400), who, as a commentator on both laws, may have been responsible for introducing the distinction into the civil law. Whatever the case, its subsequent appearance in a range of documents, publicistic as well as legal and quite various in provenance as well as type, suggest that its use was by no means uncommon.[137]

By the beginning of the sixteenth century, then, the legal version of the distinction, with its affirmation of a presently (if only extraordinarily) active *potestas absoluta* pertaining to popes, emperors and kings, had become current among canonists and civilians alike. And it was poised to enjoy a career of service in the sixteenth and seventeenth centuries at the hands of Romanizing jurists exploring the range (and limits) of the prerogatives enjoyed by the kings of France, Hungary, Spain and England.[138] Thus Innocent de Gentillet (d. 1595),

---

[136] Summarizing here Aegidius Romanus, *De eccesiastica potestate*, Lib. III, caps. 2, 3 and 9; Lib. IV, cap. 7, ed. Richard Scholz (Weimar, 1929), pp. 149–52, 156–59, 181–82, 190–95. Note that Courtenay, *Capacity and Volition*, p. 100, citing a sentence from Lib. III, cap 7 (181–82) concerning the pope's temporal jurisdiction claims that "Giles does not equate *plenitudo potestatis* with *potentia absoluta* either for pope or God." But here Randi, *Il sovrano e l'orologiaio*, pp. 92–3, strikes me as accounting in more satisfactory fashion for all the pertinent passages in Aegidius's treatise and esp. for III, cap. 9.

[137] I draw here and in what follows from Oakley, "Jacobean Political Theology," (see above, ch. 8), to which reference should be made for the works cited. In addition to the pertinent literature cited in that article, see also Almain, *Expositio circa decisiones Magistri Guilielmi Occam super potestate ecclesiastica et laica*, in Dupin, II, 1091–92, 1095, *idem*, *De dominio naturali civili et ecclesiastico*, *ibid.*, 968, and the pertinent canonistic texts cited in K.W. Nörr, *Kirche und Konzil bei Nicolaus de Tedeschis* (Cologne, 1964), pp. 47–49, 51.

[138] For the use of the distinction in relation to the power of the fifteenth-century

Bartholomaeus de Chasseneuz (d. 1541), and Jean Bodin himself (d. 1596) all made full use of the distinction, discriminating between those acts which the king did of "his absolute power" and those which he did of his "ordinary," "civil" or "regulated" power or in accordance with his "ordinary right." Thus invoking in support of his own use of the distinction the authority of no lesser a canonist than Pope Innocent IV (d. 1254), Bodin spoke of the prince as being able by his "absolute power" to "derogate from the ordinary right" (i.e. "the laws of his country") though not from the laws of God or of nature.[139] And the fact that Lambert Daneau, queasy enough about the theological version of the distinction, felt it necessary to reject outright the validity of the legal version is perhaps indicative of the extent to which it was current.[140]

Certainly, such students of the Roman law as the expatriate Scot, William Barclay (d. 1608), or in England, James Cowell (d. 1611) and Albericus Gentilis (d. 1608), did not hesitate to deploy the distinction in their own analyses of regal power. The less so, it may be, in that by the early seventeenth century it had long since (and somewhat more surprisingly) established a presence among practitioners of the English common law.[141] And, as the distinction between the "absolute" and "ordinary" powers of the king that has so puzzled (and exasperated) English constitutional historians, it moved to the center stage of English politics in the great Stuart state trials of the first half of the seventeenth century—Bate's Case (1606), the Post-Nati Case (1608), Darnel's Case (1627), and the Ship-Money Case (1637).[142]

Hungarian monarchs, see Joseph Holub, "Ordinaria potentia—absoluta potentia," *Revue historique de droit français et étranger*, 4th ser., 28 (No. 1, 1950), 92–99. And for its use and rejection (as *potestas absoluta/ordinaria*) in relation to the prerogatives of the sixteenth- and seventeenth-century Spanish monarchs, see José-Antonio Maravall, *La Philosophie politique espagnole au xvii siècle*, trans. Louis Cazes et Pierre Mesnard (Paris, 1955), pp. 159–71.

[139] For the pertinent references, see Oakley, "Jacobean Political Theology," 329–31, nn. 35, 39, 41 (see above, ch. 8).

[140] Lambert Daneau, *Ethices Christianae Libri Tres*, Lib. II, in Daneau, *Opuscula omnia theologica* (Geneva, 1583), col. 129b. For his treatment of the theological version of the distinction, see above, p. 304 and n. 81.

[141] Oakley, "Jacobean Political Theology," 324–25. It had appeared as *potentia ordinata et absoluta* and as early as 1469 in the Year Book for that date—see YB 9 Edward IV, Trin. 9; ed. as *Les Reports des Cases en Ley du Roy Edward le Quart* (London, 1680).

[142] The most complete of these formulations is that contained in Chief Baron Fleming's judgment in Bate's Case, where he says: "The King's power is double,

Of the many English invocations of the distinction in these and related legal and political settings during the first half of the seventeenth century three stand out as being most deeply (and intriguingly) embedded in the theological tradition: those of Edward Forset in 1606, Sir John Davies, Attorney-General for Ireland and writing towards the end of James I's reign, and James I himself, speaking or writing in 1609/10 and 1616. Thus Forset:

> For as we rightly conceive of God, that albeit he worketh efficiently and . . . *naturally*, by the mediate causes, yet his potencie is not by them tied or confined, but that he often performeth his owne pleasure by *extraordinarie* meanes, drawne out of his absolute power, both *praeter et contra naturam*.

And the corollary:

> To this likeness of God . . ., let us also shape our [regal] Soveraigntie: which (because that which is regular in regiment, and from his power and goodness, imparted unto the people) hath still, and reteineth to itselfe certain prerogative rights of most ample extentions . . . whereof . . . true reverence . . . admitteth no questioning disputes.[143]

Similarly, Sir John Davies who, having told us that "by the positive law the King himself was pleased to limit and stint his absolute power, and to tye himself to the ordinary rules of the Law, in common and ordinary cases," goes on to emphasize that he retained and reserved nonetheless and "in many points that absolute and unlimited power which was given unto him by the law of Nations." So that he "doth exercise a double power, *viz.* an absolute, or *Merum Imperium* which is not bound by the positive Law; and an ordinary power of Jurisdiction, which doth cooperate with the Law." And in

---

ordinary and absolute and they have several lawes and ends. That of the ordinary is for the profit of individual subjects, for the execution of civil justice, the determining of *meum*; and this is exercised by equitie and justice in ordinary courts . . . . The absolute power of the king . . . is only that which is applied to the general benefit of the peopl" and is "*alus populi*; . . . and this . . . absolute law [varieth] according to the wisdome of the King, for the common good." The full text may be found in T.B. Howell, *A Complete Collection of State Trials* (33 vols., London, 1816–26), II, 389. Cf. Oakley, "Jacobean Political Theology," 323–24, 339–46 (above, ch. 8), and for more recent discussions of the English usage, Glenn Burgess, *The Politics of the Ancient Constitution: An Introduction to English Political Thought, 1603–1642* (University Park, Penn., 1993), esp. pp. 139–62; *idem. Absolute Monarchy and the Stuart Constitution* (New Haven and London, 1996), pp. 34–36, 92–94.

[143] Edward Forset, *A Comparative Discourse of the Bodies natural and Politique* (London, 1606), pp. 20–21.

this "he doth imitate the Divine Majesty, which in the Government of the world doth suffer things for the most part to passe according to the order and course of Nature, yet many times doth shew his extraordinary power in working miracles above Nature."[144]

But it is James I himself whose formulations are the most striking. In a letter of 1616 to the judges in the case of *commendams*, and evoking "our absolute authoritie royall," James lectured them to the following effect:

> his Majestie had a doble prerogative, whereof the one was ordinary, and had relacion to his private interest, which mought be, and was, every day disputed in Westminster Hall. The other [the absolute] was of a higher nature, referringe to his supreame and imperiall power and soveraigntie, which ought not to be disputed or handled in vulgar argument.[145]

In the same year, in a speech delivered in the Star Chamber, reiterating what he had said earlier in 1609 in a speech to both houses of Parliament, and in this following in the footsteps of the Puritan theologian, William Perkins,[146] James applied the *voluntas beneplaciti/signi* distinction to the exercise of his own royal prerogative.[147] Pursuing in those same two speeches, moreover, the logical trail already blazed by Erasmus, Luther and Hubmaier, he took the further step of conflating the *voluntas beneplaciti/signi* distinction with that between the absolute and ordained power of God.[148] The outcome? An intricate series of overlapping contrasts and analogies. First, between on the one hand what God "can doe" in the absoluteness of his power, which "it is Atheisme and blasphemie to dispute," and, on the other, "his will revealed in his word," which "Divines may

---

[144] Sir John Davies, *The Question concerning Impositions, Tonnage, Poundage* (London, 1656), pp. 30–32.

[145] *Acts of the Privy Council of England, 1615–16* (London, 1925), p. 601.

[146] Perkins had applied the *voluntas benepliciti/signi* distinction to distinguish the secret will of kings from the will they promulgated in their laws—see his *Treatise of God's Free Grace and Man's Free-will*, in *Workes*, I, 704, col. 2 A–B.

[147] James I, "A Speach to the Lords and Commons of the Parliament at White-Hall . . . Anno 1609," in *The Political Works of James I*, ed. Charles Howard McIlwain (Cambridge, Mass., 1918), 307–8; *idem*, "A Speach in the Starre–Chamber . . . Anno 1616," *ibid.*, 333.

[148] For Erasmus, Luther and Hubmaier, see above, pp. 292–93, 301 and nn. 48, 68, 69 and 70. For the argument ensuing, see Francis Oakley, "The 'Hidden' and 'Revealed' Wills of James I: More Political Theology," 365–75, and Oakley, *Omnipotence Covenant, and Order*, pp. 93–122.

lawfully and doe ordinarily dispute and discuss." Second, referring analogously to "the mysterie of the king's power," between what a King "can doe" by his "absolute Prerogative" and "in the height of his power," (which it is "presumption," "high contempt" and "sedition in Subjects to dispute") and "the Kings revealed will in his Law"—i.e. the expression of his "ordinary prerogative" which, as he had written to the judges, was "every day disputed in Westminster Hall." Third, between the deport of God in Old Testament times, when he "spoke by Oracles, and wrought by Miracles," and the freedom from legal restraint characteristic of "the state of Kings in their first originall." Fourth, between God's later governing of "his people and the Church [oracles and miracles having ceased] within the limits of his reveiled will" and the commitment of "setled Kings and Monarches ... in civill Kingdomes," by a "paction" with their people analogous to the covenant which God made with Noah after the flood, to rule in conformity with the will they have revealed to us in their laws.

Not even the evocation in these intriguing statements of a dimension of historical change is wholly without precedent in the long tradition of commentary on the absolute and ordained power of God.[149] And that tradition has to be recognized as constituting the broader intellectual context in which these controversial claims of James I should properly be read. Some years ago, arguing that James "deserves a higher place in the history of systematic political thought" than he has normally been accorded and putting on center stage the speech of 1609 which we have been discussing, W.H. Greenleaf argued that the philosophic foundation of James's whole theory of divine right was "derived from a range of metaphysical notions which collectively may be called 'the idea of order.'" That idea he regarded as "best described," even classically so, in Arthur O. Lovejoy's *Great Chain of Being*, and he viewed it as a theory justifying support for "arbitrary and absolute monarchy" bereft of any "practical or politically important" restraints on the ruler's power.[150] Once they are

---

[149] Cf. Ockham, *Quodl.* VI, qu. 1, ed. Wey, 586.

[150] W.H. Greenleaf, "James I and the Divine Right of Kings," *Political Studies*, 5 (1957), 36–48 (at 48); *idem, Order, Empiricism, and Politics: Two Traditions of English Political Thought: 1500–1700* (London, 1964), pp. 8–9, 40, 47–48, 56, 67, 96, 109, 187; *idem*, "The Thomasian Tradition and the Theory of Absolute Monarchy," *English Historical Review*, 79 (Oct., 1964), 747–60 (at 747–48).

seen, however, in the broader intellectual context we have proposed, it becomes clear that in these central theoretical statements of his James is aligning himself, not with the vision of order expressed in the notion of the great chain of being, but rather with the rival vision that was grounded in will, promise and covenant. And that vision, encapsulated in the *potentia absoluta/ordinata* distinction, while it did vindicate in both its theological and legal variants the ultimate freedom of sovereign choosing and willing, also affirmed the reliably self-binding nature of that sovereign willing and emphasized the degree to which confidence could safely be reposed in its stability. If in its legal variant it did indeed serve the cause of those who wanted to claim that on extraordinary occasions the sovereign could act apart from or even against the law, it was also invoked by those whose purpose it was to underline the existence in ordinary circumstances of legal restraints on a sovereign's exercise of his power.[151] Notwithstanding his rhetorically disastrous ascription to kings in the 1609 speech of the power to "make of their subjects like men at the Chesse," James also chose to deploy the conflated absolute/ordinary power and hidden/revealed will distinction. And that choice invites contemplation of the intriguing possibility that it was his intention by so doing to reassure his understandably edgy audience and to soften for them the otherwise uncompromising contours of what has traditionally been understood as a distressingly absolutistic effusion.[152]

---

[151] Thus compare the following two instances: (i) It was Henry VIII's opinion in relation to his own marital dilemma that "although dispensation to proceed to a second marriage" was "a thing that the Pope perhaps cannot do in accordance with the divine and human laws already written, using his ordinary power," he might possibly be able to do it "of his mere and absolute power, as a thing in which he may dispense above the law"—"Instruction to Sir Francis Bryan and Peter Vannes, sent to the Court of Rome," in *Letters and Papers, Foreign and Domestic, of the reign of Henry VIII*, ed. John S. Brewer (22 vols., London, 1862–1932), IV, part 2, 2158 (No. 4977); and (ii) The posture of the members of one oppositional group who, while conceding that "by his plenitude of power the . . . pope can act above and against the law," appealed to the pope's "ordained" or "regulated" power in order to stress the self-imposed limits within which he should ordinarily operate. For which, see *Appellation deutscher geistlichen von dem executor des vom papste geforderten zehntens an dem päpstlichen stuhl* (1352–60), in *Acta imperii Inedita*, ed. Edward Winkelmann (2 vols., Innsbruck, 1885), II, 843 (No. 1182).

[152] That was the conclusion I myself drew at the end of a much fuller analysis of these statements of James I and of the recent scholarship pertaining to them— see Oakley, *Omnipotence, Covenant, and Order*, pp. 93–118.

5. *The historical significance of the distinction*

As we draw now to a conclusion it is with a somewhat startled recognition of the fact that the trail we have been pursuing has taken us across no less than seven centuries of European intellectual history stretching from Damiani's musings in mid-eleventh century about the sad case of St. Jerome's fallen virgin, via Calvin's stern rejection of arguments pivoting on the postulation of a *potentia dei absoluta*, as also via Chief Baron Fleming's judgment in Bate's Case on the reach of the royal prerogative and Boyle's physico-theologicial explorations of the divine omnipotence, all the way down to Wolff's discussion in mid-eighteenth century of the *concursus ordinarius* and *extraordinarius*. At the end of this *longue durée* some claims and disclaimers are clearly in order, as also some comment on the overall historical significance of the extraordinarily durable historical phenomenon on which it has been our purpose to dwell. And, as is only fitting for any stubborn practitioner of a currently less-than-fashionable historiographic mode, the disclaimers should come first.

So far as the meaning and usage of the absolute/ordained power distinction are concerned, much exploratory work remains to be done. If that is true even for the medieval period, still more does it hold for the sixteenth and seventeenth centuries. In relation to those latter centuries, indeed, one can hardly claim to have done much more than sketch in the principal geographical features on what must necessarily remain a highly provisional map. The range and variety of the literature to be explored and the probing nature of the scrutiny that the pertinent texts require is likely for some time to come to preclude any pretension more ambitious than that. Similarly, and *a fortiori*, even in relation to the works actually discussed, no claim can be made to have been able in every case to assess the precise significance of the role played by the distinction. Again, the number and variety of the texts involved, the degree to which they are embedded in patterns of thought of very different kinds (theological, philosophical, scientific, legal), as well as the richness and complexity of so many of those intellectual patterns—all dictate a prudent degree of deference to the judgment and expertise of those who are specialists on the thought of one leading figure or another.

At the same time, and such considerations notwithstanding, no measure of interpretative diffidence should be permitted to preclude the confident attribution of considerable historical significance to the impressive endurance of the power distinction across so long a stretch of time, as also to its appearance in so many different intellectual arenas.[153] Not least of all, as I have argued elsewhere,[154] because it attests to the presence in so many medieval and early-modern texts, sometimes confusingly juxtaposed with intimations of the scheme of things affiliated with Lovejoy's great chain of being, of a rival vision of order. That rival vision of order—natural, moral, salvational, political, legal—was grounded not in the very natures or essences of things but rather in will, promise and covenant. Only if historians recognize that such radically different conceptions of order may be jostling side by side in the texts confronting them will the perplexities generated by some segments of early-modern legal, theological and scientific thinking be susceptible to dissipation.

To illustrate the force of this claim, two examples must suffice. First, by failing to appreciate the significance of the power distinction in James I's thinking, Greenleaf was led to align the king's political thinking with the idea of order embedded in the notion of the great chain of being. And, more recently, while critical of some of the conclusions Greenleaf had drawn from that alignment, James Daly has done likewise.[155] Long before those two scholars had entered the fray, moreover, a whole generation of English constitutional historians, operating almost totally without reference to the continental analogues, let alone theological parallels, and struggling to make sense of the baffling series of early-modern references to the king's absolute and ordinary powers, had been led to interpret them as referring to the distinction between *gubernaculum* and *jurisdictio* which Charles Howard McIlwain had earlier claimed to have found in the great thirteenth-century English jurist, Henry of Bracton. As a result, they had rejected the possibility that what was intended by such references was a claim that the king possessed an absolute power by

---

[153] Space permits me here to do no more than simply take note of the far-reaching and tenaciously-argued case made for believing that the late-medieval and early-modern preoccupation with divine omnipotence and the *potentia absoluta* played a central role in the emergence of nihilism on the European philosophical scene—see Michael Allen Gillespie, *Nihilism before Nietzsche* (Chicago and London, 1995).

[154] In *Omnipotence, Covenant, and Order.*

[155] James Daly, "The Idea of Absolute Monarchy in Seventeenth-Century England," *Historical Journal*, 21 (No. 2, 1978), 222–50; *idem, Sir Robert Filmer and English Political Thought* (Toronto, 1979), and, especially, *idem, Cosmic Harmony and Political Thinking in Early Stuart England*, in *Transactions of the American Philosophical Society*, n.s. 79, p.t. 7 (Philadelphia, 1979).

virtue of which, and for "great, just and necessary cause," he could
supersede the normal course of the common law. But in this they
were simply mistaken. And what makes it clear that they were mistaken is the recognition of the English prerogative distinction for
what it truly was.[156] Nothing other, in fact, than a manifestation of
that legal, philosophical and theological distinction whose career in
the sixteenth and seventeenth centuries I have been attempting to
trace, and whose origins are to be found in the efforts of medieval
scholastic thinkers to work out the philosophical corollaries of the
biblical notion of God, and, in the teeth of necessitarian ideas of
classical Greek and Arab provenance, to vindicate the freedom and
omnipotence of that God.[157]

The second example is also drawn from the seventeenth century.
While Boyle's physico-theological views have become of recent years
the object of increasing scholarly attention, they have also been the
focus of a good deal of misunderstanding. Thus tending it would
seem to read seventeenth-century intellectual phenomena in terms
both of eighteenth-century culminations and of nineteenth-century
religio-scientific tensions, some have been inclined to view Boyle's
theological moments as residual bric-à-brac carried over from an age
of more secure belief, witnessing at best to his piety as a believer
rather than expressing his convictions as a scientist. Hence his position on miracles has been seen as part of a somewhat demoralized
rear-guard action, a bootless attempt to reconcile his essentially biblical vision of an all-powerful, loving and personal God, from whose
providential purview not even the fall of a sparrow escapes, with his
scientific understanding of the universe as a great machine operating in accordance with those immutable and necessary uniformities
which men call the laws of nature.[158]

---

[156] Drawing, in all of this, from Oakley, "Jacobean Political Theology" (above, ch. 8).

[157] This point of view seems now to be finding some resonance among historians of English political and constitutional thinking. See Corinne Comstock Weston
and Janelle Renfrew Greenberg, *Subjects and Sovereigns: The Grand Controversy over Legal
Sovereignty in Stuart England* (Cambridge, 1981), esp. pp. 10–18; David Wootton ed.,
Divine Right and Democracy (Harmondsworth, Middlx, 1986), pp. 29, 122; J.H.M.
Salmon, "Catholic resistance theory, Ultramontanism, and the royalist response,
1580–1620," in *The Cambridge History of Political Thought: 1450–1700*, ed. J.H. Burns
and Mark Goldie (Cambridge, 1991), pp. 247–49; Burgess, *The Politics of the Ancient
Constitution*, pp. 139–62, and his *Absolute Monarchy and the Stuart Constitution*, pp. 34–36.

[158] Thus Richard R. Westfall, *Science and Religion in Seventeenth-Century England* (New
Haven and London, 1958), esp. pp. 83–92; cf. Franklin L. Baumer, *Religion and the
Rise of Scepticism* (New York, 1960), esp. pp. 79–95.

Read, however, in the context not of what came after but of what went before, of the struggle of the medieval theologians not, indeed, with any mechanical philosophy of seventeenth-century type but with no less threatening deterministic notions of Neoplatonic and Aristotelian provenance, the picture takes on a very different aspect. The more different when the pertinent texts are read also in the light of an acquaintance with the history of the power distinction—itself long since deployed, after all, as a piece of analytic weaponry on that particular front. For Boyle himself invoked that same distinction and, worrying in quite traditional fashion about the threat that Aristotelian determinism posed to God's freedom and omnipotence, put it to similar use. Indeed, pondering the old scholastic conundrum concerning God's ability to make a world better than the one he had in fact chosen to create, and citing the Aristotelian denial to God of both the creation and the providential governance of the world, Boyle was forthright enough to confess that he took "divers of *Aristotle's* opinions relating to religion to be more unfriendly, not to say pernicious to it, than those of several other heathen philosophers"—i.e. the Epicurean atomists.[159]

There is every reason to believe and no reason to doubt that Boyle knew exactly what he was talking about and meant to say precisely what he said. He was tapping, after all, into a long-established and well-recognized theological and philosophical tradition and, in so doing, was prone to employing a pertinent distinction possessed already of five centuries of history. That being so, and bold "social contextualist" claims to a "gain in historicity" notwithstanding, one has to wonder more than a little about redundant expressions of puzzlement concerning his purpose in writing *A Free Inquiry into the Vulgarly Received Notion of Nature* and in mounting the attack on Aristotelianism which it contains.[160] And one has to wonder a great deal more about the further willingness, in the teeth of

---

[159] Boyle, *A Free Inquiry*, in *Works*, ed. Birch, V, 195–96, 163–64. Given Boyle's clear sympathy with Gassendi's version of the mechanical philosophy, this remark can profitably be seen in the context of Gassendi's attempt to Christianize Epicureanism. On which, see Osler, *Divine Will and the Mechanical Philosophy*, and Lisa T. Sarasohn, *Gassendi's Ethics: Freedom in a Mechanistic Universe* (Ithaca and London, 1996).

[160] "Why," J.R. Jacob asks, "was Boyle so concerned to oppose his natural philosophy to the vulgarly received notion [of nature]? Was Aristotelian and Platonic philosophy in 1666 tainted with heresy and atheism? If so, how could this be? For centuries Aristotle had been at the foundation of orthodox Christian thought."— *Robert Boyle and the English Revolution*, pp. 4–5, 159–76.

Boyle's own perfectly comprehensible identification of Aristotelian ideas as his primary target, to insist that his quarrel in *A Free Inquiry* was "less with Aristotle and his scholastic interpreters than with certain contemporaries," people close to court circles and suspected of plotting sedition.[161]

This latter example, moreover, is particularly well-positioned to remind us, by way of conclusion and on a still more general level, that in the often abstruse theological arguments that led first to the development of the power distinction and later to its reshaping and dissemination into other realms of discourse, what we are witnessing is a phenomenon of very wide-ranging intellectual significance indeed. Nothing other, in fact, beneath the shifting play of forces less enduring, than the sort of seismic activity inevitably to be expected along the profound geologic fault that runs right across the conflicted landscape of our Western intellectual tradition, the bumping, the grinding, the subduction of those great tectonic plates of disparate Greek and biblical origin which long ago collided to form the unstable continent of our *mentalité*.

---

[161] Thus Jacob, *Robert Boyle and the English Revolution*, pp. 161–76. For some of the critical literature concerning the "social contextualist" approach and for commentary on current perspectives in Boyle studies, see above, nn. 118 and 125. Malcolm Oster concludes, I think correctly, as follows: "That Boyle (and his Oxford colleagues) in the 1650s consciously developed a new 'Anglican' synthesis crystallised around 'a metaphysics of God and matter that authorized a conservative interpretation of the social hierarchy,' erodes the epistemological, philosophical and theological roots of Boyle's philosophy of nature for a more fundamental, and unwarranted, recourse to socio-political explanation."—"Virtue, providence and political neutralism," in *Robert Boyle Reconsidered*, ed. Hunter, p. 32.

CHAPTER TEN

EPILOGUE: OAKESHOTT'S WILL AND ARTIFICE AND THE MIRROR OF ETERNITY

> To establish the connections, in principle and in detail, directly or mediately, between politics and eternity is a project which has never been without its followers. . . . Probably there has been no theory of the nature of the world, of the activity of man, of the destiny of mankind, no theology or cosmology, perhaps even no metaphysics, that has not sought a reflection of itself in the mirror of political philosophy; certainly there has been no fully considered politics that has not looked for its reflection in eternity.
>
> Michael Oakeshott

In the Introduction to this book I was at pains to distinguish between "the tradition of argument or discourse" that loosely links together Western political philosophizing taken as a whole, and those multiple and specific "traditions of thought," historically identifiable constellations of shared values and beliefs, that are lodged within it. In the wake now of the issues discussed especially in the latter chapters of the book, it is time to turn by way of conclusion to the matter raised at the end of that Introduction. Namely, the status to be accorded to the "three main patterns" or "three great traditions of thought" which Michael Oakeshott saw essentially as sub-traditions providing an element of "significant variety" within the continuous process of reflection upon the human predicament that constituted "the unity of the history of political philosophy."[1] More precisely (though it is pertinent also to the historicity in general of Oakeshott's triadic pattern), the specific matter to be addressed is the historical status to be accorded to his tradition of "Will and Artifice." For that is the tradition, after all, that intersects most intriguingly with the late-medieval and early-modern stream of voluntarist thinking whose course we have been at pains to trace, if not into political thought

---

[1] Michael Oakeshott ed., *The Leviathan of Thomas Hobbes* (Oxford, 1946), Introduction, pp. xi–xiii. The passage from which the superscript is drawn occurs at the same place. See above, Introduction, p. 24.

itself, at least through the realms of theology, epistemology, scientific thinking and ethics, and on into the neighboring territories of natural-law thinking and jurisprudence.

Oakeshott chose to call his patterns "traditions," he tells us, "because it belongs to the nature of a tradition to tolerate and unite an internal variety, not insisting upon conformity to a single character, and because, further, it has the ability to change without losing its identity."[2] Although he nowhere discusses these traditions at any length, he appears to be at one with others evoking comparable triadic patterns or traditions in conceding that "nowhere in the history of political philosophy do we find the three traditions in a 'pure' form," and in giving the impression, therefore, that he was inclined to view them as some sort of "ideal characterization."[3] And historians commenting on such triadic patterns have inclined to concur in that appraisal, bracketing them as "discrete organizing principles" on the part of the historian rather than treating them as features appearing in "genuinely historical narratives." Or again, as "analytic exercises" rather than as "references to historically discriminated patterns of persistence and change," their status, as a result, being "not self-evidently historical."[4] Their persistently triadic character, moreover,

---

[2] *Ibid.*, p. xii.

[3] David Boucher, *Texts in Context: Revisionist Methods for Studying the History of Ideas* (Dordrecht, 1985), p. 137, reports that as communicated to him by Oakeshott in a private letter. In the same place, citing also Dilthey, David Cameron and W.H. Greenleaf, Boucher adds: "The writers who recognize the existence of these traditions seem at once to want to assert that they are historical entities because they are inferred from the evidence, but they also want to suggest that they depart from the conventional form of history insofar as the traditions are, in effect, ideal characterizations." So that, "although this triadic conception of the organization of past political thought is supposed to aid enquiry, the status of the conception itself is not self-evidently historical." Similarly, in response to a query of my own Oakeshott noted (in a private letter dated 23 April, 1959) that he had not chosen to develop elsewhere the brief delineation of the three traditions set forth in his introduction to *Leviathan*, not because he had come "to doubt the usefulness, at a certain level, of this way of speaking about the history of political philosophy, but because I have come to recognize it as an over-bold generalization which would have to be qualified in all sorts of ways in order to be made to stand up satisfactorily."

[4] Andrew Lockyer, "'Traditions' as Context in the History of Political Theory," *Political Studies*, XXVII (No. 2, 1979), 201–17 (at 203); John G. Gunnell, *Political Theory: Tradition and Interpretation* (Cambridge, Mass., 1979), p. 86; Boucher, *Texts in Context*, p. 137. Cf. Francis Oakley, "Medieval Theories of Natural Law: William of Ockham and the Significance of the Voluntarist Tradition," *Natural Law Forum*, VI (1961), 65–83 (at 78); *idem, Omnipotence, Covenant, and Order: An Excursion in the History of Ideas from Abelard to Leibniz* (Ithaca and London, 1984), p. 121.

with its (implicity or explicitly) Hegelian echoes of a dialectical unfolding of the course of history via thesis, antithesis and synthesis, also suggests that their genesis lies in an inspiration that is philosophical rather than historical in nature. So, too, the difficulties one encounters if one attempts to ground some versions, at least, of these traditions—Greenleaf's "Empirical Tradition," for example—in unambiguously historical "principles of influence and explicitness."[5] And yet my own explorations of the late-medieval and early-modern tradition of thought which I have called "voluntarist," (and the historicity of which is, I believe, incontestable"),[6] incline me to view Oakeshott's cognate tradition of Will and Artifice as possessing greater coherence than Greenleaf's analogous "Empirical Tradition," and, Oakeshott's own hesitations notwithstanding, better historical credentials that it seems usual to accord it.

Part of the difficulty involved in coming to terms with the matter springs from the fact that Oakeshott's description of the tradition is a cursory one and has to be reconstructed from references embedded in his commentary on Hobbes, whose *Leviathan* he regarded as the tradition's masterwork. While he appears to have seen its roots as engaged in Greek (Epicurean) soil, he portrays it as drawing its nourishment also from the Roman conception of law and from "the Judaic-Christian conception of will and creation," emerging as a "living tradition" only in the Middle Ages in the thinking of Duns Scotus, William of Ockham and the later-medieval nominalists and voluntarists, before receiving a clear articulation at the hands of Hobbes, who elaborated a "comprehensive system where before there were only scattered aphorisms."[7] And characteristic of that Hobbesian

---

[5] See W.H. Greenleaf, *Order, Empiricism, and Politics: Two Traditions of English Political Thought* (London, 1964), esp. pp. 8–13, 157–206. In this work, as its title suggests, he focused his attention on two antithetical traditions. Later on, however, he sought to embed them in a triadic pattern analogous to that made familiar by his former teacher, Oakeshott. For my comments on this quintessentially idealist mode of shaping the history of political thought, I am especially indebted to the account in Boucher, *Texts in Context*, pp. 118–42.

[6] See Francis Oakley, "Medieval Theories of Natural Law;" *idem*, "Christian Theology and the Newtonian Science: The rise of the concept of the Laws of Nature," *Church History*, XXX (1961), 433–57; *idem*, *The Political Thought of Pierre d'Ailly: The Voluntarist Tradition* (New Haven and London, 1964); *idem*, *Omnipotence, Covenant and Order; idem.* "Lovejoy's Unexplored Option," *Journal of the History of Ideas*, XLVIII (No. 2, 1987), 231–45. Cf. above, chs. 7, 8, 9.

[7] Oakeshott ed., *The Leviathan of Thomas Hobbes*, Introduction, pp. xx–xxi, xxvi–ix, xliv–vi, lii–lv.

system, the thought, as it were, that pervades its parts, is (according to Oakeshott) the understanding of the universe as the contingent creation of an omnipotent divine will and of the "civil order," analogously, as an artificial creation of a concatenation of individual acts of autonomous human willing; the understanding of philosophical knowledge, accordingly as "conditional, not absolute," for "there is no effect which the power of [the omnipotent] God cannot produce in many several ways;"[8] the definition of law, divine and natural no less than human, as the mandate of a sovereign will—the effect, that is, of an efficient cause; the understanding of the civil order no less than the world at large on the analogy of a machine "where to explain an effect we go to its immediate [efficient] cause, and to seek the result of the cause we go to its immediate effect;"[9] and the concomitant banishment from the realm of politics no less than from the natural world of those age-old teleological preoccupations that ill accord with so mechanistic an understanding of reality.

Although by 1945 Oakeshott had become accustomed to schematizing the history of political philosophy in terms of his three traditions, and although he himself "connected . . . [that triadic pattern] more closely with the history of the theory of knowledge" than with that of natural philosophy,[10] the appearance in that year of R.G. Collingwood's *Idea of Nature* served to suggest the intriguing presence of a comparable triadic pattern in the history of human attempts to conceptualize the world of nature. In that book it was Collingwood's argument that "in the history of European thought there have been three periods of constructive cosmological thinking," each of which, the Greek, the early-modern and the modern, produced its own distinctive ideas of nature. And the contrasts between these ideas, he suggests, spring from the differences between their analogical approaches to nature. Whereas the Greek view of nature as an intelligent organism was based on an analogy between the world of nature and the individual human being, the modern was based upon the analogy between the process of the natural world as studied by scientists and the vicissitudes of human affairs as studied by historians. In contrast with both, the early-modern view conceived the world analogically as a machine. Instead of being regarded, Greek-fashion,

---

[8] The words are those of Hobbes, cited by Oakeshott, *ibid.*, p. xxvii.
[9] Oakeshott, *ibid*, p. xxi.
[10] Here citing again Oakeshott's letter to me of 23 April, 1959.

as capable of ordering its own movements in a rational manner and according to its own immanent laws, the motions which it exhibits are imposed from without, and "their regularity . . . due to 'laws of nature' likewise imposed from without" by the omnipotent will of a cosmic sovereign. Collingwood concludes, therefore, that this particular view of nature presupposes both the human experience of designing and constructing machines and the Christian idea of a creative and omnipotent God.[11]

Although Collingwood himself does not use the term "tradition" with reference to these three ideas of nature, the parallelism with Oakeshott's three traditions is an arresting one and certainly deserving of comment. So much so, indeed, that it is hard not to indulge the temptation to describe those traditions as representing, in effect, the reflection which Collingwood's cosmologies find in the "mirror of political philosophy." The parallelism is nowhere closer, it may be, than in the unmistakable alignment between Collingwood's early-modern idea of nature and Oakeshott's tradition of Will and Artifice.[12] And what that alignment strongly suggests is that in any coherent philosophical system, given the connections we have seen in the last three chapters to exist, either by logical implication or by intellectual affinity, among the positions a thinker adopts in natural theology, epistemology, natural, moral, legal and political philosophy, an historian would be wise to keep an eye out for the others when *any* one of the following is present: a biblical (or Qu'ranic) view of God which stresses above all his utter freedom and omnipotence; a nominalist epistemology; a natural philosophy of mechanistic sympathies which stresses the conditional nature of all knowledge based on observation of a created and contingent world; an understanding of the uniformities of nature as (natural) laws grounded in the mandate of a legislating divine will; a similarly voluntaristic conception of the (moral) natural law and of human positive law; and, finally, an essentially "mechanistic" understanding of political society as an artifice based on a specific type of consent, the creation, in effect, of a concatenation of individual (atomistic) acts of human willing.

---

[11] R.G. Collingwood, *The Idea of Nature* (Oxford, 1945), pp. 1–13.
[12] Evoking here the line of argument I first pursued in "Medieval Theories of Natural Law," esp. 78–83. Cf. "Christian Theology and the Newtonian Science," *Omnipotence, Covenant, and Order*, and, above, chs. 7, 8 and 9.

All of these elements are, of course, present in Hobbes, whom Oakeshott describes as the "head and crown" of his tradition of Will artifice and who cannot be fully understood without reference to the late-medieval and early-modern nominalist/voluntarist tradition. But the danger for an historian of approaching less systematic thinkers with the expectations inevitably generated by the intellectual model outlined above is that one may fall into the trap, as Skinner puts it, of being too "*set* in approaching the ideas of the past" and prone, accordingly, to propagating some variant of what he calls "the mythology of coherence."[13] Or, put differently, the danger is that we may be tempted to forget that people in the past did their thinking (as, perforce, do we today) not necessarily as, logically speaking, they *should*, or even as in an ideal philosophical world they *would*, but rather (within their own intellectual limits, and given the customs, challenges, complexities and confusions of their time) simply as they *could*.

That danger can be well illustrated if one turns one's attention back in time to thinkers closer to the headwaters of what I have called the voluntarist tradition. Here controversy has swirled around more than one aspect of Ockham's thinking, but not least of all about his political thinking in general and, more particularly, about his allegedly crucial role in the emergence of a subjective notion of individual rights. In the case of Ockham, the commitments we have seen to be characteristic of the tradition of Will and Artifice are evident in his natural theology, epistemology, natural, moral and legal philosophy—though this last is not particularly well developed. But although some intriguing gestures have recently been made in the direction of approaching the issue in comparatively novel ways,[14] the earlier attempts by such as Georges de Lagarde and Michel Bastit to align Ockham's complex political thinking with his more fundamental theological and philosophical commitments cannot be said to

---

[13] Quentin Skinner, "Meaning and understanding in the history of ideas," in *Meaning and Context: Quentin Skinner and his critics*, ed. James Tully (Oxford, 1988), pp. 38–43.

[14] I.e., from the angles of epistemology and theory of language. See Janet Coleman *Ancient and Medieval Memories: Studies in the reconstruction of the past* (Cambridge, 1992), pp. 500–537; Jesse M. Gellrich, *Discourse and Dominion in the Fourteenth Century* (Princeton, 1995), pp. 39–78. For a helpful discussion of these approaches, see Cary J. Nederman, "The Politics of Mind and Word, Image and Text: Retrieval and Renewal in Medieval Political Theory," *Political Theory*, XXV (No. 5, 1997), 716–32.

have met with success,[15] and it was the conclusion of one of the
century's leading experts on Ockham that his "political ideas in their
great outlines could have been developed, so far as we can see, from
any of the great classical metaphysics of the thirteenth century."[16] A
similar fate had overtaken the related claims by Michel Villey that
Ockham was the first to introduce the conception of subjective, individual rights and that it was his philosophical nominalism and the
radical individualism attendant upon it that alone accounts for that
fact.[17] And when I myself, nudged largely, let it be confessed, by the
brilliance of De Lagarde's analysis of Ockham, was moved to suggest (however tentatively) that the political ideas of Pierre d'Ailly
(d. 1420), one of Ockham's more faithful followers, bore the impress
of his fundamental philosophico-theological view of the world, I found
my scholarly knuckles gently rapped by John Morrall and somewhat
less gently by the distinguished Ockham scholar, H.S. Offler.[18]

I now find it possible to concede that their strictures, however un-
welcome at the time, were probably warranted. In his natural theology,

---

[15] Georges de Lagarde, *La naissance de l'esprit laïque au déclin du moyen-âge*, first edition (6 vols., Paris, 1942–46), IV–VI; Michel Bastit, *Naissance de la loi moderne* (Paris,
1990). Also Richard Scholz, *Wilhelm van Ockham als politischer Denker und sein "Breviloquium
de Principatu Tyrannico"* (Stuttgart, 1953; reprint of the 1944 Leipzig edition), Lagarde,
Naissance, V, 27, is careful to stress that there can be no *deduction* of Ockham's political views from his general philosophical position, but that has not saved him from
criticism by J.B. Morrall, who has insisted on "the discontinuities between Ockham's
philosophical and political thinking"—"Some Notes on a Recent Interpretation of
William of Ockham's Political Philosophy," *Franciscan Studies*, IX (1949), 355–69.
See also Arthur S. McGrade, *The Political Thought of William of Ockham: Personal and
Institutional Principles* (Cambridge, 1974), pp. 28–46. Cf. the analysis of Brian Tierney,
"Natural Law and Canon Law in Ockham's *Dialogus*," in *Aspects of Late Medieval
Government and Society*, ed. J.G. Rowe (Toronto, 1986), 3–24, which emphasizes the
formative influence on some dimensions of Ockham's moral and political thinking
exerted by standard canonistic teachings rather than by his own more abstract philosophical commitments.

[16] Philotheus Boehner, "Ockham's Political Ideas," *Review of Politics*, V (1943), (at
465–66).

[17] Michel Villey, *La formation de la pensée juridique moderne* (Paris, 1962), esp. pp.
225–72. For the dissenting voices, see esp. Arthur S. McGrade, "Ockham and the
Birth of Individual Rights," in *Authority and Power: Studies on Medieval Law and Government
presented to Walter Ullmann on his seventieth birthday*, ed. Brian Tierney and Peter Linehan
(Cambridge, 1980), pp. 149–65. Brian Tierney, *The Idea of Natural Rights: Studies on
Natural Rights, Natural Law and Church Law, 1150–1625* (Atlanta, 1997), esp. pp. 1–9,
195–203, and, more generally, Charles Zuckerman, "The Relationship of Theories
of Universals to Theories of Church Government: A Critique of Previous Views,"
Journal of the History of Ideas, XXXIV (No. 4, 1973), pp. 579–90.

[18] Oakley, *The Political Thought of Pierre d'Ailly*, pp. 23–40. See the reviews by John
B. Morrall in the *Catholic Historical Review*, LII (No. 2, 1966–67), pp. 285–86, and

epistemology, natural, moral and legal philosophy, d'Ailly was a faithful representative of the voluntarist tradition. He was most clearly and forthrightly so in his extended analysis of the nature of law—divine, natural, human—which is much more fully and coherently developed than is Ockham's.[19] But when we turn to his political thinking, theological and philosophical considerations tend to be nudged to one side by legal. Like many another late-medieval constitutionalist, his theory of consent derives, not immediately from any philosophical premise, but from Romano-canonistic corporational thinking. Its emphasis, accordingly, is on *community* consent; it is not impregnated with the voluntarism and the preoccupation with autonomous individuality that later come to be so prominent in Hobbes and Locke, that distinguish modern theories of legitimation by consent, and that constitute the "thread which holds the modern [social contract] tradition together."[20] In order to portray him, then, as a fully-fledged representative of Oakeshott's tradition of Will and Artifice one would have to place more emphasis than an historian properly should on what are, in his political writings, no more than fleeting intimations of his fundamental theological and philosophical commitments.

The reluctance of historians to concede full historical credibility to traditions of the Oakeshottian type is, then, readily comprehensible. The drawbacks and interpretative dangers attending on them are clear enough. The trouble, however, is that those drawbacks are *so* clear as to threaten to deflect our rueful gaze from the presence also of some attendant benefits. Not least among those benefits is the degree to which the study of such traditions can help us surmount the formidable barriers to understanding erected by the customary periodization of European history into ancient, medieval and modern—an increasingly Ptolemaic system that can be made to function only by recourse to a veritable embarrassment of enabling epicycles. Having in my own historical work, moreover, drawn inspiration

---

by H.S. Offler in the *English Historical Review*, LXXXI (July, 1966), pp. 560–62. Finding no obvious interconnection between d'Ailly's political thinking and his "voluntarism in ethics and law," Offler commented tartly: ". . . if this be so, we must not put one there."

[19] For a brief discussion of this last, see above, ch. 7, pp. , and for a fuller treatment, Oakley, *The Political Thought of Pierre d'Ailly*, pp. 163–97.

[20] The words are those of Patrick Riley. "How Coherent is the Social Contract Tradition?", *Journal of the History of Ideas*, XXXIV (No. 4, 1973), pp. 543–62 (at 561). For the differences between medieval and subsequent theories of consent, see above, ch. 4.

from the philosophico-historical promptings, not only of Oakeshott himself, but also of philosophers like A.N. Whitehead, Michael Foster and Collingwood,[21] perhaps I might also be permitted to indulge, and by way of conclusion, the robustly "internalist" hope that the history of ideas, currently so very preoccupied with contextualist issues of one sort or another, will not contrive somehow to ignore the context that is the most immediate and intimate of all—namely, that constituted by the totality of a given author's thinking. That as a discipline it may prove, in effect and in the end, to be a big enough tent, or sufficiently broad-church in its sensibilities, to accommodate the type of creative, intuitive insight that such philosophers generated in so stimulating a profusion. If, even in their more "historical" moments, rather than proceeding in more earthbound historical fashion, they often moved quasi-deductively to assert what in terms of the internal logic of ideas *must* have been the case, we should not miss the fact that their intuitions not infrequently turned out to have been, historically speaking, quite accurate, and their emphasis on the internal interconnections and affinities among ideas almost always illuminating. That emphasis usefully encourages a heightened sensitivity toward what Lovejoy called "the particular go" of ideas, the logical pressure they are capable of exerting on the minds of those that think them.[22] And it serves to draw attention also to the complex network of internal intellectual communications that we have seen linking together realms of discourse (theological, epistemological, scientific, moral, legal, political) that might otherwise have seemed quite disparate. In its absence, certainly, and of this I have no doubt, it would be much harder to sense the intimations of eternity in the sublunary world of political thought, and harder still to glimpse the reflection of politics in the inevitably refracting mirror of eternity.

---

[21] I have in mind here the Collingwood of *The Idea of Nature* not the Collingwood who, in his role as expert on the history of Roman Britain, contributed a distinguished volume to the Oxford History of England. For the contribution of Michael Foster to our understanding of the roots of the early-modern science of nature, see the articles (along with those of a series of commentators) now gathered together in Cameron Wybrow ed., *Creation, Nature, and Political Order in the Philosophy of Michael Foster: 1903–1959* (Lewiston, 1992)

[22] For an illustration from the history of early-modern science, see Oakley, "Christian Theology and the Newtonian Science," and *idem, Omnipotence, Covenant, and Order*, pp. 67–92.

INDEX OF NAMES AND PLACES

SUBJECT INDEX

SELECT BIBLIOGRAPHY

Bibliographical

For the history of medieval and early-modern political thought in general, extensive and up-to-date listings of both primary and secondary sources, along with useful biographical sketches of the leading thinkers, are to be found in the *The Cambridge History of Political Thought: c. 350–c. 1450*. Ed. J.H. Burns. Cambridge, Engl., 1988. Pp. 653–777. Also *The Cambridge History of Political Thought: 1450–1700*. Ed. J. H. Burns and Mark Goldie. Cambridge, Engl., 1991. Pp. 657–776. For works on John Locke in particular, see Roland Hall and Roger Woolhouse. *80 Years of Locke Scholarship: A Bibliographical Guide*. Edinburgh, 1983. Bibliographical data on the Conciliar ecclesiology, its canonistic origins and subsequent career are to be found in Brian Tierney, *Foundations of the Conciliar Theory: The Contributions of the Medieval Canonists from Gratian to the Great Schism*. Cambridge, Engl., 1955. Remigius Bäumer, "Die Erforschung des Konziliarismus," in *Die Entwicklung des Konziliarismus: Werden und Nachwirken der Konziliaren Idee*. Ed. Remigius Bäumer. Darmstadt, 1976. Pp. 3–56; Hans Schneider. *Der Konziliarismus als Problem der neueren katholischen Theologie*. Berlin, 1976; Giuseppi Alberigo. "Il movimento conciliare (xiv–xv sec.) nella ricerca storica recente," *Studi Medievali*, 3rd series, 19(1978) 213–50; Francis Oakley. "Natural Law, the *Corpus Mysticum*, and Consent in Conciliar Thought from John of Paris to Matthias Ugonius." *Speculum* 40 (1981) 786–810. Much of the literature generated by recent metahistorical and methodological debates concerning the history of political thought in particular and the history of ideas in general is listed and reviewed in *Meaning and Context: Quentin Skinner and His Critics*. Ed. James Tully. Cambridge, Engl., 1988, and John E. Toews, "Intellectual History after the Linguistic Turn: The Autonomy of Meaning and Irreducibility of History," *American Historical Review*, 92 (1987) 879–907. For the growing body of scholarly literature on matters pertaining to the divine omnipotence and the voluntarist tradition, see Gijsbert van den Brink. *Almighty God. A Study of the Doctrine of Divine Omnipotence*. Kempen. 1993. Pp. 276–95.

Metahistorical and Methodological

Bevir, Mark, "The Errors of Linguistic Contextualism," *History and Theory*, 31 (1992) 276–98.

Boucher, David. *Texts in Context: Revisionist Methods for Studying the History of Ideas*. Dordrecht-Boston-Lancaster, 1985.

Condren, Conal. *The Status and Appraisal of Classic Texts: An Essay on Political Theory, Its Inheritance, and the History of Ideas*. Princeton, N.J., 1985.

Dunn, John. *The History of Political Theory and Other Essays*. Cambridge, Engl., 1996.

Gadamer, Hans-Georg. *Truth and Method*. Trans. Garrett Barden and John Cumming. New York, 1986.

Hermerén, Goran. *Influence in Art and Literature*. Princeton, N.J., 1975.

Janssen, Peter L., "Political Thought as Traditionary Action: The Critical Response to Skinner and Pocock," *History and Theory*, 24 (1985) 115–46.

La Capra, Domenick. *History and Criticism*. Ithaca and London, 1985.

Lovejoy, Arthur O. *The Great Chain of Being: A Study of the History of an Idea*. Cambridge, Mass., 1936.

——. "The Historiography of Ideas," *Proceedings of the American Philosophical Society*, 78 (1938) 529–43.

——. "Reflections on the History of Ideas," *Journal of the History of Ideas*, 1 (1940) 3–23.

Mandelbaum, Maurice. "The History of Ideas, Intellectual History, and the History of Philosophy," *History and Theory*, 5 (1965) 34–42.

Meaning and Context: Quentin Skinner and His Critics. Ed. James Tully. Cambridge, Engl., 1988.

Modern European Intellectual History: Reappraisals and New Perspectives. Eds. Domenick La Capra and Steven L. Kaplan. Ithaca and London, 1982.

Oakley, Francis. *Omnipotence, Covenant, and Order: An Excursion in the History of Ideas from Abelard to Leibniz*. Ithaca and London, 1984. Pp. 15–40.

Pocock, J.G.A. *Politics, Language and Time: Essays on Political Thought and History*. New York, 1971.

Richter, Melvin, "Opening a Dialogue and Recognizing an Achievement," *Archiv für Begriffsgeschichte*, 39 (1996) 19–26.

Schulin, Ernst. *Traditionskritik und Rekonstruktionsversuch*. Göttingen, 1979. Pp. 144–62.

The History of Ideas: Canon and Variations. Ed. Donald R. Kelley. Rochester, N.Y., 1990.

The Meaning of Historical Terms and Concepts: New Studies in Begriffsgeschichte. Eds. Hartmut Lehmann and Melvin Richter. Washington, D.C., 1996.

Toews, John E., "Intellectual History after the Linguistic Turn: The Autonomy of Meaning and Irreducibility of History," *American Historical Review*, 92 (1987) 879–907.

Veyne, Paul. *Comment on écrit l'Histoire*. Paris, 1978.

Philosophical and Theological

Adams, Marilyn. *William Ockham*. 2 vols. Notre Dame, Ind., 1987.

Collingwood, R.G. *The Idea of Naure*. Oxford, 1945.

Courtenay, William J. *Covenant and Causality in Medieval Thought*. London, 1984.

——. *Capacity and Volition: A History of the Distinction of Absolute and Ordained Power*. Bergamo, 1990.

Creation, Nature, and Political Order in the Philosophy of Michael Foster: 1903–1959. Ed. Cameron Wybrow. Lewiston, 1992.

Creation: The Impact of an Idea. Ed. Daniel O'Connor and Francis Oakley. New York, 1969.

De Lagarde, Georges. *La naissance de l'esprit laique au déclin du moyen-âge*. 2d ed. 5 vols. Paris, 1956–63.

De Lubac, Henri. *Corpus Mysticum: L'Eucharistie et l'église au Moyen Âge*. Paris, 1944.

Funkenstein, Amos. *Theology and the Scientific Imagination from the Middle Ages to the Seventeenth Century*. Princeton, 1986.

Hamm, Bernd. *Promissio, Pactum, Ordinatio: Freiheit und Selbstbindung Gottes in der Scholastischen Gnadenlehre*. Tübingen, 1977.

John Locke: Critical Assessments. Ed. Richard Ashcraft, 4 vols. London and New York, 1991.

John Locke: Symposium Wolfenbuttel 1979. Ed. Reinhardt Brandt. Berlin and New York, 1981.

Kenny, Anthony. *The God of the Philosophers*. Oxford, 1979.

Kleutgen, Joseph. *Institutiones Theologicae in usum scholarum*. Ratisbon, 1881.

Leff, Gordon. *William of Ockham: The Metamorphosis of Scholastic Discourse*. Manchester, 1975.

Locke, John. *Essays on the Law of Nature*. Ed. and trans. W. Van Leyden. Oxford, 1954.
Mackie, J., "Evil and Omnipotence," *Mind*, 64 (1955) 200–12.
Oakley, Francis. *Omnipotence, Covenant, and Order: An Excursion in the History of Ideas from Abelard to Leibniz*. Ithaca and London, 1984.
Oberman, Heiko A. *The Harvest of Medieval Theology: Gabriel Biel and Late Medieval Nominalism*. Cambridge, Mass., 1963.
Osler, Margaret J. *Divine will and the Mechanical Philosophy: Gassendi and Descartes on contingency and necessity in the created world*. Cambridge, 1994.
Randi, Eugenio. *Il sovrano e l'orologiaio: Due immagini di Dio nel debattito sulla "potentia absoluta" fra XIII e XIV secolo*. Firenze, 1987.
Robert Boyle Reconsidered. Ed. Michael Hunter. Cambridge, Engl., 1994.
Shanahan, Timothy, "God and Nature in the Thought of Robert Boyle," *Journal of the History of Philosophy*, 26 (1988) 549–69.
Steinmetz, David C. *Calvin in Context*. New York and Oxford, 1995.
Tachau, Katherine H, "Robert Holcot on Contingency and Divine Deception," in *Filosofia e Teologia nel Trecento: Studi in ricordo di Eugenio Randi*. Ed. Jole Agrimi et al. Louvain-la-Neuve, 1994. Pp. 157–96.
——— "Logic's God and the Natural Order in Late Medieval Oxford: The Teaching of Robert Holcot," *Annals of Science*, 53 (1996) 235–67.
The Leviathan of Thomas Hobbes. Ed. Michael Oakeshott. Oxford, 1946.
The Power of God: Readings on Omnipotence and Evil. Ed. Linwood Urban and Douglas N. Walton. New York, 1978.
The Pursuit of Holiness in Late Medieval and Renaissance Religion. Ed. Charles Trinkaus and Heiko A. Oberman. Leiden, 1974.
Van den Brink, Gijsbert. *Almighty God: A Study of the Doctrine of Divine Omnipotence*. Kempen, 1993.
Wojcik, Jan W. *Robert Boyle and the Limits of Reason*. Cambridge, 1997.

Legal, Political, Ecclesiological

Alberigo, Giuseppe. *Chiesa conciliare: Identità e significato del conciliarismo*. Brescia, 1981.
Bäumer, Remigius. *Nachwirkungen des Konziliaren Gedankens in der Theologie und Kanonistik des frühen 16. Jahrhunderts*. Münster, 1971.
Becker, Hans-Jürgen. *Die Appellation vom Papst an Allgemeines Konzil. Historisches Entwicklung und kanonistische Diskussion im späten Mittelalter und der frühen Neuzeit*. Vienna, 1988.
Beskow, Per. *Rex Gloriae: The Kingship of Christ in the Early Church*. Uppsala, 1962.
Black, Antony. *Council and Commune: The Conciliar Movement and the Fifteenth-Century Heritage*. London, 1979
———. *Monarchy and Community. Political Ideas in the Later Conciliar Controversy: 1430–1450*. Cambridge, Engl., 1970.
———. *Political Thought in Europe: 1250–1450*. Cambridge, Engl., 1992.
Bloch, Marc. *Les rois thaumaturges: Étude sur le caractère surnaturel attribué à la puissance royale particulièrement en France et en Angleterre*. Strasbourg and Paris, 1924.
Burns, J.H. *Lordship, Kingship, and Empire: The Idea of Monarchy, 1400–1525*. Oxford, 1992.
Cam, H.M., Marongiu, A., Stökl, G., "Recent Work and Present Views on the Origins and Development of Representative Assemblies," in *Relazioni del X Congresso Internazionale di Scienze Storiche*. 3 vols. Florence, 1955. I, 1–101.
Chabod, Federico. *La Politica di Paolo Sarpi*. Venice and Rome, 1962.
Church, William F. *Constitutional Thought in Sixteenth-Century France: A Study in the Evolution of Ideas*. Cambridge, Mass., 1941.
Congar, Yves M.J., "Quod omnes tangit ab omnibus tractari et approbari debet," *Revue d'histoire de droit français et étranger*, 4th series, 36 (1958) 210–59.

Das Königtum: Seine geistige und rechtlichen Gründlagen. Ed. Th. Mayer. Lindau and Konstanz, 1956.

Das Konzil von Konstanz: Beiträge zu seiner Geschichte und Theologie. Ed. A. Franzen and W. Müller. Freiburg, 1964.

D'Entrèves, Alexander Passerin. *The Notion of the State: An Introduction to Political Theory.* Oxford, 1967.

De la Brosse, Olivier. *Le Pape et le Concile: La comparaison de leurs pouvoirs à la veille de la Réforme.* Paris, 1965.

De Vought, Paul. *Les pouvoirs du concile et l'autorité du pape au Concile de Constance.* Paris, 1965.

Dunn, John. *The Political Thought of John Locke.* Cambridge, Engl., 1969.

Dvornik, Francis. *Early Christian and Byzantine Political Philosophy.* 2 vols. Washington, D.C., 1966.

Fasolt, Constantin. *Council and Hierarchy: The Political Thought of William Durant the Younger.* Cambridge, Engl., 1991.

Figgis, John Neville. *Political Thought from Gerson to Grotius: 1414–1625. Seven Studies.* New York, 1960.

Fink, Karl August, "Zur Beurteilung des grossen abendländischen Schismas," *Zeitschrift für Kirchengeschichte,* 73 (1962) 335–43.

Gewirth, Alan. *Marsilius of Padua: The Defender of Peace.* 2 vols. New York, 1952–56.

Gierke, Otto. *Political Theories of the Middle Age.* Ed. and trans. F.W. Maitland. Cambridge, Engl., 1900.

Greenleaf, W.H. *Order, Empiricism, and Politics: Two Traditions of English Political Thought.* London, 1964.

Höfler, Otto, "Der Sakralcharakter des germanischen Königtums," in *The Sacral Kingship: Studies in the History of Religions,* 4 (Leiden, 1959) 716–33.

Izbicki, Thomas M., "Papalist Reaction to the Council of Constance: Juan de Torquemada to the Present," *Church History,* 55 (1986) 7–20.

Jedin, Hubert. *Bischöfliches Konzil oder Kirchenparlament? Ein Beitrag zur Ekklesiologie des Konzilien von Konstanz.* 2nd ed. Basel and Stuttgart, 1965.

———. *A History of the Council of Trent.* Trans. Ernest Graf. 2 vols. London, 1957–61.

Kantorowicz, Ernst. *The King's Two Bodies: A Study in Medieval Political Theology.* Princeton, N.J., 1957.

Küng, Hans. *Strukturen der Kirche.* Freiburg, 1962.

Marongiu, Antonio, "Il principio della democrazia e del consenso nel XIV secolo," *Studia Gratiana,* 7 (1962) 555–75.

———. *Medieval Parliaments: A Comparative Study.* Trans. S.J. Woolf. London, 1968.

Martimort, Aimé-Georges. *Le Gallicanisme de Bossuet.* Paris, 1953.

Mayer, Thomas P. *Thomas Starkey and the Commonweal: Humanist Politics and Religion in the Reign of Henry VIII.* Cambridge, Engl., 1989.

McGrade, Arthur S. *The Political Thoughts of William of Ockham: Personal and Institutional Principles.* Cambridge, Engl., 1974.

McIlwain, Charles H. *Constitutionalism: Ancient and Modern.* Rev. ed. Ithaca, 1958.

Meuthen, Erich, "Das Basler Konzil in römisch-katholischer Sicht," *Theologische Zeitschrift,* 38 (1982) 274–308.

Meyjes, G. Posthumus. *Jean Gerson: Zijn kerkpolitiek en ecclesiologie.* The Hague, 1963.

Morrall, John B. *Gerson and the Great Schism.* Manchester, 1960.

Oakley, Francis. *Natural Law, Conciliarism and Consent in the Late Middle Ages.* London, 1984.

———. *The Political Thought of Pierre d'Ailly: The Voluntarist Tradition.* New Haven and London, 1964.

Post, Gaines. *Studies in Medieval Legal Thought.* Princeton, N.J., 1957.

Salmon, J.H.M. *Renaissance and Revolt: Essays in the intellectual and social history of early modern France.* Cambridge, Engl., 1987.

Sarpi, Paolo. *Lettere ai Gallicani*. Ed. Boris Ulianich. Wiesbaden, 1961.

Schneider Hans. *Das Konziliarismus als Problem der neuren Katholischen Theologie*. Berlin, 1976.

Sieben, Hermann Josef. *Die Konzilidee des lateinischen Mittelalters (847–1378)*. Paderborn, 1984.

Sigmund, Paul E. *Nicholas of Cusa and Medieval Political Thought*. Cambridge, Mass., 1963.

Skinner, Quentin. *The Foundations of Modern Political Thought*. 2 vols. Cambridge, Engl., 1978.

Somerville, Johan. *Politics and Ideology in England: 1603–1640*. London, 1986.

The Cambridge History of Political Thought: c. 350–c. 1450. Ed. J.H. Burns. Cambridge, Engl., 1988.

The Cambridge History of Political Thought: 1450–1700. Ed. J.H. Burns and Mark Goldie. Cambridge, Engl., 1991.

Tierney, Brian. *Foundations of the Conciliar Theory: The Contributions of the Medieval Canonists from Gratian to the Great Schism*. Cambridge, Engl., 1955.

Ullmann, Walter. *Principles of Government and Politics in the Middle Ages*. 2nd ed. London, 1966.

——. *A History of Political Thought: The Middle Ages*. Harmondsworth, 1965.

——. *The Individual and Society in the Middle Ages*. Baltimore, 1966.

Wilks, Michael. *The Problem of Sovereignty in the Later Middle Ages*. Cambridge, Engl., 1963.

Wormuth, Francis D. *The Royal Prerogative 1603–1649: A Study in English Political and Constitutional Ideas*. Ithaca, 1939.

Studies in the History
of Christian Thought

EDITED BY HEIKO A. OBERMAN

54. GIAKALIS, A. *Images of the Divine*. The Theology of Icons at the Seventh Ecumenical Council. With a Foreword by Henry Chadwick. 1994. ISBN 90 04 09946 8

55. NELLEN, H. J. M. and RABBIE, E. (eds.). *Hugo Grotius – Theologian*. Essays in Honour of G. H. M. Posthumus Meyjes. 1994. ISBN 90 04 10000 8

56. TRIGG, J. D. *Baptism in the Theology of Martin Luther*. 1994. ISBN 90 04 10016 4

57. JANSE, W. *Albert Hardenberg als Theologe*. Profil eines Bucer-Schülers. 1994. ISBN 90 04 10071 7

59. SCHOOR, R.J.M. van de. *The Irenical Theology of Théophile Brachet de La Milletière (1588-1665)*. 1995. ISBN 90 04 09961 1

60. STREHLE, S. *The Catholic Roots of the Protestant Gospel*. Encounter between the Middle Ages and the Reformation. 1995. ISBN 90 04 10203 5

61. BROWN, M.L. *Donne and the Politics of Conscience in Early Modern England*. 1995. ISBN 90 04 10157 8

62. SCREECH, M.A. (ed.). *Richard Mocket, Warden of All Souls College, Oxford, Doctrina et Politia Ecclesiae Anglicanae*. An Anglican Summa. Facsimile with Variants of the Text of 1617. Edited with an Introduction. 1995. ISBN 90 04 10040 7

63. SNOEK, G.J.C. *Medieval Piety from Relics to the Eucharist*. A Process of Mutual Interaction. 1995. ISBN 90 04 10263 9

64. PIXTON, P.B. *The German Episcopacy and the Implementation of the Decrees of the Fourth Lateran Council, 1216-1245*. Watchmen on the Tower. 1995. ISBN 90 04 10262 0

65. DOLNIKOWSKI, E.W. *Thomas Bradwardine: A View of Time and a Vision of Eternity in Fourteenth-Century Thought*. 1995. ISBN 90 04 10226 4

66. RABBIE, E. (ed.). *Hugo Grotius, Ordinum Hollandiae ac Westfrisiae Pietas (1613)*. Critical Edition with Translation and Commentary. 1995. ISBN 90 04 10385 6

67. HIRSH, J.C. *The Boundaries of Faith*. The Development and Transmission of Medieval Spirituality. 1996. ISBN 90 04 10428 3

68. BURNETT, S.G. *From Christian Hebraism to Jewish Studies*. Johannes Buxtorf (1564-1629) and Hebrew Learning in the Seventeenth Century. 1996. ISBN 90 04 10346 5

69. BOLAND O.P., V. *Ideas in God according to Saint Thomas Aquinas*. Sources and Synthesis. 1996. ISBN 90 04 10392 9

70. LANGE, M.E. *Telling Tears in the English Renaissance*. 1996. ISBN 90 04 10517 4

71. CHRISTIANSON, G. and T.M. IZBICKI (eds.). *Nicholas of Cusa on Christ and the Church*. Essays in Memory of Chandler McCuskey Brooks for the American Cusanus Society. 1996. ISBN 90 04 10519 0

72. MALI, A. *Mystic in the New World*. Marie de l'Incarnation (1599-1672). 1996. ISBN 90 04 10606 5

73. VISSER, D. *Apocalypse as Utopian Expectation (800-1500)*. The Apocalypse Commentary of Berengaudus of Ferrières and the Relationship between Exegesis, Liturgy and Iconography. 1996. ISBN 90 04 10621 9

74. O'ROURKE BOYLE, M. *Divine Domesticity*. Augustine of Thagaste to Teresa of Avila. 1997. ISBN 90 04 10675 8

75. PFIZENMAIER, T.C. *The Trinitarian Theology of Dr. Samuel Clarke (1675-1729)*. Context, Sources, and Controversy. 1997. ISBN 90 04 10719 3

76. BERKVENS-STEVELINCK, C., J. ISRAEL and G.H.M. POSTHUMUS MEYJES (eds.). *The Emergence of Tolerance in the Dutch Republic*. 1997. ISBN 90 04 10768 1

77. HAYKIN, M.A.G. (ed.). *The Life and Thought of John Gill (1697-1771)*. A Tercentennial Appreciation. 1997. ISBN 90 04 10744 4

78. KAISER, C.B. *Creational Theology and the History of Physical Science*. The Creationist Tradition from Basil to Bohr. 1997. ISBN 90 04 10669 3

79. LEES, J.T. *Anselm of Havelberg*. Deeds into Words in the Twelfth Century. 1997. ISBN 90 04 10906 4

80. WINTER, J.M. van. *Sources Concerning the Hospitallers of St John in the Netherlands, 14th-18th Centuries*. 1998. ISBN 90 04 10803 3

81. TIERNEY, B. *Foundations of the Conciliar Theory*. The Contribution of the Medieval Canonists from Gratian to the Great Schism. Enlarged New Edition. 1998. ISBN 90 04 10924 2

82. MIERNOWSKI, J. *Le Dieu Néant*. Théologies négatives à l'aube des temps modernes. 1998. ISBN 90 04 10915 3

83. HALVERSON, J.L. *Peter Aureol on Predestination.* A Challenge to Late Medieval Thought. 1998. ISBN 90 04 10945 5

84. HOULISTON, V. (ed.). *Robert Persons, S.J.: The Christian Directory (1582).* The First Booke of the Christian Exercise, appertayning to Resolution. 1998. ISBN 90 04 11009 7

85. GRELL, O.P. (ed.). *Paracelsus.* The Man and His Reputation, His Ideas and Their Reputation. 1998. ISBN 90 04 11177 8

86. MAZZOLA, E. *The Pathology of the English Renaissance.* Sacred Remains and Holy Ghosts. 1998. ISBN 90 04 11195 6

Prospectus available on request

BRILL — P.O.B. 9000 — 2300 PA LEIDEN — THE NETHERLANDS